The Japanese Economy

THE
JAPANESE
ECONOMY

David Flath

OXFORD

UNIVERSITY PRESS

OXFORD

UNIVERSITY PRESS

Great Clarendon Street, Oxford OX2 6DP

Oxford University Press is a department of the University of Oxford.
It furthers the University's objective of excellence in research, scholarship,
and education by publishing worldwide in

Oxford New York

Athens Auckland Bangkok Bogotá Buenos Aires Calcutta
Cape Town Chennai Dar es Salaam Delhi Florence Hong Kong Istanbul
Karachi Kuala Lumpur Madrid Melbourne Mexico City Mumbai
Nairobi Paris São Paulo Singapore Taipei Tokyo Toronto Warsaw

with associated companies in Berlin Ibadan

Oxford is a registered trade mark of Oxford University Press
in the UK and in certain other countries

Published in the United States
by Oxford University Press Inc., New York

British Library Cataloguing in Publication Data

Data available

Library of Congress Cataloging in Publication Data

Data available

ISBN 0–19–877504–0
ISBN 0–19–877503–2 (Pbk)

10 9 8 7 6 5 4 3 2 1

Typeset by BookMan Services
Printed in Great Britain
on acid-free paper by
Bookcraft Ltd.
Midsomer Norton, Somerset

To Carol, Nick, and Maggie

Preface

Very few universities outside of Japan offer courses on the Japanese economy. I wrote this book out of the conviction that many more of them would offer such courses, if only a suitable text were available. If courses on Japan are to become a regular part of the economics curriculum in English-speaking colleges and universities, as I believe they should, then the subject has to be made accessible to students and faculty who presently have little familiarity with Japanese history or institutions.

This is less of a leap to make than one might suppose. Anyone who understands the principles of economics already knows a lot about the Japanese economy without necessarily even realizing it. Many specific topics on the Japanese economy invite uncomplicated explanations based on standard bits of economic logic, such as the axiom of revealed preference, the Ricardian theory of comparative advantage, the Solow growth model, the life-cycle model of saving, the quantity theory of money, the purchasing power parity theory of exchange rates, public goods, Coase's law, the welfare losses resulting from monopoly, analysis of company specific skills, the Modigliani–Miller theorem, and so on. Anyone now teaching economics courses at university level should find enough in this book that is familiar, along with guideposts toward the unfamiliar, to teach a solid course based on the book. The book itself supplies the relevant facts about Japan that economic arguments can illuminate, and also explains the logic of the arguments.

For those not already versed in economics, this book will afford a broad and, I hope, enticing introduction to the economic way of reasoning. This is a book not only for specialists in economics, but also for political scientists, historians, and others interested in Japan. For undergraduate students taking a course based on this book, a prior course on the principles of economics may be helpful, but is possibly not essential.

There may be more here than one should attempt to include in a one-semester course. The chapters proceed from macroeconomic topics toward microeconomic ones, but this is somewhat arbitrary and the chapters can be taken in just about any order, and any of them can be skipped without rendering the remaining chapters incomprehensible. The first chapter assesses Japan's current status as a developed nation with a high standard of living, and the next three chapters describe the sequence of events that produced this result. The remaining chapters are divided by subject area rather than chronologically. Many of these "subject area" chapters refer to historical events, but their main focus is on contemporary topics. A course emphasizing economic history and development should include the first four chapters and the chapter on industrial policy. A course emphasizing Japanese business should include the last five chapters. A course emphasizing government policy should include Chapters 8–12 and 16. A course emphasizing macroeconomics should include the first chapter and Chapters 3–7.

Very many people have helped me in this project in myriad ways, with comments on earlier drafts, copies of their own articles, conversations, mentoring, editing, and other forms of support. I am grateful to all of them and especially the following. *Colleagues at NCSU*: Steve Allen, Bob Clark, Lee Craig, Bob Fearn, Douglas Fisher, Tom Grennes, Tony Moyer, Doug Pearce, John Seater, Walt Wessels. *Colleagues at Osaka University*: Hayashi Toshio, Charles Yuji Horioka, Colin McKenzie, Royama Shoichi, Takagi Shinji. *Friends and colleagues at other universities*: Jeff Bernstein, Hanai Satoshi, Hayashi Fumio, Iida Takao, James Nakamura, Nakata Yoshihiro, Nariu Tatsuhiko, Hugh Patrick, Tish Robinson, Gary Saxonhouse, Paul Sheard, Richard Sylla, Takeuchi Nobuhito, Yishai Yafeh, Yumoto Yuji, and David Weinstein.

I would also like to thank John Sylvester (former director of the NC Japan Center), A. Scott Voorhees (of US EPA), Fujiwara Masahiko (of MITI), and my editor at Oxford, Andrew Schuller, who faithfully conveyed the comments of anonymous reviewers. I would like to acknowledge my mentors at UCLA, Harold Demsetz and Armen Alchian—whatever economics I know I learned from them. Thanks also to my first Japanese teacher, Kataoka Hiroko, who introduced me to Japan. I also acknowledge the contributions of the many students in the classes in which I tested the materials that became this book: students at North Carolina State University, Osaka University, Sapporo University, and those from all over the world who took my classes at the Harvard Summer School.

Many institutions have assisted me while writing the book and I thank them also: North Carolina Japan Center, North Carolina State University, Osaka University and Osaka Gas Company, and Nanzan University.

Finally, I am proud to thank my wife Carol and children Nick and Maggie for supporting me in this long and involved project.

D.F.

Raleigh, April 1999

Contents

Figures

Tables

I have ordered the names of Japanese persons last name first, except in citations of English-language works, where I adopted the usual conventions pertaining to authors' names, regardless of their nationality.

Introduction

Why should a university course be devoted to the economy of Japan, a small archipelago on the edge of the Pacific rim inhabited by only 2.4 percent of the world's population? Not because Japan is the unique example of a "non-Western" country achieving an equal standard of living with North America and Western Europe. (Surely, Japan should not elicit singular treatment merely because of the skin color of its inhabitants.) Not even because of the emergence of Japan as an "economic superpower", whatever that much overworked catchphrase might mean. Not because Japan contributes much to the Western standard of living. (It does not.) And certainly not because Japan causes or greatly exacerbates whatever economic ills afflict the Western countries. (Again, it does not.)

Why do we need a university course on Japan's economy? Because too many people "know" things about Japan's economy that are pure moonshine. They "know", for instance, that Japanese businesses disdain profits, that Japanese workers forgo leisure, and that Japanese consumers forgo consumption, all for reasons that are inscrutable. They "know" that the economy of Japan is only nominally capitalist, and in fact is something more akin to a centrally planned economy in which the affairs of private businesses are severely circumscribed by the directions of a pervasive government bureaucracy. They "know" that Japan's persistent trade imbalances prove that it is "closed to imports", and further they "know" that this is good for Japan and bad for its trading partners.

None of this is true. All of it is nonsense. The goal of this text is to demonstrate this, and in the process of doing so to reveal something more fascinating even than the Japanese economy of popular misconception: Japan's economy as it truly is, made coherent through the logic of modern economics.

The principles of economics apply in Japan as they do elsewhere

In the following pages we shall encounter some of the most famous contributions to modern economics. Without them, convincing explanations for many of Japan's economic peculiarities would be impossible. The economic peculiarities include the famous Japanese employment practices (lifetime employment, seniority-based wages), Japan's "miraculous" postwar rapid economic growth, Japan's currently high national saving rate, Japan's evolving patterns of international trade, the allocation of public resources in Japan, the patterns of regulation of Japanese industries, special contractual arrangements between Japanese firms and the wholesale and retail distributors of their products, and much else. The Japanese economy is a kind of test case that validates modern economic thought.

More specifically, Solow's model of a growing economy correctly accounts for Japan's rapid recovery from the devastations of the Pacific war (Chapter 4). Modigliani's life-cycle model of saving correctly predicts that postwar Japan's youthful demographic profile and rapid economic growth will precipitate an enlarged national saving rate (Chapter 5). The

Ricardian model correctly anticipates that resource-poor, skilled-labor-rich Japan will import oil and export manufactures (Chapter 8). Becker's theory of investment in company-specific skills and Lazear's theory of mandatory retirement together form a coherent explanation of Japanese employment practices (Chapter 15). Nor is this all. Samuelson's theory of revealed preference clarifies the logical difficulties we encounter in comparing the economic well-being of citizens of Japan with those of other nations (Chapter 1). Coase's exposition of the problem of social cost affords the indispensable framework for evaluating the achievements and limitations of Japan's environmental policies (Chapter 11). The modern theory of industrial organization offers convincing interpretations of the many contractual arrangements linking Japanese firms and their suppliers or customers (Chapter 12), and linking marketing channel members to one another (Chapter 14). All of these explanations fit squarely in the mainstream of modern economics. In spite of the country's fascinating strangeness, the principles of economics apply in Japan as they do elsewhere.

Major themes

The book follows a progression of topics, beginning with those that focus on Japan's economy as a whole and proceeding to those that focus on particular institutions or sectors of the economy, or aspects of Japanese business. The order is somewhat arbitrary, as I have attempted to compose each chapter so that it could stand alone, independently of the others. Thus, the reader may alter the order or skip from one chapter to another and not lose the thread of discourse. Even so, four threads do run through all the chapters: Japan's economic growth and development, Japan's integration with the world economy, government policies and their effects, and peculiar economic institutions and practices. Here are some brief previews of each of these major themes.

Japan's economic growth and development

Japan today enjoys one of the highest standards of living of any nation, a state of economic well-being comparable to that of the United States. The Japanese people live long, healthy lives, eat well, are well

educated, and have accumulated a substantial stock of durable goods. Japan's phenomenal economic growth since the end of World War II is only a part of a much longer account of how the nation achieved its current high standard of living. The story of Japan's economic development begins long before this century. It is a fascinating story, and is not well enough known outside of Japan.

When Europeans reached Japan in the sixteenth century, they beheld a country engulfed in civil wars. Soon after the end of that eventful century, the wars ended and the victors, led by Tokugawa Ieyasu, imposed on Japan a highly regimented, caste-based, political–economic regime that retained its essential features for the next two hundred and fifty years. The political system of the Tokugawa era (1603–1868) has been described as feudalistic. The country and its population were under the divided suzerainty of military rulers whose political status was determined by the taxable yield of the lands under their control. The overlord in this scheme was the *shogun*, the mantle assumed by Tokugawa Ieyasu and passed to his descendants. The shogunal domains, known as the *tenryō*, encompassed the most fertile lands and the largest cities, Edo (now Tokyo), Osaka, and Kyoto the imperial capital. Directly under the *shogun* stood the *daimyō*, the military rulers of the next largest suzerains, known as *han*, and below them still others of the samurai class, warriors with no wars to fight—in effect, an hereditary and hierarchical civil bureaucracy. The Tokugawa capital, Edo, grew from a small fishing village of no consequence in 1600 to a city of one million in 1700, a direct result of the shogunal decrees obliging all of the two to three hundred *daimyō* to reside there in alternating years and their families to remain there year round as quasi-hostages. With *daimyō* under the watchful eye of the shogunate, they were effectively prevented from forming dissenting coalitions.

The policy that most epitomized the Tokugawa political outlook was the closure of the country. The point was to forestall change altogether and perpetuate the status quo indefinitely. Contact with foreigners was an unwanted disruption and a potential source of instability. Under decree of the third *shogun* of the Tokugawa dynasty, in 1642, foreigners were expelled and Japan was closed to the outside world, with the minor exception of limited official trade with the Dutch and Chinese, conducted through the southern port of Nagasaki.

Almost the entire productive effort of Japan in the Tokugawa era was devoted to feeding the nation, which meant that the overwhelming majority of the population, around 80 percent, were of the agrarian caste, and mainly engaged in the cultivation of rice. Most of the remainder of the population, other than the 7 percent or so who were of the samurai caste, were merchants and artisans, both of which were held in lower esteem than farmers under the Confucian ideology embraced by official doctrines of the country's rulers. The farmers were obliged to pay rice taxes to the samurai under a scheme that made land inalienable, but ceded responsibility for managing the local affairs of agricultural communities to the inhabitants themselves.

With the civil wars ended and the *daimyō* secure in their right to impose taxes on the lands under their official control, land reclamation and irrigation proceeded apace in the seventeenth century, and the population of Japan grew commensurately, expanding from about 20 million in 1600 to 30 million in 1700. Then, for the next 150 years, the population grew hardly at all. A fundamental reason for population stability was that, once land reclamation had approached the limits of Japan's mountainous geography, families of all castes began deliberately to limit their offspring, including by resort to infanticide, in calculated attempts to raise their own living standards. Moderate technological advance and increased commercial activity also contributed to growth in Japanese living standards over this period.

Outside Japan, the world had undergone much more dramatic changes by the beginning of the nineteenth century. The industrial revolution in Europe rendered Japan technologically backwards. Nevertheless, Japan had indigenously developed sophisticated economic and political institutions, including fractional reserve banking, futures markets, wholesaling and retailing networks, double-entry accounting, and the mechanisms of local self-government. In these ways, Japan carried the seeds of its later rapid economic development.

The dispatch of American warships to Japan in 1853 ended Japan's two centuries of near seclusion from the outside world. Commodore Perry's demand that Japan should open its ports to foreigners set in motion a chain of events that culminated in the 1868 Meiji Restoration, a political revolution that ended shogunal rule and established in its place an oligarchy of energetic young reformers intent on transforming Japan into a military power capable of dealing with the Americans and Europeans on more equal terms. The Meiji oligarchs quickly dismantled the far-reaching Tokugawa era controls on economic activity, freeing powerful market forces that soon provided a dramatic stimulus to Japan's economic development. Japan's seclusion had already ended with the establishment of foreign treaty ports in 1858. Now the Meiji oligarchs abolished the caste system, abolished the system of feudal suzerains, dispossessed the samurai, and replaced the system of rice taxes payable in kind with a monetary land tax that for the first time in Japan rendered agricultural land alienable. Soon after the implementation of the land tax, the Meiji government was able to forgo inflation, and under the capable direction of the finance ministry by Matsukata Matsuyoshi, secured the convertibility of its currency into silver after 1886 and into gold after 1897. Private commercial banks facilitated the private financing of new industrial enterprises, and in 1885 a central bank the Bank of Japan was founded. Much has been made of the Meiji government's official promotion of industry under the political slogan *kokusan shōgyō* (increase production, encourage industry), but, actually, the government pilot plants established under this set of policies were small elements of the national economy. The spirit of the age was one of *laissez-faire*, not government planning and direction. The first mechanized industry to develop on a large scale in Japan was cotton spinning, and it prospered in the final decade of the nineteenth century with little direct government support.

Another Meiji era (1868–1912) political slogan, *fukoku kyōhei* (rich country, strong army), identifies the central preoccupation of Japanese government leaders near the dawn of the twentieth century: imperialist expansion and warfare. The Sino-Japanese War of 1895 was concluded swiftly with a Japanese victory, and left Japan with colonial possessions (Taiwan and the Pescadores) and a sizable indemnity. Japan's victory in its 1905 war with Russia cost it 100,000 war dead, and required an expenditure of about half of its national income in that year. The Portsmouth treaty ending the conflict conferred no financial indemnity on Japan, but expanded the Japanese empire to include a colony on the southern part of the island of Sakhalin, and internationally recognized spheres of Japanese influence in the Korean peninsula and in China's Kwantung peninsula. Japan annexed Korea in 1910. The following year, the 1858 commercial treaties that had established extra-territorial settlements of foreign traders in Japanese ports and limited Japanese tariff rights were fully retired, bringing to fruition a cherished goal of the Meiji political leaders.

Japan entered World War I as an ally of Britain but managed largely to avoid actual hostilities. Japan took advantage of the world-wide rise in interest rates attending the war by switching from being a net international borrower to being a net lender and expanding aggregate output. The resulting real depreciation of the yen stimulated foreign demand for Japanese goods and switched domestic demand from foreign imports to domestic goods. The business groups known as the *zaibatsu* expanded from their initial strongholds in mining, banking, and brokerage of foreign trade into shipbuilding, iron and steel, and insurance. Nevertheless, the zaibatsu form of organization, in which a few families maintained concentrated ownership in diverse holdings through the pyramiding of shares, was at no time the only viable way of financing and administering businesses in Japan. Cotton-spinning companies were among the largest corporations in Japan in the first decades of the twentieth century and were, for the most part, diversely held joint-stock enterprises. Also, about half the labor force of Japan continued to work as self-employed farmers, and another quarter of the labor force worked in small enterprises.

The 1920s was a time of economic malaise in Japan, partly owing to mistaken macroeconomic policies, but also exacerbated by the 1923 Tokyo earthquake. Japan took important strides toward establishing parliamentary democracy in those years, enjoying alternating rule by two political parties, the conservative Seiyūkai and more liberal Kenseikai–Minsetō. Japan joined Britain and the USA in arms limitation agreements, diplomatic treaties, and the establishment of an open world trading regime anchored by the gold standard. In pursuit of these aims, Japan sought to rejoin the gold standard at the same parity it had maintained from 1897 to 1917. To accomplish this the government authorities had

to reverse the substantial inflation that had occurred in Japan in the intervening years. The Tokyo earthquake dealt a devastating blow to a Japanese economy already seriously weakened by deflationary monetary policies, ultimately leading to a severe banking crisis in 1927. An unwise and unfortunately timed deflationary drive restored Japan's prewar gold parity in January 1930 just as the world-wide great depression began. Then, in September 1931, the Japanese army, without the authorization of Japan's elected government, undertook the occupation of Manchuria, a province of China in which Japan had maintained a sphere of influence since 1905. A Japanese puppet state was quickly established there and the Japanese army set about to experiment with central planning in the province, deriving few lessons from its abject failure.

Under the able counsel of the brilliant Takahasi Korekiyo as finance minister, Japan abruptly abandoned the gold standard in December 1931, and then instituted the expansionary monetary and fiscal policy that effectively insulated Japan from the world-wide great depression; but it was too late. After the assassination of the prime minister in May 1932, the Japanese military insinuated itself into the choosing of prime ministers and cabinets and in conducting Japan's foreign affairs. Democracy and cooperation with Britain and America were effectively ended from that time. Takahashi, too, the "Keynes of Japan", fell before assassins in the failed coup of February 1936. In July 1937 Japan initiated war with China, and the government of Japan began to switch the economy to a war footing, increasing arms purchases dramatically. A series of diplomatic blunders led Japan in 1941 to the disastrous war with the allies which it could not win and which left the Japanese economy in ruins.

For six years and eight months after the war, the government of Japan was completely subservient to that of the United States. This was the period of American Occupation. The Americans drafted a new constitution that permanently established democracy, dissolved the zaibatsu, redistributed agricultural land, and had laws enacted that legitimized labor unions. Additionally, the Americans allowed or directed the continuation of wartime price controls and rationing, embargoes on foreign trade, and inflation-financed subsidies of industrial firms.

Japan's postwar recovery did not begin until

these disastrous policies were suspended as part of America's "reverse course" from a punitive Japan policy toward a reconstructive policy, beginning in 1949. The rapid economic growth of the Japanese economy, from this time until the mid-1970s, is a triumph of unfettered capitalism. The ongoing process of saving and investment eventually restored the stock of wealth that Japan had dissipated in the war. The elevation of the growth path of Japan's aggregate output above the trajectory extrapolated from the prewar years reflects the dramatic enlargement of Japan's national saving rate compared with the prewar era. In fact, Japan's national saving rate continues to be among the world's largest, which accounts for its persistent trade surpluses.

Japan's integration with the world economy

After its opening to trade in 1858, Japan immediately began to export the goods that, before then, had lower prices at home than elsewhere, including silk and tea, and to import the goods that previously had higher prices at home, including cotton and wool, just as Ricardo's theory of comparative advantage would have predicted. Japan's integration into the world economy contributed to the international division of labor and thereby expanded the consumption possibilities of both Japan and other countries.

This continues to be true today. Japan's major imports include the oil and other natural resources that it lacks, and that would surely command high prices in Japan were it to forgo international trade. Similarly, Japan exports manufactures that intensively employ the capital and skilled labor that it has in abundance and, through foreign direct investment in lesser developed nations, exports the services of entrepreneurs and managers that it also has in abundance. Japan is the supreme example today validating the Ricardian theory of comparative advantage.

But this very fact has been viewed by some as anomalous; for the other developed nations, but not Japan, engage in substantial intra-industry trade, the import and export of like products. Intra-industry trade does not comport easily with notions of comparative advantage. If a nation exports the goods that it has relatively low incremental costs of producing, and imports the goods it has high incremental costs of producing, then how can it both export and import like goods? Newer theories point to pursuit of oligopoly profit as a motivation for intra-industry trade. Even if nations have the same incremental costs of producing a good so that none has a comparative advantage, they may still each supply goods in all of the nations' respective markets, simply to capture a share of the profit that accompanies competition among the few.

A lot of intra-industry trade arises as intra-company shipments of *multinational enterprises*, companies that produce goods in more than one nation. Possibly this reflects the fact that multinational enterprises include many of the world's largest companies, and are characteristic of the oligopolistic industries most apt to invite intra-industry trade. One reason for the small extent of Japan's intra-industry trade is that foreign multinational enterprises control relatively few assets in Japan. The Japanese government once restricted foreign control of domestic assets, but that policy ended with enactment of the Foreign Exchange and Investment Control Law of 1980. The limited presence of foreign multinationals in Japan now, almost two decades after *de jure* restrictions on inward foreign direct investment were lifted, mostly reflects the fact that peculiarities of the Japanese language and culture make it a difficult place for foreigners to live and work. Government protectionism has little to do with Japan's low stock of inward foreign direct investment or the small extent of its intra-industry trade.

Protectionist interferences with trade generally constrict a nation's consumption possibilities, even though they enrich the protected industry. Protectionism is, on net, harmful to the nation that imposes it, and thus represents the triumph of a narrow special interest over the broader national interest. Special interests seeking protection are more likely to prevail in industry-by-industry referenda than in economy-wide referenda. This is why international treaties were necessary to prevail upon Japan and the other developed nations to reduce their tariff rates; the treaties broadened the political question of free trade versus protection in a way that undercut the special interests within each nation. As a full participant in the rounds of multilateral agreements to reduce tariff rates, Japan has joined the developed nations in liberalizing its trade policies. The continuing instances of protectionism by Japan have analogues in other nations. For instance, Japan's restrictions on rice imports can be compared to America's restrictions on sugar imports. The sad saga of Japan–USA trade friction is not about Japan's "closed" markets or "unfair" practices: it is about how best to deal with or deflect the political pressure inside the USA for protection from expanded Japanese imports. Partly, the expanded imports from Japan have reflected the rapid growth of Japan's economy. But the most vituperative trade disputes between Japan and the USA surfaced in 1985, after several years in which extreme real appreciation of the US dollar relative to the yen had added further stimulus to American purchases of Japanese goods.

Nations gain not only from their exchange of one another's commodities and services, but also from their exchange of claims on one another's future incomes, sometimes referred to as *intertemporal trade*. A nation's extent of intertemporal trade equals its imbalance of trade in commodities and services. If a nation exports more than it imports, then it necessarily accumulates claims on the future incomes of foreigners, for the exports had to have been exchanged for something. The converse is also true. One expects a nation such as Japan with a high national saving rate to accumulate foreign assets, that is, to lend to other nations or accumulate IOUs issued by trading partners, and so to export more than it imports, incurring a trade surplus, as indeed Japan now does. In the past, Japan, like other countries, has also resorted to foreign borrowing, and has incurred temporary trade deficits, to maintain consumption when confronted with the windfall losses of a natural disaster such as the 1923 Tokyo earthquake or an event such as the first oil shock. Some adjustments of trade balances reflect not autonomous shifts such as these in nations' propensities to save, but prior movements in exchange rates. Economists have not succeeded very well in explaining short-term movements in exchange rates, but they have had a little more success in identifying the underlying bases for long-term trends in exchange rates. For instance, the gradual real appreciation of the yen relative to the US dollar which was evident throughout the 1950s and 1960s exemplifies a phenomenon known as the *Balassa–Samuelson effect*. Short-term movements in exchange rates are a lot less well understood. Probably they exhibit the influence of macroeconomic policies, but often in a somewhat complicated way. Exchange rate movements do bring about consistent changes in trade balances but with a lag of up to two years. For instance, the very sharp real depreciation of the yen relative to the dollar since 1996 is likely soon to precipitate enlarged exports from Japan to the USA, and renewed pressures for protectionism by US industries that compete with Japanese imports.

Government policies and their effects

Monetary and fiscal policy, trade policy, public spending, environmental policy, government regulation, and other government policies are significant elements of any nation's economy, and Japan is no exception. That said, the government of Japan has a smaller presence in its economy than is often recognized. Government employees comprise a mere 6 percent of Japan's labor force. With the recent privatization of telecommunications and the national railway, there no longer exist large public enterprises in Japan. Government spending, including transfers, amounts to about one-third of the nation's aggregate output, which is comparable to the USA and less than for many of the European nations. The national government in Japan controls almost all public expenditures either directly or indirectly. Centralization of control economizes on administrative costs but limits the range of choices available to citizens willing to move from one local jurisdiction to another. The objects of public expenditure are largely the same in Japan as in other nations. They include defense, education, health insurance, and social security pensions.

The scale of the public sector is a measure of only one dimension of government's role in the economy. Another dimension is regulation, the setting of rules that private firms must obey. There is little that is extraordinary about the government regulation of industry in Japan. The national government has asserted explicit control over the pricing and entry of firms in the public utilities, transport, telecommunications, and financial services industries, as have almost all other nations of the world. Antimonopoly law pertains to firms in all industries. Japan's anti-monopoly law is a legacy of the American Occupation, and has survived to the present day but without the vigorous support of the elected governments. Resources devoted to the enforcement of anti-monopoly laws are limited and penalties for violations are quite small. It is fair to say that anti-monopoly law has imposed fewer constraints on the practices of corporations in Japan than in the USA. Furthermore, the patent laws of Japan afford only weak protection for inventions, promote the early revelation of discoveries, and encourage the licensing of inventions on terms favorable to users. All of this is quite sensible from the point of view of promoting the rapid diffusion within Japan of foreign innovations and, perhaps for that reason, was optimal, given the country's status as a late developer.

The preceding remarks are quite at variance with the popular notion that a coterie of elite government bureaucrats direct the allocation of resources in Japan's economy. Proponents of that view focus particular attention on the public-sector financial intermediaries of Japan. The postal saving system of Japan, founded in 1875, allows individuals to make time deposits and purchase life insurance at post office establishments throughout the country. It may be the largest depository institution in the world. Postal savings deposits now comprise a whopping 20 percent of households' financial assets in Japan. In a process known as the Fiscal Investment and Loan Program, these postal deposits and other public funds are transferred to government financial institutions, including the Japan Development Bank and the Export–Import Bank of Japan, which issue loans to local governments and to private businesses. By manipulating the process just described, it seems that the government of Japan might have redirected the allocation of loanable funds toward favored industries that would have been shunned by profit-seeking financial intermediaries. Favored sectors in Japan have also enjoyed special tax breaks and subsidies, and special exemptions from anti-monopoly laws, but these have not really had much bite. During the 1950s, and continuing until 1964, comprehensive foreign exchange rationing conferred *de facto* government control of the pattern of imports into Japan. This control was exercised by the Ministry of International Trade and Industry, the same ministry that directs the policies of the key government financial intermediaries.

This is what the much vaunted industrial policy of Japan really amounts to, which is to say, it doesn't amount to much. The Japanese industries that have benefited the most from public loans, other subsidies, and protectionism are mostly politically powerful but economically anemic ones such as coal mining, textiles, and shipbuilding. Japan has prospered in spite of government experiments with industrial policy, not because of them.

The record of monetary and fiscal policy in Japan includes both successes and failures. Japan has endured twelve business recessions since 1950, temporary downward deviations from the economy's long-term growth path. They have almost all been growth recessions. That is, aggregate output continued to rise, but at a temporarily slower rate. Avoiding all of these recessions would have been equivalent to about a 1 percent permanent rise in Japan's national income. To put this in perspective, consider that technological advance accomplishes two or three times more than this every year in Japan.

The overall picture here is that Japan's macroeconomic policy has been a stunning success. But there have been mistakes. Contractions in the rate of growth of the money supply in Japan have invariably been followed by downturns in the growth of aggregate output. Such monetary contractions are perfectly avoidable and should be judged policy mistakes whenever they occur. Japan's Heisei recession, which so weakened the asset positions of commercial banks there, followed the unnecessary and sharp monetary contraction of 1990 directed by the Bank of Japan governor Mieno.

Economic institutions and practices peculiar to Japan

A lot of the fascination with Japan's economy, and the greatest challenge for economists, arises from the many unique institutions and practices, and peculiar features, of the Japanese economy. These include the Japanese employment system (lifetime employment, seniority-based wages, and enterprise unions), the self-organization of Japanese firms into business groups, the special arrangements between Japanese banks and their client firms, and the complex and fragmented Japanese marketing system. Satisfying economic explanations for such structures can take a variety of different forms. They can relate the peculiarities to underlying givens like geography. They can identify the apparent peculiarities as somewhat illusory, in the sense that the Japanese arrangements solve a universal problem in a no less satisfactory way than alternatives might. And finally, they can relate the peculiarities to a confluence of historical events unique to Japan. The best explanations fit more than one of these patterns.

Japan's distribution system, though frequently labeled "inefficient", manifestly is not. Japan's proliferation of small stores reflects its geography. The ubiquity of stores affords households the added convenience of next-door shopping, which they particularly value because it enables them to shop frequently, maintain low household stocks of daily necessities, and economize on scarce living space. Japan's distribution system evolved this way, in part, because the geographic centricity of the country means that the added costs of restocking a superabundance of small stores, as opposed to a smaller number of large ones, are relatively small. From these pivotal observations many others follow. For instance, the large number of small retail shops, and shopowners, tipped the political balance in favor of regulations protecting small stores from competition with larger ones. Japan's Large Store Law, which placed significant legal obstacles to the opening of stores with large floor space, contributed further toward the proliferation of small stores, but probably would not have been tolerated in Japan if it had imposed very large costs or tended to run counter to the economic forces already shaping Japan's distribution sector. The complexity of marketing channels in Japan, for instance the large number of wholesale steps, is also derivative of the ubiquity of small stores; explain the one, and the other follows.

The employment practices that pertain to the regular male employees of the large companies, about one-third of Japan's labor force, represent a sophisticated response to the universal problems inherent in recruiting, training, organizing, and motivating workers. These practices include seniority-based pay and promotion ladders, mandatory retirement, and on-the-job training. The seniority-based pay schemes discourage quits and, at the same time, enlarge the onerousness to employees of early dismissal, which enables the employers to economize on the costs of training workers in company-specific skills, while preserving performance incentives. Training in company-specific skills became valuable and prevalent in postwar Japan partly because rapid

innovation outpaced the formal system of general education and led each company to develop its own idiosyncratic ways of doing things. Other features of Japan's labor markets follow from the ones just noted. For instance, Japan's low unemployment rates largely reflect the infrequency with which the regular male employees of the large companies experience bouts of unemployment. The organization of workers into enterprise unions rather than industry-wide unions has also received some encouragement from the strong attachments of workers to their incumbent employers.

In Japan, banks have long played a dominant role in financial intermediation, collecting deposits from households and extending loans to private businesses and to government. In the USA and some other nations, securities markets are a more important source of funds and banks less important. Here the Japanese peculiarity may be less consequential than is often supposed. The universal problems that financial intermediaries must face invite a range of possible solutions, none necessarily superior to the others. Government regulations play an important role in determining which specific arrangements emerge in any particular nation, but there is a fundamental arbitrariness to it, in the sense that one set of arrangements solves the problems about as well as some others might have done. The dominant role of banks in Japanese financial intermediation owes a lot to government regulations that effectively cartelized and protected the banks, but insured deposits. When Japanese regulatory constraints on euromarket finance were lifted in the mid-1980s, the Japanese domestic banking cartel began to unravel. With decartelization, Japanese banks' profits eroded and their lending grew reckless. This was particularly so under the expansionary Japanese monetary policy following the February 1987 Louvre Accord. The resulting run-up in asset prices in 1988–9 was followed by a crash in 1990–1 that left the Japanese banks' net worth in a precarious state. And the 1990s slowdown in macroeconomic growth and investment has worsened the situation of Japanese commercial banks still further. In spite of all this, bank loans remain the most important source of external funds to Japanese businesses. Even though Japanese companies are now relatively free to issue securities rather than only relying on bank loans for funds, many of them have nevertheless retained their strong attachments to particular banks. Japanese banks are apparently able, in an economical fashion, to intermediate funds to their important client firms, with whom they have developed close relationships over the years.

The self-organization of Japanese firms into business groups originated with the zaibatsu. The zaibatsu were vast commercial empires, each controlled by a wealthy family through the pyramiding of closely held shares; they reached their fullest development soon after World War I. The zaibatsu represented a form of corporate governance, highly effective and successful in some industries, but absent and apparently unnecessary in others, for example cotton-spinning. With the appropriation and disbursal of the zaibatsu founding families' shares by the American Occupation government of Japan, the zaibatsu were dissolved. But when the Occupation ended, the constituent member firms of the old zaibatsu soon re-established their former alliances. The members of each one of the new groups, called *financial keiretsu*, traded with one another and were linked by cross-shareholding. With the demise of the zaibatsu founding families, the large banks now insinuated themselves into the governance of the former zaibatsu member corporations. Perhaps this was natural, given the important role of the banks as suppliers of funds to the companies, as discussed above.

A final comment

Courses on the centrally planned economies of the Soviet bloc were once a regular fixture of the economics curriculum at American colleges and universities, but the breakup of the Soviet Union and demise of central planning eroded student interest in these courses and caused their enrollments to plummet. Courses on the Japanese economy can, and should, fill that void in the curriculum. Japan—because of its unique history, its prolonged and strained process of integration with the world economy, its varied government policies, and its peculiar economic practices and institutions—now represents the best foil for the comparative study of American and European economies. Courses on Japan that are firmly grounded in mainstream economics are also the essential antidote to the rampant nonsense about the Japanese economy that is prevalent at present and often seems rooted in nothing more substantial than air.

Incomes and Welfare of the Japanese Today

1

A surprisingly wide range of opinions abounds concerning the economic well-being of the Japanese compared with the citizens of other countries. This reflects in part the ambiguities inherent in all measures of economic well-being, of which national income and GDP may be the most familiar but are by no means perfectly satisfactory. Japan's national income per person is now comparable to that of the USA and Western European countries evaluated at current exchange rates; but so what? Social critics both inside and outside of Japan are fond of pointing out that, in spite of high GDP, the Japanese still enjoy less leisure time, have fewer parks, spend longer hours commuting, and generally live in less satisfactory dwellings than do citizens of many other countries. Running counter to these criticisms are the long life expectancy of the Japanese, the low incidence of crime, and the relatively low expenditures for national defense, which have seemed not to impair Japan's security.

What is the correct interpretation of national income statistics, and what do such statistics omit or overlook? Furthermore, are meaningful comparisons of the economic welfare of Japan and other nations even possible?

GDP and National Income

The starting points for assessing economic welfare are the national income and product accounts, which are tabulated by many countries including Japan using comparable methods. *Gross domestic product* (GDP) is the value at current market prices of all final goods and services produced by a nation in a given year. Here, the nation is defined as encompassed by the geographic borders. *Gross national product* (GNP) is the analogue of GDP corresponding to the definition of the nation as the citizens of the country, whether or not resident within the country's borders. We shall refer alternatively to GDP and GNP as is convenient; as a practical matter, the figures do not differ much. The restriction to final sales is to avoid a problem of double counting that would arise if intermediate transactions were aggregated. For example, wheat is sold first to the miller, then as flour is sold to the baker, and finally as bread is sold to the household; only the final sale—that of the bread—needs to be included for a complete accounting.

Spending for final sales of goods and services (spending on domestic output by citizens, government, and foreigners) either contributes to the maintenance of existing production facilities, or contributes to the payment of sales taxes (or other indirect taxes), or contributes to the incomes of citizens from whom goods are purchased.[1] *National income*, the income of all citizens, is therefore computed by subtracting depreciation expenses and indirect taxes (net of subsidies) from gross domestic product. In fact, national income and gross domestic product are highly correlated from one year to

---

[1] To be complete we must add to this list unilateral transfers to foreigners. These include foreign aid payments. In relation to GDP this is trivial for Japan, for example 2/371 in 1988.

the next and in macroeconomic theories the distinction between the two is seldom important. Here we will follow convention and presume that the two are opposite views of the same economic activities. As commonly stated, "spending by one is income for another".

Spending is either for consumption, investment, or accumulation of foreign wealth

National income is disposed as either consumption, investment, or purchase of foreign assets. That is, either it is traded for goods and services used up by households in the immediate period (consumption); or it is used to accumulate machines, tools, and other durables that will add to the economy's capacity to produce goods and services in future periods (investment); or it is used to buy land, property, or securities from foreigners (accumulation of foreign wealth).

In the national income and product accounts, spending by businesses for final goods and household spending for new houses is labeled investment while other spending by households is labeled consumption. Most consumption services of houses arise from spending in earlier periods. Consequently a price must be imputed to the services of owner-occupied housing. A similar imperfect imputation could be made for other household durables but in the official statistics of Japan (and other nations) is not.

In the national income and product accounts of Japan, government purchases of final goods are identified as either consumption or investment, but in the accounts of the USA (until quite recently) and many other countries, such an explicit allocation of government purchases is not indicated. Of course, individual researchers may make their own conjectures about the extent of government purchases that should be counted as investment and consumption. In the Japanese national accounts, government purchases of buildings, roads, and other public works are counted as investment, while purchases for national defense and compensation of government employees are counted as consumption.

It may seem a bit odd to count defense spending as consumption; military weapons purchased in one year will presumably continue to be used to deter foreign attacks in future years. These purchases thus represent investments in an economic sense, rather than consumption. The reason for treating the entirety of defense spending as consumption in Japan's national accounts is that the national government is prevented by law from issuing bonds in excess of that needed to finance investment (kensetsu, lit. construction), except in extraordinary circumstances. Counting defense spending as consumption thus nominally restrains appropriations for defense.[2] The point here is that the economic distinction between consumption and investment in principle guides the presentation of national income accounts, but in fact it does so only imperfectly. The relationship among the various components of national income and gross domestic product is indicated in Figure 1.1 on page 12.

Investment contributes to sustainable consumption

The level of economic well-being inherent in the national income and product accounts is the portion of national income devoted to consumption. Investment of course raises the possible future level of consumption; but, by an argument we will encounter in Chapter 4, an economy can be expected to approach a steady state in which consumption per person either no longer changes or rises only with technological advance. In this argument higher fractions of national income devoted to investment will sustain higher steady-state levels of consumption. Japan's high saving rate and correspondingly high investment rate enables a higher sustainable consumption level. To argue as some have that Japan's high saving lowers economic well-being because it takes away from immediate consumption is to adopt a myopic view that places little weight on future consumption possibilities.

Consumption levels and national income

Table 1.1 reports the per capita GDP of Japan and other countries for 1996, partitioned into consumption and saving according to similar principles. Of

2 In fact, in every year since 1974 the national government has issued bonds in excess of that needed for investment. Special deficit-covering bonds had to be authorized in each year by the Diet. It seems that extraordinary circumstances have in fact become ordinary.

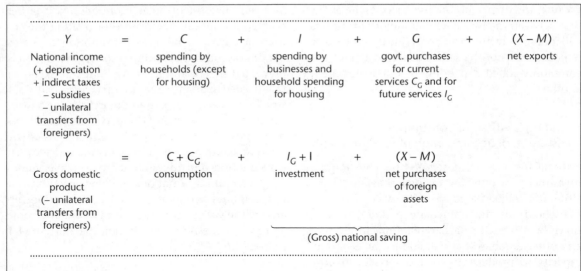

Figure 1.1. The basic equations of the national income and product accounts

course, the national income accounts are computed in the domestic currency of each respective country. International comparisons of consumption per person based on these accounts must make some assumption about the rate of conversion between currencies. The simplest procedure is to use current exchange rates, and that is what we have done in the first column of the table.

This procedure (conversion at current exchange rates) is justified by the *purchasing power parity (PPP) thesis*. Under the strongest form of this thesis, the price of each good will be the same in all countries that trade freely with one another if reckoned in the currency units of any one of the countries using current exchange rates. In a trivial sense the PPP thesis is true, for divergences from PPP can always be associated with some barrier to trade that is the result of either government interferences with trade

Table 1.1. Gross domestic product per capita and its composition, Japan and selected other nations, 1996

Country	Exchange rate	Y^a ($)	C (%)	C_G (%)	I_G (%)	I (%)	X (%)	M (%)
JAPAN	108.8 ¥/$	36,535	59.8	9.8	9.1	20.8	9.9	9.4
USA		28,755	68.2	15.5	2.9	14.6	11.4	12.6
Germany	1.505 DM/$	28,736	57.6	19.6	2.3	19.2	24.3	23.0
UK	0.641 £/$	19,700	63.8	21.0	1.4	14.5	29.3	30.0
France	5.116 Fr/$	26,361	60.6	19.6	3.1	14.1	24.0	21.4
Italy	1543 Lr/$	21,126	62.2	16.6	n.a.	n.a.	38.3	35.3
Canada	1.364 C$/$	19,520	60.5	18.6	2.1	15.6	38.3	35.3
OECD[b]		18,577	63.7	15.7	n.a.	n.a.	20.0	19.6

[a] Y = GDP per person. $C + C_G + I_G + I + X - M$ differs slightly from 100% of Y because of rounding errors.

[b] The Organisation for Economic Cooperation and Development is a consortium of 25 of the developed countries including the seven also listed here separately, the "G–7".

Sources: exchange rates: OECD Economic Outlook, no. 61 (June 1997), table a37, p. a40; *population: OECD Quarterly Labour Force Statistics*, no. 3 (1997), p. 96; *GDP and its composition: OECD Quarterly National Accounts*, no. 2 (1997).

or natural impediments. Consumption activities that use land tend to have higher relative prices within Japan than elsewhere, which is no doubt a reflection of the obvious difficulties of international trade in these items.

Comparison of national incomes or consumption levels converted into common currency units at current exchange rates imperfectly accounts for the cross-country differences in relative prices. For instance, the dramatic appreciation in the yen from 260 yen/dollar in 1985 to 135 yen/dollar in 1990, a period in which domestic inflation rates in Japan and the USA were roughly the same, certainly did not have a great effect on the relative consumption possibilities ("purchasing power") of Japanese and Americans. There are many consumption goods in both countries that are not easily traded internationally. This fall in the yen price of dollars meant a fall in the yen prices of goods that Japanese bought from Americans relative to the yen prices of goods in Japan not traded internationally, including land. The rise in Japanese purchasing power was not as great as if yen prices of all goods bought by the Japanese had fallen in the same proportion as the change in the exchange rate.

Real income indices and revealed preferences

Another way of ranking the consumption possibilities of citizens of different countries is to determine for the representative citizen of each whether her income is sufficient to have purchased a comparable consumption bundle to that chosen by the others given the prices in her own country. If another's chosen bundle was attainable, then the one reveals by her choice a preference for her own bundle. If for example an American could have purchased a similar consumption bundle to that chosen by the Japanese but did not, then the American must prefer her own bundle. This procedure requires us to determine the value of each one's consumption bundle in the domestic prices of every other country. Kravis, Heston, and Summers have done this for 34 countries including Japan in 1975 and for 60 countries, again including Japan, in 1980.[3] Some of the data from the earlier study are depicted in Table 1.2.

In 1975 the representative Japanese could have

Table 1.2. Revealed preferences, 1975

Country	Value of Japanese bundle at prices of respective country ÷ income of respective country	Value of foreign bundle at Japanese prices ÷ Japanese income
Revealed preferred to Japanese bundle		
USA	0.76	1.70
West Germany	0.87	1.36
France	0.86	1.48
Ambiguous		
Spain	1.33	1.03
Italy	1.25	1.00
UK	1.10	1.15
Revealed dispreferred to Japanese bundle		
Ireland	1.74	0.80

Source: Irving B. Kravis, Alan Heston, and Robert Summers, *World Product and Income: International Comparisons of Real Gross Product*, Johns Hopkins University Press, 1982, table 76–2, pp. 230–1.

purchased the consumption bundles of Ireland, but not those of the USA, UK, Germany, France, Italy, or Spain. (For instance, the value of the US bundle at Japanese prices was 1.70 times that of the Japanese bundle.) But neither could the representative citizen of Italy, Ireland, the UK, or Spain have purchased the consumption bundle of the Japanese. The USA, Germany, and France could have purchased the Japanese bundle. (For instance, at US prices the value of the Japanese bundle was 75.5 percent the value of the US one.) From this we conclude that the representative citizens of the USA, France, and Germany each had a revealed preference for his bundle over that of the Japanese. The representative Japanese had a revealed preference for her bundle over that of the representative Irishman. But the representative Japanese did not reveal a preference for her bundle over that of the Italian, Spaniard, or Britishman; nor vice versa.

It could have happened that this procedure would

---

[3] Irving B. Kravis, Alan Heston, and Robert Summers, *World Product and Income, International Comparisons of Real Gross Product*, Johns Hopkins University Press, 1982; and UN and Commission of the European Communities, *World Comparison of Purchasing Power and Real Product for 1980* (Phase IV of the International Comparison Project), Part One: *Summary Results for 60 Countries, 1986*, and Part Two: *Detailed Results for 60 Countries, 1987*.

have produced the startling conclusion that the representative citizens of two countries each had a revealed preference for their own chosen bundle over that of the other. This would indicate a difference in tastes. In fact, Kravis *et al.* found little evidence of taste differences between any of the pairs.

The index number problem

The ambiguous comparisons (in 1975) for Japan and Italy, Japan and Spain, and Japan and the UK reflect what is called the *index number problem*. This is the problem or impossibility of constructing a single statistic or index based only on the quantities and prices of the goods that will in all cases correctly rank consumption bundles in order of preference. That the representative Japanese cannot have purchased the Italian bundle does not allow us to infer whether she prefers the Italian bundle or her own.

Too much has been made of the fact that exactly duplicating American standards of suburban living in Japan is beyond the means of all but the very wealthiest Japanese. For it may well be the case that the reverse is also true: exactly duplicating the Japanese bundle while in the USA may be beyond the means of most Americans. In each country some items are relatively more scarce than in the other country. In Japan, compared with the USA and other countries, consumption activities that use land tend to be relatively scarce. On the other hand, items of consumption that are relatively less scarce (can be obtained at lower real marginal cost) in Japan than elsewhere include public health and safety, public order, and national defense.

Substitution

Scarcity of some goods relative to others can be offset in inventive ways. In Japan land is scarce and expensive, but the Japanese economize by living in smaller dwellings than they would if land were less scarce, and by keeping smaller stocks of food and daily necessities but making more frequent shopping trips. Further economies are achieved by conducting social activities in shared spaces outside the home, either at eating and drinking establishments or the workplace. Except for these substitutions, both in production—substitution of shopping time for household storage space—and in consumption—

substitution of social activates in shared spaces outside the home for social activates at home—the Japanese would feel the pinch of land scarcity far more than they do.

Many cultural differences between the Japanese way of daily life and that of Americans and others are merely time-honored ways of adapting to persistent scarcity of land and other goods, and are not, as it might superficially appear, the result of fundamental differences in preferences.[4] For instance, most Japanese sleep on futons that are folded and put away each morning, rather than on beds that permanently occupy space. The futons allow the same space that is used for sleeping at night to be used for other activities during the day. The traditional diet, which derives protein from soybeans, fish, or sea products, is a natural adaptation to the scarcity of red meat in a mountainous island nation with little pasture land. The beautiful but compact Japanese garden and miniature bonsai afford a touch of nature but without occupying much space. The ubiquitous coffee shops and small bars and restaurants enable social activities to use shared public spaces, further economizing on scarce land. All the cultural items just mentioned and perhaps others as well are examples of substitution in response to relative scarcity. For instance, Susan Hanley even goes so far as to suggest that the ubiquity in Japan of multigenerational living arrangements and relatively small family sizes are further adaptations to the scarcity of space.[5]

Nonmarket goods

Comparison of the Japanese consumption bundle with those of other countries based on national income and product accounts encompasses only market goods, including those purchased by governments. Many important contributors to economic well-being are omitted in such a comparison. These are *nonmarket goods*, goods that are enjoyed but not

---

[4] For a formal statement of this view of culture, see Gary Becker and George Stigler, "De Gustibus Est Non Disputandum", *American Economic Review*, vol. 67, no. 2 (March 1977), pp. 76–90.

[5] Susan B. Hanley, "Traditional Housing and Unique Lifestyles: The Unintended Outcomes of Japan's Land Policy", in John O. Haley and Kozo Yamamura (eds.), *Land Issues in Japan: A Policy Failure?* Society for Japanese Studies, 1992, pp. 195–222.

bought and sold. Though such goods are not traded directly, actions can result in their diminution and augmentation and the goods are in that sense objects of choice. The most important nonmarket goods are household production, leisure, and amenities.

Household production

"Household production" refers to goods produced and consumed within the household. These include preparation of meals at home, child-rearing, care of aged parents at home, cleaning one's own house, shopping, and so on. Notice that only goods consumed at home as well as produced there are nonmarket goods. Commuting to work is among the productive activities of households, but it does not directly result in consumption. Commuting to work is an intermediate good rather than a final one. The other examples of household production just mentioned are final goods, but they are nonmarket goods. They are not traded directly and are not included in GNP in any way, a significant omission.

Amenities

"Amenities" are present in the environment, and are not the result of human artifice. These are sunshine, beautiful scenery, clean air, and the like. There is a growing awareness that human actions are eroding amenities. The process of urbanization and industrialization converts natural areas into displeasing pollution zones. Amenities are scarce goods. Their presence contributes to economic well-being and their diminution erodes it. But they are nonmarket goods, neither produced nor traded directly and not counted as income in the national income and product accounts. Environmental damage reduces economic well-being but does not reduce the GDP.

Leisure

"Leisure" is idleness from economic pursuits. Leisure is valued just as commodities are. One may have more commodities and less leisure and consider oneself worse off than before. The national income and product accounts measure the economic value of commodities only, not leisure.

Shadow prices of nonmarket goods

Nonmarket goods are traded only in a very indirect or roundabout fashion, so their prices too can only be observed indirectly. These "shadow prices" are the marginal values that optimizing individuals place on the nonmarket goods.

Home production is gauged to economize on the household resources. One decides to clean or shop for one's self or one's family on consideration of the price of paying someone else to do it. The principle cost of home production is forgone leisure, which is itself a nonmarket good.

Leisure itself may be had only at the sacrifice of other goods. More leisure means less of other goods are produced. The shadow price of leisure is the value of output lost when an increment of labor is withheld either from home production or from outside employment, what economists call the *value of marginal product of labor*. In the competitive economy the wage rate also equals the value of marginal product of labor. For this reason, the shadow price of leisure and of home production can be approximated by wage rates.

Amenities would seem to entail no choice and thus command no price in any meaningful sense. What is the price of a beautiful day? But in fact, even beautiful days have a price. Some geographic regions have more sunshine than others. As the pursuit of sunshine congests these areas, the price of land there is bid up and the wages are driven down. Migration will cease only when the marginal individual finds all living places and their attending employment opportunities equally agreeable, given the land prices and wages. The places with more amenities will come to have higher land prices and lower wages than those lacking amenities. From these compensating differentials in land prices and wages, one can infer the marginal values that individuals place on the amenities. These represent the hypothetical contribution to economic well-being that would result if amenities could be augmented so that there were fewer rainy days or cleaner air. Using this method, Blomquist, Berger, and Hoehn find that in the United States the shadow price of reducing average humidity by 1 percent is $30 a year, that of raising sunshine by 1 percent is $309 a year, that of being on a coastline is $100 a year, and so on.[6]

---

6 Glenn C. Blomquist, Mark C. Berger, and John Hoehn, "New Estimates of Quality of Life in Urban Areas", *American Economic Review*, vol. 88 (March 1988), pp. 89–107.

Comparing the value of nonmarket goods in Japan and the United States

Much of what has been written about the quality of life in Japan compared with other countries amounts to an enumeration of nonmarket goods in Japan and elsewhere.[7] Such lists are informative but difficult to incorporate into systematic evaluations of overall economic well-being. For this it is necessary to construct shadow prices of the nonmarket goods. There have been two careful attempts to consider the contribution of nonmarket goods to economic well-being in the USA: one by Nordhause and Tobin,[8] and the other by Eisner.[9]

Nordhause and Tobin proposed adjustments to the national income and product accounts to reflect the economic value of nonmarket goods. These adjustments include an imputation of the value of household services, the value of leisure, the opportunity costs of educating students, and changes in the value of environmental amenities (which they infer as the difference in wage rates between urban and rural places). Their adjustment for annual degradation of the environment amounts to 6 percent of GNP. They also propose elimination of the US defense budget from the national product on the grounds that it represents procurement of intermediate goods only.

Eisner proposed a different set of adjustments from those of Nordhause and Tobin but in the same general spirit. Eisner makes no adjustment for the eroding value of amenities. He does impute an opportunity cost to student education and household work. Eisner treats the defense budget as only partly intermediate.

The Nordhause–Tobin attribution of a large negative value to amenities is not well supported by the Blomquist *et al.* study mentioned previously. In that study the average value of all amenities studied was a mere $186 per year, and these included the incidence of crime and the quality of public schools, which are related to government provision of services, not "amenities". The range of amenity values across locales was in fact great, however—from –$1,857 per year for the worst (East St Louis, Illinois) to $3,289 per year for the best (Pueblo, Colorado).

Similar adjustments for Japan to the Nordhause–Tobin and Eisner ones for the USA produce quantitatively similar additions to the estimated national income (see Table 1.3). Some differences may nevertheless be worth noting. First, the Japanese have apparently enjoyed fewer leisure hours. Leisure is a normal good. As people become wealthier they demand more of it. Over the decades, the average work week has gradually shrunk in all the developed economies, more in the USA than elsewhere. In Japan the typical work week still includes Saturday morning. F. Thomas Juster and Frank P. Stafford have accumulated data on the allocation of time across countries which is reported in Table 1.4. It is apparent from the figures in the table that Japanese men and women both enjoy about one hour less of leisure each week than do American men and women.

Table 1.3. Estimated value of nonmarket goods as a percentage of GNP, Japan and the United States

	USA		Japan
	Nordhause and Tobin 1965	Eisner 1981	Kanamori–Muto 1980
Household production			
Household chores	48%	33%	11%
Student time		10%	
Leisure	101%		28%
Amenities	–6%		–5%

Sources: William D. Nordhause and James Tobin, "Is Growth Obsolete?" in NBER Fiftieth Anniversary Colloquia Series, *Economic Research: Retrospect and Prospect*, v, *Economic Growth*, Columbia University Press, 1972; Robert Eisner, "The Total Income System of Accounts", *Survey of Current Business*, vol. 65, no. 1 (January 1985), pp. 24–35; Hisao Kanamori, "Japanese Economic Growth and Economic Welfare", in Sheigeto Tsuru (ed.), *Growth and Resources Problems Related to Japan*, New York: St Martin's Press, 1980 (updated to 1980 by Hiromichi Muto *et al.*, "Nihon no keizai seicho to fukushi", in Futo *et al.*, *Sofutoka to GNP tokei: sofutonomkusu shirizu*, vol. 2, Tokyo: Okurasho, 1985).

[7] See e.g. Naomi Maruo, "The Levels of Living and Welfare in Japan Reexamined", *Japanese Economic Studies*, vol. 8, no. 1 (Fall 1979), pp. 42–93.

[8] William D. Nordhause and James Tobin, "Is Growth Obsolete?" in *NBER Fiftieth Anniversary Colloquia Series, Economic Research: Retrospect and Prospect*, v, *Economic Growth*, Columbia University Press, 1972.

[9] Robert Eisner, "The Total Income System of Accounts", *Survey of Current Business*, vol. 65, no. 1 (January 1985), pp. 24–35. For a critique of Eisner's analysis, see Richard Ruggles, "Review of *The Total Incomes System of Accounts* by Robert Eisner", *Review of Income and Wealth*, series 37, no. 4 (December 1991).

Table 1.4. Hours per week devoted to various activities by men and women in Japan, Sweden, and the United States in the 1980s

Activity	Men			Women		
	USA 1981	Japan 1985	Sweden 1984	USA 1981	Japan 1985	Sweden 1984
Total work	57.8	55.5	57.9	54.4	55.6	55.5
Market work	44.0	52.0	39.8	23.9	24.6	23.7
Commuting	3.5	4.5	3.8	2.0	1.2	2.1
Housework	13.8	3.5	18.1	30.5	31.0	31.8
Personal care	68.2	72.4	70.9	71.6	72.1	73.8
Sleep	57.9	60.0	55.3	59.9	57.0	56.9
Leisure	41.8	40.3	39.0	41.9	40.3	38.5
Adult education	0.6	1.2	1.0	0.4	2.2	1.0
Social intercourse	14.9	8.0	9.6	17.6	7.0	11.2
Active leisure	5.6	5.3	7.2	4.2	3.6	8.4
Passive leisure	20.8	25.5	21.2	19.8	27.5	17.9
TV	12.7	17.3	13.4	11.5	21.4	10.8
Total	168.0	168.0	168.0	168.0	168.0	168.0

Source: F. Thomas Juster and Frank P. Stafford, "The Allocation of Time: Empirical Findings, Behavioral Models, and Problems of Measurement", *Journal of Economic Literature*, vol. 29, no. 2, pp. 471–522, table 1, p. 475. (The primary sources for these data are surveys conducted either by official government organs or by private researchers; for instance, the Japanese data are drawn from the NHK survey of time allocation.)

Second, household production may in some ways be more significant in Japan. A relatively large fraction of Japanese women who participate in the labor force are employed in small family businesses that are often complementary with home production. A further indication of significant home production is the larger percentage of the aged cared for at home by their grown children. In Japan, as in the USA, payments to retirement homes add to the national income as reported in the national income and product accounts, but care for the aged at home is a nonmarket good and is not reflected. This omission is more serious for Japan than for the USA or other countries. In spite of this, the estimate of value of household production in Japan produced by Kanamori and Muto is less than those for the USA produced by Nordhause and Tobin and by Eisner. The reason is that Muto has adopted a much less expansive definition of household production. Muto considers only full-time housewives as performing any household production, whereas Eisner and Nordhause and Tobin count all time devoted to household production activities by all persons in the economy, including those who are employed, or

are unmarried, and of all ages and both sexes. Notice in Table 1.4 the dramatic imbalance of time devoted to housework by men and women in Japan—31 hours per week for women compared with just 3.5 hours per week for men. American men performed 13.8 hours per week compared to American women's 30.5 hours per week. Notice the implication that American men and women together devote more hours to housework than do Japanese men and women together.

Other items of home production tend to be smaller in Japan than in the USA and elsewhere. The ubiquity of stores in Japan shifts some costs of household storage and shopping from the households to the retail sector. Trips to the store are more costly in the USA because of the relative paucity of stores, yet shopping time is not reflected in the national income accounts. Presumably, time devoted to shopping is included in "housework" in the Juster–Stafford data of Table 1.4.

Third, the amenities are most seriously eroded by urban congestion. A somewhat higher fraction of Japan's population resides in cities. Perhaps this implies that the representative Japanese enjoys fewer amenities than does the representative American. Neglecting the value of urban amenities would then overstate Japan's relative economic well-being. (A study of the shadow prices of urban amenities in Japan using similar methods to that of the Blomquist *et al.* study for the USA, however, finds that density of population has a positive shadow price there— thus it is claimed that Tokyo has the best amenities of all cities in Japan.[10])

The distribution of wealth

In the above discussion we have referred repeatedly to the representative Japanese and representative American. Of course, economic well-being is not shared equally. A more global comparison would rank the economic well-being of all individuals in the two countries being compared.

Generally speaking, the distribution of wealth is less skewed in Japan than in the USA. Japanese society does not encompass the same extremes of wealth and poverty found in America. Consequently a ranking of the personal wealth of all individuals in Japan and the USA would have more Americans near the top and bottom and more Japanese concentrated in the middle. Perhaps the statement that the "representative" Japanese has more economic well-

being than that of the "representative" American should mean that a Japanese chosen randomly probably has more economic well-being than an American chosen randomly. This could be true even if the average economic well-being were greater in the more skewed America. There is implicit in this kind of notion the Rawlsian theory of justice, in which the quality of a society is judged from the view of a disembodied spirit about to be injected at random into the person of one individual in the society.[11]

Table 1.5 describes the distribution of income within Japan and other countries. The *Gini coefficient* is the minimum percentage of national income that would have to be redistributed if all of a nation's citizens were to have equal income. The Gini coefficient of Japan is not appreciably different from those of other OECD countries; the Gini coefficient of the USA is relatively high. The data in the table reveal that the wealthiest 20 percent of the popula-

---

[10] Kato Takafumi, "Toshitsu seikatsu no shitsu no sihyoka" (Indicators of quality of urban life), *Hitotsubashi Ronso*, vol. 103, no. 6 (June 1990).

[11] John Rawls, *A Theory of Justice*, Harvard University Press, 1971. For a thoughtful commentary on Rawls's argument, see Kenneth J. Arrow, "Some Ordinalist–Utilitarian Notes on Rawls's Theory of Justice", *Journal of Philosophy*, vol. 70 (1973), pp. 245–63.

Table 1.5. International comparisons of income distribution, after taxes

		Gini coefficient	Shares of total income by quintile of population, ordered by income				
			Lowest I	II	III	IV	Highest V
JAPAN	1986	0.356	5.6	11.6	17.1	23.9	41.8
USA	1991	0.379	4.5	10.7	16.6	24.1	44.1
Germany	1984	0.322	6.6	12.8	18.0	23.8	38.9
UK	1979	0.365	4.9	10.9	18.2	25.3	40.5
France	1984	0.349	6.6	12.4	16.7	22.3	42.0
Italy	1991	0.322	8.4	13.2	17.7	23.3	37.4
Canada	1991	0.276	7.7	13.7	19.0	24.8	34.8
OECD	1970	0.350	5.9	11.8	17.2	23.3	41.8

Sources: Klaus Deninger and Lyn Squire, "A New Data Set Measuring Income Inequality", *World Bank Economic Review*, vol. 10, no. 3 (September 1996), pp. 565–91 (http://www.worldbank.org/html/prdmg/grthweb/absineq.htm); Malcom Sawyer, *Income Distribution in OECD Countries*, Paris, 1976; Terasaki Yasuhiro, "Sekai no shotoku kosai" (World income inequality), *JCER Economic Journal*, no. 20 (1990), p. 27.

tion absorb 41.8 percent of private income in Japan compared with 44.1 percent in the USA, while the poorest 20 percent absorb 5.6 percent of the national income in Japan compared with 4.5 percent in the USA.

The underground economy

Much of the previous discussion has focused on conceptual omissions from the national income and product accounts. A somewhat different concern is whether the national income accounts accurately measure the items that in principle already are included in the definition of national income. Spending that is for illegal activities, or on which taxes are owed but not paid, contributes to the value of final goods and services but is deliberately concealed from government authorities and thus is not reflected in the national income and product accounts. Such activities constitute the *underground economy*. How large is the underground economy of Japan, compared with that of the USA and other countries?

The major components of Japan's underground economy include the illegal activities of organized crime (*yakuza*), the activities of petty criminals, and the unreported incomes of small businesses and the self-employed. The *yakuza* operate in a surprisingly open manner, given the nature of their business: drug smuggling, prostitution, gambling, and extortion. Their meeting halls are identified by logo. Their individual members can often be identified by their lapel pens, the tattoos that they alone favor, their missing fingers, and the fact that they and few others in Japan drive large American cars. Their annual income in Japan has been estimated to be in excess of a trillion yen in 1980, just under half a percent of GNP.[12]

The other components of Japan's underground economy include the 2–3 trillion yen annual unreported incomes of the more than 35,000 "love hotels", and the 1.8 million yen unreported incomes of religious organizations.[13]

The under-reporting of income by small businesses and the self-employed is summarized as "10–7–5", meaning that all of the tax owed on wage and salary incomes is paid, but only 7/10 of that owed on business incomes and 5/10 of that owed on farm incomes.[14] Given the ubiquity of small businesses in all sectors of Japan's economy, this adds up to a potentially larger distortion of the national income accounts than do all the other components of the underground economy. For Japan, the total size of the hidden national income may be as high as 5 percent of reported national income. In the United States, the underground economy has been estimated to be of a similar magnitude.[15] In other countries it may be quite a bit larger.

Conclusion

The national income and product accounts of Japan and other nations comprise errors, and omit important contributors to economic well-being including leisure, amenities, and household production. Conversion of the various countries' national income and product accounts to common currency units, using market exchange rates, imperfectly reflects international differences in relative prices. Furthermore, the choices of the representative citizens of the various countries may very well fail to reveal preference orderings of the various nations' respective bundles. Where this is so, we may not by any device infer which of two nations has the higher average standard of living, even were we to observe national income statistics totally free of errors and omissions. And the average standard of living may not be the decisive factor in judging a nation's economic performance anyway. The skewness of wealth distribution within each nation is a further consideration in comparing nations' overall states of economic well-being. Who would envy an anonymous person to be chosen randomly from a nation in which the average standard of living was high but the vast majority lived amid squalor and poverty?

What then can we say about the relative economic well-being of the Japanese people? Quite a lot actually. Japan's sixteen-fold increase in national income per person over the last century is orders of

---

12 Tatsuya Yasukochi, "The Underground Economy", *Japanese Economic Studies*, vol. 15 (Winter 1986–7), pp. 66–89.

13 Ibid.

14 M. Homma, T. Maeda, and K. Hashimoto, "Japan", in Joseph A. Pechman (ed.), *Comparative Tax Systems: Europe, Canada, and Japan*, Arlington, Va.: Tax Analysts, ch. 9, pp. 403–40, at 420.

15 Carol S. Carson, "The Underground Economy: An Introduction", *Survey of Current Business*, vol. 64, no. 5 (May 1984), pp. 21–37.

magnitude larger than any discrepancies between measured income and actual economic welfare. The national income statistics confirm what the most casual observation of life in Japan suggests: Japan's state of economic development is on a par with that of the United States and the nations of Western Europe and vastly surpasses that of the lesser developed and non-industrialized nations including many of Japan's Asian neighbors. In the eighteenth century, Adam Smith sought sources of the wealth of nations in his native British Isles. In the twentieth century, Smith's modern disciples may discern the same sources of wealth in the Pacific island nation of Japan.

FURTHER READING

■ M. Bronfenbrenner and Y. Yasuba, "Economic Welfare", pp. 93–136 in K. Yamamura and Y. Yasuba (eds.), *The Political Economy of Japan*, i, *The Domestic Transformation*, Stanford University Press, 1987. Covers many of the same topics as this chapter.

■ Steve Dowrick and John Quiggin, "International Comparisons of Living Standards and Tastes: A Revealed Preference Analysis", *American Economic Review*, vol. 84, no. 1 (March 1994), pp. 332–41. Shows that cross-country comparisons of consumption bundles only rarely identify international differences in tastes.

■ Robert Eisner, *The Misunderstood Economy*, Harvard University Press, 1994. Thoughtful analysis of the conceptual flaws in the national income and product accounts.

■ Irving B. Kravis, "Comparative Studies of National Incomes and Prices", *Journal of Economic Literature*, vol. 22 (March 1984), pp. 1–39. Careful dissection of the analytic problems in comparing the national incomes of differing nations.

Economic History, Part 1:
The Tokugawa Period (1603–1868) and the Meiji Era (1868–1912)

Japan's current status as a wealthy nation is the culmination of a process of economic development that continues still. Too often in the past, economic development has been equated with industrialization. By this definition, Japan's economic development began only with its forced opening to the West by Perry in 1853 and the consequent dramatic political, social, and economic changes that followed in Japan throughout the remainder of the nineteenth century. But economic historians now understand that Japan's industrialization and growth in the Meiji era (1868–1912) were possible only because of the political and economic institutions that had already evolved in Japan, particularly during the two and half centuries of autocratic government, economic controls, and seclusion that immediately preceded the Meiji era, referred to (interchangeably) as the Tokugawa Period, the Edo Period, or the Early Modern Period (1603–1868).

Japan was, in superficial respects, an economically backward country at the time of Perry's visits in 1853 and 1854. Nearly all the country's resources were devoted to agriculture, and there was little evidence in Japan of the technological advances of the industrial revolution. But there were many features that differentiated the Japan that Perry saw from lesser developed countries of today. There already existed sophisticated institutions of capitalism such as wholesaling, futures markets, and an infrastructure of roads and waterways financed through widely levied taxes collected by a pervasive and dedicated civil bureaucracy. Large numbers of ordinary people were functionally literate. Japan's

backwardness in the mid-nineteenth century was really a technological backwardness only. In many other respects, Japan was as advanced as the countries of Europe which were then seeking to establish colonial empires.

Tokugawa Period (1603–1868)

We begin our consideration of Japan's economic history by identifying parallels with that of Europe. China was the Greece and Rome of Japan, the source of its system of writing, religion, ideas about government, and much else. But although the golden ages of China's civilization coincided roughly with the classical ages of Europe, China's greatest cultural influence on Japan was not until much later, in the seventh century AD. The manor economy of medieval Europe has its counterpart in Japan's *shōen* estates of the eighth through twelfth centuries AD.[1] And, just as the manorial system that had flourished under the Carolingians gradually devolved into anarchy, so Japan in the twelfth through sixteenth centuries became one great field of battle for mounted warriors. But there was no analogue in Japan to the Renaissance of Europe. In the seventeenth century, as Europe pursued trade, exploration, and discovery, Japan became insular and

---

[1] On the basic facts about *shōen*, see Elizabeth Sato, "The Early Development of the *Shōen*", in John W. Hall and Jeffrey P. Mass (eds.), *Medieval Japan: Essays in Institutional History*, Yale University Press, 1974, pp. 91–109.

self-isolated. The policies of the Tokugawa dynasty, founded in 1603, brought an end to war but segregated Japan from the scientific, technological, and cultural changes that were to sweep through Europe and America during the subsequent two and a half centuries.

Precursors of the Tokugawa hegemony

The anarchy into which Japan had sunk with the emergence of mounted warriors in the twelfth century was interrupted by two lengthy periods of relative peace, the first referred to as the Kamakura Period (1185–1333) and the later as the Muromachi or Ashikaga Period (1336–1573). Each was a period of ascendancy of one coalition of warriors over others. But the hegemony proved impermanent in both instances. The Kamakura government was mortally weakened by the drain on the country's resources by successfully repelling the Mongol invasions (1274 and 1281). The contest for power was resumed and, for a time, won by Ashikaga Takauji[2] and his familial successors and their regents (1336–1468). Though nominally still the seat of government in Japan until 1573, the Ashikaga shogunate ceased to hold anything more than local power in the vicinity of the capital at the time of the Onin war of 1469–77. The ensuing period of the warring states (*sengoku jidai*), culminating in ascendance of the overlord Oda Nobunaga[3] in 1568, most clearly resembles the period of feudalism in Europe: political authority resides almost completely in locally powerful warriors, bound to one another by no more than loose confederations.[4] Before the Onin war there had continued to be at least the semblance of a central authority, not unlike the Carolingian empire of medieval Europe.

In the civil wars that engulfed Japan in the late fifteenth and early sixteenth centuries, there gradually emerged locally powerful rulers known as *daimyō* (lit. "great names"). Eventually the *daimyō* came to exert control over ever more extensive territories. The coming of the Europeans in 1543, and their introduction of firearms, enabled technological advances in warfare that accelerated this tendency. Massed formations bearing lances were no match for those bearing muskets. The new ways of making war elicited new defenses. Castle cities surrounded by deep moats and high stone walls became the fortress headquarters for the contending factions.

These changes had fortuitous consequences for economic development. As a *daimyō*'s authority became more secure and encompassed a wider region, he became more inclined toward policies that had long-lasting benefits and enabled him to draw resources away from neighboring rivals.[5] Guild monopolies (*za*) were abolished, new roads and irrigation systems were built, and new lands were reclaimed. Standardized systems of weights and measures were introduced—by each *daimyō* separately. These activities were all either socially beneficial additions to the stock of public goods or eliminations of deadweight losses.

By the middle of the sixteenth century, the *daimyō* had come to assume all functions of government within their respective domains called *han*. The ruthless tyrant Nobunaga forged a grand coalition including the most powerful of the *daimyō*, and sealed his ascendance by occupying Kyoto in 1568. Nobunaga was assassinated in 1582 and succeeded by his lieutenant Hideyoshi.[6] Hideyoshi himself died in 1598 while pursuing an unsuccessful campaign of conquest in Korea. The descent into another civil war was averted in 1600 by the victory at Sekigahara of forces led by Tokugawa Ieyasu,[7] who emerged as the unrivaled overlord, founder of the dynasty that was to rule Japan in peace for the next two and a half centuries.

The *baku-han* system

Under Tokugawa Ieyasu and his heirs, Japan at last achieved whatever economic gains reside in a regime of stable and powerful government. In 1603 Ieyasu took for himself the title *shogun*, a revival of an ancient title assigned to Yoritomo,[8] founder of

---

2 Ashikaga Takauji (1305–1358).

3 Oda Nobunaga (1534–1582).

4 On parallels between feudalism in Europe and in Japan, refer to the excellent little book by Peter Duus, *Feudalism in Japan*, Alfred A. Knopf, New York, 1969. Regarding the onset of "full feudalism" in Japan which was precipitated by the devolution of the Kamakura government, see his ch. 4 (pp. 61–84).

5 This is the basic argument of Kozo Yamamura, "The Agricultural and Commercial Revolution in Japan, 1550–1650", *Research in Economic History*, vol. 5 (1980), pp. 85–107.

6 Toyotomi Hideyoshi (1536–1598).

7 Tokugawa Ieyasu (1542–1615).

8 Minamoto no Yoritomo (1147–1199).

the first warrior government in 1185, and claimed also by the Ashikaga in the fourteenth century. The political authority vested in Ieyasu and his heirs is referred to in English as the shogunate or the *bakufu* (lit. "tent government"), terms also used to refer to the earlier warrior governments of Japan. In principle, Ieyasu was merely the most powerful of the *daimyō*, each of whom was the sovereign of his respective *han*. In fact, Ieyasu reserved to himself alone certain rights, including the right to establish foreign policies, the right to issue national currency, the right to establish national standards of measurement, and the right to remove other *daimyō* who threatened the hegemony of the *bakufu* or otherwise gave offense to the *shogun*. All *daimyō* including the *shogun* were dynastic in character; as a general rule, each *daimyō* was succeeded by his eldest son.

The *daimyō* were divided by Ieyasu into distinct groups. *Tozama daimyō*, or "outside" *daimyō*, were those who had accepted Tokugawa hegemony only after the battle of Sekigahara; some of them had fought on the losing side, others had remained neutral. The *fudai daimyō*, or "house" *daimyō*, had been allied with Ieyasu at Sekigahara. And the *shinpan daimyō* were blood relatives of Ieyasu and represented a collateral line of ascent should the main line fail to produce an heir. Ieyasu exercised his prerogative as the victor of Sekigahara by reassigning some of the *tozama daimyō* to less prosperous *han* than the ones they had earlier controlled, conferring their original *han* upon *fudai daimyō*. Ieyasu himself controlled the most prosperous *han* of all, called the *tenryō* (lit. "emperor's realm"), which in theory he administered on behalf of the emperor, the symbol of political authority but in effect only a figurehead. The *tenryō* encompassed about a fifth of the entire land area of Japan. It included the major cities of Edo (now Tokyo), Osaka, and Kyō (now Kyoto), the ancient capital and site of the imperial court. Eventually about a third of the population of Japan came to reside in the *tenryō*.[9]

Ieyasu made his headquarters at Edo (renamed Tokyo in the nineteenth century). Prior to this time Edo had been a minor fishing village of little significance, but by 1700 it had perhaps a million residents and was the most populous city in the world at that time. Its importance as a center of culture and government is indicated by reference to the two and a half centuries of Japanese history during the Tokugawa dynasty as the "Edo Period".

The sources of revenue both for the *bakufu* and the *daimyō* were mainly rice taxes collected from the cultivators. Official *han* monopolies of the production of goods like sake, rapeseed oil, crafts, and the like were additional minor sources of revenue for many *daimyō*. Also, city dwellers were obliged to pay a head tax. There did not exist free commercial intercourse among the *han*. Rather, *daimyō* introduced protectionist policies, charging tolls to travelers passing through, taxing imports from other *han*, or even banning such imports altogether where these competed with official local monopolies. The *daimyō* were not required to remit taxes to the *bakufu* but were occasionally called upon to assist in the building of public works (*tetsudai*) and were also expected to supply guard contingents to imperial and *bakufu* facilities. Neither obligation was an important permanent drain upon the *daimyō* finances.

This *baku-han* (i.e. *bakufu* and *han*) political system initiated by Ieyasu was perpetuated with few changes by his dynastic heirs. The stability of the system was due in large part to various control measures which came to have an important bearing on the economic development of Japan. These included the caste system, alternate attendance, the system for collecting rice taxes, and the seclusion policy.

The caste system (*shi-nō-kō-shō*)

During the Tokugawa era, the Japanese population was stratified into social castes by shogunal decree. Shinto and Buddhist priests, and doctors, were outside the caste system, but nearly everyone else fell into one of four groups: samurai, farmer, artisan, and merchant (*shi-nō-kō-shō*). There were other categories as well, the emperor and his family and the court nobles at one extreme and the outcasts at the other, but these groups did not include a significant fraction of the general population. Assignment to a particular caste was according to birth: only the children of samurai were samurai, and any child of

---

9 On the details of the Tokugawa governmental system and the ancillary political controls that perpetuated it, see T. G. Tsukahira, *Feudal Control in Tokugawa Japan: The Sankin Kotai System*, Harvard University Press, 1966, pp. 5–27.

a merchant would also be a merchant. As a popular saying of the day had it, "The offspring of a toad is a toad." The natural unit of social organization was not the individual but rather the *ie* (lit. "house"). The *ie* typically consisted of an extended family, a group of persons related to one another by ties of blood or marriage and with a single patriarchal head. The head of an *ie* without natural heirs could adopt an heir from outside the *ie*, often someone who was already an adult, but this practice afforded only a modest prospect that individuals of merit and ambition could attain a caste above that of their own parents.

The social classes were distinguished not only by occupation but also by privilege and status. Of the four major classes, the samurai were at the top. Samurai included the *daimyō* themselves as well as their retinues of vassals, advisers, and military retainers. Only samurai were permitted to wear swords or to take on surnames. Sumptuary manifestos reserved favored consumption items and articles of fashionable clothing for members of the samurai class. Ostensibly, the samurai's role in society was that of soldier, but with no wars to fight the samurai assumed the tasks of civil bureaucracy, mainly tasks associated with the enforcement and collection of taxes. Each samurai *ie* was assigned by the *daimyō* a set annual income to be paid in rice out of the taxes collected. The percentage of the population that comprised the samurai class was probably only about 7 percent throughout the Edo Period. The great majority of people, 80 percent, were farmers, followed by 13 percent artisans and merchants.

Merchants were held in the lowest esteem of the four major classes according to the Confucian ideology embraced by the Tokugawa. It is clear that these social rankings of the four classes were not based on their relative wealth—by the nineteenth century some famous merchants had become quite prosperous and more than a few of the samurai class had become practically destitute.[10] Still, according to the official ideology, it was more desirable to be even a poor farmer than a prosperous merchant.

By imposing the caste system, the rulers of the country attempted to freeze the social order with themselves and their descendants for ever occupying the top place. Yet there were economic costs arising from the caste system. It blocked the complete exploitation of comparative advantages in choices of occupation. For instance, individuals with an aptitude for commerce and trade would not become merchants unless they had been born to that class, a loss to society as well as to the individuals themselves. On the other hand, by choking off any avenue of social advance other than the accumulation of *ie* assets, the caste system contributed to the incentive of families of all classes to delay marriage, and in the event of pregnancy to resort to either abortion or infanticide, at least in the period after 1700,[11] thereby restricting population growth.

Each of the respective castes was charged with duties. For the samurai these included observance of correct behavior, administration of the government, and, for the highest samurai, the *daimyō*, the observance of a peculiarly Japanese institution known as "alternate attendance".

Alternate attendance (*sankin kōtai*)

The political measure adopted by the Tokugawa that had the most immediate impact on economic development was the requirement that the *daimyō* spend half their time in Edo and that their families reside there year round. *Daimyō* whose *han* were close to Edo were required to rotate back and forth at six-month intervals, while those whose *han* were remote rotated at longer intervals of up to two years in length. This institution was formally proclaimed in 1635 and was continued until 1862, the very brink of the Meiji Restoration. It is referred to as *sankin kōtai* (lit. "alternate attendance"). The *sankin kōtai* requirement assured that the families of the *daimyō* were perpetual hostages against any *daimyō* activities offensive to the *shōgun*. It also ensured that the Tokugawa could at a minimum cost to themselves preserve their hegemony by carefully monitoring *daimyō* activities and associations, wherever necessary playing one faction off against others, or seeking a quick compromise in the event that opposition threatened.

---

10 On the evolving fortunes of merchants during the Edo Period, see Charles D. Sheldon, "Pre-Modern Merchants and Modernization in Japan", *Modern Asian Studies*, vol. 5, no. 3 (1971), pp. 193–206.

11 This is the basic argument of James I. Nakamura and M. Miyamoto, "Social Structure and Population Change: A Comparative Study of Tokugawa Japan and Ch'ing China", *Economic Development and Cultural Change*, vol. 30 (1982), pp. 229–69.

The economic effects of alternate attendance were many. The first consequence was a massive migration of persons from every part of Japan to Edo. Because *daimyō* families were the wealthiest in the country, Edo became a major consumption center. Extensive commercial activity developed in Edo to supply the *daimyō*, their families, and retainers with the daily necessities in exchange for the rice taxes collected in the various *han*. The most prosperous *han* were located in the western part of the country. Consequently a pattern of trade emerged in which rice collected as taxes in the western *han* was shipped to Osaka where it was stored in warehouses and sold, and bills of trade issued in payment for the rice were exchanged for consumption items in Edo.[12] Osaka thus became a great entrepot for the entire country. There developed in Osaka sophisticated commercial institutions such as a kind of fractional reserve banking based on the issuance of warehouse receipts for rice, wholesaling networks, and even futures markets.[13] If as a result of *sankin kōtai* Edo had become the city of samurai, then Osaka had become the city of merchants. The two cities exhibit some of these same ambiences even today.

Besides contributing to the development of Edo and Osaka, *sankin kōtai* had significant economic effects in many of the *han*. Some *han*, particularly those to the west of Osaka, were favorably situated to benefit from the expenditures by *daimyō* processions from more distant *han*. These processions were strictly governed by shogunal decrees to be commensurate in all details to the social rank of the *daimyōs* that led them. The processions of the highest ranking *daimyō* (the *hatamoto*, lit. bannermen) were quite elaborate, and typically included hundreds of servants, retainers, advisers, and so on. If spending by these processions stimulated the economies of some *han*, it is equally true that they acted as a drain on other less favorably situated *han*. Those *han* located in the far reaches of Tohoku (the north-east of the main island) had to pay taxes to finance spending in other *han* and in Edo without themselves gaining any such commerce.

An additional consequence of the *sankin kōtai* institution is that it added impetus to the development of roads and coastal waterways connecting Edo and Osaka to the farther reaches of the country. The famous Tokaido, depicted in the masterful woodblock prints of Hiroshige, was among the well traveled roads that originally had been developed to accommodate the *daimyō* processions.

Just as the high and mighty had duties to fulfill, so too did the low and common. And for the farmers, or peasants, the most important duty was the payment of taxes.

The *honbyakushō* system

Though the *daimyō* were ostensibly the sovereign rulers of their respective *han* with independent powers to set taxes on their subjects, there did exist a system of collecting land taxes that was quite uniform throughout Japan, referred to as the *honbyakushō* (lit. original farmers) system. In 1582–98 Hideyoshi had undertaken a cadastral survey of all the arable land and recorded the name of the head of each *ie* responsible for paying taxes on each specific parcel. These *honbyakushō* and later their familial successors were divided into groups of five members. Within each such group, all members were held responsible for shortcomings in tax payments by any one of them. Each village had a designated headman, in some instances elected and in others hereditary, who was the official tax collector and intermediary between the samurai and all the groups in the village. In fulfilling the various duties associated with the payment of taxes, villagers evolved a remarkable facility for enforcing advantageous rules of social behavior, and as a result grew more productive and more governable.[14]

The base for the land tax was output, so that the amount of rice collected varied from year to year with the state of the harvest. There was a natural incentive to understate the true size of the harvest, but by test plots and unannounced inspections the state of the harvest was independently measured by

---

12 On the details of these remarkably advanced institutions, see E. S. Crawcour, "The Development of a Credit System in Seventeenth Century Japan", *Journal of Economic History*, vol. 20, no. 3 (September 1961), pp. 342–60.

13 The indigenous development and evolution of cotton futures markets in Osaka during the Tokugawa period is described in some detail by William B. Hauser, *Economic Institutional Change in Tokugawa Japan, Ōsaka and the Kinai Cotton Trade*, Cambridge University Press, 1974.

14 On this point see James I. Nakamura, "Human Capital Accumulation in Premodern Rural Japan", *Journal of Economic History*, vol. 41, no. 2 (June 1981), pp. 263–81.

samurai assigned to this task. The tax rate was in principle 40 percent but in fact varied from place to place and over time. The *kokudaka*, the aggregate officially assessed annual average rice yield of the land one was authorized to tax, became a status token for the *daimyō* and some lesser samurai, for by shogunal design the size of each's *kokudaka* comported with his place in the social hierarchy. The units of measurement were *koku*; 1 *koku* = 180 liters (5.1 bushels), nominally, the amount of rice thought necessary to sustain an adult for one year.

The highly controlled, even repressive, social and economic system embodied in the various institutions so far reviewed exhibited little change over the two and a half centuries of the Edo Period. Nor was it intended by Japan's rulers that the system should change. To assure stasis, a further measure was required, one that, more than any other, conveys the essence of the Tokugawa era, the closure of the country.

The seclusion policy (*sakoku*)

The third *shōgun*, Iemitsu,[15] grandson of Ieyasu, issued in 1642 an order for the closing of the country (*sakoku*). The Dutch and Chinese were allowed continued contact through the southern port at Nagasaki but were not allowed free transit within Japan. The Dutch were restricted to a minor settlement on the small island of Dejima in Nagasaki harbor, while the Chinese were restricted to a part of Nagasaki proper, and trade with both of them was reserved to the *bakufu* alone. All foreigners of any nationality other than Dutch or Chinese were denied entry into Japan under threat of death, and Japanese abroad were, initially, allowed two years to return to Japan safely or else were ordered to remain as permanent exiles under threat of death upon repatriation. These draconian decrees were strictly enforced for two centuries, with the minor exceptions of some authorized trade with Korea by the Sō clan of Tsushima and some illicit traffic between the southernmost *han* and Chinese traders, by way of the Ryukyus (later to become Okinawa).

The principal reason for the seclusion policy was to prevent military alliances between the European countries and the *daimyō*. In the wars leading to unification, putative alliances between *daimyō* and rivalrous European powers had already set what was,

for the Tokugawa, an alarming precedent. Suppression of Christianity was an additional motivation of the *bakufu*, not necessarily distinct from the desire to prevent military alliances with Europeans. The seclusion order and the official outlawing of Christianity represented an attempt to embargo weapons and subversive ideas both at the same stroke. A final motivation for the seclusion order was to reserve for the Tokugawa a quasi-monopoly of imports into Japan, including imports of precious metals.

Economic development during the Tokugawa era

Japan achieved significant industrialization and rising per capita income only after the precipitous demise of the Tokugawa regime and the dismantlement of the *baku-han* system in the mid-nineteenth century. Scholars of Japan's economic history remain divided on whether the draconian economic and political controls of the Tokugawa era retarded Japan's economic development or, in some curious and roundabout way, hastened it. Proponents of either view must reconcile themselves to the mass of evidence that the steady accumulation of human capital in Tokugawa Japan was an antecedent to the nation's rapid economic expansion following its later opening to the West.

From the founding of the Tokugawa dynasty by Ieyasu in 1603 until the Genroku era[16] a century later, the economy of Japan grew significantly. The population increased from about 20 million in 1600 to about 30 million in 1700. The arable lands were expanded commensurate with this. The great cities, particularly Edo, grew and prospered. However, from 1700 until the Meiji Restoration in 1868, the population grew hardly at all. There was some migration from the cities back to the countryside. The remarkable changes in the political and economic order that had taken place in the early Tokugawa period had no counterparts in the later period.

The extensive growth in the seventeenth century derived from the more secure and durable rights of

---

15 Tokugawa Iemitsu (1604–1651).

16 Genroku era (1688–1704). Japanese dates are identified by the reign year of the successive emperors; for instance, 1997 is Heisei 9, the ninth year of the reign of the Heisei emperor. The Genroku era marks the apogee of Edo culture.

the samurai class to the taxable output of the economy. Prior to the establishment of the Tokugawa hegemony, *daimyō* and their forerunners perceived a smaller expected return from land reclamation and irrigation projects because of the possibility of its forfeiture in the vicissitudes of civil war. Under the *baku-han* system *daimyō* were secure in their exclusive rights to levy taxes on the lands within their own *han*. To induce the cooperative efforts of farmers in land reclamation, *daimyō* proffered temporary exemptions from taxes for newly reclaimed rice fields (*shinden*). By the end of the seventeenth century this process had approached the fundamental limits imposed by the mountainous geography of the nation. Further economic expansion would require either the discovery and diffusion of superior methods of production, or the accumulation of physical and human capital. The historical record of the late Tokugawa era affords evidence of both technical change and capital accumulation.

From 1700 to 1850 Japan's population seems to have grown hardly at all, remaining at about 30 million persons. The view, once dominant among historians, that these statistics bespeak famine, pestilence, and human misery has fallen under the weight of evidence that Japanese families in the late Tokugawa era voluntarily limited their size, to accumulate per capita wealth. Restriction of marriage to the first-born son, who was the only one to inherit family property, and delayed age at marriage were characteristic of samurai and peasant families alike in the late Tokugawa era. Infanticide afforded further controls on family size, particularly for peasants. Thomas C. Smith examined Japanese village registers and determined that the recorded sex ratio (ratio of male to female registered births) frequently diverged from one, indicating sex-selective population control, i.e. infanticide.[17] Smith focuses on infanticide, roundly condemned even in Tokugawa Japan, because its incidence can be measured indirectly through the recorded sex ratio, not because that was necessarily the most important or prevalent method of family planning in early modern Japan. But if infanticide reflects economic calculation, so too must have other methods of restraining family sizes. Smith found that the variation in the recorded sex ratio over time and across geographic locales reflected the presence or absence of female by-employment opportunity and the relative difficulty

of partitioning holdings among male heirs, both of which would be logically associated with economic incentives of families to exercise sex-selective population control.

The rational attempts of late Tokugawa Japanese families to accumulate wealth and raise living standards, and not only through population control, seem to have achieved a modicum of success. Increasing commercial activity, including farm family by-employments (spinning, weaving, pottery making, etc.), increasing trade within Japan, increasing improvements in irrigation and fertilization, and the selection and diffusion of improved strains of rice are all characteristic of eighteenth-century Japan. These developments progressed more rapidly and more completely in regions of Japan that contained the most fertile lands, and which afforded relatively greater opportunity to evade onerous government restrictions on productive activity.[18] The geographic regions around the shogunal capital of Edo (now Tokyo), the major cities of Osaka and Kyō (now Kyoto), and in much of the western parts of Japan fared rather better economically in the Tokugawa era than did the regions of the north-east (Tohoku).

By the early nineteenth century, rice taxes, head taxes on city dwellers, and franchised monopolies were becoming less and less effective at maintaining the samurai's share of Japan's rising national income.[19] *Daimyō* and *bakufu* alike resorted to debasement of the currency to enhance fiscal resources, with the inevitable result that prices rose and barter displaced monetary trade. Price controls only worsened the state of affairs. Repeated unsuccessful attempts to ban or discourage farmers from engaging in by-employments also failed to enlarge the collection of rice taxes. Attempts to raise the rice tax rates met with stiff resistance and occasional armed insurrection.

---

[17] Thomas C. Smith, *Nakahara: Family Farming and Population in a Japanese Village, 1717–1830*, Stanford University Press, 1977.

[18] For details, see Kozo Yamamura, "Towards a Reexamination of the Economic History of Tokugawa Japan, 1600–1867", *Journal of Economic History*, vol. 33, no. 3 (September 1973), pp. 509–46.

[19] In a careful study, Kozo Yamamura demonstrates that the bannermen (*hatamoto*), among the highest ranking samurai other than *daimyō*, maintained relatively constant real income throughout the Edo Period, but grew increasingly discontented as the incomes of peasants and others rose relative to their own. See Kozo Yamamura, "The Increasing Poverty of the Samurai in Tokugawa Japan, 1600–1868", *Journal of Economic History*, vol. 31, no. 2 (June 1971), pp. 378–406.

Significant political and economic transformation of the Japanese system may ultimately have occurred in the nineteenth century even without the intrusion of foreigners; but we shall never know, for intrude they did.

The Meiji era (1868–1912)

By the dawn of the nineteenth century, Russian, American, and European trade with China was beginning to result in incidental Japanese contacts with foreign vessels, apart from the long sanctioned visits of Dutch and Chinese vessels to Nagasaki. In 1792 Catherine II dispatched a naval envoy to request an opening of trade with Japan, but little came of it. And in 1832 the US president Andrew Jackson sent a naval envoy to China with instructions also to open trade with Japan if feasible, but the envoy died en route and matters went no further at that time. Twenty years later, another US president, Millard Fillmore, dispatched a naval flotilla under the command of Commodore Matthew C. Perry with instructions to demand coal depots and supply stations for American ships, permission for American vessels to enter Japanese ports (to be designated by treaty) for the purpose of trade, and amicable treatment of any Americans marooned on Japan.

Perry reached Uraga harbor near Edo in 1853 and presented the American demands, promising to return for the answer a year later. After unprecedented consultation with the leading *daimyō*, the *bakufu* agreed in 1854 to the treaty of Kanagawa which allowed American ships to obtain provisions at Shimoda (on the Izu peninsula south of Edo) and Hakodate (in the northern island of Ezo, now called Hokkaido), and also provided for an American consul posted in Japan to negotiate further trade relations between the two nations.

Perry's visits initiated a political crisis in Japan that ultimately proved fatal to the *bakufu*'s authority. There was much sentiment among the *daimyō* in favor of armed resistance to the Americans, yet the shogunate acceded to the American requests. In 1858 representatives of the shogunate signed a Treaty of Amity and Commerce with the United States establishing extraterritoriality and American trade in Kanagawa (now known as Yokohama), Nagasaki, Niigata, and Hyōgo (now Kobe), as well as Shimoda and Hakodate. Britain, France, Russia, and the Netherlands signed nearly identical treaties with Japan later that same year.

As foreigners came to the treaty ports and trade commenced on a large scale, Japan's two centuries of seclusion finally ended. During these early years of open trade, foreigners gained an unsavory reputation in Japan for sharp practices and exploitative behavior. It did not help matters that in the Treaty of Amity and Commerce the shogunate had yielded to the American consul Townsend Harris's stubborn insistence that the official foreign exchange rate between Japanese and foreign coins should equal the coins' relative contents of precious metal. Silver coins circulating in Japan in the 1850s held far less value as precious metal than the coins' exchange value in terms of other goods. This was less true of the gold coins then circulating in Japan. The price of Japan's gold coins in terms of its silver coins in 1858 was such that, by trading Japanese silver coins for gold coins, one obtained gold of 3.45 times greater value on the world market than the silver metal given up. The Mexican silver dollars that were the predominant international currency of the Orient at that time were virtually a commodity money, the equivalent of bullion. To forestall foreigners' trading Mexican silver dollars to the *bakufu* for Japanese silver coins at the unfair exchange rate stipulated in the treaty, and trading the Japanese silver coins for gold ones, the *bakufu* at first, in June 1859, attempted to remint Japan's silver coins, increasing their value relative to gold, and, under the terms of the treaty as understood by the *bakufu*, thereby increasing their foreign exchange value. But a month later, after foreign protests, it had to abandon this scheme and proceeded instead to make the best of a bad situation by reminting the gold coins, greatly inflating their issue and thereby degrading their value relative to indigenous silver coins (which it also allowed to depreciate in value in terms of domestic goods). This eliminated the unfair foreign arbitrage but also led to a four-fold increase in Japanese domestic prices between 1860 and 1866.[20]

---

[20] For the details of this episode, refer to Peter Frost, *The Bakumatsu Currency Crisis*, Harvard East Asian Monographs, Harvard University Press, 1970. Also see T(akehiko) Ohkura and H(iroshi) Shimbo, "The Tokugawa Monetary Policy in the Eighteenth and Nineteenth Centuries", *Explorations in Economic History*, vol. 15 (1978), pp. 101–24.

The massive inflation can only have exacerbated the already tense relations between Japanese and foreigners and further tested the shogunate's increasingly tenuous hold on power. In 1858 the reigning *shogun* had died without an heir, and in the succession dispute and aftermath there ensued purges, executions, and assassinations. Amidst this turmoil, the opening of the treaty ports soon provoked terrorist activity directed against foreign residents. In retaliation, the British navy in 1863 bombarded Kagoshima, a harbor city in Satsuma (in south-west Kyushu, today's Kagoshima prefecture), and the following year it destroyed a coastal battery in Chōshū (at the extreme western tip of the main island of Japan, today's Yamaguchi prefecture). Delay in implementing the terms of the 1858 treaties provoked the threat of a further armed response. In 1865 an allied flotilla entered Hyōgo (today's Kobe) and succeeded in gaining imperial, rather than *bakufu*, ratification of the treaties, now revised so that Japanese tariff rates (tax rates on imports) would be subject to ceilings averaging about 5 percent, not 20 percent as before. These "unequal" treaties, forced on Japan at gunpoint, would be honored by subsequent Japanese governments, but not without rancor.

By 1867 the end of the shogunate was assuming an aura of inevitability. On January 3, 1868, armies of several *han* from the south-west of Japan entered Kyoto and announced the establishment of direct rule by the Meiji emperor, then a boy of fifteen, a "restoration" of the form of government historically assumed to have existed in Japan of the seventh century. In fact, the new government was a virtual oligarchy primarily comprised of the leading figures of the Satsuma and Chōshū *han* governments which had spearheaded the rebellion. Armed resistance to the new government was feeble and unsuccessful.

Early steps of the new government, 1869–1871

Immediately following the 1868 Meiji Restoration, the newly proclaimed ruling council of government, the *dajōkan*, acted quickly to consolidate its authority. At first the Meiji leaders merely usurped the position previously occupied by the Tokugawa *bakufu*, continuing both to collect rice taxes and to pay samurai stipends, and allowed *han* governments to do likewise and function largely as before. During this very early period they had no way of augmenting finances to meet the continuing threat of internal military crisis except to issue inconvertible paper money, and this they proceeded to do.

Under the earlier regime, gold-based currency had circulated in Edo (which the Meiji oligarchs now renamed Tokyo) and silver-based currency had circulated in Osaka and elsewhere. In 1868 the *dajōkan* ordered the conversion into newly issued paper notes of all indigenous silver-based currency. In the treaty ports silver "trade dollars" continued to circulate. The money of various kinds in circulation now included inconvertible notes (*hansatsu*) previously issued by the *daimyō*, as well as gold, silver, and copper coins issued by the *bakufu*, and Mexican silver circulating in the treaty ports. To these were now added the inconvertible notes of the Meiji government, optimistically labeled "gold notes" (*kinsatsu*). The nominal money stock in Japan was expanded by approximately 100 percent in the first year after the restoration. In 1869 prices rose to one and a half times their levels of the previous year.[21] The gold notes were in fact never convertible into gold. Silver trade dollars now began to circulate throughout Japan, not only in the treaty ports as before. Attempts to establish a gold standard by fiat had resulted in what the government of Japan later referred to as a "de facto silver standard".[22] Actually, the paper money that continued to circulate was not made fully convertible even into silver until 1886.

In July 1871, the Meiji government, in a promulgation known as *haihan chiken*, abolished the *han*, and replaced them with new political units, three *fu* and 302 *ken*, both called "prefectures" in English. In November the same year it consolidated these into three *fu* and 72 *ken*. Japan today has 48 prefectures. With *haihan chiken*, the *dajōkan* assumed all debts and obligations of the *daimyō* rulers of the 260 *han*. It discharged these claims by the forced conversion of notes previously issued by the *han* governments into interest-bearing paper notes (*dajokansatsu*) denominated in the newly defined unit of account, the "yen". The gold notes previously issued by the

---

21 Shimbo Hiroshi, "Kinsei no bukka to keizai hatten" (Economic development and the price level in pre-modern Japan), *Toyo keizai shinpo sha* (1978), table 5–9, p. 282.
22 Matsukata Masayoshi, *Report on Adoption of the Gold Standard*, Tokyo, 1899, sect. 3, p. 38.

dajokan itself were also withdrawn in exchange for the new interest-bearing yen-denominated notes.

The *han* had been the sovereign domains of the *daimyō*, the samurai feudal lords of the Tokugawa era. The new prefectures were to be ruled by governors, appointed by the Meiji government in Tokyo. Under the earlier regime, *daimyō* had established local monopolies and levied custom duties on imports into their *han*. There was now to be uninterrupted commerce within Japan, and rice taxes, instead of being paid to local authorities, were to be remitted to the government in Tokyo.

Land tax reform

The main sources of revenue both to the *bakufu* and to the *han* governments had been rice taxes. In July 1873, the government moved to replace the rice tax with a monetary land tax (a reform known as *chiso kaisei*). To that end, the government undertook the assessment of all arable land, a process not completed until 1880.[23] As this process developed, the land taxes became the major source of revenue to the government. The Meiji land tax reform established, for the first time in Japan, private ownership of agricultural land, improving the economic incentives to allocate land efficiently. The land was initially assigned to the officially registered taxpayers under the previous regime, many of whom were in fact well-to-do former peasants already entering lease arrangements with the true cultivators.

The Tokugawa rice tax had entailed wasteful incentives for cultivators to divert effort from rice cultivation to less productive but less taxed by-employments. Figure 2.1 depicts the waste as the area of a triangle. Samurai overseers, by imposing minimum-effort stipulations and exacting penalties for noncompliance, could have counteracted the distortion and raised national income; but they had little incentive to do so, for their own stipends could not easily have been made to depend upon the diligence of their overseeing efforts and as a general rule were not so dependent. Soon after the Meiji land tax reform, many private landowners entered share tenancy contracts with cultivators which superficially resembled the earlier rice tax in that the share tenants were obliged to remit a percentage of the crop to the landowners. But under the share tenancy arrangements, any improved value of output added directly to the landowner's wealth rather than merely enlarging the remissions to a distant and poorly informed government bureaucracy. Private landowners are more diligent than tax collectors at monitoring cultivators. For this reason, private ownership of land induced higher national output.

Once land became alienable, share tenancy con-

---

[23] For concise descriptions of the Tokugawa rice tax and the methods of assessing land value under the 1873 land tax reform, see James I. Nakamura, "Appendix A: Tokugawa and Meiji Land Taxation", in *Agricultural Productivity and the Economic Development of Japan 1873–1922*, Princeton University Press, 1966, pp. 177–97.

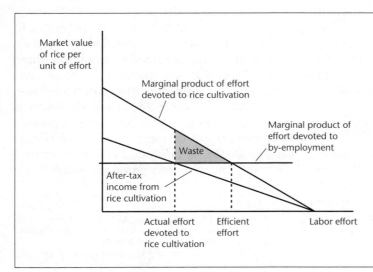

Figure 2.1. Effects of the Meiji land tax reform

The Tokugawa rice tax placed a wedge between cultivators' productivity and earnings, diverting effort away from rice cultivation toward less productive but less taxed by-employments. Meiji landowners collected a share of the rice crop from tenant cultivators, but, unlike samurai overseers of the Tokugawa era, themselves benefited directly from enforcing minimum effort stipulations.

tracts dominated alternative arrangements because they shifted a portion of the risk of unforeseen and uncontrollable fluctuations in output from poor cultivators to wealthy landowners, while contributing to the direct incentives of the cultivators to enlarge the crop size. Wage labor, compared with share tenant labor, would have required more intense monitoring by the landowner. And land rental would have obviated labor monitoring altogether but would have unduly burdened the cultivators qua land lessees with risk, and lowered their demand to rent land. This is why attempts to eliminate share tenancy by forced transfer of land, as occurred in Japan in 1948, were doomed to fail.

Dispossession of the samurai

Besides acting to consolidate sources of revenue, the Meiji government also moved to curtail expenses. The major government expense early on was the payment of stipends to the samurai or warrior caste. The samurai had comprised about 7 percent of the population of Japan throughout the Tokugawa era, compared with the 80 percent who were farmers and the 13 percent who were artisans and merchants. As the effective rulers of the country, the samurai had diverted the taxes to their own consumption. Because they also constituted the civil bureaucracy, a portion of this pay amounted to the expenses of government administration, but a larger portion of it simply represented a transfer. Though the earliest proclamations of the Meiji government (for instance the "Charter Oath", a statement of principles issued by the architects of the new government) had foreshadowed the abolition of the caste system, the government continued to pay the samurai stipends, lacking the temerity not to. However, beginning with the conscription law of 1873, the Meiji government amassed a largely non-samurai force armed with modern weapons, and this may have emboldened it to act. In a series of three steps, the government divested itself of the major drain on public finances which the samurai stipends had at first represented. (These steps are referred to as *chitsuroku shobun*, lit. "stipend measures".) The sequence of actions was:[24]

■ December 1873: voluntary commutation of samurai stipends under 100 *koku*, six years for hereditary stipends, four years for life stipends, one-half paid in cash

and one-half paid in bonds bearing 8 percent interest (*chitsuroku kōsai*);

■ November 1874: voluntary commutation of stipends greater than 100 koku on similar terms;

■ August 1876: suspension of all pension payments, compulsory commutation, issuance of "capitalized pension bond certificates [*kinroku kōsai*]".

Voluntary commutation necessitated outlays totaling 19.3 million yen of cash and 16.6 million yen in capitalized stipend bonds (*chitsuroku kōsai*) over 1875–6.[25] In contrast, the initial 1876 issue of compulsory commutation bonds (*kinroku kōsai*) was in excess of 173 million yen (which amounted to around 40 percent of Japan's 1876 national income).[26] Only about a third of those eligible had accepted voluntary commutation.

Those who accepted voluntary commutation must have anticipated the subsequent termination of the stipends. Consider the following. The present value of an hereditary stipend equals the annual stipend divided by the interest rate. It would be rational to accept commutation in return for a lump sum equal to four times the annual stipend only if the real interest rate were greater than 25 percent ($4a > a/i$ only if $i > 0.25$). In fact, the real interest rate was probably closer to 5 percent than to 25 percent. (In 1873 the Japanese government issued pound-denominated bonds on the London market at 7 percent.[27]) It would therefore have been irrational to accept commutation on the terms offered unless the stipend was thought soon to be terminated unilaterally anyway.

In light of all this, it is no surprise that compulsory commutation was strenuously opposed by the former samurai, some of whom in the south-west parts of Japan began to form private armies. In February–September 1877 the unrest culminated in the unsuccessful Satsuma rebellion or Seinan war. The

---

24 A good reference in English on the chronology of events pertaining to the commutation of samurai pensions is W. G. Beasley, *The Meiji Restoration*, Stanford University Press, 1972, pp. 379–404.

25 Yoshio Ando (ed.), *Kindai nihon keizai shi yoran* (Handbook of the economic history of modern Japan), 2nd edn, University of Tokyo Press, 1979, p. 51.

26 Ibid.

27 For a table detailing foreign borrowings of the Japanese government up until 1930, see Harold G. Moulton, *Japan: An Economic and Financial Appraisal*, Brookings Institution, Washington, DC, 1931 (reprint edn 1944), p. 376.

precipitating event was the government's bungled attempt secretly to remove arms from Satsuma and place them beyond the reach of the potential rebels, but clearly the real issue was the dispossession of the samurai class. The costs of suppressing the rebellion included 42 million yen for extraordinary expenses (around 10 percent of Japan's 1878 national product), covered by a 25 million yen loan from the Fifteenth National Bank and 27 million yen new note issue.[28] The result was further inflation, with the ironic outcome that the samurai pension bonds became worth even less.

Fiscal crisis followed in the wake of the war–tax inflation of 1878. Responding to protests (actually, riots), the government had already lowered the nominal land tax rate from 4 to 3 percent (January 1877). Now the real tax rate was eroded further by inflation. As the land tax was the major source of revenue, a fiscal crisis ensued. Proposals to base the land tax in whole or in part on the price of rice were considered and rejected.[29] The finance minister Ōkuma Shigenobu[30] proposed a new foreign loan (the government had floated loans in London in 1870 to finance railway construction and in 1873 to finance a portion of the samurai pensions), but this was successfully opposed on the grounds that it would jeopardize Japan's independence from the European powers. In the end, further inflation of the currency was the expedient chosen to defray government expenditures.

Administration of the Finance Ministry under Matsukata, 1881–1886

Three of the leading figures in the Restoration had died within a year of one another in 1877–8, of illness (Kido), battle suicide (Saigō), and assassination (Ōkubo),[31] leaving the future direction of Japanese politics unclear. Throughout 1879 and 1880, debate continued without resolution. Then, in the famous Political Crisis of 1881 the finance minister, Ōkuma, proposed the early establishment of representative democracy and was driven from office.[32] The winning view advanced by Itō Hirobumi[33] and his followers favored continued autocratic rule at home and military adventurism abroad.[34] This would require military and naval forces equipped with the latest weapons, including expensive ships. The rapid establishment of fiscal soundness and a fully

convertible currency now headed the political agenda. In conjunction with these developments, Matsukata Masayoshi[35] was appointed Minister of Finance in October 1881. As Vice Minister of Finance, Matsukata had been one of the architects of the land tax reform, and after an observation tour of European capitals had advocated a number of further reforms which would now be implemented.

Matsukata introduced several measures, all pitched

---

[28] Motokazu Kimura, "Fiscal Policy and Industrialization in Japan, 1868–95", in Kenneth Berrill (ed.), *Economic Development with Special Reference to East Asia*, New York: Macmillan, 1966, pp. 273–86 (at p. 280).

[29] For a discussion of this exchange, see Inoki T(akenori), "Meiji zenki zaisei seiri ni okeru ichi sowa: Godai Tomoatsu no chiso beino ni tsuite" (An episode in the public finances of the early Meiji period: the proposal by Godai Tomoatsu that land taxes be paid in rice), *Kikan gendai keizai*, vol. 47 (1982), pp. 93–105.

[30] Ōkuma Shigenobu (1838–1922) was later prime minister (1898 and 1914–16) and founder of Waseda, the most prestigious of Japan's private universities. For a biographical essay on Ōkuma, see Yoshitake Oka, *Five Political Leaders of Modern Japan*, University of Tokyo Press, 1986, pp. 45–84.

[31] Kido Koin (1833–1877) was a political leader of the Choshu province and major participant in the Restoration. Ōkubo Toshimichi (1830–78) was a leader of the government of the Satsuma *han* and with Kido and Iwakura (Tomomi) a leader of the mission to America and Europe in 1871–3 to seek treaty revision. He was also a key figure in the Meiji government after 1873. Saigō Takamori (1828–77) was a military man, a leader of the Satsuma *han*, a senior official of the Meiji government and ultimately the leader of the unsuccessful Satsuma rebellion. For a riveting essay on the enigmatic Saigō, see Ivan Morris, *The Nobility of Failure: Tragic Heroes in the History of Japan*, Tokyo: Charles E. Tuttle, 1975, pp. 217–75.

[32] Ramseyer and Rosenbluth speculate that Ōkuma's affinity for democratic government derived from the fact that he himself was rather popular, and therefore likely to gain election: see J. Mark Ramseyer and Frances M. Rosenbluth, *The Politics of Oligarchy: Institutional Choice in Imperial Japan*, Cambridge University Press, 1995, p. 27.

[33] Itō Hirobumi (1841–1909) from Chōshū province had studied in London in 1863–4; he became a high-level bureaucrat in the Meiji government, visited Europe in 1882–3 to study constitutional law, led the drafting of the Meiji constitution, and served as Japan's first prime minister 1885–8; he again served as prime minister 1892–6, 1898, and 1900, and as resident general of Korea in 1906–9. His assassination by a Korean nationalist in 1909 afforded the pretext for Japan's final annexation of Korea the following year.

[34] Albert M. Craig, "Central Government", in Marius B. Jansen and Gilbert Rozman (eds.), *Japan in Transition: From Tokugawa to Meiji*, Princeton University Press, 1986, ch. 2, pp. 61–2.

[35] Matsukata Masayoshi (1835–1924) had been a bureaucrat in the Satsuma *han*; he became chief of taxation of the Meiji government in 1871, traveled to Europe in 1878 as head of the Japanese delegation to the Paris exhibition, was later prime minister (1891–2 and 1896–7) and elder statesmen (*genro*) (1896–1924), but is most famous as minister of finance (1881–91, 1895–6, and 1898–1900). For a biography of Matsukata, see Haruko Matsukata Reischauer, *Samurai and Silk*, Harvard University Press, 1988.

at establishing, and maintaining, convertibility of the currency into specie. Convertibility of paper money into specie simply means that the government supplies precious metal in exchange for paper money, at a fixed price, to anyone who requests it. If, as in Japan of the 1870s, government reserves prove inadequate to maintain convertibility, the price of precious metal in terms of the paper money becomes freely determined in the marketplace. Any speculative attack that exhausts the government's reserves forces this result. Speculators refrain from supplying currency for specie if exhaustion of government specie reserves would cause specie to depreciate relative to currency, but they rush to do so the instant they deduce that it would have the opposite result.[36] A speculative attack will occur sooner, the greater is the rate of inflation of the currency, or the smaller the government's holding of liquid reserves. Take a moment to understand why.

On the first point, inflation of the currency pushes up the prices of goods in terms of currency and makes it more likely that ending convertibility would also push up the price of *specie* in terms of currency. Regarding the second point, the amount of liquid reserves the government commits to maintaining convertibility affects the timing of a speculative attack, for a subtle reason. It cannot be known with certainty whether an end to convertibility will cause the currency to depreciate relative to specie, or to appreciate. For a speculative attack to end convertibility, it must exhaust the government reserves. The larger those reserves are, the more of the speculators' own wealth must be committed to the attack, and the greater the risk to which the speculators are exposed. If the government's reserves are larger, the speculators will proceed more cautiously, attacking only when supremely confident that an end to convertibility will cause the currency to depreciate relative to specie. Maintenance of convertibility thus represents a highly credible signal that a government holds substantial liquid reserves and commands adequate fiscal resources without resorting to inflation of its currency. For this reason, a government that maintains convertibility of its currency is presumed to hold a richer war chest than one that does not, and represents a more fearsome military adversary. The Meiji oligarchs well understood this. In short, the early establishment of a convertible

currency comported perfectly with a prominent political slogan of Meiji Japan: "rich country, strong army" (*fukoku kyōhei*).

Japan was proscribed from raising tariff rates above 5 percent on most goods as a result of commercial treaties of 1866, the so-called "unequal treaties"; so tariffs could not be used as a source of added government revenue. Instead, Matsukata accelerated a policy initiated by Ōkuma, to sell government-owned factories, including replicas of manufacturing establishments copied from Europe and America,[37] retiring the proceeds and contracting the money supply.

Figure 2.2 illustrates the movement in the price of silver both in terms of Japanese currency and in terms of gold on the London exchange, from 1868 to 1897. The "Matsukata deflation" completely reversed the previous inflation. It would have been

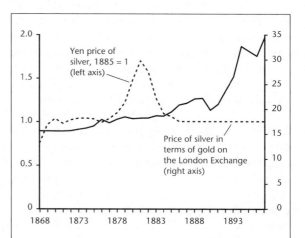

Figure 2.2. Price of silver in terms of Japanese currency and in terms of gold on the London exchange, 1868–1897

Source: Asakura K(okichi) and Nishiyama C(hiaki), *Nihon no kaheiteki bunseki* (Monetary analysis of Japan), Tokyo: Shobunsha, 1974, pp. 35–41.

---

36 For an elegant model that represents these ideas, refer to Paul R. Krugman, "Speculative Attacks on Target Zones", in Paul Krugman and Marcus Miller (eds.), *Target Zones and Currency Bands*, Oxford University Press, 1991.

37 The most complete account of the pilot plants or "model factories" is Thomas C. Smith, *Political Change and Industrial Development in Japan: Government Enterprise, 1868–1880*, Stanford University Press, 1955. The plants produced textiles, ships, bricks, cement, and glass.

possible to establish convertibility of the currency at a new par, avoiding deflation, but this would have required a smaller cache of reserves and precisely for this reason would have been a less effective signal of military might.

The Matsukata deflation induced a business recession in the 1880s[38] but raised the real value of the land tax receipts, unburdened the government of the annual losses which the government factories had invariably sustained, and restored fiscal balance. The deflation, of course, also raised the real value of outstanding samurai commutation bonds, but the bonds constituted a much smaller claim on government resources than the stipends they had replaced.

Some of the former samurai had used their voluntary commutation bonds as collateral for chartering national banks under an 1873 law patterned after the contemporary US national banking regulations. But because the right of note issue was severely restricted in Japan (in contrast to US national banks), only four national banks had been chartered, and these had all floundered. In 1876 new national banks were authorized under more liberal charters, and by 1879, 153 national banks had been founded, most of which prospered.[39] These national banks were the first joint-stock, limited liability companies in Japan. This soon became the predominant form of organization for newly founded manufacturing firms in cotton spinning and other industries.

Just before his appointment as Minister of Finance, Matsukata had advocated the complete revamping of Japan's banking system, so that a government-controlled central bank with the sole right of issuing bank notes would supplant national banks, completing the set of measures assuring government control of the money supply and maintenance of convertibility. At Matsukata's initiative a central bank, the Bank of Japan, was founded in October 1882. At that time the charters of the national banks were shortened from thirty years to twenty and made nonrenewable. New private commercial banks were now chartered in great numbers.[40]

In 1886, full silver convertibility of government paper money was established, a policy maintained until 1897 and the switch to gold. As Figure 2.2 illustrates, in the last decade of the nineteenth century silver appreciated in value relative to gold as a consequence of new gold discoveries (in Transvaal, South Africa), an unexpected windfall for Japan

and other silver standard nations. This windfall, and the sizable indemnity Japan received in the Sino-Japanese War (which is discussed in the next section), ultimately provided the needed reserves for Japan's adoption of the gold standard.

Industry, trade, and imperialism in the late Meiji era

As the end of the nineteenth century approached, the Japanese economy underwent a permanent transformation. It began to industrialize. From the last decades of the nineteenth century, Japan has numbered among the fortunate nations experiencing what Nobel laureate Simon Kuznets dubbed "modern economic growth",[41] a sustained rise in per capita output, made possible by the continual application of scientific advances to the technology of manufacturing. The hallmark of modern economic growth is the expansion of industry.

In Japan, the industries that mechanized and grew first were cotton spinning and silk reeling. The scale of these industries in Japan of the 1890s should not be exaggerated. In 1893 Japan had forty cotton spinning factories and all together these employed 25,448 persons, only about one-tenth of a percent of the nation's labor force. But cotton and silk goods in 1893 accounted for about a third of the net product in Japan's factories. (Food and beverages, mostly produced in the traditional ways, accounted for another third.) Factory output in the 1890s represented only about 15 percent of Japan's value-added in manufacturing and perhaps 3 percent of net national product. More significantly, cotton spinning

---

38 The Matsukata deflation happened to coincide with a world-wide slump, and it is difficult to disentangle the effects of the one from those of the other. So argues Teranishi J(ūrō), "Matsukata defure no makuro keizaigakuteki bunseki" (Macroeconomic analysis of the Matsukata deflation), *Kikan gendai keizai* (Spring 1982), pp. 78–92.

39 Kozo Yamamura has developed evidence that samurai commutation bonds comprised between one-third and one-half of the paid-in capital of Japanese banks in the 1880s, but in specific cases much less. See Kozo Yamamura, "The Role of the Samurai in the Development of Modern Banking in Japan", *Journal of Economic History*, vol. 27 (1967), pp. 198–220.

40 On the early development of private commercial banking in Japan, see Hugh T. Patrick, "Japan 1868–1914", in Rondo Cameron (ed.), *Banking in the Early Stages of Industrialization*, New York: Oxford University Press, 1967, pp. 239–89.

41 Simon Kuznets, *Economic Growth of Nations: Total Output and Production Structure*, Harvard University Press, 1971.

firms were among the first large joint-stock enterprises to succeed in Japan (banks were the first), and in the subsequent decades there would be many more. As Figure 2.3 illustrates, manufacturing output was now growing at a faster rate than agriculture and would eclipse it by around 1930.

Textiles carried a much greater weight in Japan's foreign trade than in its output. Cotton yarn and raw silk, together, accounted for about half of Japan's exports in the last decade of the nineteenth century. Raw cotton accounted for a third of Japan's imports. Clearly, a substantial portion of Japan's gains from specialization arose from the manufacture of cotton yarn and raw silk. The profitability of these industries derived partly from the fact that their mechanization required only an incremental change in long existing cottage industries. In the Edo Period, cotton spinning and silk reeling had both become significant by-employments of farmers using hand tools and primitive methods. Furthermore, even after mechanization in the 1880s and 1890s, both cotton spinning and silk reeling were relatively labor-intensive (often therefore described as "light" industries). In short, both employed readily available, indigenous resources.

A further, unusual, development had contributed

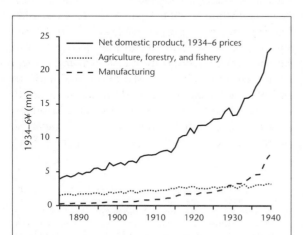

Figure 2.3. Net value-added in manufacturing and mining versus that in agriculture, forestry, and fisheries, all in 1934–6 prices, 1885–1940

Besides manufacturing and agriculture, Japan's net national product comprised outputs of construction, services, transport, and telecommunications.

Source: *LTES*, vol. 1 (1974), table 24, p. 226.

to the growth of silk reeling in Japan. A blight known as pébrine afflicted the silkworms of Europe beginning in 1852 in the south of France and continuing in the early 1860s in Italy, wiping out sericulture in Europe precisely at the point when Japan opened to foreign trade. The resulting increase in world price of silk products contributed greatly to Japan's gains from specializing in silk production. Beginning in 1865, Louis Pasteur, already famous for his studies on beer and wine leading to the development of pasteurization, was set to the task of researching the silkworm disease. Pasteur did in fact discover a way of detecting pébrine-infected silkworm eggs and thus preventing the disease. He published these findings in 1871 and effectively ended the European blight, but by then Japan's silk industry was well established on world markets and ripe for mechanization.

Meiji Japan's direct gains from foreign trade should not be overstated. From the opening of treaty ports in 1858, Japan began to export goods having lower relative prices in Japan than in the world outside (raw silk, coal), and to import goods having higher prices in Japan (cotton cloth, wool), certainly achieving gains from pure exchange.[42] And, by expanding its output of the export goods, specializing, it compounded these gains. However, from 1885 to 1910 foreign trade amounted only to about 10–15 percent of Japan's national output, and the direct gains from it were probably a lot less than this, small in comparison to the gains associated with economic growth. The opening of Japan to knowledge of foreign technology did more than free trade to hasten the country's advance toward the industrial age.

The Meiji government actively encouraged the infusion of foreign technology. Under the slogan "increase production, encourage industry" (*shokusan kōgyō*), the Meiji government hired foreign advisers to set up model factories, including mechanized cotton spinning factories and silk filatures, though just how important such factories were to the development of these industries has been seriously questioned. This matter is taken up again in the

---

[42] For some details on price differences between Japan and the outside world prior to Japan's opening, see Chapter 8 below, and also J. Richard Huber, "Effect on Prices of Japan's Entry into World Commerce After 1858", *Journal of Political Economy*, vol. 79 (May/June 1979), pp. 614–28.

chapter on industrial policy (Chapter 9). Here, suffice it to say that other government steps taken to promote foreign ways had a broader impact on daily life than did the government factories. With the help of foreign advisers, the government set up agricultural experiment stations, established a modern rail system, a telegraph network, a postal system, police forces, and schools and universities.[43] Japan also adopted another foreign institution that eventually proved disastrous: imperialism.

Foreign expansion was a major preoccupation of the Meiji oligarchy. In 1876, two decades after Japan's own forced opening by Perry, the Japanese leaders coerced Korea into opening three of its ports to Japanese traders. From this point, Japan was a rival to the Western powers in pursuit of Asian empire, even though its very own waters encompassed trade ports established by unequal treaties. Korea had historically maintained a tribute relation with its larger neighbor China which the Japanese initiative, by design, threatened to eclipse. The ensuing diplomatic disputes between China and Japan erupted into outright warfare in August 1894. The Sino-Japanese War ended quickly with China's capitulation in February 1895, and in the end proved to be as much an economic success for Japan as a military one.

Expenditures in conducting the Sino-Japanese War totaled 200 million yen, easily more than double the annual government spending up to that time (and about one-eighth of Japan's 1895 GNP). These expenditures were partially defrayed by placing a 43 million yen loan at 5 percent and a 10 million pound sterling loan at 4 percent, both on the London market. Along with this, the Japanese government once again resorted to the inflation tax. The spoils of war outweighed the economic sacrifice, at least if one takes a rather pecuniary view of the matter. The indemnity from China provided in the Treaty of Shimonoseki of 1895 totaled 32 million pounds sterling (equivalent to 362 million yen at the current exchange rate, about one-fifth of Japan's 1896 GNP), and along with this Japan was awarded control of Taiwan and the nearby Pescadores, and promised access to treaty ports on the Chinese mainland on a par with the European powers. In the "Triple Intervention", France, Russia, and Germany jointly pre-empted Japan from also taking control of the Kwantung peninsula of South Manchuria as

agreed under the original terms of the Shimonoseki treaty. Then three years later (in 1898) Russia itself took control of the Kwantung peninsula under a twenty-five-year lease, and began to construct a rail line connecting the newly opened trans-Siberia line to the year-round ports there, Darien and Port Arthur. (Vladivostok freezes every winter.)

In the anti-foreigner Chinese rebellion of 1900 (called the "Boxer" rebellion[44]) the Russian-built Manchurian rail line came under attack, and Russian troops occupied the whole of Manchuria. A combined relief expedition of foreign troops, including a large contingent of Japanese troops, marched on Peking and suppressed the rebellion. Russia agreed at that time to withdraw its troops from Manchuria but was slow to act on it and seemed to threaten Japanese designs on Korea. Tensions between Japan and Russia led to war in February 1904. Japanese land forces attacked Russian positions in South Manchuria, sustaining large casualties but prevailing. Then in May of the following year (1905) the Russian fleet was intercepted en route to Vladivostok and destroyed by a Japanese fleet comprised mostly of warships purchased from Britain. Both sides accepted American mediation and the US President Theodore Roosevelt successfully negotiated a mutually acceptable treaty at Portsmouth, New Hampshire, in 1906. Japan obtained the Russian lease on the Kwantung peninsula and control of the Russian-built Manchurian rail line, recognition of Japan's pre-eminent position in Korea, and control of the southern half of the island of Sakhalin (north of Hokkaido); Japan recognized China's sovereignty over Manchuria. Japan received no financial indemnity as it had after the war with China. Japanese deaths in the war with Russia totaled more than

---

[43] On the agricultural experiment stations, see Yujiro Hayami *et al.*, *A Century of Agricultural Growth in Japan: Its Relevance to Asian Development*, University of Minnesota Press, 1975 (esp. pp. 44–59). On the educational system, see Richard Rubinger, "Education: From One Room to One System", in M. Jansen and G. Rozman (eds.), *Japan in Transition: From Tokugawa to Meiji*, Princeton University Press, 1986, ch. 8, pp. 195–230. On the police force and post office, see D. Eleanor Westney, *Imitation and Innovation: The Transfer of Western Organizational Patterns to Meiji Japan*, Harvard University Press, 1987. On the rail and telegraph networks, see Thomas C. Smith, *Political Change and Industrial Development in Japan: Government Enterprise, 1868–1880*, Stanford University Press, 1955 (esp. pp. 42–46).

[44] The rebellion drew inspiration from a special kind of martial art, resembling boxing, but infused with mysticism.

100,000. Moreover, military expenses totaling 1,639 million yen (approximately half of Japan's 1905 GNP) had necessitated massive foreign loans and special taxes.

Assassination by a Korean patriot of the Japanese resident general in Korea (Itō Hirobumi, then one of the leading survivors among the Meiji oligarchs) afforded the pretext for Japanese annexation of Korea in 1910. Japan's formal empire now included Taiwan and the Pescadores, the southern half of the island of Sakhalin (called Karafuto by the Japanese), Korea, a long-term lease on Port Arthur in South Manchuria, and concessions in selected treaty ports on the Chinese mainland.[45] Extraterritoriality had ended in Japan itself in 1894. In 1911 commercial treaties with the United States and other nations completely restored to Japan control of its own tariffs. Less than fifty years after the Restoration, all of the immediate aims of the Meiji oligarchs had been realized.

Meiji industrialization in light of the Gerschenkron thesis

Scholars and others have wondered whether the Meiji transformation of Japan's economy was *sui generis* or, in subtle respects, resembled the experiences of other developed nations. In a series of essays, the famous Harvard economic historian Alexander Gerschenkron argued that the European process of industrial development during the nineteenth century exhibited some coherent patterns that comport well with economic logic.[46] It seems quite natural to place Japan within the framework of that argument, and we shall close our discussion of Meiji industrialization by attempting to do so. The Gerschenkron thesis holds that, as a general tendency,

[t]he more delayed the industrial development of a country, the more explosive was the great spurt of its industrialization, if and when it came. Moreover, the higher degree of backwardness was associated with a stronger tendency toward larger scale of plant and enterprise . . . Finally, the more backward a country, the more likely its industrialization was to proceed under some organized direction; depending on the degree of backwardness, the seat of such direction could be found in investment banks, in investment banks acting under the aegis of the state, or in bureaucratic controls.[47]

The economic sense behind these patterns, and some of the evidence, can be briefly sketched. Gerschenkron argued that in the nineteenth century, compared with England, which had the most advanced economy, France was more backward economically, followed in order by Germany, Austria, Italy, and Russia. Here, "backwardness" refers to an amalgam of factors including low per capita output, small extent of urbanization, low degree of literacy, absence of sophisticated business institutions and practices, and so on. In Gerschenkron's characterization, backward countries exhibited relative scarcity of skilled and disciplined workers so that their most economical manufacturing methods employed labor-saving machines and tools, which required capital investment. But financing such investment was problematic because backwardness was apt also to be associated with factors that inhibited the process of financial intermediation. For instance, in order to succeed, private banks themselves require trustworthy borrowers, willing depositors, and managers and clerks with business acumen. Lack of trust in lending could be overcome if banks themselves controlled the businesses to which they lent, but where backwardness was such that banks lacked sufficient expertise to do this or failed to attract depositors, then if industrial development occurred at all it was likely to draw on government direction and public funds. In France, private banks supplied most of the investable funds for industrial development but played little role in the actual management and direction of the businesses to which they lent. In Germany, which took longer to develop and at the time was more backwards than France, private banks themselves organized and managed new businesses in emergent industries. In the still more backward nations that did industrialize, government subsidy and direction of banking and industry was more prominent. In Russia, even before the revolution, the state both

---

[45] For details on Japan's concessions in China outside Manchuria, see Mark R. Peattie, "Japanese Treaty Port Settlements in China, 1895–1937", in Peter Duus, Ramon H. Myers, and Mark R. Peattie (eds.), *The Japanese Informal Empire in China, 1895–1937*, Princeton University Press, 1989, pp. 166–209.

[46] Alexander Gerschenkron, *Economic Backwardness in Historical Perspective: A Book of Essays*, Belknap Press of Harvard University Press, 1962.

[47] Ibid. p. 44.

managed and financed railroads and other industrial ventures.

Where does Japan fit into this framework? Japan fits Gerschenkron's framework only if we regard it as one of the *less* backward nations at the time of its first industrialization rather than more backward. Except in the lateness and rapidity of its industrialization, Japan's economic development process more resembles that of England or France than Italy or Russia. Let us consider Japan in reference to each portion of the Gerschenkron quotation.

1. "The more delayed the industrial development of a country, the more explosive was the great spurt of its industrialization, if and when it came."

Recent scholarship has blunted some of the sharp edges in Gerschenkron's characterizations of European experience. Gerschenkron probably overemphasized the tendency for more backward nations' first industrializations to occur in great spurts.[48] We have already learned that the growth of manufacturing in Japan was steady, but undramatic. Nevertheless, in the initial decades of modern economic growth, Japan exhibited a faster rise in per capita GNP than any of the nations that industrialized before it did. Table 2.1 represents Maddison's imputations of the per capita GNP of Japan and selected other nations at their initial point of modern economic growth as judged by Kuznets and in the ensuing fifty years. The nations are arranged in the table in order of the lateness of modern growth. Japan was the latest to experience modern economic growth and also enjoyed the most rapid initial growth. Britain, the first to experience an industrial revolution, grew more slowly in initial stages than any country that came after it. The other nations lie between these two extremes in no discernible pattern.

2. "Moreover, the higher degree of backwardness was associated with a stronger tendency toward larger scale of plant and enterprise . . ."

Before World War I, industry in Japan was overwhelmingly "light" industry; silk reeling and cotton spinning were the two leading examples, not heavy, capital-intensive manufacturing. Moreover, factory labor was relatively abundant in Meiji Japan, not scarce, as Gerschenkron found to be true of the relatively backwards European nations. Efficient methods substituted labor for capital rather than the reverse. The profitable early ventures in cotton spinning applied round-the-clock work shifts. Most of the workers were young, single women living in company dormitories. In 1912 Japanese cotton mills employed four times as many workers as American mills of the same size using the same equipment.[49] Further, a kind of cottage industry and putting-out system persisted in these textile industries well into the twentieth century in Japan, workers using hand looms or small machines and working at home rather than in factories. The profitable ventures in silk-reeling used machinery that substituted where possible endogenously obtainable wooden machine parts for imported metal ones, yet another example of substitution of labor for capital.[50]

Gary Saxonhouse has estimated a(n hedonic) supply of labor schedule based on data from a comprehensive government survey of cotton spinning factories in 1897.[51] Although the 71,000 workers in these factories exhibited high absenteeism and short tenures, they did value safety, rest periods, short work shifts, dormitory space, and personal freedom, as reflected in the compensating wage differentials identified by Saxonhouse. In short, Japanese factory workers responded to economic incentives in a sophisticated way. Perhaps the relative abundance of factory labor manifests the fact that Meiji Japan was not economically backwards in Gerschenkron's sense, even though its per capita GNP was indeed low. For estimates of per capita GNP in Japan and other countries at the start of modern economic growth, refer again to Table 2.1. The table also includes crude figures on the extent of adult illiteracy and degree of urbanization of many of the countries near the starting points of their modern growth. Japan in 1890 was undistinguished from the other nations (except for Italy) in its degree of adult

---

48 The other basic points of his framework survive. For a recent assessment of Gerschenkron's thought, see Richard Sylla and Gianni Toniolo, *Patterns of European Industrialization: The Nineteenth Century*, New York: Routledge, 1991.

49 David S. Landes, "Japan and Europe: Contrasts in Industrialization", in William Lockwood (ed.), *The State and Economic Enterprise in Japan*, Princeton University Press, 1965, pp. 93–182.

50 Thomas C. Smith, *Political Change and Industrial Development in Japan: Government Enterprise, 1868–1880*, Stanford University Press, 1955, p. 57.

51 Gary R. Saxonhouse, "The Supply of Quality Workers and the Demand for Quality in Jobs in Japan's Early Industrialization", *Explorations in Economic History*, vol. 15 (1978), pp. 40–68.

Table 2.1. Conditions at the start of modern economic growth, Japan and selected other nations

	First 50 years of modern economic growth[a]	Per capita GNP in first year of modern economic growth (1985 US$)[b]	Adult illiteracy near the start of modern economic growth (%)		Urbanization near the start of modern economic growth[e] (%)		Annual average growth rate in real per capita GNP in first 50 years of modern economic growth[b] (%)
JAPAN	1886–1936	738	50[c]	1890	13.1	1887/90	1.8
Canada	1870–1920	1347	n.a.		18.8	1871	1.7
Denmark	1865–1915	1461	< 30[d]	1850	13.8	1860	1.2
Norway	1865–1915	1148	< 30[d]	1850	5.3	1845	1.3
Australia	1861–1911	2954	n.a.		22.1	1861	0.8
Italy	1861–1911	1153	75–80[d]	1886	25.2	1861	1.1
Sweden	1861–1911	1110	10[d]	1850	7.6	1860	1.5
Germany	1850–1900	1050	< 30[d]	1850	26.8	1849	1.4
USA	1840–1890	1461	n.a.		8.5	1840	1.5
Belgium	1830–1880	1053	51[d]	1843	5.4	1846	1.6
France	1830–1880	1077	53[d]	1832	11.2	1836	1.0
Great Britain	1780–1830	1210	46[d]	1800	21.3	1801	0.4

[a] Dating of modern growth phase based on Simon Kuznets, *Economic Growth of Nations: Total Output and Production Structure*, Harvard University Press, 1971, p. 24, table 2; and Ryōshin Minami, *The Economic Development of Japan: A Quantitative Study*, London: Macmillan, 1986, table 1.1, p. 13.

[b] GNP (based on International Comparison Project estimates for 1985 projected into the past) and population from Angus Maddison, *Dynamic Forces in Capitalist Development*, Oxford University Press, 1991, appendices A and B.

[c] Japanese illiteracy rates from Koji Taira, "Education and Literacy in Meiji Japan", *Explorations in Economic History*, vol. 8 (July 1971), pp. 371–94, at p. 377.

[d] Adult illiteracy rates of European countries based on Carlo M. Cipolla, *Literacy and Development in the West*, Harmondsworth, Middx (UK): Penguin, 1969: Denmark, Norway, and Germany, table 23, pp. 113–14; Sweden and Italy, table 24, p. 115; Belgium and France, table 25, p. 117 (illiterates among army recruits); Great Britain, p. 62 (% newly married persons unable to sign their names).

[e] Urbanization rates (% of population residing in cities of 10,000 inhabitants or more, except where otherwise noted) from Adna F. Weber, *The Growth of Cities in the Nineteenth Century: A Study in Statistics*, New York: Macmillan (for Columbia University), 1899: Japan, p. 129; Canada (cities larger than 1,500), p. 130; Denmark, p. 113; Norway, p. 112; Australia (capital cities), p. 139; Italy (cities larger than 6,000), p. 118; Sweden, p. 119; Germany (Prussia), p. 82; USA (cities larger than 8,000), p. 22; Belgium, p. 116; France, p. 71; Great Britain (England and Wales), p. 43.

illiteracy. Neither was it significantly less urbanized than most other nations at the starting point of modern economic growth.

3. "Finally, the more backward a country, the more likely its industrialization was to proceed under some organized direction; depending on the degree of backwardness, the seat of such direction could be found in investment banks, in investment banks acting under the aegis of the state, or in bureaucratic controls."

Japan's industrialization was accomplished with little organized direction by government, and only limited intermediation by banks. As will be sketched out in a bit more detail in the chapter on industrial policy (Chapter 9), government encouragement of industry was more a political slogan than a reality. The government set up pilot plants with the assistance of foreign contractors to demonstrate new mechanical devices for silk reeling, cotton spinning, and the like, but the factories were not profitable and were eventually sold. The Meiji government was also a heavy investor in railroads and telecommunications, and in 1906 amalgamated the extant private rail lines into a government enterprise. Further, the government subsidized ocean shipping and shipbuilding, and established the first integrated steel factory in Japan, the Yawata iron works, which produced its first steel in 1901. But it is hard to view any of these efforts as essential. As Nobel laureate Robert Fogel famously demonstrated in the American case,[52] substitute modes of transport greatly diminish the incremental value of a rail system, and even in the Edo Period Japan had developed an extensive infrastructure of post roads and intercoastal waterways. The government promotion of steel and shipbuilding may have served a military purpose but was largely irrelevant to the main thrust of entrepreneurial activity in Japan.

The thirty or forty major cotton spinning companies were established as limited partnerships or joint-stock companies with the equity participation of hundreds of investors. They were independent companies, not closely tied to banks, and they dominated the ranks of the largest companies in Japan right up to the 1930s. The principle sources of raw cotton were foreign as were the markets for the final product. Entrepreneurs in the cotton spinning industry were thus pursuing an economic opportunity made possible by the removal of a government barrier, the Tokugawa seclusion policy. Not only this, the factory workers themselves, and indeed also the entrepreneurs and managers, might have been constrained by the caste system even had the seclusion policy been abandoned but the other Tokugawa controls remained in place. The spirit of the Meiji era was one of *laissez-faire*, not government control. The economist Koji Taira has, with good reason, described the Meiji transformation of Japan as a "revolution of markets", an opening of Japan to the powers of trade, not only internationally but also internally.[53] In short, Japan industrialized without organized direction, similar to the experience of less backward nations such as England or France, rather than the more backward ones such as Italy or Russia.

Conclusion

In the early seventeenth century the Tokugawa shogunate, which ruled Japan from 1603 to 1868, ended for ever the civil wars that had long ravaged the nation, but imposed far-reaching controls including a caste system, the forced concentration of underlords and their families in the Edo capital, a structure of taxes that made land inalienable, and the seclu-

sion of Japan from the outside world. Within this highly controlled political–economic system, the feudal lords of Japan, secure in their rights to levy taxes in perpetuity on the lands under their suzerainty, promoted the reclamation of new rice fields throughout the seventeenth century. The population of Japan rose from around 20 million persons in 1600 to 30 million persons a century later. The Tokugawa capital, Edo, became the consumption center of the rentier class, the samurai, warriors with no wars to fight—in effect, an hereditary and hierarchical civil bureaucracy. Osaka, the city of merchants, became an entrepot for the rice collected in taxes throughout the fertile regions in western Japan, and evolved sophisticated institutions of capitalism including wholesaling networks, futures markets, and a system of issuing warehouse receipts for rice that resembled fractional reserve banking.

The population of Japan grew hardly at all from 1700 to 1850 as land reclamation approached the natural limits of the nation's mountainous geography and families of all castes limited their offspring in order to endow each heir with greater wealth. A modicum of technological advance in the cultivation of rice, increasing commercial activity, and increasing trade within Japan all contributed to moderate growth in living standards further. But perhaps inevitably, given the forced isolation of the country, the wonders of the industrial revolution that had first appeared in Britain near the end of the eighteenth century were nowhere in evidence in the Japan that Commodore Perry demanded in 1853 should open its ports to foreigners. Perry's demands precipitated a political crisis in Japan that culminated in a revolution, the Meiji Restoration of 1868, which replaced the highly conservative *baku-han* political system of the Tokugawa with an oligarchy of forward-looking and energetic reformers from the south-west periphery of the nation.

The Meiji oligarchs proceeded to dismantle the elaborate controls of the Tokugawa era. Foreign treaties had already forced an end to the seclusion

---

[52] Robert W. Fogel, *Railroads and American Economic Growth*, Johns Hopkins University Press, 1964.

[53] The apt phrase "revolution of markets" is from the conclusion of Taira's monograph on the historical evolution of Japanese employment practices and labor relations: Koji Taira, *Economic Development and the Labor Market in Japan*, Columbia University Press, 1970.

policy. Now the oligarchs abolished the caste system, replaced the Tokugawa rice tax with a monetary land tax that assured the alienability of land for the first time, and pensioned off the samurai. The feudal fiefdoms that under the earlier regime had taxed and interfered with domestic trade within Japan itself were abolished, and were replaced by prefectures, mere sub-units of a single, economically integrated national polity, within which free trade and migration were permitted. The steps freeing markets of government controls were joined by others that assured a stable monetary unit and facilitated the capitalization of business. Japan had a central bank from 1885, and a currency convertible into silver from 1886 and convertible into gold from 1897. By the turn of the century, Japan had a proliferation of commercial banks and joint-stock companies. Furthermore, private manufacturing businesses, led by cotton spinning and silk-reeling, had begun gradually to displace agriculture.

FURTHER READING

Data

■ Ando Yoshio (ed.), *Kindai nihon keizai shi yoran* (Handbook of the economic history of modern Japan), 2nd edn, University of Tokyo, 1979. Data on Japan's economic development since Perry's visit in 1853, including quotations from official documents and chronologies, time series and other quantitative items, culled from many sources.

■ K(azushi) Ohkawa and M(iyohei) Shinohara (with Larry Meissner) (eds.), *Patterns of Japanese Economic Development: A Quantitative Appraisal*, Yale University Press, 1979; based on Ohkawa K(azushi), Shinohara M(iyohei), and Umemura M(ataji) (series eds.), *Chōki keizai tokei, suikei to bunseki* (Long-term economic statistics, estimates and analysis), 14 vols., Tokyo: Toyo Keizai Shinposha, 1974. The authoritative source of economic time-series data for Japan from the late nineteenth century to 1945.

General historical background

■ William G. Beasley, *The Rise of Modern Japan*, New York: St Martin's Press, 1990. Focuses on the history of Japan since the Meiji Restoration, particularly good on political history.

■ John K. Fairbank, Edwin O. Reischauer, and Albert M. Craig, *East Asia, Tradition and Transformation*, Boston: Houghton Mifflin, 1978. The textbook developed for use at Harvard in the course introducing undergraduates to Asian history.

■ John Whitney Hall, *Japan From Prehistory to Modern Times*, New York: Dell, 1970. Very readable, concise history of Japan.

■ Harry Wray and Hilary Conroy (eds.), *Japan Examined: Perspectives on Modern Japanese History*, University of Hawaii Press, 1983. Leading historians contribute thoughtful and engaging opinion pieces on the big questions about Japan's economic and political development since the Edo Period.

Tokugawa Period

■ Charles J. Dunn, *Everyday Life in Traditional Japan*, Rutland, Vt: Charles E. Tuttle, 1969. A popular treatment of life in the Edo Period.

■ Susan B. Hanley and Kozo Yamamura, *Economic and Demographic Change in Pre-Industrial Japan, 1600–1868*, Princeton University Press, 1977. Argues that population control after 1700 contributed to a sustained rise in Japanese living standards.

■ Marius B. Jansen (ed.), *The Cambridge History of Japan*, v, *The Nineteenth Century*, Cambridge University Press, 1989 (especially essays by Gilbert Rozman (ch. 8), and E. Sydney Crawcour (ch. 9)). Summarizes the results of historical scholarship on the late Tokugawa period.

■ Thomas C. Smith, *Native Sources of Japanese Industrialization, 1750–1920*, University of California Press, 1988. Collection of essays by the most respected scholar of Tokugawa economic history.

Meiji Period

■ Marius B. Jansen and Gilbert Rozman (eds.), *Japan in Transition: From Tokugawa to Meiji*, Princeton University Press, 1986. Essays on the government policies of the early Meiji period.

■ M. Miyamoto, Y. Sakudo, and Y. Yasuba, "Economic Development in Preindustrial Japan, 1859–1894", *Journal of Economic History*, vol. 25 (December 1965), pp. 541–64. Argues that Japan's rapid industrialization was premised on its having already developed sophisticated market institutions, indigenously.

■ Hugh Patrick, "External Equilibrium and Internal Convertibility: Financial Policy in Meiji Japan", *Journal of Economic History*, vol. 25 (June 1965), pp. 187–213. Discusses the steps taken by the Meiji government in placing Japan on the silver standard in 1886 and the gold standard in 1897.

■ Henry Rosovsky, "Japan's Transition to Modern Economic Growth, 1868–1885", in H. Rosovsky (ed.), *Industrialization in Two Systems*, 1966. Argues that the Meiji government promoted Japan's economic development by facilitating and supporting private enterprise.

Economic History, Part 2:
The Twentieth Century (1912–1945)

As the Meiji era closed in 1912, Japan's economy exhibited many features that would have struck an Edoite of a hundred years earlier as completely alien but would be familiar to a Tokyoite of today. In incipient form, the modern Japanese economy could be clearly glimpsed. Joint-stock companies, managed by trained professionals, operated mechanized factories under regimented work schedules. The agrarian population enjoyed alienable farm land and education for the masses, and urban amenities had come to include streetcars, telegraphs, and electric lights. The standard of living was still low by the standards of today, but rising steadily.

During World War I Japan enjoyed an unprecedented economic boom, from which emerged in full splendor the business groups known as the *zaibatsu*. Nevertheless, half of the nation's labor force continued to work as self-employed farmers, and another fourth of the labor force as small shopkeepers, independent craftsmen, and the like. In other words, large enterprises, though prominent, remained atypical. The 1920s, Japan's decade of government by political parties and cooperation with the West, brought financial crises and slowed growth, both greatly exacerbated by the 1923 Tokyo earthquake and the misguided policy of returning to the gold standard at the same parity that held when it was abandoned in 1917. The two years in which Japan succeeded in re-establishing the gold standard, January 1930–December 1931, coincided with the start of the world-wide depression. Fiscal and monetary expansion under the guidance of the famous finance minister Takahashi Korekiyo (1932–6)

effected a rapid recovery, but it was not rapid enough to forestall the hijacking of the Japanese government by a military bent on war. From the outbreak of war with China in 1937, Japan's economy was placed on a war footing, which entailed a widening web of government command and control of productive resources, a dramatic departure from the essentially *laissez-faire* regimes of the immediate past.

World War I boom

Japan entered World War I as an ally of Britain. The Anglo-Japanese treaty of 1902, renewed in 1911, required either nation to defend the other in the event it was attacked by more than one enemy. Under these stipulations Japan might have remained neutral when Britain, France, and Russia declared war on Germany, but the government of prime minister Ōkuma chose not to and declared war itself the same month (August 23, 1914). During the first three months of hostilities Japanese forces occupied the German concession in China (in Shantung, across the Yellow Sea from Korea and directly south of the Kwantung peninsula), and also occupied the German-held islands north of the Equator in the South Pacific (the Mariana, Palau, Caroline, and Marshall groups[1]). Except for these actions and the

---

[1] The names of selected islands in these groups may be noted: Saipan and Guam (both Mariana), Yap (Palau), Truk (Caroline), and Bikini Atoll (Marshall).

dispatch of a small flotilla to the Mediterranean, Japan's role in the European conflict was limited to that of an interested bystander. As such, it enjoyed an unprecedented economic boom, a small nation experiencing an exogenous improvement in its intertemporal terms of trade.

Japan had accumulated massive foreign debt to finance its 1905 war with Russia. When World War I came, Britain began to divest its own vast holdings of foreign wealth in order to finance armaments expenditures, and the other combatants did likewise. The resulting dramatic rise in world real interest rates induced Japan to become a net international lender, in fact accumulating by 1920 more claims on foreigners than in 1914 Japan itself had owed them.

Table 3.1 describes Japan's approximate international debt and investment position just prior to and immediately after World War I. Its net foreign

Table 3.1. Japan's international debt and investment position, end-1913 and 1919 (¥100 million)

	Net indebtedness (surplus, +)/ net asset-holdings (deficit, –)			
	1913		1919	
Foreign loans to Japanese entities				
National government	16.0		13.7	
Municipal governments	1.8		1.5	
Private corporations	1.9		2.0	
		19.7		17.2
Loans by Japan to foreigners				
Japanese government loans to allied governments				
Britain			–1.8	
France			–1.3	
Russia			–2.4	
Japanese government loans to China			–2.7	
Private loans	–0.6		–1.5	
		–0.6		–9.7
Foreign investments in Japan		1.0		1.0
Japanese investments abroad				
South Manchuria Railroad	–1.0			
China (other than SMR)	–3.5			
Hawaii and the USA	–0.5			
Other	–0.4			
		–5.4		–8.8
Foreign exchange reserves				
Japanese specie holdings abroad	–2.5		–13.4	
Japanese specie holdings at home	–1.3		–7.0	
		–3.8		–20.4
Totals		+10.9		–20.5[a]

[a] In 1913 yen, approximately –11.5.

Source: Harold G. Moulton, *Japan: An Economic and Financial Appraisal*, Washington, DC: Brookings Institution, 1931, pp. 390–7.

indebtedness at the end of 1913 of 1.09 billion yen represented about 22 percent of its 1913 GNP (= 5.01 billion yen). Most of Japan's foreign debt at that time consisted of Japanese national government bonds denominated in pounds and francs (used to finance railway construction and to cover extra-ordinary expenses arising from the 1905 war with Russia). The table shows the outstanding amounts, valued at par in terms of yen. Some of the foreign loans matured during the war years and were paid off, so the outstanding amount diminished from 1.92 billion yen at the end of 1913 to 1.72 billion yen at the end of 1919. Also during the war years, the government of Japan itself issued considerable medium-term (3 to 5-year maturity) loans to allied governments and to China. A large portion of the loans to China were issued without security and ulti-mately represented unilateral transfers.[2] In addition, the Russian revolution rendered the loans to Russia uncollectable. Nevertheless, by the end of 1919 Japan had become a net international creditor, its nominal asset-holdings of 2.05 billion yen amount-ing to approximately 13 percent of its 1919 GNP (= 15.45 billion yen).

A nation that is a net international debtor will generally suffer from a small rise in world interest rates, but can gain from a very large rise in world interest rates, that is, a rise large enough to induce it to become a lender. A moment's reflection reveals why. A rise in real interest rates enlarges the cost of borrowing but, equally, adds to the profitability of lending. For a nation that initially is a debtor, a small rise in real interest rates simply means greater costs of its continued borrowing. But if the real interest rate rises so much it induces the nation to become a lender, the profits from that lending can leave it better off. This seems to describe Japan's experience during the World War I years.

The Japanese accumulation of foreign assets during World War I had implications for Japan's exchange rate and industrial structure. In switching from the position of a net international borrower to a net international lender, Japan supplied more of its own currency, the yen, in exchange for foreign currency. To ensure an offsetting net increase in the quantity of yen demanded, and thus maintain equilibrium in the foreign exchange market, the Japanese exchange rate depreciated in real terms, so that the relative price of Japanese goods as perceived

by foreigners fell, leading them to buy more, to spend more, and to increase their demand for Japanese currency.[3] Symmetrically, this also meant that Japanese citizens had to pay higher prices for foreign goods, and therefore switched their demand toward domestic suppliers of substitute products, further contributing to equilibrium in the foreign exchange market. In other words, during Japan's World War I boom, Japanese producers of export goods enjoyed an increase in foreign demand, while Japanese producers of goods that had competed with imports enjoyed an increase in domestic demand for their output. And both phenomena reflected the real depreciation in Japan's currency resulting from Japanese accumulation of foreign assets in response to the temporarily enlarged world-wide real interest rate. Figure 3.1 illustrates the movement in Japan's real exchange rate or "terms of trade", an index of the price of exports relative to imports. Real depreci-ation of the yen is particularly evident in the inter-val 1916–18, as is its abrupt reversal in 1919, the abnormal international conditions having abated.

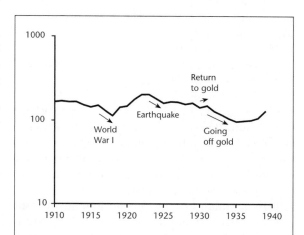

Figure 3.1. Japanese terms of trade, 1885–1940 (1934–6 = 100)

Price of Japanese exports in terms of imports, based on price indices for Japan's trade other than with its own colonies
Source: *LTES*, vol. 14 (1979), table 4–3, p. 87.

---

[2] Some significant portion of the loans to China, called "Nishi-hara" loans after the Japanese government official responsible, were later exposed as little more than naked payments to Chinese warlords in exchange for diplomatic considerations.
[3] This presumes that the elasticity of foreigners' demand for Japanese goods was greater than 1.

During the boom, Japanese entrepreneurs rushed to expand production of exportables including metals, machinery, and raw silk, and also to expand production of goods that substituted for the now higher priced imports, including dyestuffs, ships, iron and steel, and finished textiles. The government-owned Yawata steel works continued to account for the major part of Japan's domestic steel output, but now Japan's private shipyards expanded at a rapid clip as did the private production of chemicals for industrial use including dyes, fertilizers, paper-making, and the like. At the war's end, world interest rates returned to their prewar level, reversing also the aberrant Japanese exchange rates and precipitating a slump in the same industries that had prospered during the boom.

From 1914 to 1919, Japan's real GNP exceeded its secular trend by 3–5 percent per year. The abnormal increase in real GNP over the years 1914–19 has both a Keynesian and a neoclassical interpretation. The Keynesian one holds that the wartime increase in aggregate demand led to expanded employment of otherwise idle resources. Under the alternative neoclassical interpretation, the temporary increase in real interest rates induced Japanese workers voluntarily to forgo leisure to accumulate more wealth than they could achieve by reallocating their asset portfolios alone. These explanations are actually not mutually exclusive.

The expansion in Japan's output during World War I was further spurred by technological advance, not directly related to the abnormal economic conditions of the period. In particular, an important permanent change contemporaneous with the World War I boom was the reticulation of electric power, largely accomplished by private investment, but also with loans from the government-affiliated Industrial Bank of Japan. Electric power generation in Japan dates from establishment of the Tokyo Electric Light company in 1883, which over the following two decades was joined by more than fifty more electric companies. By 1920, five private hydroelectric generating companies generated most of the electric power in Japan, selling it wholesale to the numerous smaller distribution companies, almost all of which were also private companies. The availability of electric power significantly lowered the costs of producing chemical fertilizer, which was now poised to become a significant industry.

By the war's end, large manufacturing and commercial enterprises using sophisticated technology had become fairly prominent in Japan, though not by any means displacing small family enterprises employing traditional methods. It was only at this time that the famous Japanese zaibatsu reached their full development.

Zaibatsu

Each zaibatsu (lit. "property agglomeration") was a set of interrelated and interlocked commercial enterprises, closely held by the same family. The four most prominent zaibatsu—Mitsui, Mitsubishi, Yasuda, and Sumitomo—had varied origins, but the founding families of each acquired existing enterprises and established new ones throughout the Meiji era, all the while maintaining close ownership, and ultimately consolidating controlling-share interests in a family-owned holding company. As their commercial empires expanded, the zaibatsu families exercised control by selecting and monitoring the professional managers of the constituent enterprises, rather than themselves acting as managers.

The zaibatsu founders are as famous in Japan, and were as colorful, as their American analogues and contemporaries Carnegie, Rockefeller, and Vanderbilt. The founder of the Mitsubishi zaibatsu Iwasaki Yatarō (1834–1885) started as the manager of a trading company set up by his home Tosa domain (in Shikoku). After the Restoration, the trading company and its ancillary ocean shipping fleet reverted to Iwasaki's private ownership. By providing ships for military expeditions including the Taiwan expedition[4] and the Satsuma rebellion, Iwasaki eventually garnered generous government favors, subsidies, and protection while artfully evading onerous government restrictions on his operations. By the time of Iwasaki's death in 1885, Mitsubishi Mail Steamship Company was the largest and most profitable shipping line in Japan and had provided the capital necessary to purchase from the government the Takashima Coal Mine and Nagasaki Shipyard. In the ensuing decades, the expanding Mitsubishi empire

---

[4] In 1873 a contingent of 54 shipwrecked Japanese sailors were attacked and killed on Taiwan and the following year the Meiji government conducted a retaliatory raid.

came under the direction of Iwasaki's brother, son, and grandson, successively. The last of these, Iwasaki Koyata (1879–1946), who directed the Mitsubishi zaibatsu from 1916 until 1945, was particularly able.

Both the Mitsui and Sumitomo zaibatsu have as antecedents merchant houses founded in the late seventeenth century. Each owed its successful metamorphosis into a leading zaibatsu to the agency of hired managers with business acumen and political connections. The house of Mitsui operated dry goods shops in Edo and Osaka and dealt in currency exchange, including the discounting of government notes based on rice collected in taxes and stored in Osaka warehouses. Under the direction of Minomura Rizaemon (1821–1877), hired by the eight Mitsui founding families to manage their affairs (a post referred to as *bantō*, lit. "clerk"), the house of Mitsui performed lucrative banking services for the Meiji government, eventually leading to the establishment of the Mitsui Bank in 1876. The other Mitsui businesses did not fare so well under the new regime at first, but all began to change when in 1876 a collateral branch of the Mitsui family acquired a new company with influential political connections, renaming it Mitsui Bussan (lit. "Mitsui products"). Government procurement and marketing contracts soon brought a stream of profits on foreign transactions, for example selling the coal from government mines to China, obtaining provisions abroad for Japan's new conscript army, and so on.

In 1888 Mitsui Bussan acquired the government's Miike Coal Mine, the beginning of extensive diversification. In 1892 the founders of Mitsui Bussan were welcomed back to the Mitsui fold, combining Mitsui Bank and its related enterprises with Mitsui Bussan under the joint control of eleven families. As Japan's cotton textile industry boomed in the last decade of the nineteenth century and first decade of the twentieth, Mitsui Bussan's business also expanded. Soon it had spread into ocean shipping. By 1910 the company, in addition to its substantial domestic business, was brokering one-fifth of Japan's exports and a sixth of its imports.

The Sumitomo family had specialized in copper trading and operated the shogunate's Besshi Copper Mine (in Shikoku) from 1691. After the restoration, Hirose Saihei (1828–1914), the delegated agent (*bantō*) of the Sumitomo family, persuaded the *dajokan* that the Besshi Copper Mine belonged to the family rather than to the government. Hirose successfully adapted superior foreign technology for use in the mine and developed effective channels of foreign trade, but resisted diversification of Sumitomo investments into banking and finance up until his forced retirement in 1894.

Yasuda Zenjirō (1838–1921)[5] amassed a personal fortune as a money-changer during the chaotic final years of the shogunate, then parlayed it further as a fiscal agent of the Meiji government. He used his wealth to found a banking empire that became the Yasuda zaibatsu, which was never as diversified into industry as were the other major zaibatsu.

Table 3A.1 at the end of this chapter gives the four major zaibatsu's principal enterprises as well as the date at which each was founded or acquired. The entries give a fair representation of the pattern of zaibatsu development. Each of them began in the 1870s and 1880s in a specific industry or activity as already mentioned:

Mitsui:	banking and brokerage of international trade
Mitsubishi:	shipping
Yasuda:	banking
Sumitomo:	copper mining

Profits in the original zaibatsu lines of business in the 1890s and 1900s financed diversification into related lines:

Mitsui:	mining, textiles, iron and steel
Mitsubishi:	shipbuilding and mining
Yasuda:	insurance
Sumitomo:	banking, coal mining, steel, and copper wire

During the World War I boom the major zaibatsu reaped immense profits, emerging as the dominant forces in a wide range of industries. By around 1920, the owner families of the major zaibatsu had configured their respective commercial empires as disparate enterprises controlled by a holding company, a company whose assets consisted of equity shares in other companies. The principal enterprises so controlled, themselves, had numerous subsidiaries.

---

[5] For a biographical sketch of the venal yet frugal Yasuda, see Kozo Yamamura, "A Re-examination of Entrepreneurship in Meiji Japan (1868–1912)", *Economic History Review*, vol. 21 (April 1968), pp. 144–58.

Some idea of the overall place of the major zaibatsu in the economy can be gauged by the numbers of firms in the zaibatsu orbits and their paid-in capital. Table 3.2 indicates the scale of the major zaibatsu empires in 1928. Paid-in capital refers to the cumulative receipts from the issue of equity shares. It represents a crude measure of the economic scale of enterprise at best, but here affords an approximate meter of the major zaibatsu's importance in the economy. In the 1920s employment and output were still rather heavily concentrated in agriculture and textile manufacturing, neither of which much engaged the zaibatsu. In the remaining sectors, the zaibatsu must have been rather dominating indeed.

The distinguishing features of the zaibatsu were their diversification and their close control by the founding families. By these criteria, there existed zaibatsu other than the four major ones: these include Furukawa, Asano, Ōkura, Suzuki, Nomura, Fujita, Yasukawa, Kawasaki, Iwai, and Kuhara. Behind each of them was an entrepreneur-founder,[6] who upon success in one enterprise branched into others, all the while maintaining close control. We can differentiate the zaibatsu from the numerous enterprises in Japan that were in fact closely held but did not spawn other ventures.[7] We can further differentiate the zaibatsu from diversified businesses that were not closely held. These included the so-called "new zaibatsu", spawned by military procurement spending in the 1920s and 1930s, and coaxed

[6] These lesser zaibatsu and the names of their respective founders include: Asano—Asano Sōichirō (1848–1930); Ōkura—Ōkura Kihachirō (1837–1928); Furukawa—Furukawa Ichibei (1832–1903); Nakajima Kumakichi; Yasukawa—Yasukawa Keiichiro (1849–1934), founder of Yasukawa zaibatsu, which he developed from coal mines in northern Kyushu; Fujita—Fujita Denzaburō (1841–1912), grew rich from government supply contracts, and went on to found a business empire centering on mining, land reclamation and forestry; Kawasaki—Kawasaki Shozo (1837–1912), vice president of Japanese government mail steamship company "YJK", unsuccessful rival of Mitsubishi mail steamship co., founder of Kawasaki shipyard company 1886; Matsukata Kōjirō (1865–1950), third son of the famous finance minister, took over Kawasaki shipbuilding in 1896 and the Kawasaki empire ultimately passed to the control of the Matsukata family; Suzuki—Suzuki Iwajiro (?–1894); Kaneko Naokichi; Nomura—Nomura Tokushichi (1878–1945); Iwai—Iwai Katsujiro; Hitachi/Kuhara—Kuhara Fusanosuke (1869–1965).

[7] Some of the most famous entrepreneurs and the companies they founded are: Itō Denhichi, Mie textile company; Tomiji Hirano, Ishikawajima shipyard; Suzuki Tōzaburo, Japan sugar refining company; Morinaga Taichiro, Morinaga candy; Toyoda Sakichi (1867–1930), Toyota weaving looms, forerunner of the famous automobile company.

Table 3.2. Scale of the major zaibatsu, 1928

	Mitsui	Mitsubishi	Sumitomo	Yasuda	Total
(a) Numbers of firms in the orbit of each zaibatsu					
Directly controlled firms[a]	6	10	13	12	41
Related firms[b]	11	11	5	18	45
Subsidiaries of directly controlled firms	34	14	6	12	66
Subsidiaries of related firms	24	12	0	3	39
Quasi-controlled firms	21	13	3	—	—
Total	96	60	27	—	—
(b) Paid-in capital of firms in the orbit of each zaibatsu (¥mn)					
Directly controlled firms[a]	242	225	132	159	758
Related firms[b]	204	181	47	67	499
Subsidiaries of directly controlled firms	179	84	8	18	289
Subsidiaries of related firms	75	47	24	45	215
Quasi-controlled firms	54	57	1	113	225
Total (% of national total)	849 (6.5%)	588 (4.5%)	188 (1.4%)	361 (2.8%)	1936 (15.2%)

  [a] Directly controlled firms are mainly the firms whose names, or their antecedents, are given in capital letters in Table 3A.1 below.
  [b] Related firms include those denoted by superscript in Table 3A.1 and others not shown in the table.

Source: Takafusa Nakamura, *Economic Growth in Prewar Japan*, Yale University Press, 1971, p. 208 (based on Takahashi Kamekichi, *Nihon zaibatsu no kaibō* (An analysis of Japanese zaibatsu), Tokyo: Chūō Kōronsha, 1930).

by the army into investing in the occupied areas beginning with Manchuria.[8]

Close ownership was not an inevitable feature of business in Japan at the end of the nineteenth century and first half of the twentieth. The numerous large cotton spinning companies were diffusely held, and remained outside the orbit of the zaibatsu. The same is true of the private railroads that predated the 1906 nationalization of rail in Japan. Zaibatsu enterprises, too, might have been diffusely held, enabling the owner-families more fully to diversify their wealth portfolios. Instead, the families chose to maintain close control, perhaps because the particular advantages of close control were more pronounced or its costs less in the industries in which the zaibatsu emerged than others.

The advantages of close ownership reside in the superior economic incentives to monitor managers that such ownership entails. This monitoring benefits all shareholders in proportion to their holdings. Small shareholders have little to gain from actively aligning the interests of corporate managers with their own interest, and they rationally defer to large shareholders who have more of their own wealth at stake. Diffuse shareholding is viable where other considerations, such as the possibility of interruption or termination of managers' careers owing to company bankruptcy or adverse labor market reputation effects, adequately constrain managerial behavior without the active intervention of shareholders. To the extent that zaibatsu enterprises prospered *because* they were closely held firms, rather than *in spite of* that fact, they must not have exhibited the aforementioned characteristics.

The principal economic cost of maintaining concentrated share interests arises from the risk entailed in holding an incompletely diversified wealth portfolio. It is very natural, if not inevitable, that the specialists in close ownership of companies will be the wealthiest investors, for they can attain significant diversification of personal wealth even while maintaining large blocks of stock in specific enterprises. Not all zaibatsu prospered. Notable failures include Furukawa and Suzuki, neither of which survived the financial crises of the 1920s, which illustrates that the zaibatsu fortunes were subject to a degree of risk.

After the end of World War II, the American Occupation authorities directed the dismantling of the zaibatsu. These measures included the divestiture of share interlocks, the dissolution and abolition of holding companies, and the appropriation and disbursement of shares held by the zaibatsu families. By 1960, however, many of the constituent companies of the major zaibatsu had re-formed their earlier alliances. The new groups, known as the *financial keiretsu*, include many of the largest publicly owned corporations in Japan. At the center of each of the six financial keiretsu is a single commercial bank that is the largest debtholder and a significant stockholder in most of the other large firms affiliated with the keiretsu group. In some ways these banks fulfill the same economic role of monitoring investments that the founding families undertook in the zaibatsu.

Small firms

As impressive as the zaibatsu empires became, they never employed a very large fraction of Japan's labor force. Cumulatively, very small firms employed far more Japanese workers in 1920 than did large firms. And, indeed, the proliferation of small firms remains a distinctive aspect of Japanese economic organization even today. Tables 3.3(*a*) and 3.3(*b*) on page 50 present some relevant data.

A proliferation of small firms can reflect either an absence of vertical integration or a lack of horizontal concentration. That is, small firms may supply intermediate inputs to an oligopolistic industry of final goods producers, or, alternatively, an industry of final goods producers may itself be atomistic, comprised only of small firms. Japan has long had examples of both sorts of industrial organization. In the former category are the now ubiquitous subcontractors supplying parts to producers of machinery and equipment. In the 1920s there were relatively few of these. Most small enterprises belonged to atomistic final goods industries. In Japan of the 1920s, examples of final goods industries dominated by small firms and

---

8 The founders of the so-called "new zaibatsu" were: Ayukawa Yoshisuke (1880–1967), Nissan; Mori Nobuteru (1884–1941), Shōwa fertilizer, later Shōwa electric manufacturing company; Nakajima Chikuhei (1884–1949), Nakajima aircraft; Nakano Tomonori (1887–1965), Nihon soda company; Noguchi Shitagau (1873–1944), Japan nitrogen fertilizer company; Ōkochi Masatoshi (1878–1952), Riken, inc.

Table 3.3. Employment in Japan, by sector

(a) Employment by sector, 1880–1970 (millions of persons)

	1880	1890	1900	1910	1920	1930	1940	1950	1960	1970
Agriculture and forestry	15.9	15.9	16.1	16.1	14.2	14.1	13.8	17.4	13.9	8.4
Fishing				0.6	0.5	0.6	0.5	0.7	0.6	0.4
Mining				0.2	0.4	0.3	0.6	0.5	0.5	0.2
Construction				0.6	0.8	1.0	1.0	1.2	2.4	3.9
Manufacturing				2.9	4.6	4.8	7.0	6.2	9.5	13.8
Public utilities and transport				0.7	1.2	1.3	1.5	1.7	2.4	3.5
Retail and wholesale trade				2.6	3.4	5.1	4.9	3.7	8.5	11.4
Services including banking				1.7	2.2	2.6	4.8	4.1	6.8	9.1
Total	21.9	23.0	24.4	25.5	27.1	29.6	34.2	36.2	45.1	51.5

*(b) Self-employed workers or employees of small factories
(those with fewer than 5 employees), by sector, 1920–1950 (%)*

	1920	1930	1940	1950
Agriculture and forestry	97.1	96.8	97.5	96.5
Fishing	n.a.	n.a.	n.a.	n.a.
Mining	n.a.	n.a.	n.a.	n.a.
Construction	n.a.	n.a.	n.a.	n.a.
Manufacturing	37.3	39.6	21.3	21.7
Public utilities and transport	29.7	16.4	8.1	5.6
Retail and wholesale trade	75.0	68.8	63.6	64.0
Services including banking	83.1	82.9	61.3	n.a.
Total	60.5	67.7	58.1	60.4

Sources: Kazushi Ohkawa and Miyohei Shinohara (eds.), *Patterns of Japanese Economic Development*, Yale University Press, 1979, tables A53 and A54; Koji Taira, "Economic Development, Labor Markets and Industrial Relations in Japan, 1905–1955", in Peter Duus (ed.), *The Cambridge History of Japan*, vi, *The Twentieth Century*, Cambridge University Press, 1988, p. 610.

the self-employed included agriculture, retailing and wholesaling, and production of traditional handicraft items such as laquerware, baskets, pottery, hand-sewn kimonos and other clothing, handmade furniture, straw mats, and the like.

Agriculture was the occupation of roughly half the workforce in Japan of the 1920s and 1930s and these were overwhelmingly self-employed, many of them share tenants. Japan's relative scarcity of arable land and abundance of labor induced the development of labor-intensive methods of production. In the first half of the twentieth century, technological innovation in Japanese agriculture focused on improvements in fertilizers and on the introduction of hybrid varieties complementary to the use of fertilizer, rather than on labor-saving mechanical devices which would have been impractical for use in intensively cultivated small plots.[9] Organizing the farmers as employees of large enterprises would have necessitated direct monitoring and oversight by managers, only to achieve the same discipline that market incentives impose on self-employed farmers. And because agriculture in Japan employed relatively little capital and exhibited no significant economies of scale, the organization of farmers into large productive units would not have achieved benefits that warranted these added costs.

[9] Yujiro Hayami and V. W. Ruttan, "Factor Prices and Technical Change in Agricultural Development: The United States and Japan, 1880–1960", *Journal of Political Economy*, vol. 78 (September 1970), pp. 1115–41.

Turning from agriculture to manufacturing, the persistence of small firms in Japan in the 1920s and 1930s can be attributed to the extreme refinement of traditional handicrafts. In fact, the advent of mass production has never yet completely displaced the demand for consumption goods produced in the traditional ways by individual craftsmen. And the crafts are distinctive to Japan, a legacy of the country's historical isolation. The artisans that produce these wares exhibit remarkable skill, require relatively little capital equipment, and are themselves the best governors of their own enterprises. Some of this applies to small retailers and wholesalers, too. In addition, the proliferation of small retailers even today reflects some peculiarities of Japanese geography.

Small stores provide the convenience of next-door shopping, which large stores cannot. On the other hand, fragmented retail outlets are more costly to restock. Retail stores proliferate where households place a high value on shopping convenience and where the cost to the distribution sector of supplying such convenience is relatively modest. Japan's ubiquity of stores has always reflected the fact that Japanese households' storage and transport costs are relatively high in comparison with those of the distributors. The close proximity in Japan of point of production to point of consumption means that the costs of restocking retailers are less than they would be in a more continental economy like that of America. The complexity of wholesale marketing channels and the implied ubiquity of wholesalers is a corollary of the economic considerations that favor a proliferation of stores.

A contrary interpretation to those just offered concerning the persistence in Japan of small firms informs much academic writing on Japan's economic history. A claim, often asserted as fact if only implicitly, holds that Japan has or had a dual economy, that is one with two sectors, only one of which—the modern sector—exhibits a sensitive response to economic incentives. According to this line of thinking, Japan's small firms belong to a backwards sector of its economy, in which sentimental attachments to traditional ways of living have attenuated the pursuit of economic gain. One very precise representation of this argument is Nobel laureate W. Arthur Lewis's theory of disguised unemployment.[10] In Lewis's theory, family enterprises in the traditional sector of a dual economy award their individual members equal shares, which amounts to payment according to each's average product of labor. Enterprises in the modern sector pay market wages equal to the value of the marginal product of labor. The migration of workers from the traditional sector to the modern one assures that the individual rewards are equal in each; but if, in the traditional sector, the average product of labor is greater than the marginal product of labor, then the traditional sector exhibits wasteful overemployment ("disguised unemployment"). The source of this distortion is the adoption of an equal shares rule in the traditional sector; perhaps such a rule follows some cultural norm that predates the evolution of modern industry. Minami, and Fei and Ranis, have applied the Lewis model to Japan, arguing that migration of labor from agriculture to manufacturing accounts for much of the country's economic growth in the twentieth century.[11]

The 1920s: party politics and deflation

World War I ended with armistice on November 11, 1918, followed by the Treaty of Versailles the following June. Japan had remained on the gold standard until September 1917, when it embargoed gold exports and allowed the international price of gold in terms of yen to float freely.[12] From that point, the

---

[10] W. A. Lewis, "Economic Development with Unlimited Supplies of Labour", in Amar Narain Agarwala and Sampat Pal Singh (eds.), *The Economics of Underdevelopment*, Oxford University Press, 1958, pp. 400–49; and W. A. Lewis, "Unlimited Labour: Further Notes", *Manchester School of Economics and Social Studies*, vol. 26 (January 1958), pp. 1–32.

[11] Ryōshin Minami, "The Supply of Farm Labor and the 'Turning Point' in the Japanese Economy", in K. Ohkawa, B. F. Johnston, and H. Kaneda (eds.), *Agriculture and Economic Growth: Japan's Experience*, Princeton University Press, 1970, ch. 11, pp. 270–99; and J. C. H. Fei and Gustav Ranis, *Development of the Labor Surplus Economy: Theory and Policy*, Illinois: 1964. Also see Ryōsin Minami, *The Economic Development of Japan: A Quantitative Study*, New York: St Martin's Press, 1986, esp. ch. 9, "Labour Market and Dual Structure".

[12] Maintaining a gold standard means pegging the price of gold in terms of home currency on international markets, thereby pegging the exchange value of the home currency in terms of the currencies of other gold standard nations. With Japan's embargo of gold exports, international arbitrage in gold was effectively disallowed, and the price of gold in terms of the yen on international markets floated freely, even though the Japanese financial authorities continued to peg the domestic gold price. Technically, in September 1917 the Japanese government authorities pro-

financial authorities in Japan allowed money prices to rise, maintaining a roughly stable nominal exchange rate between the yen and the US dollar. Britain had effectively ceased to maintain the international price of gold in terms of the pound from 1915 onward, and the United States had entered the war and gone off gold in April 1917. Britain and America financed their war expenditures, in part, by inflating their currencies, and Japan matched this inflation. Wholesale prices in Japan roughly doubled between 1917 and the beginning of 1919.

At the war's end, the abnormal boom abated and Japan's national output slumped, inducing a further temporary rise in money prices as implied by the quantity theory of money.[13] Many Japanese businesses that had depended on the wartime conditions, or that did not anticipate their abrupt end, failed. In March 1920 the Tokyo stock market crashed. The Fujita and Kuhara zaibatsu numbered among the business failures, but the larger zaibatsu emerged from the war boom stronger than ever, and proceeded to absorb many of the failing businesses.

In conferences at Brussels in 1920 and Genoa in 1922, the central banks of Britain, France, Italy, and Japan, along with those of other nations, agreed in principle to re-establish the gold standard. Germany in 1924, France in 1926, and Italy in 1927 went back on gold at new parities that reflected the inflation they experienced during the war years. Britain re-established its prewar gold parity in 1925, having effected a substantial reversal of its wartime inflation. The United States had already returned to the gold standard at prewar parity in June 1919.

Return to the gold standard at prewar parity was an avowed goal of Japanese cabinets throughout the 1920s, and the goal was finally attained on January 11, 1930, only to be abandoned once again on December 13, 1931. Britain's return to gold at the prewar parity was famously critiqued at the time by Keynes as unnecessarily subjecting the nation to costly dislocations and high unemployment.[14] In retrospect, Japan's return to gold at prewar parity, too, seems like a costly error, for it necessitated a contractionary monetary policy that contributed to anemic economic conditions in Japan throughout the 1920s.[15] Japan's troubled economic conditions during the 1920s occurred precisely at the delicate time when it was striding toward parliamentary democracy.

The Meiji constitution promulgated in 1889 had provided for a bicameral assembly (the Diet), including an elected Lower House and non-elected House of Peers; but most essential powers of government reposed in a prime minister, nominally appointed by the emperor but in actual practice selected by the Meiji oligarchs themselves, both extra-legally as *genrō* (elder statesmen) and in their formal capacity as an advisory council to the emperor (*sūmitsuin*, the Privy Council). The army and navy chiefs of staff were also nominally appointed by the emperor. The constitution required fiscal proposals to be ratified by the Diet, with the proviso that, should the Diet fail to act, the previous year's budget would be automatically repeated. The proviso, by design, enfeebled the Diet, but not as much as some of the oligarchs would have preferred.

In the first decades under the Meiji constitution, the surviving oligarchs alternated as prime minister, each vying to widen and secure his own base of support. The charismatic Ōkuma sought political strength in party alliances, becoming a bit of an outcast among the other oligarchs, who adopted the principle that the prime ministership should alternate between an oligarch of Chōshū (Itō or Yamagata[16]) and one

---

hibited only exports of gold, and even remained willing to buy gold from foreigners at the same price in terms of yen as before; but, because that price was now below the prevailing international price, nobody took them up on the offer.

13 The quantity theory holds that nominal national income is proportionate to the nation's money stock. If real output falls and the money stock remains stable, prices rise.

14 John Maynard Keynes, "The Economic Consequences of Mr Churchill" (1925); reprinted in J. M. Keynes, *Essays in Persuasion*, New York: Harcourt, Brace, 1932.

15 This is the main thrust of Hugh Patrick, "The Muddle of the 1920s", in J. W. Morley (ed.), *Dilemmas of Growth in Prewar Japan*, Princeton University Press, 1971, ch. 7, pp. 211–66. More recent scholarship argues that price deflation before 1929 was anticipatory of Japanese currency revaluation, not the direct result of contracting the money supply. See Riccardo Faini and Giani Toniolo, "Reconsidering Japanese Deflation during the 1920s", *Explorations in Economic History*, vol. 29 (1992), pp. 121–43.

16 Yamagata Aritomo (1838–1922), son of a low ranking samurai, first rose to prominence as a military leader in Chōshū in the years just prior to the Restoration. War minister at the time of the Satsuma rebellion, he developed Japan's system of conscription. Yamagata was a field commander in the Sino-Japanese war, chief of general staff during the Russo-Japanese war, and twice prime minister, in 1889–91 and 1898–1900, achieving apotheosis in later years as the most powerful of the *genrō* (elder statesman, lit. "founding elder"), an *eminence grise* of Japanese politics. For a fairly sympathetic political biography of Yamagata, see Roger F. Hackett, *Yamagata Aritomo in the Rise of Modern Japan, 1838–1922*, Harvard University Press, 1971.

from Satsuma (Kuroda[17] or Matsukata); Ōkuma was from Hizen (at the western tip of Kyushu, today's Saga prefecture). A list of Japan's prime ministers and the dates of their administrations may be found in Table 3A.2 at the end of this chapter.

As the years passed, electoral politics exerted a stronger force in government affairs, even though the franchise was, until 1920, limited essentially to the wealthy.[18] Matsukata and Itō at first avoided party alliances, but ultimately found it impossible to govern without them. The second Matsukata administration (1896–7) and the third Itō administration (1898) both failed to gain Diet ratification for enlarged military budgets and ended in disarray, allowing Ōkuma to form a party coalition cabinet which, as his rivals had hoped and expected, collapsed from internal disputes after only four months. Yamagata, whose second administration succeeded Ōkuma's first one, now emerged as the most powerful of the oligarchs, in firm control of the army, and with a cadre of followers in the provincial governments and in the House of Peers. He acted to entrench his position by conferring upon the military chiefs of staff *de facto* veto powers over the choice of prime minister. Under the new rules, in order to form a cabinet a prime minister needed serving military officers as army and navy ministers, and this required the assent of the army and navy chiefs of staff. By refusing to delegate a minister, the army or navy chief of staff could pre-empt formation of a cabinet and bring down the government.

Opposition to the Yamagata faction coalesced under the leadership of Itō as president of a new political party, the Rikken Seiyūkai (lit., "political friends of constitutional government"), in 1900. The Seiyūkai was able to secure control of the lower house of the Diet for about twelve years, 1900–12, and remained a major force long after that. With the conclusion of the fourth Itō administration, 1900–1, Itō (who was assassinated in 1909) and Yamagata (who lived until 1922) contrived to assure that their respective proxies alternated as prime minister, Saionji Kimmochi[19] as proxy for Itō, and Katsura Tarō[20] as proxy for Yamagata. This arrangement ended in 1912 when Katsura broke with the Yamagata faction and established his own political party, called the Rikken Dōshikai (lit. "kindred spirits of constitutional government"). Katsura was driven from office in February 1913 and died of

stomach cancer the following year. Yamagata, until his death in 1922, continued to participate in political machinations, but his faction in the Diet and in the bureaucracy now defected to the political party formed by his late protégé. The other established party, the Seiyūkai, also emerged stronger than ever, at last reaping the benefit of efforts by home minister Hara Kei[21] to channel government spending for rail and telegraph lines toward lower house districts represented by party members. In 1913 Hara managed to get the rule that army and navy ministers be appointed from the ranks of active officers set aside, and it was not reinstated until 1936.

---

[17] Kuroda Kiyotaka (1840–1900) was a leader of the government forces that suppressed the Seinan rebellion, succeeding Saigō and Ōkubo as the *de facto* leader of the Satsuma faction among the Meiji oligarchs. He was serving as prime minister at the time the Meiji constitution was promulgated (1889), and gave voice to the principle, widely shared among the oligarchs other than Ōkuma, that the prime minister and his cabinet should remain aloof from party politics.

[18] Originally, only males over 25 who paid more than ¥15 in direct taxes could vote, i.e. 1.3% of the total population. In 1902 the tax limit was lowered to ¥10, expanding the eligible to 2.2% of the population, and in 1920 it was lowered to ¥3, encompassing 5.5% of the population. In 1928 the tax requirement was abolished and 20% of the population was eligible to vote. Women did not obtain the right to vote until after World War II.

[19] Saionji Kimmochi (1849–1940), born to a family of court nobles, graduated from the Sorbonne in Paris where he became a friend of Clemenceau. In 1880 he founded the university that became Meiji university, still among Japan's leading private universities. He also founded and directed a newspaper and editorialized in support of wider political freedom until being asked by the Emperor Meiji himself to give it up. He accompanied Itō to Europe in 1882 to study alternative constitutions, and later served in the upper house of the Diet, eventually (with Itō) co-founding the Seiyūkai political party in 1900. Saionji served as prime minister in 1906–8 and 1911–12, and headed Japan's delegation to the Versailles conference. In later years he served as *genrō* and, from 1924 until his death in 1940, as the only one.

[20] Katsura Tarō (1847–1913), like Yamagata, a general from Chōshū, was thrice prime minister, in 1901–5, 1908–11, and 1912–13.

[21] Hara Kei (also known as Hara Takashi and as David Hara) (1856–1921), of a samurai family from Tohoku, was a newspaper reporter and editor who entered government in 1882, serving in a variety of capacities including posts in the ministry of agriculture and commerce, and foreign ministry. Hara assisted Itō in forming the Seiyūkai political party, served as minister of communications in the fourth Itō cabinet (1900), and as minister of home affairs in the first and second Saionji cabinets (1906–8, 1911–12) and first Yamamoto cabinet (1913–14). He succeeded Saionji as president of the Seiyūkai and became prime minister in 1918 after the Seiyūkai gained a majority of Diet seats in election, an unprecedented development in Japan. His assassination in 1921 deprived Japan of an able and respected leader, more a pragmatist than an idealist. For analysis of Hara's political career, see T. Najita, *Hara Kei and the Politics of Compromise, 1905–1915*, Harvard University Press, 1967.

The third Katsura administration was succeeded by that of an admiral, Yamamoto Gombei,[22] not himself affiliated with a party but well supported by the Seiyūkai. When the Yamamoto administration was brought down by a bribery scandal, Ōkuma was returned as prime minister, having been persuaded out of retirement to lead the Dōshikai. Then, Ōkuma's vigorous campaigning as the incumbent prime minister garnered a majority of the Diet seats for the Dōshikai in the 1915 election. The era of party government was nearly at hand.

Ōkuma's second administration was followed by a non-party government supported by the Seiyūkai, but when in the general elections of 1917 the Seiyūkai gained a majority, Hara, as the party's president, formed a government. Tragically, Hara Kei was assassinated three years later, a setback for the principle of democratic government. Hara was immediately succeeded by the Seiyūkai's Takahashi Korekiyo,[23] later famous for his adept service as minister of finance in 1932–6, but not nearly as able a politician as Hara had been. There followed a sequence of rather weak governments based on coalitions of forces outside either of the major parties, the Seiyūkai and the Kenseikai (lit. "constitutional government association"), the latter formed from a merger of the Dōshikai and two other parties in 1916. Finally, in the 1924 election the parties united to embrace the principle of party government. The Kenseikai won a plurality and its leader Katō Takaaki[24] became prime minister. From that time until the advent of military governments in 1932, cabinets alternated between the Seiyūkai and Kenseikai (in 1927 renamed the Minseitō, lit. "populist party", upon merger with another party, the Seiyū-hontō).

The Seiyūkai and Kenseikai–Minseitō actually differed little in their political platforms, as is commonly true of political parties vying for electoral majorities, but some differences may nevertheless be noted. The Seiyūkai prospered from blatant pork barrel politics, steering government spending toward friendly electoral districts. For this reason, the Seiyūkai continued to favor government investment in rail lines, bridges, harbors, roads, and telegraph and telephone networks, even when it necessitated tax increases. The Seiyūkai enjoyed its strongest support in rural districts. The Kenseikai–Minseitō was the party of fiscal austerity and limited taxation,

and found its strongest support in the urban districts. Both parties garnered political contributions and candidates for office from the various zaibatsu; but, largely because of personal connections between zaibatsu families and party leaders, the Seiyūkai became closely connected in the public mind with the Mitsui zaibatsu and the Kenseikai–Minseitō with the Mitsubishi zaibatsu.

Many leaders of both major parties had experienced life in the West and had acquired a cosmopolitan outlook. In foreign affairs, both parties

---

[22] Yamamoto Gombei (1852–1933), of Satsuma, became a staff officer in the navy, rising to the post of navy minister, and served twice as prime minister, in 1913–14, and 1923–4.

[23] Takahashi Koreikiyo (1854–1936) was adopted into a family of low-ranking samurai in Sendai, learned English as a house servant in Yokohama in 1865–6 and in California in 1867, returning to Japan the following year and serving as an English instructor, college student, a clerk in the Ministry of Finance, and private speculator. In 1881 Takahashi assumed a post in the ministry of education, and later in the ministry of agriculture and commerce, was sent to America in 1887–8 to study the monopoly trademark system and returned to Japan as the first director of the Patent Office in 1887. Leaving government service, he was financially ruined in a failed attempt to open a silver mine in Peru but in 1892 entered employment in the Bank of Japan, where he displayed exceptional talent, supervising the flotation of sovereign debt to finance the Russo-Japanese war expenditures and rising to the post of governor of the Bank of Japan in 1911. He joined the Seiyūkai in 1913 and served as finance minister in the first administration of Yamamoto Gombei 1913–14, and the Hara Kei administration in 1918–21, succeeding to the prime ministership upon Hara's assassination. He served as minister of agriculture and commerce, and after the ministry's division that same year as minister of commerce and industry in 1924–5. Following the 1927 financial crisis he came out of retirement to again serve as minister of finance under Tanaka Giichi, departing after four months, and he left retirement again in 1931 to serve as finance minister in the administrations of Inukai in 1931–2, Saitō in 1932–4, and Okada in 1934–6, overseeing Japan's abandonment of the gold standard and adoption of expansive fiscal and monetary policies widely credited with ending the great depression in Japan. Takahashi was assassinated in the February 26, 1936 attempted military coup.

[24] Katō Takaaki (1860–1926) graduated from Tokyo Imperial University in 1881 and began his career in the Mitsubishi company, studying in England for two years in 1883–5, and in 1886 marrying the eldest daughter of the company's founder, Iwasaki Yatarō. Katō entered government service in 1888 as the secretary of the foreign minister Ōkuma, and later served as minister of finance in the fourth Itō administration in 1900–1, as foreign minister in the first Saionji cabinet in 1909, as ambassador to England in 1909–13, and as minister of foreign affairs in the second Ōkuma administration of 1914–16. It was Katō who pushed hardest for war on Germany and authored the Twenty-One Demands, in pursuit of both widened Japanese political and commercial privileges in China. A founder of the Kenseikai in 1916, Katō became a promoter of party government and served as prime minister based on Kenseikai plurality in the 1924 election; he died in office, of natural causes, and was succeeded by his home minister Wakatsugi.

supported cooperation with the western powers, and integration of Japan with the world economy, but they asserted special prerogatives for Japan in Asia. The 1911 republican revolution in China had thrown the old treaty port system there into permanent disarray. The second Ōkuma administration, with Katō Takaaki as foreign minister, had aggressively sought to exploit this situation, in 1914 by entering World War I mainly in order to take over the German concessions in China, and then in 1915 by demanding the Chinese republican government's recognition of special Japanese commercial and political privileges in China, the so-called "Twenty-One Demands". But at the war's end, Japan joined the movement toward internationalism and peaceful coexistence championed by the American president Woodrow Wilson, withdrawing from Shantung, and accepting something less than colonial status for the formerly German-held islands of the South Pacific. Both parties maintained a pragmatic rather than principled opposition to foreign military adventures, objecting on grounds of ineffectiveness and high costs, rather than from any pacifistic inclinations. Following the Russian revolution of 1918, Japan had joined a multinational force in Siberia, a costly and fruitless attempt to displace the Bolsheviks. The Hara administration began a withdrawal of the Japanese forces from Siberia but this was not completed until 1925. Both political parties supported the maintenance of a Japanese sphere of influence in Manchuria. None of this implied any departure from the basic policy supported by both, of cooperation with the western powers, mainly Britain and the United States. Cooperation with the West entailed, first, the maintenance of an open world trading regime, anchored by the gold standard, and, second, the conclusion of arms limitation agreements and diplomatic treaties. The Washington Conference in 1921–2 resulted in a treaty that set strict limits on warships. The 1930 London Conference continued and expanded restraints on warships. Additionally, Japan was a member of the League of Nations from 1919 until 1933, and a signatory of the Nine Power Agreement of 1922 recognizing the sovereignty of China, and the Pact of Paris (August) 1928 renouncing war.

Japan's return to the gold standard, as promised at the 1922 Genoa conference, required that it amass a stock of official reserves sufficiently great to pre-empt

speculative attack. This was more consonant with the fiscal austerity of the Kenseikai–Minseitō than with the pork barrel politics of the Seiyūkai. The Kenseikai governments of Katō Takaaki (1924–5) and Wakatsugi Rejirō[25] (1926–7) failed to re-establish gold parity only because of the continuing financial legacy of the Tokyo earthquake in 1923. The earthquake and ensuing fires had wreaked havoc in Tokyo and Yokohama. Total damages have been estimated at 5.5 billion yen,[26] roughly 42 percent of Japan's 1923 GNP. About 100,000 persons died, including 40,000 who had gathered in a single spot after the quake and were consumed in fire. Government relief efforts virtually depleted Japan's remaining specie reserves accumulated during the World War I boom, and even necessitated international borrowing, including 545 million yen in Japanese government bonds issued in London and New York in February 1924.

Up until the earthquake, Japan's financial authorities had maintained rough parity between the yen and the dollar. With the depletion of the government's international reserves in disaster relief, speculators anticipated an indefinite postponement of Japan's return to the gold standard at the old parity. For this reason, in the months after the earthquake the yen depreciated sharply against the dollar and other foreign currencies. For Japan's international traders, this compounded the losses arising from the earthquake itself, a contributing factor in the banking panic of 1927 which ended the Wakatsugi administration and returned the Seiyūkai to power.

The earthquake actually had occurred during the period in which non-party government had temporarily reasserted itself following the assassination of Hara Kei. At that time, Yamamoto Gombei was called to a second term as prime minister to oversee

---

[25] Wakatsugi Reijirō (1866–1949) graduated from Tokyo Imperial University in 1892 and entered government service, rising to the posts of minister of finance in the second Ōkuma administration of 1914–16, and home minister under Katō Takaaki in 1924–5, succeeding Katō as prime minister upon his death. Wakatsugi headed the Japanese delegation to the London disarmament conference of 1930 and, following the mortal wounding of Hamaguchi that same year, succeeded him as president of the Minseitō and prime minister. The Manchurian incident ended his administration, and he entered the upper house of the Diet.

[26] Ando Yoshio (ed.), *Kindai nihon keizai shi yoran* (Handbook of the economic history of modern Japan), 2nd edn, University of Tokyo, 1979, p. 110.

the earthquake relief effort with Innou Junnosuke[27] as finance minister. The liberal issue of government loans to make up business losses resulting from the earthquake prevented an instant collapse of the banking system but created trouble later on. The immediate relief was accomplished by the Bank of Japan paying cash to banks in exchange for discounted commercial bills which were uncollectable because of the earthquake.

Discounted bills come about when the holder of an IOU of some kind (a "bill") signs over payment to a bank in exchange for immediate funds. Banks "discount" such bills; that is, they pay out less than the amount promised by the bill itself, because the bills promise only a future cash receipt which has a discounted present value. By purchasing these discounted bills from the banks, that is by "rediscounting" the bills, the Bank of Japan, for the time being, effected full reimbursement for IOUs that were uncollectable, supposedly because of the earthquake. (In fact, a lot of the bills stamped "earthquake bills" by banks and presented to the Bank of Japan for rediscounting were unrelated to the earthquake.) In all, the Bank of Japan rediscounted 431 million yen of "earthquake bills". Of this, approximately 230 million yen was repaid by the issuers of the notes, leaving another 200 million yen unrecovered and essentially worthless.

Whether these losses would be absorbed by the government or by the banks became a matter of intense political debate in 1926 and 1927, with the ruling Kenseikai favoring the former and the opposition Seiyūkai the latter. In Diet debates on this matter it became public knowledge that a number of banks, including the quasi-official Bank of Taiwan, held a disproportionate share of the questionable notes and would be subject to collapse in the event that the legislative relief was not enacted.[28] When it became clear that the Seiyūkai would prevent a government bailout of the Bank of Taiwan, panic ensued. Bank runs, in which depositors attempted en masse to withdraw funds, precipitated the collapse of the Bank of Taiwan and eleven private banks, including the prestigious Fifteenth Bank, closely linked to the imperial household and whose president was the eldest son of the late finance minister Matsukata. The Wakatsugi cabinet resigned and the Seiyūkai returned to power with Tanaka Giichi[29] as prime minister.

The Seiyūkai now presided over essentially the same bailout of commercial banks that, as the party out of power, it had opposed. The Seiyūkai failed to hold a legislative majority and thus could not prevent the enactment of a Kenseikai-sponsored bank law that imposed minimum capital requirements on banks and effected the closure or amalgamation of many smaller banks in Seiyūkai rural strongholds.[30]

The Tanaka administration ruled for a little over two years and was ultimately unseated over its mishandling of an incident in which Japanese army troops assassinated the Chinese warlord in control of Manchuria (Zhang Tso-lin). The Kenseikai, which soon after the fall of the Wakatsugi cabinet had merged with the Seiyūhontō to form the Minseitō, returned to power under Hamaguchi Osachi[31] in

27 Innoue Junnosuke (1869–1932) graduated from Tokyo Imperial University in 1896 and joined the Bank of Japan, assuming posts in Britain in 1897–9 and America in 1908–11, becoming president of the Yokohama Specie Bank in 1913, governor of the Bank of Japan in 1919, and finance minister in the second Yamamoto administration in 1923. Innoue joined the upper house of the Diet in 1924, and again served as governor of the BOJ for 13 months in 1927–8. In 1929 he joined the Minseitō and again served as minister of finance, this time under Hamaguchi in 1929–30, engineering the return to the gold standard at the prewar parity. Innoue was assassinated in the February 1932 *ketsumeidan* (blood oath league) incident.

28 The Bank of Taiwan held about 100 million yen of the unrecoverable earthquake notes, and 70 million yen were owed by a single company, the Suzuki trading company.

29 Tanaka Giichi (1863–1929) was born in Chōshū and, like Katsura Tarō, was a protégé of Yamagata Aritomo. He entered the army in 1883, serving as a staff officer in Manchuria during the Russo-Japanese War of 1905, as minister of war in cabinets of Hara in 1918–21 and Yamamoto in 1923. Tanaka became president of the Seiyūkai in 1925 and prime minister in 1927, at the same time also serving as foreign minister and minister of colonial affairs. His administration collapsed in the wake of controversy over assassination of the Chinese warlord Chang Tso-lin by Japanese army officers in Manchuria. For an analysis of Tanaka's political thought and career, see William Fitch Morton, *Tanaka Giichi and Japan's China Policy*, New York: St Martin's Press, 1980.

30 On the political calculations of the established parties with regard to the indemnity of earthquake bills, the 1927 banking law, and the return to the gold standard at prewar parity, see J. Mark Ramseyer and Frances M. Rosenbluth, *The Politics of Oligarchy: Institutional Choice in Imperial Japan*, Cambridge University Press, 1995 (esp. ch. 8).

31 Hamaguchi Osachi (1870–1931) graduated from Tokyo Imperial University in 1895 and entered the ministry of finance, rising to the posts of vice minister in the second Ōkuma administration in 1914–16 and minister in the Katō Takaaki administrations in 1924–5, and as minister of home affairs in the first Wakatsugi administration in 1926. Hamaguchi was elected to the lower house of the Diet in 1916 for the Kenseikai, and in 1927 became president of the Minseitō (as the Kenseikai was renamed), succeeding Tanaka Giichi as prime minister in 1929. After mortal wounding by an assassin, he turned over his party and administration to Wakatsugi and died the following year.

July 1929, with Innoue Junnosuke again serving as minister of finance. The Minseitō was now determined to see through Japan's return to the gold standard at the prewar parity of ¥100 = $49.85. In late 1929 the yen–dollar rate stood around ¥100 = $44–$46. Returning to the prewar parity would require an upward revaluation of about 10 percent, a real currency appreciation and a domestic price deflation. Innoue first directed fiscal austerity and contraction of the money supply, then announced on November 21, 1929, that beginning January 11, the following year, the government would buy and sell gold on demand in international markets at the prewar parity, removing the embargo on gold exports from Japan that had been operative since September 1917, and re-establishing the gold standard.

The Innoue announcement followed the New York stock market crash (of October 24, 1929) by only a month. Innoue's fiscal and monetary contraction hit Japan just as the United States and Europe entered the Great Depression. In retrospect, Innoue's policies were likened to "opening a window in the middle of a typhoon".[32] As Figure 3.2 depicts, through 1930 and 1931 Japan's real GNP remained level, displaying neither growth nor contraction, while domestic prices dropped precipitously.

Farmers were caught unawares, unable to repay money loans at the newly deflated prices. A bumper harvest of rice in 1930 and collapse of American demand for raw silk exacerbated the economic distress of Japan's agricultural sector which continued to employ about half of the nation's labor force.[33] The real appreciation of the yen inhibited foreign demand for Japanese goods and switched domestic demand toward foreign suppliers. A number of businesses went bankrupt. As the economic and political situation in Japan deteriorated, speculators began to enlarge their holdings of specie, seriously depleting Japan's official reserves. Amidst this political turmoil, in November 1930 Prime Minister Hamaguchi was shot by a lone fanatic. Wakatsugi was once again called upon to serve as prime minister, continuing with the same cabinet and same policies as Hamaguchi, who lingered for a few months before finally succumbing to his wounds.

On March 1931, a group of right-wing extremist army officers called the Sakurakai (lit. "cherry blossom society") plotted unsuccessfully to engineer a coup and install the army minister (Ugaki Kazushige) as the prime minister. The plot was foiled before it could be implemented, but foreshadowed worse things to come. On September 18, 1931, field grade officers in Japan's Kwantung army led by Lieutenant Colonel Ishihara Kanji (1889–1949) set off a small explosion on the tracks of the South Manchuria Railway north of Mukden (today's Shenyang), claimed that it was an act of sabotage, and took that as the pretext for attacking Chinese troops there. The Wakatsugi cabinet decided the following day on a policy of nonexpansion of hostilities, but the army in the field ignored this and proceeded to quickly occupy the whole of Manchuria, an event incongruously dubbed the "Manchurian incident". In October, yet another coup attempt by the Sakurakai was discovered and foiled. Unable to control the army and unable to decide on a course of action, the Wakatsugi cabinet resigned in December, and was succeeded by a Seiyūkai cabinet headed by Inukai

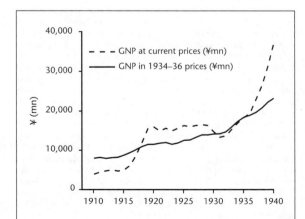

Figure 3.2. Real and nominal GNP, 1910–1940

Source: Kazushi Ohkawa and Miyohei Shinohara (eds.), *Patterns of Japanese Economic Development*, Yale University Press, 1979, tables A1 and A3.

---

[32] The retort of Muto Sanji, president of Kanebo, Japan's largest cotton spinning company at the time.

[33] Ironically, farmers are impoverished by a large harvest; for, given the relatively price-inelastic demand for agricultural staples, an expansion of the supply depresses revenue. In 1930 Japan produced 67 million *koku* of rice compared with 60 million *koku* in 1929, while the value of the crop fell from 1,585 million yen in 1929 to 1,118 million yen in 1930 (*LTES*, vol. 9) (1 *koku* = 4.96019 bushels). The GNP deflator fell by about 11.6% from 1929 to 1930.

Tsuyoshi,[34] with 77-year-old Takahashi Korekiyo as finance minister. This was to be Japan's last government headed by a political party until after the end of World War II. Takahashi immediately took Japan off of the gold standard and introduced an expansionary monetary and fiscal policy, with salutary effects on Japan's economy, but the die was already cast. The Seiyūkai proved no more effective than the Minseitō at curbing the army. Inukai and Takahashi were both to fall before assassins, as would the former finance minister Innoue. Ishihara would be promoted and given important new responsibilities in preparing the nation of Japan for total war.

Military government and the wartime economy, 1931–1945

The Japanese military occupation of Manchuria marked an abrupt departure from Japan's policy of conciliation of the Western powers, widely referred to as "Shidehara diplomacy", after Shidehara Kijūrō,[35] foreign minister in Kenseikai–Minseitō cabinets 1924–7 and 1929–31. Both Seiyūkai prime ministers of the early Showa era, Tanaka Giichi and Inukai Tsuyoshi, opposed certain elements of Shidehara diplomacy, but not its basic thrust. Tanaka Giichi argued for a more forceful insistence on special Japanese prerogatives in China, and Inukai argued that the terms negotiated by the Kenseikai's Wakatsugi at the London conference of 1930 jeopardized Japan's security. More radical critiques of Shidehara diplomacy emanated from political factions within the military forces. Where the established parties embraced Japan's participation in an open world trading system, the political factions in the army and navy sought instead the establishment of an autarkic Japanese trading bloc in Asia, anchored by the colonial empire and expanded through military conquest if necessary. In the end, the militaristic position won out, not by democratic election but by assassination, by the threat of armed coup, and by *fait accompli*. Toward the end of the decade, popular support for the policy of cooperation with the West began to erode anyway. The economic distress induced by Japan's return to the gold standard figures in this, but other factors loom larger. The 1928 advance north by the Kuomintang (lit. "national people's party") forces of Chiang Kai-shek was widely

believed to threaten Japanese commercial interests in Manchuria. Furthermore, the conciliatory attitude of Japan toward the West appeared less reciprocal in the face of the 1924 US law excluding Japanese immigration, Britain's abandonment of the gold standard on September 21, 1930, and its Import Duties Act of 1931, and America's Smoot–Hawley tariff of 1930. This was the setting in which the Seiyūkai returned to office for the last time.

Immediately upon assuming power in December 1931, the Inukai–Takahashi administration abandoned the gold standard and allowed the yen to depreciate in real terms, that is to depreciate relative to foreign currencies by more than the difference in domestic and foreign rates of change inflation. The real yen depreciation, by lowering the foreign price of Japanese goods, stimulated demand for Japanese exports, but provoked foreign enmity and attempts to organize boycotts of Japanese goods in America and Britain, which in 1932 were both nearing the trough of the Great Depression. The real yen depreciation also induced Japanese demanders to switch from foreign suppliers to domestic ones, further reviving Japan's sagging economy. Abandonment of the gold standard, or at the least devaluation of the exchange rate, may have been inevitable anyway by the end of 1931, simply because of the dramatic depletion of Japan's official holdings of specie in the two years it was back on the gold standard, but this

---

[34] Inukai Tsuyoshi (1855–1932) began as a journalist, and entered politics in 1885, serving first as a member of the Tokyo prefectural assembly, then as a representative in the lower house of the Diet from his home district in Okayama. He was a political ally of Ōkuma, and a leader of splinter parties including the Kakushin Karuba (reform club), which merged with the Seiyūkai in 1925, and upon the death of Tanaka Giichi in 1929 succeeded him as president of the Seiyūkai, ending a four-year retirement. Inukai succeeded Wakatsugi as prime minister and was assassinated in the May 15 (1932) incident half a year later.

[35] Shidehara Kijūrō (1872–1951) of Osaka, was married to the daughter of the founder of Mitsubishi (Iwasaki Yatarō) who was also the younger sister of the wife of Kenseikai leader Katō Takaaki. Shidehara graduated from Tokyo Imperial University and entered the diplomatic corps in 1896, serving as vice minister of foreign affairs in 1915–19, ambassador to the USA in 1919–22, foreign minister under Katō and Wakatsugi in 1924–7 and again under Hamaguchi in 1929–31, and for four months acting prime minister after Hamaguchi's mortal wounding, continuing as foreign minister in the second Wakatsugi administration. Shidehara also had served as a member of the upper house of the Diet from 1926. Later he was the first postwar prime minister (October 1945–April 1946), served as foreign minister under Yoshida Shigeru, was elected to the lower house in 1947, and served as speaker from 1949 until his death in 1951.

was only one element of "Takahasi finance". Besides abandoning the gold standard, Takahashi also initiated expansionary monetary and fiscal policies, which have earned him the sobriquet "the Keynes of Japan".

Perhaps, as suggested by Dick Nanto and S(hinji) Takagi,[36] Takahashi had read and assimilated Keynes's pre-*General Theory*[37] writings. In any case, Takahashi asserted, in the manner of Keynes, that, by deficit financing and accommodative monetary policy, the government could stimulate private economic activity. Takahashi wrote that, by spending ¥2,000 rather than saving it, an individual contributes to the income of others, who in turn spend some portion of it and so on, ultimately raising the national income by some multiple of the original ¥2,000, and that the same would hold if government were to initiate the process by spending the ¥2,000.[38] Takahashi speculated that the multiplier effects of added spending might range between 20 and 30, which, as every modern economics student will perceive, requires a marginal propensity to consume of between 0.95 and 0.97, and also presumes that added output absorbs otherwise idle resources.[39]

The Takahashi fiscal expansion rested upon enlarged military spending and upon a package of public investments labeled "emergency relief expenditures" (*jikyoku kyōkyūhi*), largely comprising

land reclamation, irrigation, drainage, dykes, roads, and river repairs. Rather than levy new taxes to finance these measures, the national government issued bonds, at prices supported by an accommodative Bank of Japan. That is, the Bank of Japan lowered its official discount rate and expanded its credit to commercial banks. (The *discount rate* is the interest rate at which the Bank of Japan loans funds to commercial banks.) This policy reversed the sharp contraction in Japan's money stock that had accompanied the return to the gold standard.

Figure 3.3 depicts the course of monetary policy in relation to growth in output and prices from 1910 to

---

[36] Dick K. Nanto and Shinji Takagi, "Korekiyo Takahashi and Japan's Recovery from the Great Depression", *American Economic Review*, vol. 75 (May 1985), pp. 369–74; an excellent and concise description of Takahashi's career, the origin of his economic ideas, and some of the details of his policies as minister of finance in 1932–6.

[37] John Maynard Keynes, *The General Theory of Employment, Interest and Money*, London: Macmillan, 1936.

[38] Takahashi Korekiyo, *Zuisōroku* (essays), Tokyo: Chikura shobō, 1936, p. 247; cited by Nanto and Takagi. The particular essay anticipating Keynes's spending multiplier was originally published in 1929.

[39] The "marginal propensity to consume" is the percentage of each dollar of added income that is devoted to consumption. If, as Keynes presumed, added consumption spending enlarges final demand and, by drawing into service otherwise idle resources, expands output by the same amount, then an autonomous increase in spending ultimately expands output by a factor known as the *spending multiplier*, i.e. 1/(1 – marginal propensity to consume).

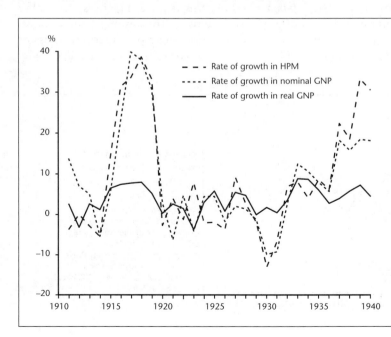

Figure 3.3. Annual rates of growth in high-powered money (HPM) and real GNP, 1910–1940

Sources: *real GNP*: Kazushi Ohkawa and Miyohei Shinohara (eds.), *Patterns of Japanese Economic Development*, Yale University Press, 1979, table A2; *high-powered money*: Harada and Horiuchi, "Senzenki nihon no kinyū: pafuōmansu to sono hyōka" (Prewar Japanese finance: an evaluation of its performance), *Yūsei kenkyū rebyū*, vol. 3 (March 1993), pp. 57–74.

1940. Growth in prices is represented as the difference between growth of nominal GNP (the dotted line) and growth in real GNP (the solid line). The dashed line represents the annual percentage change in "high-powered money", sometimes referred to as the monetary base, consisting of currency held by the public, banks' vault cash, and deposits at the Bank of Japan. By raising its official discount rate and constricting credit to commercial banks, the Bank of Japan effects a contraction of high-powered money, and this induces a contraction of bank deposits, as the banks call in their own loans. A reduction in the discount rate accomplishes the reverse. The contraction in the money stock from 1927 to 1930, as intended, reduced prices in Japan, enabling a restoration of the prewar gold parity of the yen; but also it may have contributed to the leveling off of Japan's real GNP from 1929 to 1931. Takahashi's abandonment of the gold standard and expansion of the money supply reversed the deflation and was followed by rapid growth in real GNP.

Fiscal policy over these years was also expansionary. Under Takahashi's direction, government spending expanded from around one-fifth of GNP in 1927–31 to one-fourth of GNP in 1932 and 1933, consistent with a pattern set by earlier Seiyūkai administrations. Figure 3.4 depicts annual changes in real government spending over 1910–40 as percentages of the previous year's real GNP. The Seiyūkai administrations—Hara–Takahashi (1919–21) and Tanaka (1927–8)—expanded government spending, while the Kenseikai–Minseitō administra-

tions—Katō–Wakatsugi (1925–6) and Hamaguchi–Wakatsugi (1929–31)—contracted it, consonant with the rural pork barrel politics of the former and the urban tax relief politics of the latter. Only the 1931 fiscal expansion during the last Minseitō administration deviates significantly from this pattern, largely reflecting the decline in the price level from the previous year—appropriations of the national government were actually less in nominal terms in 1931 than in 1930. The military governments after 1936 greatly expanded government spending compared with the earlier governments of either political party.

Whether because of "Takahashi finance" or the natural resiliency of Japan's market economy, the economic malaise, in which the last Seiyūkai administration assumed office, abated rapidly. The political turmoil did not abate. In February 1932, right-wing civilian fanatics dubbing themselves the "blood oath league" (Ketsumeidan) assassinated the former minister of finance Innoue, and the following month assassinated the top manager of the Mitsui zaibatsu (Dan Takuma). Then, in the May 15 incident of 1932, a group of young naval officers confronted Prime Minister Inukai in his official residence and shot him to death. On the same day, their co-conspirators attempted to sabotage Tokyo's electric power station and attacked the Bank of Japan building, Seiyūkai headquarters, and other official installations. In the ensuing military trials, the prosecutors and judges permitted the assassins of Inukai and their co-conspirators to deliver long-

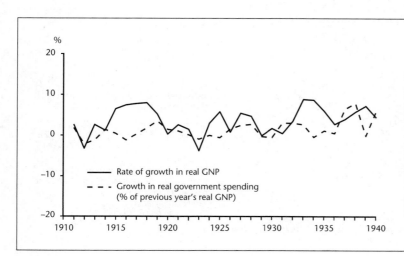

Figure 3.4. Changes in real government spending as a percentage of previous year's real GNP, 1910–1940

Sources: government spending = government consumption (Kazushi Ohkawa and Miyohei Shinohara (eds.), *Patterns of Japanese Economic Development*, Yale University Press, 1979, table A3) + government investment (*Patterns*, table A39); real GNP: same as figure 3.6.

winded harangues claiming patriotic motivations for everything, and then meted out shockingly lenient sentences, for example four years' imprisonment for the assassination of the prime minister. Civilians among the conspirators were given sentences up to life imprisonment by civil courts.

The assassination of Inukai effectively ended government by the political parties. The Inukai administration was immediately succeeded by two coalition governments headed by admirals not affiliated with political parties, but holding moderate views, that is in broad agreement with the terms of the Washington and London naval treaties: Saitō Makoto[40] (prime minister May 1932–July 1934) and Okada Keisuke[41] (prime minister July 1934–March 1936). Takahashi Korekiyo continued as finance minister and enhanced his posthumous reputation by defying the armed forces' insistence on increased appropriations. About all that the military was able to wring from the government in these years were special subsidies for defense industries: subsidies for production of vehicles for military use (1932); subsidies for shipbuilding (1933); and tax credits, subsidies, and protection of the oil refining industry and amalgamation of steel producers into Nippon *seitetsu*, the government-owned successor to Yawata (1934).

Meanwhile, another struggle for political control was under way within the armed forces themselves. Army officers aligned into two opposing factions. The "imperial way faction" (Kōdōha), led by Araki Sadao,[42] the army minister in the Inukai and Saitō cabinets in 1932–4, foresaw the coming war with the Soviet Union, was virulently anti-communist, and seriously entertained possibilities of completely revamping the government as a military dictatorship. The Kōdōha traced its roots to the Satsuma political clique, viewed Saigo Takamori, leader of the doomed Satsuma rebellion of 1877, as its founding figure, and steeped itself in romantic notions of the spiritual purity and innate superiority of the Japanese warrior. The "control faction" (Tōseiha), had a more pragmatic outlook, and viewed Japan's military strength as dependent upon modern weapons and a large national economy geared toward manufacturing such weapons in great quantities. Ultimately, the Tōseiha sought to establish a planned economy under martial law, but within the existing constitutional framework. The Tōseiha traced its roots to the Chōshū political faction, originally dominated

by Yamagata Aritomo. It is a great irony that the pragmatic politics championed by the Tōseiha led Japan toward alliance with Nazi Germany. The "pragmatists" in Japan's government in 1940 judged incorrectly that Germany would conquer Britain and that alliance with Germany would forestall American intervention in Japan's war of conquest in China. But this runs a bit ahead of our story.

In the parliamentary elections of February 1936, the Minseitō emerged with a majority of seats in the Lower House, after campaigning on the principle of parliamentary government and against fascism. One week later, on February 26, 1936, young officers of the Kōdōha, leading 1,400 troops, attempted a *coup d'état*. They conducted a wave of assassinations, and occupied a number of government offices in the center of Tokyo. The victims of assassination in the "February 26 incident", as it came to be known, included the finance minister Takahashi, the former prime minister Saitō, and the brother-in-law of the prime minister Okada who was mistaken for Okada himself. The coup attempt was suppressed after three days, and the thirteen leading perpetrators were secretly tried and (in July) hanged. From this point until near the end of the Pacific war, the "control faction" held a firm grip on the army.

After the February incident, the prime ministership went to Hirota Kōki,[43] a former diplomat. Under Hirota's administration, the rule requiring army and navy ministers to be appointed from the

---

40 Saitō Makoto (1858–1936) rose through the officer corps of the navy, and became a protégé of prime minister Yamamoto Gombei, serving as naval minister in 1906–14, governor general of Korea in 1919–27 and 1929–31, prime minister in 1931–4, and Lord Keeper of the Privy Seal 1934–6. Saitō was assassinated in the February 26 (1936) incident.

41 Okada Keisuke (1868–1952) was a career naval officer who rose to the post of navy minister in the 1927 Tanaka Giichi cabinet and the Saitō Makoto cabinet of 1931–4, and was called to serve as prime minister in 1934–6 after a financial scandal brought down the Saitō cabinet. Okada survived an assassination attempt in the February 26 (1936) incident, after which he resigned.

42 Araki Sadao (1877–1966), a career army officer, was forced out of active duty following the attempted coup of February 1936 but returned as minister of education in the first Konoe cabinet 1938, in charge of military indoctrination of Japanese youth. After the war Araki was tried as a war criminal and sentenced to life imprisonment, but was later pardoned.

43 Hirota Kōki (1878–1948) was a career diplomat, rising to the posts of minister to Holland in 1923, ambassador to the Soviet Union in 1930, foreign minister under Saitō in 1933, and prime minister after the February incident. After the war Hirota was hanged as a class-A war criminal.

active ranks was reinstated, and new legislation was enacted removing the remaining protections for political dissent. The Hirota administration was succeeded ten months later by that of a general, Hayashi Senjūrō,[44] who was in turn forced to resign after four months when the militaristic political party he favored (the Shōwa-kai) was soundly trounced in the 1937 Diet elections.

Now that army and navy ministers had to be drawn from the ranks of active officers, the military chiefs of staff held effective veto power over any proposed choice of prime minister. The elderly Saionji, last of the *genrō*, hoped to preserve Japan's amicable relations with Britain and America, but faced the dilemma of having to recommend to the emperor a prime minister who was acceptable to the army and navy leadership. After the fall of the Hayashi cabinet, the prime ministership was bestowed in June 1937 upon 45-year-old Konoe Fumimaro,[45] like Saionji, an aristocrat of the court nobility, with experience of the West. Konoe was also acceptable to the military, having long argued that the post-World War I Anglo-American hegemony, although couched in the idealistic rhetoric of pacifism and democracy, was actually intended to preserve a disproportionate share of the world's resources for America and Britain, unfairly depriving Japan of its proper role as the leading colonial power in Asia and the Pacific.

The hostilities in Manchuria had led, in February 1932, to the creation of a new state, known as "Manchukuo", with a puppet government completely subordinate to Japanese influence, a move condemned by the League of Nations, precipitating Japan's withdrawal from that body in March 1933. Later that same year an economic construction program for Manchukuo placed key industries under state control, each one a government monopoly, managed by the Japanese army.

Despite the army's best efforts, central planning of colonial enterprise proved disastrously ineffective in Manchukuo, and in 1936 the army invited private firms to enter Manchukuo with government guarantees. These so called "new zaibatsu" included Nippon sangyō (antecedent of today's Nissan) and Nakajima aircraft (antecedent of Fuji heavy industries). The new zaibatsu were diffusely held, not closely controlled by their founders. In this sense, the new zaibatsu may be distinguished from the others; they were in fact not really zaibatsu at all.[46] The new zaibatsu prospered on the basis of government procurement contracts and special subsidies, rather than entrepreneurship and business acumen. Few of them other than Nissan and Fuji heavy industries survived the upcoming war in any form. The resident population of Japanese citizens in Manchuria/Manchukuo swelled from 190,000 in 1936 to 418,000 in 1937, out of a total population of Manchukuo around 35 million.[47] Such was the state of affairs in China as Prince Konoe assumed the prime ministership for the first time. Matters were about to change, dramatically.

On July 7, 1937, one month after Konoe's assumption of office, an unplanned exchange of gunfire between Japanese and Chinese troops at the Marco Polo bridge near Peking quickly escalated into full warfare. The government had only recently officially adopted the army chief of operations Ishihara Kanji's "concept" of postponing war—with China, with the Soviet Union—for five years, until, it was argued, heavy industry could be expanded sufficiently to assure military success. But now that war with China had come, the time to establish the militarized, planned economy long envisioned by the army's reigning "control faction" was at hand.

The first of the industrial policies placing Japan's economy on a war footing, the 1931 Major Industries Control Law, had officially identified existing trade associations, the oldest and most famous of these being the Japan Cotton Spinners Association, as nexuses of government control.[48] Many approved

---

[44] Hayashi Senjūrō (1876–1943) was an army general who served as army minister in the Saitō and Okada cabinets in 1932–4.

[45] Konoe Fumimaro (1891–1945) was of noble birth. From 1916 he was the holder of a seat in the upper house of the Diet, a member of the Japanese delegation at the Versailles Peace conference. He was prime minister at the time of the outbreak of the China war in 1937–8, and again at the signing of the tripartite pact, the outlawing of political parties, attempts to institute a command economy, and the setting of a course toward war with the Allied forces in 1940–1. Konoe committed suicide by taking poison, after the issue of an order for his arrest as a possible war criminal.

[46] For a list of the new zaibatsu and their founders, see fn. 8.

[47] E. B. Schumpeter, "Population of the Japanese Empire", in E. B. Schumpeter *et al.* (eds.), *The Industrialization of Japan and Manchukuo, 1930–1940*, New York: Macmillan, 1940, pp. 41–79.

[48] See Takeo Kikkawa, "Functions of Japanese Trade Association before World War II: The Case of Cartel Organizations", in Hiroaki Yamazaki and Matao Miyamoto (eds.), *Trade Associations in Business History: The International Conference on Business History (Fuji Conference)*, vol. 14, University of Tokyo Press, 1988, pp. 53–83.

activities of the control associations were means of effecting cartel restrictions in output. To the extent that these measures succeeded, they freed resources for war production, the intended aim. The industries designated in this law, which was renewed for a second five-year term in 1936, were ultimately forced to produce weapons or shut down. Then, in September 1937, several laws dramatically extended the scope of government control over economic activity of all kinds.

Under the Temporary Capital Adjustment Law, long-term lending controls were placed in effect. Industries deemed inessential to the war effort, that is most civilian industries, including textiles, were now barred altogether from seeking bank loans or other external funding. The Emergency Shipping Management Law empowered the government to commandeer private vessels. Strict government controls over all imports and exports were enforced by the Law Relating to Temporary Export and Import Commodities Measures. And the Armaments Industry Mobilization Law, which had been enacted in 1918, was also finally invoked. Now the management and investment plans of virtually all private factories in Japan were nominally subject to direct government control. In October 1937 the Cabinet Planning Board was established, to draw up materials mobilization plans and administer controls on foreign trade.

In 1938 the National General Mobilization Law nationalized electric power generation. Most war materials were produced by private firms, but these were subject to increasing government control. The 1936 Automobile Industry Law, 1937 Synthetic Oil Industry Law, 1938 Machine Tool Industry Law, 1938 Aircraft Industry Law, 1939 Shipbuilding Law, 1939 Light Metal Industry Law, and 1941 Important Machines Manufacturing Law all placed these industries under government guidance.

By 1939 the China war had developed into one of attrition. Japanese forces had captured the major cities including Hangkow, Canton, Shanghai, Peiping (as the nationalist Chinese renamed Peking in 1928), and the nationalist government capital of Nanking (in December 1937). The murder and pillage that followed in the wake of these "successes" sickened and outraged the entire world. The nationalist government led by Chiang Kai-shek had departed from Nanking and continued the struggle from the natural redoubt at Chungking, far to the west, which the Japanese forces proceeded to bomb indiscriminately from the air. Meanwhile, the Japanese established puppet governments in Peiping (December 1937) and Nanking (March 1938). The Japanese army now firmly controlled the major cities and transportation arteries, but not the vast and heavily populated Chinese countryside. As Ishihara had anticipated, Japan's economic resources were inadequate for the rapid subjugation of China. If, under these circumstances, Japan were attacked by the Soviet Union or the western nations, the results could be disastrous for it. Japanese diplomacy now focused on preserving the country's ability to prosecute the war of conquest against China while discouraging any other nation from joining China as a belligerent.

In January 1939 Konoe stepped aside as prime minister but continued as president of the Privy Council and minister without portfolio in the cabinet of his successor Hiranuma Kiichirō,[49] a former bureaucrat and one-time minister of justice. During Hiranuma's short tenure, Japanese diplomats focused on cementing a defensive alliance with Germany against the USSR, and were completely surprised when in August 1939 Nazi Germany concluded a nonaggression pact with the Soviet Union. Hiranuma was now replaced by Abe Nobuyuki,[50] a former general. Almost immediately after the formation of the short-lived Abe cabinet, in September 1939, Germany invaded Poland, initiating war with Britain. Abe was succeeded as prime minister by an admiral with pro-British and pro-Western inclinations, Yonai Mitsumasa,[51] but the German blitzkrieg of France and the Low Countries in May and June 1940 once again strengthened the pro-German factions among

---

[49] Hiranuma Kiichirō (1867–1952) rose through the ranks of the justice ministry, serving as prosecutor general and in 1923 as minister. He was highly critical of the London naval agreement. Before assuming the post of prime minister in 1939 he had served for three years as president of the Privy Council. After the war he was tried as a class A war criminal and sentenced to life imprisonment.

[50] Abe Nobuyuki (1875–1953).

[51] Yonai Mitsumasa (1880–1948) advanced through the naval officer corps, serving as navy minister in 1937–9. His brief tenure as prime minister in January–July 1940 ended when the army declined to appoint a cabinet minister because of his opposition to a Japanese pact with Germany and Italy. After July 1944 Yonai again served as navy minister in the cabinets that concluded the war and negotiated Japan's final surrender.

the Japanese military leadership and returned Konoe to office as prime minister in July 1940. In September of that year the Japanese government signed the Tripartite Pact with Germany and Italy, and in April the following year it concluded a neutrality pact with the USSR. Then, in a stunning and unexpected development, in June 1941 Germany unilaterally abrogated its own nonaggression pact and invaded the Soviet Union. In July 1941 Japanese forces advanced into the southern parts of Indochina. The United States, which had never recognized Manchukuo as an independent nation and instead had insisted on Japanese withdrawal from China, now, at last, embargoed all exports to Japan, including oil. As the German forces stalled that autumn before Moscow, the Japanese government under Konoe decided to maintain its own neutrality agreement with the USSR and, if the American export embargo was not lifted, to advance southward to expropriate the oil-rich resources of the Dutch West Indies, in effect initiating war with isolationist America and beleaguered Britain.

As the months passed, negotiations between Japan and America proved intractable. In October, the army minister Tōjō Hideki[52] replaced Konoe as prime minister and began the final preparations for war with the United States and its allies. The war came on the morning of December 7, 1941, with the Japanese attack on Pearl Harbor.

Japan's war policy had been accompanied by measures, already mentioned, to divert resources from civilian goods to weapons. Figure 3.5 depicts the result of these policies. From 1937, the initial year of the war with China, military expenditures rose dramatically while expenditures on civilian goods declined by a corresponding amount, beginning a trend that continued until the war's end in total defeat. The combinations of weapons and civilian goods in Japan from 1936 to 1942 in fact trace out the "guns versus butter" production possibilities boundary of the principles of economics textbooks. Similar, but less profound, arms buildups coincident with the 1894 Sino-Japanese War and the 1905 Russo-Japanese War demark the earlier production possibilities boundaries from which, in 1937, growth in labor force, wealth accumulation, and technological advance had moved the nation. The effect of

---

52 Tōjō Hideki (1884–1948) rose through the army officer corps to become chief of staff of the Kwantung army in 1937, vice minister of the army in 1938, army minister in 1940, and prime minister in 1941–4. Tōjō was forced to resign as prime minister in July 1944 after the fall of Saipan and the beginning of allied bombing of Japan's major cities. Demonized in allied propaganda and hanged as a war criminal, Tōjō was in fact not a charismatic and all-powerful dictator such as Hitler or Mussolini.

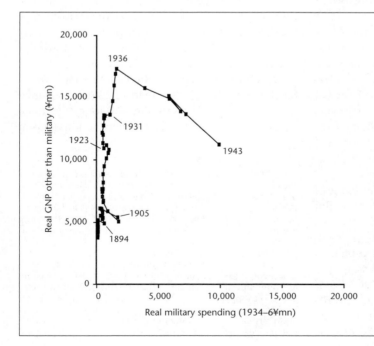

Figure 3.5. Movements along the boundary of Japan's production possibilities, 1885–1942

Producing more military goods—as in the Sino-Japanese War (1894), Russo-Japanese War (1905), the occupation of Manchuria (1931) and the Pacific war (1936–45)— diverted resources away from the production of civilian goods.

Sources: real GNP (calendar year): 1885–1939: Kazushi Ohkawa and Miyohei Shinohara (eds.), Patterns of Japanese Economic Development, Yale University Press, 1979, tables A1 and A3; 1940–43: Patterns, tables A2 and A4; military spending (fiscal year): 1885–1939: LTES vol. 7, table 10, col. 9, pp. 186–9; 1940–43: LTES vol. 7, table 3–1b, col. B, p. 22.

the 1923 earthquake in displacing the production possibilities boundary back toward the origin is also evident in the diagram.

With the outbreak of war in Europe in September 1939, the rather heavy government controls on economic activity already in place in Japan (such as the rationing of foreign exchange and government designation of many civilian businesses as unqualified for bank loans), were joined by still further controls including a widening of conscription, comprehensive wage–price controls, and the forced closure of small businesses not producing war materials. Even more draconian controls were introduced after Japan's early successes in the war itself were followed by dramatic reversals and defeats. The November 1943 Munitions Company Law designated company managers as government employees and financial institutions as lead banks. To administer these rather sweeping controls, a Munitions Ministry was formed by consolidating the Cabinet Planning Board and the Ministry of Commerce and Industry. In spite of it all, many private companies in Japan retained a surprising degree of actual autonomy right up to the war's end, the simple explanation being that the burden of administering a centrally planned economy proved no more tractable in Japan than it had in Manchukuo.

Conclusion

As Japan's economy grew, its political rulers invested a portion of the nation's wealth in foreign conquests. From the Sino-Japanese War of 1895, Japan acquired colonies (Taiwan and the Pescadores) and a foreign sphere of influence (Korea). In the first years of the new century, Japan regained tariff autonomy and achieved an end to extraterritorial foreign settlements on its own soil. With its victory over Russia in 1905 and the annexation of Korea in 1910, Japan joined the European nations as a political rival in pursuit of empire. Japan entered World War I as an ally of Britain, largely in order to expand its empire to include the formerly German South Sea Islands and Chinese concessions.

Japan prospered during World War I by taking advantage of the wartime boost in world interest rates to switch from being a net international borrower to a net lender, and it compounded its gains from doing so by expanding output. In this boom, the business groups known as the zaibatsu expanded from their initial strongholds in mining, banking, and the brokerage of foreign trade into new and diverse activities, including shipbuilding, iron and steel, and insurance. Still, in the 1920s and 1930s more than one-half of Japan's labor force continued to work in very small enterprises or were self-employed. Also, many of the leading large firms in Japan, including the cotton spinning firms, remained outside the zaibatsu orbit and were diffusely held, not closely held. The zaibatsu form of organization, in which a few families maintained concentrated ownership of diverse commercial holdings, was never the only viable way of financing and administering businesses in Japan.

In the decade after World War I, Japan joined Britain and the United States in arms limitation agreements, diplomatic treaties, and pursuit of an open world trading regime, anchored by the gold standard. For Japan to re-establish the gold standard at the same parity as it had maintained from 1897 until 1917, it had to accumulate a stock of international reserves and to reverse the inflation it had experienced from 1917 to 1920. The achievement of these goals was delayed by the 1923 Tokyo earthquake, which drained government resources and ultimately led to a severe banking crisis in 1927. The final deflationary drive to re-establish the prewar international price of gold in terms of yen, in January 1930, happened to coincide with the advent of the world-wide Great Depression. Amidst the economic distress attending these events, in September 1931 the Japanese army, acting without orders and against the policy of Japan's elected government, proceeded to occupy the whole of Manchuria, a province of China in which Japan had maintained a sphere of influence since 1905. The economic malaise abated when Japan abandoned the gold standard in December 1931, inflated its currency, and expanded government expenditures, all under the direction of Minister of Finance Takahashi Korekiyo, dubbed the "Keynes of Japan" for his articulation of such Keynesian principles as the expenditure multiplier. But the established political parties, the Seiyūkai of Takahashi and its rival Kenseikai–Minseitō, never managed to constrain the Japanese military forces, which, by assassination and the threat of armed coup, from this point onward, insinuated themselves into the dominant position in choosing prime ministers and cabinets, and in conducting Japan's foreign affairs.

Japan's final course toward war was set after the unsuccessful military coup of February 1936, which greatly debilitated the remaining champions in Japan of freedom and democracy. From July 1937 Japan was at war with all of China, and after December 1941 was at war with the United States, Britain, and their allies. Beginning in 1937, government appropriations for arms purchases had increased dramatically, and comprehensive economic controls over foreign exchange, bank loans, and production and pricing in selected industries were all coordinated so as to divert resources away from civilian goods and toward weapons. After 1939, to these controls were added comprehensive wage and price controls, and after 1943 the managers of munitions companies—essentially all the manufacturing concerns still operating in Japan—were designated as government employees. None of these measures was enough. The production capabilities of Japan were simply inadequate to the test of arms with the allies arrayed against it. Japan's leaders had miscalculated badly, sacrificing much of the nation's material wealth on a losing bid for foreign conquest.

Appendix

Table 3A.1 on pages 67–9 describes the formation and development of the four major zaibatsu.

Table 3A.2 on page 70 presents a list of Japanese prime ministers.

FURTHER READING

■ Akira Irie, "The Failure of Economic Expansionism: 1918–1931", in Bernard S. Silberman and H. D. Harootunian, *Japan in Crisis: Essays in Taishō Democracy*, Princeton University Press, 1974, ch. 9, pp. 237–69. A leading historian explains how economic malaise in 1920s Japan undercut support for democratic government and for cooperation with the west.

■ Takafusa Nakamura, *Lectures on Modern Japanese Economic History, 1926–1994*, Tokyo: LTCB [Long Term Credit Bank (of Japan)] International Library Foundation, 1994. By Japan's leading non-Marxian economic historian; covers many of the same topics as this chapter.

■ Hugh Patrick, "The Muddle of the 1920s", in J. W. Morley (ed.), *Dilemmas of Growth in Prewar Japan*, Princeton University Press, 1971, ch. 7, pp. 211–66. Discusses Japan's interwar monetary and fiscal policies.

■ J. Mark Ramseyer and Frances M. Rosenbluth, *The Politics of Oligarchy: Institutional Choice in Imperial Japan*, Cambridge University Press, 1995. Discusses Meiji and Taisho political history from the standpoint of rational calculation by the leading politicians.

Table 3A.1. Formation of the four major zaibatsu: principal affiliated enterprises and their dates of entry into the zaibatsu orbits

	Mitsui	Mitsubishi	Yasuda	Sumitomo
Banking	Money Exchange Shops (1691) = MITSUI BANK (1876) MITSUI TRUST (1924)	119th National Bank (1885) = MITSUBISHI BANK (1895) MITSUBISHI TRUST (1927)	Yasuda shoten (1866–87) + Third national bank (1876) = Yasuda bank (1880) Yasuda trust (1925)	SUMITOMO BANK (1895) SUMITOMO TRUST (1925)
Insurance	Taishō Marine & Fire Insurance[a] (1918) MITSUI LIFE INSURANCE (1926)	Tokyo Marine & Fire Insurance[b] –1944) Meiji Life Insurance[b] MITSUBISHI MARINE & FIRE INSURANCE (1919)	Tokyo Fire Insurance Company, Ltd (1893); Imperial Marine Insurance Company, Ltd (1893) Kyōsai Life Insurance (1894) = Yasuda Life (1929)	Fusō Marine & Fire Insurance (1917) = SUMITOMO MARINE & FIRE INSURANCE (1940) SUMITOMO LIFE INSURANCE (1925)
General trading companies	MITSUI BUSSAN (1876)	Bōeki shōkai (1880) = Dōshin kaisha (1886) = MITSUBISHI TRADING COMPANY (1918)	Yasuda motojime yakuba (1874) = Yasuda Trading (1899)	
Mining	Miike Coal Mine* (1888) + Kamioka Metal Mines (1886) = MITSUI MINING COMPANY (1892) Yamano Coal Mine (1895) Tagawa Coal Mine (1900) Hokkaido Colliery & Steamship[a] (1913) Ishikari Coal (1916)	Yoshioka Copper Mine (1878) Takashima Coal Mine* (1878) Shinnyū Coal Mine (1889) Namazuda Coal Mine (1889) Hashima Coal Mine (1890) Osarizawa Metal Mine (1887) Makimine Metal Mines (1889) Sado Gold Mine* (1896) Osaka Copper Refinery* (1896) Ikuno Silver Mine* (1896) Kyomip'o Iron Mine (1911) (consolidated as MITSUBISHI MINING 1918)	Kushiro Sulfur Mine (1888–98)	Besshi Copper Mine (1691) = SUMITOMO BESSHI MINING (1927) Shōji Coal Mine (1893–1903) Tadakuma Coal Mine (1894) = Sumitomo Kyushu Colliery (1928) + Sumitomo ban colliery (1921) = SUMITOMO COAL MINING (1930)
Construction				
Foods		Kirin Brewery[b] (1907) Koiwai Farm (1904)		
Textiles	Kanegafuchu cotton spinning[a] (1890s) Maebashi silk spinning mill Shinamachi silk filature* Tomioka silk filature* (1894) Mie and Nagoya silk filatures (all sold 1900s) Tōyō rayon (1926)		Nishinari Cotton Spinning (1899–1905)	

Table 3A.1. (*cont.*)

	Mitsui	Mitsubishi	Yasuda	Sumitomo
Paper and pulp	Oji paper[a] (founded 1873)	Mitsubishi Paper Mills[b] (1897)		
Chemicals	First Nitrogen Industries (1926) Claude-process Nitrogen Industries (1929–35) = Miike nitrogen (1931–37) + oriental high pressure (1933) + synthetic industries (1938) = MITSUI CHEMICAL INDUSTRIES (1941) Dai Nippon Celluloid[a] Electrochemical Industries[a] Miike Petroleum Synthesis (1934)	Nippon Nitrogen Fertilizer (1908) Nippon Tar Industries (1934) = Nippon Chemical Industries (1936) + Shinko Rayon (1942) = MITSUBISHI CHEMICAL INDUSTRIES (1944)		Sumitomo Fertilizer Mfg. (1925) = SUMITOMO CHEMICAL INDUSTRIES (1934)
Oil and coal products		MITSUBISHI OIL (1931)		
Rubber goods				
Cement, glass, ceramics	Onoda Cement[a]	Asahi Glass[b] (1907) (consolidated with MITSUBISHI CHEMICAL INDUSTRIES 1944)		Nichibei Sheet Glass (1918) = Nippon Sheet Glass[c] (1922)
Iron and steel	Nippon Steelworks[a] (1907) Kamaishi Kōzan Company (1924–34)	Makiyama Coke Factory (1896) MITSUBISHI IRON AND STEEL (1917–34)	Yasuda Seichōsho (1897)	Sumitomo Steel Works (1901) = Sumitomo Steel (1915) + Sumitomo Copper and Steel (1926) = SUMITOMO METAL INDUSTRIES (1935)
Nonferrous metals				Sumitomo Copper Rolling (1897) SUMITOMO ELECTRICAL WIRE (1911) Sumitomo Aluminum Refining (1934)
Machinery	Shibaura Engineering Works[a]		Tenma tekkōjo (1900)	
Electrical equipment		MITSUBISHI ELECTRIC (1921)		Nippon Electric Company[c] (1899)
Shipbuilding	MITSUI SHIPBUILDING (1942)	Nagasaki Shipyard* (1884) Kobe Shipyard (1905) Hikoshima Shipyard (1914) = Mitsubishi Shipbuilding and Engineering (1917) = MITSUBISHI HEAVY INDUSTRIES (1934)	Toba zōsensho (1911–13)	

Sector	Companies
Other transport equipment	Mitsubishi Internal Combustion Engine Works (1920) = Mitsubishi Aircraft (1928) (absorbed by MITSUBISHI HEAVY INDUSTRIES, 1934)
Precision machinery	
Real estate	Maronouchi Land (1890) = MITSUBISHI ESTATE COMPANY LTD (1937)
Transport	Mitsubishi Mail Steamship Company (1872) = Nippon Mail Steamship Company, "NYK"[b] (1885); Osaka shōsen kaisha (1884)
Shipping related businesses	Mitsubishi Ship Repair Facility (1875); Mitsubishi Exchange Office (1876–85)
Warehousing	Tokyo Warehouse Company (1887) = MITSUBISHI WAREHOUSING AND TRANSPORTATION (1918); Toshin Warehousing (1909); Yasuda unpan jimusho (1894)
Services	Mitsui Dry Goods (1673) = Mitsukoshi Dry Goods[a] (1904); Kobe Copper Sales (1871–82)
Utilities	Senkawa Water (1880–1908)
Holding companies; central control organs	Mitsui gumi (1866) = Mitsui motokata (1893) = Mitsui board of directors (1896) = Mitsui gōmei kaisha (1909) (absorbed by Mitsui bussan 1940); Mitsubishi Company (1886) = Mitsubishi Ltd (1893) = Mitsubishi Inc. (1937) = Mitsubishi Head Office (1943); Hozensha (1887); Sumitomo honten = Sumitomo sōhonten (1909) = Sumitomo Ltd (1921) = Sumitomo Head Office (1939)

Notes

Companies whose names appear in capital letters were directly controlled subsidiaries of the holding company. In the table, "+" denotes amalgamation, and "=" denotes a new company name. Superscripts denote the following:

* purchased from the government.

[a] Independent company in which Mitsui gōmei kaisha was a major shareholder.

[b] Independent company in which the Iwasaki family was a major shareholder.

[c] Independent company in which Sumitomo Ltd was a major shareholder.

Source: based on Hidemasa Morikawa, *Zaibatsu: the Rise and Fall of Family Enterprise Groups in Japan*, University of Tokyo Press, 1992.

Table 3A.2. Japanese prime ministers

Name		Initial date	Notes, factional affiliation
Itō	1st	Dec. 1885–	*Hanbatsu* government, alternating control between Chōshū and Satsuma:
Kuroda	1st	Apr. 1888–	Chōshū
Yamagata	1st	Dec. 1889–	Satsuma
Matsukata	1st	May 1891–	Chōshū
Itō	2nd	May 1892–	Satsuma
Matsukata	2nd	Sept. 1896–	Chōshū
Itō	3rd	Jan. 1898–	Satsuma
Ōkuma	1st	June 1898–	*Kenseitō* coalition of parties: Shinpotō ("progressives") headed by Ōkuma, and Jiyūtō ("liberals") headed by Itagaki. Alternating control by Yamagata faction and Itō's Seiyūkai:
Yamagata	2nd	Nov. 1898–	Yamagata
Itō	4th	Oct. 1900–	Seiyūkai
Katsura	1st	June 1901–	Yamagata
Saionji	1st	Jan. 1906–	Seiyūkai
Katsura	2nd	July 1908–	Yamagata
Saionji	2nd	Aug. 1911–	Seiyūkai. Eclipse of Yamagata faction:
Katsura	3rd	Dec. 1912–	Dōshikai
Yamamoto	1st	Feb. 1913–	Seiyūkai
Ōkuma	2nd	Apr. 1914–	Dōshikai
Terauchi		Oct. 1916–	Seiyūkai. First prime minister appointed as leader of party winning an election:
Hara		Sept. 1918–	Seiyūkai
Takahashi		Nov. 1921–	Seiyūkai. Coalition governments drawing on support in upper house of the Diet:
Katō Tomosaburō		June 1922–	Kenkyūkai
Yamamoto	2nd	Sept. 1923–	
Kiyoura		Jan. 1924–	Party cabinets:
Katō Takaaki	1st	June 1924–	Kenseikai
Katō Takaaki	2nd	Aug. 1925–	Kenseikai
Wakatsugi	1st	Jan. 1926–	Kenseikai
Tanaka		Apr. 1927–	Seiyūkai
Hamaguchi		July 1929–	Minseitō (new name for Kenseikai)
Wakatsugi	2nd	Apr. 1931–	Minseitō
Inukai		Dec. 1931–	Seiyūkai. Military governments
Saitō		May 1932–	
Okada		July 1934–	
Hirota		Mar. 1936–	
Hayashi		Feb. 1937–	
Konoe	1st	June 1937–	
Hiranuma		Jan. 1939–	
Abe		Aug. 1939–	
Yonai		Jan. 1940–	

Name		Initial date	Notes, factional affiliation
Konoe	2nd	July 1940–	
Konoe	3rd	July 1941–	
Tōjō		Oct. 1941–	
Koiso		July 1944–	
Suzuki		Apr. 1945–	Occupation era
Higashikuni		Aug. 1945–	Member of Japan's royal family
Shidehara		Oct. 1945–	Shinpōtō
Yoshida	1st	May 1946–	Liberal party
Katayama		May 1947–	Socialist party
Ashida		Feb. 1948–	Democratic party
Yoshida	2nd	Oct. 1948–	Liberal Democratic Party
Yoshida	3rd	Feb. 1949–	Liberal Democratic Party
Yoshida	4th	Oct. 1952–	Liberal Democratic Party
Yoshida	5th	May 1953–	Liberal Democratic Party dominance
Hatoyama	1st	Dec. 1954–	
Hatoyama	2nd	Mar. 1955–	
Hatoyama	3rd	Nov. 1955–	
Ishibashi		Dec. 1956	
Kishi	1st	Feb. 1957–	
Kishi	2nd	June 1958–	
Ikeda	1st	July 1960–	
Ikeda	2nd	Dec. 1960–	
Ikeda	3rd	Dec. 1963–	
Satō	1st	Nov. 1964–	
Satō	2nd	Feb. 1967–	
Satō	3rd	Jan. 1970–	
Tanaka	1st	July 1972–	
Tanaka	2nd	Dec. 1972–	
Miki		Dec. 1974–	
Fukuda		Dec. 1976–	
Ōhira	1st	Dec. 1978–	
Ōhira	2nd	Nov. 1979–	
Suzuki		June 1980–	
Nakasone	1st	Nov. 1982–	
Nakasone	2nd	Dec. 1983–	
Nakasone	3rd	May 1986–	
Takeshita	1st	Nov. 1987–	
Takeshita	2nd	Dec. 1988–	
Uno		June 1989–	
Kaifu	1st	Aug. 1989–	
Kaifu	2nd	Feb. 1990–	
Miyazawa		Nov. 1991–	Coalition governments
Hosokawa		Aug. 1993–	Nihon shintō + 7
Hata		Apr. 1994–	Shinseitō + 7
Murayama		June 1994–	Socialist party +2
Hashimoto	1st	Apr. 1996–	LDP + Socialist party
Hashimoto	2nd	Sept. 1997–	LDP
Obuchi		July 1998–	LDP + Liberal Party

Economic History, Part 3:
Postwar Recovery (1945–1964)

The time chart of aggregate output (real gross national product) in Japan from 1885 to the present (Figure 4.1) is marked by a deep valley, representing the devastations of the Pacific war. Its trough is 1945, the year of the war's end. The ensuing steep ascent out of that trough has been widely hailed as the "Japanese miracle".

When the war ended in 1945, the allied forces led by the United States occupied Japan and took firm control of its government, restoring sovereignty only in 1952. The Occupation government promulgated a number of economic reforms, including land reform, the breakup of the zaibatsu, and important additions to Japan's labor legislation. Additionally, the Americans extended direct economic assistance to the Japanese, and during the Korean War (1950–2) further stimulated Japan's economy with procurement spending. However, Japan's phenomenal postwar economic growth owes far more to the resilience of its market economy than it does to any government policies.

The ongoing process of saving and investment inevitably guides the market economy to a set, "steady-state" path that is determined by the expansion of the labor force, the pace of technological advance, and the nation's desire to accumulate wealth. The war's devastations eliminated buildings, factories, ships, and tools but did little to alter the determinates of the Japanese economy's steady-state path. Japan's aggregate output was therefore destined eventually to return to the same trajectory it would have followed had there been no Pacific war.

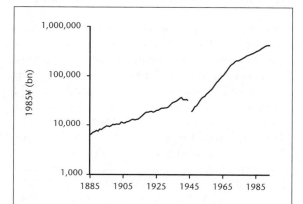

Figure 4.1. Real gross national product, 1885–1992

Figures are on a calendar-year basis, 1885–1944, and a fiscal-year basis 1946–93. Note that the Ohkawa–Shinohara GNP deflator, 1941–54, differs somewhat from that reported by the Japanese government. In linking the prewar and postwar GNP deflator, I have preserved the Ohkawa–Shinohara estimate of annual percentage increase in real GNP for 1954–5.

Sources: 1885–1954: Kazushi Ohkawa and Miyohei Shinohara (eds.), *Patterns of Japanese Economic Development*, Yale University Press, 1979: nominal GNP (1885–1940), table A1, pp. 251–3; (1941–54), table A8, pp. 269–70; GNP deflator (1885–1940), table A50, pp. 387–8; (1940–54), table A51, p. 389; *1955–89*: Economic Planning Agency, *Report on National Income and Product Accounts, 1955–1989*, 1991; *1990–3*: Economic Planning Agency, *Report on National Accounts*, 1995.

These preliminary remarks may leave the impression that Japan's rapid postwar recovery was inevitable. Few regarded it as such prior to the actual event. Government policies may not have been strictly necessary to Japan's postwar economic growth, but they certainly could have impeded that process. Some of the other nations devastated by World War II, particularly those falling into the Soviet bloc, were a lot slower than Japan to rebuild. In the final days of the war, the Soviet Union entered hostilities against Japan, occupying much of Manchuria, Sakhalin, and the Kuril Islands and parts of Korea. But the USSR played essentially no role in the postwar occupation of Japan. The centrally planned economic system of the Soviet bloc was not therefore imposed on any region of Japan, as it was on the less fortunate nations of Eastern Europe. Japan's postwar recovery is a triumph of unfettered capitalism.

The American Occupation, 1945–1952

With Japan's acceptance of the Potsdam Declaration on August 15, 1945,[1] its government became, for a time, completely subordinate to that of the United States. The six years and eight and a half months from Japan's capitulation until the April 28, 1952 restoration of national sovereignty under the terms of the San Francisco Treaty (signed in September 1951) is referred to as the American Occupation era. Although the United States was not the sole occupying power, the Supreme Commander of Allied Powers (SCAP)—from August 1945 to April 1951, General Douglas MacArthur, and from April 1951 to April 1952, General Mathew B. Ridgway—was in each instance an American and subservient only to Washington, the existence of multinational advisory bodies[2] notwithstanding. The overwhelming majority of occupying troops, ultimately totaling about half a million, were also American.

At an early point, the American government opted not to abolish the existing organs of government in Japan or to impose martial law, as had been done in Germany after its defeat, but instead to allow the existing Japanese government to function as the ratifier and implementer of policies dictated to it by Washington, through the office of the SCAP. The policies so introduced in the initial three years of the Occupation were labeled "democratization", both in the sense of strengthening representational government and in the sense of promoting social equality by redistributing wealth and widening economic opportunity.

Democratization

In the eventful first three years of the American Occupation, Japan was completely disarmed, its armed forces were disbanded, and war criminals were arrested, tried, and punished. Japan was given a new constitution, which remains in effect to this day without amendment, and a constellation of economic reforms were implemented including land reform, dissolution of the zaibatsu, and enactment of legislation supporting the unionization of labor. Our focus here is largely upon the economic reforms, but we first digress briefly to describe the new constitution, by far the most significant legacy of the American Occupation.

At the behest of General MacArthur, the government section of the office of the SCAP drafted a new Japanese constitution in the astonishingly short period of one week, and presented it to Japanese officials, including the foreign minister Yoshida Shigeru,[3] on February 13. The Shidehara cabinet soon decided to endorse the basic tenets of the draft

---

[1] The Potsdam Declaration, of July 1945, was a statement of allied aims toward Japan issued in the form of an ultimatum. On August 9, the day of the atomic bombing of Nagasaki, Japan informed the USA of its acceptance of the Potsdam terms, conditional on retention of the Emperor as sovereign ruler. The USA insisted on unconditional surrender and continued the intensive bombing of Tokyo. On August 15, as a result of an unprecedented intervention in the war council by the Emperor himself, Japan accepted the Potsdam Declaration without condition and the hostilities ended. On August 28 a small advance party of American servicemen entered Atsugi air base near Tokyo, followed by General MacArthur and his party two days later. Formal surrender ceremonies on the deck of the battleship Missouri in Tokyo Bay occurred the morning of September 2, followed immediately by the rapid deployment of a large contingent of Allied troops throughout Japan.

[2] These included the short-lived Far Eastern Advisory Commission (Oct. 1945–Feb. 1946) and its successors the Far East Commission meeting in Washington (Feb. 1946–Apr. 1952), and the Allied Council for Japan meeting in Tokyo (Apr. 1946–Apr. 1952).

[3] Yoshida Shigeru (1878–1967) graduated from Tokyo University in 1906 and entered the foreign ministry, rising to the post of vice minister of foreign affairs in the Tanaka Giichi cabinet, 1928. Yoshida joined former prime minister Konoe in unsuccessfully attempting to arrange a peace settlement near the war's end and was briefly imprisoned for it. He served as foreign minister in the Higashikuni-no-miya and Shidehara cabinets, 1945–6. After the 1946 election he rose to the post of president of the victorious Liberal Party (succeeding Hatoyama Ichirō, who was purged from that post by SCAP) and becoming prime minister. After the brief coalition government under the Socialist Party president Ashida Hitoshi, 1947, Yoshida returned to office, serving until 1955. Yoshida was the leading Japanese political figure of the Occupation era.

constitution. Meetings between Japanese officials and the Occupation staff on March 4 and 5 substituted the provision of a bicameral legislature for a unicameral one but effected no other substantive changes. The Constitution, with a few minor alterations, was passed with near unanimity by the Diet in September 1946, was promulgated by the emperor on November 3, 1946, and took effect May 3, 1947.

The Constitution enfranchised women for the first time and lowered the voting age from 25 to 20 (the age of majority in Japan). It provided for a bicameral Diet. The lower house (House of Representatives, Shūgi-in) comprises representatives elected for four-year terms. The lower house elects the prime minister and can be dissolved at any time the prime minister calls a new election. The upper house (House of Councilors, Sangi-in) comprises a smaller number of members, who serve for six-year terms, half of them standing for re-election every three years. Under the rules enacted by the Diet, three-fifths of the upper house members are elected by the various prefectures and the remainder are elected by national vote, while all members of the lower house represent local districts. The prime minister and a majority of the Cabinet must be Diet members. Any amendments to the Constitution require a two-thirds majority in both houses, ratified by majority vote in a national referendum. All other legislation is enacted by a majority vote of both houses, and the lower house may override the upper house by a two-thirds majority. A Supreme Court, appointed by the Cabinet, serves as the court of last appeal and appoints all lower judges. The Constitution officially recognizes the emperor as "the symbol of the state", but explicitly asserts that he "shall not have powers related to government".

One of the more curious features of the Constitution is its Article 9, which "renounces war as a sovereign right of the nation and the threat or use of force as a means of settling international disputes", and asserts that "land, sea, and air forces as well as other war potential, will never be maintained". In spite of Article 9, Japan has, since 1954, maintained "self-defense forces" (*jieitai*), directed by the Defense Agency, the head of which holds Cabinet rank. Japan's participation in multinational military coalitions, such as the one formed in the Persian Gulf War, provokes questions of constitutionality that do not arise for any other nation. In the immediate aftermath of World War II, such eventualities were far from anybody's consideration.

Whatever else, the new Constitution firmly established in Japan parliamentary democracy, free of domination by military leaders, a significant accomplishment and the major aim of United States policy toward occupied Japan. Besides promoting political democracy, the Occupation authorities sought also to promote economic democracy, that is social equality, and they did this largely through redistributing land and shares of stock, and by seeking to encourage labor unions. We next take up each of these policies.

Land reform

Land reform, of a sort, was first initiated by the government of Japan itself, with no special encouragement by SCAP. The First Land Reform measure, passed December 28, 1945, and implemented the following year, sought to institutionalize the changes in agricultural land rental wrought by wartime controls, which had benefited tenant cultivators at the expense of landlords. Land rentals and land sales had become subject to the sweeping price controls that were instituted on many items in Japan beginning in 1939, and continued in effect after the war at the direction of SCAP. Consumer prices of rice and other agricultural commodities were also subject to price ceilings; and to prevent these controls from eroding production incentives, the government, under stipulations of the 1942 Food Control Law, purchased rice and other staples from cultivators at inflated prices and itself distributed these items directly to consumers at the lower, controlled, retail prices.[4] Cultivator-tenants thus paid land rentals not in kind, but in money, and at a controlled level corresponding to the unchanging retail prices, not the gradually escalated producer prices. In November 1945 the official retail price of rice stood at 55 yen per *koku*, while the producer price had been raised to 300 yen per *koku*. (1 *koku* of rice = 5.1 bushels, or 331.5 lbs., of brown rice; traditionally, 1 *koku* of rice was considered sufficient to nurture an adult for a year.) In other words, tenant cultivators of rice were paying landlords only about one-sixth of the monetary value at producer prices of the

---

4 Amazingly, for rice this system remains in effect in Japan to this very day.

corresponding shares of their crops stipulated in their original lease contracts. The First Land Control Law stipulated that land rents would continue to be paid in cash only, rather than in kind, institutionalizing this windfall for tenant cultivators. The law further limited the ownership of arable land to 5 *chō* (12.25 acres), but there were actually very few agricultural landowners in Japan whose holdings exceeded this limit.

The Diet debate on the First Land Control Law engaged the attention of the SCAP staff as well as that of General MacArthur himself, and precipitated American insistence on a more thoroughgoing redistribution of wealth from landlords to cultivator-tenants. The Second Land Reform Law, enacted in March 1946, disallowed absentee landlordism (ownership of agricultural land by anyone not residing in close proximity to it), permitted resident landlords to retain ownership of at most 1 *chō*[5] (4 *chō* in Hokkaido), and disallowed owner cultivation of more than 3 *chō* (12 *chō* in Hokkaido). To reach compliance with these stipulations, the government was to purchase land and resell it to tenants, not at market prices, but at the controlled prices that had prevailed since 1939, unadjusted for the ensuing massive inflation. By the end of 1949, retail prices in Japan were on average more than 150 times greater than their level in 1939, so this really amounted to outright confiscation of land. An elaborate system of local land commissions, delegated by local elections, was to adjudicate the process. With the implementation of these laws, a process begun in 1947 and completed only in 1950, share tenancy, which had been known in Japan in some form since time immemorial, was drastically curtailed. In 1946 nearly half the agricultural land area was cultivated by tenants rather than by owners, whereas in 1955 only about one-tenth was cultivated by tenants.

It is occasionally suggested that the Second Land Reform measure caused a jump in agricultural productivity. In fact, it almost certainly did not. There is almost no measurable difference in productivity between land under share tenancy and land under owner cultivation, either in 1934–6 or in 1951–4.[6] Nor did the rise in agricultural productivity in Japan over the immediate postwar period correspond in detail to the implementation of land reform. It occurred contemporaneously in the prefectures of Japan in which land reform was first implemented

and last implemented.[7] In Japan, the productivity of agricultural land increased by as much as 56 percent between 1939 and 1949, but this was due to more intense application of labor, diffusion of chemical fertilizers, and selection of hybrid varieties of seed, none of which can be easily connected to the abolition of tenant cultivation.[8] In short, the Second Land Reform may have transferred wealth from landlords to cultivators, but it did not stimulate agricultural production, or eliminate wastes and inefficiencies. Further measures even introduced new inefficiencies that continue to this day.

The 1952 Agricultural Land Law codified and perpetuated the severe restrictions on land ownership and land use already then in effect. Under this law, agricultural land could only be sold to one already cultivating at least 0.3 *chō* of land, and any one person's combined ownership of agricultural land could not exceed the limits imposed by the Second Land Reform Law. Furthermore, the terms of land leases were placed under strict government control, and were held at very low levels. Government controls on land use, similar in effect to this, have remained in force and continue to distort the allocation of land in Japan. As a result, small rice fields are still cultivated in the now densely inhabited suburbs of Osaka, Nagoya, and Tokyo, even though this clearly is not the highest valued use of that land. The owner-cultivators cannot, without penalty, divert it to any other use or sell it to anyone except another cultivator. The political support for maintaining these costly and distorting land use controls is to be found among the owners of nonagricultural land, rendered artificially scarce by the designation of other land as reserved exclusively for agriculture.

In the melodramatic prose of Douglas MacArthur, the object of land reform was "to insure that those who till the soil of Japan shall have more equal op-

---

5 1 *chō* = 2.45 acres.

6 S(higeto) Kawano, "Effects of the Land Reform on Consumption and Investment of Farmers", in Kazushi Ohkawa, Bruce F. Johnston, and Hiromitsu Kaneda (eds.), *Agriculture and Economic Growth: Japan's Experience*, Princeton University Press, 1970, ch. 15, pp. 374–97.

7 H(iromitsu) Kaneda, "Structural Change and Policy Response in Japanese Agriculture after the Land Reform", in Lawrence H. Redford (ed.), *The Occupation of Japan: Economic Policy and Reform, the Proceedings of a Symposium Sponsored by the MacArthur Memorial, April 13–15, 1978*, Norfolk, Va: The MacArthur Memorial, 1980, pp. 133–146.

8 Kaneda, "Structural Change".

portunity to enjoy the fruits of their labor".[9] By the time of this proclamation (December 1945), government controls had already greatly attenuated the private ownership rights of landlords, to the enrichment of tenant-cultivators, and the First Land Reform measure had institutionalized these changes. The Second Land Reform, instigated by SCAP, expropriated most of the remaining holdings of absentee landlords and large landholders, and formally awarded these to small cultivators, but the distributional effects of even this were less than many have claimed. The number of landlords dispossessed by the Second Land Reform amounted to 3.7 million—not a wealthy few, but instead a portion of the middle class, at best a kind of *petite bourgeois*.[10]

Land reform was not the only wealth redistribution measure of the Occupation era. Shares of stock in the zaibatsu were also confiscated and redistributed.

Dissolution of the zaibatsu

The owners and managers of Japan's zaibatsu incurred the special wrath of the American Occupation authorities. American antagonism was directed both toward the founding families and leaders of the original zaibatsu, and also toward those of the so-called "new zaibatsu" that had been induced by government subsidies to invest in Manchuria and other territories subdued and occupied by Japan's military forces. To put it bluntly, Americans in 1945 embraced the notion that Japanese industrialists bore special responsibility for Japan's turn toward military government and armed aggression in the 1930s. In retrospect, this attitude seems to have emanated from passions aroused by the war itself rather than from objective consideration of the facts. The major zaibatsu, Mitsui and Mitsubishi in particular, actually had maintained close connections with the major political parties during the 1920s, the Seiyūkai and Kenseikai–Minseitō. The military fanatics who wrested control of the Japanese government from the political parties after 1932 would therefore hardly seem the natural allies of Mitsui and Mitsubishi. The new zaibatsu did enjoy a close association with Japan's armed forces, and, initially, profited from that association. Most of the new zaibatsu were effectively dissolved by the forced transfer of assets in place outside of Japan, to the governments of the respective nations formerly oc-

cupied by Japanese troops, including the colonies Taiwan and Korea, which were declared independent at war's end. But the two largest of the new zaibatsu, Nissan and Nakajima, also had numerous installations in Japan itself.

The measures directed at owners and managers of Japan's large industrial firms proceeded in a sequence of three steps: (1) expropriation of all the securities holdings of designated individuals and companies, the latter including all the zaibatsu holding companies and their leading affiliates; dissolution of the main holding companies; and resale of shares in the remaining companies to individuals other than the zaibatsu founding families or top managers; (2) purge of management personnel; and (3) forced liquidation of selected tangible assets of particular large companies. The last two of these steps became politically controversial in America itself and were scaled back as a result. SCAP fully implemented the first step.[11]

As a result of consultations between SCAP and Japanese government officials, the Japanese Cabinet in November 1945 proposed a law, enacted with modifications by the Diet in April 1946, that mandated the formation of a "Holding Company Liquidation Commission" to oversee the expropriation and redistribution of corporate equities. This commission expropriated all the securities held by fifty-six designated zaibatsu family members,[12] and also expropriated all the securities held by any of eighty-three designated companies, including the main holding companies and leading subsidiaries of the big four zaibatsu (Mitsui, Mitsubishi, Sumitomo, and Yasuda), four of the lesser zaibatsu (Asano, Okura, Furukawa, and Nomura), and the two largest new zaibatsu (Nissan and Nakajima). The main holding companies, nexus of family control of the

---

[9] SCAP, "Memorandum concerning rural land reform", Dec. 9, 1945.

[10] This point is raised by Yutaka Kosai, *The Era of High Speed Growth: Notes on the Postwar Japanese Economy*, University of Tokyo Press, 1986, p. 21.

[11] For details of these policies related in the next paragraphs, I have drawn upon two sources: T. A. Bisson, *Zaibatsu Dissolution in Japan*, University of California Press, 1954; and Eleanor Hadley, *Antitrust in Japan*, Princeton University Press, 1970.

[12] The owners of shares in pure holding companies, including members of the zaibatsu founding families, received partial compensation in the form of non-negotiable, 10-year Japanese government bonds, ultimately rendered almost worthless by the rise in prices from war's end to 1950.

original zaibatsu, were all completely dissolved. The expropriated shares of companies not dissolved were mostly sold to the public through underwriting dealers between May 1948 and December 1950. Finally, other companies in which the eighty-three designated companies had held a 10 percent or greater stock position, 1,120 companies in all, were required by SCAP in 1949 to divest their own stock-holdings in all other companies, eliminating the remaining vestiges of zaibatsu shareholding interlocks.

SCAP also initiated political and economic purges. In January 1946 it issued a directive barring selected present and former political, military, and bureaucratic officials from further political or government posts, more than 200,000 persons (including about 180,000 former military officers). In conformity with the American position that industrialists, too, bore responsibility for Japan's military aggression, the following year, in January 1947, 1,535 officers of twenty-eight government economic organs, about sixty industry control associations, fifty-three private economic associations, and 283 private companies (of which eighty-five had been based in Manchuria, Taiwan, Korea, and elsewhere), including most of the larger companies in the orbit of the original zaibatsu or new zaibatsu during the years 1937–45, were identified by name and barred from holding any of the vacated positions in any of the companies for ten years.[13] Finally, in January 1948 a similar purge was extended to members of zaibatsu founding families and 2,798 additional persons who, before the war's end, had held high-level managerial positions in an extended list of 1,681 companies.[14] Initially, all these individuals were barred from any of the vacated positions for ten years, but the ten-year limit on purgee activity was ultimately much shortened for most of the individuals affected; for in May, June, and July 1951 the Japanese government, with the approval of SCAP, removed purge restrictions on about half of the political purgees, and removed the restrictions on nearly all of the economic purgees, including all of the zaibatsu family members.

Even though the economic purges were short-lived, they elevated young and vigorous junior executives to top-level managerial positions in nearly all of Japan's leading companies. Many have suggested that this was a disguised blessing. And, in fact, most companies in Japan thereafter voluntarily adopted

relatively low ages of mandatory retirement (55 years), institutionalizing the elevation of the young to top positions, so there might actually be something to the notion of a blessing in disguise.

SCAP's original attempt at the widespread reorganization of large Japanese firms was derailed about the same time that the purges were overturned. The policy and its ultimate denouement are worth a mention. SCAP had already, in July 1947, forced the liquidation of most of the assets of Japan's two large trading companies, Mitsui Trading Company and Mitsubishi Trading Company, immediately spawning more than 200 much smaller successor companies of these two. The next step was to empower the Holding Company Liquidation Commission to extend similar measures to Japan's other large companies. At the behest of SCAP, in December 1947 the Diet enacted a law empowering the Holding Company Liquidation Commission (HCLC) to order the divestiture of tangible assets of any firm judged by it as having an "excessive concentration of economic power". And in February 1948, after close consultation with SCAP, the Commission publicly identified 325 companies as targets for reorganization under the new statute.

The deconcentration policy differed fundamentally from the zaibatsu dissolution and economic purge in that its aim was not punishment, but wealth redistribution, to allow wider economic opportunity for smaller rivals of large firms. Perhaps this is why, unlike the measures directed specifically at the zaibatsu, this one became politically controversial in the United States itself. How could large firms in Japan have an unfair advantage over smaller rivals, unless an analogous statement also applied to large firms in the United States? This was a policy that should be nipped in the bud before it got grafted onto home soil. *Newsweek* magazine editorialized against the deconcentration policy, and US Senator William Knowland of California, with a critical eye on MacArthur's candidacy in the 1948 Republican presidential primaries, spoke out against

---

13 All of the 85 companies based outside Japan, all of the economic associations and the like, and a number of the companies based in Japan were dissolved with no successors, leaving only 187 companies, of the approximately 400 named entities, still in operation at the time of the purge order: see Bisson, *Zaibatsu Dissolution*, table 8, p. 163.

14 Ibid., table 11, p. 175.

it.[15] Both *Newsweek* and Senator Knowland argued, among other things, that by impeding economic reconstruction, the deconcentration measure, and the economic purge, might prolong or enlarge the burden on US taxpayers of humanitarian aid for Japan. Ultimately, in May–June 1949 the HCLC directed that eleven large Japanese companies be reorganized into twenty-six smaller ones; it ordered two other companies to divest factories, and five more companies to divest securities.[16] None of this had much effect on market concentration in Japan.[17] And in 1954, the surviving remnants of the Mitsui Trading Company and Mitsubishi Trading Company were re-amalgamated. These two firms resumed their dominant positions in the brokerage of Japan's foreign trade, and have also come to play a major role in the intermediation of funds to small and medium-sized Japanese businesses. So it appears that the zaibatsu dissolution was the only one of the Occupation era policies to alter Japan's industrial organization significantly. The alterations were not necessarily for the better.

Zaibatsu dissolution disrupted an effective mechanism of corporate governance, based on concentrated ownership in holding companies, and a pyramiding of control through interlocking shareholding. This probably had detrimental effects on the performance of the affected firms. For instance, Yishay Yafeh has shown that, the greater the percentage of a firm's outstanding shares expropriated and resold by the HCLC, all else the same, the worse was its performance during the years 1951 to 1953.[18] To just that extent, zaibatsu dissolution retarded Japan's economic recovery from the war rather than hastening it. But the disruption of corporate governance was only temporary. Beginning soon after the Occupation ended, and continuing until about 1960, many of the firms previously affiliated with the major zaibatsu, or the successors of such firms, re-established their old shareholding interlocks. The large commercial banks among these firms became major stockholders in most of the other members of their respective reconstituted groups, occupying the same role in monitoring investments and governing enterprises once performed by the zaibatsu founding families. None of the founding families of the zaibatsu ever reasserted a controlling interest in any of these reconstituted business groups, today known as the financial keiretsu, and,

under the Anti-monopoly Law enacted by the Diet at the behest of SCAP in April 1947 (amended June 1949 and amended again September 1953), holding companies were prohibited.[19]

The Anti-monopoly Law just mentioned was loosely modeled on America's antitrust statutes. It is one of the remaining traces of America's, largely unsuccessful, attempt to remake Japan in its own image. Japan's Anti-monopoly Law, unlike America's antitrust statutes, proscribes little, broaches many exceptions, is weakly enforced and rather inconsequential. Japan's labor legislation, also enacted during the Occupation era, has had more noticeable effects.

Labor legislation

The office of SCAP, under instruction from Washington, took early steps to encourage labor unions. The aim of the Americans was partly political. Labor unions with elected leaders afford an outlet for free political expression, even where the official organs of government are not democratic. Perhaps for this reason, Japan's military government banned labor unions altogether in 1940, the same year it abolished political parties, and the ban remained in effect at the war's end. But labor unions, of course, serve an economic purpose as well as a political one. The economic purpose of unions is to extract higher wages for members, by first either effecting contrived scarcities of labor services or providing valued services, and then bargaining successfully for a share in the resulting economic rent. The valuable services that unions can provide include collective negotiation of employment contracts, monitoring of employers' compliance with such contracts, and

15 Excerpts from both the *Newsweek* piece and a speech by Senator Knowland are reprinted in Jon Livingston, Joe Moore, and Felicia Oldfather (eds.), *Postwar Japan: 1945 to the Present*, New York: Random House, 1973, pp. 107–15.

16 For a list of the companies affected by these directives, see Hadley, *Antitrust in Japan*, table 9–1, pp. 178–80.

17 On this point, see Masu Uekusa, "Effects of the Deconcentration Measures in Japan", *Antitrust Bulletin*, vol. 22, no. 3 (Fall 1977), pp. 687–715.

18 Yafeh measures corporate performance by the price–cost margin (i.e. the profit-to-sales ratio), and controls for the effect of market share and capital intensity: see Yishai Yafeh, "Corporate Ownership, Profitability, and Bank-Firm Ties: Evidence from the American Occupation Reforms in Japan", *Journal of the Japanese and International Economies*, vol. 9 (1995), pp. 154–73.

19 Under amendments to the anti-monopoly law enacted in 1997, holding companies are once again permitted in Japan.

identification of skilled and disciplined workers. Whether unions monopolize labor or provide valuable services, their insistence on higher wages for members will achieve little unless it is buttressed by the credible threat to impose losses on a recalcitrant employer by striking.

In every country where unions have succeeded economically, the unions' right to strike is legally protected. In Japan, Article 17 of the Police Regulations enacted in 1900, did exactly the opposite, explicitly outlawing coercive acts connected with strikes and barring union organizing activities. As interpreted by the courts and law enforcement officials, this amounted to a blanket prohibition of strikes. But strikes did occur anyway. In spite of Article 17, in the first two decades of this century Japanese labor unions organized selected industries including the merchant marine, railroad operation, printing, and coal mining. These same industries were among the earliest to be unionized in America and Europe. They are all industries in which strikes are particularly costly to employers, either because workers represent a unique resource (those who reside near a mine) or exhibit unique skills and are therefore not easily replaced (printers, locomotive engineers), or because they are industries in which employers are dependent on unions to identify productive workers (a ship's operators are often a motley crew).

In the World War I economic boom, Japanese labor unions gained economic strength from the expanded demand for industrial labor. Strike activity also increased, even though it frequently meant incarceration of union leaders. The growing economic strength of unions led to political concessions. In July 1926 the Diet repealed Article 17 and enacted a new law providing for police conciliation of labor disputes. This statute was a step toward legitimizing unions, but it interfered little with union-busting dismissals by employers. Under this regime, Japanese labor unions mainly succeeded in organizing some of the workers in small firms. Union membership as a percentage of the industrial workforce peaked in 1931 at a mere 8 percent. The Minseitō administration of Hamaguchi, in 1929 and 1931, proposed additional labor legislation that would have gone farther to protect unions' right to strike, and to organize the employees of large firms, but failed to enact it.[20] The subsequent Japanese admin-

istrations regarded the socialistic political agenda of the leading unions as anathema, and imprisoned many of the leaders. In November 1940, the second Konoe administration abolished independent labor unions altogether, and at the same stroke itself organized all industrial workers into company-by-company political cells called *sangyō hōkokukai* (or *sanpō* for short; lit. "industrial patriotic associations"). These cells, as intended, completely preempted the formation of autonomous labor unions, suppressing labor disputes in order to advance the war effort. The *sanpō* associations of Japan were explicitly modeled on the German Nazi government's labor associations known as the National Labor Front. At the war's end, no effective independent labor unions existed in Japan. Ending this state of affairs became an early priority of SCAP.

Under the broad guidance of SCAP, Japan's Diet enacted three basic laws pertaining to labor unions and industrial relations. The Labor Union Law, enacted December 1945, officially recognizes labor unions with elected leaders as the collective bargaining agents of their voluntary members, and explicitly recognizes a right-to-strike. For example, it disallows employers from collecting indemnities from unionized workers to compensate for the employer's own losses arising from strikes. The law also disallows employers from discriminating against workers who participate in unions. It *ipso facto* extends the terms of union agreements to other employees of the same factory if three-fourths of the employees are members of the particular union. Finally, it provides for national and prefectural labor relations commissions, staffed by appointees of the government, to conciliate, mediate, and arbitrate labor disputes, including those arising from employee complaints of unfair practices such as employer discrimination against union members.

The Labor Relations Adjustment Law, enacted September 1946, details the procedures for the labor relations commissions to follow in conciliating, mediating, and arbitrating labor disputes, of which there had been quite a large number in the months

---

[20] Japanese labor unions and their supporters both in the government bureaucracy and in the political parties, including the Kenseikai–Minseitō, struggled unsuccessfully throughout the prewar era to legitimize union strike activity. These events are described in detail by Sheldon Garon, *The State and Labor in Modern Japan*, University of California Press, 1987.

since the Labor Union Law took effect. Under the terms of this statute, *conciliation* entails the participation in negotiations of a presumably impartial, but expert, third party, chosen from a panel appointed by the relevant labor relations commission. Also under the terms of the Labor Relations Adjustment Law, *mediation* is the proposal of resolution of a labor dispute by an appointed panel, some members of which represent employers and some, workers. The recommendations of a mediation committee are non-binding. The disputing parties themselves may, in the end, choose to disregard them. Finally, *arbitration* entails the referral of a labor dispute to a three-person committee designated by the relevant labor relations commission and agreed upon by both disputants, which, after consideration of the matter, issues a binding recommendation.

In addition to these stipulations, the Labor Relations Adjustment Law also prohibited strikes by policemen, firemen, government bureaucrats, and the like. In July 1948, this was broadened (by ordinance 201) to prohibit strikes by all public employees including the workers in government enterprises, the largest of which was the national railroad. These strike prohibitions were subsequently made permanent by amendments of the National Public Service Law (December 1950) and Public Corporations Labor Relations Law (July 1952).

The last of the three basic labor laws of the Occupation era, the Labor Standards Law, enacted April 1947, stipulates terms of employment including 25 percent added wages for overtime work (initially, work in excess of eight hours in a day, six days in a week). It establishes a mechanism for imposing legal minimum wage stipulations; it prohibits child labor; it provides for thirty-day notice of dismissal; it provides for employer compensation for on-the-job accidents; and it requires that minimal standards of workplace safety and sanitation be observed.

Besides the three laws just described, the new Constitution, promulgated in November 1946, includes a stipulation (Article 28) guaranteeing "the right of workers to organize and to bargain and to act collectively". Whether this stipulation carries any force is unclear. For instance, the prohibitions against strikes by government employees have been upheld by the courts in Japan, Article 28 notwithstanding.

Unionization of workers in Japan proceeded quite rapidly immediately following the December 1945

implementation of the Labor Union Law. By year's end 1949, 55.8 percent of the nation's non-farm labor force belonged to unions, which numbered 34,688. By 1955, the unionized fraction of the industrial workforce had declined to around one-third, where it remained until the mid-1970s. Since then, unionization has steadily decreased in Japan. Currently, about one-fourth of Japan's industrial workforce are union members. Most of the unions formed from 1946 to 1949 simply organized the employees of a single company or business establishment. They could therefore be described, for the most part, as enterprise unions, not industrial unions or craft unions. Many of these unions joined together in national confederations, but many more did not. In the early postwar years, two national confederations of labor unions in particular vied with one another for national prominence. The one known as Sanbetsu (shorthand for Zen nihon sangyōbetsu rōdō kumiai kaigi, lit. "Japan-wide Congress of Industrial Unions") was closely allied with the Communist Party, while its main rival, originally known as Sōdōmei (short for Nihon rōdō kumiai sōdōmei, lit. "Confederation of Japanese Labor Unions"), was allied with the Democratic Socialist Party (not to be confused with the larger Japan Socialist Party). The purposes of Sanbetsu and Sōdōmei were to advance national political agendas, not to organize workers into broader collective bargaining units than one enterprise.

The high water mark of the national confederations of labor unions came when Sanbetsu called for a general strike to occur on February 1, 1947, and was joined by its main rival Sōdōmei and by a number of large, unaffiliated public employees' unions. In all, labor leaders claiming to represent about two-thirds of Japan's nonfarm labor force joined the call for a general strike. Their demands included not only wage hikes for public employees, but the resignation of the Yoshida cabinet. The situation became especially tense when, two weeks before the strike date, the president of Sanbetsu was mortally wounded in an attempted assassination.

The strike never occurred. At the very last moment MacArthur issued a directive prohibiting it, and the vast majority of workers complied with the directive. Afterwards, Sanbetsu shrank to insignificance. Sōdōmei too suffered diminished ranks, and in 1954 merged with several other national labor organizations to form Dōmei (short for Zen-nihon rōdō kumiai sōdōmei, lit. "Japan-wide Confederation of Labor Unions"). Dōmei was for a long time the second largest national labor organization in Japan. The largest was Sōhyō, (short for Nihon rōdō kumiai sōhyōgikai, lit. "General Council of Japanese Labor Unions"), formed in March 1950, its ranks greatly swelled in reaction to the so-called "red purge" of June 1950 that it opposed, in which thousands of persons identified as communists were barred from private employment. Communists had been purged from the civil service the previous year. In 1987 Dōmei merged with another labor federation to form a new organization known as Rengō, which in 1989 also absorbed Sōhyō. The full name of Rengō is now Nihon rōdō kumiai sō-rengō kai (lit. "General Alliance of Japanese Labor Unions").

The rationale and essential activities of the national confederations have always been political, and they have not been very effective. Sōhyō, and since 1987 Rengō, have been the main supporters of the Japan Socialist Party, for many years the leading opposition party in Japan. The Japan Socialist Party has formed only two cabinets in the entire postwar period, the Katayama Tetsu cabinet of 1947, and the coalition cabinet led by Murayama Tomiichi in 1994–5. The real political battles in contemporary Japan have occurred mainly within the ranks of the Liberal Democratic Party (LDP), which despite its name is rather conservative, and not very sympathetic to labor unions. The LDP was formed in 1955 by the merger of the Liberal Party led by Yoshida with the Democratic Party, the leading conservative opposition party, led by Hatoyama Ichirō, successor to Yoshida as prime minister, 1954–6. The LDP prevailed in every general election from the time of its formation until 1993, when the party fragmented over the issue of money scandals. In other words, the leftist political parties supported by organized labor in Japan have been largely shut out of the government.

It is the individual labor unions, not the national confederations, that are the effective bargaining units in wage negotiations. That these are mostly enterprise unions, whose respective members are employees of a given company, does not preclude their having succeeded in raising members' wages. Industry unions and craft unions are probably more effective than enterprise unions at monopolizing the supply of labor, but unions can also create economic rents by providing valuable services related to labor contracting. And enterprise unions probably economize on the costs of negotiating and enforcing labor contracts as well as or better than industry or craft unions, particularly in Japan's large companies, where long tenures of employment have become the norm since the 1950s.

The various Occupation era measures toward labor did legitimize unions, both as bargaining units on behalf of the employees of large companies and as political organizations, but they prohibited strikes by public employees, and did not lead to the establishment of effective labor monopolies. In the early postwar years, policies that ended distorting government subsidies, halted inflation, loosened price controls, and reopened foreign trade, none of which was fully accomplished until after 1949, ultimately contributed far more than unions to Japanese workers' standards of living.

The rise and fall of government controls over the postwar economy

At the war's end, the Japanese government hastened to fulfill its outstanding financial obligations to businesses and individuals, including indemnities of war losses, mustering out pay to servicemen, compensation for canceled munitions contracts, and other such items. It did this by issuing new currency, which inevitably resulted in price inflation. In the two weeks between capitulation and formal surrender alone (August 15–September 2, 1945), wholesale prices in Japan approximately doubled. By the end of the Occupation in 1952 they had increased a hundredfold from the August 15, 1945 level. The Americans considered, but rejected, proposals to substitute US military scrip for the indigenous currency, and, especially in the early years of the Occupation, allowed inflation of the currency and inflation of prices to continue. SCAP had directed the Japanese government to continue the system of wartime price controls, first erected in 1939, but enforcement was now half-hearted at best. By December 1945, black market prices exceeded official prices by a factor of thirty. In a futile attempt to halt the inflation, the Japanese government mandated that all private money holdings, other than currency of the smallest denominations, be deposited in commercial banks on February 16, 1946 (after which it would cease to be legal tender), and thereafter limited withdrawals. By placing limits on private expenditures, it was hoped that inflation of prices could be checked, but in the months that followed, the limits on personal withdrawals were widely flouted, then relaxed, and finally removed altogether.[21]

Strengthening of government price controls also failed to halt inflation. The Price Control Ordinance of March 1946 authorized a new system of price controls, to finally replace the wartime mechanism. Price controls necessitate some form of rationing, and under the wartime system in Japan rationing was carried out by designated consortia of leading producers in selected industries, dubbed "control associations". These control associations were now to be dissolved. The Economic Stabilization Board, set up in August 1946 to directly administer economic regulations and facilitate abolition of the control associations, was placed above fifteen new public corporations (*kodan*), which would actually carry out the rationing of major commodities (initially, thirty-four producer goods and fifty-two consumer goods). The *kodan* would purchase the commodities from producers at controlled prices, and resell in rationed amounts to demanders at lower prices. In other words, the *kodan* operated at a loss, adding still further to the fiscal burdens of the Japanese government.

In spite of the price controls, inflation continued. Black markets flourished, to the extent that official price indices were based, in part, on black market prices. And the controlled prices themselves were adjusted upwards a couple of times, from initial positions in March 1946 averaging eight times the 1934–6 base-year level to, in July 1947, sixty-five times the base-year level (government wages were, at that time, set at twenty-eight times their base-year level) and, in June 1948, 110 times the base-year level. (Government wages were then set at fifty-seven times their base-year level.) Price controls were having little effect on inflation.

The only sure way of halting the inflation would have been to curb government expenditures and obtain new sources of government revenue. SCAP, somewhat cautiously, and not out of concern about inflation, directed that the Diet take both kinds of step. The Americans took a rather dim view of the

Japanese government's continuing payment of war debts, quite apart from the inflationary consequences, and in October 1946 had the Diet enact a special measure that effectively dissolved all private claims against the Japanese government arising from wartime procurement, war indemnities, and so on. (Outstanding bonds would still be honored, although inflation was eroding their value.) It was feared by Japanese and American authorities alike that this repudiation of private claims against the Japanese government could force many businesses, including banks, into financial insolvency, greatly disrupting the process of economic recovery. In light of these concerns, two laws were enacted in October 1946 to enable businesses and financial institutions to restructure: the Business Reconstruction and Adjustment Law, and the Financial Institutions Reconstruction and Adjustment Law. These measures allowed companies to shield a portion of their assets from creditors by transferring them to new secondary companies set up to conduct on-going operations, and to pay off debts gradually, eventually dissolving the original companies. The ongoing inflation hastened the resolution of wartime private debts, and by the end of 1949 few of these debts remained outstanding.

A step was also taken in 1946 that enlarged government revenues, however temporarily. To punish war profiteers, SCAP had the Diet exact, in November 1946, a capital levy, a graduated tax on personal assets exceeding ¥100,000 (approximately equal to ¥1.5 million in 1995 prices, or about US$15,000 in 1995 prices), including financial assets such as bank balances and securities, as well as real assets such as houses and other property. The tax rate ranged from 10 percent on the first ¥10,000 of taxable assets up to 90 percent on taxable assets in excess of ¥15 million, and raised approximately ¥43.5 billion in revenue.[22] However, the capital levy did little to

---

21 Frozen deposits as a percentage of the money supply (currency in circulation plus deposits of all banks including postal savings system) were: 1946.3, 70.0; 1946.6, 61.0; 1946.9, 53.8; 1946.12, 43.8; 1947.3, 35.5; 1947.6, 29.5; 1947.9, 23.5; 1947.12, 17.3; 1948.3, 11.4; 1948.6, 9.2; 1948.9, 0. (*Source*: Juro Teranishi, "Inflation Stabilisation with Growth: The Japanese Experience, 1945–50", in Juro Teranishi and Yutaka Kosai (eds.), *The Japanese Experience of Economic Reforms*, New York: St Martin's Press, 1993, table 3.4, p. 71.)

22 Jerome Cohen, *Japan's Economy in War and Reconstruction*, University of Minnesota Press, 1949, p. 429.

close the massive fiscal deficits that had been necessitating an ongoing inflation tax, because, even after the suspension of indemnities, the Japanese government continued to pump money into the private economy. It did this in a circuitous fashion, through a new government financial institution called the Reconstruction Finance Bank, authorized by the Diet in October 1946 and first operative in January 1947.

The Reconstruction Finance Bank (RFB) provided subsidized loans to private companies, and was itself financed by borrowing from the Bank of Japan. Almost all the loans were fully repaid, but their interest rates were so far below the rate of inflation that the loans really amounted to unilateral transfers. The RFB was little more than a subterfuge for diverting new currency directly to government outlays, circumventing altogether the process of legislative appropriations, and, for the time being, also avoiding the scrutiny of American officials. The bulk of the RFB loans went to the coal mining, electric power, steel and chemical fertilizer industries, based on principles enunciated by then finance minister Ishibashi Tanzan[23] and his advisers, and labeled by them the "priority production scheme" (*keisha seisan hōshiki*). Private commercial banks, under the aegis of the Emergency Financial Measures Ordinance of February 1946, were also directed by government edict to allocate 50 percent of their own loans to the same "priority" industries favored by the RFB. The priority production scheme really was a kind of industrial policy, for it purported to single out, for subsidy and government promotion, industries meeting a particular criterion: they provided "essential" raw materials for other industries. "Essential" industries were any labeled as such by the government authorities, in this instance the inaptly named Economic Stabilization Board. It should not have surprised anyone when a private company (Shōwa Denkō), in pursuit of RFB loans, was caught attempting to bribe cabinet officers. The scandal felled the Ashida Hitoshi administration in October 1948, after a mere five months in power. Yoshida Shigeru returned as prime minister, a post he would retain until December 1954, forming three successive cabinets.

Price controls, subsidies, and government regulation actually compounded the adverse effects of inflation by impeding market forces and hampering the flow of resources to most valued uses. These government policies were getting in the way of economic recovery. So was another one: state control of Japan's foreign trade. In the first two years of the Occupation, virtually all of Japan's foreign trade was on a government-to-government basis. SCAP did authorize some private imports in July 1947, but all Japanese exports and most imports remained on a government-to-government basis until April 1949. The way this functioned, international trade was channeled through an agency of the Japanese government set up for that purpose, and called the Board of Trade (Boeki-Cho). The Board of Trade purchased domestic goods for export, as authorized by SCAP, and sold imported foreign goods, both at controlled prices, debiting and crediting a yen-denominated revolving fund. Similarly, SCAP, operating through agencies of the US government, handled the foreign sale of Japanese export goods, and the foreign purchase of selected goods for importation to Japan, crediting and debiting a special dollar-denominated fund. In this scheme, the Board of Trade supplied SCAP with all exports from Japan and obtained from SCAP all imports into Japan. A complicated schedule of artificial exchange rates, varying from item to item in an idiosyncratic and arbitrary way, determined the exact terms of each transaction between the Board of Trade and SCAP.

In aggregate, during the Occupation years imports into Japan exceeded exports from Japan, and this trade deficit was financed by US aid. Specifically, a lot of the imported food, petroleum, fertilizer, and medicine proffered to the Board of Trade for sale in Japan was a gift to the government of Japan from that of the United States, under aid programs labeled GARIOA (government and relief in occupied areas) and EROA (economic rehabilitation of occupied areas). Because of the Japanese trade deficit, one might have expected the revolving fund of the Board of Trade to attain a net surplus, but in fact it remained near balance, for the Board purchased domestic goods for export at inflated prices and sold imported foreign goods at artificially low prices. In

---

[23] Ishibashi Tanzan (1884–1973) was a journalist, who rose to the post of president of Tōyō Keizai Shinpō in 1941, and served on government committees during the war years. After the war he served as finance minister in the first Yoshida administration, as minister of trade and industry in the three Hatoyama cabinets 1954–6, and briefly as president of the Liberal Democratic Party and prime minister, 1957.

this way, almost every transaction between the Board of Trade and a Japanese citizen entailed a subsidy.[24] This policy virtually assured failure to exploit comparative advantage.

Government regulation and control of every aspect of economic activity was never stronger in Japan than in the early years of the American Occupation. These misguided policies delayed Japan's economic recovery. Things began to change with the arrival in Tokyo of Joseph M. Dodge,[25] President Truman's new special emissary to Japan. The fiscal austerity measures and reforms introduced at his suggestion became known as the Dodge line.

The Dodge line

The relaxation of government controls over Japan's economy forms the major part of a "reverse course" in American policy. The initial goals of Occupation policy had been to punish the guilty (as defined by the United States!) and to strengthen political democracy. As the Americans set about achieving these aims, they regarded Japan's rapid economic recovery indifferently, at best. Perhaps this is why, in the first three years after the war, SCAP did little to curb the Japanese government's inflationary finance, rampant subsidies, and highly distorting regulations. Then, in 1949, the American government's official attitude toward Japan changed. US relations with the Soviet Union had deteriorated and the Communist revolution had succeeded in mainland China, so it had become clear that Japan could be an important US ally in Asia. If Japan's economy failed to recover, the Japan–USA alliance would perpetually drain US government resources. Washington politics thus dictated that SCAP should no longer regard Japan's economic recovery with indifference, but should actively promote it. To accomplish this, Truman dispatched Joseph M. Dodge to Tokyo, to review economic policies and carry out necessary changes.

Dodge arrived in Tokyo on February 1, 1949, and went immediately to work. In discussions with the Yoshida cabinet, including finance minister Ikeda Hayato,[26] he spelled out the necessary changes, and in some memorable press conferences he indicated to the Japanese public that America was insisting on austere measures and was leaving the ruling Liberal Party little choice but to comply. The Dodge line included an end to inflation-financed subsidies,

restoration of private foreign trade at a single exchange rate, and eventual elimination of US aid.

Dodge had the Reconstruction Finance Bank shut down. It extended no new loans after September 1949. The RFB had been one major conduit of inflation-financed government subsidies, and the *kodan*, the public corporations charged with administering price controls, were another. Dodge had the number of items subject to price controls greatly reduced and their corresponding *kodan* shut down. The deficit trading activity of the remaining *kodan* was severely curtailed by requiring that they, along with all other government enterprises and agencies, be consolidated into the general account of the Japanese government, and requiring that the general account balance. Further subsidies would now have to draw upon tax revenues, not borrowing from the Bank of Japan. To attain fiscal balance, the ruling Liberal Party had to forgo its campaign promise to reduce the statutory tax rates. (The recent inflation had bumped many individuals into higher tax brackets.) Many government employees were laid off, including 100,000 railway workers and 20,000 telephone workers. Proposed government construc-

---

[24] Hiroshi Yoshikawa and Tetsuji Okazaki, "Postwar Hyper-Inflation and the Dodge Plan, 1945–50: An Overview", in Juro Teranishi and Yutaka Kosai, (eds.), *The Japanese Experience of Economic Reforms*, New York: St Martin's Press, 1993, ch. 4, pp. 86–104. For discussion of the operations of the Board of Trade, see their pp. 98–100 and tables 4.9 and 4.10.

[25] Joseph M. Dodge (1891–1964) was not a college graduate, but nevertheless rose to the post of president of the Detroit Bank and served on the boards of directors of Chrysler and several other important companies, and during World War II served in Washington as chairman of the War Contracts Board and of the Price Adjustment Board. After the war he served with distinction as the financial adviser of the American Occupation government of Germany, and, based on that, was appointed as the leader of a US mission to review and alter the financial policies of the Japanese government, taking a three-month leave of absence from the Detroit Bank. The fiscally austere policies he implemented became known as the Dodge line. For a very revealing essay on Dodge and the Dodge line, see Howard B. Schonberger, *Aftermath of War: Americans and the Remaking of Japan, 1945–1952*, Kent State University Press, 1989, ch. 8. According to Schonberger, the granite-like, no-nonsense Dodge was, in the words of his private diary, "angered by the many 'smartees,' 'do-gooders,' and 'hobby-riders' he encountered in SCAP . . ." (p. 201).

[26] Ikeda Hayato (1899–1965) was a career bureaucrat in the finance ministry, rising to the post of finance minister in the third Yoshida administration, 1949, and later also serving as minister of international trade and industry in the same administration, then again as finance minister in the cabinets of Ishiabshi and his successor Iwata 1960, and finally as president of Liberal Democratic party, serving as prime minister 1960–3, forming three cabinets.

tion projects, including new school buildings, had to be postponed.

The subsidies extended through the Board of Trade had been financed not with new currency or taxes, but by diverting US aid. Dodge sought to end this by directing that the yen proceeds from the sale of items proffered to Japan under US aid programs no longer be placed in the Board of Trade's revolving account, but in a new account, called the counterpart funds account, under the control of SCAP. Japanese requests for counterpart funds were granted only on a case by case basis. US financing of Japanese trade deficits was no longer automatically assured.

Dodge took steps to restore Japan's foreign trade to private hands, at market-determined prices. From April 25, 1949, the terms of all transactions between SCAP and Japan's Board of Trade were determined by applying the same exchange rate to the original purchase price of every item, ¥360 = $1. In May 1949 the Board of Trade was reconfigured as a bureau within the Ministry of Commerce and Industry, now renamed the Ministry of International Trade and Industry (MITI). In the ensuing months, the Japanese government withdrew altogether from participating directly in foreign trade. From December 1949, all Japanese exports were on a private basis rather than a government basis, and from January 1950 all Japanese imports were on a private basis. The Japanese government did continue to regulate private imports by rationing foreign exchange rights.

The December 1949 Foreign Exchange and Foreign Trade Control Law, which remained in effect until its repeal in 1980, prohibited Japanese citizens from holding foreign exchange except where permission was explicitly granted by government authorities. By bestowing foreign exchange upon selected industries and withholding it from others, MITI was enabled to effect selective import restrictions even without statutory tariffs or other legislated barriers to imports. This became an important aspect of Japanese industrial policy, particularly during the 1950s. Foreign exchange remained artificially scarce in Japan until the 1960s.

Annual rates of change in Japan's money stock (M2), real and nominal GNP, and GNP deflator, 1946–55, are depicted in Figure 4.2. As is very evident in the figure, under the Dodge line, the rapid inflation at last ground to a halt. Ending the issue of new currency by the RFB and the *kodan* checked the growth in Japan's money supply. Demand for money also increased, as belief that inflation would slow made individuals more inclined to hold wealth in the form of money. As people sought to accumulate money holdings, they refrained from spending and thereby removed some of the upward pressure on market prices. Some of this effect could be observed in Japan even before full implementation of Dodge's measures, perhaps in anticipation of the measures' likely effects on inflation. General expansion of the supply of goods in response to

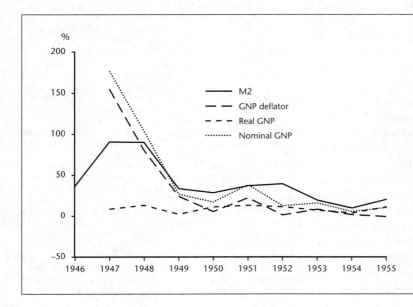

Figure 4.2. Annual percentage increases in money stock (M2), prices (GNP deflator), and real GNP, 1946–1955

Source: Ōkurashō zaiseishi-shitsu hen, *shōwa zaisei shi: shūen kara kōwa made* (Financial history of the Showa era: from war's end to peace), vol. 19 (data), *Tōyō keizai shinpō sha*, 1978.

strengthened market incentives served as an additional restraint on price inflation.

Whether the Dodge line, in and of itself, had salutary effects on Japan's macroeconomic performance, or, as many have claimed, led to a jump in unemployment and an idling of productive resources is difficult to judge; for the Korean War boom ensued before the full effects of the Dodge line could be observed.

The Korean War began on June 25, 1950, with a surprise attack on South Korea by North Korea. The USA intervened in defense of South Korea with the support of the United Nations. Following the brilliantly successful Inchon landing in September 1950, led by General MacArthur, allied forces quickly occupied large portions of North Korea. Then in November 1950 Chinese troops entered the conflict, recapturing the northern half of the Korean penin-

sula, and producing a military stalemate. MacArthur argued publicly for an allied invasion of China, and in April 1951 was dismissed by President Truman and replaced as SCAP by Mathew Ridgeway. Truce talks commenced in July 1951, and resulted in armistice two years later. During the first two years of the Korean War, Japan became a major staging area for US troops and a major supplier of military goods. US procurement spending in Japan produced an economic boom.

Figure 4.3 graphs annual magnitudes, in billions of 1934–6 yen, of the *kodan* price subsidies, RFB loans, US government aid payments received by Japan, and US procurement spending in Japan (including private spending in Japan by US service personnel). As already discussed, the price subsidies and much of the RFB loans represented inflation-financed transfer payments of the Japanese govern-

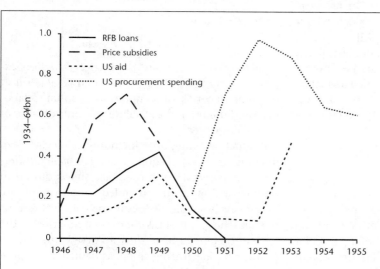

Figure 4.3. Japanese government subsidies, US aid, and US procurement spending in Japan, 1946–1955

All figures converted to 1934–6 prices using GNP deflator. Japan's GNP in 1954 equaled approximately ¥12bn in 1934–6 prices. Also, 1934–6¥0.50bn approximately equals 1985¥7.41bn (about US$100m).

Sources: *GNP deflator*: same as Fig. 4.2; *price subsidies*: Andō Yoshio (ed.), *Kindai nihon keizai shi yoran* (Handbook of the economic history of modern Japan), 2nd edn, University of Tokyo Press, 1979, table 7.25 (primary source: Economic Stabilization Board, *Bukka yōran* (price level survey), July 1952, p. 26); *RFB loans*: Miyazaki Masayasu and Itoh Osamu, "Senji-sengo no sangyō to kigyō", in Nakamura Takafusa (ed.), *Nihon keizaishi* (Japanese economic history), vii, *"Keikaku-ka" to "minshūka"* (Democratization and planning), Iwanami Shoten, 1989, table 4–3, p. 185 (primary source: Fukkō kinyū kinko (Reconstruction Finance Bank), *Fukkin yūshi no kaiko* (Recapitulation of RFB disbursements), 1950); *US aid*: 1946–9, estimated subsidies extended through Board of Trade: Hiroshi Yoshikawa and Tetsuji Okazaki, "Postwar Hyper-inflation and the Dodge Line", in Juro Teranishi and Yutaka Kosai (eds.), *The Japanese Experience of Economic Reforms*, New York: St Martin's Press, 1993, table 4.10, p. 100; 1950–3, Japanese spending of Counterpart Account funds: Andō, *Kindai nihon keizai shi yoran*, table 7.25, p. 153 (same primary source as for price subsidies); *US procurement spending*: Takafusa Nakamura, *Lectures on Modern Japanese Economic History, 1926–1994*, LTCB International Library Foundation, 1994, table 4.6, p. 166, converted from US dollars to yen using average exchange rates pertaining to Japanese imports calculated by Yoshikawa and Okazaki, "Postwar Hyper-inflation", table 4.9, p. 100. This includes private spending by US service personnel posted to Japan as well as US government spending.

ment. The US aid payments represented transfers from the US government to Japan, and the US procurement spending directly expanded aggregate demand for Japanese output. Thus, the different items are not directly comparable in their likely effects on aggregate demand for Japanese output. The inflation tax probably negated whatever expansionary effects might otherwise have attended the price subsidies and RFB loans, so one supposes that US aid and spending had a larger impact on Japan's real GNP. It is clear from the figure that the increase in US procurement spending during the Korean War occurred precisely when US aid was being choked off by the Dodge line. By the time sovereignty was restored to Japan in April 1952, its recovery from the Pacific war was in full stride.

The most striking characteristic of Japan's postwar economy was its phenomenal growth rate, and about this we have so far said little. In fact, the various government policies that have engaged our attention, and the many others we will take up in the chapter on industrial policy and elsewhere, probably contributed very little to rapid economic growth. To see why requires an informed acquaintance with the Solow growth model, the one indispensable framework for discussing the Japanese miracle.

The Solow growth model

Economic growth represents the core problem in macroeconomics. Why some economies grow and others do not, why the growth rates of a particular economy have been higher in some decades than in others, and what government policies might influence economic growth have long engaged the best intellects in economics. Although it is far from true that all the conundrums have convincing answers, there does indeed exist a body of thought on economic growth that is an essential starting point for any informed opinion on the matter. It is referred to as the neoclassical growth model, or the Solow growth model.

Basic premises of the model

As argued by the economist and Nobel laureate Robert Solow, there are three facts about an econ-omy that together would imply a tendency for its real GNP and capital stock to follow specific, easily characterized, paths: (1) constant returns to scale, (2) a constant saving rate, and (3) a constant rate of growth of labor.[27]

Constant returns to scale

By "constant returns to scale" is meant that proportionate increases in capital and labor enable equiproportionate changes in output. And here the abstraction "output" can be taken to mean real gross national product (henceforth GNP), the aggregate of goods and services produced in the economy in a year, valued at constant prices. Under constant returns to scale, GNP depends upon employment of capital and labor according to an aggregate production function, f(capital, labor), such that

$$\lambda GNP = f(\lambda capital, \lambda labor),$$

or, for $\lambda = 1/labor$,

$$GNP/labor = f(capital/labor, 1).$$

That is, if the aggregate production function exhibits constant returns to scale, then GNP per unit of labor depends only upon the capital-to-labor ratio and not upon the absolute amounts of labor or capital employed.

Production functions, including aggregate production functions, conform to the *law of diminishing marginal returns*. That is, the successive additions to output arising from expanded employment are progressively smaller.[28] Presuming constant returns to scale, the graph of *GNP/labor* as a function of the capital-to-labor ratio is thus a curved line with a positive but decreasing slope, as depicted in Figure 4.4.

Constant national saving rate

We presume that national saving is a constant fraction of national income. Saving means wealth accumulation. Wealth is the present value of assets, and income is the amount of wealth that, if con-

---

[27] Robert M. Solow, *Growth Theory: An Exposition*, Oxford University Press, 1970.

[28] In mathematical notation, the law of diminishing marginal returns holds that:

$$\partial GNP/\partial labor > 0, \quad \text{and} \quad \partial^2 GNP/\partial labor^2 < 0;$$
$$\partial GNP/\partial capital > 0, \quad \text{and} \quad \partial^2 GNP/\partial capital^2 < 0.$$

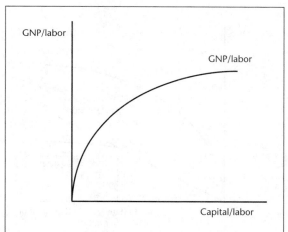

Figure 4.4. The per capita production function under constant returns to scale

sumed in a year, would leave wealth unchanged. National income measured in units of output, sometimes called *net national product* (NNP), is the gross output of the economy (GNP) less depreciation. (Depreciation is the physical wearing out of capital.)

$$NNP = GNP - \delta \cdot capital,$$

where δ is the depreciation rate, $0 < \delta < 1$.

The assumption that national saving is a constant fraction of national income means that

$$saving = s \cdot NNP,$$

where s is the (net) national saving rate, $0 < s < 1$.

Here we should emphasize that national saving is more inclusive than the more familiar concept, private saving. *National saving* is the portion of NNP devoted to uses other than consumption. For the nation, consumption includes final consumption expenditures of government as well as those of private individuals. *Private saving* is the portion of individuals' after-tax income (including business income) not devoted to household consumption. National saving exceeds private saving by an amount that is the accumulation of publicly owned wealth, i.e. government assets. It remains an open question of great importance for the public finances what relation between national saving and private saving is imposed by the logic of choice. For instance, do individuals view government saving as interchangeable with their own private saving, so

that, if government saving decreases, households increase their own personal saving by the same amount? We shall defer such questions until the following chapter. For our present purpose, the assumption of a constant national saving rate need not be based on anything more than the empirical tendency of national saving rates to vary far less from year to year for any one country than they do across countries—even though each country's saving rate is rather sensitive to changes in the business cycle. The saving rate is low during recessions and high during expansions. In this sense the assumption of constant national saving rate means a relatively stable secular average.

Japan's national saving rate in the postwar era has fluctuated between 20 and 30 percent of national income, and in the prewar era between 0 and 10 percent (see Figure 4.5). That of the USA has fluctuated between 2 and 10 percent of national income. Japan's national saving rate is among the highest of all the countries of the world. In the next chapter, we will explore some of the reasons and implications. Here, the presumption only that a country's national saving rate is some unspecified constant is sufficient for developing the logic of steady-state growth, needed to understand Japan's postwar economic recovery.

In the simplest case, the economy maintains balanced trade; that is, it finances its imports through the sale of exports and neither borrows nor lends internationally. Then the annual net additions to the nation's stock of capital (in other words, net investment) must exactly equal saving:[29]

$$\Delta capital = s \cdot NNP.$$

The annual net additions to the stock of capital per unit of labor may thus be represented by a

---

[29] The simple presumption that investment equals saving has empirical validity for open economies as well as closed ones. Feldstein and Horioka have pointed out that, empirically, each developed nation's investment–GDP ratio approximately equals its saving–GDP ratio and that the two ratios move together over time, even for nations whose economies are presumptively open, not closed: see Martin Feldstein and Charles Horioka, "Domestic Saving and International Capital Flows", *Economic Journal*, vol. 90 (June 1980), pp. 314–29. A vast literature has developed that explores the possible origin of this pattern. For a recent example, see Roger H. Gordon and A. Lans Bovenberg, "Why is Capital So Immobile Internationally? Possible Explanations and Implications for Capital Income Taxation", *American Economic Review*, vol. 86, no. 5 (December 1996), pp. 1057–75.

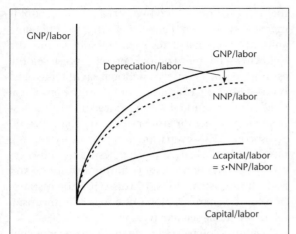

Figure 4.5. The per capita production function and annual net investment per unit of labor at each alternative capital–labor ratio, under constant returns to scale, constant rate of saving, balanced trade, and constant rate of depreciation

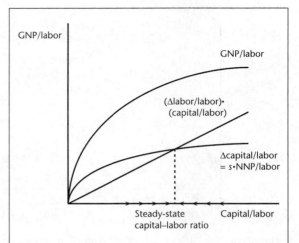

Figure 4.6. The steady state

If the capital–labor ratio is such that actual investment per unit of labor (= Δcapital/labor) is greater than (Δlabor/labor)·(capital/labor), then the capital–labor ratio rises over time. In the opposite circumstance, the capital–labor ratio decreases over time. In either case the capital–labor ratio approaches the same steady-state level.

curved line proportionate in height to the graph of the NNP/labor. The graph of NNP/labor resembles that of GNP/labor, only displaced downward by the extent of depreciation per unit of labor. This is depicted in Figure 4.5.

Constant growth rate of labor

If, in addition to the above, the labor supply is growing at some constant given rate, then the economy has an inherent tendency to follow an equilibrium path along which capital and real gross national product grow at the same exogenous rate as labor. The word "equilibrium" in the previous sentence means that, if the economy should veer off this path, then the ongoing process of saving and investing will, over time, direct capital and real gross national product back to their path values.

To see that these claims are true, note the following. In a steady state, capital is growing at the same rate as labor and thus the capital–labor ratio is unchanging. There exists a unique capital–labor ratio for which this is true. The unique capital–labor ratio for which capital is tending to grow at the same rate as labor is that for which

$$\Delta capital/labor = (\Delta labor/labor)(capital/labor);$$

for, if the left-hand side of this equation is greater than the right, then the growth rate of capital (de-

fined as Δ*capital*/*capital*) must be greater than that of labor (defined as Δ*labor*/*labor*, by assumption, a constant). And in the reverse case the opposite is true.

Under our assumption of a constant growth rate of labor, the graph of (Δ*labor*/*labor*)(*capital*/*labor*), the net addition to capital per unit of labor such that capital will grow at the same rate as labor is a straight line ray from the origin as depicted in Figure 4.6. Should the capital–labor ratio momentarily be less than its steady-state value, then actual net additions to the capital stock are more than would be sufficient for capital to grow at the same given rate as labor, and the capital–labor ratio will rise. In the reverse case, the capital–labor ratio will fall. There exists, then, an inherent tendency for the capital–labor ratio to move toward the steady-state value (as in Figure 4.6).

Technological change

The assumption of a static production function has meant that our model economy can grow only to the extent that its labor force is growing. But growth in labor might mean not only growth in the labor force, in the sense of an expanding population, but also growth in effective human effort resulting from technological advance. That is, labor might be measured in "efficiency units", so that a twentieth-century workman equipped with modern tools and the knowledge of their use is in some sense the equivalent of a multiple of his nineteenth-century counterparts. The assumed constant growth rate of labor should be understood as the sum of a constant growth in population *and* a constant rate of technological progress α:

$$\Delta labor/labor = \Delta population/population + \alpha.$$

Then in the steady state there is still an unchanging GNP–labor ratio, but its corollary is a continually rising GNP–population ratio, continually rising at the rate α. The standard of living is perpetually advancing according to the rate of technological progress.

The Solow growth model and Japan

The Japanese production function

Except for the years of the Pacific war, Japan's growth in output and in population have both been fairly stable over long periods of years. The figures in Table 4.1 indicate growth rates in real GNP and in population, by decade, for 1885–1995. The long-term trend rates of growth can be taken to indicate the steady-state growth rate. By this reasoning, Japan's steady-state growth rate in the prewar era, i.e. 1885–1935, was approximately 3 percent per year, of which 1 percent per year represented growth in population and 2 percent per year, persistent technological advance. Since 1935, the pace of technical advance seems to have risen from 2 percent per year up to around 3 percent per year. Population growth continues at about 1 percent per year. These long-term trends are interrupted by the war's devastations, 1935–46, and by the postwar recovery, 1946–65.

We can discover further details of Japan's aggregate production function by analyzing the portion of Japan's national income realized as payment for labor services. Profit-maximizing firms employ workers to the extent that the incremental contribution to the firms' output ($\partial GNP/\partial labor$), referred to as the *marginal product of labor*, just equals the *real*

Table 4.1. Average annual growth rates in real GNP and population, 1885–1995 (%)

	Annual growth rate of real GNP[a]	Annual growth rate of population[b]	Difference = annual growth rate in per capita real GNP
1885–1895	4.25	0.82	3.43
1895–1905	1.54	1.16	0.38
1905–1915	2.43	1.24	1.19
1915–1925	3.67	1.25	2.42
1925–1935	3.91	1.49	2.42
1885–1935	3.15	1.19	1.96
1935–1946	−4.89	0.82	−5.71
1946–1955	10.56	1.84	8.72
1955–1965	9.51	0.96	8.55
1935–1965	4.38	1.17	3.21
1965–1975	7.85	1.31	6.54
1975–1985	4.41	0.78	3.63
1985–1995	2.97	0.39	2.58
1885–1995	3.92	1.10	2.82

[a] Same source as for Figure 4.1.
[b] Government of Japan, *Nihon tōkei nenkan* (Statistical yearbook of Japan).

wage rate (w/P), the money wage rate divided by the price level (that is, the wage expressed in units of output of equivalent market value to the money wage). A corollary is that, in the competitive economy, the equilibrium real wage rate equals the marginal product of labor. That is, the wage rate attains precisely the level at which the available labor force is fully employed. Analogously, the equilibrium *real rental price of capital* (r/P) equals the *marginal product of capital* ($\partial GNP/\partial capital$).

If the aggregate production function exhibits the characteristic of constant returns to scale, then, by the rules of calculus (Euler's theorem[30]), we know that

$$GNP = labor \cdot \partial GNP/\partial labor + capital \cdot \partial GNP/\partial capital,$$

which, by the reasoning of the previous paragraph, implies that

$$GNP = labor \cdot w/P + capital \cdot r/P.$$

---

[30] Euler's theorem holds that, if $y = f(\lambda x_1, \lambda x_2) = \lambda f(x_1, x_2)$, then $f(x_1, x_2) = (\partial f/\partial x_1)x_1 + (\partial f/\partial x_2)x_2$. To prove the theorem, write out the expressions for $dy/d\lambda$ and evaluate them at $\lambda = 1$.

The entirety of output is paid out either as wages or as a return to capital.

Further, *labor's share*, that is the fraction of output paid as real wages, equals the *elasticity of output with respect to labor*:

$$(labor \cdot w/P)/GNP = \partial GNP/\partial labor \cdot labor/GNP.$$

Capital's share equals the *elasticity of output with respect to capital* and is also equal to one minus labor's share when the production function exhibits constant returns to scale.

Now labor's share, in most countries, has exhibited fair stability from year to year, which argues for a production function in which elasticities of output with respect to labor and with respect to capital are constants. The production function exhibiting this characteristic is the *Cobb–Douglas production function*.

$$GNP = A \cdot labor^{\theta} \cdot labor^{(1-\theta)},$$

and $\theta = \partial GNP/\partial labor \cdot labor/GNP$ is the (constant) elasticity of output with respect to labor.

Historical data on labor's share in Japan is highly

suspect, but in recent decades seems to lie around 3/4, as depicted in Figure 4.7. The problem in measuring labor's share is that the earnings of sole proprietors are not easy to separate into wages and implicit returns to other inputs. Where proprietorships are numerous, as in Japan, this problem particularly confounds accurate assessment of an overall measure of labor's share.

Presuming that labor's share in Japan of recent decades averages 3/4, we infer that a Cobb–Douglas production function with parameter $\theta = 3/4$ accurately represents Japan's aggregate output. Over time, population, technology, and capital evolve, which accounts for the secular trend of Japanese real GNP as well as transitory deviations from the trend:

$$1/GNP \cdot dGNP/dt = \theta \cdot 1/labor \cdot dlabor/dt$$
$$+ (1 - \theta) \cdot 1/capital \cdot dcapital/dt$$

$$\begin{array}{l} \text{growth rate} \\ \text{of real GNP} \end{array} = \theta \cdot \left(\begin{array}{l} \text{growth rate} \\ \text{of population} \end{array} + \alpha \right)$$
$$+ (1 - \theta) \cdot \left(\begin{array}{l} \text{growth rate} \\ \text{of capital} \end{array} \right)$$

Growth in technology and growth in capital are both far more difficult to measure than either growth of population or output (GNP). But it does appear, from the substantial variability in aggregate expenditures for investment and from the persistent long-term trends in growth of per capita GNP already noted, that year-to-year variability in growth of capital is far greater than year-to-year variability in technological progress.

Return to steady state

The idea that an economy could have a steady-state path is fundamental to our comprehension of the Japanese miracle. A large component of Japan's rapid growth in real GNP during the postwar years should be considered a return to such a steady-state path.

During the Pacific war, as many as 2.68 million Japanese citizens (including 690,000 civilians) lost their lives, 3.67 percent of the 1945 national population of 75 million. Additionally, at the war's end the ranks of the jobless were swelled by Japan's 7.61 million troops now mustering out, by the 1.5 million Japanese civilians repatriated from abroad, and by

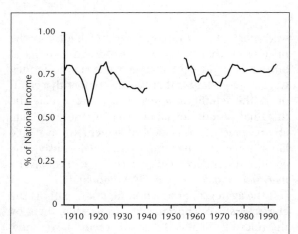

Figure 4.7. Labor's share in Japan, 1906–1940 and 1955–1993

The prewar estimate equals wages paid by corporations, other than those engaged in primary industries, as a percentage of corresponding corporate income; the postwar estimate equals all wages, as a percentage of the portion of National Income not arising from sole proprietorships.

Sources: 1906–40: Kazushi Ohkawa and Miyohei Shinohara (eds.), *Patterns of Japanese Economic Development*, Yale University Press, 1979, table A47, pp. 379–80; *1955–93*: EPA, *Report on National Accounts from 1955–1989*, pp. 118–25; and EPA, *Annual Report on National Accounts 1995*, p. 141.

the 4 million workers formerly engaged in military production.[31] In the war's aftermath, then, more than one-fourth of the labor force had become structurally unemployed.[32] But the surge in unemployed workers was quite temporary. Many found work in agriculture; others engaged in self-employed commerce. The unemployment rate averaged a mere 1 percent between 1946 and 1950.[33] Thus, Japan's employed labor force emerged from the war nearly intact. The country's capital stock did not.

Historical estimates of Japan's gross national product show that the real output of Japan's economy in 1946 stood at a mere 50 percent of its 1939 level.[34] If, as the evidence of the preceding paragraph perhaps suggests, this fall in output were due strictly to the destruction of capital, then the destruction must have been nearly total. Consider the following. A Cobb–Douglas production function with parameters that are consistent with Japan's national income statistics (labor's share ≈ 3/4) is reduced by half only if the stock of capital is reduced by 94 percent. If

$$GNP_{1946}/GNP_{1939} = (AL.^{3/4}K_{1946}^{1/4})/(AL.^{3/4}K_{1939}^{1/4}) = 1/2,$$

then

$$K_{1946}/K_{1939} = (1/2)^4 = 1/16.$$

Occupation era surveys of war damage concluded that one-fourth of the real value of total national assets had been destroyed, including 81 percent of the aggregate tonnage of ships, 34 percent of the value of industrial machinery, and 25 percent of the dwellings.[35] But these estimates vastly understate the percentage of the physical capital stock that had been rendered effectively useless. Destruction of one-fourth of the physical capital would have reduced output by only 7 percent, again assuming labor's share = 3/4. The discrepancy between postwar damage assessments and the indirect estimate of percentage destruction of capital stock must largely reflect the fact that much of the capital that had apparently withstood the war's onslaught was nevertheless unusable, because fuel, spare parts, or essential transportation links were either nonexistent or temporarily incapacitated. Additionally, much surviving capital could not quickly be redirected from the manufacture of weapons to the manufacture of civilian goods.

If Japan's economy could be viewed as following a

steady-state path before the war, then by the time of the war's immediate aftermath it had veered rather far from the steady-state path. The capital stock was far below its steady-state path, and consequently so was real GNP. But, as already described, the ongoing process of saving and investing would inexorably cause a rate of growth of capital that was at first very rapid, then less rapid, as capital again approached its steady-state path. And as the capital–labor ratio increased toward its steady-state value, the GNP–labor ratio too would rise.

Figures 4.8 and 4.9 depict the actual growth rate in real GNP in Japan from 1947 to 1970, and implied rates of growth in capital, based on the assumption

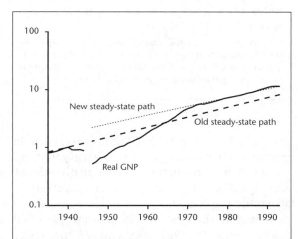

Figure 4.8. Growth path of Japan's real GNP, 1935–1993

The trend line labeled "Old steady-state path" is projected from the 1940 value at an annual growth rate of 4 percent.

31 Takafusa Nakamura *The Postwar Japanese Economy: Its Development and Structure*, University of Tokyo Press, 1981, p. 21.

32 In 1954 the labor force of Japan stood at approximately 40mn persons, in 1947 at 33.329mn (comparable to the number gainfully employed in Japan in the 1930s: 32.198mn in 1939).

33 Yutaka Kosai, *The Era of High-Speed Growth: Notes on the Postwar Japanese Economy*, University of Tokyo Press, 1986, table 9–1, p. 4.

34 Japan's GNP in 1934–6 prices stood at 22bn yen in 1939 and 11bn yen in 1946: from Kazushi Ohkawa and Miyohei Shinohara (eds.), *Patterns of Japanese Economic Development*, Yale University Press, 1979, table A4, p. 259.

35 Tatsurō Uchino, *Japan's Postwar Economy: An Insider's View of its History and its Future*, Kodansha International, 1978, pp. 14–15. These figures are quoted from a government report: Economic Stabilization Board, *Taiheiyō sensō ni yoru waga kuni no higai sōgō hōkokusho* (Comprehensive report on damage to our country from the Pacific war), 1949.

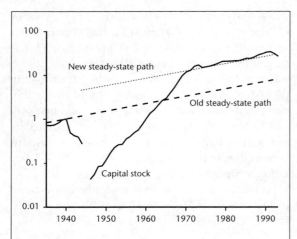

Figure 4.9. Imputed growth path of Japan's capital stock, 1935–1993 (1940 = 1)

Implied growth in capital is based on a Cobb–Douglas aggregate production function in which labor's share is 3/4, capital's share is 1/4, and the annual exogenous growth in labor, measured in efficiency units, is 4 percent.

that capital's share is 1/4 and the annual exogenous growth rate in labor measured in efficiency units is 4 percent. Notice that in the war's aftermath real GNP and capital both grew at annual rates substantially above the projected steady state growth rate of 4 percent, but that the old steady-state path was reached only in 1964, the year of the Tokyo Olympics, widely heralded as marking Japan's recovery from the war and return to the community of nations.

Japan's real GNP surpassed its old steady-state path, and since about 1974 seems to have followed a new path, about 1.4 times higher than the old one. In the main, this reflects the increase in Japan's net national saving rate during the postwar decades, in comparison with the prewar era. Japan's net national saving rate 1885–1945 averaged between 5 and 10 percent. Since 1945, it has generally averaged between 20 and 30 percent. (Figure 5.2 below depicts annual movements in the net national saving rate.) If the entire shift in the steady-state path of real GNP is attributed to the postwar increase in the national saving rate, then, as depicted in Figure 4.9, the imputed new steady-state path of Japan's capital

stock lies at about four times above its old steady-state path.[36] In other words, the net national saving rate would have had to have quadrupled, which it approximately did do, moving from 6 percent before the war to 24 percent afterwards, say. Any shift in the steady-state path of real GNP not explained by the increase in saving rate would have to be attributed to a discrete technological advance. As just related, there is no compelling reason to search for such a discrete technological leap in postwar Japan; the enlargement of the saving rate explains all or nearly all of the apparent upward shift in steady-state path of real GNP.

This begs the question why Japan's national saving rate became higher after the war. It is a question that merits an extended treatment, and is the main subject of the next chapter.

Conclusion

Japan still bears the stamp of laws and regulations enacted during the American Occupation. The Constitution, written by MacArthur's military staff and promulgated in 1946, remains in effect without amendment. So do the labor laws enacted in 1946 and 1947, which legitimized unions and provided mechanisms for resolving labor disputes, and detailed standard terms of employment. So do anti-monopoly laws, land use controls, regulation of the production and distribution of rice, and regulations of banking and securities. But the extensive price controls, inflation-financed government subsidies, and state control of foreign trade that bedeviled Japan's early postwar years, thankfully, did not survive the reverse course in American policy. The Japanese miracle began the day in February 1949 that Joseph Dodge went to work dismantling government control of the Japanese economy. Once free of government restraint, Japan's citizens set about replacing the wealth destroyed during the war. Nevertheless, the capital stock and aggregate output of Japan reached their postwar steady-state paths only in the mid-1970s.

---

36 If $GNP = AL^{3/4}K^{1/4}$, then $\lambda^{1/4}GNP = AL^{3/4}(\lambda K)^{1/4}$, and if $\lambda^{1/4} \doteq 1.4$, then $\lambda \doteq 4$.

FURTHER READING

■ Robert J. Barro and Xavier Sala-i-Martin, *Economic Growth*, New York: McGraw-Hill, 1995. A recent, detailed survey of theoretical and empirical studies of macroeconomic growth.

■ Edward Denison and William Chung, *How Japan's Economy Grew so Fast*, Washington: Brookings Institution, 1976. Empirical analysis of the sources of economic growth in Japan, 1952–1971.

■ MacArthur Memorial, *The Occupation of Japan: Economic Policy and Reform*, Norfolk, Va: The MacArthur Memorial, 1980. Proceedings of a symposium, April 13–15, 1978, attended by historians, economists and former SCAP officials.

■ Juro Teranishi and Yutaka Kosai (eds.), *The Japanese Experience of Economic Reforms*, New York: St Martins Press, 1993. A collection of papers on different aspects of the Occupation era economic reforms, written by economists.

Saving | 5

Japan's national saving rate ranks among the world's greatest. Over the last four decades Japan's (net) national saving rate has fluctuated between 20 and 30 percent of national income; by way of comparison, that of the USA ranged between 5 and 10 percent over the same interval. Japan's high saving rate accelerated its recovery from the war's devastations and has transformed Japan into a major international creditor, a country that exports more than it imports. In this sense, Japan's high saving propensity has indirectly contributed to its trade friction with other nations. Indeed, saving underlies many important facets of Japan's economic development and integration with the world economy. It is not therefore surprising that economists interested in Japan have devoted much attention to Japanese saving.

The high national saving rate of Japan is characteristic of the postwar era, not the prewar one. This exemplifies the correspondence between a high rate of macroeconomic growth and a high national saving rate that is implied by the life-cycle model of saving, developed by Nobel laureates Franco Modigliani and Milton Friedman. This chapter considers the life-cycle model, its applicability to Japan, and the leading alternative theory of saving known as the Ricardian theory. The Ricardian theory focuses on the desire to leave a bequest for one's heirs as an important motivation for saving. If the Ricardian theory is true, then adjustments in taxes and government transfers including social security benefits have little effect upon private consumption or national saving.

Measurement of saving

First, some basic definitions. *Wealth* is the present value of owned assets, and *income* is the value of goods and services that, if consumed in a year, would leave wealth unchanged from its level in the previous year. *Consumption* is the portion of one's wealth devoted to the satisfaction of wants over the current year, and *saving* is the increase in wealth from one year to the next. According to these definitions, saving equals income less consumption.

National saving is the sum of private saving and government saving, the accumulation of private wealth and public wealth, respectively.[1] In the national income and product accounts, national saving is computed by subtracting government and private consumption expenditures from national income. *National income at market prices* (sometimes referred to as *net national product* or NNP[2]) is gross national product less depreciation, plus unilateral transfers from foreigners. *Depreciation* is the wearing out of machinery, buildings, and tools, an ineluctable reduction in wealth that must be made up out

---

[1] Often, private saving is partitioned into personal saving and business saving, the latter defined as profits not distributed as dividends. This partitioning is chimerical: any wealth accumulated as business assets is in fact owned by individuals, and is perfectly fungible with other components of their personal wealth. In this sense, all private saving should be regarded as "personal" saving.

[2] National income at factor prices is NNP less indirect taxes. Indirect taxes impose a wedge between the amount spent (at market prices) and the amount received as after-tax (factor) income. "Factors" are productive inputs including labor services.

of current production before any net increase in national wealth may be judged as having occurred. Unilateral transfers from foreigners of course add to national wealth directly.

Before proceeding further, we should recognize that much national wealth reposes in the knowledge and skills of workers but that the measures of saving based on national income and product accounts reflect increases in physical wealth only, not human wealth.[3] Changes in the value of human capital, the present value of future services of the labor force, are excluded from the measures of saving only because of the difficulty of measuring them. The difficulty arises because much accumulation of human capital is the result of implicit acts of saving. The earnings of students are typically less than their incomes, as incomes are defined above, i.e. the maximum one could consume in a year without depleting wealth. By attending school instead of working at a job, a student is implicitly diverting a portion of his income from consumption to saving. Students forgo earnings now, hoping that the knowledge they acquire will enable them to achieve greater future earnings. Much wealth is in the form of human capital,[4] and much accumulation of human capital entails implicit acts of saving of this sort, unrecorded in the national income and product accounts.

Even changes in the value of physical wealth are imperfectly reflected in the national income and product accounts. The value of physical wealth is in principle detectable from the market prices of assets, but many assets are traded only infrequently so their market prices are not fully revealed. For this reason, the general approach taken in the national income and product accounts is to measure the income associated with ownership of assets by observing the current rental payments for the use of the assets, rather than to measure changes in the market value of such assets. For example, the dramatic rise in land prices in Japan in the 1980s "bubble economy" is reflected in estimates of Japan's national income— but only to the extent that current payments for the use of land were enlarged. Such phenomena probably induce errors in the measures of saving.

Further measurement errors arise because in the national income and product accounts some expenditures labeled consumption are in fact saving. The purchase of an appliance one expects to use in future years, or the purchase of dental services that will enable one to maintain a bright smile or a strong bite in future years, add to one's future consumption possibilities, that is to one's wealth. In the national income and product accounts these expenditures are typically included in the aggregate labeled "consumption", though they should in large part be counted as saving. Several scholars over the years have attempted to correct this bias in the measurement of consumption. Hayashi F(umio) has developed indirect techniques for inferring which personal expenditures should be regarded as saving rather than consumption and applied the techniques to Japanese panel data.[5] He concludes that only expenditures on food are purely consumption. Even expenditures on entertainment have a component of saving. Individuals act as though the future recall of the experience is at least the partial motivation even for attending a movie. (That is, they are likely to expend on such entertainment a temporary windfall, which implies that they regard this as a way of spreading the enjoyment of the windfall over the remainder of their lives.) But the bias that results when consumption is proxied by expenditures may not be so large, at least for Japan in recent years. Large expenditures on durable appliances by a household in one year are apt to be followed by low expenditures in the next year. Aggregation of expenditures over all households tends to average out these opposing biases and produces a reasonable approximation of true consumption. In another article, Hayashi imputes a service flow to household durables in Japan's national income and product accounts (based on measures of the stock of such durables and presumptions about the depreciation rate), and confirms that the service flow

---

[3] To regard physical wealth *per se* as an object of economic optimization, one must presume that accumulation of wealth in the form of human capital is an exogenous process, one removed altogether from the domain of choice. For instance, this is very much the spirit of the Solow growth model examined in the last chapter, in which technological advance was viewed as an exogenous and continuous expansion of the effective labor force and national saving was viewed as accumulation of machinery, buildings, and tools (physical capital inputs) only.

[4] In contemporary Japan, as much as 3/4 of national income is paid as wages. The value of human capital probably comprises a similar fraction of total wealth.

[5] Fumio Hayashi, "The Permanent Income Hypothesis and Consumption Durability: Analysis based on Japanese Panel Data", *Quarterly Journal of Economics*, vol. 100, no. 4 (November 1985), pp. 1083–1114.

matches aggregate expenditures on durables fairly closely.[6] The bias in measuring saving that results from treating all household expenditures as consumption is perhaps not large enough to pose serious problems for those who use unadjusted national income and product accounts data to gauge the accumulation of physical wealth.

Finally, a problem arises from the discrepancy between accounting measures of depreciation of business assets and the true economic depreciation. For instance, in Japan's national income and product accounts depreciation is based on historical costs, which grossly understate economic depreciation in the event of a rising inflation rate, as experienced by Japan in the years 1973–4. Again, the problem, though troublesome, probably results in only a small error in the measurement of income for most years.

Trends and fluctuations in Japanese national saving

Figure 5.1 charts national saving of Japan as a percentage of national income over 1885–1996. Japan's national saving rate fluctuated between 0 and 20 percent before the Pacific war, and has fluctuated between 20 and 30 percent in the years since the end of the war. Many of the fluctuations in Japan's national savings rate correspond to windfall gains and losses in national wealth. For instance in 1897, two years after the Sino-Japanese War, Japan received a sizable indemnity from China (payable in British pounds equivalent to 362 million yen, 20 percent of Japan's 1897 national income), a unilateral transfer and a significant increase in national wealth that accounts for the jump in national saving in that year.

In 1905 Japan dipped into its national wealth to wage the Russo-Japanese War, which accounts for the fall in national saving in that year. During the World War I years Japan experienced a prolonged boom which enabled it rapidly to accumulate foreign wealth, a windfall gain, much of which went into national saving. The windfall losses arising from the 1923 Tokyo earthquake precipitated a decumulation of Japan's foreign assets. This shows up as a sharp decrease in national saving. The years immediately before and during the Pacific war are marked by the persistent government accumulation of military assets.

Japan's national saving rate since the war has been dramatically higher than before it. Not only this, but Japan's national saving rate in the postwar era dramatically exceeds the national saving rates of other countries. Many explanations for postwar Japan's high national saving rate have been offered and we shall review some of them. For the moment, setting aside the question of the average level of postwar Japan's national saving rate, the postwar fluctuations in national saving rate have continued to reflect windfall gains and losses in national wealth. For example, the peaks in saving rate in 1948 and 1952 correspond respectively to the receipt of American foreign assistance and American procurement spending during the Korean War, each of which was a windfall gain for Japan, sizable relative to Japan's then substantially depleted national wealth in the aftermath of the Pacific war.

The subsequent peaks and troughs in national saving mirror the business cycle. A major recession in 1965, for instance, depressed the saving rate, and a prolonged boom from then until the mid-1970s fueled by inflation-induced US demand for Japanese goods, precipitated heightened Japanese national saving rates. The 1973 Arab oil embargo and the ensuing increase in world oil prices brought an economic recession to Japan, a major importer of oil, imposing on Japan a windfall loss. As already mentioned, Hayashi has argued that in the immediate aftermath of this event Japan's national income and product accounts significantly overstate national saving by failing to adjust depreciation expenses for inflation. Perhaps the actual dip in the national saving rate at the time of the first oil shock was greater than the figure indicates.

Government saving

Our analysis of the fluctuations in Japan's national saving implicitly accepted that individuals regard the public wealth (i.e. government owned assets)

---

[6] Fumio Hayashi, "Why Is Japan's Saving Rate So Apparently High?" *NBER Macroeconomics Annual 1986*, Cambridge, Mass.: MIT Press, pp. 147–210; see fig. 2, p. 154, and discussion on p. 155 on imputation of service flow to household durables.

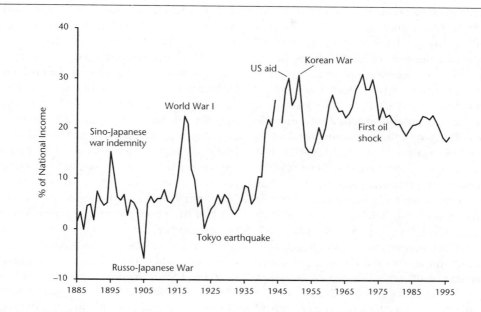

Figure 5.1. Net national saving relative to national income at market prices, 1885–1996

Sources: *National Income at market prices*: 1885–1954: Kazushi Ohkawa and Miyohei Shinohara (eds.), *Patterns of Japanese Economic Development*, Yale University Press, 1979, table A7, pp. 266–8, and table A8, pp. 269–70; 1955–89: Economic Planning Agency, *Report on National Accounts from 1955–1989*, pp. 102–9; 1990–3: Economic Planning Agency, *Report on National Accounts, 1995*, pp. 138–49; 1994–6: Bank of Japan, *Economic Statistics Annual* (1997), table 127, pp. 350–1; *net national saving*: 1885–1954: Ohkawa and Shinohara, *Patterns*, table A5, series A, pp. 261–3, and table A6, pp. 264–5; 1955–93: National Income at market prices, minus private final consumption expenditures and government final consumption expenditures from EPA, *Report on National Accounts*.

and their private wealth as interchangeable. Many contentious issues in macroeconomics revolve around whether that is indeed so. If it is not, then public wealth accumulation and private wealth accumulation need to be examined separately rather than lumped together. Government saving is the name for the portion of national saving that is the accumulation of public wealth.

Government saving may be calculated as government income minus government consumption. *Government consumption* is government spending for final goods and services used up during the current year. *Government income* consists of (1) tax receipts net of government transfer payments (which include interest payments, social security payments,[7] and subsidies), *plus* (2) profits from government enterprises, *plus* (3) increases in the amount of currency held by the public and by commercial banks, *plus* (4) any inflation-induced diminution in the value of previously issued government debt, *minus* (5) de-

preciation of government-owned physical assets. The first, second, and fifth items require no immediate comment. The third item is also straightforward: the stock of currency held by the public or by commercial banks is sometimes called "high-powered money" or "base money" (as distinct from "deposit money", which consists of deposits at commercial banks). Issuing high-powered money enables the government to acquire goods directly without collecting tax revenues or issuing debt. For this reason, additions to the stock of high-powered money augment government income.

---

[7] Not only the current year's social security payments but also any increase in the present value of promised future social security payments diminish the current year's government income. But the "promised" future social security benefits are sufficiently nebulous in Japan, as elsewhere, that changes in them may not be accurately computed and are generally ignored in constructing estimates of government income and saving.

The fourth item in computing government income involves some minor subtleties. Notice that government saving is related to the government's fiscal surplus (the opposite of fiscal deficit). In the absence of inflation, depreciation, or government investment, the government budget deficit equals government dissaving. That is, to the extent that government consumption expenditures outstrip tax receipts, the government accumulates debt; it amasses liabilities against whatever stock of assets it owns, reducing government wealth. But inflation, depreciation, and investment break the close link between the fiscal deficit and government dissaving. Consider the effects of inflation. In years of high inflation, even though government spending may exceed tax receipts, necessitating new debt issuance, the diminution in the real value (i.e. value reckoned in terms of goods) of previously issued monetary debt may more than offset the new debt issuance. In this event, all else the same, though the government issues new debt, its outstanding debt (in nominal and real terms) is lower than in the previous year, not higher!

The nominal increase in year t in privately held government debt, net of inflation-induced diminution of the value of previously issued debt (in other words, the nominal government deficit) is

$$B_t - B_{t-1} - B_{t-1}(P_t - P_{t-1})/P_{t-1},$$

where B_t is the nominal amount of outstanding debt at the end of year t, and P_t is the price level in year t. The third term comprises the inflation adjustment, the inflation-induced diminution in real value of previously issued debt, expressed in monetary equivalent units at current prices in year t. The peculiar phenomenon described in the previous paragraph, of the government issuing new debt but experiencing a reduction in the amount of debt outstanding, resides in the fact that the inflation adjustment term can oppose and more than offset the other two terms.

The inflation-adjusted nominal increase in government debt may also be expressed as

$$(B_t/P_t - B_{t-1}/P_{t-1})P_t,$$

i.e. as the difference in real value of outstanding debt between this year and the previous, multiplied by this year's price level. Quite intuitively, the increase in outstanding government debt measured in current prices is the change in value of outstanding debt in terms of real goods, times the current monetary price of a unit of real goods.

Figure 5.2 depicts movements in the government saving rate as a percentage of national income in Japan from 1955 to 1996. In the chart, the government sector includes central and local government but not the Bank of Japan (BOJ) or government financial intermediaries. (The latter consist of the Postal Savings System, Japan Development, the Export–Import Bank of Japan, and other public intermediaries of the Fiscal Investment and Loan Program.) In other words, the annual change in stock of high-powered money is not here included in the disposable income of the government (though it should be included). And annual interest payments on BOJ holdings of government bonds are subtracted from the disposable income of the government (though these should not be subtracted). These errors, we presume, are approximately offsetting. The precise implications of consolidating the accounts of the public financial intermediaries with the other components of the government sector are harder to fathom. In any case, we ignore those implications here.

The government saving ratio of the figure is adjusted for the effects of inflation on the net financial liabilities of the government as described in the previous section. The size of this inflation adjustment is also represented in the figure. As a practical matter, the inflation adjustment is relatively small. Before 1965 the stock of outstanding government debt was virtually zero, and it became substantial only after 1974. But except for 1974, in which the CPI grew by about 23 percent, inflation rates have remained fairly low in Japan, so the inflation adjustment in computing government saving is still relatively small.

The most noticeable features of the figure are the sharp drop in government saving around 1974 and gradual rise until 1991, after which government saving again declines. The revenues of the government of Japan were insufficient to cover the substantial increase in social security and health benefits beginning in 1974. The increase in government transfer payments were financed with new debt issue rather than taxes. In part, this was a calculated policy. But the necessity of resorting to debt finance was enlarged by the unanticipated 1974 recession,

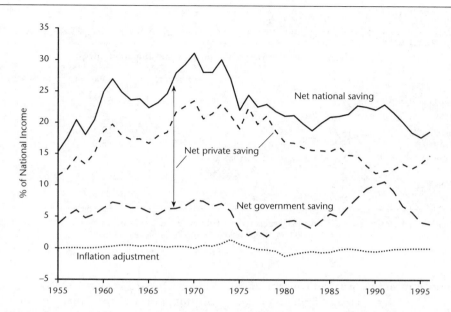

Figure 5.2. Net national saving and net government saving relative to National Income at market prices, 1955–1996

In this chart, the government sector comprises central and local government but not the Bank of Japan or government financial intermediaries.

Sources: *government saving gross of inflation adjustment*: 1955–69: Economic Planning Agency, *Report on National Accounts from 1955–1969*, pp. 86–7; 1970–9: Economic Planning Agency, *Report on National Accounts*, 1985; 1980–93: Economic Planning Agency, *Report on National Accounts*, 1995, pp. 88–9; *inflation adjustment* (amount subtracted from gross government saving) = financial assets of general government minus liabilities of general government, times percentage increase in consumer price index from previous year: 1955–69: Economic Planning Agency, *Report on National Accounts from 1955–1969*, pp. 446–9; 1970–93: Economic Planning Agency, *Report on National Accounts*, 1995, pp. 340–51; 1994–6: set equal to zero (consumer price index: Management and Coordination Agency, widely available from many sources); *net national saving*: same as Figure 5.1.

which greatly reduced tax receipts of the government.[8]

The decline in net government saving after 1991 reflects the fiscal deficits of the Japanese government that have attended the decline in tax receipts since the 1991–3 recession, and the enactment of fiscal stimulus measures (tax cuts and government spending increases) to address the recession.

In spite of the fact that the government was in a state of fiscal deficit from the late 1970s through the 1980s, and again in the 1990s, government saving remained positive. This is because a significant component of government spending was devoted to investment rather than consumption. The government's net borrowing was less than its net investment in all years; consequently there was a continual net accumulation of public wealth.

Saving rates of Japan versus other countries

In the postwar era the net national saving rate of the United States has varied between 5 and 10 percent, which is far lower than the net national saving rate of Japan. In fact, the national saving rates of most developed countries are closer to that of the USA than that of Japan. The data in Table 5.1 are illustrative.

The high national saving rate of Japan has transformed it into one of the world's largest creditors,

[8] Yukio Noguchi, "Public Finance", in Kozo Yamamura and Yasukichi Yasuba (eds.), *The Political Economy of Japan*, i, *The Domestic Transformation*, Stanford University Press, 1987, pp. 186–222.

Table 5.1. Net national saving rates of Japan and selected other nations, 1960–1994

	Net national saving (% of national income at market prices)				
	1960–73	1974–79	1980–89	1990–94	1960–94
JAPAN	26.3	23.1	21.1	21.3	23.6
USA	10.8	8.8	5.2	3.3	7.8
Germany	17.6	11.5	10.1	10.5	13.5
France	19.5	15.2	9.0	8.0	14.3
Italy	19.4	15.5	11.1	7.3	14.7
UK	11.1	6.2	5.4	3.0	7.5
Canada	11.5	13.0	9.5	2.7	10.0
OECD	14.7	12.2	9.3	7.9	11.8

Source: computed from gross saving as a percentage of GDP and net saving as a percentage of GDP, from OECD, *Historical Statistics 1960–1994*, Paris: OECD, 1996, table 6.15, p. 77, and table 6.17, p. 78.

which is the real meaning of Japan's overall trade imbalances of recent years. Japan's high saving rate has attracted more attention from academic specialists over the years than any other single aspect of its economy. Before describing this literature, we need first to sketch the most important economic theories of saving. Theories of saving belong to either the life-cycle, the Ricardian, or the Keynesian paradigms.

Theories of saving

Life-cycle paradigm

The life-cycle paradigm, developed by Nobel laureate Franco Modigliani, envisions individuals as arranging their lifetime patterns of consumption so as to completely exhaust their available wealth.[9] So if for instance, as might be typical, individuals earn labor income while young but retire upon becoming aged, then under the life-cycle hypothesis they would choose to save while young and dissave after retirement, so that they could enjoy balanced consumption throughout life and leave nothing to their heirs.

The essence of the life-cycle paradigm is that each individual consumes the entirety of her own wealth herself, at the end of life having saved nothing. However, paradoxical as it may seem, a nation of such individuals will, in the aggregate, save in each year if the nation's economy is growing. For instance, in the event of population growth, the young who are saving to support their own later consumption will perpetually outnumber the aged who are dissaving. The savers outnumber the dissavers, so in aggregate there is net saving. In the case of technological advance, the young will perpetually be wealthier than the aged and will save more to support their own relatively lavish future consumption than the currently old, who enjoy only modest consumption, will be dissaving. Again, aggregate saving outweighs aggregate dissaving. Japan's high saving rates, high growth, and youthful demographic profile in the postwar years have frequently been offered as evidence in support of the basic tenets of the life-cycle paradigm.

The *permanent income hypothesis* of Milton Friedman, yet another Nobel laureate, also belongs to the life-cycle paradigm.[10] The essence of the permanent income hypothesis is that individuals desire to arrange their lifetime patterns of consumption as the life-cycle paradigm maintains, but can do so only imperfectly because of their limited ability to foresee the extent of their own lifetime wealth. Friedman argued that a best estimator of wealth was the present value of a lifetime stream of income following a trend extrapolated from past years' incomes, plus any projected increase in physical

---

[9] Albert Ando and Franco Modigliani. "The Life Cycle Hypothesis of Saving: Aggregate Implications and Tests", *American Economic Review*, vol. 53 (March 1963), pp. 55–84.

[10] Milton Friedman, *A Theory of the Consumption Function*, Princeton University Press, 1957.

wealth arising from the current period's saving. Corresponding to this wealth estimator is an expectation of the next period's income, which Friedman labeled "permanent income". A deviation from the permanent income would be regarded as transitory, either a windfall gain or windfall loss—a random, one-time change in wealth. For this reason, a deviation from permanent income would precipitate a revision of the lifetime consumption plan: to consume slightly more than had previously been planned throughout the remaining years of life if the deviation were a windfall gain, slightly less if a windfall loss.

Ricardian paradigm

The Ricardian paradigm highlights the desire to leave a bequest for one's heirs as a motivation for saving. Conspicuously absent from the life-cycle paradigm is any sense that individuals might behave altruistically toward their own children. If such an impulse is present, and few parents would deny it, then parents will share their wealth with their own children and will not selfishly exhaust it on their own consumption. This seemingly innocuous presumption has some startling implications. First, the planning horizon is essentially infinite. If parents care about their own children, who in turn care about their children, and so on, then indirectly they must care about all of their descendants. Second, government programs that transfer private wealth across generations could precipitate offsetting voluntary transfers within families, and therefore be largely ineffectual. Such programs include social security and the issuance and retirement of government debt.

Social security is the name for government programs that transfer income to retired persons, financed largely by wage taxes. Social security policies have been adopted by nearly all the developed countries, including Japan. In Japan as elsewhere, taxes and benefits have been adjusted so that each successive cohort has derived a net benefit from participation. That is, the present value of lifetime wage taxes is less than the value of post-retirement benefits. This can be true for each successive cohort if the economy is growing and the distorting effects of the wage taxes are sufficiently small, which may account for the wide political support social security

has elicited throughout the world's developed countries. Social security amounts to a government-administered transfer of private wealth from succeeding generations to current ones. Because the establishment of a social security system raises the private wealth of those currently living, the life-cycle thesis holds that they will increase their lifetime consumption, on net reducing the aggregate savings that the life-cycle theory predicts will exist in a growing economy. The Ricardian paradigm, however, indicates that individuals might not adjust their consumption if a social security system is established, but instead might return the social security windfall to their descendants by adding it to their bequests.

Though Japan has had some form of social security system since 1941, pension benefits were rather modest until 1973. In that year benefits were raised to levels commensurate with those of the social security system of the USA, a dramatic windfall for those in Japan already retired or near retirement.

The issuance and retirement of government debt, like social security, represents a government-administered transfer of wealth across generations. For example, if the government sells bonds to finance lump-sum transfers to those currently living, it incurs an obligation to levy taxes in the future either to pay the interest on the debt or to retire it. However, if individuals have essentially infinite planning horizons, as the Ricardian paradigm presumes, then the incipient tax liabilities offset the lump-sum transfers and people will not alter their own consumption. If the future taxes are to be paid by the descendants of those now living, they will merely add the lump-sum transfers to their bequests, returning the expected net wealth of succeeding generations to the level they had originally chosen. In the life-cycle paradigm, in contrast, people disregard any future taxes likely to fall on their descendants (they do not disregard future taxes likely to fall on themselves!); they consider a lump-sum transfer financed by the issuance of government debt a windfall, and use it to finance greater lifetime consumption.

Keynesian views on saving

The Keynesian paradigm views individuals as "liquidity-constrained" so that their consumption is tied to their own current income, rather than to lifetime or permanent income. If enough individuals are so constrained, then changes in aggregate spending have "multiplier effects", which arise because consumption spending by one person is income for another. Changes in spending beget changes in income which beget still more changes in spending, and so on, ad infinitum. An autonomous increase in spending thus ultimately precipitates an increase in income that is a multiple of the original increase in spending.[11]

Estimates of the aggregate income of households in Japan that act as though liquidity-constrained, as a percentage of all personal income in Japan, range from 16 percent (Hayashi[12]) to 30 percent (Takenaka[13]), greatest during recession, lowest during booms. Similar estimates for the United States generally lie above this.

The Keynesian theory is by itself an incomplete model of saving, for it begs the question of what determines the saving behavior of the individuals who are not liquidity-constrained. In this sense, it is perhaps better to regard it as an addendum to the other two paradigms of saving, rather than as a third paradigm.

Analysis of Japanese saving patterns

Analysts of Japanese saving patterns have been largely preoccupied with explaining why postwar Japan's private saving rate has substantially exceeded the private saving rates of other countries. In a recent survey of the vast literature on this topic, Charles Horioka identifies no less than thirty-five different hypotheses for explaining postwar Japan's high rate of private saving.[14] Many of these hypotheses can be placed within either the life-cycle or the Ricardian paradigm.

In the life-cycle paradigm, individuals save while young and dissave when old. Societal savings arise because the young either outnumber the old or else perceive themselves as wealthier than the currently old did while they were young. Within this paradigm, *postwar Japan's high growth rate*[15] would seem to contribute to its high saving rate, as would the *youthful demographic profile*[16] of Japan; for throughout the last half of the twentieth century the percentage of Japanese who are relatively young will

have been less than would be true in a steady state. Japan's surfeit of young persons in recent decades is the combined result of a postwar baby boom and the delayed but rapid adoption in Japan of modern nutrition and scientific medicine, too late to greatly prolong the lives of those already beyond youth in the 1950s.

Also within the life-cycle paradigm, factors that exaggerate the tendency to save while young or dissave when old would exaggerate the effect on the societal saving rate of Japan's high growth rate and peculiar demographic profile. These factors include the *high cost of housing, land, and (children's) weddings*,[17] the *early average age of retirement*,[18] and the *long life expectancy*[19] of Japanese people. Before 1974

---

11 Denote the marginal propensity to consume out of income as b. In equilibrium, income y equals expenditures $c_0 + by$, and so $y = c_0/(1 - b)$. An autonomous increase in expenditures Δc_0 ultimately precipitates an increase in income $\Delta y/\Delta c_0 = 1/(1 - b)$, and $1/(1 - b)$ is called "the multiplier".

12 Fumio Hayashi, "The Effects of Liquidity Constraints on Consumption: A Cross-Sectional Analysis", *Quarterly Journal of Economics*, vol. 100, no. 1 (November 1985), pp. 183–206.

13 Heizo Takenaka, *Contemporary Japanese Economy and Japanese Economic Policy*, University of Michigan Press, 1991, p. 51.

14 Charles Yuji Horioka. "Why Is Japan's Household Saving Rate So High? A Literature Survey", *Journal of the Japanese and International Economies*, vol. 4 (1990), pp. 49–92.

15 Franco Modigliani and A. Sterling, "Determinates of Private Saving with Special Reference to the Role of Social Security", in F. Modigliani and R. Hemming (eds.), *The Determinates of National Saving and Wealth*, London: Macmillan, 1983, pp. 24–55; Martin Feldstein, "International Differences in Social Security and Saving", *Journal of Public Economics*, vol. 14 (1980), pp. 225–44.

16 Charles Yuji Horioka, "The Determinates of Japan's Saving Rate: The Impact of the Age Structure of the Population and Other Factors", *Economic Studies Quarterly*, vol. 42, no. 3 (September 1991), pp. 237–53; Franco Modigliani, "The Life Cycle Hypothesis of Saving and Intercountry Differences in the Saving Ratio", in W. A. Eltis, M. F. G. Scott, and J. N. Wolfe (eds.), *Induction, Growth and Trade: Essays in Honor of Sir Roy Harrod*, Oxford University Press, 1970, pp. 197–225.

17 T. Ishikawa, "Chochiku: kakei chochiku no kōzō yōin to kinyū zeisei" (Saving: structural determinants of household saving and the financial and tax systems), in K. Hamada, M. Kurond, and A. Horiuchi (eds.), *Nihon keizai no makuro bunseki* (Macroeconomic analysis of the Japanese economy), Tokyo: Tōkyō daigaku shuppan-kai, 1987, pp. 177–210; Charles Yuji Horioka, "The Cost of Marriages and Marriage-Related Saving in Japan", *Kyoto University Economic Review*, vol. 57 (1987), pp. 47–58.

18 Michael J. Boskin, "Issues in the Measurement and Interpretation of Saving and Wealth", in Ernst R. Berndt and Jack E. Triplett (eds.), *Fifty Years of Economic Measurement: The Jubilee of the Conference on Research in Income and Wealth*, NBER Studies in Income and Wealth, vol. 54, University of Chicago Press, 1990, pp. 159–93.

19 Charles Yuji Horioka, "The Applicability of the Life-Cycle Hypothesis to Japan", *Kyoto University Economic Review*, vol. 54 (1984), pp. 31–56.

Japan's relative *paucity of social security benefits*[20] meant that, within the life-cycle paradigm, the Japanese consumed less and saved more than other nations because less private wealth was shifted from future generations than was true of nations with generous social security benefits.

The Ricardian paradigm focuses attention on bequests as a motivation for saving. Within the Ricardian paradigm, factors that tend to increase a nation's saving rate include individuals' heightened degree of altruism toward their children, and the fact that their current familial wealth is low relative to some steady-state target value. The relatively *large extent of bequests*[21] in Japan might indicate the strength of familial altruism as a motivation for saving. Additionally, the relative *ubiquity in Japan of extended families living together*[22] might further evidence a heightened sense of familial altruism. Of course, the extended family is not a new aspect of life in Japan, and so its significance for explaining higher national saving rates in Japan only in the postwar era and not before is rather diminished. Not only this, but bequests might arise for other than altruistic reasons, perfectly consistent with the life-cycle paradigm. First, "accidental bequests" might arise because mortality is unpredictable.[23] Second, the promise of a bequest can be a means of inducing favors from children. Such a "strategic bequest" is granted for selfish reasons; it really amounts to a form of consumption expenditure.[24] Evidence for Japan is mixed. If the first explanation for bequests is the main one, then those with fewer children ought to have as large bequests as those with more children. In fact, this appears to be so for Japan.[25] However, except for bequests of the childless, this same evidence could also reflect the incidence of strategic bequests in Japan.

Proponents of the Ricardian paradigm argue that the *devastations of the war reduced the wealth of Japanese families significantly below target levels*,[26] which precipitated a temporarily high propensity to save. Also, the Japanese' relatively *low expectation of nuclear war*[27] and *greater expectation of natural disasters*[28] such as earthquakes have been cited as contributing toward their inclination to save for the bequest purposes.

Within both the Ricardian paradigm and the life-cycle paradigm for a growing economy, factors that increase the real return to saving tend to increase societal saving. The *depleted stock of capital in the war's aftermath*[29] might indicate a relatively high real return to saving in Japan. Also, aspects of the Japanese tax system, including *effective tax exemption on personal interest income*,[30] might result in a smaller tax wedge separating the rate of return on investment and that on saving.

Many have attempted to relate Japan's high private saving rate to the fact that *a substantial portion of wage income in Japan is paid in the form of bonuses*[31] twice yearly. This seems to be a confused notion. The sizes of the individual bonuses are not predetermined but nevertheless are somewhat predictable. It is not therefore correct to infer that because of these

---

20 Y(ukio) Noguchi, "Problems of Public Pensions in Japan", *Hitotsubashi Journal of Economics*, vol. 24 (1983), pp. 43–68; G. Kopits and P. Gotur, "The Influence of Social Security on Household Savings: A Cross-Country Investigation", *IMF Staff Papers*, vol. 27 (1960), pp. 161–90.

21 F(umio) Hayashi, A. Ando, and R. Ferris, "Life Cycle and Bequest Savings: A Study of Japanese and US Households based on Data from the 1984 NSFIE and the 1983 Survey of Consumer Finances, *Journal of the Japanese and International Economies*, vol. 2 (1988), pp. 450–91.

22 J. A. Lucken, "Consumption and Saving Behavior", *Kodansha Encyclopedia of Japan*, ii, Kōdansha Ltd, 1983, pp. 18–19.

23 Andrew B. Abel, "Precautionary Saving and Accidental Bequests", *American Economic Review*, vol. 75, no. 4 (September 1985), pp. 777–91.

24 Douglas B. Blenheim, Andrei Shleifer, and Lawrence H. Summers, "The Strategic Bequest Motive", *Journal of Labor Economics*, vol. 4, no. 3 (July 1986), pp. s151–s182.

25 Robert Dekle, "Do the Japanese Elderly Reduce their Total Wealth?" *Journal of the Japanese and International Economies*, vol. 4, no. 3 (September 1990), pp. 309–17.

26 M. Shinohara, "The Determinates of Post-War Savings Behavior in Japan", in F. Modigliani and R. Hemming (eds.), *The Determinates of National Saving and Wealth*, London: Macmillan, 1983, pp. 201–18; Fumio Hayashi, "Why is Japan's Saving Rate so Apparently High?" *NBER Macroeconomics Annual 1986*, i, Cambridge, Mass.: MIT Press, 1986, pp. 147–210.

27 Joel Slemrod, "Fear of Nuclear War and Intercountry Differences in the Rate of Saving", *Economic Inquiry*, vol. 28, no. 4 (October 1990), pp. 647–57.

28 Martin Bronfenbrenner and Y. Yasuba, "Economic Welfare", in Kozo Yamamura and Y. Yasuba (eds.), *The Political Economy of Japan*, i, *The Domestic Transformation*, Stanford University Press, 1987, pp. 93–136; at p. 121.

29 L. Christiano, "Understanding Japan's Saving Rate: The Reconstruction Hypothesis", *Federal Reserve Bank of Minneapolis Quarterly Review* (Spring 1989), pp. 10–25.

30 John B. Shoven and T. Tachibanaki, "The Taxation of Income from Capital in Japan", in John B. Shoven (ed.), *Government Policy towards Industry in the United States and Japan*, Cambridge University Press, 1988, pp. 51–96.

31 T. Ishikawa and K(azuo) Ueda, "The Bonus Payment System and Japanese Personal Saving" in M. Aoki (ed.), *The Economic Analysis of the Japanese Firm*, Amsterdam: North-Holland, 1984, pp. 133–92.

bonuses wage incomes are substantially less predictable in Japan than in other countries. If the bonuses were wholly transitory, then in the logic of the permanent income hypothesis those who receive them would devote them mainly to saving. Is this the source of the confusion—incorrectly regarding the bonuses as transitory income?

This is not an exhaustive list of explanations for Japan's high saving rate, but it does include most of the explanations that have been given serious consideration. The weight one attaches to each of them may depend on whether one judges the life-cycle paradigm or the Ricardian paradigm more convincing. Empirical investigation of the Ricardian versus life-cycle theories has spawned a vast but inconclusive literature exploring US data.[32] M. Homma et al. apply some of the same methods to Japanese aggregate data.[33] The basis for these investigations is that in the Ricardian model private consumption is unrelated to government debt and taxation, whereas in the life-cycle model current private consumption is inversely related to taxes net of transfers and is positively related to public debt. To determine reliably whether private consumption is sensitive to the public finances requires that one control for all other things on which private consumption might depend: wealth, the composition of private and publicly held assets, the distorting effects of the tax system, and so on. Homma et al. estimate aggregate private consumption functions for Japan over 1960–83, replicating the US study of Feldstein,[34] for Japan in 1952–82 replicating the US study of Kormendi,[35] and for Japan in 1957–82 replicating the US study of Seater and Mariano.[36] The sample periods include the years of significant accumulation of government debt in Japan that began with the expansion of social security benefits in 1974. The results are no more conclusive than the US studies on which they are based. For selected sub-periods, particularly before 1965, Homma et al. find significant inverse relationships between government taxes net of transfers and private consumption, which is consistent with the life-cycle model and contrary to the Ricardian one. However, for estimates based on the full time period they generally fail to discover statistically significant interdepend-

encies between government finances and private consumption. And for none of the sub-periods do they identify a statistically significant interdependence between public debt and private consumption. On these grounds, the Homma et al. study may be viewed as failing to reject the Ricardian paradigm, but perhaps it represents only a weak test of it. The Homma et al. findings are not decisive one way or the other.

Conclusion

Much of the physical wealth of Japan was dissipated in the great obscenity known as World War II. Since then, the nation of Japan has again diligently amassed a stock of private and public wealth. There are two interpretations of this process. The first, based on the life-cycle model of saving, emphasizes that societal saving is due to the saving of the young, who in postwar Japan have continually been both more numerous and more prosperous then their older contemporaries, the result of rapid economic growth and an aberrant national demographic profile. The second interpretation of Japan's high saving, based on the Ricardian model, emphasizes the desire of Japanese living in the postwar era to raise the incomes of their descendants. Whichever interpretation is true, Japan's sizable national saving rate during the postwar era is not the result of government policy or social engineering. It is the aggregate result of individuals' choices about living and working in a market economy.

---

32 For a recent review, see John J. Seater, "Ricardian Equivalence", *Journal of Economic Literature*, vol. 31, no. 1 (March 1993), pp. 142–90.

33 M. Homma, Y. Mutoh, T. Ihora, A. Abe, M. Kandori, and M. Atoda, "Kōsai no chūritsusei meidai: riron to sono jisshō bunseki" (The proposition of neutrality of public debt, theory and evidence), *Keizai bunseki* (February 1987), Tokyo: Economic Planning Agency, Government of Japan.

34 Martin Feldstein, "Government Deficits and Aggregate Demand", *Journal of Monetary Economics*, vol. 9 (1982), pp. 1–20.

35 Roger Kormendi, "Government Debt, Government Spending, and Private Sector Behavior", *American Economic Review*, vol. 73, no. 5 (1983), pp. 994–1010.

36 John J. Seater and Robert S. Mariano, "New Tests of the Life Cycle and Tax Discounting Hypothesis", *Journal of Monetary Economics* (March 1985), pp. 195–215.

FURTHER READING

■ Fumio Hayashi, *Understanding Savings: Evidence from the United States and Japan*, Cambridge, Mass.: MIT Press, 1997. Argues that the Ricardian, altruistic bequest motive is a major factor contributing to Japan's national saving.

■ Charles Yuji Horioka, "Saving in Japan", in Arnold Heertje (ed.), *World Savings: An International Survey*, Oxford: Blackwell, 1993, ch. 7, pp. 238–78. Argues that the life-cycle model explains Japan's high postwar saving rate better than the Ricardian model.

■ Charles Yuji Horioka, "Why is Japan's Household Saving Rate so High?" *Journal of the Japanese and International Economies*, vol. 4 (1990), pp. 49–92. Surveys the vast literature on private saving in Japan.

Macroeconomics | 6

Japan, like other developed countries including the United States, has from time to time experienced slowed growth in output, or even falling output. Since 1950, Japan has experienced twelve recessions. Macroeconomists argue that recessions devolve from either declines in aggregate demand or declines in aggregate supply, or both.

Aggregate demand is the economy-wide demand for output at each given price level. Aggregate demand depends on the size of the nation's money stock and on the willingness of the nation's citizens to hold wealth in the form of money rather than other assets. Governments determine the sizes of their nation's money stocks but may subordinate control of money to other goals, such as pegging the nation's foreign exchange rate or stabilizing interest rates. *Monetary policy* refers to the government's adjustments in the rate of growth of the nation's money stock. For instance, contractionary monetary policy in Japan generally means that the nation's central bank the Bank of Japan either reduces its ongoing purchases of securities from the private sector or constricts its lending to commercial banks, or both. As commercial banks' reserves accumulate less rapidly, the banks in turn constrict the flow of loans to their own clients, contracting the growth of bank deposits. As less money circulates, aggregate demand falls. Expansionary monetary policy is the opposite of contractionary in its meaning and implications. *Fiscal policy* refers to changes in government spending and taxation. Fiscal policy generally causes fluctuations in aggregate demand by inducing changes in interest rates.[1] If interest rates get bid up, citizens become less willing to hold wealth in the form of non-interest-bearing money, and this leads to an increase in aggregate demand if the nation's money stock is unchanging. If interest rates fall, citizens become more willing to hold wealth in the form of money, and aggregate demand decreases.

Aggregate supply is the economy-wide supply of goods and services at each given price level. Aggregate supply reflects the state of technology and depends also on the nation's employment of productive inputs including labor. Technological advance increases aggregate supply, an ongoing process in all the developed countries, but one that is also subject to random jumps and starts. Some contractions in aggregate supply result from changes in the relative scarcity of inputs. For instance, in 1973 the Arab oil embargo induced a steep rise in the world price of oil and reduced aggregate supply in all countries that use oil as a productive input, including Japan; the rise in world oil prices coincident with the 1979 Iranian revolution had a similar effect. Finally, aggregate supply may also reflect temporary misallocation of productive inputs, including labor. For

---

[1] There is one qualification to this statement. In the Keynesian "liquidity trap", citizens are satiated with money-holdings in the sense that they have no attractive alternative repositories of their wealth, so that aggregate demand can increase, and citizens draw down their cash balances, even without a rise in the interest rate. This has long been regarded as a theoretical curiosity only, but recently Paul Krugman has suggested that Japan may have actually entered such a liquidity trap in 1997 or 1998: Paul R. Krugman, "It's BAACK: Japan's Slump and the Return of the Liquidity Trap", *Brookings Papers on Economic Activity (Macroeconomics)*, vol. 2 (1998), pp. 137–205.

instance, if misinformation or mistaken predictions distort the calculations of employers and workers, and lead to a mistaken amount of hiring, then employment either rises or falls, depending on the direction of error, and aggregate supply either swells or shrinks. Such mistakes can result from confusion about the true price level, which is most likely to occur if aggregate demand is shifting in some unsystematic or unpredictable fashion.

Economists are divided as to the relative importance of each of the factors just described in understanding actual business cycles. The key issues are these. Do monetary and fiscal policy have systematic, predictable influences on aggregate demand, and if so which kind of policy has stronger effects? Do shifts in aggregate demand have predictable influences on price and output? That is, what is the relation between aggregate supply and the price level? And finally, are specific business cycles the result of shifts in aggregate demand or shifts in aggregate supply, and are most business cycles the result of only one of these?

There are at least three discernible schools of thought on these issues. Most prominent academic macroeconomists in Japan have been proponents of the *Keynesian* school; they argue that fiscal policy has strong and systematic influences on aggregate demand and that monetary policy has weak effects, that expansions in aggregate demand precipitate fluctuations in either output or prices but not both, and that business cycles generally result from shifts in aggregate demand and not from shifts in aggregate supply.

Proponents of the *monetarist* view, including Nobel laureate Milton Friedman[2] (and economists in Japan including Suzuki Yoshio[3]), have argued that fluctuations in the price level and in output are closely related to monetary policies, that fiscal policy has been ineffectual, and that monetary policy has either caused or exacerbated most business cycles.

Proponents of a third school, which has been labeled the *rational expectations* or market-clearing paradigm and is closely associated with University of Chicago Nobel laureate Robert Lucas and Harvard's Robert Barro, argue that fiscal policy has little discernible effect on aggregate demand but that monetary policy does influence aggregate demand and mainly induces changes in the price level but

not in output. They further hold that business cycles are nearly exclusively the result of shifts in aggregate supply. The monetarists and rational expectationists are both claimants of the label "neoclassical", which in economics means the basing of argument on the logic of individual choice.

Exhaustive analysis of American business cycles has failed to resolve the many contentious issues that divide the three major camps. Macroeconomists of all persuasions might well seek new evidence and fresh insights in the record of Japanese business cycles.

Business cycles in Japan

Business cycles are the economy's temporary deviations from its long-term growth path. Peaks and troughs in economic activity, called business cycle turning points, delineate the successive periods of economic expansion and contraction. Contractions, periods from peaks to next troughs, are also called *recessions*. The Economic Planning Agency of the government of Japan (EPA) has identified twelve recessions in the postwar era. The last turning point was a peak, reached in March 1997. Table 6.1 identifies business cycle turning points in Japan from 1888 to the present.

The Economic Planning Agency bases its dating of business cycle turning points in Japan on a "diffusion index" of leading, coincident, and lagging indicators of economic activity. The EPA first constructed the diffusion index in 1957 and used it to date Japan's postwar business cycle turning points prior to that. In the intervening years, the EPA has about a half dozen times added new indicators to the diffusion index and has deleted others, to maintain its concordance with the turning points

---

[2] Milton Friedman gave a series of lectures in Japan in 1980 arguing that monetarism well explained Japan's postwar macroeconomy, published with commentary as M. Friedman, C. Nishiyama, T. Uchida, and H. Kanamori, *Furiidoman no nihon shindan* (Friedman's diagnosis of Japan), Kodansha, 1981.

[3] As an economist at the BOJ in 1979–89, Suzuki Yoshio became an influential proponent of monetarist policies in Japan. Suzuki now serves in the lower house of the Japanese Diet as a member of the Liberal Party and maintains an informative and entertaining web page called the "Suzuki Journal" (http://www.suzuki.org/indexe.html). A representative academic work is *Money, Finance, and Macroeconomic Performance in Japan*, Yale University Press, 1986.

Table 6.1. Business cycle turning points, 1888–1998

Peak	Contraction (no. of months from peak to next trough)		Trough	Expansion (no of. months from trough to next peak)	
Mar. 1888	13		Apr. 1889	15	
July 1890	15		Oct. 1891	27	
Jan. 1893	5		June 1893	23	Sino-Japanese War
May 1895	11		Apr. 1896	18	
Nov. 1897	12		Nov. 1898	13	
Dec. 1899	19		June 1901	23	
Apr. 1903	8		Dec. 1903	18	Russo-Japanese War
June 1905	13		July 1906	10	
May 1907	20		Jan. 1909	21	
Dec. 1910	5		May 1911	13	
Apr. 1912	12		Apr. 1913	5	
Sept.1913	15		Dec. 1914	24	World War I boom
Dec. 1916	3		Mar. 1917	12	World War I boom
Mar. 1918	13		Apr. 1919	12	
Apr. 1920	12		Apr. 1921	12	
Apr. 1922	9		Nov. 1922	14	
Jan. 1924	25	Kanto earthquake	Dec. 1926	27	
Mar. 1929	19	Worldwide depression	Nov. 1930	20	
July 1933	2		Sept.1933	48	Takahashi finance
Sept.1937	7		Apr. 1938	20	
Dec. 1939	17		May 1941		
June 1951	4	Post-Korean War recession	Oct. 1951	27	Consumption boom
Jan. 1954	10	1954 recession	Nov. 1954	31	Jimmu boom
June 1957	12	Bottom-of-the-pot recession	June 1958	42	Iwato boom
Dec. 1961	10		Oct. 1962	24	Olympic boom
Oct. 1964	12	1965 recession	Oct. 1965	57	Izanagi boom
July 1970	17		Dec. 1971	23	Retto kaizo boom
Nov. 1973	16	First oil shock	Mar. 1975	22	
Jan. 1977	9	1977 recession	Oct. 1977	28	
Feb. 1980	36	Second oil shock	Feb. 1983	28	
June 1985	17		Nov. 1986	51	Bubble economy
Feb. 1991	32	Heisei recession	Oct. 1993	41	
Mar. 1997	?	Asian financial crisis			

Sources: *prewar*: S. Fujino, *Nihon no keiki junkan* (The Japanese business cycle), Tokyo: Keiso shobo, 1965, table 2–4, p. 35; *postwar*: Keizai kikakucho (Economic planning agency), *Nihon keizai shiso* (Japanese economic indicators), Tokyo: Keizai kikakucho, annual.

identified by an official committee of experts. Table 6.2 lists the indicators currently included by the EPA. The value of the index is the percentage of these indicators that have improved over the corresponding previous three months. In computing the value of the index, any two indicators displaying no change over the previous three months are treated as equivalent to any one indicator showing improvement. Business cycle turning points are, in principle, months in which the diffusion index breaks the 50 percent mark, a trough if the diffusion index is rising and a peak if the index is falling.

The business cycle is not a new phenomenon in Japan. A variety of Japanese economic indicators are available on a monthly or quarterly basis even as early as the Meiji period. The macroeconomist

Table 6.2. Components of the EPA diffusion index used for dating turning points of the business cycle

Leading indicators (13)

1. Producer inventories of finished goods, ratio to shipments (index)*
2. Manufacturers' raw materials inventories, ratio to consumption (index)*
3. New job offers (excluding recent graduates)
4. Real machinery orders received (private demand except from shipbuilders and electric power companies; 280 companies): value of orders deflated by wholesale price index
5. Building construction starts: total floor space (mining and mfg, commerce, and service industries)
6. Housing starts: total floor space
7. Construction backlogs during the month
8. Durable goods shipments (rate of growth; annualized rate of growth for the month, compared with the corresponding figure for the same month of the previous year)
9. Nikkei index of commodity prices (42 commodities, end of month; annualized rate of growth for the month, compared with the corresponding figure for the same month of the previous year)
10. Money supply (M2 + CDs, annualized rate of growth for the month, compared with the corresponding figure for the same month of the previous year)
11. Manufacturers' earnings index (utilization rate × shipments price index/investment price index)
12. Investment index (operating profit rate on assets × rate of return on NTT bonds)
13. Outlook for small and medium enterprise in the coming period; opinion survey of businesses

Coincident indicators (11)

1. Index of industrial production (mining and mfg industries)
2. Raw materials consumption index (mfg industries)
3. Electrical power usage (9 power companies)
4. Manufacturing capacity utilization rate (index)
5. Manpower procurement index (actual hours worked index × index of number of employees)
6. Investment goods shipments index (excluding transportation equipment)
7. Department store sales (annualized rate of growth for the month, compared with the corresponding figure for the same month of the previous year)
8. Wholesale sales index (annualized rate of growth for the month, compared with the corresponding figure for the same month of the previous year)
9. Operating profits (all industries)
10. Small and medium mfg firms' sales (= small and medium firms' shipments index × wholesale price index for small and medium firms' producer goods)
11. Ratio of job offers to applicants (excluding recent graduates)

Lagging indicators (8)

1. Index of final producers' goods inventories
2. Index of raw materials inventories (mfg industries)
3. Regular employees in manufacturing (index)
4. Real plant investment by corporations
5. Household consumption expenditures (all worker households; annualized rate of growth for the month, compared with the corresponding figure for the same month of the previous year)
6. Corporate income tax receipts
7. Unemployment rate*
8. All banks' average contracted interest rate on loans and discounts

* Statistics for which a decrease indicates an improvement.

Source: Toyo Keizai, *Keizai tokei nenkan 1993* (Economic statistics yearbook 1993), p. 338.

Fujino Shōzaburō used such indicators to identify turning points of the prewar Japanese business cycles.[4] He compiled a monthly diffusion index based on month-to-month changes in fifty-six indicators from January 1888 to June 1941. The indicators include exports, imports, bank clearings, interest rates, bank deposits, loan volumes, various price indices, money supply, warehouse inventories, silk production, rail shipments, coal and cement inventories, paper production and inventory, copper production and inventories, and others. Not all of the series are available from 1888. Fujino's turning points from January 1868 to December 1888 are based on a single economic indicator: the month's percentage increase in wholesale prices compared with that of the same month of the previous year, which is in fact highly correlated with the diffusion index in the years 1888–1940. Table 6.1 reports Fujino's turning points only for the years 1888–1940. Quite clearly, the frequency and duration of Japan's business cycles were as great in the prewar era as in the modern era.

In the United States, a widely respected nonprofit organization known as the National Bureau of Economic Research (NBER) identifies business cycle turning points. The economists of the NBER consider a broad set of measures of economic activity in making these judgments, not unlike the procedure adopted by Japan's EPA. It usually takes several months after a turning point is reached before the data supporting an official designation become fully available, in both Japan and the USA. For example, the March 1997 peak in Japan was officially designated by the EPA only on June 22, 1998. American journalists do not wait for the NBER announcement that the US economy has entered a recession. Journalists proclaim that the American economy is in a recession at any time when seasonally adjusted real GDP have declined in two successive three-month periods, and the journalists are almost always later confirmed in that judgment by the NBER. This journalistic rule of thumb would have identified Japan's last two recessions (Feb./91–Oct./93 and Mar./97–), but none of its previous postwar recessions. In other words, often Japan's economy has continued to grow even during officially designated recessions. We may well ask, just how severe have Japan's business recessions been?

Severity of Japan's recent recessions

We can judge the severity of temporary economic slowdowns by comparing the actual trajectory of aggregate output with interpolated trend values. Table 6.3 presents estimates of the shortfall in real GDP during the final year of each of Japan's recent

---

[4] Fujino Shōzaburō, *Nihon no keiki junkan* (The Japanese business cycle), Keiso Shobo, 1965.

Table 6.3. Real GDP during Japan's recent recessions

Benchmark years for log linear interpolation	1956	1961	1964	1970	1973	1976	1979	1985	1991	1996
Final year of recession	1958	1962	1965	1971	1974	1977	1982	1986	1993	Ave.
Interpolated growth rate of real GDP (%)	9.66	9.52	10.24	6.69	2.13	5.04	3.72	4.45	1.82	5.86
Real GDP in final year of recession (1985¥bn)	52,721	79,162	101,109	198,981	207,183	232,550	285,002	328,816	419,765	
Predicted real GDP based on interpolation	55,204	79,718	105,411	183,145	212,913	233,274	287,161	334,654	427,205	
Shortfall	2,483	556	4,628	4,164	5,730	724	2,158	5,838	7,440	
Percentage shortfall in real GDP	4.71	0.70	4.25	2.33	2.79	0.31	0.76	1.74	1.74	2.1

Sources: real GDP: Economic Planning Agency, *Report on National Accounts from 1955 to 1989*, and *Annual Report on National Accounts 1998*.

recessions, based on a comparison of actual real GDP with interpolated trend lines. The benchmark growth rates in real GDP are higher in the 1950s and 1960s than in the 1970s and 1980s. The high growth rates in the earlier years reflect both the recovery from the war and the convergence of technology. The very low interpolated growth rate between 1973 and 1976 (2.13 percent per year) can be understood as a transition to a lower and flatter steady-state path, following the sharp increase in world oil prices. Until the current recession that began March 1997 (not shown in the table), the 1974 recession was often described as Japan's worst postwar recession. But according to Table 6.3, percentage shortfalls in real GDP were greater in the 1958 and 1965 recessions, and absolute shortfall in real GDP was greater in the 1986 recession, than in the 1974 one. Of course, identification of the 1974 recession as particularly severe is based on the low absolute growth rate of Japan's real GDP in that year. But Japan's economic growth rate would probably have been low in 1974 anyway, even if no recession had occurred as Figure 6.1 illustrates. It is too early to know whether the same applies to the current recession. Preliminary figures indicate that Japan's real GDP actually grew 1.4 percent in calendar year 1997 and then shrank 2.8 percent in calendar year 1998.

The shortfalls in real GDP, based on a comparison with the interpolated benchmarks, are plotted in Figure 6.2. If these shortfalls were distributed across the years in proportion to benchmark real GDP, they would altogether hold an equivalent value to a

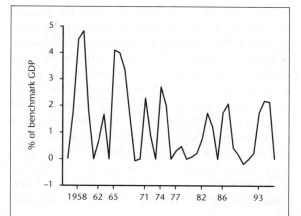

Figure 6.2. Shortfalls in real GDP as percentages of benchmark real GDP, 1956–1996

The figure shows deviations from the interpolated benchmark real GDP. Each of the peaks corresponds to a different recession. If spread over the entire span of years in proportion to benchmark real GDP, the shortfalls would amount to about 1 percent of real GDP in every year.

Source: calculated by the author; for details of the interpolation intervals and sources of raw data, refer to the previous figure.

stream of income near 1 percent of the benchmark GDP in each respective year. This can be placed in further perspective by recalling that technological advance has been raising the steady-state path of real GDP in Japan by about 1 percent per year. In other words, permanent elimination of Japan's recessions would contribute to the nation's wealth about as much as any one year's technological advance. From this perspective, Japan's recessions have indeed been rather mild.

Japan's recessions of the postwar era have been mostly "growth recessions", in which real GDP continues to grow but at a slowed rate. The experience of the United States has been quite different—so much so that, as already mentioned, successive quarters of decline in real GDP represents the journalistic rule-of-thumb for identifying business cycle peaks in the USA. Japan's postwar recessions, except for the 1973–5 first oil shock recession, the 1991–3 Heisei recession, and the ongoing 1997–8 recession, have been growth recessions. In America, growth recessions have been the rare exceptions to the usual pattern, just the opposite of Japan.

Why the difference? For one thing, Japan's benchmark growth rate has generally exceeded America's,

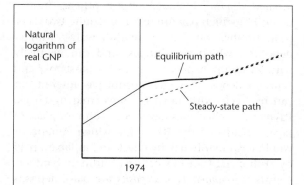

Figure 6.1. Rate of growth along the equilibrium path
This is temporarily low in the transition to a new, lower and flatter, steady-state path.

because of both the recovery from wartime destruction and the closing of the technology gap between Japan and the United States. But additionally, some economists have argued that Japan's business recessions have been mild because of efficacious monetary and fiscal policies, and because of structural features that act as automatic stabilizers. For these reasons, the Japanese case holds particular significance in the ongoing academic debate about macroeconomic policy. We shall return to these issues presently, but only after closely analyzing the determinates in Japan of aggregate demand and aggregate supply. We begin with aggregate demand.

Aggregate demand: money and monetary policy

Aggregate demand is the economy-wide demand for output at each price level. As in Figure 6.3, it may be represented by an *aggregate demand curve*, a locus of points indicating the price levels at which different real GDPs would be willingly purchased. Generally speaking, aggregate demand depends upon the size of the national money stock, which government authorities control through monetary policy, and on the willingness of the nation's citizens to hold wealth in the form of money. In the concise language of macroeconomics, aggregate demand depends upon the supply and demand for money.

Japan's money stock

Money consists of currency held by the public, bank balances, and other liquid financial assets used as media of exchange. The money aggregates regularly reported by the Bank of Japan and their amounts for 1996, in trillions of yen, are listed below. (The figures for "M3 + CDs" and "base" represent the amount outstanding at the end of the year; all other figures are averages over the year.) For reference, Japan's 1997 nominal GDP = 507 trillion yen.

M1	=	163.4	= *currency* held by the public (40.8) plus *demand deposits* of the public at commercial banks (122.6)
M2	=	538.9	= M1 plus *time deposits* of the public at commercial banks (375.5)
M2 + CDs	=	553.8	= M2 plus *certificates of deposit* (14.9)

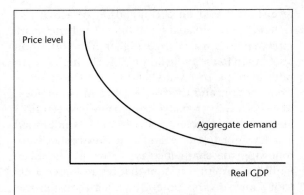

Figure 6.3. An aggregate demand curve

This comprises a locus of points indicating the economy-wide demand for goods and services at each given price level.

M3 + CDs	=	1,001.8	= M2 + CDs plus deposits at post offices, cooperatives, and credit unions, as well as trust accounts
Broadly defined liquidity	=	1,154.2	= M3 + CDs plus bank debentures, government bonds, foreign bonds, bonds with repurchase agreements (*gensaki*), and investment trusts
Base	=	57.8	= currency held by the public and vault cash of banks plus *official bank reserves* held against M2

In Japan, *currency* includes coins and paper currency (Bank of Japan notes) held by the public (in other words, not by financial institutions). *Official bank reserves* consist of commercial banks' deposits at the central bank, the Bank of Japan. In Japan *demand deposits* include, among others, "notice deposits", which pay interest and require two days' prior notification prior to withdrawal, "ordinary deposits", which pay interest and can be freely withdrawn upon presentation of a passbook, and "current deposits", which do not pay interest but can be freely withdrawn or transferred by check. Payment by check has never been commonplace in Japan. Many of the items for which Americans would customarily pay by check are, in Japan, paid by authorized transfers between ordinary bank accounts (*furikomi*). *Time deposits* are bank deposits that, in principle, are for a fixed term. *Certificates of deposit* (CDs) are very large-denomination negotiable bank notes held mainly by corporate investors. Banks have been permitted to issue these CDs only since 1979. The market return on CDs represents one of the longest series of unregulated, nearly riskless, interest rates in Japan. All of the monetary aggregates are highly correlated with one another, especially over short observation periods. Currently, analysts of monetary policy in Japan follow M2 + CDs most closely. The longest continuous series (available from 1868 (Meiji 1)) is the monetary base.

Figure 6.4 indicates the path of Japan's money stock (M2 + CDs) and nominal and real GNP from 1900 to 1997. In the figure the vertical difference between nominal GNP and real GNP equals the natural logarithm of the GNP deflator. The GNP deflator is a broad measure of the average movement in money prices of all goods produced in a nation. That inflation is caused by expansion of the money stock, clearly evident from the figure, is the most widely confirmed macroeconomic phenomenon. Its algebraic representation is known as the quantity equation.

The quantity equation

Expansion of the nation's money supply precipitates inflation because the nation's citizens spend money and bid up prices if their money holdings exceed the amount they demand. In thinking clearly about this phenomenon, one must be careful to distinguish between money and wealth. The *demand for money* refers to the portion of the nation's wealth that its citizens desire to hold in the form of money. The demand for money depends upon national income, interest rates, and the technology of banking. The holding of money facilitates transactions but generally offers a lower return than the holding of other assets. Deposit money accumulates at a lower interest rate than do stocks, bonds, or other assets, and currency actually depreciates in real value as the money price level rises. A rise in the return on non-monetary assets induces businesses and individuals to hold more of their wealth in such assets and less in the form of money, absorbing the higher costs of transacting that accompany the loss in liquidity. For instance, with smaller money holdings relative to wealth, an individual might have to make more frequent trips to the bank or more frequent sales of other assets just to fulfill ongoing purchases. The advent of automatic teller machines has lowered these costs and lowered the demand for money, but this process has been fairly gradual, not marked by abrupt shifts.

When the money demand is a stable function of

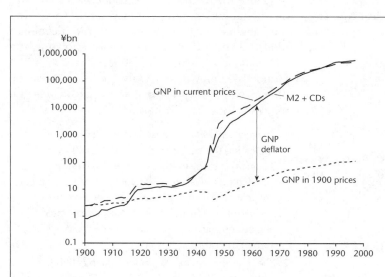

Figure 6.4. Money stock, nominal GNP, and real GNP, 1900–1997

Sources: *money stock*, pre-1955: Harada and Horiuchi, "Senzenki nihon no kinyū pafōmansu to sono hyōka" (Prewar Japanese finance: an evaluation of its performance), *Yūsei kenkyū rebyū*, vol. 3 (March 1993), pp. 57–74; 1955–97: Bank of Japan web page: http://www.boj.or.jp/en/down/long/data/hms.txt; *nominal and real GNP*: pre-1955: Kazushi Ohkawa and Miyohei Shinohara (eds.), *Patterns of Japanese Economic Development*, Yale University Press, 1979, tables A1 and A2; 1955–97: Economic Planning Agency web page: http://www.epa.go.jp/e-e/eri/menu.html.

interest rates and income, there will exist an equilibrium relation between money supply, the price level, and real income known as the *quantity equation*. Equilibrium of domestic asset markets requires that the quantity of money demanded equal the money supply:

$$M = K(i)Py, \quad \text{and} \quad \partial K/\partial i \leq 0,$$

where M is the nominal money supply, i is the nominal interest rate, P is the price level, y is real GDP, and $M_d/P = yK(i)$ is the real demand-for-money function. Notice that this formulation presumes that the real demand for money is proportional to real GDP.

The value of the function $K(i)$ in the quantity equation is sometimes referred to as the "Cambridge K", after an influential group of Cambridge University economists including Alfred Marshall, who once argued that, for their contemporary England of the early twentieth century, it was a constant; that is, that real money demand was proportionate to real GDP and independent of the interest rate. The result of such an assumption is the "quantity theory":

$$M = KPy,$$

which states that the nation's nominal GDP is proportionate to its money stock. Its logical corollary, that the rate of change in the money supply is the sum of rates of change in the price level and in real GDP, is sometimes referred to as the "dynamic quantity theory":

$$d\ln M/dt = d\ln P/dt + d\ln y/dt.$$

Given that trend growth in real GDP is predetermined (by the nation's growth in labor force, technological advance, and saving behavior), movements in the money stock will, according to the quantity theory, eventually lead to proportionate movements in money prices.

The quantity equation and the aggregate demand curve

In the simplest macroeconomic model, based on the quantity theory, the aggregate demand curve is a perfect hyperbola, the graph of $P = ay^{-1}$, where $a = M/K$, i.e. nominal money stock divided by the Cambridge K. In the simple quantity theory, then,

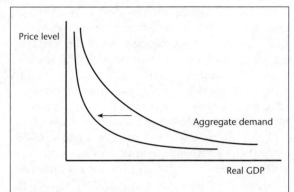

Figure 6.5. A contraction of the money supply or expansion of money demand

This reduces the aggregate demand at each alternative price level.

only changes in the nominal money stock shift the aggregate demand curve. Figure 6.5 displays a shift in aggregate demand curve as might be induced by a contraction of the money supply.

In fact, contrary to the simple quantity theory, the real demand for money depends upon the interest rate. Consequently, the position of the aggregate demand curve depends upon all the factors that influence the interest rate, and not just on the size of the nation's nominal money stock. This is the fundamental logic expressed by the Keynesian model of the economics textbooks, known as the IS–LM model or, in its open economy version, as the Mundell–Fleming model. Only a brief sketch will be offered here.[5] The essential elements include the following functional relations.

1. *the real demand-for-money function, $L(r + \pi^*, y)$,* indicating the dependence of desired real cash balances (money holdings expressed in terms of purchasing power) on real national income y, and on the real rate of interest plus the expected rate of inflation $r + \pi^*$ (equal to the money rate of interest, the opportunity cost of holding real wealth in the form of money);

2. *the consumption function, $c(y - T)$,* indicating the

---

5 For a detailed elaboration of the IS–LM model, the following are excellent: N. Gregory Mankiw, *Macroeconomics*, 2nd edn, Worth Publishers, 1994; Paul R. Krugman and Maurice Obstfeld, *International Economics: Theory and Policy*, 2nd edn, London: Harper Collins, 1991.

dependence of private consumption expenditures on income, net of taxes and other transfers between the government and private sectors;

3. *the investment function, i(r)*, indicating dependence of domestic private investment on the real interest rate; and

4. a relation *nfi(r)*, that is *the* inverse *of the function indicating the dependence of the world-wide real interest rate*[6] *on the nation's own net foreign investment*, i.e. its net accumulation of claims on the future incomes of foreigners (capital account deficit). A small economy has no influence upon the world-wide interest rate and this relation becomes $nfi(r) = \overline{nfi}$, but an open economy as large as that of Japan's today does influence the world's interest rates. A surge in Japanese net foreign investment as occurred in the late 1980s depresses interest rates in America and elsewhere as well as in Japan.

These functional relations determine the unique levels of real GDP (or national income) and real rate of interest that fulfill two conditions of economic equilibrium: first, that real demand for money equals the real stock of money (the LM condition), and, second, that (planned or intended) investment subtracted from saving equals net foreign investment (the IS condition). Algebraically, where signs above variables indicate the signs of the corresponding partial derivatives of the functions in which the variables are arguments, the LM and IS conditions are the following:

$$\text{LM: } M/P = L(\overset{+}{y}, \overset{-}{r + \pi^*}),$$

$$\text{IS: } y - c(\overset{+}{y - T}) - G - i(\overset{-}{r}) = nfi(\overset{-}{r}).$$

The predetermined variables here are: money supply M, price level P, expected rate of inflation π^*, government purchases G, and taxes net of transfers T. The IS condition is an inverse relation between real income y and real rate of interest r. The LM condition is a positive relation between real income y and real rate of interest r.[7]

Each of the relations on which the IS and LM conditions depend widens the set of factors capable of shifting the aggregate demand curve. Because increases in the interest rate lower the real demand for money, factors that raise the interest rate corresponding to any given real GDP—such as an exogenous increase in domestic private investment

(an upward shift in $i(r)$), an exogenous increase in foreign real interest rates (and upward shift in $nfi(r)$), or an increase in government purchases G or reduction in taxes T—increase aggregate demand at each price level.

The neoclassical paradigms, including both the monetarist and the rational expectationist, emphasize the importance of fluctuations in the money stock in explaining movements in aggregate demand. The Keynesian paradigm identifies the wider set of factors as accounting for fluctuations in aggregate demand, factors that include changes in government spending and taxation (fiscal policy). To put matters bluntly, the neoclassical view emphasizes money supply as the pre-eminent immediate influence on aggregate demand, while the Keynesian view emphasizes money demand as pre-eminent but also regards money demand itself as responsive to numerous influences. The interest sensitivity of money demand occupies a crucial link in the Keynesian chain of logic.

According to Hamada and Hayashi's[8] estimates of the money demand function for Japan over 1974–82, if the interest rate (on interbank loans) rose, say, from 4 to 4.4 percent (and the interest rate on time deposits did not change), then the real demand for money would within three months fall by around 0.2 percent, and ultimately would fall by 1 percent—a rather inelastic response in each case (short-run elasticity = 0.02 and long-run elasticity = 0.10). These estimates closely resemble similar estimates of the interest elasticity of the US money demand function. Hamada and Hayashi's estimates of the elasticity of real money demand with respect

---

6 Here we make the simple presumption known as "relative purchasing power parity", which implies that foreign and domestic real rates of interest are made equal by arbitrage. See Ch. 7 for more details on the relative purchasing power parity thesis.

7 A commonly encountered extension of the IS–LM model incorporates a relation $nex(y, e)$, describing the dependence of the nation's net exports (exports minus imports, also known as the current account surplus) upon domestic real income y and the real exchange rate e. Introducing the exchange rate as a third variable to be determined by the model requires adding a third equilibrium condition, that net exports equal net foreign investment: $nex(y, e) = nfi(r)$. This equation, together with the IS and LM conditions, determines the equilibrium national income y, the world real interest rate r, and the exchange rate e.

8 Koichi Hamada and Fumio Hayashi, "Monetary Policy in Postwar Japan", in Albert Ando, Hidekazu Eguchi, Roger Farmer, and Yoshio Suzuki (eds.), *Monetary Policy in our Times*, Cambridge, Mass.: MIT Press, 1985, table 4.5, p. 100.

to real GDP range from 0.7 to 1.5. The elasticity of real money demand with respect to changes in real GDP cannot be estimated precisely because both real money demand and real GDP exhibit strong upward trends. That real money demand at any given interest rate is proportionate to real income cannot easily be refuted.

These estimates, and others like them,[9] establish that Japan's money demand is measurably sensitive to movements in interest rates as the Keynesian paradigm requires. However, as an empirical matter, fluctuations in money supply and not in money demand do account for many of the major fluctuations in aggregate demand in Japan in the decades since the war's end. Monetary policy has played a crucial role in the Japanese business cycles.

Instruments of monetary policy in Japan

Monetary policy refers to government measures that influence the growth path of the nation's stock of money. The agent of monetary policy in most nations today is the central bank, the government bank authorized to issue currency usable as bank reserves (base money). Japan's central bank, the Bank of Japan, was founded in 1882, America's central bank, the Federal Reserve, in 1914. The instruments of monetary policy that can be exercised by a central bank include changes in its own lending

to private banks at its official discount rate, open-market operations (sales and purchases of assets by the central bank), and changes in reserve requirements (stipulated minimum bank reserve holdings per unit of deposit accounts of differing kinds). The Bank of Japan's principle instruments for controlling Japan's money stock are its discount window lending and open market operations, not its required reserve ratios. The Bank of Japan did not even introduce reserve requirements until 1959. In October 1991 the BOJ reduced its required reserve ratios from an average effective rate of 0.72 percent to one of 0.43 percent (The average effective rate equals required reserves divided by bank liabilities subject to reserve requirements.) Except for this episode and a couple of others like it, the BOJ has only ever changed the required reserve ratios slightly, and has relied instead upon its other instruments to effect changes in the stock of base money.

Figure 6.6 depicts the Bank of Japan's cumulative discount window lending and purchase of securities

---

9 For other estimates refer to the following: T(omō) Yoshida, "On the Stability of the Japanese Money Demand Function: Estimation Results using the Error Correction Model", *BOJ Monetary and Economic Studies*, vol. 8, no. 1 (January 1990), pp. 1–48; Robert H. Rasche, "Equilibrium Income and Interest Elasticities of the Demand for M1 in Japan", *BOJ Monetary and Economic Studies*, vol. 8, no. 2 (September 1990), pp. 31–58; Colin R. McKenzie, "Money Demand in an Open Economy", *Journal of Japanese and International Economies*, vol. 6 (1992), pp. 176–98.

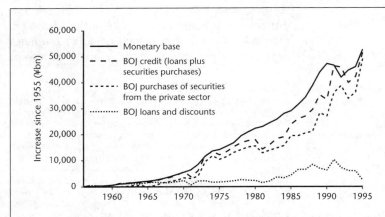

Figure 6.6. Bank of Japan loans and discounts (discount window lending) and purchases of securities from the private sector (open market operations), 1956–1995

Changes in the monetary base result from the Bank of Japan's discount window loans and open market operations, and also from BOJ receipts and payments of the Japanese government's Treasury accounts, including its foreign exchange fund special account.

Source: Bank of Japan, *Economic Statistics Annual*: items "BOJ total credit" and "lendings outstanding" (= loans and discounts) in the table "Supply and Demand of Funds", and item "reserve money" (= base) in the table "Monetary Survey".

from the private sector since 1955. Almost the entire outstanding stock of base money in Japan in 1955 was the result of the BOJ's previous purchase of securities directly from the government, the inflationary finance of the government's wartime and early postwar era expenditures. From the advent of the Dodge line in 1949 to the present, the Bank of Japan has eschewed the overt monetization of government debt. In the first decade following the restoration of Japanese sovereignty, 1952–62, virtually the entire increase in Japan's stock of base money was the result of BOJ discount window lending to private banks. Out of concern at the growth in size of outstanding BOJ loans and discounts, the Bank in 1962 adopted the so-called "New Scheme for Monetary Control" in which it determined to restrain the growth in its outstanding lending and instead to expand the stock of base money through its purchases of securities from the private sector. This process was at first very much inhibited by the small amounts of outstanding Japanese government debt.

In 1965 the Japanese government issued long-term bonds for the first time since the Pacific war. Until 1978, the government did not sell its long-term bonds at auction, but instead placed them directly with a syndicate consisting of virtually all the private financial institutions of Japan, at controlled, below-market prices. And, one year after issue, the BOJ purchased the long-term government bonds from these same financial institutions, also at controlled prices. (The 1947 Fiscal Law prohibits the Bank of Japan from purchasing Japanese government bonds sooner than one year after issue.) These operations enabled the BOJ to expand the supply of base money without enlarging its outstanding discount window loans, as depicted in Figure 6.6, but the discount window remained the essential instrument of day-to-day and week-to-week control of the stock of bank reserves at least until the mid-1970s. With the explosion of Japanese government debt after 1974, the earlier system of indirectly placing long-term government bonds with the BOJ through the forced intermediation of private financial institutions was no longer viable, and since 1978 selected issues have been sold at auction by the government.

BOJ open-market operations are not confined to government securities, and this is particularly relevant for short-term securities. Because the out-standing amounts of short-term government debt instruments (government financing bills (FBs) with sixty-day maturities and, since 1986, treasury bills (TBs) with six-month and three-month maturities) have always been small, the Bank has also transacted in other kinds of short-term security. It has conducted open-market operations in the short-term securities known, respectively, as discounted bills (since 1972), *gensaki* (since 1983), and commercial paper (since 1995). These are, in the order listed, bank certificates with promissory notes as attached collateral, short-term loans with long-term bonds as attached collateral, and short-term negotiable promissory notes issued without collateral by high-grade corporations. The first of these, discounted bills, are traded in the interbank market through six broker–dealers. These same broker–dealers also act as intermediaries for very short-term interbank loans (from a half-day to one week), referred to as "call loans". The call market is the Japanese analogue of the "federal funds market" of the United States. The BOJ conducts anonymous trades in the call market as part of its discount window lending.

Discount window lending is now waning in importance for the Bank of Japan, but even as recently as 1991, outstanding loans and discounts of the BOJ equaled about one-fifth the size of Japan's monetary base. Discount window lending entails commercial banks offering their own promissory notes to the BOJ, secured by various sorts of high-quality collateral including government securities, designated debentures, and commercial bills of selected blue-chip companies. The collateral falls into one of two categories, each subject to a different discount rate (a system initiated in 1973). The lower of these two rates, the one applicable to loans with the superior collateral, is more frequently cited as "the" official discount rate. In September 1995 it was lowered from 1.0 to 0.5 percent, its lowest level ever, at which it remains as of March 1999. Changes in the official discount rate have generally accompanied, and heralded, changes in monetary policy. But, in the past, the precise level of the official discount rate did not itself directly influence the level of commercial bank reserves because the BOJ limited its lending to each commercial bank, and banks borrowed up to the limit.

In the past, the Bank of Japan assured that the call rate was nearly always slightly above the official discount rate. This afforded a riskless arbitrage opportunity to any bank able to borrow from the BOJ and lend on the interbank market, an arbitrage opportunity that the BOJ did not allow the banks to fully exploit. But the BOJ lent more to the banks that complied with its moral suasion than to those that did not, a practice known as "window guidance". It is widely thought that window guidance was implemented in such a way as to channel loanable funds toward industries favored by the government and away from others. Evidence that window guidance significantly influenced the allocation of credit in this way is indirect, ambiguous, and disputed. We shall return to this topic when we take up the analysis of Japan's industrial policy. Window guidance was officially suspended as of June 1991. And, recently, the Bank has even allowed the call rate to fall below the official discount rate. (In February 1999 the overnight call rate reached the level 0.15 percent, compared with the official discount rate equal to 0.50 percent.) For the time being, it seems, the BOJ limits on bank lending no longer even bind, a further manifestation of the Bank's increasing reliance on open-market operations rather than discount window lending to influence the monetary base, and thereby control the size of money stock.

There is a fairly straightforward and, in the short-run, stable relation between the money supply and the monetary base, which consists of bank reserves plus currency held by the public. Here, "reserves" refer not only to official reserves R that are bank deposits at the BOJ, but also vault cash V, the portion of the nation's stock of currency that banks hold in order to meet the daily obligations of their transactions with customers. The banks' desired holding of reserves relative to deposits is stable:

$$(R + V)/D = r,$$

and the public's preferred holdings of currency CU relative to deposits D also exhibits a lot of inertia:

$$CU/D = k.$$

Therefore the *money multiplier* μ, the ratio of the money supply to the monetary base (bank reserves plus currency), is also stable and predictable:

$$\mu \equiv (M2 + CDs)/(CU + R + V) = (CU + D)/(CU + R + V)$$
$$= (k + 1)/(k + r).$$

By controlling the level of the monetary base, whether by discount window lending or by sale and purchase of securities, a central bank can precisely effect particular levels of monetary aggregates.

Figure 6.7 illustrates movements in the components of the money multiplier in Japan from 1955 to 1997. Though the money multiplier does exhibit secular movement, mainly caused by secular changes in the public's desired currency–deposit ratio, it does not fluctuate wildly. The Bank of Japan, through its discount window lending and through open-market operations, controls bank reserves, and, because the money multiplier is rather predictable, it thereby controls the monetary aggregates. This means only that the BOJ could have adopted particular levels of the money supply as an operating target, not that it actually did so. In fact, the BOJ has adopted a variety of operating targets other than the size of the money supply, including the interbank lending rate (the call rate), the level of foreign exchange reserves, and the exchange rate between the yen and the US dollar. When, in pursuit of these or other objectives, the BOJ has constricted the rate of growth of the money stock, it has generally precipitated changes in Japan's aggregate output and employment.

The precise locus of decision-making authority within the BOJ is the Policy Board, which until April 1998, when a revised Bank of Japan Law took effect, was effectively under the control of the governor of the BOJ, appointed to a five-year term by the Cabinet and approved by the Diet, and removable by the same procedure. The new law expands the number of voting members of the Policy Board (from five including the governor to nine, all appointed by the Cabinet and approved by the Diet as before), and explicitly prohibits removal of the governor or other Policy Board members because of their official decisions. The minutes of the Board meetings are made public shortly after they occur. The Board meets every other week.

Monetary policy and Japanese business cycles

Contractions of the rate of growth of the money stock have generally but not always accompanied Japan's recent recessions. Table 6.4 is a compilation of data describing growth in money, prices, and output during Japan's recent recessions. The first row of the table reports the shortfalls in real GDP as

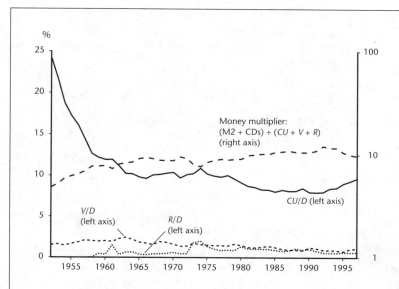

The money multiplier components include: vault cash ÷ private deposits in banks (*V/D*); official reserves of banks ÷ private deposits in banks (*R/D*); and currency held by the public ÷ private deposits in banks (*CU/D*). Official reserves are bank deposits at the Bank of Japan. Because the components of the money multiplier exhibit a great deal of inertia, so does the multiplier itself; by controlling the monetary base (*CU* + *V* + *R*), the Bank of Japan is able to control the stock of money (M2 + CDs). The money multiplier equals:

$$(CU/D + 1)/(CU/D + V/D + R/D).$$

Source: Bank of Japan, *Monetary Survey*. The following are the BOJ English terms of reference for the various aggregates:

    CU = cash currency in circulation (asset account of the consolidated balance sheet of monetary authorities and banks)
    D = deposit money plus quasi-money (liability accounts of deposit money banks)
  R + *V* = reserves at Bank of Japan (liability account of monetary authorities)
  CU + *V* = cash currency issued (liability account of monetary authorities)
    R = deposits from deposit money banks (liability account of monetary authorities)

Figure 6.7. The money multiplier and its components, 1952–1997

calculated in Table 6.3. The other rows in the table describe the behavior of the monetary base and the GDP deflator. We extrapolate growth in the monetary base at the annual average log linear growth rate in the five years preceding the benchmark year prior to the recession. In the final year of each recession, the extrapolated value of the monetary base is compared with its actual value. On average, the monetary base lay 5.4 percent below its extrapolated value in the final year of recession, and was below its extrapolated value in the final year of seven of the nine recessions (1962 and 1986 are the two anomalies).

The price level during the last year of each recession is compared with a value extrapolated from a pre-recession benchmark in the same manner as the values of the monetary base just described. In seven of the nine cases, the price level was below the extrapolated value. In 1974, on the other hand, the price level was significantly above its extrapolated value. The phenomenon of recession combined with rising inflation experienced by Japan, the USA, and other developed countries around 1974 was described as "stagflation", a portmanteau word combining *stag*nant economy and in*flation*.

The data in the table suggest that monetary policy contributed to Japan's recent recessions. In other words, by constricting growth in aggregate demand, Japan's monetary authorities seem to have constricted the growth of the nation's output. To complete the picture, however, we need to take into account aggregate supply, focusing in particular on movements in employment over the business cycles. This is our next task.

Table 6.4. Real and nominal variables during Japan's recent recessions

Benchmark years for log linear interpolation/ extrapolation	1956	1961	1964	1970	1973	1976	1979	1985	1991	1996
Final year of recession	1958	1962	1965	1971	1974	1977	1982	1986	1993	Ave.
% shortfall in real GDP	4.71	0.70	4.25	2.33	2.79	0.31	0.76	1.74	1.74	2.1
M: monetary base in final year of recession (bn)	933	1,868	2,786	7,096	14,278	17,482	25,034	32,119	45,279	
Average annual growth rate over 5 years preceding earlier benchmark (%)	9.91	13.95	18.71	17.35	22.81	18.42	8.67	5.31	8.13	
M^0: extrapolation at the above rate (from previous benchmark) in final year of recession	981	1,765	3,025	7,269	15,097	19,105	27,692	31,282	55,171	
$M^0 - M$	48	<103>	239	173	819	1,623	2,658	<837>	9,898	
Percentage shortfall in M	4.9	<5.8>	7.9	2.4	5.4	8.5	9.6	<2.7>	17.9	5.4
P: GDP (GNP) deflator in final year of recession	21.89	27.72	32.51	45.09	64.79	79.82	94.95	101.76	108.57	
Average annual growth rate in deflator over five years preceding earlier benchmark (%)	2.77	5.34	6.19	5.62	7.24	10.84	5.86	2.12	1.31	
P^0: extrapolation at the above rate (from previous benchmark) in final year of recession	21.67	27.99	32.81	45.13	57.87	83.14	102.12	102.13	111.43	
$P^0 - P$	<0.22>	0.27	0.30	0.04	<6.92>	3.32	7.17	0.37	2.86	
% shortfall in P	<1.0>	1.0	0.9	0.1	<12.0>	4.0	7.0	0.4	2.6	0.3

Sources: shortfalls in real GDP from Table 6.3; GDP (GNP) deflator: Economic Planning Agency, *Report on National Accounts from 1955 to 1989*, and *Annual Report on National Accounts, 1995*; monetary base: Bank of Japan, *Monetary Survey*: currency held by the public + vault cash of banks + commercial bank deposits at the Bank of Japan.

Aggregate supply: output and employment

Aggregate supply is the economy-wide supply of goods and services at each given price level. As in Figure 6.8, it may be represented by an *aggregate supply curve*. The intersection of the aggregate demand curve and aggregate supply curve determine the actual price level and real GDP of the economy in each given period. Trajectories in price level and output reflect shifts in one curve or the other or shifts in both.

Movements in the aggregate demand curve can adequately account for business cycles only if the aggregate supply curve is not vertical. If the aggregate supply curve *is* vertical, then movements in aggregate demand will cause fluctuations in the price level but not in real GDP. But as we have just learned, in Japan retardation of aggregate demand induced by contractionary monetary policy has seemed to constrict real GDP. It appears from this that Japan's aggregate supply curve is, in fact, usually not vertical, but upward-sloping from left to right. If that is the case, then the stagflation phenomenon—declines in real GDP coinciding with rising inflation—must reflect leftward shifts in the aggregate supply curve itself, not shifts in aggregate demand.

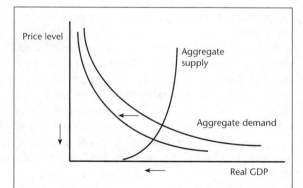

Figure 6.8. An aggregate supply curve

A locus of points indicating the economy-wide supply of output at each alternative price level. The intersection of the aggregate demand curve and aggregate supply curve determines the actual price level and real GDP of the economy. Retardation in aggregate demand precipitates declines in both the price level and the real GDP only if the aggregate supply curve is upward-sloping as depicted here.

Table 6.5. Unemployment rates, selected countries, 1965–1997 (% of labor force unemployed)

	1965–1990	1991–1997
JAPAN	1.1–2.8	2.1–3.6
USA	3.4–9.5	4.6–7.5
Germany	0.2–7.7	6.2–10.3
France	1.5–10.5	8.9–12.6
Italy	5.3–11.0	8.8–12.4
UK	2.3–12.4	6.4–10.2
Canada	3.3–11.8	8.6–11.3
OECD	2.5–8.5	6.6–8.0

Source: OECD, *Economic Outlook*, no. 50 (Dec. 1991), table R–18, p. 208; no. 29 (July 1981), table H–12, p. 142, and no. 61 (June 1997), annex table 21, p. a24. For latest figures available see the OECD web page: http://www.oecd.org/news_and_events/new-numbers/sur/surlist.htm.

Recent developments in macroeconomic theory have expanded our understanding of the ways in which fluctuations in aggregate demand induce distortions and misallocation in the economy, accounting for the apparent positive slope of aggregate supply curves. Labor markets and unemployment constitute the central issues.

Unemployment rates in Japan

Japan's unemployment rate has been relatively low from the 1950s to the present. The unemployment rate of Japan varied from 1.1 to 3.6 percent over the thirty years from 1965 to 1997. In contrast, that of the United States varied between 3.4 and 9.5 percent over the same interval. However, in the months since then, Japan's unemployment has risen while America's has fallen. In February 1999 Japan's unemployment rate reached a postwar high at 4.6 percent, while America's unemployment rate stood at a twenty-nine-year low of 4.2 percent, reflecting the fact that Japan was still mired in recession while America's economy was expanding. Japan has a low natural rate of unemployment, that is a low rate of unemployment when not experiencing a cyclical episode.

The precise definitions of employment status that underlie official unemployment rates vary some-

what from country to country. An appendix to this chapter details some of the idiosyncrasies of the Japanese unemployment statistics. In any case, Japan's low, and stable, unemployment rates in comparison with most other developed nations are more than a statistical illusion. The OECD adjusts data on unemployment rates to a common definition that is rather close to that underlying the US official unemployment rate statistics. These unemployment rates for selected countries in recent years are presented in Table 6.5. The unemployment rates of the major European countries have tended to lie somewhere in between those of Japan and America. Japan's unemployment rate has consistently been among the lowest of all the OECD countries. (Sweden's unemployment rate has been the lowest.)

The natural rate of unemployment

The unemployment rate is determined by the rate of entry into the pool of unemployed and the rate of exit. Both rates are affected by the business cycle. In a business downturn, dismissals increase and fewer of the unemployed succeed in finding jobs. As a result, the number of unemployed rises. In an upturn, the opposite occurs and the pool of unemployed persons shrinks. These phenomena are transitory. In the normal course of economic activity, there will be some particular rates of entry into the pool of unemployed workers and of exits from that pool. If these rates remain stable long enough, the size of the pool will attain an equilibrium size in relation to the labor force and the unemployment rate will be stable. Such an unemployment rate is referred to as the *natural rate of unemployment*, signifying that it is the unemployment rate consistent with acyclic economic activity.

Japan has experienced low unemployment rates because the rate of job separation is low there. A simple example illustrates the connection between the unemployment rate and job separation rate.[10] Let ϕ be the percentage of the employed who separate from their jobs and become unemployed in a given normal month, and let π be the percentage of the unemployed who find jobs (or exit from the labor force) in a given month. Then the monthly change in the number unemployed is

$$\Delta U = \phi N - \pi U,$$

where N and U are the previous month's numbers of employed and unemployed, respectively. If the flow of persons into the pool of unemployed, ϕN, exceeds the flow out of that pool πU, then the number unemployed and the unemployment rate are rising. In the opposite case, the unemployment rate is falling. An equilibrium is eventually approached in which the flows into and out of the pool of unemployed persons are equal and the unemployment rate is unchanging. This "natural rate of unemployment" is

$$U/(N + U) = \phi/(\pi + \phi).$$

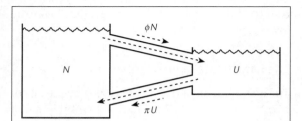

Figure 6.9. Flows into and out of the pool of unemployed workers

These determine a natural rate of unemployment:

$$U/(N + U) = \phi/(\pi + \phi).$$

(Flows into and out of the labor force are approximately offsetting and are ignored here.)

Figure 6.9 illustrates the mechanism just described.

Table 6.6 reports data on the rates of flow out of and into the unemployment pools of selected countries and also the implied natural rates of unemployment for each. As the data illustrate, the main reason for Japan's low natural rate of unemployment is the very small percentage of the Japanese labor force who become unemployed in a given normal month —Japanese workers experience bouts of unemployment far less frequently than do their counterparts in most other developed countries. The flow out of the unemployment pool in Japan is also low (which means that the representative unemployed person in Japan waits longer before accepting a job than do his or her counterparts in other countries), and by itself this would imply higher unemployment rates in Japan. But the effects on unemployment rates of the slow flow out of the unemployment pool are more than offset by the slow flow into it. The infrequency with which the typical worker experiences unemployment is the essence of Japan's low natural rate of unemployment.

Underlying reasons for Japan's low natural rate of unemployment

We can identify several factors that contribute to the relative infrequency with which the typical Japanese worker experiences unemployment, and that therefore account for Japan's low natural rate of unemployment. The most important is the system of lifetime employment; but additionally, minimum wage laws, unemployment compensation, and the demographic structure of the labor force each have a bearing on the country's natural rate of unemployment.

Lifetime employment
Low rates of flow into the pool of the unemployed are a clear manifestation of Japan's lifetime employment system, as is Japan's low natural rate of unemployment.

The lifetime employment system refers to the fact

---

10 The example is loosely based on Michael R. Darby, John Haltiwanger, and Mark Plant, "Unemployment Rate Dynamics and Persistent Unemployment under Rational Expectations", *American Economic Review*, vol. 75, no. 4 (September 1985), pp. 614–37.

Table 6.6. Monthly flows into and out of the unemployment pool and natural rates of unemployment, selected countries and years

		π Monthly flows out of the unemployment pool as a % of the unemployed		ϕ Monthly % of employed who separate from their jobs		$\phi/(\pi+\phi)$ Implied natural rate of unemployment (%)	
	Left-hand figures[a]		1988[b]		1988[b]		1988[b]
JAPAN	(1979–80)	24	20	0.5	0.5	2.0	2.4
USA	(1976)	38	33	2.7	2.2	6.6	6.2
Canada	(1976–80)	43	33	3.1	2.6	6.7	7.2
UK	(1979)	18	10		0.9		8.2
West Germany	(1977)	30	6		0.4		6.2
Australia	(1979–80)	38	17	2.2	1.4	5.5	7.6

Note: Expected duration of unemployment = $1/\pi$ months, and expected frequency of unemployment = once every $1/\phi$ months. *Proof*: The expected duration of unemployment (in months) = $\pi + 2(1-\pi)\pi + \ldots + n(1-\pi)^{n-1}\pi + \ldots = 1/\pi$—summation of the likelihood of finding employment after one month times 1, after two months times 2, etc.; and the expected interval between bouts of unemployment (in months) equals an identical formula with ϕ replacing π—summation of the likelihood of becoming unemployed after one month times 1, after two months times 2, etc.

[a] Akira Ono, "On Recent Studies of Unemployment in Japan", *Japanese Economic Studies* (Fall 1985), table 1, p. 87 and table 4, p. 94.

[b] Richard Layard, Stephen Nickell, and Richard Jackman, *Unemployment: Macroeconomic Performance and the Labour Market*, Oxford University Press, 1991, table 1, p. 222.

that Japanese companies avoid dismissals and have adopted wage schemes that discourage quits. The representative Japanese worker can expect to hold fewer than five different jobs over his lifetime, his American counterpart as many as eleven. The lifetime employment system became prevalent only in the postwar era. In the 1930s the rate of job separation was more than twice as high in Japan as it is currently,[11] and unemployment rates too were significantly higher, averaging 4.4 percent in that decade and reaching a maximum 6.8 percent in 1936.[12]

The lifetime employment system appears to have evolved in order to protect companies' investments in training their employees. Such training investments are most common for skills that are specific to the company. Company-specific skills are characteristic of methods of production that are innovative, and this may be why the rapid technological changes of postwar Japan were accompanied by changes in the employment practices of Japanese companies. These issues are more fully explored in Chapter 15, which focuses on labor markets in Japan.

Minimum wage laws

Japan, like most developed countries, has laws that stipulate minimum legal wage rates for many categories of work. For workers whose labor services would otherwise command wages below these limits, the effect of minimum wage laws is to prolong the search for employment. This slows the net flow out of the pool of unemployed workers, and raises the aggregate natural rate of unemployment. However, it is unlikely that the effect of minimum wage laws on the American natural unemployment rate is very great,[13] and it is even less likely that the effect on Japan's natural unemployment rate is great. In Japan minimum wages are lower, their coverage of industries less universal, and enforcement less strict

[11] Jacob Mincer and Yoshio Higuchi, "Wage Structures and Labor Turnover in the United States and Japan", *Journal of the Japanese and International Economies*, vol. 2, no. 2 (June 1988), pp. 97–133; figure 1, p. 100.

[12] B. R. Mitchell, *International Historical Statistics, Africa and Asia*, New York University Press, 1982, table c-2, p. 97.

[13] Charles Brown, "Minimum Wage Laws: Are They Overrated?" *Journal of Economic Perspectives*, vol. 2, no. 3 (Summer 1988), pp. 133–45.

than in the United States. Rather than a single minimum wage that is the same for all industries and locales, as in the USA, Japan's statutes empower the prefectural governments to set separate, differing, industry-specific minimum wages.

Unemployment compensation

Among the social insurance programs of most governments is provision for unemployment compensation. More generous unemployment benefits encourage quits, and lower the costs of prolonging job search. Higher unemployment compensation can thus be expected to raise the natural rate of unemployment. The level of unemployment compensation is measured by the so-called *replacement rate*, the ratio of initial maximum allowable unemployment compensation to the previous wage income of an unemployed person. Countries also differ in the duration for which unemployment benefits may be collected. Japan's replacement rate of 60 percent and maximum duration of benefits of six months are commensurate with the unemployment insurance benefits of other developed countries as described in Table 6.7.

Demographic structure of the labor force

Our analysis of the natural rate of unemployment has thus far treated the labor force as though it consisted of workers with identical probabilities

Table 6.7. Unemployment insurance in Japan and selected other countries, 1985

Country	Replacement rate (%)	Maximum duration of benefits (yrs)
JAPAN	60	0.5
Canada	60	0.5
USA	50	0.5
France	57	3.75
Germany	63	indefinite
Italy	2	0.5
UK	36	indefinite

Source: Richard Layard, Stephen Nickell, and Richard Jackman, *Unemployment: Macroeconomic Performance and the Labour Market*, Oxford University Press, 1991, table 5, p. 51. (Primary sources: US Dept of Health and Social Services, *Social Security Programs throughout the World, 1985* (Reserve Report No. 60); and OECD *Employment Outlook* (Sept. 1988), tables 4.3 and 4.4.)

of experiencing unemployment, and whose unemployment bouts would be of identical expected duration. Actually, in Japan as elsewhere, the youth unemployment rate is higher than the adult unemployment rate. Youths are more frequently unemployed than older workers. They are less likely than mature workers to have discovered a superior match between the needs of a particular employer and their own tastes and talents; their attachment to a particular job is correspondingly less; and they are more likely to quit or be dismissed than are mature workers. These factors explain why rates of unemployment for youths are higher than those for mature workers. As the age structure of the workforce changes, the aggregate natural rate of unemployment too can be expected to change. Also, in Japan fewer teenagers work as employees than in the USA and elsewhere and this, along with the system of lifetime employment, is another reason why Japan's natural rate of unemployment is so low.

The employment patterns of women may also be distinguished. Women are more frequently unemployed but experience shorter unemployment bouts than men. The reasons are partly economic. Women are more inclined than men to exit the labor force in order to tend their young children; consequently they invest less in marketable labor skills and earn lower wages than men, and to just that extent the net gains from prolonging unemployment to find a more agreeable or rewarding job are less for women than men. For instance, Japanese women are far less likely than men to be employees, more likely to be self-employed. Because women have less opportunity to accumulate company-specific skills, their attachment to a particular job is rather less on average than is true of men. The effects of these opposing influences on the unemployment rates of women are ambiguous. Frequent unemployment would imply high rates of unemployment, but short duration of unemployment implies the opposite. Unsurprisingly, the women's unemployment rate in Japan has been, over the years, at times higher than that of men, and at other times lower.

The foregoing paragraphs pertain to Japan's relatively low natural rate of unemployment. Japan's unemployment rate also exhibits less sensitivity to business cycles than do the unemployment rates of many other nations.

Business cycles and employment in Japan

A temporary increase in job dismissals or a temporary increase in the average length of unemployment spells enlarges the unemployment pool and increases the unemployment rate above its natural level. And it may well take some months after the temporary condition has abated for the unemployment rate to return to its natural level. For this reason, the unemployment rate represents a lagging indicator of economic activity (as in Table 6.2), even though in the USA and most developed nations other than Japan, unemployment rates tend very much to swell during recessions.

Table 6.8 on page 126 describes the behavior of employment, total hours of work, and unemployment rates during Japan's recent recessions, including the current one. The cyclical component in these variables is estimated by comparing the actual annual value in the final year of each recession with a benchmark value. The benchmark values of employment and total hours are extrapolations from the most recent previous year used in interpolating the benchmark path of real GDP. Employment is extrapolated at the annual rate 1.21 percent and hours at the annual rate of 0.66 percent, the respective averages over the interval 1955–92. The benchmark value of the unemployment rate is simply the unemployment rate prevailing in the most recent

previous year used in interpolating the benchmark path of real GDP.

The estimate of total hours of employment used in the table is the best available for the full period but is nevertheless flawed. We multiply the total employment by the average number of hours per worker in manufacturing establishments employing 30 or more. Average hours per worker in smaller establishments are unavailable for the earlier years.

Quite apparently, from the entries in the table, the number unemployed and the unemployment rate in Japan have exhibited little sensitivity to the business cycle. However, total hours of employment have diminished fairly consistently during recessions. Based on the final column of the table, the current recession is unprecedented in the severity of its effects on employment, hours, and the unemployment rate.

Of course the precise figures in the table depend upon the method of computation and choice of interpolation points. For instance, the unemployment rate was higher in 1958 than in 1957, though not higher than in 1956, our benchmark year. Figure 6.10 plots the unemployment rate gap, as calculated in Table 6.8, against the real GDP gap for all the years 1956–96.

In the USA, rises in the unemployment rate typically do accompany shortfalls in real GDP, a relation named Okun's law after its discoverer, Arthur Okun. For example, it is often claimed that, for the United States, each rise in the unemployment rate of 1 percent is associated with a diminution of real GDP by 2 percent, an "Okun coefficient" of 2. If an analogous relation between Japan's unemployment rate and output exists at all, it is rather unstable and requires that much smaller changes in the unemployment rate correspond to any given percentage change in real GDP than is apparently true for the USA. For instance, Hamada and Kurosaka assert an Okun coefficient for Japan for 1953–82 equal to 18.[14] In another study, Kurosaka and Goto estimate an Okun coefficient for Japan for 1960–85 equal to 36.9.[15]

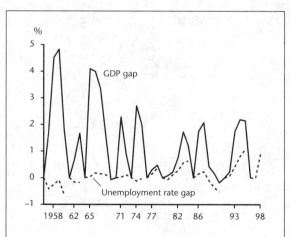

Figure 6.10. Unemployment rate gap and GDP gap, 1956–1996

Unemployment rates have risen only slightly if at all during recessions in Japan.

14 Koichi Hamada and Yoshio Kurosaka, "The Relationship between Production and Unemployment in Japan: Okun's Law in Comparative Perspective", *European Economic Review*, 25 (1984), pp. 71–94.
15 Kurosaka Yoshio and Goto Akira M., "Sōkyokyū kyokuse koubai ni kasuru kokusai hikaku" (International comparisons concerning the slopes of aggregate supply curves), *Keizai Kekyū*, vol. 38, no. 2 (April 1987), pp. 110–20.

Table 6.8. Output, employment, and unemployment during Japan's recent recessions

Benchmark year for comparison	1956	1961	1964	1970	1973	1976	1979	1985	1991	Ave.	1996
Final year of recession	1958	1962	1965	1971	1974	1977	1982	1986	1993		1998
% shortfall in real GDP	4.71	0.70	4.25	2.33	2.79	0.31	0.76	1.74	1.74	2.1	unavailable
Number employed (mns)											
N actual	42.98	45.56	47.30	51.21	52.37	53.42	56.38	58.53	64.50		65.14
N^0 extrapolated from benchmark*	43.24	45.43	47.02	51.45	53.12	53.32	56.37	58.65	65.24		66.44
$N^0 - N$	0.26	-0.13	-0.28	0.24	0.75	-0.10	-0.01	0.12	0.74		1.30
% shortfall in employment	0.60	-0.29	-0.61	0.47	1.40	-0.19	-0.02	0.21	1.1	0.3	2.0
Total hours (bns)											
H actual	103.9	108.5	108.9	113.3	108.9	111.9	119.8	125.2	133.6		126.7
H^0 extrapolated from benchmark**	105.3	110.9	110.4	115.7	116.0	111.3	120.0	126.5	126.5		130.8
$H^0 - H$	1.4	2.4	1.5	2.4	7.1	-0.6	0.2	1.3	7.1		4.1
% shortfall in total hours	1.3	2.2	1.4	2.1	6.2	<0.5>	0.2	1.0	5.3	2.1	3.2
Unemployment rate (% of labor force)											
U actual	2.05	1.28	1.19	1.14	1.28	2.03	2.36	2.77	2.51		4.11
U^0 benchmark	2.30	1.45	1.15	1.12	1.40	1.88	2.09	2.62	2.09		3.35
$U - U^0$	-0.25	-0.17	0.04	0.02	-0.12	0.15	0.27	0.15	0.04	0.01	0.76

* For total hours we extrapolate from the most recent benchmark using the growth rate of 0.66%, which is the average growth rate from 1955 to 1992.
** For employment we extrapolate from the most recent benchmark using the rate 1.21%, which is the average from 1955 to 1992.

Sources: Shortfall in real GDP from Table 6.3; employment, total hours and unemployment rate from Ministry of Labor, *Monthly Labor Force Survey*; total hours estimated by multiplying employment times hours per worker of manufacturing establishments employing 30 or more.

These large and divergent estimates simply reflect the fact that Japan's unemployment rate exhibits little movement from year to year. In Japan, total hours of work are far more responsive to the business cycle than is the unemployment rate.

Figure 6.11 plots annual rates of *decrease* in employment and hours against the real GDP gap. Correlations between the real GDP gap and annual percentage decrease in hours are, in fact, rather evident. Employment appears rather less sensitive than total hours to the business cycle, in broad conformity with the picture one gets from Table 6.9.

Cyclical movement in unemployment rates, employment, and total hours constitute the central topics in recent macroeconomic models of aggregate supply. We next explain short sketches of these models, and consider their relevance to Japan.[16]

The earliest models of aggregate supply evolved from the Keynesian presumption that *labor contracts impart a degree of stickiness to money wages*.[17] Under this hypothesis, workers, perhaps negotiating through unions, agree to contracts that stipulate particular wage rates but that allow the employers to determine the levels of employment and hours. If the general price level should fall below the level anticipated when the contracts were negotiated, the real wage—that is, the wage rate expressed in terms of purchasing power rather than money—would be temporarily high, discouraging firms from employing labor until after the next round of contract negotiations. In other words, if the price level falls below its anticipated level, firms employ less labor and produce less output than otherwise.

A further model of aggregate supply focuses on the possibility that *workers misperceive current levels of money prices*.[18] Perhaps workers are slow to recognize a deviation in the general price level from its recent path. In the event that the growth in the general price level slows but workers fail to perceive it, the workers would regard any particular money wage rate as having lower purchasing power than it in fact does. Such misperceptions would lead unemployed workers to mistakenly prolong their search for a job or exit the labor force, and would lead employed workers to mistakenly decline opportunities to extend their hours of work. Again, an unexpected, and therefore misperceived, drop-off in the price level precipitates smaller levels of employment, and smaller aggregate supply.

---

[16] These sketches draw upon N. Gregory Mankiw, *Macroeconomics*, 2nd edn, Worth Publishing, 1994, ch. 11, pp. 289–320.

[17] Stanley Fischer, "Long-term Contracts, Rational Expectations, and the Optimal Money Supply Rule", *Journal of Political Economy*, vol. 85 (February 1977), pp. 191–205.

[18] Milton Friedman, "The Role of Monetary Policy", *American Economic Review*, vol. 68 (March 1968), pp. 1–17.

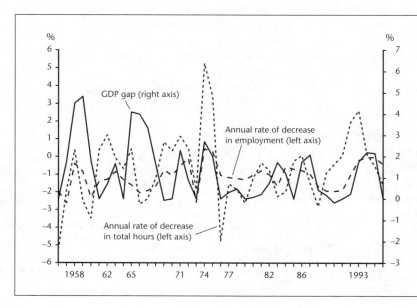

Figure 6.11. Annual rates of decrease in total hours and employment, and GDP gap, 1956–1996

Total hours have grown at slower rates or even decreased during Japan's recent recessions. Employment decreases have not accompanied every recession.

127

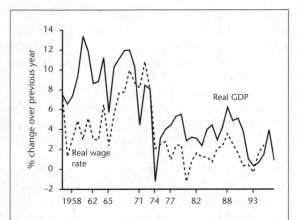

Figure 6.12. Annual growth in real wage rate and in real GDP, 1956–1997

The real wage rate is decidedly pro-cyclic in Japan; it grows less rapidly during recessions, and more rapidly during expansions.

Sources: *real wage rate*: average cash earnings including bonuses of all establishments with 30 or more regular employees in all industries except for services, divided by the consumer price index, and averaged over the 12 months of the calendar year, Ministry of Labor, *Monthly Labor Statistics*; *real GDP*: same as Figure 6.4.

Both of the arguments just related imply that the real wage rate should move counter-cyclically, reaching abnormally high levels during recessions and the opposite during expansions. In Japan, however, the real wage rate is decidedly pro-cyclic. As Figure 6.12 illustrates, the real wage rate in Japan has generally grown less rapidly during recessions, and more rapidly during expansions. In America, the real wage rate is generally neither pro-cyclic nor counter-cyclic.[19]

There are a couple of reasons why the sticky wage argument might be less applicable to Japan than to America or other nations. The first of these is the practice, widespread in Japan, of awarding a substantial portion of compensation in the form of bonuses. Bonuses are paid in June or July and in December, and generally amount to between one-fourth and one-third of total labor earnings. Because the bonuses are not set in advance, they impart a degree of flexibility to wages. But the firm is not free to set the bonus at any level it chooses, for workers will not be fooled more than once. If a firm or industry encounters adversities, its bonuses will be less generous, and employees expect that. But in the opposite case, workers anticipate larger bonuses than usual and invariably get them. The wage flexibility imparted by the bonuses tempers the employment effects of labor contracts that fail to anticipate subsequent events. (For more on bonuses, refer to Chapter 15 on labor markets.)

Besides bonuses, the fact that wage negotiations in Japan are synchronous imparts a degree of flexibility to wage contracts that would not be present if the contracting periods were staggered, as is typical of the USA. Since the 1950s in Japan, the labor unions have entered collective bargaining agreements at the same time each year, a process referred to as *shuntō* (lit., the spring struggle). With staggered contracts, if workers in one enterprise or industry previously over-predicted the price level, so that their real wage rate is higher than they had intended, this will increase the demand for labor in rival enterprises or industries, and will prompt their employees to seek higher wages, too, when their current contracts expire. Synchronicity assures that, if workers in one enterprise or industry over-predict the price level, so that their real wage rate is higher than they had intended, then at least it will not have influenced the real wage in rival firms or industries producing substitute products. The employment effect of such errors will accordingly be attenuated by the synchronicity of labor agreements.[20] Perhaps the synchronicity of labor contracts and the payment of a substantial portion of wages in the form of bonuses, by contributing to the flexibility of wages, account for Japan's absence of counter-cyclic real wages and also explain some of the weakness in the effects of the business cycle on Japanese employment.

Two additional models of aggregate supply behavior imply that real wages should move pro-

[19] For an extremely thorough dissection of the evidence pertaining to the cyclicity of the real wage rate in the USA, see Katherine G. Abraham and John C. Haltiwanger, "Real Wages and the Business Cycle", *Journal of Economic Literature*, vol. 33, no. 3 (September 1995), pp. 1215–64.

[20] This line of argument is developed in some detail by Stanley Fischer, "Long-term Contracts, Rational Expectations and the Optimal Money Supply Rule", *Journal of Political Economy*, vol. 85 (1977), pp. 191–205; John B. Taylor, "Aggregate Dynamics and Staggered Contracts", *Journal of Political Economy*, vol. 88 (1980), pp. 1–23; and John B. Taylor, "Differences in Economic Fluctuations in Japan and the US: The Role of Nominal Rigidities", *Journal of the Japanese and International Economies*, vol. 3 (June 1989), pp. 127–44.

cyclically, as in Japan. First, *suppliers of output, too, can misperceive movements in the general price level.*[21] For instance, if a drop-off in the general price level is mistaken for a decline in the relative price of a firm's output, then the firm would, wrongly, contract output and employment, not recognizing that the prices of its inputs, too, have dropped off so that its marginal cost of producing has moved *pari passu* with the price of output. As in the other arguments, an unanticipated dip in the general price level leads to a contraction of output and employment.

Yet further, *some suppliers may find it convenient to commit themselves to fulfill demand at posted prices, not unlike restaurants that fill any orders at the prices on their menus, which they change rather infrequently.*[22] Suppliers who in this manner post prices in advance will, if the general price level falls below its anticipated level, find that their own prices have risen relative to other prices in the economy, including those charged by some rivals, and so will experience a dip in demand for their own output. As in the other cases discussed, a drop-off in the general price level elicits a contraction of aggregate supply and a decline in employment.

That Japan's unemployment rates and employment seem to respond weakly if at all to the business cycle has led many to speculate that, compared with other nations, not only wages but also prices in Japan exhibit greater flexibility and have a generally smaller influence on employment and output.[23] These conjectures remain tentative, but some institutional features of Japanese markets support them. First, the ubiquity of long-term trading arrangements in the Japanese economy probably weakens the influence of prices on output. Prominent examples of long-term arrangements include the business groups, both the financial keiretsu that are the consortia of large companies, including those historically affiliated with the prewar zaibatsu, and the enterprise groups, i.e. the large manufacturing companies and their families of suppliers, subcontractors, wholesalers, and retailers. But even households in Japan are somewhat loathe to abandon neighborhood shops in pursuit of a temporary bargain, and to that extent fall into *de facto*, long-term trading arrangements. The upshot is that, where "menu pricing" or supplier misperceptions lead to temporarily aberrant pricing, this induces less customer switching, and a smaller aggregate

supply response, than would be true in a regime with less durable long-term relationships.

Finally, the behavior of employment over the business cycle in Japan must also reflect the practice known as lifetime employment. Perhaps employers in Japan are particularly reluctant to dismiss workers during a temporary business downturn because the workers have acquired company-specific skills, and it would be more costly to train new replacements after the inevitable next business upturn than to hoard the trained workers during downturns. All of this remains a bit speculative. The truth is that Japanese labor markets still hold many mysteries.

On this note of humility, we close our survey of aggregate demand and aggregate supply in Japan. Our final task in this chapter is to consider the postwar record of Japanese business cycles in light of what we have learned.

Macroeconomic policy and performance in Japan

Japan's monetary policy differed markedly under the pre-1971 Bretton Woods international monetary regime of fixed exchange rates and under the current, floating exchange rate regime. Under the Bretton Woods system, control of the money supply in Japan was completely subordinated to the goal of maintaining a fixed nominal exchange rate of ¥360 = $1. If the United States adopted a tight monetary policy, then Japan was obliged to do likewise in order to forestall the need for devaluation of the

---

21 Robert E. Lucas, Jr, "Understanding Business Cycles", in *Stabilization of the Domestic and International Economy*, vol. 5 of the *Carnegie–Rochester Conference on Public Policy*, Amsterdam: North-Holland, 1977.

22 Laurence Ball, N. Gregory Mankiw, and David Romer, "The New Keynesian Economics and the Output–Inflation Tradeoff", *Brookings Papers on Economic Activity*, vol. 1 (1988), pp. 1–65.

23 See T(oshiaki) Tachibanaki, "Labour Market Flexibility in Japan in Comparison with Europe and the US", *European Economic Review*, vol. 31 (1987), pp. 647–84; K(oichi) Hamada and Y. Kurosaka, "The Relationship between Production and Unemployment in Japan: Okun's Law in Comparative Perspective", *European Economic Review*, vol. 25 (1984), pp. 71–94; Robert J. Gordon, "Why US Wage and Employment Behaviour Differs from that in Japan", *Economic Journal*, vol. 92 (March 1982), pp. 13–44; R. Komiya and K. Yasui, "Japan's Macroeconomic Performance since the First Oil Crisis: Review and Appraisal", *Carnegie–Rochester Conference Series on Public Policy*, vol. 20 (Spring 1984), pp. 69–114.

yen. The Japanese recessions of 1954, 1958, 1962, and 1965 have all been attributed to the contractions in the growth rate of Japan's money stock dictated by this logic.[24]

The US inflation of the late 1960s doomed the Bretton Woods fixed exchange rate international monetary regime. Japan, like some of the European nations, resisted either revaluing its currency or matching the high inflation rate of the USA. Rather than devalue the dollar relative to virtually all other currencies, the Nixon administration, in August 1971, opted instead to unilaterally abandon participation in the fixed exchange rate system. Specifically, the government of the United States announced that it would no longer maintain the international price of gold in terms of the dollar at a fixed level. After this announcement, referred to ever since in Japan as the "Nixon shock", the international monetary system fairly quickly dissolved into one of floating exchange rates. The Bank of Japan persisted for a short time in attempting to maintain the yen–dollar rate near the Bretton Woods level, but by year's end 1971 had given it up for good. For the first time since the Pacific war, Japan was now completely free to manage its own monetary policy, independent of explicitly acknowledged, international constraints. A severe test for Japan's monetary authorities was not long in coming.

In the months following the Middle Eastern War of October 1973, the Organization of Petroleum Exporting Countries (OPEC), led by the oil-rich Arab states, effected a doubling of world oil prices. This event is now referred to as the "first oil shock". The dramatic and sustained rise in petroleum prices induced a contraction of aggregate supply in Japan, the United States, Europe, and virtually all the nations that were net importers of oil rather than net exporters. Quite simply, the enhanced scarcity of oil, whether contrived, merely to transfer wealth from consumers to producers, or real, the belated recognition of the true incremental costs of oil depletion, resembled a technological regress in its effects on the oil-consuming nations. With the same labor and capital as before, less output could now be produced.

As aggregate supply and real GDP contracted in Japan, prices rose at a faster rate, just as the dynamic quantity theory of money would predict. But at the time, few informed observers recognized how severe

the effects of heightened oil prices would be on output. The rise in the inflation rate throughout 1974 was therefore regarded as a mystery, in Japan as elsewhere. The Japanese monetary authorities reacted to the abnormal inflation by inducing a monetary contraction. Now aggregate demand as well as aggregate supply were being constricted. It is not possible to identify precisely the adverse effects on output of this monetary episode. Although real GDP in Japan suffered its first actual decline of the postwar era in 1974, it is impossible to assert convincingly that this was because of the monetary contraction, rather than a consequence of transition to a lower, flatter steady-state path.

Also in the eventful year 1974, the government of Japan began to accumulate debt at an unprecedented rate. The recession of 1965 had so depleted government revenues that the Diet had authorized the issue of deficit-covering national bonds for the first time since the Pacific war, but these remained of modest extent relative to national income until the fiscal crisis of 1974. In 1973, the government led by Prime Minister Tanaka Kakuei had authorized a significant enhancement of social security benefits and national health insurance coverage, without enacting commensurate tax increases. As the government debt flooded into the tightly regulated financial system, it crowded out the flow of funds to private businesses. The eventual political response was an opening of access to foreign financial markets in 1980, and the gradual dismantlement of interest rate controls and other government restraints on domestic financial markets in Japan. The actual consequences of any of this for the business cycle in Japan are quite difficult to fathom. The traditional, Keynesian interpretation of a debt-financed enhancement of government transfer payments holds that it would expand private consumption, reduce national saving, and expand national income. In other words, it would have been fortuitously counter-cyclical in 1974.[25] The Ricardian view

---

[24] For a development of this view, see esp. Michael W. Keran, "Monetary Policy and the Business Cycle in Postwar Japan", in David Meiselman (ed.), *Varieties of Monetary Experience*, University of Chicago Press, 1970, ch. 3, pp. 165–248.

[25] For a traditional interpretation of the episode, see Kazumi Asako and Takatoshi Ito, "The Rise and Fall of Deficit in Japan, 1965–1990", *Journal of the Japanese and International Economies*, vol. 5 (1991), pp. 451–72.

would attribute no such effects to the debt-financed expansion of government transfer payments. The ambiguous actual effects of the run-up in government debt on Japan's private saving and national saving have been discussed in the previous chapter.

From 1975 to 1985, the Bank of Japan gradually reduced the rate of growth of the money supply M2 + CDs, avoiding erratic movements. This period encompasses the 1979 Iranian revolution, which precipitated yet another dramatic rise in world oil prices, the so-called "second oil shock". Monetarists argued that the second oil shock had less severe effects in Japan than in the United States and Europe because Japan pursued relatively more stable monetary policy than did the USA or the European nations.[26] It may also matter that, as the BOJ gradually reduced the rate of monetary growth over these years, it began to announce narrow ranges within which it expected the monetary aggregate M2 + CDs to move in ensuing months. These announcements,

by reducing the possibility of monetary surprises, probably mitigated the effects on aggregate supply of the contractionary drift in the rate of growth of the money supply.

The monetary policy record of Japan from 1955 to 1998 is depicted graphically in Figure 6.13. Contractions in the growth of real GDP mirror contractions in the growth of M2 + CDs of the previous year fairly closely.[27] The "stop–go" monetary policy of the 1950s and 1960s, supporting the Bretton Woods fixed exchange rate between the yen and the dollar, is evident in the erratic behavior of Japan's money supply in those years. So is the dramatic contraction of monetary growth in 1974 and the gradual reduc-

---

[26] See e.g. Yoshio Suzuki, "Why is the Performance of the Japanese Economy So Much Better?" *Journal of Japanese Studies*, vol. 7, no. 2 (Summer 1981), pp. 403–13.

[27] This pattern has been noted by many others, including the most famous monetarist of them all: Milton Friedman, *Money Mischief*, New York: Harcourt Brace, 1992, esp. pp. 229–32.

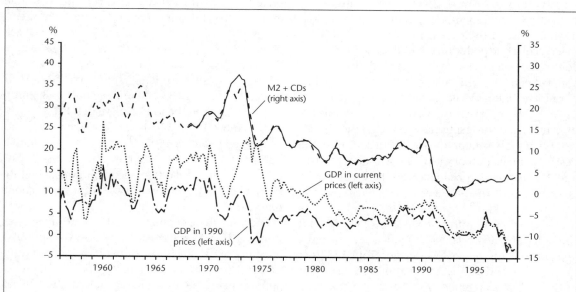

Figure 6.13. Growth rates in money, real GDP, and nominal GDP, first quarter 1956–last quarter 1998

The chart shows the percentage increase over the corresponding quarter of the previous year in each of the three series. Money is measured by average of M2 + CDs over the previous three months (based on end-of-month observation 1956(I)–1994(IV), and upon average over entire month 1968(I)–1998(III)). Notice how the business recessions of 1958, 1962, 1965, 1971, 1975, and 1991 were all preceded by sharp contractions in the growth rate of the money stock. The most recent recession, beginning in March 1997, was apparently not preceded by tightened monetary policy.

Sources: M2 + CDs: Bank of Japan, *Monetary Survey*; GDP in current prices and 1990 prices: EPA, *National Income and Product Accounts*.

tion in monetary growth in the decade following that episode. The vertical difference between the dotted line indicating growth rate in real GDP and the solid line indicating growth rate in nominal GDP indicates the rate of inflation in Japan. As monetary growth slowed, so did inflation. After the September 1985 Plaza Accord, the Bank of Japan switched its policy focus away from gradual reduction in the rate of growth of Japan's money supply, and toward attempts to influence exchange rates.

The Plaza Accord (so named because of its venue, the Plaza Hotel of New York City) was an agreement among representatives of the monetary authorities of the USA, Japan, the UK, West Germany, and France (the "G-5", or group of five) to coordinate their monetary policies so as to effect a depreciation of the US dollar relative to other currencies.[28] The major impetus for the Plaza Accord was the sharp and persistent real appreciation of the dollar during the early 1980s that had invited a flood of Japanese imports into the United States, fueling anti-Japan protectionist sentiment in the Congress. The fundamental cause of the strong dollar had been the US macroeconomic policy mix, specifically, the Reagan administration's ongoing expansionary fiscal policy coupled with the anti-inflationary monetary policy of the Federal Reserve Bank under the chairmanship of Paul Volker. Rather than attempt the politically difficult task of reversing these policies, the Reagan administration sought instead to accomplish the desired depreciation of the dollar by inducing Japan and the major European powers to contract the growth rates of their money supplies. This was the essence of the Plaza Accord.

In the twelve months following the Plaza Accord, the dollar did depreciate sharply. For instance, the yen price of the dollar fell steadily from ¥237 per dollar at the end of August 1985 to ¥154 per dollar at the end of September 1986. Yet at that time the depreciation of the dollar relative to the yen seemed to have little inhibiting effect on imports into the USA from Japan. Now American diplomats reversed course, imploring the government of Japan to institute expansionary monetary policy and strengthen the dollar relative to the yen. In an October 1986 agreement with the US Treasury Secretary James Baker, the Japanese Minister of Finance Miyazawa Kiichi agreed that Japan would do essentially as America requested. This new international policy regime was widened and perpetuated at the February 1987 Louvre conference, in which the central banks of the G-7 nations (Japan, the USA, the UK, West Germany, and France—the G-5—plus Canada and Italy) agreed to take concerted actions to effect a further appreciation of the dollar.

In accordance with the Baker–Miyazawa agreement and the Louvre agreement, the BOJ began in late 1986 to allow more rapid growth in Japan's money supply. Following the October 1987 New York Stock Exchange "Black Monday" crash, the government of Japan, with American encouragement, became even more firmly committed to the policy of monetary expansion. The growth of Japan's money supply fueled massive increases in land and equity prices, and the years 1987–90 are widely referred to in Japan as the period of the "bubble" economy. A speculative bubble is a situation in which an asset price gets pushed upward by purchasers who expect to resell at an even higher price for no particular reason except the plausible existence of still other purchasers just like themselves. When the bubble bursts, the price crashes back down to the level supported by non-speculative demand. The Nikkei Stock Index, a broad average of Japanese share prices, rose from 22,621 in November 1987, to 38,130 in December 1989, only to slide rapidly in the following year, hitting 23,740 in December 1990, 22,304 in December 1991, and 17,390 in December 1992. If there was a speculative bubble—which is not certain by any means—it had burst. Land and real estate prices followed a roughly similar course to equity prices, with a lag of about one year.

The immediate reason for the 1990–1 drop in asset prices is that Mieno Yasushi, who was appointed governor of the BOJ in December 1989, had abruptly halted the expansionary monetary policy. Upon his appointment, he immediately raised the official discount rate and, after March 1990, effected a very sharp contraction in monetary growth, quite evident in Figure 6.13. In the twelve months ending March 31, 1990, Japan's money supply (M2 + CDs)

---

28 On the details of the Plaza Accord (and the Baker–Miyazawa agreement and the Louvre agreement), see Yoichi Funabashi, *Managing the Dollar: From the Plaza to the Louvre*, 2nd edn, Washington, DC: Institute for International Economics, 1989.

grew by 12.6 percent; in the subsequent twelve months it grew by 6.9 percent, and in the twelve months after that by only 0.7 percent. Mieno's rationale for this dramatic monetary contraction? In an interview he declared that the late 1980s boom in Japan's asset markets had "hastened a decline in morals", fostered "inequalities in the distribution of wealth", and "undermined the stability . . . of Japanese society by weakening the ethos of labor, the notion of working by the sweat of your brow".[29] Governor Mieno's misguided monetary contraction engendered the Heisei recession, and wreaked particular havoc on the commercial banks of Japan that were left holding the greatly depreciated collateral on their defaulted loans. The recession reached its official trough in October 1993, and Mieno's five-year term as BOJ governor ended in December 1994. Even though the business cycle was now in expansion, growth in aggregate output remained slow compared with the previous decade, except for the one year, 1996. Japan's real GDP, after having grown 5.1 percent in 1990, 3.8 percent in 1991, 1.0 percent in 1992, and 0.3 percent in 1993, grew 0.6 percent in 1994, 1.5 percent in 1995, and 3.9 percent in 1996.

And from March 1997, Japan's economy was again in recession. Asset prices once again spiraled downwards. In September 1998 the Nikkei average had fallen below 14,000 for the first time since 1986, to a mere one-third of its November 1987 peak level. This recession is generally regarded as a continuation of the previous one, its root cause the reining in of consumption spending engendered by the windfall losses in the land and equities markets, losses that ultimately represent the economic costs of imprudent bank lending during the bubble era.

The current recession is said by many observers and some government spokesmen to be Japan's most severe of the postwar era. But this judgment is, for now, based upon the recent and unprecedented absolute declines in Japan's real GDP, not upon comparison between actual and potential growth in real GDP, for the potential growth is not yet knowable. From April 1997 to March 1998, Japan's real GDP edged downward at the rate –0.7 percent, and, judging by preliminary figures, it continued downward over April–December 1998 at the annual rate of –2.4 percent. Japan's unemployment rate in

March 1999 was at a postwar high of 4.6 percent. Money prices in Japan are exhibiting mild deflation (less than 1 percent, based on the CPI or the GDP deflator) and interest rates are at unprecedentedly low levels. The call rate in March 1999 was near zero at 0.04 percent, while the short-term prime lending rates of the largest banks have remained at 1.5 percent since September 1998 and for the three years prior to that stood at 1.625 percent. The long-term prime rate edged downward to 2.2 percent in December 1998 before rising sharply to 2.9 percent in the first months of 1999. In September 1998 the yield rate on the benchmark ten-year Japanese government bond reached 0.76 percent, said to be the lowest long-term interest rate ever, not only for Japan but for any nation in history. (It rose sharply to 2 percent in December 1998 and remained near that level in the first months of 1999.) Japan's combination of low aggregate output and near-zero interest rates has many economists thinking anew about the Keynesian "liquidity trap", long regarded as a merely theoretical curiosity.

A *liquidity trap* is a situation in which expansion of the money supply simply enlarges the money holdings of the nation's citizens, and does not therefore stimulate aggregate demand. In a much cited and provocative essay, Paul Krugman develops a logical framework within which, if any current expansion of the money supply is expected to be reversed in the subsequent year, a liquidity trap will arise should the money rate of interest reach zero (its lowest conceivable level).[30] Krugman argues that Japan's currently very low money rates of interest, and the BOJ's reputed commitment to price stability, place Japan in this situation. He advocates a sustained expansion of the rate of growth of Japan's money supply sufficient to engender an expectation of inflation and allow Japan's real rates of interest to sink lower, i.e. to break the liquidity trap, stimulate investment spending, and end the recession.

Others have proposed expansionary fiscal policy as a solution to Japan's current dilemma. In fact, in

---

29 These quotes are taken from "Yen Master: Japan's Central Banker Begins to Win Praise for Saving its 'Soul'", *Wall Street Journal*, June 15, 1993, p. A1.

30 The original essay, a follow-up answer to critics, and other related pieces on Japan by Paul Krugman may be found at his web site: (http://web.mit.edu//krugman/www/jpage.html).

every year from 1990 to 1998 the Japanese government actually has enacted supplementary budgets that included special increases in government purchases and special tax reductions. Some Keynesian economists claim these have not gone far enough.[31] Figure 6.14 describes the fiscal policy of the Japanese government from 1968 to 1997. The "government surplus" is the difference between government purchases and taxes net of transfers (from the government to the private sector). Government purchases equal government consumption plus government investment. The annual percentage change in real GDP is also plotted in the figure. All entries are for the calendar years.

The supplemental budgets in 1991–7 included special government appropriations for public works spending, which in the figure appears as the bulge in government investment during those years. The greatest of the supplementary spending measures, enacted in October 1995 and ultimately amounting to around 1 percent of 1995 GDP, was for rebuilding the public resources damaged by the January 1995 Kobe earthquake. The earthquake had killed more than 5,000 persons, toppled buildings, and destroyed large sections of the major traffic artery connecting

Kobe to Osaka (the Hanshin expressway). Other recent supplemental spending measures (besides the October 1995 one) have included rural development projects and the like, decried by the political opposition in Japan as wasteful pork-barrel spending. But in the Keynesian framework, even "make-work" government spending can stimulate aggregate demand and boost output and employment—with a multiplier effect, if consumers are liquidity-constrained and monetary policy is accommodative. The ruling LDP has offered this Keynesian argument in support of the special measures, each of which it has dubbed as an "economic stimulus package" when first proposing it.

Also within the Keynesian framework, tax cuts can stimulate aggregate demand by enlarging private after-tax income and increasing the private spending of liquidity-constrained consumers, i.e. those unable to finance current consumption by borrowing. The purchases of consumers who are not liquidity-constrained will reflect the perceptions of

---

[31] See e.g. Adam S. Posen, *Restoring Japan's Economic Growth*, Washington, DC: Institute for International Economics, September 1998.

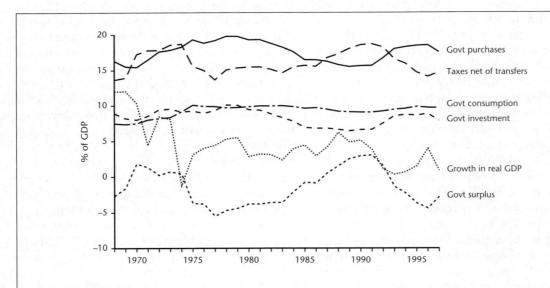

Figure 6.14. Fiscal policy, 1968–1997

Sources: *government surplus*, including social security surplus (= net lending by government as a percentage of GDP): OECD, *Economic Outlook* (no. 63, June 1998), and OECD *Historical Statistics* (1988, 1995, and 1997); *government consumption and government investment*: EPA, National Income and Product Accounts (http://www.epa.go.jp/e-e/eri/menu.html).

their own after-tax wealth, which are apt to be little affected by changes in taxes. Forward-looking individuals perceive that government purchases must ultimately be financed by taxes, if not in the current year, then in some future year. Only a permanent change in the flow of government purchases, and not any change in current taxes, will much alter perceptions of private wealth. Prime Minister Hashimoto was excoriated as the Herbert Hoover of Japan for pressing forward with fiscal austerity measures in 1996–7, including a hike in personal income taxes and a long-scheduled increase in Japan's national sales tax from 3 to 5 percent in April 1997. Sales of big-ticket consumer items such as cars jumped upwards in the first quarter of 1997 only to decline thereafter, reflecting a hastening of planned purchases in anticipation of the sales tax increase, but there seemed to be few other effects. Similarly, a belated tax rebate, approved by the cabinet in December 1997 and enacted in March 1998, temporarily reversing the previous increase in personal income taxes and equal to about half a percent of GDP, seemed to have little effect on private consumption. In other words, tax cuts and tax hikes, like changes in spending on public works, have had little effect on aggregate demand in Japan, contrary to the Keynesian notion.

An early end to Japan's current recession is important to the fate of the other nations in Asia now reeling from economic crises of their own. In summer 1997 successful speculative attacks on the Thai baht, the Indonesian rupiah, and the Malaysian ringgit, and severe depreciation of the Korean won, led to massive defaults on the foreign debts of these nations and sent their economies into turmoil. Indonesia and Malaysia in particular have now entered deep recessions. Korea and Thailand have suffered less serious setbacks. These nations are populous (Indonesia, 193 million; Thailand, 58 million; Malaysia, 20 million; Korea, 45 million), but the output of goods and services of each is small compared with that of Japan. According to estimates of the World Bank, the 1995 aggregate outputs of virtually all the East Asian and South-east Asian economies other than Japan and China, if valued at "purchasing power parities", equaled about one-twelfth of the total world output, which was about three-fourths as great as Japan's output.[32] The adverse effects upon Japan, the United States, and Europe of loan defaults or the loss of export opportunities in these troubled nations should not be exaggerated. The Asian financial crisis represents a severe contraction of the South-east Asian economy, but not of the world economy.

Conclusion

Japan's enviable record of macroeconomic performance during the last half of the twentieth century probably owed little to efficacious government policies. Its rate of unemployment remained low and inflexible compared with that of other nations because of institutional features of Japanese markets, not because of the soundness of monetary or fiscal policies. The high benchmark rate of growth in Japan of the 1950s and 1960s meant that deviations from a smooth growth path generally did not effect absolute contractions of output in Japan.

The current recession that began in March 1997 has had unprecedented adverse effects on Japanese employment, hours of work, and unemployment rates. Whether this will instill permanent changes in Japanese labor market institutions or will turn out to be an aberration is still too early to know. It is also too early to judge the precise extent of current shortfall in output owing to the wasteful idling of labor and other resources. However, even if the current recession turns out to have been the most severe of Japan's postwar history, its impact should not be exaggerated. The temporary deviations of Japanese output from its long-run growth path in the last forty years taken as a whole do not amount to much. The same is true of the USA and the other developed nations.

In Japan as elsewhere, contractions of the growth rate of the nation's money stock have been consistently followed by business recessions. The monetary authorities of Japan have seemed no more, or less, disciplined at maintaining a steady course than have the central banks of other nations.

---

32 These data are from World Bank, *World Development Report 1997*, Oxford University Press, 1997. The often-repeated statement that Japan's real GDP represents "seventy percent of that of Asia" is based on conversion of GDPs at current exchange rates in 1995.

Macroeconomics

Appendix   Unemployment statistics of Japan

Japan's Ministry of Labor publishes unemployment rates based on monthly surveys of the workforce. These series are the basis for tracking cyclical changes in the unemployment rate of Japan. The precise definitions of unemployed and employed that underlie these statistics are not the same definitions that the US Department of Labor adopts in computing US unemployment rates.

The Japanese Ministry of Labor survey defines the labor force as consisting of all those aged 15 years and older usually residing in Japan other than foreign military or diplomatic corps. Members of Japan's military are counted as employed members of the workforce. In the United States only those 16 years or older may be counted as members of the labor force, and military personnel were not officially counted as members of the US workforce until 1983. In Japan only those either employed or actively seeking employment in the previous week are counted as being in the labor force; in the USA, one need only have sought employment in the previous month to be considered a member of the labor force. In Japan unpaid family workers who work fewer than fifteen hours a week are counted as employed, though in the USA such individuals are not considered members of the labor force. Those waiting to start jobs within the month are counted as already employed in Japan, but as unemployed in the USA. And finally, the statistics are presented differently:

Japan's official unemployment rate is the ratio of unemployed to the labor force, whereas for the United States it is the ratio of unemployed to employed.

None of these differences has a very great bearing on the overall annual rates of unemployment reported by the respective governments, though they have a somewhat greater impact on sex-based unemployment rates.[33] If the US presumptions were applied to Japan's survey data, the result would be annual unemployment rates that are from 0.1 to 0.4 percentage point above the rates reported by Japan's Ministry of Labor. But a substantial number of female respondents in Japan are not employed although they have sought work in the previous month (though not in the previous week); the labor ministry of Japan excludes such respondents from its enumeration of the labor force, whereas in America such respondents would be classified by the Bureau of Labor Statistics as unemployed. Applying the American criteria nearly doubles Japan's March unemployment rate for women compared with the official statistics. (But March is an unusual month in Japan, the beginning of the school year and the usual time of first entry into employment for graduates.)

---

[33] Constance Sorrentino, "Japan's Low Unemployment: An In-Depth Analysis", *Monthly Labor Review*, March 1984, pp. 18–27.

FURTHER READING

Data

■ Data from Japan's national income and product accounts, in current prices and constant prices, along with deflators, all of which is presented quarterly (both seasonally adjusted and not) and annually (both by fiscal year and calendar year), from 1955 to the present, may be downloaded from the web page of the Economic Planning Agency of the Japanese government: http://www.epa.go.jp/e-e/eri/menu.html.

General

■ Yukio Noguchi and Kozo Yamamura (eds.), *US–Japan Macroeconomic Relations: Interactions and Interdependence in the 1980s*, University of Washington Press, 1996. Economists dissect the reasons and implications of the misguided policies that led to the Heisei recession in Japan.

■ Yoshio Suzuki, *Money, Finance, and Macroeconomic Performance in Japan*, Yale University Press, 1986. A monetarist view of BOJ policies and their effects, by the longtime director of economic research of the BOJ.

■ Kurosaka Yoshiou and Hamada Kouichi, *Makuro keizaigaku to niho keizai* (Macroeconomics and the Japanese economy), Niho hyorosha, 1984. An eclectic, textbook treatment of many of the same topics of this chapter.

■ Hiroshi Yoshikawa, *Macroeconomics and the Japanese Economy*, Oxford University Press, 1995. A Keynesian interpretation of recent business cycles in Japan.

International Finance   7

When a nation exports more than it imports, it necessarily accumulates claims on the future incomes of foreigners. After all, the exports had to have been exchanged for something—if not imports, then foreign assets, perhaps IOUs of some sort, either promises to pay in the future or forgiveness of one's own prior promises of future payment. The converse is also true. When one nation lends to others, or acquires ownership rights in foreign assets, it experiences a trade surplus—it exports more than it imports. One expects a nation that has a relatively high saving propensity, as Japan now does, to be accumulating claims on the future incomes of foreigners and so to export more than it imports. Of course, imbalances of trade with any one other country need not have this interpretation; they may merely reflect the international division of labor. Japan imports oil and other natural resources from the Middle East and South-east Asia, and exports manufactured goods to Europe and North America. Such a triangular trade pattern is perfectly consistent with overall balance between Japan's exports to all nations and imports from all nations. But Japan's trade has frequently not been in a state of overall balance. A lot of the largest imbalances in Japan's trade through the years can be associated with extraordinary events that conferred enormous windfall losses (the Tokyo earthquake, the first oil shock, the Persian Gulf War) and led to temporary spurts in foreign borrowing, or that conferred windfall gains (the World War I boom, the Korean War boom) which were largely added to Japan's holdings of foreign assets.

Some adjustments of trade balances are associated not with autonomous shifts in the nation's propensity to save, but with previous movements in exchange rates. Changes in the price of foreign currency in terms of home currency that are not in proportion to changes in the nation's price levels, by definition, alter the price of foreign goods in terms of home-country output and alter the price of home goods in terms of foreign output. Such "real" exchange rate movements induce substitution in demand toward the goods whose relative prices have fallen, and induce expanded supply of goods whose relative prices have risen. These responses to exchange rate movements are not instantaneous and can take as long as two years to occur. However, the evidence is overwhelming that real appreciation of the yen relative to other currencies, as occurred in 1985–7 for example, is eventually followed by a constriction of Japan's exports and an expansion of its imports; conversely, real depreciation of the yen, as occurred in 1996, is within a couple of years followed by expansion of Japanese exports and constriction of imports.

Economists have not succeeded very well in explaining short-term movements in real exchange rates. There exist elegant models describing the real exchange rate dynamics arising from monetary or fiscal shocks, but the models have not proved all that helpful in understanding actual exchange rate movements. Attention has therefore turned from specific short-term exchange rate movements themselves to attempts at identifying generic reasons for exchange rate volatility. Some progress along these lines is evident in our understanding of the phenomena known, respectively, as overshooting, the J-curve, and hysteresis. Furthermore, some of the long-term trends in real exchange rate movements have also been understood. In particular, the gradual real appreciation of the yen relative to the US dollar, evident throughout the 1950s and 1960s, has been convincingly explained by Balassa and Samuelson.

International finance encompasses many topics pertinent to Japan's economy. We begin our discussion of them with the balance of payments.

Balance of payments

The basic accounts of transactions between citizens of one country and those of others are referred to as the one country's *balance of payments accounts*. Each transaction is an exchange of one item for another and is recorded by accounting entries for both items, a double entry system. One side of every transaction (what is given up) entails either the tendering of an asset or the incurring of a liability and is recorded by a "credit" entry, and the other side (what is obtained) entails either the receipt of an asset or the resolution of a liability and is recorded by a "debit" entry.[1] The annual balance of payments reflects the net effects on each account of all international transactions during the year. Net credit balances are referred to as "surpluses" and net debit balances as "deficits". For instance, a surplus of the merchandise account means that more merchandise was tendered to foreigners than was received (an asset was reduced—credit balance); i.e., more merchandise was sold to foreigners than was purchased—merchandise exports exceeded merchandise imports. A deficit of the long-term loan account means that, on net, either long-term loans *from* foreigners were resolved (a liability was reduced—debit balance), or new long-term loans were extended *to* foreigners (an asset increased—debit balance). Table 7.1 summarizes the basic argot of double-entry accounting.

The accounts of the balance of payments are grouped into two broad categories: current accounts and capital accounts. The *current accounts* are those in which activity affects current income. Such activity includes the sale or purchase of items produced in the current year, and unilateral transfers. The sale of items produced in the current year gives rise

Table 7.1. Double-entry accounting

	Assets	Liabilities
Credit	Decrease	Increase
Debit	Increase	Decrease

Surplus: credit balance
Deficit: debit balance

directly to domestic income. And the purchase of such items from foreigners, when viewed in an unabashedly superficial way, diminishes home-country income compared with the level of such income if the items were purchased domestically. Current accounts include merchandise, services, and unilateral transfers. Dividends and interest payments on foreign assets are treated as rental payments for the services of the assets (investment income) and so are reflected in the current accounts.

The *capital accounts* are those in which activity represents the sale and purchase of claims on future income, in the form of either financial assets, that is nonproduced assets, or real assets produced in a previous year rather than the current one. Capital accounts include securities, currency, real estate, shares of stock, and so on.

The subset of the capital accounts designated *official reserves* requires special discussion. These accounts record the international financial transactions of the nation's monetary authorities. And in the balance of payments of Japan, changes in the international capital accounts of the private commercial banks are also categorized as official reserve transactions, as though the transactions were at the behest of the government or under its direct control —which at one time they indeed were. Under the Bretton Woods system of fixed exchange rates (1944–71), the monetary authorities of participating countries maintained fixed exchange rates between their national currencies and the US dollar by trading in dollar-denominated financial assets. If a nation's reserve holdings were depleted, exchange rate movements could no longer be prevented. Move-

---

[1] Unilateral transfers including foreign aid payments, reparations, and pensions paid to foreigners are recorded as though the nation receiving the transfer incurs a (current) liability in the account "unilateral transfers".

ments in official reserve accounts therefore elicited special attention, distinct from the other capital accounts. In the balance of payments of Japan (and also France and Italy) the international assets (i.e. net dollar-denominated claims) of private commercial banks are treated as though they are under the regulatory control of the monetary authorities and are therefore a component of the nation's stock of international reserves usable to maintain a fixed exchange rate. But since the early 1980s in Japan, financial market deregulation has largely freed the international capital transactions involving Japanese citizens and corporations, including commercial banks. The international holdings of private banks in Japan should probably no longer be considered official reserves, but in the official presentation of Japan's balance of payments they still are. Since the 1971 demise of the Bretton Woods system and its replacement with a regime of floating rates, central banks, including the Bank of Japan, continue to intervene in international currency markets but not nearly to the same extent as before.

Table 7.2 represents the official accounts of the balance of payments for Japan for 1991. In that year merchandise exports exceeded merchandise imports by $103.1 billion, the net surplus of the merchandise trade account. A more inclusive measure of Japan's imbalance of trade is the current account, which in 1991 stood in surplus of $72.9 billion. The current account balance is the net balance on merchandise, services, and unilateral transfers.

Now let us turn our attention to the capital accounts. *Direct investment* refers to the acquisition or enlargement of a controlling interest in a tangible asset, including such items as a business establishment or a corporation in its entirety. In 1991, Japanese citizens' net direct investments in foreign countries (for Japan, "outward direct investment") totaled $30.7 billion. Foreigners' net direct investments in Japan (for Japan, "inward" direct investment) totaled $1.4 billion. Investments that do not confer control of tangible assets are referred to as portfolio investments. *Portfolio investments* include loans of greater than one year's maturity, corporate bonds, and shares of stock insufficient in extent to confer significant corporate control (say, less than 10 percent of outstanding shares of a corporation). The short-term capital account in Japan's official balance of payments indicates the net balance of

individuals' and nonfinancial corporations' transactions in loans of shorter maturity than one year, foreign currency, and other relatively liquid international assets held outside the Japanese banking system. (Recall that banks' international transactions are recorded in the official reserves accounts.) In 1991 the Bank of Japan on net sold $8.1 billion of foreign currency reserves—perhaps in an attempt to alter the exchange rate between the yen and foreign currencies. The banking system of Japan on net acquired $84.5 billion of international financial claims, including foreign currency, securities denominated in foreign currency, loans to foreigners, and so on.

In 1991 the net balance of the capital accounts for Japan including the official reserves accounts was a deficit of $65.1 billion. This indicates a net accumulation of foreign asset holdings by Japanese citizens including the central bank and government. The $72.9 billion excess of Japanese sales of goods and services to foreigners over purchases from foreigners was largely offset by net lending to foreigners. In fact, but for the inevitable incompleteness in the accounting of international transactions, the offset would be exact—this follows from the principle of double entry. Each transaction has two equal sides: what is given up (credit), and what is obtained (debit). A current account surplus must be accompanied by a capital account deficit, and a current account deficit by a capital account surplus. The account "net errors and omissions" records the fact that, in 1991, missing debit and credit entries had a net deficit balance of $7.8 billion, the difference between the recorded current account surplus of $72.9 billion and the recorded capital account deficit of $65.1 billion.

Current account imbalance

Setting aside the inevitable errors and omissions in recording international transactions, imbalances of imports and exports—current account imbalances—correspond to equal and offsetting imbalances of international trade in assets. This is tautological, but has some important implications, because prices, exchange rates, and interest rates adjust so that exports, imports, and net accumulation of foreign assets also equal their intended or desired levels. That is, if interest rates and so on are such that the

Table 7.2. Accounts of the balance of payments of Japan, 1991 (US$bns)

	Debits	Credits	Deficit (−) or surplus (+)
(A) Current account			
1. Goods			
Exports		306.6	
Imports	203.5		
Net balance on merchandise trade			+103.1
2. Services			
(*a*) Transportation	29.9	19.6	
(*b*) Travel	24.0	3.4	
(*c*) Investment income	113.8	140.6	
(*d*) Other	38.4	24.8	
Net balance on goods and services			+85.4
3. Unilateral transfers	13.7	1.2	
Net balance on current account			+72.9
(B) Capital account			
1. Long-term capital			
(*a*) Direct investment			
Inward (net)		1.4	
Outward (net)	30.7		
(*b*) Portfolio investment	90.7	157.1	
2. Short-term capital (net)	25.8		
Net balance on non-reserve capital accounts			+11.3
3. Official reserves			
(*a*) Monetary gold (net)			
(*b*) Other reserve assets of the government (net)		8.1	
(*c*) Financial assets and liabilities of authorized foreign exchange banks (net)	84.5		
Net balance on official reserves accounts			−76.4
Net balance on capital accounts			−65.1
Net errors and omissions			−7.8

Source: Bank of Japan, *Kokusai shūshi geppō* (Monthly report on the international balance of payments).

nation desires on net to lend to foreigners, and does so, i.e. has a capital account deficit, then exchange rates and prices will have to adjust so that the nation also desires to export more than it imports, and does in fact do so; there is a current account surplus. The point is essential but is too often overlooked. Japan's current account balance in no way meters its openness to imports. It is far more usefully regarded as an indicator of Japan's changing inclination to borrow from foreign nations or lend to them. Japan's recent current account surpluses indicate that Japan as a nation is increasing its net loans to foreigners and otherwise accumulating foreign asset holdings. The Japanese lack of openness to imports, for example the severe government restrictions on imports and/or high tariff rates (high tax rates on imported goods), can well be expected to reduce the nation's expenditures on imports. But if the fundamental determinates of the desired capital account balance remain unaffected, then any factors that constrict imports will precipitate exchange rate movements that induce an equal reduction in exports.

Figure 7.1 charts the current account balance of Japan relative to its GNP from 1885 to 1997. The first thing to notice is that current account deficits and surpluses are about equally common over spans of many decades. This is unsurprising. Loans must, after all, eventually be repaid. Continual borrowing or continual lending is unsustainable.

Second, many of the prominent peaks indicating large current account surpluses, and troughs indicating large current account deficits, have ready explanations. The trough of the late 1890s coincides with Japan's (1897) adoption of the gold standard (i.e., adoption of the policy of officially maintaining a fixed price of gold in terms of the nation's currency, the yen). It was necessary for the government authorities to accumulate official reserves to maintain the gold standard. Initially, a sizable indemnity from China, an outcome of the 1895 Sino-Japanese War, was diverted to this purpose. The accumulation of international reserves is a capital surplus, the opposite side of the late 1890s current account deficit. The large current account deficit of 1905 co-

incides with the Russo-Japanese War. The national government floated substantial international loans to cover its military expenses, a capital account surplus. During World War I, Japan, as an ally of Britain but not a major combatant, became a major international creditor for the first time. The increased willingness of Britain and the other allies to borrow to finance their own war expenditures pushed up international interest rates and induced Japan to lend, giving rise to capital account deficits. This shows up in the figure as the large current account surpluses of Japan's World War I years. The large current account deficit of the mid-1920s represents Japan's international borrowing (capital account surplus) in the aftermath of the 1923 Tokyo earthquake.

Through the 1950s and 1960s the government of Japan maintained exchange controls, limiting international capital transactions. The immediate purpose was to facilitate maintenance of the fixed exchange rate of ¥360 = $1, the key point in Japan's participation in the Bretton Woods international monetary regime. In implementing the controls— limits on the ability of Japanese citizens to borrow from foreigners, limits on the ability of foreigners to accumulate wealth in Japan, limits on the rights to import foreign goods—the government authorities

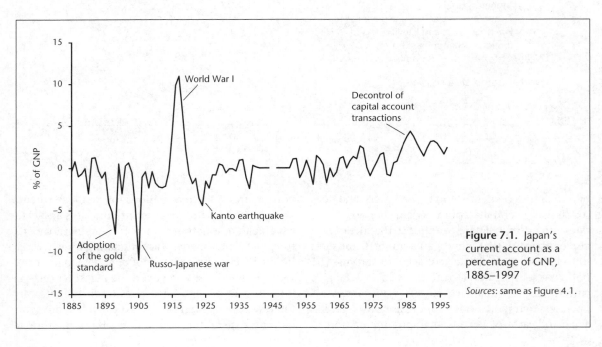

Figure 7.1. Japan's current account as a percentage of GNP, 1885–1997

Sources: same as Figure 4.1.

in Japan (Ministry of Finance and Ministry of International Trade and Industry) did not allow large capital account imbalances and current account imbalances to persist. The Bretton Woods fixed exchange rate system survived until the "Nixon shock" of August 1971—unilateral termination of US cooperation with the maintenance of fixed exchange rates, suspension of the US government's willingness to trade gold for the holdings of US dollar-denominated financial assets of foreign central banks. But Japan's strict government control and regulation of international capital transactions continued for another decade, ending in mid-1981.

It is quite natural that, in the years after Japan's 1981 deregulation of international capital transactions, the country experienced gaping capital account deficits (current account surpluses). Japan's high national saving rate had fueled the postwar recovery, but was now depressing effective interest rates in Japan below international levels. With the removal of government regulations that had inhibited it, Japanese citizens were free to take advantage of the relatively higher interest rates in the United States and elsewhere. The massive capital account deficits (current account surpluses) of the 1980s signify the surge of Japanese world lending. The surge was abating by the decade's end, only to reappear in the early 1990s.

In short, a lot of the peaks and valleys in Japan's current account can be understood as autonomous movements in the willingness of the nation to lend or borrow. Such an understanding casts exchange rates to the periphery of our attention. Our next task is to reverse the focus and treat exchange rate movements themselves as the object of scrutiny.

Exchange rates and terms of trade

We begin with the basics. An *exchange rate* is the price of one nation's currency in terms of another nation's currency. A currency is said to *appreciate* relative to another when its price in terms of the other rises, and to *depreciate* relative to another when its price in terms of the other falls. A rise in the yen–dollar rate is an appreciation of the dollar (relative to the yen) and a depreciation of the yen. A fall in the yen–dollar rate is a depreciation of the dollar and an appreciation of the yen. Because the reciprocal of an exchange rate is also an exchange rate, references to "rises" and "falls" in exchange rates are often confusing and should be avoided in favor of the unambiguous "appreciation" or "depreciation" of one currency relative to another. Currency appreciation is also sometimes referred to as currency strengthening and currency depreciation as weakening.

The nominal exchange rate, just defined, needs to be distinguished from the *real exchange rate*, an index of the quantity of goods produced in a country that can be exchanged for one unit of goods produced in another country. Real exchange rates are nominal exchange rates e_f (price of foreign currency in terms of domestic) divided by the ratio of the price level in the home country to that in the foreign country P/P_f. A unit bundle of foreign goods can be exchanged for P_f units of foreign currency; a unit of foreign currency can be exchanged for an amount of home currency which equals the exchange rate e_f; and a unit of home currency can be traded for home goods having value $1/P$. So a unit bundle of foreign goods can be traded indirectly for $P_f \times e_f \times 1/P$ units of home goods. The real exchange rate is: $q_f = e_f/(P/P_f)$. Movements in real exchange rates are referred to as "real currency appreciation" or "real currency depreciation". Real currency appreciation means that one unit of foreign goods trade for a smaller quantity of home goods and real currency depreciation means the opposite.

A related concept, the *terms of trade*, refers to an index of the price of exports in terms of imports—operationally, the ratio of export price index to import price index. (To see that a ratio of prices indicates the price of one good in terms of the other, consider for instance that, if transistors are priced at ¥100 each and apples at ¥50 each, then the price of transistors in terms of apples is 2 apples per transistor: ¥100 per transistor ÷ ¥50 per apple.) The terms of trade differ from the real exchange rate in that the bundles of goods on which the real exchange rate is based include imports, exports, and nontrade goods of the respective countries, whereas terms of trade are based only on the imports and exports of the one country. Real currency appreciation and improvements in a country's terms of trade often accompany one another. For example, if the prices of foreign imports fall while all other prices remain unchanged, then the country's terms

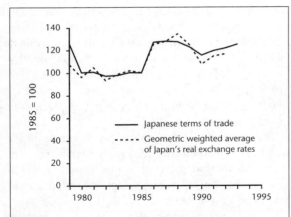

Figure 7.2. Japanese terms of trade and real exchange rates, 1979–1992

The figure plots annual averages of Japan's terms-of-trade and effective real exchange rate, both normalized so that 1985 = 100. Real appreciation of the yen relative to foreign currencies, as occurred in the late 1980s, also entailed improvement in terms of trade, a rise in the price of Japan's exports relative to the price of its imports.

Sources: *terms of trade*: Economic Planning Agency, *Annual Report on National Accounts*, 1994, 1995 (implicit price deflator of exports divided by implicit price deflator of imports); *real effective exchange rate*: International Monetary Fund, *International Financial Statistics*, 1994, 1995 (real effective exchange rate, based on value-added deflators).

of trade will have improved and its currency will have appreciated in value.

Figure 7.2 nicely illustrates the close correspondence between Japan's terms of trade and a geometric weighted average of its real exchange rates over 1979–92,[2] with weights matching the composition of trade across nations. However, close correspondence between secular movement in Japan's terms of trade and in its real exchange rates was not characteristic of the 1950s, 1960s, and 1970s, and we will examine some of the reasons for this below (in the section discussing the Balassa–Samuelson effect). First, however, we will explore some basic economic principles that govern movements in exchange rates, beginning with the interest parity condition that results from arbitrage in international financial markets.

Interest parity

When purchasing an asset denominated in foreign currency, one is mindful not only of its nominal interest rate but also of anticipated movements in the exchange rate. For, if converting domestic currency into foreign currency upon the purchase of an asset and the reverse upon its maturity, in addition to compounding at the nominal foreign interest rate, one can expect the investment to have been further compounded at the rate of appreciation of the foreign currency relative to the domestic currency. If these respective rates are expressed as continuously compounded[3] annual rates of increase, then investment in the foreign asset is expected to yield a nominal return on investment of domestic currency that is equal to the foreign nominal interest rate plus the expected rate of appreciation of foreign currency relative to domestic currency. Where international capital flows are unimpeded by government regulations or by the costliness of transacting, then arbitrage will assure that the expected returns on identical domestic and foreign assets are the same. To put it succinctly, equilibrium in frictionless international capital markets results in *interest parity*:

$$i_h = i_f + \dot{e}_f^*,$$

where i_h and i_f are the continuously compounded nominal home and foreign interest rates on equivalent assets, and $\dot{e}_f^*$ is the expected average continuous rate of appreciation of the foreign currency relative to the domestic currency over the period of maturity of the assets (the expected rate of decrease in the price of home currency in terms of foreign currency). The market's expectation of the rate of appreciation of foreign currency relative to home currency is implicit in the forward exchange rate, i.e. the current price in terms of one currency of promised future delivery of a single unit of another currency. The market's expectation is presumably unbiased but often inaccurate. Substitution of the actual subsequent rate of appreciation of foreign currency relative to home currency for the expected

---

[2] A geometric weighted average of items x_i is computed as $\sum x_i e^{wi}$, where $\sum w_i = 1$.

[3] The continuously compounded rate of increase is an exponential rate of growth. The initial amount A grows at the continuously compounded annual rate r, to equal Ae^{rt} after t years, where e is the base of the natural logarithm, the transcendent number approximately equal to 2.7182. For a detailed exposition, consult Deborah Hughs-Hallett, Andrew M. Gleason, Patti Frazer Lock, Daniel Flath, *et al.*, *Applied Calculus for Business, Social Science and Life Sciences*, New York: John Wiley, 1996, sect. 1.6.

rate, in the above expression, gives a relation known as *uncovered interest parity*, that is parity of domestic and foreign interest rates even without hedging in forward markets for foreign exchange. The former expression is therefore symmetrically described as the *covered interest parity* condition. There is no presumption that international arbitrage should assure uncovered interest parity, only covered interest parity, and even that presumes that arbitrage is unimpeded by government regulations or transactions cost.

Before 1980, the government of Japan exercised strict control over the international financial transactions of its citizens. These capital controls blocked arbitragers from fully exploiting international differences in asset prices. Figure 7.3 plots the difference in yen-denominated nominal returns on comparable Japanese and American financial assets from January 1972 to December 1984. Covered interest parity holds persistently only after December

1980, the point of significant deregulation of arbitrage transactions. The departures from covered interest parity prior to that indicate that Japanese government capital controls imposed significant constraints; they allowed interest differentials that free arbitrage would have erased.

That covered interest parity applies to the yen–dollar rate, and presumably also to other Japanese exchange rates since 1980, links expected movements in Japan's nominal exchange rates to differences between nominal interest rates in Japan and in foreign nations. All the factors, including monetary and fiscal policy, that precipitate sharp movements in nominal interest rates can thus be expected to influence exchange rates. A curious example of this is the phenomenon of *exchange rate overshooting*, caused by monetary policy. Sustained, contractionary monetary policy, as occurred in Japan in the early 1990s—that is, a one-time, permanent reduction in the rate of growth of the money stock—at first raises domestic nominal interest rates,[4] but after a time (two to four years) lowers nominal interest rates below their initial levels, once money prices fully adjust and a lower inflation rate comes to be expected.[5] Consider the expected effects on exchange rates of such a contraction in the growth of Japan's money stock, based on covered interest parity. The initial rise in Japan's nominal interest rate can be consistent with covered interest parity only if the yen is expected to depreciate relative to other currencies. If the expected ultimate real exchange rate is unaltered, then it must also be expected that the yen will, in the end, nominally appreciate relative to other currencies as the Japanese inflation slows, compared with what it would have done. Covered interest parity requires the yen to approach this new trajectory by at first sharply appreciating and thereafter gradually depreciating; that is, the exchange rate is expected at first to overshoot its new ultimate trajectory.

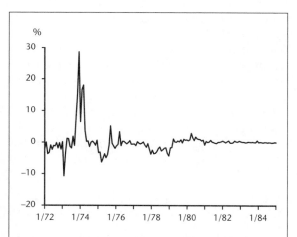

Figure 7.3. Deviations of the Japan–US forward exchange rate from covered interest parity, 1972–1984

The figure plots the difference between the three-month interest rate in Japan (the *gensaki* rate) and the three-month yen rate of return on dollar-denominated bank deposits (eurodollar deposits swapped into yen at the forward exchange rate). It represents the expected rate of appreciation of the yen relative to the dollar, in excess of the interest rate differential between the USA and Japan:

$$-\dot{e}^* - (i_{US} - i_{Japan}).$$

Source: Takatoshi Ito, "Capital Controls and Covered Interest Parity between the Yen and the Dollar", *Economic Studies Quarterly*, vol. 37, no. 3 (September 1986), pp. 223–41.

---

[4] Contractionary monetary policy at first raises nominal interest rates because money prices exhibit substantial inertia, and the money stock therefore has, at first, a smaller value in terms of real goods than it otherwise would have had. This is sustainable only if market forces cause the nominal interest rate to rise, for that is the opportunity cost of holding real wealth in the form of money rather than interest-bearing assets. Once money prices of goods fully adjust, this effect disappears.

[5] The link between nominal interest rates and expected inflation is described by Fisher's equation, discussed in fn. 8 below.

Because we know that covered interest parity holds now (refer again to Figure 7.3), and because we know that monetary policy influences nominal interest rates in a particular way, we know that exchange rate overshooting should be expected to occur. But does it actually? We are so far unable to relate, in a detailed manner, measures of the relative ease or tightness of monetary policy to the actual subsequent trajectories of exchange rates. There have been many attempts to do so employing sophisticated statistical methods, and the results are disappointing.[6] Perhaps the very same volatility in exchange rates that the overshooting model predicts, and that, more fundamentally, the stickiness of money prices predicts, makes it impossible to account accurately for the actual short-run trajectories of exchange rates, using any model. When our focus changes from the short run to the long run, economic theories of exchange rate movements are a little more helpful. Purchasing power parity is the core idea underlying long-run models of exchange rates.

Purchasing power parity

Recall that the real exchange rate is the nominal exchange rate (price of foreign currency in terms of home currency) divided by the ratio of home price level to foreign price level. Accordingly, the continuous rate of real depreciation in the home currency relative to the foreign currency can also be expressed as the continuous rate of nominal depreciation in the home currency relative to the foreign currency, plus the continuous rate of domestic inflation minus the continuous rate of foreign inflation:

$$\dot{q}_f = \dot{e}_f + \dot{p}_h - \dot{p}_f.$$

The rational person should therefore expect a rate of real depreciation in the home currency that equals her expectation of the future rate of nominal depreciation in the home currency plus the difference in her expectation of the future rate of inflation in the home country and in the foreign country.

The hypothesis that the expected rate of real depreciation in the home currency is zero is referred to as the *relative purchasing power parity* thesis. Under this thesis, the home currency, as just related, is expected nominally to depreciate relative to foreign currency at a rate equal to the expected domestic rate of inflation minus the expected foreign rate of inflation. Where covered interest parity holds, relative purchasing power parity implies that real rates of interest are equal across nations.[7] In other words, a frictionless international capital market, the underlying premise of covered interest parity, is not sufficient to equalize domestic and foreign real interest rates: absence of expected movement in real exchange rates (that is, relative purchasing power parity) is also required.

The relative purchasing power parity thesis is a corollary of the stronger *absolute purchasing power parity* thesis, which holds not only that the expected movement in the real exchange rate between a pair of countries is zero, but that the level of the real exchange rate is precisely such as to equalize the market values of equivalent baskets of goods in both countries, reckoned in the currency of either. Absolute purchasing power parity is sometimes referred to as the *law of one price*, but this law's domain is clearly limited. International arbitrage will not assure that prices of (nontrade) goods like haircuts or restaurant meals are the same in each country, and even the prices of tradables are subject to incomplete international arbitrage. Table 7.3 illustrates the variability across nations in the retail prices of a number of standard consumer items, converted to yen at the current (1993) exchange rate.

Of course, the real exchange rate could still exhibit absolute purchasing power parity over the entire market basket of goods, even though the law of one price fails on many individual items. But, as

---

6 For a recent survey of the empirical literature exploring exchange rate overshooting and other such transitory exchange rate phenomenon, see Jeffrey A. Frankel and Andrew K. Rose, "Empirical research on Nominal Exchange Rates", in Gene M. Grossman and Kenneth Rogoff (eds.), *Handbook of International Economics*, iii, Amsterdam: North-Holland, 1995, ch. 13, pp. 1689–1729.

7 Where the real rate of interest r, the nominal rate of interest i, and the expected rate of inflation $\dot{p}^*$ are all expressed as continuously compounded annual rates, their market equilibrium relation will be $i = r + \dot{p}^*$. This is referred to as "Fisher's equation", after the famous American economist of the early twentieth century, Irving Fisher. Fisher's equation enables us to restate the covered interest parity condition as the following, using subscripts h and f for the home and foreign countries, respectively: $r_h + \dot{p}^* = r_f + \dot{p}_f^* + \dot{q}_f^* + \dot{p}^* - \dot{p}_f^*$, which reduces to $\dot{q}_f^* = r_h - r_f$. The expected rate of real depreciation of the home currency relative to the foreign currency equals the domestic real interest rate minus the foreign real interest rate. For a brief introduction to the basic principles of interest rates, see David Flath, "Interest Rates", in Richard C. Dorf (ed.), *The Handbook of Technology Management*, CRC Press, 1998.

Table 7.3. International variation in retail prices, 1993

Item	Units	Price in Tokyo (¥)	Local price as a % of price in Tokyo*			
			New York	London	Paris	Berlin
Rice	10 kg	3,814	51	58	44	56
Bread	1 kg	413	106	40	153	91
Spaghetti	300 kg	160	64	44	74	98
Sake	100 g	279	95	82	65	87
Broccoli	1 kg	631	53	71	71	55
Onion	1 kg	174	104	70	82	92
Orange	1 kg	448	57	44	44	60
Banana	1 kg	247	78	83	111	60
Milk	1 ltr.	210	58	54	68	61
Egg	1 kg	295	84	127	152	112
Tea	25 bags	343	59	33	65	66
Cola drink	1 can	109	77	58	54	50
Granular sugar	1 kg	274	57	51	61	66
Hamburger	1 serving	217	64	82	92	105
Men's winter suit		53,760	78	74	68	88
Women's fall–winter skirt		12,680	66	78	80	86
Men's long-sleeved dress shirt		4,245	113	78	131	64
Men's underwear		483	168	167	137	233
Men's leather shoes	1 pair	11,670	105	75	108	93
Tissue paper	5 boxes	535	146	212	208	204
Disposable diapers	pack of 36	2,087	105	77	99	75
Compact disk		2,886	66	93	113	88
Magazine		380	98	88	126	139
Gasoline	1 ltr.	129	43	84	96	84
Parking fee	1 time	487	51	76	56	40
Laundry fee (men's dress suit)		1,052	93	144	178	127
Hotel lodging	1 night	12,390	194	197	131	116
Movie theater admission		1,716	55	92	63	53
Film developing	1 roll	32	216	188	294	144
Haircut		3,276	109	92	85	92
Permanent wave		6,512	196	172	126	100
Beer	1can	240	40	80	50	54

* The comparisons are based on 1992 average exchange rates: $1 = ¥126.65, £1 = ¥223.60, FrFr1 = ¥23.93, DM1 = ¥81.09.

Source: Economic Planning Agency, *Bukka repōto '93* (Price level report '93).

it turns out, even this is not so, for real exchange rates evolve in a manner inconsistent with the stationarity implied by (both relative and absolute) purchasing power parity. In very long time-series, real exchange rates seem only gradually to revert to their mean values. Deviations of real exchange rates from purchasing power parity seem to have a half-life of about four years, which, given the observed annual variability in real exchange rates, means that convergence of real exchange rates to purchasing power parity levels is so slow as to be hardly de-

tectable in time-series shorter than seventy-two years![8] James Lothian analyzed annual movement in the real yen exchange rates *vis à vis* the US dollar,

[8] For a discussion of the extensive empirical literature on purchasing power parity, see the following excellent survey: Kenneth A. Froot and Kenneth Rogoff, "Perspectives on PPP and Long-Run Real Exchange Rates", in Gene M. Grossman and Kenneth Rogoff (eds.), *Handbook of International Economics*, iii, Amsterdam: North-Holland, 1995, ch. 32, pp. 1647–88. The comment that 72 years of data are needed for tests of PPP to have adequate statistical power occurs at pp. 1656–7.

British pound, and French franc from 1874 to 1987 and found evidence of convergence to the mean in all of them, with half-lives of deviations ranging roughly between two and four years.[9]

The prices of nontrade goods may in fact never converge to purchasing power parity levels. This presumption is a key to understanding a secular trend in Japan's real exchange rates, based on an argument due to Bela Balassa and Paul Samuelson.

The Balassa–Samuelson effect

In the postwar period, the yen has exhibited a gradual but persistent real appreciation relative to the US dollar, as depicted in Figure 7.4. Some small portion of this secular tendency may be caused by growth in productivity of the export sector of Japan's economy relative to the productivity of its nontrade sectors. If capital accumulation and technical advances meant that Japan, more than its major trading partners, could produce manufactured goods at a steadily lower unit cost, but continued to produce services in the same unchanging fashion,

then one would expect that the relative supplies of goods would shift so that services rose in price relative to manufactures. And if, further, the prices of tradable manufactures were pegged to international purchasing power parities by arbitrage but the prices of nontradable services were not, then the prices of services would continually rise relative to their international purchasing power parity levels, strengthening the home currency in real terms, that is, causing home prices (of nontrade goods) to appear higher to foreigners in terms of real goods, and foreign prices (of nontrade goods) to appear lower to home citizens in terms of real goods. This phenomenon is known as the Balassa–Samuelson effect after its discoverers.[10] The economist Richard Marston has constructed indices of the labor productivity differentials between sectors producing nontradables and those producing tradables for Japan and the USA over 1973–83. He finds that, as the Balassa–Samuelson effect presumes, the productivity gap between the two nations narrowed much more for tradables than it did for nontradables. Marston judged this phenomenon to have caused real appreciation of the yen relative to the US dollar of about 1 percent per year over the sample period.[11]

Further observations make the existence of a Balassa–Samuelson effect even more convincing. First, notice in Figure 7.4 that the steady real appreciation of the yen relative to the dollar through the 1950s and 1960s seems to have had little influence on Japan's terms of trade. This is consistent with real appreciation of the yen relative to the dollar having been largely confined to the nontrade sector and therefore not reflected in the index prices of exports or imports, the ratio of which defines the terms of trade.

Also, throughout Japan's high growth era, its consumer price index rose decidedly more rapidly than its wholesale price index, again, consistent

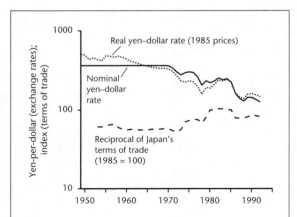

Figure 7.4. Nominal and real yen-per-dollar exchange rates, and reciprocal of Japan's terms of trade, 1949–1993

The real yen–dollar rate is based on the GNP deflators of the respective nations.

Sources: GNP deflators: Japan, EPA, *Report on National Accounts*; USA, Dept of Commerce, Bureau of Economic Analysis, *Survey of Current Business*; nominal yen-per-dollar rate: 1949–70 = 360 yen/dollar; 1971–92: Bank of Japan, *Economic Statistics Annual*; terms of trade: 1953–4, Kazushi Ohkawa and Miyohei Shinohara (eds.), *Patterns of Japanese Economic Development*, Yale University Press, 1979, p. 331; 1971–, same as Figure 7.2.

9 James R. Lothian, "A Century Plus of Yen Exchange Rate Behavior", *Japan and the World Economy*, vol. 2 (1990), pp. 47–70.

10 Bela Balassa, "The Purchasing Power Parity Doctrine: A Reappraisal", *Journal of Political Economy*, vol. 72 (December 1964), pp. 584–96; and Paul A. Samuelson, "Theoretical Notes on Trade Problems", *Review of Economics and Statistics*, vol. 46 (May 1964), pp. 145–54.

11 Richard C. Marston, "Real Exchange Rates and Productivity Growth in the United States and Japan", in Sven W. Arndt and J. David Richardson (eds.), *Real Financial Linkages among Open Economies*, Cambridge, Mass.: MIT Press, 1987, pp. 71–96.

with the Balassa–Samuelson presumption that Japan's nontrade goods would rise in price relative to other goods. Nontradable service goods tend to be consumption goods, not producer goods. The fact that service goods rise in price relative to manufactured goods is characteristic of all the developed nations including the United States, the technology leader. This, as argued by Baumol and Bowen, is because the rate of technological advance seems to be greater for manufactured goods than for service goods.[12] For the Balassa–Samuelson effect to manifest itself in this setting, the technology gap between countries must have originally been relatively large but grown smaller for tradable manufactures, while remaining negligent for nontradable services. As depicted in Figure 7.5, the US consumer price index (CPI) has also risen faster than its wholesale price index (WPI), but the difference between these two inflation rates is smaller than for Japan, clear evidence of a Balassa–Samuelson effect as well as a Baumol–Bowen effect. The gradual disappearance of the Balassa–Samuelson effect is predicted by the steady closing of technology gap between Japan and foreign nations. And, indeed, movements in the real

yen–dollar rate and in Japanese terms of trade do seem to have converged in recent years. (Again, refer to Figure 7.4, and also Figure 7.2.)

Our understanding of real exchange rate movements is modest in the extreme. As elegant as the theories might be, they account for only some portion of the secular trend in real exchange rates and explain almost none of the year-to-year variation in them. It might therefore come as a surprise that we are on rather firm ground in predicting the effects of real exchange rate movements on the trade balance. For example, sustained real depreciation of the yen relative to the dollar, as occurred 1995–6, is very typically followed within two years by an improvement of Japan's bilateral current account balance with the USA. (This, of course, does not apply to the autonomous movements in the current account such as follow from wars, natural disasters, or unexpected windfalls!).

Exchange rate movements and the current account

Exchange rate movements exert a complicated set of influences on the current account. In discussing them, it is important to be clear about whether or not an exchange rate movement is accompanied by changes in import prices (pass-through effects). Here, *import prices* refer to the prices in terms of output of the importing nation. Understand that import prices, like all prices, are determined by the law of supply and demand. If, in the first instance, an exchange rate movement is unaccompanied by any supply response, then the import price and quantity demanded will remain unchanged. But, even so, the effective demand schedule in terms of foreign output *is* changed, for the identical payment in terms of the importing nation's output now has a different exchange value in terms of the exporting nation's output. If the suppliers respond to the shift in demand schedule by proportionately expanding or contracting their output, an infinitely elastic supply response, then the resulting new equilibrium will have the same price in terms of the domestic output of the exporting nation as before the ex-

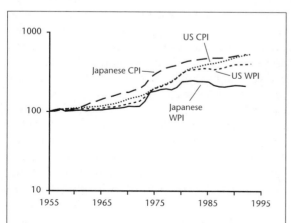

Figure 7.5. Movements in the Wholesale Price Index (WPI) and Consumer Price Index (CPI), Japan and the United States, 1955–1993

From 1955 to 1975, Japan's CPI rose steadily relative both to Japan's WPI and to America's CPI and WPI, as predicted by the Balassa–Samuelson effect. This phenomenon is less evident in more recent years.

Sources: *Japan*: WPI, Bank of Japan, Price Indexes Annual (prewar basis overall wholesale price index); CPI, Management and Co-ordination Agency, Retail Price Survey (general consumer price index for all Japan); *USA*: Bureau of Labor Statistics.

12 William J. Baumol and W. Bowen, *Performing Arts: The Economic Dilemma*, New York: Twentieth Century Fund, 1966.

change rate movement; and, assuming, as here we shall, that the law of one price is maintained,[13] the import price will have changed exactly in proportion to the exchange rate movement. To put it another way, if elasticity of supply is infinite, real exchange rate movements are fully passed through to import prices. If, on the other hand, supply elasticities are less than infinite, real exchange rate movements induce less than proportionate changes in import prices (are incompletely passed through to import prices).

The Marshall–Lerner condition

To see the precise implications for current account movements of a change in real exchange rate that is fully passed through to import prices, first write the current account balance in units of output of the home country in the following way:

$$
\begin{array}{ccccc}
\text{Real} & & \text{real} & & \left(\begin{array}{c}\text{real}\\\text{exchange} \times \\ \text{rate}\end{array}\times\begin{array}{c}\text{real}\\\text{imports}\end{array}\right)
\end{array}
$$

$$
\text{Real current account} = \text{real exports} - \left(\text{real exchange rate} \times \text{real imports}\right)
$$

$$
CA = X - (q \times M)
$$

Notice that, in order to express imports in units of domestic output, it suffices to multiply the real quantity of goods imported times the real exchange rate, for with full pass-through, a real exchange rate movement corresponds exactly to a change in the import price in terms of the importing nation's output, and implies no change whatever in the export price in terms of the exporting nation's output. (To consider cases of incomplete pass-through, it would be necessary to express the real current account as a more complicated function of the real exchange rate.)

Now the elasticity of the real current account with respect to real depreciation of the home currency (increase in real exchange rate q) is

$$
\frac{dCA}{dq}\frac{q}{CA}=\left(\frac{dX}{dq}\frac{q}{X}-\frac{Mq}{X}-\frac{dM}{dq}\frac{q}{(X/q)}\right)\frac{X}{CA}.
$$

And if the current account is initially in a state of balance so that $Mq = X$, then the expression in brackets, the sign of which is the same as that of the left-hand side of the equation, becomes

$$
\left(\frac{dX}{dq}\frac{q}{X} - 1 - \frac{dM}{dq}\frac{q}{M}\right).
$$

However, real depreciation of a nation's currency (that is, a rise in real exchange rate q), with full pass-through, implies an equiproportionate rise in the domestic relative price of its imports and, as viewed by foreigners, an equiproportionate fall in the relative price of its exports. Consequently this expression equals the following (where elasticities are in absolute value):

Elasticity of demand by foreigners for the nation's exports $- 1 +$ elasticity of demand by the nation for imports.

This implies the *Marshall–Lerner proposition*:

From an initial state of balanced trade, a real depreciation of the home currency that is fully passed through to import prices improves the current account, if and only if the nation's elasticity of demand for imports plus the elasticity of demand by foreigners for the nation's exports is greater than one. A real appreciation of the home currency that is fully passed through to import prices worsens the current account under the same condition.[14]

If demands for imports and exports are both price-inelastic (i.e. if the Marshall–Lerner condition fails to hold), then a real depreciation of the home currency that is fully passed through to import prices can improve a country's current account balance even though it leads to less export of home output and greater import of foreign output. The reason is actually quite simple. A rise in import price (depreciation of home currency) induces an increase in expenditures on imports if demand for imports is price-inelastic, that is if the quantity demanded of imports is relatively insensitive to price changes. Then, if foreign demand for exports, too, is sufficiently price-inelastic, the export quantities demanded will increase by too little to offset the rise in

---

13 We presume that the law of one price holds for trade goods but not for nontradables. In the analysis that follows, we imagine that tradables represent only a small element of each economy's output and consumption, so that the international differences in relative prices of nontradables determine real exchange rates. This is approximately true for large economies like those of Japan or the USA, but not for small open economies like those of Singapore or Liechtenstein.

14 We ignore any changes in real national income that accompany real exchange rate movements. For a careful dissection of the many qualifications implicit in the Marshall–Lerner proposition, see Rudiger Dornbusch, "Exchange Rates and Fiscal Policy in a Popular Model of International Trade", *American Economic Review*, vol. 65, no. 5 (December 1975), pp. 859–71.

expenditures on imports, and the current account worsens.[15]

Based on estimates of the relevant elasticities of demand, this perverse response is in fact regularly observed as the initial impact of a change in the real exchange rates of Japan and other nations, a phenomenon referred to as the J-curve.

The J-curve

Demanders' substitutions in response to relative price changes are often costly to effect, and may be judged worth the costs only if the price changes are seen to be permanent. For this reason, the price elasticities of the home country's demand for imports and of foreigners' demand for its exports are smaller the shorter is the time since prices have changed. A real exchange rate movement, fully passed through to import prices, implies an equiproportionate change in the domestic relative price of home-country imports and, as viewed by foreigners, an opposite but also equiproportionate change in the relative price of home country exports. However, in the initial period after full pass-through of a sustained change in real exchange rate, demands are rather unresponsive to the respective price changes and the quantities imported and exported will thus exhibit little change (i.e., the Marshall–Lerner condition will fail to hold). Consequently, a real depreciation of the home currency, fully passed through to import prices, at first worsens the current account balance (the nation spends more domestic output on the same quantity of imports and faces unchanged demand for its exports); and a real appreciation of the home currency, fully passed through to import prices, at first improves the current account (for a symmetric reason). After a period of time has passed, however, the demands for exports and imports do respond to the changes in prices (i.e. the Marshall–Lerner condition holds), and the current account moves in the opposite of its initial direction. This pattern, in which real depreciation of the home currency, fully passed through to import prices, at first worsens the current account balance but after a year or more improves it, is referred to as the J-curve phenomenon because of the implied shape of a time graph of a country's real current account following such an event. The J-curve is depicted in Figure 7.6.

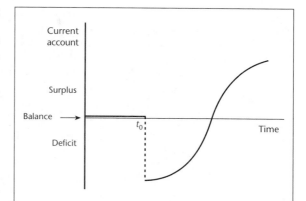

Figure 7.6. The J-curve

A real depreciation of the home currency, occurring at time t_0 and fully passed through to import prices, at first worsens the current account but eventually improves it.

We can gain some notion of the length of the J-curve from empirical estimates of the lagged effect of prices on quantities demanded for Japan's imports and exports. Some recent estimates are detailed in Table 7.4. The estimates of short-run and long-run price elasticities of import and export demand for Japan are close in magnitude to similar estimates for other developed countries. None of the estimates reported in the table implies a J-curve lasting longer than two years, and the Corker and Meredith studies that use quarterly data find J-curves of only six months and nine months, respectively.

After the Plaza Accord of September 1985, the yen sharply appreciated in real terms relative to the US dollar, but this seemed, at first, to have little effect on the sizable Japanese current account surplus. The association between strong yen and sizable Japanese current account seemed too persistent to have been caused only by lagged demand responses to changed import prices. It therefore occurred to many analysts that lags in the response of suppliers, i.e. "hysteresis" in supply, might be impeding the pass-through of yen-strengthening to import prices and delaying the process of demand adjustment.

---

[15] In terms of the equations, when the price of imports q rises, the quantity demanded M is contracted, but if contracted by only a little (i.e. if price elasticity of demand for imports is less than 1), then the product, $q \times M$, rises. Now if X expands by only a little (i.e. if price elasticity of foreign demand for home country exports is "small"), then the current account worsens.

Table 7.4. Estimates of the short-run and long-run price elasticities of demand for Japanese imports and exports

Study	Sample period	Short-run		Long-run	
		Imports	Exports	Imports	Exports
Ueda (1988)	1970–1987	sum = 0.69		0.41	0.92
Krugman (1989)	1971–1986	0	0.35	0.42	0.88
Corker (1989)	1975(I)–1987(IV)			0.55	1.09
	First quarter	0.27	0.37		
	Second quarter	0.41	0.62		
	Third quarter	0.48	0.78		
	One year	0.52	0.89		
Meredith (1993)	1975(I)–1985(IV)			0.61	0.93
	First quarter	0.13	0.26		
	Second quarter	0.23	0.44		
	Third quarter	0.31	0.57		
	One year	0.37	0.67		

Sources: Kazuo Ueda, "Perspectives on the Japanese Current Account Surplus", *NBER Macroeconomics Annual*, vol. 3 (1988), pp. 217–56; Paul R. Krugman, "Differences in Income Elasticities and Trends in Real Exchange Rates", *European Economic Review*, vol. 33 (1989), pp. 1031–54; Robert Corker, "External Adjustment and the Strong Yen: Recent Japanese Experience", *IMF Staff Papers*, vol. 36, no. 2 (June 1989), pp. 464–93; Guy Meredith, "Revisiting Japan's External Adjustment Since 1985", *IMF Working Paper* no. 52, June 1993.

Hysteresis in the supply of imports and exports

Expansion in supply of both imports and exports requires investment in new plant and equipment, development of new marketing channels, and so on. Such investments entail non-recoverable expenditures (sunk costs), so firms will be reluctant to undertake them in response to merely transitory real exchange rate movements, and will prudently wait to confirm that the real exchange rate movement is permanent.[16] And once firms have made investments that entail sunk costs, they will be slow to abandon them for the same reason—an adverse movement in the real exchange rate might also be temporary. In each case, if the inherent volatility in the real exchange rate is greater, a firm will wait longer before concluding that a permanent change has occurred. In other words, noisiness in real exchange rates weakens their effectiveness at signaling permanently changed underlying conditions.

Real exchange rate movements that elicit only a weak supply response are incompletely passed through to import prices. In the case of no pass-through (extreme hysteresis of supplies), when the home currency appreciates in real terms, the nation receives proportionately less, in terms of its own output, from the sale of its exports; and when the home currency depreciates in real terms the nation receives proportionately more, while its expenditures on imports, in terms of its own output, are unchanged in either case. A real appreciation of the home currency thus worsens the current account and real depreciation improves it, though by less in each instance than if pass-through were more complete and demands were highly price-elastic. With extreme hysteresis of supplies, a J-curve does not appear even if demand elasticities are small. But supplies of imports and exports are likely eventually to respond to a permanent change in the real ex-

---

16 The decision rules regarding investments that give rise to sunk cost, appropriate for stochastic environments, have been worked out with great mathematical elegance by Avanish Dixit and others. The upshot of these rules is that irreversible investments exhibit hysteresis. Firms are slow to undertake them and then slow to abandon them, ever mindful that current conditions may prove impermanent. For a good overview of this topic, see Avanish Dixit and Robert S. Pindyck, *Investment under Uncertainty*, Princeton University Press, 1994.

change rate, and as this occurs, the real exchange rate movement gradually gets passed through to import prices. Then the process of adjustment in the home country's demand for imports and foreign demand for its exports will begin to work, perhaps eventually manifesting a J-curve, but possibly not, even if a J-curve would have appeared had hysteresis of supplies been fully absent.[17] In other words, hysteresis in the supply of imports and exports slows the pass-through of real exchange rate movements to import prices, and prolongs the process of current account adjustment, but softens the J-curve effect. Things become even more complicated when hysteresis of supply is asymmetric across nations. This is relevant here because Japanese exporters may have exhibited more extreme hysteresis than the exporters of other nations selling products to Japan.

A frequent claim is that movements in Japan's real exchange rates have gotten passed through to import prices within Japan, but not to the prices of imports from Japan in other nations. For instance, when in 1985–6 the yen appreciated sharply relative to the US currency, the dollar prices of Japanese goods in the United States exhibited little increase, even though the yen prices of American goods sold in Japan fell dramatically.[18] Such asymmetry in pass-through of real yen appreciation to the import prices of Japan and its trading partners should mean that current account adjustment is faster and a J-curve more likely than if foreign exporters to Japan also behaved hysteretically, but that current account adjustment is slower and a J-curve less likely than if Japanese exporters did not behave hysteretically.

Many academic studies have explored the underlying reasons why Japanese exporters, in particular, should have behaved hysteretically. One conjecture, much worked over, centers on the oligopolistic character of Japanese export industries, focusing on the possibility that real exchange rate movements, under a variety of complicated assumptions, might influence profit-maximizing price discrimination across countries, or otherwise induce oligopolies to effect contrived scarcities or relax them.[19] But as the trade economist Jagdish Bhagwati has pointed out, there is a much simpler explanation for the unresponsiveness of Japanese exports to yen appreciation in 1985.[20] At that time, a significant fraction of Japan's exports were subject to government-enforced restraints, agreed upon in trade negotia-

tions with other countries. Automobiles, televisions, textiles, steel, and other Japanese export products were subject to such restraints. If the government export restraints were binding, then it is unsurprising that the Japanese producers subject to the restraints should contract the export quantities little or not at all when the yen appreciated. In other words, the elegant theory of lagged supply responses to noisy changes in the exchange rate may actually have had very little to do with the incomplete pass-through of yen appreciation to US import prices.

Low elasticities of supply in response to real exchange rate movements, whether the result of government interferences with foreign trade, hysteresis, or something else, contribute to exchange rate volatility. For, logically, any factor that weakens sensitivity of the current account to changes in real exchange rate must also increase the sensitivity of real exchange rates to autonomous movements in the current account. Here, then, is another reason (along with the overshooting response of exchange

---

[17] Hysteresis in the supply of exports and imports interacts in a subtle way with price elasticity of demand in determining current account responses to real exchange rate movements. A rather complicated expression (known as the Bickerdike–Robinson–Metzler condition, and which generalizes the Marshall–Lerner condition) determines the qualitative relation between movements in the real exchange rate and movements in the current account when supply elasticities are less than infinite. On this point refer to G. Harberler, "The Market for Foreign Exchange and the Stability of the Balance of Payments: a Theoretical Analysis", *Kyklos*, vol. 3 (1949), pp. 193–218.

[18] Ohno carefully develops statistical evidence that, from 1979 to 1987, Japanese exporters did not fully pass through real exchange rate movements but US exporters did: see Kenichi Ohno, "Export Pricing Behavior of Manufacturing: A US–Japan Comparison", *IMF Staff Papers*, vol. 36, no. 3 (September 1989), pp. 550–79.

[19] Marston develops evidence that low pass-through by Japanese exporters, from February 1985 to December 1988, was accompanied by widening differences between US import prices and domestic Japanese prices of the same products, that is by departures from the law of one price. Hysteresis alone does not require this, and it raises the suggestion that some additional factor was present, possibly having to do with profit-maximizing price discrimination by oligopolies: see Richard C. Marston, "Price Behavior in Japanese and US Manufacturing", in Paul R. Krugman (ed.), *Trade with Japan: Has the Door Opened Wider?* University of Chicago Press, 1991, ch. 4, pp. 121–41. Also see Paul R. Krugman, "Pricing to Market when the Exchange Rate Changes", in S. W. Arndt and J. D. Richardson (eds.), *Real–Financial Linkages among Open Economies*, Cambridge, Mass.: MIT Press, 1987.

[20] Jagdish Bhagwati, "The Pass-through Puzzle: The Missing Prince from Hamlet", in Jagdish Bhagwati, *Political Economy and International Economics*, Cambridge, Mass.: MIT Press, 1991, ch. 5, pp. 116–25.

rates to monetary disturbances, and the J-curve) why real exchange rates exhibit such remarkable volatility that economists' attempts to predict or explain their movements have, so far, met with abject failure.[21]

Conclusion

The necessary corollary of an excess of exports over imports is an equal excess of national saving over domestic investment, in other words a net accumulation of claims on the future incomes of foreigners. Japan's persistent trade surpluses of recent decades reflect its growing presence as an international creditor, and not its relative lack of openness to imports—if, indeed, it is relatively more closed to imports than are the other trading nations. The final removal in 1980 of most remaining government obstacles to financial transactions between Japanese and foreigners actually enriched the world economy, even though it contributed to enlarged Japanese trade imbalances and added new sources of volatility to exchange rates, for international financial transactions are no less a source of gains from foreign trade than the international exchange of commodities. Still, the complex interactions between the two kinds of international trade—the financial and the real—continue to harbor many mysteries.

---

[21] For an artful explication of this view, see Paul R. Krugman, *Exchange-Rate Instability*, Cambridge, Mass.: MIT Press, 1989.

FURTHER READING

- Richard E. Caves, Jeffrey A. Frankel, and Ronald W. Jones, *World Trade and Payments: An Introduction*, 7th edn, New York: Harper Collins, 1996. The latest edition of a venerated college text on international finance (and international trade).

- William R. Cline, *International Economic Policy in the 1990s*, Cambridge, Mass.: MIT Press 1994. Discusses the influence of exchange rate movements on current account balances, in general and with specific reference to Japan, in chapters 2 and 4, respectively.

- Paul De Grauwe, *International Money: Postwar Trends and Theories*, 2nd edn, Oxford University Press, 1996. Discusses in detail the many economic theories for predicting or explaining exchange rate movements, their applicability to specific events, and their relevance for government policy; a small book that covers a broad set of topics very well.

- Takagi Shinji, *Nyūmon kokusai kinyū* (Introduction to international finance), Tokyo: Nihon hyōron sha, 1992. Textbook treatment of many of the same topics in this chapter and more, with many specific references to Japan.

International Trade   8

Those who assert that Japan is more protectionist than its trading partners (it isn't) usually also imply that protectionism necessarily benefits Japan. The opposite is true. Foreign trade pushes out the national boundary of consumption possibilities, just as technological advance does. Interferences with trade constrict the nation's consumption possibilities. Protectionism thus represents the triumph of a narrow special interest over the broader national interest, an occurrence not unknown in Japan, or elsewhere.

From the aftermath of World War II right up to the early 1960s, Japan's protectionist interferences with foreign trade were quite extreme. Since then, however, Japan's participation in multilateral agreements has drawn it toward more liberal trade policies. Japan ended its system of current account foreign exchange rationing in 1964 and, along with the other developed nations, reduced its tariffs on manufactured imports substantially after 1967; in 1980, somewhat later than other developed nations, it relaxed most remaining controls on inward foreign direct investment. In spite of these major liberalizations of Japan's trade policy, it has often been embroiled in trade friction with the United States. The reason is simple, and is not widely enough appreciated. Growth of Japan's exports provoked protectionist political pressure by import-competing American industries. Japan–US trade friction is really about how best to appease or deflect that political pressure. It is not about Japan's "closed" markets or "unfair" trading practices.

Japan's trade patterns do exhibit peculiarities, but not necessarily ones that reflect the hand of government. Japan is a geographically small and mountainous country lacking natural resources but endowed with an abundance of skilled workers and substantial physical capital. For these reasons, Japan has relatively low marginal costs of producing manufactured goods, which it exports, and has rather high marginal costs of producing agricultural commodities, petroleum and other natural resources, all of which it imports. Japan is the supreme example today validating the Ricardian theory of comparative advantage. But the Ricardian theory did not predict the growing importance of intra-industry trade, the name for one country's import and export of apparently similar goods. Newer trade theories point to the pursuit of oligopoly profits as a basis for intra-industry trade. Yet Japan, which is no less dominated by oligopolies than other developed nations, engages in significantly less intra-industry trade than does America or the countries of the European Union. This is indeed a peculiarity.

A lot of intra-industry trade arises as intra-company shipments of multinational enterprises, the name for companies that produce goods in more than one nation. Japan's small extent of intra-industry trade is, in part, a manifestation of the relative absence within its borders of facilities controlled by foreign multinationals. Japan's *de jure* restrictions on inward foreign direct investment ended with enactment of the Foreign Exchange and Investment Control Law of 1980. That the stock of such investment should remain small nearly two decades later probably reflects the fact that Japan is an inherently difficult place for foreigners to live and work—not because of any government barriers, but because the language and the local culture are insanely difficult for foreigners to master. In that respect, Japan is different from other nations.

Gains from trade

Japan of the mid-nineteenth century is the clearest historical example of a nation rapidly switching from autarky to free trade. From 1640 until the coming of Commodore Perry's "black ships" in 1853, the Tokugawa *bakufu* had (with the minor exceptions of the Dutch settlement at an island in Nagasaki harbor (Dejima), and a Chinese enclave in Nagasaki proper) attempted to seclude Japan from international contact. Except for the Dutch trading ship arriving every other year, the Chinese ships, and some illicit trade reaching Satsuma *han* via the Ryūkyu islands (now known as Okinawa), Japan was autarkic and self-sufficient, a closed country. Perry's visit precipitated the abandonment of these policies. In 1858, five years after Perry delivered the American ultimatum (Allow American vessels to make port in Japan or else), Japan had concluded treaties with the United States, Britain, the Netherlands, France, and Russia, granting sweeping concessions that included free access of foreigners to designated "treaty" ports including Yokohama and Kobe, and drastic limitations on Japan's ability to levy tariffs on imports. In a very short span of years, Japan had gone from a policy of enforced autarky to nearly free international trade. For this reason, Meiji Japan has become the textbook illustration of the gains to be had from international trade.

How much did Japan gain from abandoning autarky in the mid-nineteenth century? How much does it gain from its international trade today?

The compensation principle

Trade is voluntary. Consequently, trade occurs only if each party gains, in the sense that the value placed on the object received surpasses the party's valuation of the object tendered. But the claim that a nation gains from international trade does not immediately follow from the fact that those of its citizens who enter into trade with foreigners do so

voluntarily. For if a nation moves from autarky to free trade, as Japan did in the mid-nineteenth century, the resulting changes in prices at which domestic trades occur may in fact leave some citizens worse off (those with a relatively great preference for the now higher-priced items). Nevertheless, as is demonstrated below, there does exist a net national gain in moving from autarky to free trade; or, equivalently, some constellation of lump-sum transfers from gainers to losers would leave all enriched by a move from autarky to free trade.

Of course, such lump-sum transfers generally do not, and as a practical matter probably could not, accompany a shift in trade regime. But the *compensation principle*, embraced by most economists and some philosophers, holds that policies which, if implemented along with some pattern of lump-sum transfers, would elicit unanimity should be adopted even without the lump-sum transfers. One rationale for this is that, because there are many unrelated issues before the nation's political bodies, the lump-sum transfers needed to elicit unanimity on each one of them separately are likely to offset one another when considered cumulatively. So it is indeed the net national gain cumulated over all citizens that matters in comparing alternative regimes, and it is on this we shall focus. The following example demonstrates that a nation of citizens, on net, values more the consumption it attains under free trade than under autarky, explains why, and supports some educated guesses regarding the magnitude of Japan's national gains from foreign trade over the years.

National gains from trade in a world of two goods

Let us divide the amalgam of goods the nation produces and trades into two composite goods, one called "agricultures" and the other, "manufactures". In Figure 8.1 the value to the nation's citizens of manufactures (reckoned in units of agricultures) is indicated by the area under the demand curve, and the agricultures that they necessarily must forgo to obtain additional manufactures are indicated by the area under the supply curve. This is because the height of the demand curve indicates the highest price in terms of agricultures at which each successive unit of manufactures would be willingly pur-

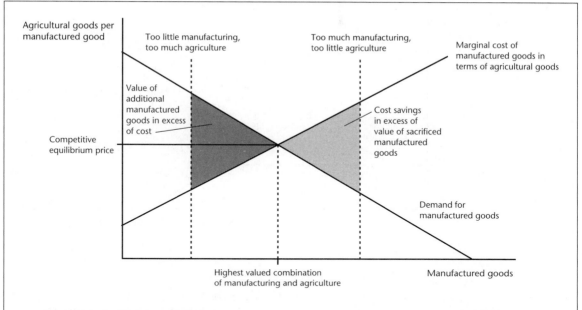

Figure 8.1. Equilibrium under autarky

Production and exchange at the competitive equilibrium price attains the (autarkic) nation's most highly valued feasible combination of the two types of good, agricultural and manufactured. Production and exchange of any other combination, besides failing to equilibrate supply and demand, entails production of combinations less valued than the competitive allocation by amounts such as the areas of the labeled regions.

chased and—assuming, as here we shall, that profits are fully competed away—the height of the supply curve indicates the incremental cost in terms of agricultures of each successive unit of manufactures. (For simplicity, we ignore any effects of trading itself on the positions of the curves.) As the figure demonstrates, the domestic competitive equilibrium allocation of manufactures and agricultures is the most valued of those feasible under autarky; the production of any other combination would leave open the possibility of producing additional units of one good more highly valued than the necessary sacrifice of units of the other good. Adam Smith's invisible hand guides profit-seeking individuals to the economically efficient allocation of the nation's productive resources. But all this presumes that the nation is completely closed to foreign trade. And, as we shall next see, by exploiting foreign trade opportunities, the nation attains combinations of manufactures and agricultures that it values even more than any combination feasible under autarky.

Figure 8.2 illustrates the national equilibrium that

ensues under free international trade. None will buy manufactures at the previous autarkic equilibrium price if given the opportunity to purchase from foreigners at the lower, world, price. None will supply agricultures at the previous autarkic equilibrium price if given the opportunity to sell to foreigners at the more remunerative world price. Thus, the equilibrium price of manufactures in terms of agricultures under free trade is the world price, and the domestic imbalance of supply and demand at that price—or "excess demand"—indicates equilibrium imports of manufactures. The areas of the labeled triangular regions of the figure indicate the national gains from international trade, i.e. the difference in each citizen's valuation of the consumption enjoyed under free trade and that enjoyed under autarky, cumulated over the entire population. These gains arise from two sources. First, even if the nation produces the same combination of goods as under autarky, it gains from acquiring additional manufactures at the world price (It values the manufactures it acquires more than the agricultures it gives up:

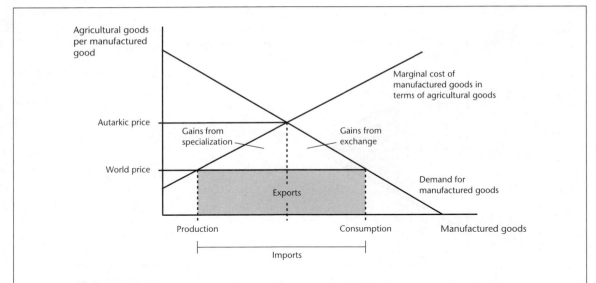

Figure 8.2. Equilibrium under free trade

By *exchanging* at the world price a portion of the agricultural goods it produces, the nation acquires manufactured goods which it values more than the agricultural goods it forgoes. Additionally, by further *specializing*, diverting its own production from manufactured goods to agricultural goods and exporting the agricultural goods, the nation acquires yet more manufactured goods than it forgoes producing.

gains from pure exchange). Additionally, by diverting production from manufactures to agricultures and selling the increased output of agricultures on the world market, the nation obtains more manufactures than it has forgone producing (*gains from specialization*[1]).

Net gains from international trade exist under more general conditions than those of the two-good example.[2] Quite generally, there exists some combination of lump-sum transfers such that every citizen of the small economy under free trade could, if they wished, purchase the same consumption bundle they had enjoyed under autarky. To put it another way, the national income of a small economy under free trade equals or exceeds the amount needed to purchase, at free-trade prices, the nation's autarkic consumption. This is because the competitive economy produces an output having the highest market value of any feasible, given the equilibrium vector of prices.[3] The autarkic consumption vector is feasible to produce, but is not necessarily the equilibrium output at the free-trade prices, and so its value at those prices can at most equal, but not exceed, the value of the equilibrium output. Not

everyone may, in fact, be left better off if the nation moves, as Japan did in the mid-nineteenth century, from autarky to free trade; but on the basis of the argument related here, the gainers could, in principle, purchase the consent of the losers. Opening to foreign trade pushes out the national boundary of consumption possibilities, just as technological advance does.

---

1 In economics "specialization" refers to production of more of a good than one consumes oneself, that is, production for other people's consumption.

2 The reasoning in this paragraph follows that of Paul Samuelson, "The Gains From International Trade", *Canadian Journal of Economics and Political Science*, vol. 5 (1939), pp. 195–205.

3 A competitive economy is one in which, among other things, no individual producer is large enough to influence prices. With given input prices, and given quantities of inputs (labor and capital), producers attain maximum aggregate profits only when the output having highest market value is produced. (Profit is the difference between market value of output and expenditures on inputs.) If aggregate profit is less than the maximum feasible, given the output prices, then there remains an unexploited opportunity to profit from by withdrawing productive resources from some activity and redeploying them elsewhere, and so the existing allocation of productive resources is not an equilibrium.

Measuring Japan's gains from international trade

A nation's net gains from foreign trade depend upon the shapes of its supply and demand curves for the goods it exports and imports. Assume, as in the stylized example, that these shapes are unaffected by the pattern of trade, and assume also that they can be well approximated by straight lines. Continue also to regard the import goods as a single composite commodity and likewise for the goods the nation exports. Then the nation's gains from international trade equal about half the value of exports times the percentage by which the autarkic price of imports exceeds the free-trade price. In other words, the gains equal one-half the base times the height (that is, the area) of the triangle formed of the two regions labeled, respectively, "gains from specialization" and "gains from exchange" in Figure 8.2.

A study by J. Richard Huber[4] comparing prices in Japan under autarky (1846–53) and under free trade (1881–79) found that an index of the prices of Japan's imports fell by about 70 percent in relation to an index of the prices of its exports. In other words, the autarkic prices of the goods it was to import, relative to the prices of goods it was to export, had exceeded the corresponding world relative prices by 3.4 times ($1 \div 0.30 \approx 3.4$). By the reasoning of the previous paragraph, this implies that Japan's

annual net national gains from trade equaled about 1.7 times the value of its exports.

Figure 8.3 plots Japan's international trade in relation to GNP over the last hundred years. National income and product accounts for Japan are available only from 1885. In the last fifteen years of the nineteenth century, Japan's international trade (average of imports and exports, reckoned in units of Japanese currency) ranged between 5 and 10 percent of GNP. We thus arrive at an educated guess that the value to Meiji Japan of its international trade in each year was about 10–15 percent of the nation's GNP. Of course this represents only the static gains from trade, i.e. the net gains from exchange and specialization afforded by the divergence between Japan's autarkic relative prices and world relative prices. It does not reflect the substantial benefits that Meiji Japan no doubt realized from its widened access to foreign technology. As an historical fact, the closure of Japan to foreign trade had entailed its closure to foreign ideas and discoveries, including the application of scientific advances to methods of industry. The rapid technological advance Japan experienced in the late nineteenth century should also be regarded, in part, as an indirect benefit of its opening

---

[4] J. Richard Huber, "Effect on Prices of Japan's Entry into World Commerce after 1858", *Journal of Political Economy*, vol. 79, no. 3 (May/June 1971), pp. 614–28.

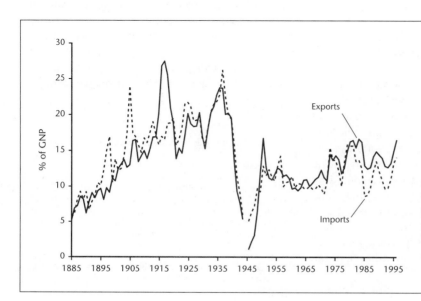

Figure 8.3. International trade in relation to GNP, 1885–1997

Here, exports include factor income received from abroad and imports include factor income paid abroad.

Sources: same as for Table 7.1.

to foreign trade, one not reflected in our estimate of the static gains from such trade. In other words, Japan had access to some foreign inventions and discoveries only because it had commercial relations with other countries. These dynamic gains to Japan from international trade may have been large in relation to the static gains, but nobody really knows for sure.

As we move away from the Meiji era toward the present, even Japan's static gains from trade become impossible to estimate, but it is natural to suppose they are of the same order of magnitude as its exports and imports. If this is so, then static gains from foreign trade account for precious little of Japan's economic development. From 1885 until 1990, Japan's real GNP per person doubled four times, rising by a factor of 16. How much of this can we attribute directly to Japan's foreign trade, which has never exceeded 25 percent of Japan's gross national product, and which in recent decades has hovered between 10 and 15 percent of its GNP (refer again to Figure 8.3)? The only sensible guess would seem to be: not much.

We shall return to the question of the nation's gains from trade when we take up the matter of Japan's trade policies, government policies that have interfered with foreign trade. But before addressing these important topics, we first consider the fundamental determinates of Japan's patterns of foreign trade. Which goods has it imported and which exported, and why?

Composition of Japanese trade

Japan's trade patterns have evolved dramatically in the century and a half since Perry's visit and the end of the Tokugawa seclusion policy. Japan's major exports in the early Meiji period were coal and silk, and its major imports were manufactured goods, wool, and cotton. From the late nineteenth century until the Pacific war, the major export was textiles, and major imports were primary products including fuel. Since 1960 Japan's major exports have been automobiles, electronic goods, and other manufactured goods. And since 1945 the country's major imports have been petroleum and other natural resources.

To explain the composition of a nation's imports

and exports is a principal task of the theory of international trade. There actually exist two theories, not mutually exclusive: the theory of comparative advantage, and the theory of scale economies.

Comparative advantage

The theory of comparative advantage was first elucidated by the nineteenth-century genius David Ricardo.[5] The theory rests on Ricardo's insight that intercountry differences in production possibilities constitute a basis for mutually advantageous trade. In Ricardo's original exposition of the idea, the constant marginal cost of producing either of two goods (cloth and wine) differs between two nations (England and Portugal)—the production possibility boundary of each country is a straight line. Under autarky, in each country the relative price of either good in terms of the other equals its marginal costs of production. The free-trade relative price lies between the autarkic prices of the two countries. Under free trade, each country exports the good for which it, of the two countries, has the lower marginal cost of producing, that is in which it has *comparative advantage*, and imports the other good, thereby obtaining a combination beyond any feasible under autarky.

Generalization of Ricardo's example to many countries and many goods is relatively straightforward.[6] Generalization to nonlinear production possibilities is problematic (how exactly should one define comparative advantage in this case?), though not intractable.[7] The essence of Ricardo's argument that survives such generalization is that *intercountry differences in autarkic prices* somewhat predict the overall pattern of trade. The nation will tend, on

---

[5] David Ricardo, *The Principles of Political Economy and Taxation*, 1817.

[6] For generalizations of the basic Ricardian model, see Ronald W. Jones, "Comparative Advantage and the Theory of Tariffs: A Multi-Country, Multi-Commodity Model", *Review of Economic Studies*, vol. 28 (June 1961), pp. 161–75; Rudiger Dornbusch, Stanley Fischer, and Paul Samuelson, "Comparative Advantage, Trade, and Payments in a Ricardian Model with a Continuum of Goods", *American Economic Review*, vol. 67 (December 1977), pp. 823–39.

[7] The discussion that follows encapsulates the reasoning of Alan V. Deardorff, "The General Validity of the Law of Comparative Advantage", *Journal of Political Economy*, vol. 88, no. 4 (October 1980), pp. 941–57.

average, to export those goods for which its autarkic prices (in terms of some numeraire good) are lower than other nations' autarkic prices, and will import goods for which its own autarkic prices are higher. The argument is worth relating for the insights it affords regarding Japan's evolving trade patterns.

Denote the vector of relative prices under autarky as p_a and the vectors of consumption and production under autarky c_a and x_a. Autarkic consumption and production are identical, i.e. $c_a = x_a$. Further denote the vectors of relative prices, and of consumption and production under free trade by p_f, c_f, and x_f. A nation in competitive equilibrium produces the combination of goods that, given the prevailing prices, has the greatest market value of any feasible. (If another feasible combination had greater market value at prevailing prices, the pursuit of profits would lead to a withdrawal of productive resources from some activities and a redirection toward others—the initial allocation could not in that case have been an equilibrium, cf. fn. 3). The nation's vector of production under free trade is feasible also under autarky. Thus, the free-trade production vector must have a lower market value at autarkic prices than the equilibrium autarkic production (and consumption) vector:

$$p_a \cdot x_f < p_a \cdot x_a = p_a \cdot c_a,$$

where "$\cdot$" denotes the inner product operator. (The inner product of two vectors is the sum of products of their corresponding elements; so for instance, $p_a \cdot c_a$ is the market value of the nation's autarkic consumption and production—it represents national income or GNP under autarky.)

If, as seems highly probable, the combination of goods the nation consumes under free trade would, under autarkic prices and income, have proved unattainable ($p_a \cdot c_f > p_a \cdot c_a$),[8] *then the nation must tend to import the goods whose prices under free trade are less than under autarkic prices and export the goods whose autarkic prices exceed free-trade prices.* To see why, denote the vector of excess demand under free trade by D, the difference between the nation's vectors of consumption and production. (Excess demand for any one good is simply the difference between the nation's consumption and production of it, in other words imports if positive and exports if negative.) And note that if, as we shall presume, trade is balanced, the market value of the excess demand vector is zero: $p_f \cdot D =$ $p_f \cdot (c_f - x_f) = 0$. Now if $p_a \cdot c_f > p_a \cdot c_a$, then, because, as already described, $p_a \cdot x_f < p_a \cdot x_a = p_a \cdot c_a$, it follows that

$$(p_a - p_f) \cdot D \, (= p_a \cdot (c_f - x_f)) > 0,$$

which establishes an overall tendency for negative elements of D to correspond to negative elements of $(p_a - p_f)$, and positive elements of D to correspond to positive elements of $(p_a - p_f)$. That is, the nation's overall tendency is to export the goods whose autarkic prices are less than free-trade prices, and to import goods whose autarkic prices are above free-trade prices.

In competitive equilibrium, prices reflect marginal costs of production. Conditions that favor lower marginal cost production of a good imply lower relative prices of the good under autarky and therefore increase the likelihood of the country exporting it. The opposite conditions increase the likelihood of its import. In this way, trade patterns will reflect nations' comparative advantages.

The Leontief paradox

Empirical analysts have sought correspondences between determinates of nations' comparative advantages and the compositions of their imports and exports. Each resource is generally better suited to the production of some goods than others. If a nation is richly endowed with arable land, for instance, its marginal costs of producing agricultural goods will tend to be low, its autarkic prices of agricultural goods will tend to be low,[9] and agricultural goods are likely to number among that nation's exports. The proposition that, in this way, the relative abundance of productive resources influences each

8 This might be advanced as an empirical observation. Alternatively, the proposition follows from the axiom of revealed preference if we regard the nation's consumption of every good as proportionate to that of a representative individual. The axiom of revealed preference holds that individuals choose combinations of goods which, among those attainable at prevailing prices, and given their income, they most prefer. For a nation's consumption to be strictly proportionate to that of a single representative individual whose choices conform to the axiom of revealed preference, redistribution of wealth within the nation must not alter aggregate consumption patterns. (For technical details, see Hal Varian, *Microeconomic Analysis*, 2nd edn, New York: W.W. Norton, 1984, pp. 150–3.)

9 That increased abundance of a resource has a biased effect on production possibilities and on autarkic prices is known as the Rybczynski effect: T. M. Rybczynski, "Factor Endowments and Relative Commodity Prices", *Economica*, vol. 22 (1955), pp. 336–41.

nation's composition of imports and exports—*the Heckscher–Ohlin theorem*—has been widely applied to the study of trade patterns, but with mixed results.

Anomalous findings have challenged trade theorists to think anew about the empirical validity of the Heckscher–Ohlin theorem. For instance, Nobel laureate Wassily Leontief famously unveiled the fact that in 1947 and 1951 the United States, though richly endowed with capital compared with other nations, was tending to export not capital-intensive manufactured goods, so much as labor-intensive agricultural goods.[10] This fact at first seemed paradoxical, and was so labeled (the *Leontief paradox*).

The Leontief paradox and other such anomalies perhaps reflect the very great extent to which government interferences with trade have impeded the efficient allocation of productive resources. But international differences in technology afford an alternative explanation; for, where technology varies from nation to nation, resource endowments need not be the decisive determinate of each country's comparative advantage.[11] The story of Japan's economic development over the last hundred years is replete with instances of adoption in Japan of technologies discovered elsewhere and already employed outside of Japan. Japan's evolving pattern of imports and exports well reflects this process, and so reveals the force of comparative advantage to a remarkable degree.

Japanese trade patterns and comparative advantage
By the nineteenth century, the relative prices of goods in Japan under autarky had become quite different from those prevailing elsewhere in the world. As the reasoning advanced earlier in this chapter would lead us to anticipate, following Japan's opening to trade it tended to import items that had higher relative prices within Japan than outside it, and to export items that had lower relative prices within Japan. The data in Table 8.1, drawn from the Huber article already cited, indicates that Japan's major exports of the 1870s including raw silk and tea had lower relative prices in Japan than outside it under the autarky that had prevailed in the 1840s immediately prior to Perry's visit. And the world price of raw silk was raised even further in the 1870s by the pébrine blight which greatly impaired silk production in Europe but spared Japan. Meiji

Japan's major imports, including cotton and wool products and sugar, had substantially higher prices in Japan under autarky than elsewhere. Rice had a higher price under autarky than under free trade and yet was exported by Japan, but this runs counter to the general tendency.

Japan's industrial boom of the last decade of the nineteenth century and the first decade of the twentieth permanently transformed the nation's productive potential. As the nation accumulated machinery, buildings, and tools and also acquired knowledge of how to use them, Japan's marginal costs of producing manufactured goods, particularly textiles, fell in terms of agricultural goods. And in the first decades of the twentieth century silk piece-goods, cotton yarn, and other textiles displaced coal, raw silk, and rice as the major exports of Japan. Steel and raw materials, including raw cotton, became the major imports, largely displacing machinery.

Cotton textiles remained an important export even after the World War I boom subsided, but in the period between the wars further capital accumulation and technological advance saw a further shift in Japan's production possibilities, now toward chemicals and heavy industry, including shipbuilding and iron and steel. In the interwar period these products assumed increasing importance in the composition of Japan's exports. As the country's heavy industry developed, derived demands for iron ore and fuel including crude oil and coal also increased, inducing wider imports of these goods, all of which comports well with the general principle of comparative advantage.

The economic depression that afflicted Europe

---

10 Wassily Leontief, "Domestic Production and Foreign Trade: The American Capital Position Re-Examined", *Proceedings of the American Philosophical Society*, vol. 97 (September 1953); reprinted in *Economia Internatinale*, vol. 7 (February 1954), pp. 3–32.

11 Besides this, where there exist three or more factors of production, the link between relative factor abundance and comparative advantage assumes added complexity. When these complexities are fully taken into account, the Leontief paradox may in fact not even contradict the principle of comparative advantage, even ignoring international differences in technology. For instance, capital-rich and labor-scarce America's comparative advantage may indeed lie in the production of labor-intensive agriculture rather than capital-intensive manufacture, because production of agricultural products is also land-intensive while production of manufactures is not, and America has an abundance of land. For a cogent statement of this view, see Edward E. Leamer, "The Leontief Paradox Reconsidered", *Journal of Political Economy*, vol. 88 (June 1980), pp. 495–503.

Table 8.1. Exports and imports of Japan in the early Meiji era (1870s)

Exports	% of Japan's exports valued in Mexican silver dollars	Autarkic price relative to world price	Imports	% of Japan's imports valued in Mexican silver dollars	Autarkic price relative to world price
Raw silk	39	0.79	Iron and nails	7	3.70
Refined copper	3	0.79	Raw cotton	1	2.50
Dried fish	3	n.a.	Cotton yarn	18	2.44
Coal	3	n.a.	Cotton shirting,		
Rice	6	1.10	cotton cloth		
Tea	25	0.67	and products	19	2.38
Other	21	n.a.	Raw and refined		
			sugar	11	2.13
			Woolen products	20	n.a.
			Kerosene	3	n.a.
			Other*	21	n.a.
Weighted average		0.77	Weighted average		2.52

* Clocks and watches, scientific instruments, rails and rolling stock, telegraph equipment, machinery, ocean-going steamships, papers and books, leather, chemicals and pharmaceuticals, armaments.

Source: J. Richard Huber, "Effect on Prices of Japan's Entry into World Commerce after 1858", *Journal of Political Economy*, vol. 79, no. 3 (May/June 1971), pp. 614–28.

and North America in the 1930s, and escalating American and European tariff rates, somewhat constrained Japanese trade, and the Pacific war ultimately interrupted Japanese trade altogether. The composition of Japan's foreign trade has continued to evolve in the decades since the end of World War II. Since the 1950s Japan's exports have shifted away from labor-intensive manufactured goods such as textiles, and toward steel, automobiles, home electronics, and heavy equipment. Imports have evolved away from raw materials used in textile manufacturing, and toward fuel, including petroleum.

Analysts have widely regarded Japan of the early 1950s as labor-abundant and capital-scarce. Perhaps, in the immediate aftermath of the war, the composition of Japan's trade should have been expected not to resemble that of the prewar era but instead to shift toward the export of relatively more labor-intensive products, and toward the import of products that would have absorbed more capital if produced in Japan than outside it; but as Japan rebuilt its lost capital stock, its composition of trade would resume whatever trajectory it might have followed but for the war's devastations, continuing the development of comparative advantage in advanced, capital-intensive technologies. Several researchers have investigated the factor content of Japan's international trade in the 1950s, 1960s, and 1970s. In analogue of the Leontief paradox, Japan in 1951, although, as just described, temporarily abundant in labor and scarce in capital, still tended to export capital-intensive goods and import labor-intensive goods.[12] Less paradoxically, this pattern of exporting capital-intensive goods and importing labor-intensive goods strengthened from 1956 to 1969.[13] And from 1967 to 1975, Japan's trade structure evolved further toward yet greater export of capital-intensive goods and import of labor-intensive goods, particularly goods the production of which used unskilled labor intensively.[14]

[12] Masahiro Tatemoto and Shinichi Ichimura, "Factor Proportions and Foreign Trade: The Case of Japan", *Review of Economics and Statistics*, vol. 41, no. 4 (November 1959), pp. 442–6.

[13] Peter S. Heller, "Factor Endowment Change and Comparative Advantage: The Case of Japan, 1956–1969", *Review of Economics and Statistics*, vol. 58, no. 4 (November 1976), pp. 283–92.

[14] Shujiro Urata, "Factor Inputs and Japanese Manufacturing Trade Structure", *Review of Economics and Statistics*, vol. 65, no. 4 (November 1983), pp. 678–84.

In summary, Japan's evolving pattern of foreign trade nicely illustrates the principle of comparative advantage. Meiji Japan did indeed tend to export goods that under autarky had lower relative prices in Japan than elsewhere and to import goods that under autarky had higher relative prices in Japan than elsewhere. As Japan industrialized and accumulated physical and human capital, its trade structure continued to evolve, exports including more of the goods in which Japan was gaining expanded production possibilities and imports including relatively more of the remaining goods. In broad terms, Japan's foreign trade illustrates and confirms the principle of comparative advantage.

More recent investigations have focused on whether the commodity composition and overall extent of Japan's trade are governed by the same underlying principles that shape the trade patterns of other countries. Do Japan's trade patterns mark it as an outlier, or are they about what one would expect, based on the trade patterns of other nations? In a series of papers, Gary Saxonhouse has explored this question in detail, examining data for the 1960s and 1970s.[15] The technique he employed in all of these papers was first to estimate, for a broad set of nations other than Japan, the relation between each country's per capita endowment of six productive factors and its net exports of a much larger number of differing items, controlling for average distance from trading partners; and then to investigate whether these same estimated relations also fit Japan. If they did not fit, then this could be taken as evidence that interferences with trade were distorting Japan's pattern of specialization. But Saxonhouse found in all the papers that, broadly speaking, Japan's factor endowments weakly but accurately predict the commodity composition of Japanese trade, and that the overall extent of Japan's foreign trade can be accounted for by presuming that factor endowments and distance from trading partners operate on Japan's trade in the same way as they do on the trade of other countries. A study by Leamer using approximately the same methods as Saxonhouse, and examining 1982 data, also found that Japan's overall extent of trade is not significantly different from what one should expect based on its particular factor endowment and distance from trading partners.[16]

Not all researchers have accepted these findings at face value. Noland made some adjustments to the Saxonhouse specification, re-estimated it using similar data, and reached an opposite conclusion.[17] Stewart, eschewing sophisticated econometrics altogether in favor of a back-of-envelope calculation, sides with Noland: Japan doesn't import enough.[18] In any case, the issue here is not the applicability of Ricardian comparative advantage to Japanese trade. It is almost trivially clear that the Ricardian principle does apply to Japan. But it is far less clear that the Ricardian principle applies very well to the trade patterns of the other developed nations. The reason is the increasing extent of intra-industry trade, the simultaneous import and export of apparently similar goods. Attempts to account for intra-industry trade have led economists recently to propose new trade theories, which identify scale economies as a basis for trade among developed countries, even in the absence of differences in technology or in relative factor abundance.

Scale economies

Even if all countries had identical technologies and factor endowments, so that comparative advantages were largely absent, there would still remain an important basis for international trade. For some goods, lower average costs of production accompany larger scales of output. This can motivate foreign trade in two ways. First, the scale economies might be so severe that the world-wide industry is a natural monopoly, an industry in which two or more suppliers cannot profitably coexist but in which a

---

15 Gary R. Saxonhouse, "Evolving Comparative Advantage and Japan's Imports of Manufactures", in Kozo Yamamura (ed.), *Policy and Trade Issues of the Japanese Economy*, University of Washington Press, 1982, pp. 239–70; Gary R. Saxonhouse, "Differentiated Products, Economies of Scale and Access to the Japanese Market", in Robert C. Feenstra (ed.), *Trade Policies and International Competitiveness*, Cambridge, Mass.: NBER, 1989, pp. 145–74. Gary R. Saxonhouse, "Economic Growth and Trade Relations: Japanese Performance in Long-Term Perspective", in Takatoshi Ito and Anne O. Krueger (eds.), *Trade and Protectionism*, University of Chicago Press, 1993, pp. 149–79.

16 Edward Leamer, "Measures of Openness", in Robert E. Baldwin (ed.), *Trade Policy Issues and Empirical Analysis*, University of Chicago Press, 1988, ch. 6, pp. 147–200.

17 Marcus Noland, "Public Policy, Private Preferences, and the Japanese Trade Pattern", *Review of Economics and Statistics*, vol. 79, no. 2 (May 1997), pp. 259–66.

18 Charles T. Stewart, "How Much Should Japan Import?" *Challenge*, January–February 1996, pp. 57–9.

single supplier does earn profits. Notice the possible arbitrariness regarding *which* nation is the natural monopolist. The nation need not enjoy a comparative advantage.

In fact, there are few if any non-trivial examples of world-wide natural monopoly. But even where scale economies are not so severe as to confer a natural monopoly on one nation, they may still give rise to foreign trade in a second way. Scale economies may mold the corresponding industries of differing nations into oligopolies that each allow product prices to rise above marginal costs. And these oligopolies of the various nations are likely to sell in one another's markets. Such "reciprocal dumping" is predicated not upon comparative advantage, but upon the contrived scarcities to which oligopolies are prone.[19] The oligopolies of the respective nations can be supplying differentiated goods, but the argument does not require it.

This so-called "new" trade theory really describes a basis for international trade that differs fundamentally from comparative advantage; for international differences in marginal costs of producing—the origin of comparative advantage—cannot explain why nations would both import and export similar or even identical products, that is, would engage in *intra-industry trade*. The new trade theory can, in principle, explain intra-industry trade. But does it in fact do so? Japan, which is thought by many to be dominated by oligopolies, exhibits strikingly less intra-industry trade than do the other developed nations.

Table 8.2 depicts broad measures of the extent of intra-industry trade for Japan and other nations, adjusted for differences in the trade balance, as computed by Gary Saxonhouse. The index is constructed on the basis of rather aggregated data. That is, the industries are defined very broadly: "transport equipment", "chemicals", "textiles", etc., the so-called two-digit SIC[20] level of aggregation. Of course, import and export of products classified in these industries need not represent import and export of virtually identical products. Nevertheless, the index identifies an important difference in Japan's trade structure compared with that of other nations. The USA, for example, is both a major exporter and a major importer of automobiles and automotive parts, while Japan is a major exporter of these products, but imports them hardly at all.

Table 8.2. Intra-industry manufacturing trade indices, Japan and selected other countries, 1981 and 1991 (%)

	1981	1991
JAPAN	31.9	48.7
USA	57.6	70.0
Germany	67.5	66.9
France	87.2	91.1
UK	82.5	88.0
EC12 (external trade only)	59.4	73.2

The index represents:

$$\sum_j \frac{w_j[(\text{exports}_j + \text{imports}_j) - |\text{exports}_j - \text{imports}_j|]}{(\text{exports}_j + \text{imports}_j) \times (1 - |\Sigma\,\text{exports} - \Sigma\text{imports}|)},$$

where j indexes two-digit manufacturing industries, and w_j is the share of the industry in the nation's total trade in manufactures. That is,

$$w_j = (\text{exports}_j + \text{imports}_j)/(\Sigma\text{exports} + \Sigma\text{imports}).$$

Source: Gary R. Saxonhouse, "What Does Japanese Trade Structure Tell Us about Japanese Trade Policy?", *Journal of Economic Perspectives*, vol. 7, no. 3 (Summer 1993), pp. 21–43, table 2, at p. 25. The raw data on which Saxonhouse computed these indices came from OECD, *Statistics on Foreign Trade*.

Much intra-industry trade arises as intra-company shipments by *multinational enterprises*, the name for companies that produce goods in more than one nation. The small extent of Japan's intra-industry trade may be a manifestation of the relatively small stock of assets within its borders controlled by foreign multinational enterprises. We next explore some of the reasons for, and further implications of, Japan's seeming inhospitality to inward foreign direct investment.

Foreign direct investment

Direct investment is the acquisition of a controlling interest in a productive asset. The asset might be an item of real estate, a business establishment, or a

---

[19] The term "reciprocal dumping" was apparently coined by James Brander and Paul Krugman, "A 'Reciprocal Dumping' Model of International Trade", *Journal of International Economics*, vol. 15 (1983), pp. 313–23.

[20] SIC stands for "standard industrial classification", a set of numerical codes for each industry in which successive digits identify finer distinctions.

business enterprise itself in its entirety. Control of productive assets encompasses activities associated with entrepreneurship, that is, the organization and operation of enterprise. Investments that confer merely a financial interest, and not control, are called *portfolio investments*. The distinction between a direct investment and a portfolio investment is fuzzy. In practical terms, anyone holding 10 percent or more of the ownership value of an asset may be judged to at least participate in its control. This is the criterion used by many governments, including those of Japan and the USA, in distinguishing between direct investment and portfolio investment in balance of payments accounting. In the UK and Germany, the criterion is maintenance of 20 percent or more of ownership value. Direct investment that crosses national borders is called *foreign direct investment*. It represents a form of international trade.

When citizens of separate nations exchange commodities, they might be viewed as indirectly exchanging the factor services embodied in them. Foreign direct investment means that some of the factor services embodied in domestic output, including those absorbed by the entrepreneurial activities inherent in the control of productive assets, are actually supplied by foreigners. In this sense, foreign direct investment is merely another way, besides commodities trade, in which factor services are exchanged internationally. The fundamental motivations for foreign direct investment are thus exactly the same as those for international trade generally, namely, exploitation of comparative advantage and pursuit of oligopoly profit. Let us examine how both motivations for trade relate to foreign direct investment, beginning with comparative advantage.

Comparative advantage as a rationale for foreign direct investment

First, notice that, even if a nation exhibits a relative abundance of entrepreneurial resources, so that it has a comparative advantage in activities that use such resources intensively, it still may be able to exploit the situation fully without foreign direct investment. If nations have the same technology and do not differ too much in their relative abundances of productive factors, then commodities trade by itself suffices to fully exhaust international gains

from trade and bring about equalization of factor prices across nations, a proposition known as the *factor price equalization theorem*.[21] But where these very stringent conditions are violated, as inevitably occurs, commodities trade fails to bring about equal factor prices across nations, and productive resources then migrate toward the nations in which their services command the highest premia. And entrepreneurial resources are at least as mobile as other productive inputs, possibly even more so. Under this logic, one expects that nations particularly well endowed with entrepreneurial resources would directly invest in others, but not the reverse.[22]

Table 8.3 describes estimates of the stocks of inward and outward foreign direct investment of Japan, the USA, the nations of the EU, all the developed nations, and the developing nations in

Table 8.3. Inward and outward stocks of foreign direct investment, Japan and selected other countries, 1995

	Foreign direct investment, 1995 (US$ trillions)		
	Inward stock	Outward stock	Net stock
JAPAN	—[a]	0.3	0.3
USA	0.6	0.7	0.1
European Union	1.0	1.2	0.2
Developed nations	1.9	2.5	0.6
Developing nations	0.7	0.2	(0.5)
World	2.7	2.7	—

Note: The developed nations are, on average, sources of direct investment and the developing nations are, on average, hosts of direct investment. This is consistent with the developed nations' presumed superabundance of factors well suited for organizing and operating enterprises, and with developing nations' profound scarcity of the same. It fits notions of comparative advantage.

[a] Japan's inward stock of FDI is estimated at the negligible amount $17.8 billion.

Source: UNCTAD, *World Investment Report 1996*, New York: UN, 1996, table 3, p. 239 and table 4, p. 245.

---

21 Paul Samuelson, "International Trade and the Equalisation of Factor Prices", *Economic Journal*, vol. 58 (1948), pp. 163–84; and Paul Samuelson, "International Factor Price Equalisation Once Again", *Economic Journal*, vol. 59 (1949), pp. 181–96.

22 Helpman has developed the comparative advantage (relative factor abundance) rationale for foreign direct investment using diagrams: Elhanan Helpman, "A Simple Theory of International Trade with Multinational Corporations", *Journal of Political Economy*, vol. 92, no. 3 (1984), pp. 451–71.

1995. It is quite evident from the figures in the table that Japan's outward direct investment vastly exceeds its inward direct investment. The natural interpretation of this is that Japan has such a super-abundance of resources well suited for organizing and operating enterprises that it can fully exploit its comparative advantage in those activities only by extending them beyond its own borders. The same is surely also true of the other developed nations, and all are net investors in the developing nations. But Japan's extreme asymmetry of inward and outward foreign direct investment—indeed, its near absence of inward direct investment—is atypical. A closer look at the foreign direct investment among the developed nations themselves is further revealing.

Figure 8.4 depicts the stocks of foreign direct investment linking the nations of the "Triad" (the USA, Japan, and the EU) to one another and to their respective regions. The diagram identifies about half the world's estimated stock of foreign direct investment. (The world's stock totaled approximately $2 trillion in 1993.) The direct investments linking the nations of the EU with one another and linking the USA to the EU and to Japan do not have the natural comparative advantage interpretation we have ascribed to the developed nations' direct invest-

ments in developing nations. The USA and the EU exhibit an approximate balance between their inward and outward foreign direct investments with one another, but Japan invests about thrice as much in each of these regions as they directly invest in Japan. The asymmetry is very much analogous to that pertaining to intra-industry trade, in which, it will be recalled, Japan is also an outlier. In fact, as already suggested, the two asymmetries may even be differing manifestations of the same phenomenon, for foreign direct investment and intra-industry trade are both very much the provenance of multinational enterprises, the name for companies that produce goods and services in more than one nation.

Multinational enterprises

The very large multinational enterprises, which include Japan's big auto-makers, electronics firms, and general trading companies, play a dominant role in foreign direct investment worldwide. Table 8.4 lists the nineteen Japanese companies among the hundred largest multinational enterprises ranked by their presumed holdings of foreign assets, and lists the ten largest multinationals regardless of home country. The hundred largest multinational enterprises, by themselves, account for about one-third of

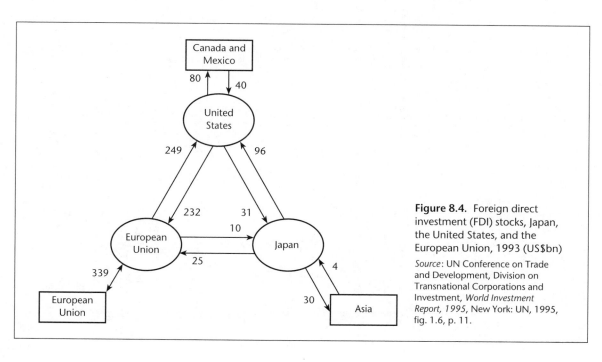

Figure 8.4. Foreign direct investment (FDI) stocks, Japan, the United States, and the European Union, 1993 (US$bn)

Source: UN Conference on Trade and Development, Division on Transnational Corporations and Investment, *World Investment Report, 1995*, New York: UN, 1995, fig. 1.6, p. 11.

Table 8.4. Japanese companies among the world's 100 largest multinational enterprises, ranked by estimated dollar value of foreign assets, 1994

Rank	Corporation	Home country	Industry	Assets (US$bn)		Employment (nos.)	
				Foreign	Total	Foreign	Total
1	Royal Dutch Shell	UK/Nether.	Petroleum	63.7	102.0	79,000	106,000
2	Ford	USA	Motor vehicles and parts	60.6	219.4	96,726	337,778
3	Exxon	USA	Petroleum	56.2	87.9	55,000	86,000
4	General Motors	USA	Motor vehicles and parts	43.9–56.2	198.6	177,730	692,800
5	IBM	USA	Computers	43.9	81.1	115,555	219,839
6	Volkswagen	Germany	Motor vehicles and parts	33.9–43.9	52.4	96,545	242,318
7	General Electric	USA	Electronics	33.9	251.5	36,169	216,000
8	TOYOTA	JAPAN	Motor vehicles and parts	27.9–33.9	116.8	27,567	172,675
9	Daimler-Benz	Germany	Transport and communication	27.9	66.5	79,297	330,551
10	Elf Aquitaine	France	Petroleum	26.2–27.9	48.9	43,950	89,500
12	MITSUBISHI	JAPAN	Diversified	25.4–26.3	109.3	11,146	36,000
14	NISSAN MOTOR	JAPAN	Motor vehicles and parts	24.8–25.4	80.8	34,464	143,310
16	MATSUSHITA ELECTRIC	JAPAN	Electronics	23.4–24.8	92.2	112,314	265,397
19	SONY	JAPAN	Electronics	22.5–23.1	47.6	90,000	156,000
22	HITACHI	JAPAN	Electronics	22.0–22.4	92.5	80,000	331,852
30	MITSUI	JAPAN	Diversified	15.8–18.0	82.5	23,560	80,000
32	NISSHO IWAI	JAPAN	Trading	15.8–18.0	55.5	2,101	7,245
38	SUMITOMO	JAPAN	Trading	14.2–15.5	59.0	n.a.	22,000
41	TOSHIBA	JAPAN	Electronics	11.7–13.0	63.2	38,000	190,000
43	ITOCHU CORPORATION	JAPAN	Trading	11.7–13.0	62.5	2,706	10,140
47	MARUBENI	JAPAN	Trading	10.4–11.2	78.8	1,915	10,006
51	HONDA	JAPAN	Motor vehicles and parts	9.6–10.2	28.3	19,668	92,800
57	NEC CORPORATION	JAPAN	Electronics	9.3	47.7	17,569	151,069
63	NIPPON STEEL CORPORATION	JAPAN	Metal	8.5–9.0	51.3	15,000	50,438
68	CANON Inc.	JAPAN	Computers	8.0	23.9	35,101	72,280
69	SHARP CORPORATION	JAPAN	Electronics	7.7–8.0	109.9	29,000	42,853
97	KOBE STEEL Ltd	JAPAN	Metals	4.8–4.9	28.3	5,522	32,485
100	BRIDGESTONE	JAPAN	Rubber and plastics	≤4.7	20.1	52,000	89,711

Source: UN Conference on Trade and Development, *World Investment Report 1996*, New York: UN, 1996, table 1.12, pp. 30–2.

the world's foreign direct investments.[23] To make the same point in a different way, foreign direct investment is more characteristic of oligopolies than it is of atomistic industries. A complete understanding of foreign direct investment requires an oligopoly-based theory. The outlines of such a theory are clear enough.

The members of an international oligopoly compete with one another in each nation, and they typically find that it economizes on transport costs to manufacture goods in the nations where they are to be sold, rather than only at home.[24] These firms could license foreigners in the respective nations to organize and manage local manufacturing operations, and thereby forgo directly investing, but very often they do not, because by retaining control themselves they avoid troublesome misalignments of incentives between licensor and licensee. These misalignments are potentially the most severe for production processes subject to rapidly changing technology, or for those requiring close attention to local variation in the preferences of demanders. For a similar reason, if, in order to compete effectively, multinational firms find it necessary to organize and operate exclusive retail outlets or dedicated wholesalers, then they often choose to do it themselves rather than delegate these tasks to foreign licensees. Products that require the sort of marketing effort just described tend to be pitched at consumers rather than businesses, and are ones that elicit special attention to the promotion, service, and maintenance of brand reputation, and so on. Consumer electronics, cameras, pharmaceuticals, and automobiles are good examples of such products, and multinational enterprises supplying these items do indeed account for a lot of the foreign direct investment hosted by developed nations.

A further locus of foreign direct investment by multinational enterprises is research and development activity. It is as important to the economic success of multinational enterprises to conduct research in many nations as it is to manufacture goods in many nations, for only then can they fully exploit the human resources of nationally based communities of scientists and engineers. Like the direction of a dedicated marketing channel, management of an applied research facility is infused with highly local information and, to that extent, is difficult to contract for at arm's length. Research

facilities are therefore usually controlled directly by the manufacturing firms that apply the fruits of their labors. Multinational enterprises, including the Japanese ones, operate laboratories in all of the developed nations, particularly in the high tech industries such as the pharmaceuticals, agro-chemicals, computers, robotics, software, telecommunications, automotive, and precision instruments industries.[25]

In light of the above, Japan's relative lack of inward foreign direct investment, like its paucity of intra-industry trade, is rather anomalous. In fact, the two anomalies are, at least in part, different manifestations of the same underlying phenomenon, for the multinational enterprises that hold the lion's share of intra-Triad foreign direct investments also account for much of the world's intra-industry trade.

Why is Japan's stock of inward foreign direct investment so low?

Direct investment by multinational enterprises supports and expands intra-industry trade in commodities, and exhibits a like pattern to it. About one-fourth of Japan's exports and one-seventh of its imports are realized as intra-company shipments by multinational enterprises, and very much of this is counted as intra-industry trade. Intra-company shipments comprise about one-third of the exports and imports of the United States.[26] From this evidence,

---

[23] The total world stock of foreign direct investment is estimated to have been between $2.3 and $2.4 trillion in 1994, and the hundred largest multinational enterprises have held about one-third of this in recent years. The foreign asset holdings of these hundred companies, including financial assets (i.e. portfolio investment), was around $1.4 trillion in 1994: UNCTAD, *World Investment Report 1996*, New York: UN, 1996, p. 29, annex table 3, p. 239, and annex table 4, p. 245.

[24] Markusen has constructed a simple model in which foreign direct investment economizes on transport costs: James R. Markusen, "Multinationals, Multi-Plant Economies, and the Gains from Trade", *Journal of International Economics*, vol. 16, no. 3/4 (May 1984), pp. 205–24.

[25] Some details concerning the European research facilities of Japanese multinationals are discussed by Robert Pearce and Marina Papanastassiou, *The Technological Competitiveness of Japanese Multinationals: The European Dimension*, University of Michigan Press, 1996.

[26] In 1993, intra-firm shipments accounted for 25% of Japan's total exports and 14% of its total imports. In the same year, intra-firm shipments accounted for 36% of the USA's total exports and 43% of its total imports: UNCTAD, *World Investment Report 1996*, New York: UN, 1996, p. 121.

it seems that Japan's relative paucity of intra-industry trade and smallness of inward foreign direct investment are, to some extent, linked. Factors inhibiting Japan's inward foreign investment must also have diminished the nation's intra-industry trade.

Two factors account for Japan's low stock of inward foreign direct investment. The first is that the Japanese government maintained policies hostile to inward foreign direct investment for the thirty years up until 1980.[27] The second factor is that the inherent peculiarities of Japan's language and culture make it a difficult place for foreigners to live and work. Perhaps the two factors just mentioned are related. Government restrictions on inward foreign direct investment would have been more costly to Japan if such investment had a higher expected return, and would have encountered more effective political resistance. Government restrictions on inward foreign direct investment may have been maintained for as long as they were precisely because they were not the decisive factor inhibiting such investment. The fact that removal of government restrictions was not soon followed by a surge of inward foreign direct investment in Japan might be confirmation of this point, though not all analysts agree. The economist Robert Lawrence has argued that, even though *de jure* government restraints on inward foreign direct investment were removed in Japan around 1980, *de facto* government restraints in the form of arbitrary and special application of local ordinances to foreign producers, particularly those involving mergers and acquisitions, continue to inhibit it.[28]

Japan's outward foreign direct investment, too, has been influenced by government measures, mostly those imposed by Japan's trading partners. For example, the 1981 imposition, at the American request, of Japanese government restraints on exports of automobiles to the USA precipitated not only a dramatic rise in the relative price of motor vehicles in the United States, but an expansion in both the scale and number of automotive production plants in the USA organized and managed by Japanese auto producers. US government measures to restrict such Japanese direct investment in America were widely discussed throughout the 1980s, but in the end were not adopted. The Japanese auto export restraints were suspended in

1994, and, for now at least, Japan–US friction on matters related to foreign direct investment seems to have abated.

The reason why government restrictions on imports of commodities induce expanded foreign direct investment is a bit subtle. Government restrictions on imports, including both tariffs and non-tariff barriers, reduce the supply of the affected product and raise its relative price. The high relative price induces domestic resource suppliers to withdraw from producing other goods and divert their efforts more toward producing just the one. There is no necessity that expanded domestic production of the protected good should be disproportionately organized and directed by foreigners, or that resources withdrawn from other activities should have been disproportionately controlled by home citizens rather than foreigners. In other words, there is no logically necessary relation between government restrictions on imports of commodities and the extent of inward foreign direct investment. But as a practical matter, there is a relation. Protectionist barriers are more likely to be erected for products in which foreigners hold a comparative advantage. And for precisely that reason, it is likely that a disproportionately large amount of the expanded domestic production that protection elicits will be organized and controlled by foreigners.[29] The severe restrictions upon inward foreign direct investment that the Japanese government imposed in the 1950s were, in this sense, a natural accompaniment to the limitations it also imposed on imports of commodities. The same domestic producers benefited from both policies. Japan's tariff and non-tariff barriers to imports were drastically reduced in the 1960s, and its restrictions on inward foreign direct investment came off in 1980. Nevertheless, Japan's trade policy continues to elicit much commentary.

---

[27] These policies and some of their implications are documented by Mark Mason, *American Multinationals and Japan: The Political Economy of Japanese Capital Controls, 1899–1980*, Harvard University Press, 1992.

[28] Robert Z. Lawrence, "Japan's Low Levels of Inward Investment: The Role of Inhibitions on Acquisitions", in Kenneth A. Froot (ed.), *Foreign Direct Investment: An NBER Project Report*, University of Chicago Press, 1993, p. 85–107.

[29] This argument may be found in Paul R. Krugman and Edward Graham, *Foreign Direct Investment in the United States*, 3rd edn, International Economic Institute, 1995, p. 50.

Japanese trade policy

Protectionism lowers the national income and economic welfare of the nation that practices it. Theoretical exceptions may be noted—the exploitation of international market power, the protection of an infant industry, or the counteraction of distorting effects of other policies—but they hold little practical significance.[30] In spite of this, Japan has adopted numerous policies that interfere with foreign trade—tariffs, import quotas (including those implicit in foreign exchange rationing prior to 1964), export restraints (at the request of foreign governments), and, until 1980, restrictions on inward foreign direct investment. But it is not alone in this. An examination of the recent trade policy of the USA or the nations of the EU reveals many more examples of protectionism. And all of these nations seem to have significantly reduced their own interferences with trade, particularly tariffs, only after negotiating international treaties that required them to do so. The first question to ask about all this is, why? Why have nations interfered with trade, deliberately forgoing gains, and why are international treaties needed for them to stop doing so?

International negotiations and Japanese liberalization

Trade policies emerge from political conflict among competing special interests, not from consensus regarding the national interest. In a representative democracy, the outcome of a political test is often determined more by the relative magnitudes of political contributions than by the simple number of persons on each side of the issue in question. The side that more clearly perceives its self-interest, and is better able to overcome free-riding among its own members, is likely to amass a larger war chest and may actually prevail, even if its desired policy confers smaller collective benefits on its own members than the losses it imposes on the rest of society. And this is why countries so often adopt self-damaging trade policies. In a referendum on protection of a single industry, domestic producers may well prevail, for the policy, if adopted, would enrich the few of them at the expense of the many demanders. The concentration of benefits on producers and the diffusion of losses among demanders makes it easy

for the producers and hard for the demanders to overcome free-riding, amass a large war chest, and mount an effective political lobby. But in a referendum on an economy-wide policy of free trade versus economy-wide protection, matters are apt to play out quite differently. Producers benefit only from their own specific exceptions to free trade but are harmed by the exceptions proffered to others. Economy-wide protection can garner little effective support.

A series of multilateral trade policy agreements has cumulatively reduced the developed nations' *ad valorem* tariff rates (averaged across dutiable imports) from 40 percent in 1947 to 4 percent in 1994. These international treaties were needed for each country to reduce its own tariff rates not because they assured reciprocity, but because they framed the question of tariff reduction as a single economy-wide issue, rather than as a multiplicity of separate issues each mostly affecting only one import-competing industry. To quote the economist Paul Krugman, "[t]he true purpose of international negotiations is arguably not to protect us from unfair foreign competition, but to protect us from ourselves."[31] It is often suggested that foreign pressure (*gaiatsu*) is an essential catalyst in the elimination of protectionist trade policies of the Japanese government. In the way just described, the same could be said of virtually every developed nation including the United States. International negotiations have drawn all of them toward more liberal trade policies.

The General Agreement on Tariffs and Trade (GATT), launched in October 1947, provided the essential starting point for the rounds of multilateral negotiations on tariffs alluded to in the previous paragraph. The cornerstone of the 1947 agreement was that signatories would accord one another *most-favored-nation* status; that is, they would not apply a higher tariff rate to imports from any of them than was applied to imports from any other, nor a lower duty on exports to one signatory nation than to another. Japan was still under American Occupation in 1947 and was not an original signatory to the

---

30 For a detailed discussion of the theoretical justifications for policies that interfere with foreign trade, see Neil Vousden, *The Economics of Trade Protection*, Cambridge University Press, 1990.

31 Paul R. Krugman, "What Should Trade Negotiators Negotiate About?" *Journal of Economic Literature*, vol. 35 (March 1997), pp. 113–20, at p. 118.

GATT. But in August 1955, three years after Japan's sovereignty was restored, it joined the Agreement in full, having obtained the approval of the required two-thirds of incumbent signatories.

Japan's accession to the GATT did not require it to abolish its rather sweeping system of foreign exchange rationing. The 1947 agreement (Article 11) prohibited the use of quantitative restrictions (quotas) except to maintain balance of payments equilibrium, promote economic development, preserve national security, or protect agriculture. Within this set of qualifications, the government of Japan discovered license to maintain its system of foreign exchange rationing, abandoning item-specific trade quotas (except those pertaining to agricultural commodities) only in February 1963, that is, converting the quotas to tariffs. Japan finally abandoned all foreign exchange restrictions on current transactions in April 1964 (and, in accordance with the IMF charter, the "rule book" for the Bretton Woods monetary regime, was bound thereafter not to reintroduce them (article 8)). The government of Japan had used its foreign exchange rationing system to nurture favored sectors of the economy, such as petrochemicals, steel, and automobiles, and to retard others. Abandonment of that tool permanently weakened Japanese industrial policy, and greatly liberalized its foreign trade.

Fourteen countries (Australia, Austria, Belgium, Brazil, Cuba, France, Haiti, India, Luxembourg, the Netherlands, New Zealand, Rhodesia-Nyasaland, South Africa, and the UK) did not assent to Japan's accession to GATT in 1955, which, under Article 35 of the 1947 agreement, meant that they were not obliged to accord Japan most-favored-nation trading status. These countries withheld most-favored-nation treatment from Japan and imposed discriminatory tariffs on it, that is, higher than they imposed on imports of like goods from other nations.[32] In contrast, West Germany acceded to GATT nearly five years before Japan with little opposition, and was accorded most-favored-nation trade status by all of the Western European nations. Soon after its accession to GATT, Japan entered bilateral negotiations with Britain, France, Australia, and the other nations invoking Article 35 against it, in pursuit of most-favored-nation status. The effective opposition to the policy in each of them appeared to emanate from economic sectors likely to be harmed by ex-

panded textile imports from Japan. Textiles had been Japan's major export in the prewar era, and would again be in the early postwar period. Few in the 1950s perceived the dramatic advances in Japan's economy that were soon to shift its comparative advantage away from textiles and toward more capital-intensive manufacturing industries.

To obtain most-favored-nation status, the government of Japan agreed to administer restraints of exports to the respective nations of selected Japanese goods, mostly cotton textiles. The precedent for this had been set by the United States, which had already elicited Japanese restraint of exports to it of tuna, beginning in April 1952, and of cotton textiles, first in 1956 and then extended for a five-year interval beginning in 1957, and for plywood, stainless steel kitchen utensils, and woodscrews, all from 1958.[33] These "voluntary export restraints" (VERs), as they were euphemistically dubbed—they were not really voluntary, but were adopted under some duress— muted the foreign opposition to Japan's participation in multilateral trading arrangements. Britain disinvoked GATT Article 35 in its policies toward Japan in spring 1963, and Australia, France, and the Benelux countries disinvoked it soon after, each of them, in doing so, extending most-favored-nation status to Japan. But the Japanese concessions to foreign seekers of protection set a troublesome precedent. By the early 1960s Japan had agreed to voluntary restraint of its exports of cotton textiles and a few other items to no less than twenty nations. Japan agreed to numerous additional VERs in subsequent years. The perpetuation or enlargement of foreign protection directed against particular Japanese industries has seemed to be an inevitable

---

[32] For details pertaining to Japan's accession to GATT and the discriminatory tariff policies of the 14 nations voting against it, see Gardner Patterson, *Discrimination in International Trade: The Policy Issues, 1945–1965*, Princeton University Press, 1966, esp. ch. 6.

[33] On the American political background surrounding the Japanese voluntary restraints of exports to the USA prior to 1970, see the short but informative work by William McClenahan, "The Growth of Voluntary Export Restraints and American Foreign Economic Policy", *Business and Economic History*, 2nd ser., vol. 20 (1991), pp. 180–90. According to McClenahan (p. 189), "VERs and bilateral restraints of Japanese products allowed the United States to continue to advocate unconditional most-favored-nation treatment in international trade while it maintained some modicum of protection for domestic industries whose opposition to liberal trade policies could jeopardize those policies and future legislation."

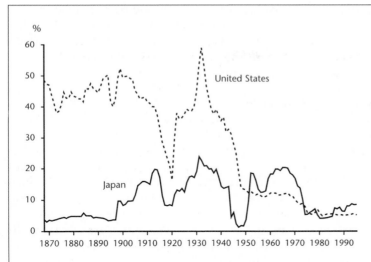

Figure 8.5(*a*). Annual average tariff rates (customs duties divided by dutiable imports) of Japan and the United States, 1868–1995

Sources: *Japan*: *LTES*, vol. 14 (1979), table 22, p. 252; and *Zaisei kinyū tōkei geppō*, no. 389 (September 1989) and no. 534 (October 1996); *USA*: US Bureau of the Census, *Historical Statistics of the United States from Colonial Times to 1970*, and *Statistical Abstract of the United States* (annual).

accompaniment to Japan's inclusion in multilateral agreements liberalizing tariffs.

The 1947 GATT included an ongoing commitment of signatories to meet annually in Geneva and also to meet at irregular intervals in special conferences like the original one, to seek further multilateral tariff reduction agreements. There have now been seven more special GATT conferences since the original one in 1947, each resulting in a further round of multilateral tariff reductions. The first four of these achieved only modest tariff reductions, but the fifth, known as the Kennedy Round (1963–7), the sixth or Tokyo Round (1973–9), and seventh,

the Uruguay Round (1986–93), each reduced tariff rates in all the developed nations, averaged over dutiable items, by about one-third. Figures 8.5(*a*) and 8.5(*b*) depict tariff rates in Japan and the United States, averaged over dutiable imports and over all imports, respectively, show the liberalizing effect of the Kennedy and Tokyo Round agreements in historical context.

The Uruguay Round, besides reducing tariff rates, also abolished voluntary export restraints, initiated a phased ten-year elimination of internationally agreed textile trade quotas, and converted many agricultural import quotas to tariffs (but not Japan's

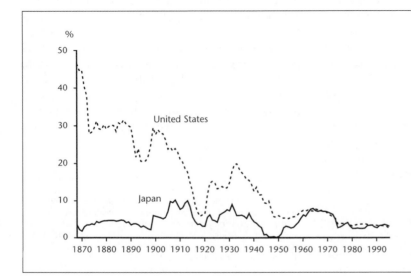

Figure 8.5(*b*). Annual average tariff rates (customs duties divided by c.i.f. imports) of Japan and the United States, 1868–1995

Sources: same as for Figure 8.5(*a*).

quota system for rice imports, which until 1995 amounted to a virtual ban on such imports). The Uruguay Round also established a body known as the World Trade Organization (WTO) to adjudicate trade disputes among members (GATT signatories), and carry forward the other activities that emanated with GATT. (The original 1947 GATT had included a provision that would have established a standing body to adjudicate international trade disputes, but the US Congress failed to ratify it and it was never implemented.) Perhaps the WTO will be the forum in which trade complaints aimed at Japan are finally defused or settled.

Trade friction

In spite of Japan's full participation in multilateral tariff reductions, it frequently has been embroiled in contentious trade disputes with the United States and, to a somewhat lesser extent, with Europe. Before 1980, most of the friction was generated by US industries seeking protection from Japanese imports, including textiles, steel, televisions, and automobiles. All of the cases just mentioned, and others, were ultimately settled when the government of Japan agreed to voluntarily restrain exports of the disputed items. And restraint of exports to the USA often led to requests by the EU, to which Japan acceded, that it also restrain exports to it. By the mid-1980s, a substantial fraction of Japan's exports to the United States were subject to Japanese government restraints. Nevertheless, protectionist pressures in the USA seemed to grow rather than dissipate. To counterbalance the protectionist pressure, American politicians and government officials attempted to shift the focus of US trade policy away from Japanese imports and toward expanded sales of US products to Japan, particularly in closed or regulated markets there. In a succession of bilateral negotiations since 1985, the US government has demanded and obtained, under threats of retaliation, many Japanese concessions benefiting American exporters to Japan. The beneficiaries of this policy include American exporters of semiconductors, beef, oranges, wood products, insurance, telecommunications, auto parts, and other items. Through it all, Japan has only rarely lodged official protests against the trade policies or practices of the United States. From the one-sidedness of the complaints, one might think that Japan–US trade friction really is about Japan's "unfair" practices and "closed" markets. It isn't. It is about how best to deal with, or deflect, the protectionist response in the USA to expanded Japanese exports.

Growth in Japanese trade and protectionist response in the USA

In a bow to the inevitable, the GATT Article 19, known as the "escape clause", explicitly recognizes the legitimacy of temporary protection against surging imports. Additionally, GATT Article 6 authorizes special protection from imports sold at lower price than in the country of origin, referred to as "dumping", and also authorizes special tariffs called "countervailing duties" to offset the effect of foreign subsidies. These GATT stipulations were modeled on corresponding stipulations in US trade laws. The 1897 Countervailing Duty Law authorized the US Treasury to impose special tariff protection equal in size to any foreign subsidy to foreign competitors. The Anti-Dumping Law of 1921 authorized the US Treasury to impose special anti-dumping penalties on foreign goods sold at lower prices in America than in the country of origin. And versions of the escape clause were appended to US trade law as early as 1934, authorizing special tariffs in the event of a finding by the US Tariff Commission, an official advisory panel in existence since 1916 (renamed the US International Trade Commission (USITC) in 1974), of substantial injury from any import competition resulting from US concessions. The political scientist I. M. Destler has argued that the US Congress established these special avenues for industries seeking protection, to deflect political pressure away from itself and preserve and expand, to the extent politically feasible, a generally liberal trade policy.[34] In other words, the "administered protection" embodied in commission recommendations and special executive orders is the lesser of two

---

34 I. M. Destler, *American Trade Politics*, 3rd edn, Institute for International Economics, 1995. Destler argues that the "root problem" of US trade policy since 1930 was the political effectiveness of special interests seeking import protection, and that the "solutions" over the years have involved various ways of "protecting Congress from trade pressures" by deferring trade policy questions either to an executive, such as the Secretary of State or the US Trade Representative, or to administrative bodies, such as the US International Trade Commission.

evils, a preferred alternative to legislated tariffs and other sweeping trade restrictions. Imports from Japan strained this US political equilibrium nearly to the breaking point in the 1970s and 1980s. It is important to understand why.

Industries facing new competition from imports are particularly effective at gaining protection. Nobel laureate Gary Becker has attributed this to the fact that the deadweight costs of protecting such industries are smaller relative to the wealth transferred than is true of other industries.[35] An industry facing an unexpected surge of competing imports will have already installed the productive capacity needed to meet the domestic demand, and will have incurred some non-recoverable sunk costs in doing so. In contrast, an industry that faces long-standing competition from imports will install the capacity needed to meet domestic demand only if protection is granted. In other words, the costs of installing new capacity add to the deadweight cost of protecting an industry only if the import competition it faces was expected. And this is why industries facing unexpected competition from imports are more able to exert influence and elicit political support. Protection of such industries imposes relatively small deadweight costs and thus encounters little effective resistance. Persistent growth in Japanese trade, particularly following the Kennedy Round tariff reductions of the late 1960s, therefore eventually incited a protectionist response in the United States that produced friction between the two countries.

An early episode of Japan–US trade friction was the "textile wrangle" that continued for the three years from 1969 to 1971.[36] Japan's exports to the United States of cotton textiles had been subject to voluntary restraint in 1956 and the restraint was extended for an additional five years, 1957–61. After that agreement expired, it was immediately succeeded by a series of multilateral agreements permitting the signatories, which included the USA, to set maximum limits on imports of cotton textiles and apparel from each other nation (the Short-Term Cotton Textile Arrangement 1961–2, and the Long-Term Arrangement regarding International Trade in Cotton Textiles 1962–74). These agreements did not encompass textiles woven of wool or synthetic fibers, and in the 1960s exports of such items from Japan to the USA increased significantly. The US government, under President Lyndon Johnson, had

requested that Japan voluntarily restrain its exports to America of synthetic fiber textiles and had been rebuffed. To secure the support of southern, textile-producing, states in the 1968 presidential election, Richard Nixon promised to insist upon Japanese restraint of synthetic textile exports to the United States and to condition the return of Okinawa to Japanese control upon it. President Nixon fulfilled this campaign pledge, and, after three years of somewhat clumsy negotiations and heavy-handed American pressure, the government of Japan consented in 1971 to administer the export restraint, and in 1972 Okinawa reverted to Japanese control. Hong Kong, Taiwan, and Korea also consented in 1971 to voluntary restraints of exports to the USA of woolen and synthetic textiles.

Ironically, very soon after the voluntary export restraint was invoked, Japan's textile industry shrunk dramatically, a manifestation of shifting comparative advantage. Japan became a net importer of textiles and the export restraints were totally redundant. Nor is this all. The export restraints would have been redundant even had Japan continued to be a net exporter of textiles, for in 1974, the year the Japanese voluntary restraint took effect, the multilateral agreement permitting GATT signatories to impose country-by-country import quotas on textiles and apparel was expanded to encompass synthetic fibers, an agreement known as the Multi-Fiber Arrangement. That arrangement has been in effect in some form ever since. (Under the terms of the Uruguay Round, it is to be phased out over a ten-year period ending in 2004.)

Steel was another of the industries in which expanding Japanese exports first incited US protectionist pressure. Imports from Japan rose from less than 1 percent of total steel consumption in the USA in 1960 to nearly 7 percent in 1968. The steel industry responded by filing numerous petitions for the imposition of countervailing duties and anti-dumping penalties upon both Japanese and European steel exporters. Under the threat of legislated

---

[35] Gary Becker, "A Theory of Competition among Pressure Groups for Political Advantage", *Quarterly Journal of Economics*, vol. 98, no. 3 (August 1983), pp. 371–400. Becker discusses industries facing unexpected competition from imports on p. 382.

[36] This episode is discussed in detail in I. M. Destler, Haruhiro Fukui, and Hideo Sato, *The Textile Wrangle: Conflict in Japanese American Relations, 1969–1971*, Cornell University Press, 1979.

quotas on steel imports into the USA, both Japan and the European Community agreed to voluntarily restrain steel exports to the United States between January 1969 and December 1971. A second series of voluntary export restraints were agreed upon for May 1972–December 1974. After the voluntary restraints lapsed, in a pattern that has been repeated many times since, the US steel producers again filed numerous petitions with the US government for special relief. To resolve matters, the US government effectively imposed a minimum price for steel imports, based on presumed Japanese production costs and costs of transport to America, the so-called "trigger price mechanism",[37] which was in effect from January 1978 to March 1980 and from October 1980 to January 1982. In return, the steel industry agreed to refrain from filing countervailing duty, anti-dumping, or escape clause petitions. The arrangement ultimately broke down when appreciation of the dollar in the early 1980s rendered the trigger price mechanism ineffective. Steel producers again began filing petitions for special protection, ultimately inducing the reinstatement of voluntary restraint of exports, not only by Japan and the EC, but also by Brazil, Mexico, South Africa, and Korea, from October 1984 to March 1992.

Steel firms have continued to file petitions for relief and to lobby for a system of multilateral export quotas similar to the Multi-Fiber Arrangement, so far unsuccessfully. US imports of steel from Japan in 1995 amounted to 2.2 million metric tons, half as much as the 4.4 million metric tons imported from Japan in 1966, a mere 2 percent of US total steel consumption and only about 10 percent of US imports of steel. As with textiles, shifting Japanese comparative advantage, and not US protection, is largely responsible for the secular decline in Japanese steel imports.

Other US industries besides steel and textiles sought special protection from Japanese imports in the 1960s and 1970s but were less successful in obtaining it. The television case is illustrative. A 1968 petition by Zenith for imposing anti-dumping penalties on Japanese exporters was decided upon favorably by the US Tariff Commission in 1971, but only in 1978 was an ($440 million) anti-dumping penalty actually assessed by the US Treasury. In 1980 a greatly reduced ($66 million) anti-dumping penalty was finally collected. Meanwhile, in Decem-

ber 1970, some American television manufacturers had initiated an antitrust suit against the Japanese competitors (charging them with violating US law by pricing their products at too low a level), which began a long, torturous, and ultimately futile progression through the US courts, failing at the Supreme Court in 1987.[38] After the USITC ruled favorably on a petition by Sylvania for special protection based on the escape clause, the government of Japan acceded to voluntarily restrain its exports of color television sets between July 1977 and June 1980. The voluntary restraint did not prevent television imports from entering the United States from countries other than Japan, such as Korea and Taiwan. Within a few years after the voluntary export restraint had expired, Zenith was the only American-owned manufacturer of televisions still in operation.

Rising imports into the United States in the 1960s and 1970s, from both Japan and Europe, brought political pressure not only to protect particularly besieged American industries such as steel and televisions, but also to make it easier, in general, for petitioners to obtain anti-dumping penalties, countervailing duties, or escape clause protection. The pressure met with an affirmative response. The 1974 Trade Act (authorizing US participation in the Tokyo Round), Section 201, relaxed the criteria for invoking the GATT escape clause, so that imports (not necessarily the result of US tariff concessions, as before), must be a "substantial" cause of injury, that is not less than any one other cause, rather than, as before, the "major cause" of injury, that is, greater than all other causes combined. The 1974 Trade Act also lowered the threshold for finding that dumping had occurred, from one of sales at lower prices in the country of origin than in the USA to one of sales "below cost" in the USA, with cost to be determined based on indirect evidence.

Before 1974, very few US petitioners for adminis-

---

[37] Imports sold below the stipulated legal minimum price would automatically trigger the imposition of special anti-dumping penalties.

[38] For a detailed account of this episode, see Kozo Yamamura and Jan Vandenberg, "Japan's Rapid Growth Policy on Trial: The Television Case", in Gary R. Saxonhouse and Kozo Yamamura (eds.), *Law and Trade Issues of the Japanese Economy: American and Japanese Perspectives*, University of Washington Press, 1986, pp. 238–84.

tered protection of any kind actually secured relief from import competition.[39] Now the number of petitions began to rise, particularly for anti-dumping penalties, and more met with an affirmative response. Further changes enacted in 1979 hastened these trends. The Trade Agreements Act of 1979, approving the Tokyo Round agreements, included stipulations shifting the administration of countervailing duties and anti-dumping penalties from the US Department of the Treasury to the Department of Commerce; it also set precise time limits on investigations, and mandated the imposition of penalties in the event of an affirmative finding. (Before that, penalties were left to the discretion of the president.)

Even after the new laws were enacted, administered protection remained elusive for many petitioners. This point was driven home quite forcefully by the denial in 1980 of petitions (by the United Auto Workers Union and by Ford Motor Company) before the USITC for escape clause protection from Japanese automobile imports. Process innovations that had been developed at Toyota in the 1950s and 1960s, and then diffused to other Japanese companies, had lowered the production costs of the Japanese auto manufacturers and boosted their exports. Then the rise in gasoline prices arising from the two oil shocks (the 1973 Arab oil embargo and the 1979 Iranian revolution) switched demand away from the large American cars and toward the Japanese imports. The USITC, in declining to recommend escape clause protection, ruled that business recession, and not imports, was the greater cause of injury to the American automobile producers, the "substantial" cause. Congressional response was swift. In February 1981 Senators John Danforth (Republican, Missouri) and Lloyd Bentsen (Democrat, Texas) proposed a bill (s.396) that would have established import quotas for automobiles. Soon afterwards, in May 1981, the government of Japan agreed to administer a system of voluntary export restraints for two years, April 1981–March 1983, with renewal possible thereafter. The restraints were renewed annually through March 1994 before finally being allowed to lapse, and this was in spite of the fact that the US government ceased formal requests for their renewal in 1985. The Japanese government had also arranged restraints of automotive exports to the UK beginning in 1977 and continuing through 1992, and to the EU beginning in 1986 and still in effect (but scheduled to lapse in 1999).

One of the curious implications of the Japanese automotive export restraints to the United States in the first two years it was in effect was the switch toward higher-quality vehicles. Because the export restraints entailed MITI assigning each manufacturer a maximum allowable number of vehicles to export, the companies naturally tended to export vehicles on which the profit margin was as great as possible, in other words higher-quality vehicles. The trade economist Robert Feenstra estimated that, as a result of the export restraint, the average inflation-adjusted retail prices of Japanese small cars sold in the USA rose by 8.4 percent in 1981 compared with the previous year, relative to the prices of American small cars (that also rose), but that a 5.3 percent rise in Japanese small car relative price could be attributed to increased average quality of Japanese cars sold.[40] In a later paper, comparing the American prices of Japanese cars (subject to VER) and trucks (not subject to VER), Feenstra found that little further quality upgrading of Japanese cars occurred in 1983–4, but that the prices of the Japanese cars rose by about another 12 percent in those years over their 1981–2 level.[41] This further price rise occurred in spite of expanded production by Japanese manufacturers' American plants, and the establishment by them of more such plants. The export restraint, by raising the American prices of Japanese cars, increased the demand in America for both American

---

[39] Of 113 Tariff Commission escape clause investigations between 1948 and 1962, it recommended relief in 41 and the president provided it in only 15; of 30 escape clause petitioners before the Tariff Commission between 1962 and 1974, only 4 obtained relief. Between 1934 and 1968, the US Treasury considered 191 petitions for countervailing duties but actually imposed them in only 30. In 1969 it imposed three more countervailing duties and between 1970 and 1974 imposed eight more. The US Treasury investigated 371 allegations of dumping over 1955–68, and imposed anti-dumping penalties in only 12 cases, but 89 others resulted in price revisions or withdrawal from the US market (Destler, *American Trade Policies* (n. 34), p. 141 and *passim*).

[40] Robert C. Feenstra, "Voluntary Export Restraint in US Autos, 1980–81: Quality, Employment and Welfare Effects", in Robert E. Baldwin and Anne O. Krueger (eds.), *The Structure and Evolution of Recent US Trade Policy*, University of Chicago Press, 1984, ch. 2, pp. 35–66.

[41] Robert C. Feenstra, "Quality Change under Trade Restraints: Theory and Evidence from Japanese Autos", *Quarterly Journal of Economics*, vol. 102 (1988), pp. 131–46.

and European cars, and induced rises in their prices.[42] American automobile manufacturers' profits soared in 1983 and 1984, as did the profits of Japanese automobile manufacturers on their American sales.

In other words, the Japanese export restraint acted as a cartelizing restriction of output. The Reagan administration's announcement in March 1985 that, because of the harm inflicted on US consumers, it would not seek renewal of the voluntary export restraint was met with a storm of protests from the American auto producers. Spurred, in part, by proposals before Congress to legislate Japanese import quotas for cars, the government of Japan announced that it would unilaterally continue to administer the export restraint, but would raise the maximum number of vehicles to be exported by 24 percent. Subsequent Japanese exports fell substantially short of the maximum limit in each year that the voluntary restraint remained in effect. In 1992 the Japanese government reduced the export limit again, but with minimal apparent effects. The restraint was finally allowed by the government of Japan to lapse altogether in March 1994.

America's machine tool industry was among the most persistent in seeking protection from Japanese imports, eventually winning voluntary export restraints. After the industry association (National Machine Tool Builders Association) failed in its 1977 petition for anti-dumping penalties, one firm, Houdaille Industries, citing a never-before invoked clause in the US tax code, petitioned the President in June 1982 to deny investment tax-credits for US purchasers of Japanese machine tools, on the grounds that the Japanese manufacturers had obtained Japanese government subsidies. The petition was not affirmed. In March 1983 the industry association again petitioned for special protection, this time on the basis of necessity to the national defense, exploiting a stipulation in the 1962 Trade Expansion Act. This petition, too, seemed headed for oblivion until a 1986 incident in which a Japanese machine tool company, Toshiba Machine Corporation, and a Norwegian one, Kongsberg Corporation, were found to have sold machine tools for milling quiet propellers for submarines to the USSR, a serious breach of Alliance security policy. In the ensuing flap, the government of Japan and that of Taiwan agreed to voluntary restraint of machine tool exports from 1987 to 1993. West Germany and

Switzerland informally agreed not to expand their US exports of machine tools in response. Machine tool prices in the USA seem to have risen slightly in 1987 as a result of the export restraint. But in 1988 the expansion of Japanese machine tool plants in the USA largely reversed this price rise.[43] Japan had already imposed voluntary restraint on machine tool exports to the EU in 1986, and these remained in effect until 1993.

The late 1980s marked the high tide of Japan's voluntary export restraints. Table 8.5 indicates the most important ones, including some not discussed here. A comprehensive listing is difficult given the non-transparent way in which such restraints often have come about. MITI estimated that in 1989, 29 percent of Japan's merchandise exports to the USA and 5 percent of its merchandise exports to the EEC were subject to restraints.[44] It might seem from the pervasiveness of voluntary export restraints, that expansion of Japan's exports to the United States in the 1960s and 1970s had met a substantial protectionist response. But, then again, perhaps not. One of the striking differences between voluntary export restraints and either import quotas or tariffs is their porousness. Diversions of trade through third countries, quality upgrading, and production in foreign plants—all afford ways around an onerous export restraint.[45] The previous discussion has included references to all of these. Voluntary export restraints, at the very least, pre-empted more severe and more permanent forms of protection. As a result of the Uruguay Round agreement, existing voluntary export restraints will be allowed to lapse and new ones will not be imposed.

By 1985, political pressure for more effective protection from Japanese imports was building in the USA. American and Japanese government leaders

---

[42] Dinopoulus and Kreinin found that American prices of European cars were raised by about one-third in 1984, as a result of the Japanese VER: Elias Dinopoulus and Mordechai E. Kreinin, "Effects of the US–Japan Auto VER on European Prices and on US Welfare", *Review of Economics and Statistics*, vol. 70, no. 3 (August 1988), pp. 484–91.

[43] Elias Dinopoulos and Mordechai E. Kreinin, "The US VER on Machine Tools: Causes and Effects", in Robert E. Baldwin (ed.), *Empirical Studies of Commercial Policy*, University of Chicago Press, 1991, ch. 4, pp. 113–29.

[44] General Agreement on Tariffs and Trade, *Trade Policy Review, Japan, 1990*, Geneva: GATT, November 1990, p. 200.

[45] Jagdish Bhagwati, "VERs, Quid Pro Quo DFI, and VIEs: Political–Economic–Theoretic Analyses", *International Economic Journal*, vol. 1, no. 1 (1987), pp. 1–14.

Table 8.5. Voluntary export restraints of Japan

Countries and affected products	Duration
USA	
Ball bearings	–Jul. 1993
Metal flatware	1962–Dec. 1994
Pottery and chinaware	1964–Dec. 1994
Textiles and clothing	Oct. 1974–1992
Passenger cars	Apr. 1981–Mar. 1994
Steel and steel products	Jan. 1969–Dec. 1971
	May 1972–Dec. 1974
	Oct. 1984–Mar. 1992
Machine tools	Dec. 1987–Dec. 1993
European Union	
Ball bearings	–Jul. 1993
Cotton fabrics	1978–
Steel products	1972–Apr. 1992
Machine tools	1986–Dec. 1993
Passenger cars	1986–Dec. 1999
Forklift trucks	1987–Dec. 1994
UK	
Pottery and chinaware	1964–
Light and heavy commercial vehicles	1975–92
Passenger cars	1977–92
Clothing	1978–Dec. 1994
Canada	
Ball bearings	–Jul. 1993
Pottery and chinaware	1964–
Polyester filament, fabrics, clothing	1982–Dec. 1994
Passenger cars	1986–88
Australia	
Ball bearings	–Jul. 1993

Source: GATT, *Trade Policy Review: Japan 1994*, Geneva: GATT Secretariat, 1995, table 1v.16, pp. 81–2.

were able to deflect the pressure only by switching the focus away from the US market and toward the expanded sale of US products in Japan.

Expanded access to the Japanese market

In 1985 anti-Japan, protectionist sentiment in Washington reached its high-water mark. Not co-incidentally, that was also the year of peak real appreciation of the dollar relative to the yen, caused by the Reagan administration's ongoing expansionary fiscal policy and the anti-inflationary monetary policy of the Federal Reserve Bank under the chair-manship of Paul Volker (1979–87). It was the strong dollar, and not the "closed" Japanese market or "unfair" Japanese trading practices, that had promoted sales of Japanese goods in the USA and inhibited the sale of US products in Japan. Nevertheless, in March 1985 the US Senate unanimously passed a non-binding resolution proposed by Senator John Danforth (Republican, Missouri) condemning Japan as an unfair trader, and imploring the President to retaliate. Senator Lloyd Bentsen (Democrat, Texas), in supporting the measure, famously remarked, "We are in a trade war, and we are losing it." Legislated protection directed specifically at Japan now seemed dangerously possible, and Congressman Richard Gephardt (Democrat, Missouri), in concert with Senator Lloyd Bentsen and Congressman Dan Rostenkowski (Democratic, Illinois), the chairman of the House Ways and Means Committee, provided the instrument, in the form of proposed legislation that, in blatant contravention of the GATT, would have imposed a 25 percent surtax on imports from any nation with a large bilateral surplus in its trade with the USA. Japan, clearly the intended target, was one of only four nations to meet the proposed criterion (the other nations were Brazil, Korea, and Taiwan). This was the background against which the G-5 financial ministers, meeting at the Plaza Hotel in New York on September 22, 1985, agreed to co-ordinate their nations' respective monetary policies to effect a depreciation of the US dollar. The ensuing real depreciation of the dollar relative to the yen, at first, seemed to have little inhibiting effect on Japanese exports to the USA. As argued in the previous chapter, this, in a delicious irony, was probably a reflection of the large portion of those exports subject to voluntary restraints.

The governments of both Japan and the United States now stepped up their ongoing attempts to deflect the growing protectionist sentiment in the USA, by shifting the focus toward expanding the sales of US products in Japan. The government of Japan had already entered a series of negotiations with the United States to remove offending regulations claimed to impede the sale of US products in four specific sectors: telecommunications, medical equipment/pharmaceuticals, microelectronics, and forest products. These negotiations, initiated at the January 1985 summit meeting between Prime Minister Nakasone Yasuhiro and President Ronald Reagan, became known as the Market-Oriented, Sector-Specific (MOSS) talks. In 1986, transportation machinery and automotive parts were added to the agenda. In these last two sectors, the Americans argued that exclusionary business practices were impeding American export sales in Japan. The MOSS talks concluded in August 1987, having achieved only modest Japanese concessions, mostly in the form of tariff reductions and some relaxation of regulations.

In October 1985, Prime Minister Nakasone empanelled a special advisory commission chaired by Maekawa Haruo, former governor of the Bank of Japan (dubbed the Advisory Group on Economic Structural Adjustment for International Harmony, but widely known as the Maekawa commission), to recommend measures that would expand foreign access to the Japanese market. The commission issued reports in April 1986 and May 1987 recommending, among other things, expansionary fiscal policy to stimulate Japanese aggregate demand, relaxation of government restrictions inhibiting the opening of large stores, and relaxation of agricultural land-use controls. The Maekawa reports, like the MOSS talks, had almost no noticeable effect on the sentiment in Congress supporting a more aggressive US government posture toward Japan–US trade. The Reagan administration, belatedly, was seeking to effect such a posture, all the while avoiding, as far as possible, seriously damaging relations with Japan. This required a delicate balancing act.

The 1974 US Trade Act included stipulations (Section 301) authorizing the president to retaliate against a foreign country that maintains "unjustifiable or unreasonable" tariff or other import restrictions or export subsidies, "substantially reducing sales of the competitive United States product". This afforded US exporters an avenue for enlisting US government leverage in their pursuit of expanded access to foreign markets; but before 1985 very few had availed themselves of it, and fewer still attained positive results. Now this would change. In September 1985, the Reagan administration, amidst much fanfare, opened some new Section 301 investigations, including one involving cigarette sales in Japan, and threatened retaliation in another long-standing but unresolved 301 case involving Japanese import quotas on leather hides and leather shoes. Japan responded to the cigarette complaint by agreeing to eliminate its tariffs on cigarettes. Sales of American cigarettes in Japan subsequently rose from less than $100 million in 1985 to more than $1 billion in 1990.[46] Also about this time, acting on its own initiatives and on earlier Section 301 petitions and dumping complaints by the Semiconductor Industry Association, the USA entered negotiations with the government of Japan that led to the August 1986 Semiconductor agreement, stipulating minimum selling prices for certain types of Japanese semiconductor chips in the United States, Japan, and third countries.[47] The agreement also included a side letter stating an expectation that foreign sales of such chips in Japan would at least double over five years, from 10 percent in 1986 to 20 percent in 1991.

In March 1987, the USA claimed that Japan had violated this agreement, both by underpricing in third countries and by failing to make ample progress toward the goal of expanded foreign market share in Japan, and it imposed sanctions in the form of retaliatory 100 percent tariffs (on laptop and desktop computers, color televisions, and power hand tools). In 1991 the semiconductor agreement was renegotiated and extended for five years; it was ultimately allowed to lapse in 1996. The semiconductor arrangement was nothing less than a Japanese international price-setting cartel instigated by the US government, a clear example that export-promoting trade policies do not always promote economic efficiency. Meanwhile, the US government continued to wrest substantive concessions on specific sectoral issues as outcomes of Section 301 investigations (abolition of Japan's import quotas of beef and citrus in July 1988), or under the threat of such investigations (relaxation of restrictions on activities of foreign lawyers in Japan in February 1987, relaxation of import quotas on fish products in March 1987, the opening to foreign firms of Japanese procurement of construction services in May 1988, and the relaxation of restrictions on foreign entry into Japan's cellular telephone business in June 1989). Cases such as these remain a prominent aspect of US trade policy toward Japan, even now.

---

[46] Thomas O. Bayard and Kimberly Ann Elliot, *Reciprocity and Retaliation in US Trade Policy*, Washington, DC: Institute for International Economics, September 1994, pp. 414–15.

[47] For details on the semiconductor agreement, the following is excellent: Kenneth Flamm, *Mismanaged Trade? Strategic Policy and the Semiconductor Industry*, Washington, DC: Brookings Institution, 1996, esp. ch. 4.

Throughout 1986 and 1987, the US Congress continued to debate measures for an even more aggressive policy toward Japan. This eventually culminated in its attaching the so-called "Super 301" provision to the 1988 Omnibus Trade and Competitiveness Act (the law authorizing US participation in the Uruguay Round). The Super 301 provision was intended to mandate the threat of trade sanctions against recalcitrant foreign nations, Japan in particular. Specifically, it required that the US Trade Representative,[48] by May 31 of each of the two succeeding years (1989 and 1990), publicly name "priority foreign countries" exhibiting numerous and pervasive "acts, policies, or practices" impeding US exports, and impose retaliatory sanctions if in the ensuing year the offending measures were not redressed. To the surprise of no one, on May 25, 1989, Japan was named (along with Brazil and India) as a priority foreign country threatened by US retaliation. On the same day, the US Trade Representative, Carla Hills, announced the beginning of special negotiations between the governments of Japan and the USA on wide-ranging economic issues, to be known as the Structural Impediments Initiative (SII).

The Super 301 agenda for 1989 included (besides Brazil's import quotas, and India's closed insurance market and restrictions on inward foreign direct investment), Japan's exclusionary government procurement of supercomputers and satellites, and its barriers to trade in forest products. Japanese government purchase of supercomputers had also been on the agenda of the MOSS talks, which had resulted in only token purchases of US supercomputers. The 1988 law enacting the Super 301 provision had included a "sense of Congress" section deploring Japan's unresponsiveness in the matter and urging the US Trade Representative to attach a high priority to it, so its designation by the USTR Hills was, in a sense, pre-ordained. In June 1990, the two countries announced an agreement abolishing discriminatory features of Japan's government procurement of supercomputers and settling the dispute.[49] Tariffs on products fabricated of wood had been a subject of US complaints at least since 1977, and had also been a topic in the MOSS talks. In the MOSS agreement, Japan had agreed to accelerate scheduled tariff reductions, and to alter building codes and product standards and testing in ways intended to benefit American exporters, but this did not go far enough to satisfy the US congressmen representing lumber-exporting states. In April 1990, the government of Japan agreed to further revisions in tariffs and building standards. Inclusion of satellites in the Super 301 designation was an oddity because the US producers of satellites had not lobbied for it. Rather, officials of the Bush administration, acting on their own counsel, had apparently concluded that it was in the US national interest to pre-empt Japanese development of commercial satellite technology. In June 1990, Japan agreed to enforce non-discriminatory and transparent procurement of commercial satellites. US Trade Representative Carla Hills announced no new priority countries in June 1990, asserting completion of the Uruguay Round to be the top priority. She again designated India, having achieved no results, but suspended the investigation and imposed no retaliatory sanctions. Having satisfactorily resolved each of the Japanese issues raised under Super 301 and the Brazilian issue, she designated neither country a continuing priority.

The joint report concluding the SII talks was also issued in June 1990. The broad-ranging SII agenda—structural impediments to trade, factors affecting the bilateral trade balance, anti-competitive practices—more or less precluded tangible results. Japan agreed to enlarged government infrastructure investment over the ensuing decade. (It probably would have done this anyway.) It agreed to enhance anti-monopoly enforcement and increase penalties for violating anti-monopoly laws. (These laws remain toothless and inconsequential, which in all likelihood means only that large firms in Japan including foreign ones are less impeded by inefficient prohibitions.) It agreed to reform the Large Store Law, expediting the process of reviewing applications to open large stores (but that law is probably not a major source of inefficiency anyway). Corresponding features of the US economy and economic

---

[48] The US Trade Representative is the USA's chief negotiator of international trade policy agreements. The position, originally titled Special Trade Representative, was created in 1962 to facilitate negotiation of the Kennedy Round. In 1974 the office was renamed and elevated from ambassadorial to cabinet-level status.

[49] On the supercomputer agreement and other Super 301 cases involving Japan, see Bayard and Elliot, *Reciprocity and Retaliation* (fn. 46), ch. 5, pp. 101–48; and Michael Mastunduno, "Setting Market Access Priorities: The Use of Super 301 in US Trade with Japan", *The World Economy*, vol. 15, no. 6 (November 1992), pp. 729–53.

policy had also been on the SII agenda. The United States agreed to reduce its federal budget deficit, increase support for research and development, and improve workforce training. SII was, at best, an earnest attempt, by both sides, to hold US protectionist pressures in check.

The Clinton administration took a somewhat different tack than had been embodied in SII, focusing its demands on precisely quantified expansions of US sales to Japan, similar to the side letter in the 1986 semiconductor agreement. The Clinton administration's Japan policy was unveiled at the July 1993, Tokyo summit meeting of the G7 nations, in the form of an announcement that Japan and the United States would enter yet another round of bilateral negotiations on trade issues, this time under the rubric of US–Japan Framework for a New Economic Partnership (known as the "Framework" talks). The talks were to focus on access to the Japanese markets for insurance, vehicles and automotive parts, telecommunications (NTT purchases), flat glass, financial services, intellectual property rights, and foreign direct investment in Japan.

The Framework talks began during a difficult period in Japanese politics. In August 1993, the month after initiation of the talks, the scandal-plagued Liberal Democratic Party fell from power after thirty-eight years of continual rule. The new prime minister, Hosokawa Morihiro, leader of the Japan New political party (Nihon Shin Tō, newly formed from a splinter faction of the LDP), assumed office as the leader of an eight-party coalition. Meanwhile, the Framework talks were at an impasse, with Japan opposed, on principal, to the setting of quantitative targets for increased Japanese purchases of US goods in designated sectors. At the rather tense February 1994 Clinton–Hosokawa Washington summit, the two leaders announced that the Framework talks were deadlocked and would be suspended indefinitely. The following month, March 1994, President Clinton, in what was widely viewed as a slap at Japan, issued an executive order reinstating the Super 301 provisions for an additional year. (The original Super 301 amendment had remained in effect for the two years 1989–90 only, and attempts in Congress to renew it had met with failure.)

The new, Clinton Super 301, which was extended thrice by executive order, then allowed to lapse in 1997–8, and again reinstated in 1999, manifests slight differences over the previous Super 301 statute, intended to soften foreign distaste. The USTR is to designate unfair practices, not countries, and is explicitly granted wider discretion than in the earlier statute, both in announcing such priorities and in deciding whether to initiate investigations or invoke retaliatory sanctions.

Prime Minister Hosokawa was forced to resign on April 8, 1994, over questions about the financing of his twelve-year previous prefectural governor campaign, and was succeeded by Hata Tsutomo of the Renaissance Party (Shinsei Tō, another splinter off the LDP), leader of the same eight-party coalition that had assumed power the previous year. The next month, on May 23, 1994, the governments of America and Japan reached an understanding that enabled a resumption of the Framework talks. However, the very next month, June 1994, Hata was forced to resign after his overly tepid response to controversial statements by the Minister of Justice about the 1937 Nanking massacre, and Murayama Tomiichi, president of the Japan Socialist Party and leader of a three-party coalition, became the fourth Japanese prime minister within twelve months. The Framework talks, which were extended for a second year in June 1995, ended in a number of sectoral accords, including an agreement in June 1995 to increase Japanese purchases of US automobiles and auto parts, concluded only after the United States threatened a retaliatory tariff on Japanese luxury cars if its demands were not met.

The era of wide-ranging demands for expanded US access to the Japanese market is, for the time being, over.[50] But it could be revived if Japan's burgeoning exports again provoke a protectionist response in the United States.

Conclusion

The composition of Japan's trade well reflects its endowment of productive resources in the way that the Ricardian theory of comparative advantage predicts. Japan imports the petroleum and other natural

---

[50] On the history, and apparent recent demise, of US aggressiveness toward Japan, see Douglas Ostrom, "US–Japan Trade Relations: Bilateral versus Multilateral Options", Japan Economic Institute Report, no. 43A, November 14, 1997.

resources that it lacks, and exports manufactures that intensively employ the skilled labor and capital that it has in abundance; and, through foreign direct investment in lesser developed nations, it exports the services of entrepreneurs and managers that it also has in abundance. Accordingly, Japan's integration into the world economy has contributed to the international division of labor and thereby has expanded the consumption possibilities of both Japan and other countries. To preserve and enlarge these gains, the nations of the world have expended much diplomatic effort in erecting and maintaining a liberal international trading regime. The protection-

ist response in America to the postwar growth of Japanese exports threatened that process but did not derail it. The political rhetoric attending these events can easily confuse us, and is often meant to do so. We should resist the confusion.

The barriers that continue to separate Japan's economy from that of the rest of the world are barriers of language and culture, not of laws and regulations. They are not the creation of government, nor are they the product of hidden conspiracies. The barriers are real, as evidenced by the paucity in Japan of establishments controlled and operated by foreigners, but they are not insurmountable.

FURTHER READING

■ Jagdish Bhagwati and Hugh T. Patrick (eds.), *Aggressive Unilateralism: America's 301 Trade Policy and the World Trading System*, University of Michigan Press, 1990. Includes thoughtful essays and comments on the American government's adoption, in the 1980s, of a more aggressive posture in its trade disputes with Japan.

■ I. M. Destler, *American Trade Politics*, 3rd edn, Institute for International Economics, 1995. Places the succession of Japan–US trade talks and trade disputes in the US political context.

■ General Agreement on Tariffs and Trade (GATT), *Trade Policy Review: Japan 1996*, 2 vols., Geneva: GATT, 1997. Fourth biennial GATT review of Japan's trade policies and agreements. GATT publishes similar biennial reviews of the trade policies of the USA, EU, and Canada, and publishes reviews of the trade policies of other nations at less frequent intervals.

■ Christopher Howe, *The Origins of Japanese Trade Supremacy: Development and Technology in Asia from 1540 to the Pacific War*, University of Chicago Press, 1996. Describes and analyzes Japan's evolving trade patterns, focusing particularly on the Meiji era and first half of the twentieth century, drawing on an extremely rich bibliography; includes many tables.

■ Paul R. Krugman, "Increasing Returns, Imperfect Competition and the Positive Theory of International Trade", in Gene M. Grossman and Kenneth Rogoff (eds.), *Handbook of International Economics*, iii, Amsterdam: North-Holland, 1995, pp. 1243–77. Recent review of the new trade theories by one of its originators.

■ Masaru Yoshitomi and Edward M. Graham (eds.), *Foreign Direct Investment in Japan*, Brookfield, Mass.: Edward Elgar, 1996. Economists address the paucity of Japan's inward foreign direct investment.

Industrial Policy | 9

Industrial policy refers to government authorities' use of subsidies, tax credits, trade restrictions, antitrust exemptions, and other such measures to direct resources toward or away from specific, targeted industries. Proponents of industrial policy argue that it has succeeded grandly in raising Japan's national income. But such arguments frequently rely upon the obviously biased testaments of high Japanese government officials or upon hypothetical arguments that establish only the logical possibility that Japan's industrial policy improved welfare. Careful empirical analyses point toward less sanguine assessments.

In the debates about industrial policy, advocates and critics alike have focused on Japan as the key example of a country that has a coherent one. Probably this is because Japan's industrial policy resides in unique institutions—so much so that "Japanese-style" industrial policy has itself become a generic category. The defining institutions of Japanese-style industrial policy include government financial intermediaries and an elite bureaucracy with broad powers. High among the industrial policy elite in Japan are the bureaucrats of the much vaunted MITI—the Ministry of International Trade and Industry. Any informed assessment of the role of government in shaping Japan's economy has got to confront industrial policy, and MITI, squarely.

Economists' analysis of Japanese industrial policy has been caricatured as holding the view that industrial policy cannot have been successful, therefore it was not.[1] As with all good caricatures, this one brings a smile of recognition, but exaggerates. Intellectually respectable arguments in support of an industrial policy do exist. Each of them derives from the premise that private investors elide some costs or benefits of industrial expansion. Where the premise is true, Smith's invisible hand fumbles and an industrial policy that improves resource allocation becomes a logical possibility.

Thinking about industrial policy

Before evaluating Japan's industrial policy, we need first to consider industrial policy generically. How do we define industrial policy? What valid arguments support it? And what sorts of industries would a wise industrial policy promote?

Industrial policy usually connotes a sort of metapolicy, a broad set of government policies all of which promote the same specific targeted industry or industries, or avert resources away from particular industries. The industries that postwar Japanese industrial policy is most often argued to have promoted include petrochemicals, steel, automobiles and semiconductors. Each at various times benefited from import restraints, subsidies, antitrust exemptions, and so on. Also, Japanese government-orchestrated merger and cartelization hastened the withdrawal of resources from aluminum smelting, shipbuilding, and textiles. And these too are widely accepted as

---

[1] Chalmers Johnson, quoting Robert Kuttner (*Atlantic Monthly*, February 1985), appreciatively: "Economics knows only that Japanese economic planning didn't help, because it couldn't have, *a priori*": Chalmers Johnson, "Studies of Japanese Political Economy: A Crisis in Theory", *Japan Foundation Newsletter*, vol. 16, no. 3 (December 1988).

instances of industrial policy. Outside of Japan, the variety of ways in which the US government has supported the production and export of advanced weaponry—including government procurement, tax credits, government enterprise (NASA), and trade protection—is often described as an American example of industrial policy.

Virtually all government policies distort the allocation of resources in some manner. The policies that together constitute an *industrial policy* divert resources in a coherent and intended fashion, toward some particular industries or sectors and away from others. But which industries should be favored? Which industries should be retrenched? Some widely repeated answers to these questions turn out to be specious, but intellectually rigorous blueprints for industrial policy do exist. Let us consider each of the most frequently offered criteria for industrial targeting.

"High value-added"

Many admirers of Japan's industrial policy assert that it favors the industries with "high value-added", as though the common sense of such a policy were self-evident. One origin of this notion may be the famous 1960 "national income doubling plan" of the Ikeda administration, which called explicitly for the promotion of high value-added industries. By value-added is meant the difference between the market value of an industry's output and its payments for intermediate goods. An industry's value-added equals its payments to the suppliers of productive factors (e.g. labor, capital, land) plus any economic profit it earns. Any industry that is a large employer of the nation's resources is apt to have high value-added. Therefore, if taken literally, diverting resources toward high value-added industries means diverting resources toward industries that are already large. Surely proponents of targeting high value-added industries have something else in mind, but what?

Perhaps by "high value-added industry" is meant an industry in which value-added per worker is relatively high.[2] An industry's value-added measures its contribution to the value of national output—GDP. So concentrating resources in industries with high value-added per worker would increase the total GDP, right? Actually, wrong! In the competitive economy profits are zero[3] and value-added corresponds to factor payments. Value-added per worker then equals (the market value of) the average product of labor. As every economics student knows, optimal allocation requires that it is the value of *marginal* product of labor that is equal across firms and industries, not that of *average* product of labor.[4] At the optimal allocation, equality of value-added per worker across industries would be a remarkable coincidence.

Nor is this all. In the competitive economy, resources already are allocated optimally, so that the value of marginal product of each input in each industry equals its price, without government direction. The reason? The value of marginal product of an input is what employing more of it adds to the competitive firm's revenues. If this exceeds the input price, then employing more of the input is profitable. Firms expand resource employment until doing so further would not add to their profits. Government direction of resources toward industries with high value-added per worker would allocate according to a wrong criterion. Smith's invisible hand allocates according to the correct criterion (setting aside for the moment important qualifications such as public goods, externalities, and other such market failures). This logic is represented diagrammatically in Figure 9.1.

Or perhaps an industry with "high value-added" is a somewhat obtuse way of referring to an industry with great economic profits, that is, high value-added relative to its overall employment of inputs. Allocating according to this criterion may be correct, but it is the same criterion that guides Smith's invisible hand. In other words, if an industry is earning profits, then one expects that private entrepreneurs will be lured to it even without

---

[2] The Japanese capitalist developmental state operates by "facilitating changes of industrial structure to keep as many high-value-added jobs in Japan as possible": Chalmers Johnson, "The People Who Invented the Mechanical Nightingale", in Carol Gluck and Stephen R. Graubard (eds.), *Showa: The Japan of Hirohito*, New York: W.W. Norton, 1992, ch. 5, at p. 74.

[3] In Japan in 1985 economic profits of all firms may have equaled about 1% of GDP. See Ch. 12.

[4] Value of marginal product of labor is the market value of the added output made possible by employment of an additional increment of labor. It is the added revenue of a competitive firm that hires an additional unit of labor, and sells output at the market price (which it takes as given because its output is such a small component of the total industry supply).

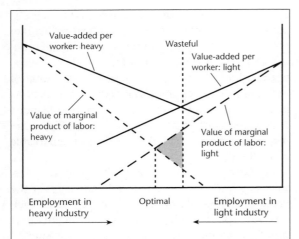

Figure 9.1. Directing resources toward an industry with high value-added per worker

In the competitive economy, resources are allocated optimally, without government direction: the (market) value of each input's marginal product is the same in every industry. Diverting workers instead toward industries with higher value-added per worker, i.e. toward "heavy" and away from "light", reduces GDP by an amount equal to the shaded triangle.

government direction. Yet an influential MITI white paper of May 1971 argued that the government should promote industries that had prospects of rapid technological advance and faced an income-elastic demand because these were destined to flourish.[5] Such insights would hardly seem beyond the ken of private investors. In fact, private investors stake their personal fortunes on such calculations, whereas government bureaucrats do not. In any event, the existence in postwar Japan of government-owned financial intermediaries made it inevitable that bureaucrats would allocate loanable funds there. To argue that government intermediaries should target industries destined to be profitable amounts to proposing that they mimic the behavior of private investors. Is there a role for industrial policy not to mimic, but to surpass, market forces acting alone? Many analysts of Japanese industrial policy seem to think so.

National defense

A lot of Japanese government support of industry from the Meiji era to the present has been predicated on its contribution to national defense. Defense is the classic example of a pure public good, one that is nondivisible and that can be consumed by many persons without congestion. Few contest the appropriateness of government provision of national defense, but why should it entail government promotion of defense-related industries? There are reasons. The reluctance of nations to arm their potential adversaries prevents international trade in weapons from extending as far as the normal forces of comparative advantage would warrant. This imparts a bias toward producing weapons rather than importing them, one that is uncharacteristic of civilian goods. And because of this, something like an industrial policy often attends the government accumulation of arms. That is, in order to accumulate arms it may be necessary to nurture a domestic arms-producing industry. The Meiji government's promotion of military-related industries has to be understood in this light. If, beginning about 1896, Japan was to accumulate military assets commensurate to its imperialistic aspirations, then government promotion of industries producing ships, steel, chemicals, and machine tools could be justified, even if it depleted the national wealth and retarded development of the civilian economy.

There is a further argument rationalizing government support of defense-related industries, which is due to UCLA economist Earl Thompson.[6] To maintain a credible defense, it may be necessary to allow naked government appropriation of private property in wartime. Conscription, commandeering of ships and factories, and price controls are familiar examples. The anticipation of such extraordinary measures in wartime discourages peacetime private investment in those assets most subject to confiscation. Broadly subsidizing defense industries might correct the distortion and improve resource allocation. This argument presumes that defense industries also serve civilian purposes and that it is efficient for them to exist in peacetime. These premises need to be carefully examined in each instance, but where they are true an industrial policy merits informed consideration. There also are other sophisticated arguments for industrial policy.

---

5 "70 nendai no tsūshō sangyō seisaku" (Industrial policy of the 1970s), *Tsūshō Jaanaru*, vol. 4, no. 3 (1971), pp. 1–67.

6 Earl Thompson, "An Economic Basis for the 'National Defense Argument' for Aiding Certain Industries", *Journal of Political Economy*, vol. 87, no. 1 (February 1979), pp. 1–36.

Marshallian externalities

Cost savings sometimes arise from the general development of an industry, and remain external to the calculations of any one firm. Economists refer to such phenomena as externalities, external effects, or spillovers. The famous economist Alfred Marshall long ago described "the advantages which people following the same skilled trade get from near neighborhood to one another. The mysteries of the trade become no mysteries; but are as it were in the air, and children learn many of them unconsciously."[7] No firm will decide to expand its output, fully because of its implied contribution to these propitious neighborhood effects, and precisely for this reason there will tend to be less output in the industry than is economically efficient. Where costs come about in the same way as the neighborhood effects described by Marshall, industries grow larger than is economically efficient. Environmental pollution is the familiar example of a cost that arises as a Marshallian externality, or spillover.

An obvious case can be made for government promotion of industries with external benefits, and for government retrenchment of industries with external costs. But Marshallian externalities may be less pervasive and less consequential than many suppose. This is because clever entrepreneurs often find ways of converting an external economy to an internal economy, or of forcing others to internalize external diseconomies. For instance, if customers drawn to one shop become more likely to patronize its neighboring shops, then entrepreneurs will establish shopping centers and rent space to merchants. Or, if polluting activity depreciates the market value of adjoining land, entrepreneurs might amass large land parcels, attach restrictive covenants that preclude polluting activity, and then subdivide and resell.[8] The external economies or diseconomies that persist, and that offer a possible rationale for government intervention, elude such internalization either because the costs of internalization are too great or the benefits are too small. The case for government intervention in such industries has to rest on arguments that whatever caused the cost of private action to be prohibitively large does not similarly afflict the costs of government administration.

There is a further important caveat. Not all externalities are Marshallian in nature. Pecuniary externalities, those that operate only through price changes, imply no economic inefficiency. Consider the following example. Expansion by any one shipbuilder leads it to demand more skilled workmen, bidding up the wage rate that must be paid by all the firms in the industry. But the shipbuilder will ignore the increases in wage payments that its own expansion indirectly imposes on the other firms in its industry. Is this externality the logical basis for government retrenchment of the shipbuilding industry? It is a pecuniary externality (not a Marshallian one) and results in no inefficiency. An increase in the wage bill reduces employers' profit, but the reduction in profit is not a cost, but a transfer: whatever the employers lose, workers gain. Transfers are correctly ignored in determining the economically efficient scale of industry, defined as the scale at which the last increment of output is just worth the added *cost*.

Pecuniary externalities recur with frequency in popular arguments for industrial policy, but they hold no sway with informed opinion. A common instance is the argument that government should promote industries that supply intermediate goods to other industries, or, as it is usually stated, that have strong "linkages" with other industries. The argument goes like this. Increased supply and lower price of computer chips benefits the many producers and consumers of products that use computer chips. Computer chip producers ignore these benefits of their expanded output and so do not produce enough, or so the argument goes. Actually, computer chip producers fail to produce enough only if they *do* ignore any reductions in price which their added output effects. If the computer chip industry is competitive, each of its members supplies a small fraction of the total, takes price as given, and supplies an economically efficient amount, such that marginal cost equals price.[9] If, on the other hand,

7 Alfred Marshall, *Principles of Economics*, 8th edn, London: Macmillan, 1947, p. 271 (1st edn 1890).

8 We take up further examples in the chapter on environmental policy of Japan.

9 Here, marginal cost needs to be carefully defined to take into account the fact that an expanded output of semiconductors entails learning which reduces future costs of producing. (For semiconductor chips, such learning effects are quite large.) See Andrew R. Dick, "Learning by Doing and Dumping in the Semiconductor Industry", *Journal of Law and Economics*, vol. 54, no. 1 (April 1991), pp. 133–59.

the suppliers form a cartel that recognizes the depressing effect on price of industry expansion, the cartel will contract output to push up the price and add to industry profit. The cartel price exceeds marginal cost and cartel output is less than the efficient amount. Competitive industries supply the efficient amount, precisely because they ignore the pecuniary externalities that their added output confers on consumers and other producers. Marshallian externalities, but not pecuniary externalities, constitute a logical case for industrial policy. International oligopolies afford additional sophisticated rationales for industrial policy.

International oligopoly

Oligopolies—industries with few firms—earn economic profits, and industrial policy might enable the nation to attain more of these economic profits. This sort of industrial policy exploits the strategic advantages of precommitment. More specifically, if government subsidy, promotion, and protection precommits a nation to a large output of some product, foreign suppliers might rationally retrench, conceding the lion's share of the world-wide industry's output and profit.[10] This sort of example well fits the businessman's view of world trade as a competition for scarce prizes, namely export profits, but in fact the "prizes" are small. By all measures, oligopoly profits account for a trivial percentage of national income in all developed nations, including Japan. Nevertheless the argument is a clever one. Its suggestion that, in an oligopoly, market power might be exploited by expanding output rather than contracting it is downright counterintuitive, but still logical.

For industries in which the nation's cumulative share of world output approaches monopoly, national welfare requires not an expansion of output as in the argument just related, but a contraction of it and thereby a rise in its price to foreign consumers. This might be accomplished by implementing an industrial policy that expands the set of goods the nation exports.[11] Subsidizing production in selected industries diverts resources away from the other industries. Therefore one way of retrenching export industries is to subsidize import industries—ideally, from the standpoint of the nation's own economic welfare, those import industries in which the

nation's comparative *dis*advantage is the smallest. If production subsidies are focused on these industries, they will become export industries rather than import industries. Nevertheless, the putative goal is greater profit in the original, monopolized, export industries. The argument amounts to rationalizing industrial policy as a way of exploiting the nation's market power in the world economy. Such a circuitous and blunt way of achieving this aim would seem justifiable only if, instead of a few industries in which the nation held a monopoly, there were many; in other words, fully exploiting international market power would require a broad retrenchment of the nation's original exports.

Thus, there exist a number of logical arguments in support of an industrial policy. Having now reviewed them, we can readily understand why proponents of industrial policy have focused particular rhetoric on the so called "high technology" industries.

High technology

The high technology industries elicit special consideration as candidates for government promotion, on the basis of just about all of the valid arguments already reviewed. These are industries in which the general progress of science gains relatively quick application, and which consequently devote more resources to invention and discovery than others and so exhibit more rapid cost-reducing innovation. Lately, the high tech industries include those producing chemicals, pharmaceuticals, and microelectronics.

Many high technology industries either contribute to the nation's production of weapons or can be rapidly converted to that purpose. This would perhaps be a sufficient reason for arguing that government should promote investments in these industries, but there are two additional justifications. First, the high tech industries' contributions to the stock of knowledge have the characteristics

---

10 James A. Brander and Barbara J. Spencer, "Export Subsidies and International Market Share Rivalry", *Journal of International Economics*, vol. 16 (1985), pp. 83–100; James A. Brander and Barbara J. Spencer, "International R&D Rivalry and Industrial Strategy", *Review of Economic Studies*, vol. 50 (1983), pp. 707–22.

11 Motoshige Itoh and Kazuharu Kiyono, "Welfare Enhancing Export Subsidies", *Journal of Political Economy*, vol. 95, no. 1 (Feb. 1987), pp. 115–37.

of Marshallian externality and arise in part as by-products of their outputs. Government encouragement of production in high tech industries thus amounts to promoting efficient innovation. Consider the argument in a bit more detail.

Those who create or discover new information often cannot prevent others from using it without paying for it. Where new products can be observed and imitated, or where new technologies can be copied to great advantage, inventive activity gives rise to external economies. Most nations, Japan included, offer broad government support for innovation, including patents and copyrights, tax credits and tax exemptions for research and development expenditures, government grants for scientific research, and support for higher education. The high tech industries benefit disproportionately from these measures, but many have argued that, on top of this, these industries merit specific targeting for promotion because some portion of their contribution to knowledge arises not from research, but as an inevitable consequence of production. The argument here is that high tech industries have given rise to national communities of scientists and engineers who share knowledge with one another, so that their cumulative experience exhibits propitious neighborhood effects.[12] In other words, as high tech industries produce more, the scientists and engineers they employ learn more and a portion of their learning arises as an external economy; any one firm's expansion of output automatically enhances the knowledge available to others. This sort of claim is difficult to prove, but it does afford a logical argument for policies that promote high tech industries.

The second additional reason for targeting the high tech industries is that they tend to be rather oligopolistic, and so earn economic profits that industrial policies might redistribute in favor of home country producers. The oligopolistic organization of high tech industries is a natural consequence of learning effects. Firms with greater cumulative output learn more and, until imitation diffuses the knowledge through the industry, enjoy lower cost functions than rivals. In other words, learning effects confer economies of scale. The large research expenditures of high tech industries represent fixed costs and so add even further to the economies of scale. For these reasons, high tech industries will each tend to be dominated by a few large firms that possess market power and earn economic profits. Industrial policies that promote high tech industries might succeed in shifting these profits away from foreign producers and toward domestic ones.

All of the foregoing is but a necessary prelude to our next task, an informed consideration of the mechanisms and patterns of Japanese industrial policy, from the Meiji era to the present. A final section of this chapter reviews some sophisticated analyses of the effects of Japanese industrial policy, all focusing on the postwar era.

History of Japanese industrial policy

Industrial policy in the century before the postwar era

Early Meiji and before, 1850–1885

The origins of industrial policy in Japan may be sought in the iron foundries, shipyards, and arsenals that the Tokugawa shogunate and several of the *han* governments established during the 1850s.[13] The Meiji government continued these operations and, under the slogan "increase industrial production" (*shokusan kōgyō*), established new enterprises in a variety of fields, so that in 1880, national government enterprises included three shipbuilding yards, five munitions works, ten mines, and fifty-two factories. The government also began the development of rail and telegraph networks. In 1872 it built the first rail line in Japan, connecting Tokyo and Yokohama, and in 1874 and 1877 it added rail lines connecting Kobe, Osaka, and Kyoto. During this time it also strung telegraph wires throughout the nation.

---

12 ". . . a new product often does not embody the entirety of a new technology. The know-how, the understanding of how the technology was developed, and the potential ways it can be used or modified, extends beyond the product into the network or community of people who developed the technology and helped to apply it": Michael Borrus, Laura D'Andrea Tyson, and John Zysman, "Creating Advantage: How Government Policies Shape International Trade in the Semiconductor Industry", in Paul R. Krugman (ed.), *Strategic Trade Policy and the New International Economics*, Cambridge, Mass.: MIT Press, 1986, ch. 5, at p. 93.

13 Thomas C. Smith, *Political Change and Industrial Development in Japan: Government Enterprise, 1868–1880*, Stanford University Press, 1955; see esp. ch. 1, "The Beginnings of Modern Industry", pp. 1–12.

The new government factories acquired or established between 1873 and 1876 included arsenals, explosive factories, and a shipyard, as well as a sheep ranch and woolen mill for making military uniforms, a beer brewery, cement plant, glass factory, sugar refinery, and canning plants, all employing imported technology and staffed with foreign advisers. But the most famous of the Meiji government's model factories was the silk reeling plant established in 1872 at Tomioka (in the Gumma prefecture in the mountains north of Tokyo), with the assistance of a French contractor. The government also operated two other mechanized silk reeling plants (one also in Gumma from 1877 and the other in Tokyo from 1873), and briefly in the 1870s operated two mechanized cotton spinning plants (in Kobe and in Kyushu). Between 1884 and 1887 the government sold almost all of its factories and mines to private investors, retaining only the arsenals, explosive factories, and one of the shipbuilding yards (Yokosuka).

The policies just described evoke several comments. First, government enterprise may have accounted for nearly the whole extent of industrial output in Japan, other than textiles and handicrafts, before 1880. In this sense, the government factories truly did represent an industrial policy. Instead of displacing private enterprise, the government factories diverted resources into new activities. The government enterprises were nevertheless small relative to overall economic activity in Japan which was still dominated by agriculture.

Second, the government plants were not profitable, but may still have been socially beneficial. The plants were a drain on the Meiji government's limited fiscal resources. The decision to sell the government enterprises came as an austerity measure in the wake of the extraordinary expenses that accompanied the Saga and Satsuma rebellions and the pensioning off of the samurai. But the unprofitability of the government factories does not establish that they were all mistakes. Some of them might have been justifiable as promoting the diffusion of foreign technology in Japan, a process inherently laden with Marshallian externalities. For example, the Tomioka and Tokyo silk reeling plants were set up as demonstration factories, where Japanese workers would be taught the use of French machinery and would then become instructors at private plants using similar machinery.[14] Admirers of Japanese

industrial policy argue that the Tomioka plant spurred the adoption of superior technology in silk reeling and defend it as a wise public investment, even though it was unprofitable.[15] When Japan's silk reeling industry did mechanize in the 1880s, it did so using machines roughly like the ones used in the Tomioka plant, only better adapted to the local conditions, for instance by substituting wooden parts for metal ones.

Government efforts to mechanize cotton spinning were less fruitful. The two government cotton spinning plants have already been mentioned. Also, in hopes of establishing small, water-powered cotton spinning factories, the government in 1879 imported ten sets of 2,000 mechanical spindles each, and resold them to private Japanese investors at a loss. Additional sets of spindles were financed with (prefectural) government loans. As it turned out, the profitable cotton-spinning factories of the 1880s used steam power not water power, were of too large a scale to employ the 2,000 spindles, and used double work shifts to exploit Japan's relative abundance of labor. Government efforts *may* in some way have facilitated the diffusion of foreign technology and been worth the relatively meager public expense, but nobody can say this for sure.

Third, and finally, military purposes are clearly evident in a lot of the government enterprise of the early Meiji period. Even the railroads and telegraph lines were so construed at the time, as were the shipyards and woolen mill, the arsenals and the explosives plants. National security concerns would continue to figure prominently in Japanese industrial policy.[16]

Late Meiji and early Taisho, 1885–1914

With the sale of the model factories and other enterprises, Japanese industrial policy for a time focused

---

14 Ibid. p. 59.

15 For a dissenting view on the Tomioka plant, see Kozo Yamamura, "Entrepreneurship, Ownership, and Management in Japan", in Peter Mathias and M. M. Postan (eds.), *The Cambridge Economic History of Europe*, vii, pt 2, Cambridge University Press, 1978, pp. 226–7.

16 Richard Samuels advances the provocative thesis that national security concerns underlay Japanese industrial policy not only in the Meiji era but throughout the 20th cent. and continuing to the present: see Richard J. Samuels, *"Rich Country Strong Army": National Security and the Technological Transformation of Japan*, Cornell University Press, 1994.

mainly on shipbuilding and coastal navigation. These policies were infused with national security concerns. The government's Yokosuka shipyard had survived the sale of government enterprises in the early 1880s, but most of Japan's shipyards were in private hands. During the 1895 Sino-Japanese War, Western nations denied Japan's request to borrow some of their naval vessels. The following year, to expand the fleet of ships potentially usable in wartime, the government enacted the Shipping Promotion Law and the Navigation Promotion Law. The first provided subsidies for the construction of vessels in private shipyards in Japan, and the second provided subsidies for the operation of vessels by Japanese companies. (In 1899 the subsidy for operating imported vessels was reduced to half that for operating domestically produced ones.) These were not the first subsidies for commercial shipping in Japan. The Mitsubishi Steamship Company had benefited greatly from government contracts, government loans, and various subsidies including the transfer of government vessels and other assets. The shipbuilding and shipping industries received 75 percent of all Japanese government subsidies from 1897 to 1913. Then, when Japan regained tariff autonomy in 1911, it immediately increased the tariff rate on foreign ships from 5 to 15 percent.

Another focus of late Meiji industrial policy, not wholly unrelated to the promotion of shipbuilding, was the development of integrated steel manufacture, that is the production of steel from molten pig iron formed in blast furnaces. In 1896 the government broke ground on the new Yawata steel mill (Yawata being the name of the village in Fukuoka prefecture in which it was located). It produced its first steel in 1901, increased its capacity through the next decade, and finally showed a profit in 1910. During the first decade of the twentieth century several private steel companies also were founded in Japan, but Yawata steel works accounted for 80 percent of total industry output as late as 1914, and remained the major Japanese steel producer into the 1930s.

A characteristically Japanese industrial policy institution that dates from this era is the *public financial intermediary*. Three special government banks founded near the end of the nineteenth century became vehicles for extending subsidized loans to private firms: the Hypothec Bank (Nippon Kangyo Ginko) (1897), the Hokkaido Colonial Bank (1900), and the Industrial Bank of Japan (1902). All of these were privately capitalized but government-controlled, their charters stipulating that the government would appoint all directors. Each of the three obtained funds from the government which they re-lent to businesses and local governments at low interest rates. The Hypothec Bank (including its affiliated prefectural banks which it absorbed in 1934) was the largest of these special government intermediaries, its outstanding loans equal to those of the other two combined and approaching a tenth of the outstanding loans of all banks. The Hypothec Bank lent primarily to farmers, local governments, and light industry including textiles. The Industrial Bank supplied funds to firms in heavy industry including shipbuilding, iron and steel, chemicals, and electric power; later on it supplied funds for colonial development in Manchuria and Taiwan.

The government's industrial policies figured prominently in the development of shipbuilding, rail, steel, and, of course, munitions, but collectively these accounted for little of Japan's manufacturing output or employment near the turn of the century. Government spending in Japan from 1885 to 1915 averaged about 10 percent of GNP but accounted for about 35 percent of capital investment, which reflects the government's prominent role in producing steel, ships, and rail lines.

What are we to make of these government efforts to promote heavy industry during an era when Japan's light industries, particularly cotton spinning and silk reeling, were expanding dramatically with little government assistance whatsoever? The point of Japanese industrial policy in the late Meiji era was to develop an armaments producing capability. The output of Japan's heavy industry in the decade after the Russo-Japanese War of 1905–15 was largely absorbed by the military.[17] Also, subsidies for coastal shipping might be viewed as offsetting the distorting effects of the Japanese government's proven inclination to confiscate private vessels in wartime.

---

[17] On the early development of heavy industry in Japan, see Yoshio Andō, "The Formation of Heavy Industry", in Seiichi Tōbata (ed.), *The Modernization of Japan*, i, Tokyo: Institute of Asian Economic Affairs, 1966, pp. 115–36.

World War I boom and interwar period, 1915–1936
During World War I, Japan exploited the temporarily high world interest rates by accumulating foreign assets, which caused the yen to depreciate in real terms, stimulating foreign demand for Japanese goods and switching domestic demand from foreign imports to domestic products. Industrial policy is little evident in the remarkable stimulus to Japanese economic activity that accompanied this process. When war ended, so did the boom in Japanese production.

After observing the economic mobilization efforts of the European powers during World War I, the leading members of the "control faction" (*tōseiha*) within the officer corps of the Japanese army, including Nagata Tetsuzan[18] and Ishihara Kanji, became advocates of a strengthened industrial policy. They argued that Japan's future success in a war of attrition would require an industrial policy that substantially expanded the nation's capacity to produce weapons. Throughout the 1920s, the established political parties avoided such measures, and sought instead to base Japanese national security upon foreign diplomacy, international arms limitations agreements, and *laissez-faire* economic policies. As a consequence, the arms buildup that immediately followed the Japanese seizure of Manchuria in 1931–2, had to rely upon government purchases in a free market. The 1931 Major Industries Control Law, recognizing extant trade associations as instruments of government control, represented a first small step toward a more intrusive form of government direction. Further steps were taken when the coalition governments that followed the May 1932 assassination of Prime Minister Inukai succumbed to the army's insistence on special subsidies for production of motor vehicles (1932), subsidies for shipbuilding (1933), tax credits, subsidies, the protection of oil refiners, and the stipulation that oil refiners hold substantial oil reserves (1934), and an amalgamation of a number of private steel producers along with the government's Yawata steel works into a new government enterprise called Japan Steel (Nippon Seitetsu) (also in 1934). One impetus for these subsidies and related measures was to discourage or counteract the withdrawal of private wealth from investments likely to be commandeered if a wider war should occur, as it soon did. The measures fell far short of the broad industrial policy advocated by the control faction.

Effectively blocked from imposing a truly sweeping industrial policy in the home islands, the Japanese army sought instead to impose one in the Japanese puppet state Manchukuo, in 1932–5. First the army attempted, with little success, to foster investment in targeted heavy industries, through state enterprises under the aegis of the South Manchuria Railway. Then, with a slightly better result, it sought to attract private investment by Nissan and other so-called "new zaibatsu", by offering them government guarantees and other subsidies.

Successful suppression of the February 1936 coup attempt left the army's control faction in a greatly strengthened political position. This immediately resulted in the so-called "quasi-wartime economy" (*junsenji keizai*), a year of inflation-financed increases in military spending, but with minimal direct controls on private economic activity. At this same time, as a result of the Major Industry Control Law (renewed for another five-year term) and related measures, including laws enacted in May 1936 to force government licensing and nominal government oversight of the automobile industry and fertilizer industry, a largely dormant apparatus of government control did exist in a number of industries, and was about to spring to life.

The wartime economy, 1937–1945
Soon after the outbreak of war with China in July 1937, the Japanese military finally succeeded in imposing a comprehensive industrial policy. The policy rested on three pillars: rationing of foreign exchange, government control of financial intermediation, and production subsidies. Using these measures, the government systematically enlarged the productive capacity of munitions industries and retrenched civilian industries. In the postwar era, virtually the same methods were used in Japan to shift resources from some civilian industries to others.

The 1933 Foreign Exchange Control Law had vested the Ministry of Finance (MOF) with authority to regulate all foreign exchange transactions. Given this, the awkwardly named September 1937 Law Relating to Temporary Export and Import Commod-

---

[18] Nagata Tetsuzan (1884–1935) rose through the ranks to become the *de facto* leader of the army's control faction, and in 1934 the army chief of staff. He was assassinated by a fellow officer affiliated with the imperial way faction.

ities Measure might seem redundant, but, in fact, it was anything but so. This is because the MOF had routinely approved foreign exchange transactions pertaining to the import and export of commodities. The 1937 law vested the government with broad powers not only to specifically restrict or prohibit the import or export of any commodity, but also to control the pricing and allocation of all imported raw materials and products that embodied the same, essentially all the manufactured goods of Japan. To exercise this broad mandate, the Diet established the Cabinet Planning Board the very next month, October 1937.

The Cabinet Planning Board has been described as an "economic general staff",[19] the central coordinator of Japan's wartime industrial policy. Under this control scheme, the Cabinet Planning Board would establish production targets for the various war materials, along with implied volumes of imports and exports needed to achieve these targets and at the same time maintain balanced trade. Then the ministries with direct responsibility for issuing licenses or approvals to the respective industries would actually execute the indicated policies; that is, they would assign import and export rights to the respective, officially recognized, trade associations of industries under their jurisdictions. The ministry charged with oversight of the heavy industries, so important in the production of munitions, was the Ministry of Commerce and Industry, which had been formed in 1925 with the brilliant Takahashi Korekiyo its first leader. The immediate antecedent of the Ministry of Commerce and Industry was the Commercial and Industrial Affairs Bureau of the Ministry of Agriculture and Commerce, the bureau that, among other things, administered the Yawata steel works. In November 1943 the Ministry of Commerce and Industry was consolidated with the Cabinet Planning Board and renamed the Munitions Ministry.

The second major thrust of the wartime industrial policy, besides government management and control of foreign trade, was government direction of financial intermediation. Under the September 1937 Temporary Capital Adjustment Law, all private bank loans and other sources of external financing, such as issuance of stocks and bonds, required government approval. Furthermore, individuals were required to maintain set portions of their earnings in the form of illiquid deposits at postal savings accounts or agricultural cooperatives. Government financial intermediaries, including the Industrial Bank of Japan, the Hypothec Bank, and the Wartime Finance Bank (created in February 1942), then re-loaned these funds to munitions companies. Private commercial banks, too, were obliged to follow government dictates, particularly in the final two years of the war. After the creation of the Munitions Ministry in November 1943, private munitions firms were each assigned to particular banks which were then required to extend them the credit needed to carry out production assignments.

Government subsidies represented the third and final element of the wartime industrial policy. Production subsidies were at first included in laws specific to each targeted industry. Through special laws, the government bestowed subsidies, tax exemptions, and protection from foreign competition upon designated industries, all producing war materials: synthetic oil (August 1937), machine tools (March 1938), aircraft (March 1938), shipbuilding (April 1939), light metals (May 1939), and machines (May 1941). The special subsidies embodied in these statutes ultimately paled in comparison with the implicit subsidies inherent in the tidal wave of wartime government procurement spending, most of it on a "cost plus" basis, with full indemnities for war damage and other extraordinary losses.

In March 1938, the Diet made the 1918 National Mobilization Law applicable to the China war, and the government subsequently invoked it in September 1939 to institute comprehensive wage and price controls and mass conscription. In November 1940, the second Konoe administration abolished political parties and labor unions, and at the same stroke proposed a "New Economic Policy" that would have virtually abolished private businesses and substituted central planning. The proposal was shelved, but, in light of the other wartime policies, private businesses and their employees enjoyed little freedom from government direction anyway.[20]

---

[19] Chalmers Johnson, *MITI and the Japanese Miracle, 1925–1975*, Stanford University Press, 1982, p. 137.

[20] For an excellent discussion of the precise ways in which wartime controls limited the autonomy of private firms, see Tetsuji Okazaki, "The Japanese Firm under the Wartime Planned Economy", *Journal of the Japanese and International Economies*, vol. 7 (1993), pp. 175–205.

The wartime industrial policy did shift resources from the production of civilian goods to the production of armaments. Whether it accomplished this more effectively than simple government procurement in a free-market economy remains highly dubious. Perhaps the army's control faction and other like-minded architects of the wartime industrial policy incorrectly perceived the true nature of a price system, that it induces economically efficient choices without the need for central direction. Or perhaps, instead, they correctly perceived the nature of politics. By erecting a broad and intrusive, but opaque, mechanism for shifting private resources to the war effort, Japan's leaders effectively removed government procurement from the arena of public debate, and veiled the true economic costs of the war behind a cloak of secrecy.

Occupation era, 1945–1952

For some period after the defeat, Japan's government, now under direction of the US-controlled office of the SCAP, continued all three elements of the wartime industrial policy: production subsidies, government financial intermediation, and foreign exchange controls. But now, instead of promoting munitions industries, these policies were used to promote specific civilian goods industries: coal, steel, fertilizer, and electricity.

During the war, the massive flow of government procurement spending had become the major source of direct subsidies. This flow continued even after Japan's unconditional surrender to the Allies. In the early months of the Occupation, the Japanese government continued to pay war indemnities and other accumulated obligations to individuals and private firms, inflating the currency to do so. Other elements of the wartime economy also survived or were revived. At the direction of SCAP, wartime price controls continued in effect and new government bureaus were created to administer them, direct analogues of the wartime structures they resurrected or replaced. In the week after Japan's capitulation, the Munitions Ministry had been hastily reassigned its old name, the Ministry of Commerce and Industry. Exactly one year later, in August 1946, the Economic Stabilization Board was established, a direct analogue of the old Cabinet Planning Board. About the same time, new public corporations (*kodan*) were established to carry out the rationing of

major commodities, made necessary by the price controls, under the direction of the Stabilization Board.

The *kodan* performed the same functions that during the war years had been performed by the now dissolved wartime control associations. But in addition, the *kodan*, very much like the special wartime government enterprises called *eidan*, purchased materials at market prices for resale to businesses at the lower, government-controlled prices. They were vehicles for extending implicit subsidies to producers. These so-called "price subsidies", in aggregate, absorbed 2.8 percent of Japan's national income from 1946 to 1948. The majority of the price subsidies (74 percent in real terms) were bestowed upon just three industries: (i) coal, (ii) iron and steel, and (iii) chemical fertilizer. Table 9.1 depicts some details of these price subsidies. Still other subsidies were implicit in loans from the Reconstruction Finance Bank (RFB), which are also given in Table 9.1.

The RFB, formed by splitting off a department of the government-controlled Industrial Bank of Japan, was a direct analogue of the now defunct Wartime Finance Bank. Its loans were little more than outright cash transfers to the fortunate private businesses that received them, for the interest rates on these loans completely failed to take into account the extremely rapid inflation of these years. As the table depicts, most of the RFB loans were bestowed on only a few, "priority" industries: the coal mining, electric power, steel, and chemical fertilizer industries, the same ones receiving the bulk of price subsidies described in the previous paragraph. Private commercial banks were also directed by government edict to allocate half of their own loans to the same industries. Although the targeting of these industries was publicly defended, that does not mean the incidence of RFB largesse lay beyond the reach of crass political patronage. The coming to light of bribes in pursuit of RFB loans by the chemical fertilizer company Shōwa Denkō felled the Ashida administration, and even resulted in the arrest of the, by then, former prime minister himself. The RFB loans of 1947–9 were, in aggregate, almost exactly as large as the price subsidies described in the preceding paragraph.

The final pillar of the Occupation industrial policy was government management of foreign trade. In the first three and a half years of the Occupation,

Table 9.1. Domestic price subsidies ("price") and Reconstruction Finance Bank loans ("RFB"), 1946–1950 (1934–6¥mn)

Fiscal year	1946		1947		1948		1949		1950
	Price	RFB	Price	RFB	Price	RFB	Price	RFB	Price
Coal	62	25	96	181	97	147	93	4	0
Iron and steel	0	7	37	15	114	9	200	96	1
Fertilizers	0	14	17	31	56	12	110	47	3
Electricity	0	7	0	24	0	104	0	0	0
Nonferrous metals	0	0	8	0	12	0	8	0	0
Soda	0	0	2	0	8	0	11	3	0
Food	158	0	53	0	3	0	0	0	0
Marine shipping	0	12	0	35	0	49	0	0	0
Other	0	81	3	228	45	64	0	0	0
Total	220	146	216	514	335	385	422	150	4
% of GNP	1.90	1.26	1.72	4.09	2.34	2.72	2.90	0.93	0.02
Real GNP, f.y. 1934–6 = 1 (¥bn)	11.59		12.57		14.21		14.52		16.12

Sources: see Figure 4.3.

nearly all Japanese foreign trade was confined to transactions between a bureau of the Japanese government set up for the purpose, called the Board of Trade, and agencies of the US government.[21] Initially, SCAP virtually curtailed Japanese exports, and imposed strict limits on Japanese imports, essentially limiting the flow of goods into the country to humanitarian relief items such as food, pharmaceuticals, fertilizer, and fuel, which the Board of Trade resold within Japan at artificially low prices. Similarly, the Board of Trade purchased Japanese goods for export at inflated prices, conferring implicit subsidies on the suppliers, and then resold the goods to SCAP. The terms of each transaction between the Board of Trade and SCAP were in these years based on the application of artificial yen–dollar exchange rates to the original purchase prices of the traded items, exchange rates that varied from item to item. In other words, SCAP and the Board of Trade exercised full control over which items were imported and exported, and each transaction between the Board of Trade and a Japanese supplier or demander conferred an implicit subsidy. In aggregate, the subsidies were of the same scale as the US aid, about half as large as the price subsidies extended through the *kodan*. The result of government

management of foreign trade in the early years of the Occupation was to retrench just about all industries in which Japan might have enjoyed an international comparative advantage (such as handicrafts, textiles, and some types of machinery) and to afford blanket protection of industries in which it did not enjoy comparative advantage (such as coal mining, steel, or rice production).

All three prongs of the industrial policy of the early Occupation—the price subsidies, RFB loans, and Board of Trade subsidies and protection—were used to promote the same few industries, i.e. the coal, electricity, iron and steel, and chemical fertilizer industries. Ishibashi Tanzan, finance minister in the first Yoshida administration and the architect of the Reconstruction Finance Bank, explicitly defended the targeting of these industries, on the grounds that they supplied essential materials to other industries, a wholly specious justification. Private advisers to the Prime Minister led by Tokyo University economics professor Arisawa Hiromi had

---

[21] After protests by Prime Minister Yoshida in fall 1946, SCAP did allow the private import of some raw materials such as cotton to be financed by private exports, including exports of textiles, but this was a minor deviation from the basic policy in place from August 1945 to April 1949.

also concocted arguments in support of this so-called "priority production" policy, a mishmash of Keynesian, Hayekian, and Marxist rhetoric, better left unexamined.[22] In any case, the priority production scheme proved to be rather short-lived.

Under the Dodge line, introduced in 1949, the government of Japan was forced, temporarily, to abandon its experiments with industrial policy. The RFB was shut down. It extended no new loans after September 1949. Also, a large number of items were freed from price controls and the *kodan* were either shut down or forced to operate on limited budgets. The days of rampant subsidies were over. With the phasing out of price controls, the Economic Stabilization Board became somewhat redundant, but survived, shifting its focus from policy implementation to policy analysis. In August 1952 it was renamed the Economic Deliberation Agency and in July 1955 the Economic Planning Agency, the name by which it is known today. It compiles Japan's national income and product accounts, constructs economic forecasts, dates business cycle turning points, and publishes economic analyses including the annual "white paper" on the Japanese economy. The Board of Trade was reconfigured as a bureau of the Ministry of International Trade and Industry (MITI), the new name for the old Ministry of Commerce and Industry.

By January 1950, all of Japan's foreign trade was returned to a private basis at fixed exchange rates pegged to the US dollar at ¥360 = $1. Although the International Trade Bureau of MITI no longer itself conducted foreign transactions, it did participate in the allocation of foreign exchange, which was kept artificially scarce until the 1960s. Indeed, control of foreign trade would again become a major element of Japanese industrial policy, as would government financial intermediation. But in the final three years of the Occupation, coinciding with the Korean War boom and the beginning of rapid economic growth, Japan's industrial policy remained a spent force.

Industrial policy in the postwar era

The high-growth era, 1953–1974

The zenith of Japanese industrial policy occurred during the twelve years between restoration of independence on April 28, 1952, and Japan's acceptance of Article 8 of the IMF Articles of Agreement on April 1, 1964, which finally freed Japanese current account transactions from all government controls. In this interval, the Japanese government, and MITI in particular, by rationing foreign exchange, wielded considerable authority to determine the composition of Japanese imports. And until the liberalization of inward direct investment in 1968, MITI also substantially determined the pattern and details of the private licensing of foreign technologies in Japan. This was the period in which the Japanese government used industrial policy to encourage private domestic investment in specific, targeted sectors, including steel, petrochemicals, and shipbuilding, and to protect them from foreign competition. Besides foreign exchange rationing, which ended in the 1960s, industrial policy instruments of the high growth era included public intermediation of funds, preferential tax stipulations, and special exemptions from anti-monopoly laws, all of which persist in some form even today.

Let us consider some details of each industrial policy instrument of the high growth era, beginning with foreign exchange rationing.

(i) The rationing of foreign exchange Under the December 1949 Foreign Exchange and Foreign Trade Control Law, which was not repealed until 1980, the government retained the authority to allocate foreign exchange. In the decade following the end of the Occupation, the government of Japan used this authority to restrict inward investment, to manage the acquisition of foreign technology by Japanese firms, and to influence the composition of Japan's foreign trade. During the years before 1964, the International Trade Bureau of MITI and the Foreign Exchange Bureau of the MOF shared responsibility for rationing foreign exchange. The foreign exchange allocations were enforced by requiring a license issued by MITI for each foreign currency transaction relating to imports or exports, and a license from the MOF for any other foreign currency transactions. In these years, MITI and MOF together drafted a semi-annual foreign exchange budget that designated for approval the sale of specified amounts of foreign exchange in the upcoming

---

22 Readers who wish to judge for themselves should consult the following (not recommended): Arisawa Hiromi, "Infurēshon to shakaika" (Socialization and inflation), *Nippon hyōron sha* 1948.

period, according to each different sort of item to be imported ("fund allocations") or, for items outside of the specified categories, according to the foreign currency involved irrespective of the specific item to be traded ("automatic approvals").[23] Given the scarcity of foreign exchange at the official exchange rate, these allocations amounted to *de facto* import restrictions in many industries. Export transactions were generally allowed, with a few minor exceptions. Direct investment transactions encountered additional obstacles.

Under the Foreign Investment Law of 1950, all instances of inward and outward foreign direct investment, including technology licensing agreements, that is the purchase of patent rights or know-how, required not only a license issued by the MOF, but also the approval of the newly created Foreign Investment Deliberation Council, dominated by the Investment Bureau of MITI. Under this regime, permission for foreigners to acquire or set up production facilities or subsidiaries in Japan proved more difficult to obtain than permission to enter technology agreements.[24] But technology agreements, too, were subject to careful scrutiny by MITI.

Many have argued that MITI used its authority to approve or deny requests to license foreign technology, to bargain for more favorable terms than an open policy would have implied. Specifically, MITI pre-empted competition among Japanese companies, and presumably improved the Japanese terms of trade in these transactions, by designating only one specific company or consortium of companies to bargain with each particular foreign supplier of technology. With the liberalization of inward investment from 1968 onwards, average royalty rates paid by Japanese purchasers of foreign technology did rise, from less than 4 percent of sales or production costs in 1963–7 to more than 5 percent of sales or production costs in 1968–71, which seems consistent with this general notion.[25] This policy of exploiting national monopsony in the purchase of foreign technology could still go awry if MITI bureaucrats failed to select the correct domestic firm to develop each foreign technology. One of the great chestnuts in the history of Japanese industrial policy is the delay in allowing Sony, then a small, young company, to negotiate with Western Electric for patent rights to the transistor, a relatively new solid state device that would later become the crucial

element in most electronic products. As told in the autobiography of Akio Morita, Sony's founder, the MITI bureaucrats were reluctant to bestow such a new technology on a small company; it took six months of argument in 1953 before MITI was convinced.[26]

The economic effects of foreign exchange rationing in Japan are quite difficult to know precisely. Certainly the policy protected industries such as coal mining, textiles, and agriculture, in which Japan had lost its comparative advantage, and thereby diminished Japan's gains from foreign trade. On the other hand, many analysts, including some economic sophisticates, argue that the *de facto* ban on imports of motor vehicles allowed Japan's domestic automobile industry to grow and realize propitious Marshallian externalities. Nobody really knows if this is true.

Besides its direct allocative effects, foreign exchange rationing enhanced MITI influence over business policies generally. Perhaps this was the origin of the notion that administrative guidance (*gyōsei shidō*), i.e. private communications between bureaucrats and businesses, has projected Japanese government influence beyond the legally prescribed domains of regulation. For example, MITI used the dependence of Japan's petrochemical firms on foreign technology, requiring its approval, also to control entry, exit, and investment in the petrochemical industry. MITI participated in the site selection, planning, and organization of the numerous petrochemical industrial complexes established in the 1950s and 1960s along the coasts of Japan.[27]

---

23 On the details of the formal process for allocating foreign exchange in Japan, 1950–64, see Shinji Takagi, "The Japanese System of Foreign Exchange and Trade Control", Working Paper no. 123, Center on Japanese Economy and Business, Columbia Business School, June 1996.

24 Mark Mason, *American Multinationals in Japan: The Political Economy of Japanese Capital Controls, 1899–1980*, Harvard University Press, 1992. Mason discusses the Foreign Investment Deliberation Council on pp. 150–61. For more details, see Dan Fenno Henderson, *Foreign Enterprise in Japan: Laws and Policies*, University of North Carolina Press, 1973.

25 Merton Peck and Shūji Tamura, "Technology", in Hugh Patrick and Henry Rosovsky, *Asia's New Giant: How the Japanese Economy Works*, Washington, DC: Brookings Institution, 1972, pp. 525–85; esp. pp. 544–58, "government controls".

26 Akio Morita with E. M. Reingold and Mitsuko Shimomura, *Made in Japan: Akio Morita and Sony*, Signet, 1988, pp. 72–3.

27 On the details of petrochemical complexes established in Japan in the high growth era, see Eleanor Hadley, *Antitrust in Japan*, Princeton University Press, 1970, pp. 301–15.

Because of the rapid growth and subsequent international prominence of the Japanese petrochemical industry, MITI involvement in these matters is often counted as an industrial policy success, but one wonders how the industry might have fared without MITI. Again, nobody really knows.

In any case, MITI's broad authority to ration foreign exchange ended when the government made the yen convertible on current account in 1964 and relaxed (but did not eliminate!) restrictions on inward foreign investment in 1968. Japanese trade protection in the years since has resided mostly in explicit tariffs and quotas, and even these have been substantially reduced and eliminated, mainly in conjunction with the various GATT agreements.

The era in which MITI was the official gatekeeper of foreign access to the Japanese market ended at least thirty years ago, in the 1960s. But another important aspect of industrial policy dating from the early postwar period still survives, and that is the public intermediation of investable funds, established in its present form as the Fiscal Investment and Loan Program in 1952.

(ii) Fiscal Investment and Loan Program   The Dodge line put an end to the Reconstruction Finance Bank in 1949, but almost immediately afterwards the Japanese government established new public financial intermediaries to take its place. The Export Bank of Japan and the Japan Development Bank, both chartered near the end of the Occupation era, became the main vehicles for expanding the flow of government credit to targeted industries.

The Export Bank of Japan (renamed the Export–Import Bank of Japan in April 1952) was chartered in December 1950 and opened in February 1951, a government bank, its initial purpose the issuing of long-term loans to Japanese exporters to cover deferred payments by foreign buyers. Its name change, a year after its opening, reflected an expansion of its activities to include loans and credits facilitating Japanese imports and supporting foreign direct investment.

The other public financial intermediary dating from this era, the Japan Development Bank, was chartered in March 1951, and opened its doors in two months later. It immediately took over the remaining outstanding loans of the RFB and also the US Aid Counterpart Fund Account, comprising proceeds from the sale of items proffered to Japan under US aid programs. The Japan Development Bank was the reincarnation of the RFB, but this time with non-inflationary sources of funds. In July 1952, only months after the Occupation ended, legislation was enacted that linked the Export–Import Bank of Japan, the Japan Development Bank, and other government financial intermediaries to the government's Postal Saving System, creating the Fiscal Investment and Loan Program (FILP).

The Fiscal Investment and Loan Program[28] (Zaisei Toyūshi) refers to the portion of Japan's public sector that engages in financial intermediation. Public financial intermediation dates from the Meiji era in Japan, but was not conducted in a fully coordinated or systematic fashion until the adoption of the FILP budgeting process in fiscal year 1953. Figure 9.2 describes schematically the main flows of funds encompassed by the FILP. The Postal Savings System lies at the core of the FILP. From its founding in 1875, the Postal Savings System has collected savings deposits from households and transferred them to the Ministry of Finance. Until 1885 the postal savings were invested exclusively in national government bonds. Later some portion of the postal deposits were diverted to local governments, and to the special government banks that, in the war years of the 1930s and 1940s, financed munitions production and funded investments in Manchuria and other occupied territories.[29] The postal savings have always been the largest original source of funds in the FILP. The other sources include social security surpluses,[30] proceeds from the issuance of government guaranteed bonds, postal life insurance trust funds, and allocations from the general account of

---

[28] For the best short description of the FILP see Yukio Noguchi, "The Role of the Fiscal Investment and Loan Program in Postwar Japanese Economic Growth", in Hyung-Ki Kim, Michio Muramatsu, T. J. Pempel, and Kozo Yamamura (eds.), *The Japanese Civil Service and Economic Development: Catalysts for Change*, Oxford: Clarendon Press, 1995, pp. 261–87.

[29] The special government banks included the Japan Hypothec Bank (founded in 1896), the Agriculture and Industry Bank (founded in 1896), the Industrial Bank of Japan (founded in 1900), and the Yokohama Specie Bank, the Bank of Taiwan, and the Bank of Korea. At the war's end, SCAP suspended the activities of the special banks, but then allowed some of them to be rechartered as private commercial banks, thus originating Japan's three long-term credit banks.

[30] The social security surplus has risen in size over the years, from being about one-third as large as postal deposits in the 1950s to around two-thirds as large as postal deposits in 1995.

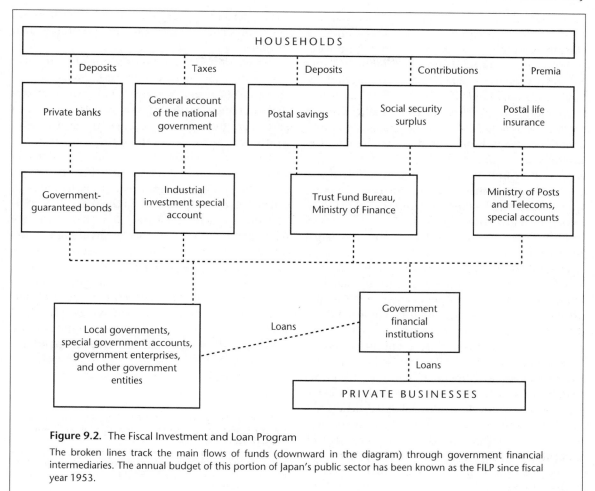

Figure 9.2. The Fiscal Investment and Loan Program

The broken lines track the main flows of funds (downward in the diagram) through government financial intermediaries. The annual budget of this portion of Japan's public sector has been known as the FILP since fiscal year 1953.

the national government. The postal life insurance trust funds are under the direction of the Ministry of Posts and Telecommunications, but all others are under direction of the MOF.

Over the years, a lot of the FILP funds have been lent either to government enterprises or to the scores of government entities and special government accounts that construct or operate toll roads, toll bridges, port facilities, airports, subways, and so on. This, the main element of the FILP fulfills the same intermediary function as the municipal bond markets of other developed nations. Some small number of the entities with direct access to FILP funds are, in fact, also authorized to issue government guaranteed bonds. But these bonds are not sold to the public. They are placed with syndicates of private

commercial banks. The government entities within the FILP orbit exhibit a bewildering variety of special designations, including *kōko* (public financial intermediaries), *kōsha* (public corporations), *jigyōdan* (enterprise units), *tokushu kaisha* (special companies), *tokubetsu kaikei* (special accounts), and *chihō kōkyō dantai* (local public entities).[31] Most of these various government entities post-date the 1953 formation of the FILP.

---

31 For a careful dissection of the taxonomy of Japanese government entities, see Chalmers Johnson, *Japan's Public Policy Companies*, Washington: American Enterprise Institute, 1978. Johnson discusses the entire range of government entities, including those that do not themselves generate flows of income and are therefore budgeted in the general account of the national government, not the FILP.

The aspect of the FILP most relevant to the conduct of industrial policy is the flow of funds to private businesses through the Export–Import Bank of Japan (ExIm) and the Japan Development Bank. Besides these, the Japan Finance Corporation for Small Business, founded September 1953, has served as a conduit for subsidized loans to smaller firms in targeted sectors, including subcontractors and subsidiaries of larger firms. The other public financial intermediaries attached to the FILP exhibit a range of specialized functions less related to industrial policy. The largest of these, the Housing Loan Corporation, holds about half the residential credit in Japan. Others extend loans to farms and fisheries, firms in less developed regions of Japan, and municipal service firms.

The scale of the FILP may be judged from the fact that in the postwar era postal saving deposits have comprised 10–20 percent of Japan's household financial assets, an immense quantity. For instance, in 1993 postal savings deposits represented 20 percent of personal savings and were about 39 percent as large as Japan's GDP. The JDB and ExIm Banks have intermediated only about a tenth of the postal deposits, but each has assets comparable in scale to Japan's largest private banks. Table 9.2 details private firms' sources of external funds during the high growth era. The JDB, in the early 1950s, provided 3.5 percent of the external funds raised by private businesses, and from 1956 to 1975 provided 1.7 percent of the external funds, very small compared with the 70–80 percent provided by private institutions. The ExIm Bank provided slightly fewer funds than the JDB.

The share of external funds supplied by the JDB may understate the bank's actual influence on the allocation of credit. Because a JDB loan indicates the willingness of the government to subsidize a particular private firm, it improves the firm's creditworthiness. To the extent this is true, the JDB acts as a "bell cow", leading private banks to particular clients.[32] But the evidence for this is mixed. Horiuchi and Sui examined data from the financial statements of Japanese firms in the years 1968–88.[33] The firms in their sample, each of which had a close relationship with one particular main bank, upon borrowing from the JDB did not experience any detectable increase in loans from private banks. Other firms that borrowed from the JDB did borrow slightly more from private sources. The bell cow effect seems to have been operative only for firms without main banks—the smaller, peripheral firms, not affiliated with the bank-centered groups known as the financial keiretsu.

---

[32] The "bell cow" tag is due to M. Higano, *Kinyū kikan no shinsa noryoku* (Credit assessments by financial institutions), University of Tokyo Press, 1986.

[33] Akiyoshi Horiuchi and Quing-yuan Sui, "Influence of the Japan Development Bank Loans on Corporate Investment Behavior", *Journal of the Japanese and International Economies*, vol. 7 (1993), pp. 441–65.

Table 9.2. Sources of industrial funds, 1946–1975 (% of external funds)[a]

	Stocks	Bonds	Loans by private financial institutions	RFB	JDB	ExIm	FCSB	Other public loans	Total external (¥bn)	Own funds (¥bn)
1946–50	13.1	3.5	72.4	5.5				2.3	1,635	654
1951–55	14.1	3.8	71.9	−0.3	3.5	0.9	0.8	6.2	4,230	3,196
1956–60	14.2	4.7	73.0		1.7	0.9	1.1	4.5	9,878	6,468
1961–65	13.9	4.4	74.7		1.6	1.3	0.8	3.3	24,168	16,775
1966–70	6.8	3.1	81.2		1.8	1.8	1.3	4.0	43,030	41,635
1971–75	5.6	3.9	81.8		1.7	1.4	1.5	4.1	95,405	67,268

a RFB = Reconstruction Finance Bank; JDB = Japan Development Bank; ExIm = Export–Import Bank of Japan; FCSB = Japan Finance Corporation for Small Business.

Source: Ministry of Finance, *Shōwa zaiseishi, shūsen kara kōwa made* (Financial history of the Showa era, from the war's end to the Peace Treaty of San Francisco) vol. 19 (1978), table 149, pp. 462–3.

It has also been frequently suggested that, in the high growth era, BOJ lending practices indirectly supported industrial policy, augmenting the efforts of the public intermediaries. In the 1950s, the Bank held its discount rate at a lower level than the interbank lending rate, and limited the amounts it loaned to each bank. These limits on BOJ discount window borrowing varied over time and from bank to bank and were conveyed to each bank privately, in the form of suggestions. In theory, the banks could have disregarded these suggestions, referred to as "window guidance" (that is, BOJ discount *window*, administrative *guidance*), but at the peril of antagonizing the Bank of Japan and its controlling ministry, the MOF. It has been widely reported that in the 1950s, through window guidance, banks were allowed to borrow more from the BOJ if their own loan portfolios included loans to the industries targeted by industrial policy, presumably the same industries favored by the JDB. And because discount window loans, and not BOJ purchases of bonds, were the main (and in fact almost the only) source of high powered money in Japan, this was, potentially, an important influence over the allocation of private credit.

But was it actually? A couple of facts suggest otherwise. First, when targeted industries such as coal mining, and in the late 1970s the shipbuilding and steel industries, went into decline, private banks withdrew funding even as the public intermediaries expanded funding. The private banks were guided in their credit allocations by the profit motive, not by government dictates. Second, the evidence, already mentioned, that the JDB did not always serve as a "bell cow" inducing the private banks to lend to particular client firms further indicates the independence of private banks. In short, the private banks in Japan are neither cows nor sheep, but profit-seeking commercial enterprises. The public financial intermediaries, on the other hand, are of course not profit-seekers, and that is precisely why they are effective instruments of industrial policy. By offering loans at special low interest rates, the JDB could induce favored industries to borrow more and invest more than otherwise. MITI's close attention to the JDB is therefore unsurprising.

From the outset, MITI bureaucrats participated in the annual drafting of the FILP budget, and insinuated themselves into the management of the JDB.

For instance, the Enterprises Bureau of MITI annually informed the JDB of the desired amount of loans to each industry in the upcoming year, based on MITI's own overall targets for the industry compared with estimates of the supplies of loans from private sector financial intermediaries.[34] In constructing these projections, MITI consulted closely with the respective industries, through an elaborate set of advisory councils (*shingikai*).

The coherent focus of Japanese industrial policy in the postwar era is due largely to the concentration of JDB and ExIm Bank loans on only a few industries. In the 1950s, loans from the JDB and the ExIm Bank were at first centered on the same industries favored under the earlier "priority production" scheme. As detailed in Table 9.3(*a*), from 1951 to 1960 more than 63 percent of JDB loans went to the electric power and marine shipping industries and another 14 percent to the coal mining and steel industries. Table 9.3(*b*) indicates the importance of public funds to these industries relative to private funds. In the late 1950s, the JDB supplied funds equaling almost one-third of the equipment purchases of the coal mining and marine shipping industries, and the JDB together with other government financial intermediaries supplied about a third of the equipment funds used by the electric power industry. Public funds were most important to the agriculture and fisheries industries, though these were not a particular focus of the JDB. The extensive subsidy and protection of agriculture in Japan, persisting since the war, may well have had a greater effect on resource allocation than any of the policies focused on the manufacturing industries. Nobody has argued that Japanese government support of agriculture is anything other than the naked transfer of wealth to influential special interests.

During the high growth era, the Export–Import Bank of Japan focused on the development of shipbuilding. As shown in Table 9.4, continually from 1950 until 1970, approximately half of the ExIm Bank's loans were to finance ship exports, and most of the rest financed plant exports. Shipbuilding in Japan falls under the purview of the Ministry of Transport, making it one of the few manufacturing industries there not assigned to MITI. As already

---

34 Johnson, *MITI*, p. 209.

Table 9.3(*a*). Composition of JDB loans, 1951–1974 (¥bn and %)[a]

	1951–55		1956–60		1961–65		1966–70		1971–74	
Electric power	117	(42.8)	118	(39.0)	112	(16.6)	101	(7.4)	136	(6.6)
Marine shipping	64	(23.4)	83	(27.3)	202	(30.0)	483	(35.4)	426	(20.7)
Coal mining	17	(6.0)	26	(8.4)	57	(3.4)	47	(3.4)	6	(0.3)
Iron and Steel	14	(5.2)	8	(2.6)	4	(0.6)	5	(0.4)	0	(0.0)
Subtotal	212	(77.4)	234	(77.3)	376	(46.6)	635	(46.6)	529	(27.6)
Total	274	(100.0)	303	(100.0)	673	(100.0)	1363	(100.0)	2061	(100.0)

[a] Percentages are given in parentheses.

Source: Akiyoshi Horiuchi and Quing-yuan Sui, "Influence of the Japan Development Bank Loans on Corporate Investment Behavior", *Journal of the Japanese and International Economies*, vol. 7 (1993), pp. 441–65, table 1 at p. 444.

discussed, JDB loans in this same era were heavily concentrated on the marine shipping industry. As these loans largely financed purchases of ships built in Japan, one could say that the ExIm Bank loans and JDB loans both heavily targeted the shipbuilding industry. In fact, this continued an explicit government program begun in 1947, called the "planned shipbuilding program". Not only were the

Table 9.3(*b*). Equipment purchases of private firms financed by government intermediaries and by the Japan Development Bank, 1954–1967

	1954–60[a]		1961–67[a]	
Electric power	32.4	(13.1)	19.7	(8.3)
Marine shipping	33.9	(29.5)	50.9	(39.0)
Coal mining	37.2	(31.2)	65.9	(45.3)
Steel	4.6	(2.5)	3.6	(1.0)
Machinery	11.3	(2.6)	9.5	(3.1)
Chemicals	8.1	(3.4)	7.1	(3.8)
Textiles	14.2	(2.1)	14.7	(2.2)
Agriculture and fisheries	52.9	(0.5)	47.9	(0.4)
Land transport	10.4	(0.7)	21.9	(2.2)
All industries	21.6	(6.8)	15.7	(4.3)

[a] Purchases by the Japan Development Bank are given in parentheses.

Source: Akiyoshi Horiuchi and M. Ohtaki, "Seifu no kainyū to ginko kashidashi no jūyosei" (Government intervention in financial markets and the importance of bank loans), in Koichi Hamada, M. Kuroda, and A. Horiuchi (eds.), *Nihon keizai no makuro bunseki* (Macroeconomic analysis of the Japanese economy), University of Tokyo Press, 1987, table 5–3, p. 128 (primary sources: Bank of Japan, *Honpou keizai tokei* (National economic statistics) and Bank of Japan, *Keizai tokei nenpō* (Economic statistics annual)).

vessels financed by loans from public intermediaries (at first the RFB and later the JDB and ExIm Bank), but the government (Shipbuilding Bureau of the Ministry of Transportation) made specific production assignments to particular firms in the industry. Under legislation enacted in the early 1950s, the government also controlled entry into the shipbuilding industry. By the early 1970s Japan had become the world leader in production of ocean shipping. Of course, this does not imply anything about the wisdom of Japan's having targeted this industry.

Loans from public intermediaries at below-market interest rates lay at the core of Japanese industrial policy in the postwar era, but during the 1950s and 1960s these loans were coordinated with other measures, including preferential tax stipulations.

(iii) Preferential tax stipulations and related measures
In the 1950s and the decades since, the Japanese Diet, to encourage exports and investment in targeted industries, enacted numerous laws stipulating preferential tax deferrals and exemptions. These measures have been coordinated with the loan allocations of the public intermediaries and have embodied industrial policy aims.

The Special Tax Measures Law, in effect from 1951 to 1961, accelerated depreciation for designated equipment purchases, deferring taxes and thereby reducing the present value of taxes for favored firms and industries. Initially, designated machinery in targeted industries qualified for 50 percent write-off of equipment purchases in the first year (and 20 percent in the next two years for experimental

Table 9.4. Composition of ExIm Bank loans, 1950–1975 (¥bn and %)[a]

	1950–55		1956–60		1961–65		1966–70		1971–75	
Exports	133	(94)	282	(85)	663	(77)	1382	(76)	1719	(44)
Shipbuilding	88	(66)	184	(56)	419	(48)	822	(45)	727	(19)
Plants	44	(33)	97	(30)	244	(28)	560	(31)	992	(25)
Imports	0	(0)	2	(1)	6	(1)	60	(3)	685	(18)
Investment	1	(1)	26	(8)	44	(5)	143	(8)	639	(16)
Economic cooperation	0	(0)	19	(6)	151	(17)	223	(12)	865	(22)
Total	134	(100)	330	(100)	866	(100)	1809	(100)	3909	(100)

[a] Percentages are given in parentheses.

Source: Seiritsu Ogura and Naoyuki Yoshino, "The Tax System and the Fiscal Investment and Loan Program", in Ryutaro Komiya, Masahiro Okuno, and Kotaru Suzumura (eds.), *Industrial Policy of Japan*, New York: Academic Press, 1988, table 5, p. 141.

equipment). Subsequent modifications of the 1951 statute reduced first-year depreciation of designated equipment to one-third of cost in 1962 and to one-fourth in 1964, expanded its coverage in 1970 and 1971, and ultimately phased out increased initial depreciation for targeted industries, completely abolishing it in 1973.

Export industries enjoyed further special encouragement from Japanese tax policy in the 1950s and 1960s. The System of Tax Exemptions for Export Income, enacted in 1953, provided 50 percent exclusion of export income (up to 3 percent of total manufacturing sales) for tax purposes. This was abolished in 1963 and replaced by special added deductions proportionate to increases in each firm's export-to-sales ratio (abolished in 1972). Also under the 1963 measure, small and medium firms could divert a portion of foreign earnings to tax-free reserves.

Besides the tax exemptions just mentioned, a bewildering variety of special tax-sheltered reserves, some of them specific to particular industries, have been authorized over the years.[35] The corporate taxes avoided by siphoning earnings into these special reserves amount to government subsidies.

Other preferential tax measures worthy of mention include Tariff Exemptions for Import of Important Machinery (1951), Initial Depreciation for Equipment Embodying New Technology (1958), Accelerated Depreciation for Equipment Purchases by Small and Medium Enterprises (1963), Initial Depreciation for Purchase of Anti-Pollution Equipment (1967), and Tax Credits for R&D Expenditures (1967).

Many of the preferential tax stipulations listed above pertained to "designated" or "important" machinery and equipment, and so on. Cabinet directives or special statutes were needed to add specifics to these sorts of adjective. The most comprehensive such statute of the 1950s was the Enterprise Rationalization Promotion Law, enacted in 1952. The Act empowered the Industrial Rationalization Council,[36] under the aegis of MITI, to formulate industry-specific packages of economic encouragements, including stipulating particular machinery for tax deferrals under provisions of the special tax measures law, but also including special property tax exemptions, subsidies, loans of government-owned plant and equipment, and government infrastructure investments (ports, highways, industrial complexes, power grids, railroads, gas lines). The "rationalization plans"—for such was the name given to these various dispensations of public largesse—also called for loans from public financial intermediaries at preferential interest rates, lower even than the interest rates on loans by these same intermediaries to firms in other, non-

---

[35] Tsuru lists no less than 26 such stipulations extant in 1975: Shigeto Tsuru, *Japan's Capitalism: Creative Defeat and Beyond*, Cambridge University Press, 1993, fn. 11, p. 105.

[36] The Industrial Rationalization Council, founded in December 1949, was an immense advisory body with, originally, 45 committees and 81 subcommittees, all staffed by bureaucrats, business executives, and academics. In 1964 it was merged with the Industrial Structure Advisory Committee (begun in 1961) and renamed the Industrial Structure Council. See Johnson, *MITI*, pp. 215–16.

designated, industries. The 1952 Act specifically targeted thirty-two industries, led by steel and coal mining; through subsequent legislation and cabinet directives, its provisions were extended to an additional eighteen. Some of the most prominent rationalization plans and related measures are listed in Table 9.5.

Special exemptions from the anti-monopoly law completed the package of industrial policy instruments of the high growth era.

(iv) Antitrust exemptions The Anti-monopoly Law of Japan (Law Relating to Prohibition of Private Monopoly and Methods of Preserving Fair Trade, enacted in April 1947), like the American statutes on which it is loosely based, prohibited cartels and price-fixing conspiracies (under its Article 3, which reads in its entirety: "No entrepreneur shall effect a private monopolization nor shall undertake any unreasonable restraint of trade"). In spite of this stipulation, the Special Measures Law for the Stabilization of Designated Medium and Smaller Enterprises, enacted immediately after the Occupation ended in August 1952, authorized government-sponsored domestic cartels of small and medium firms. Similarly, the Exports Transaction Law, also enacted in August 1952, authorized officially sanctioned export cartels of small and medium firms. (This Act was strengthened in 1955 by making the cartels compulsory.)

The September 1953 amendments to the Anti-monopoly Law provided further exceptions to the ordinary prohibitions of cartels. The relevant amendments included new articles empowering the Japan Fair Trade Commission (JFTC), on the advice of the ministry having provenance over an industry, to temporarily exempt the industry from the prohibitions against collusion and price-fixing, provided one of two sets of conditions are met. The first set of conditions pertains to the imminent bankruptcy of firms in an industry, and authorizes the sanction of a so-called *recession cartel* to "fix prices" (Article 24–3). The alternative set of conditions pertains to the benignity of collusion among the firms in an industry, and authorizes the sanction of a *rationalization cartel* to effect "technical promotion, quality improvement, cost reduction, efficiency increase or other enterprise rationalization" (Article 24–4). The concurrence of the JFTC with MITI's proposed

designations of industries for antitrust exemptions has largely proved to be a *pro forma* matter.

Scores of Japanese industries have formed recession cartels, rationalization cartels, export cartels, and so on. Yet it is unlikely that these cartels have achieved significant scarcities of industry output, or have much enriched the profits of their members. There have been two careful analyses of the price and output effects of the official sanctioning of cartels in Japan. Andrew Dick analyzed twelve Japanese export cartels formed between 1955 and 1985.[37] A few of these seem to have reduced costs or enlarged demand, perhaps by economizing on the costs of distributing products or by protecting investments in a shared reputation; but most of the export cartels analyzed by Dick lacked measurable effects.[38] Based on this, Japan's export cartels cannot be considered a major factor in industrial policy. In a second analysis, David Weinstein studied recession cartels (in eleven industries) sanctioned under Article 24–3 of the Anti-monopoly Law, and domestic cartels apparently sanctioned under special legislation such as the Special Measures Law for the Stabilization of Designated Medium and Smaller Enterprises[39] (in eighteen industries).[40] The domestic

---

[37] Andrew R. Dick, "The Competitive Consequences of Japan's Export Cartel Associations", *Journal of the Japanese and International Economies*, vol. 6 (1992), pp. 275–98.

[38] For each of the 12 commodities, Dick estimated reduced-form equations explaining price and quantity, respectively, based on structural equations of the Japanese industry export supply and world demand. The estimated coefficients on dummy variables (equal to 1 in years in which an export cartel was sanctioned for the respective commodity and equal to 0 in other years) reveal the effects on both export price and export quantity of sanctioning of a cartel. In 8 of the 12 industries analyzed, the sanctioning of cartels had no measurable effect on either price or quantity. Dick found that for paint, sanctioning of a cartel induced an increase in export price with no change in export quantity, and that for cement, glassware, and silk textiles, sanctioning of cartels expanded export quantities with no change in prices.

[39] Other special legislation sanctioning domestic cartels included the Law on Temporary Measures for Promoting and Stabilizing Specified Depressed Industries, 1978–1982, and the Law on Temporary Measures for the Structural Improvement of Specified Industries, 1983–88, both discussed below. Numerous other laws have also authorized exemptions from anti-monopoly law prohibitions of cartels and not all of them even require approval or notification of the government. For details, see Akinori Uesugi, "Japan's Cartel System and its Impact on International Trade", *Harvard International Law Journal*, vol. 27, special issue (1986), pp. 389–424.

[40] David E. Weinstein, "Evaluating Administrative Guidance and Cartels in Japan (1957–1988), *Journal of the Japanese and International Economies*, vol. 9 (1995), pp. 200–23.

Table 9.5. Rationalization plans and related measures, 1951–1974

Name of plan or statute	Year enacted, suspended	Notes
Steel Industry Rationalization Plans	First plan: 1951 Second plan: 1956 Third plan: 1960	Containing numerous stipulations such as JDB preferential loans, special depreciation allowances, tariff exemptions, property tax exemptions, approval of foreign technology imports, income tax deductions for import income, import restrictions under foreign exchange rationing
Law on Temporary Measures for Coal Mining Industry Rationalization	1955	Creating the Coal Mining Industry Rationalization Corporation, a special public body authorized to purchase inefficient mines and extend zero interest loans to surviving mines
Synthetic Fiber Five Year Development Plan	1953	Providing government procurement, tax breaks, and special allocations of electricity to makers of nylon, vinylon, and vinylidene choloride and products embodying them
Law on Temporary Measures for Promoting the Machinery (lit., Specified Manufacturing) Industries	1956, extended 1961, 1966–71	Stipulating special low-interest loans by the JDB and other public intermediaries to industries producing machine tools, auto parts and implements, mostly comprising small and medium firms
Law on Temporary Measures for Promoting the Electronics Industry	1957; revised 1964–71	Stipulating low-interest loans by public intermediaries to makers of electronic calculators and instruments for automating factories
Law on Temporary Measures for Promoting Specified Machinery Industries and Specified Electronics Industries	1971–78	Successor to the two aforementioned measures, targeting firms producing auto parts and those producing integrated circuits
Law on Temporary Measures for Promoting Specified Machinery and Information Industries	1978	Extension of the previous
Petrochemicals Promotion Measures	First measure 1955–58 Second measure 1959–64 Third measure 1964–65	Providing sale of government-owned fuel storage facilities to private firms, as well as JDB loans at preferential interest rates, accelerated depreciation, and tariff reductions on machinery imports
Law on Temporary Measures for Textile Industry Equipment	1956	Preferential public financing of purchases of modern looms tied to the scrapping of old ones; promotion of synthetic fibers, cartelization of cotton spinning
Law on Temporary Measures for Textile Industry Equipment and Related Equipment	1964	Providing accelerated depreciation of equipment and JDB financing of one new machine for each two scrapped
Structural Improvement of Specified Textile Industries	1967–73	Providing preferential financing for mergers and modernization
Law on Temporary Measures for Rationalization of Production of Small and Medium Sized Ships	1959–64	
Law Concerning the Production and Operation of Small Ships	1966	Extension of the previous
Law on Temporary Measures for Textile Industry Equipment and Related Equipment	1964	Providing accelerated depreciation of equipment and JDB financing of one new machine for each two scrapped

Source: Ryutaro Komiya, Masahiro Okuno, and Kotaro Suzumura (eds.), *Industrial Policy of Japan*, New York: Academic Press, 1988; and James Vestal, *Planning for Change: Industrial Policy and Japanese Economic Development, 1945–1990*, Oxford University Press, 1993.

cartels studied by Weinstein, like the export cartels studied by Dick, were generally ineffective either at inducing contrived scarcities or enriching their members.[41]

The ineffectiveness of antitrust exemptions in Japan is unsurprising for two reasons. First, the penalties for violating the anti-monopoly law of Japan are notoriously weak and the resources devoted to enforcing the law are minimal. Even without an official exemption, the anti-monopoly law is unlikely to have much impeded the formation of cartels among Japanese firms. Second, official sanction of cartels does not imply public enforcement of collusive agreements. And without that, cheating among the firms themselves is apt to thwart attempts at inducing contrived scarcities or resolving free-rider problems. Furthermore, administrative guidance, with no powerful sanctions to back it up, is apparently not sufficient to enforce collusive arrangements. MITI attempted without much success to cartelize the steel industry through coordinating the investment plans of the various firms, and issuing administrative guidance regarding prices. The "steel list price system", initiated with MITI assistance in 1958 and continued for many years thereafter, was largely ineffective at inhibiting price-cutting.[42] Given all this, why would industries covet official permission to form cartels? Perhaps the officially sanctioned cartels really represent the organized constituencies of firms that might qualify for targeted measures of the sorts listed in the previous sections, but this is only a hunch.

There have been only a few attempts to quantify the economic effects of the varied and numerous measures described above. In one of these, Ogura and Yoshino[43] examined data from the financial statements of large corporations. They found that in 1955–61 the automobile and steel industries benefited most from special depreciation measures, that the shipbuilding and machinery industries benefited somewhat less, and that other industries benefited very little. From 1962 to 1973, special depreciation expenses were smaller in magnitude than in the earlier period, with shipbuilding benefiting the most, but, again, with the automobile and steel industries also benefiting greatly. They calculated the present value of the special depreciation measures and found them generally to range between 0.5 and 4 percent of investment expenditures for most of

these industries in each year. Ogura and Yoshino also estimated reductions in interest burdens resulting from firms' having borrowed from public intermediaries rather than private banks. They inferred effective interest rates by dividing each enterprise's interest payments to private and public intermediaries, respectively, by its outstanding loans to same. In this calculation, interest payments to private banks include an estimated implicit interest payment due to the holding of deposits in the same bank (compensating balances).

Table 9.6 reports Ogura and Yoshino's summaries of the present value of reduced interest burden arising from loans from public intermediaries and the present value of tax deferrals arising from special acceleration of depreciation expenses, by broad sectors of the economy over 1961–80. From these estimates, one might judge the former to have been far less evenly distributed across industries, in relation to investment. As a targeting measure, the preferential tax stipulations may not have amounted to much.

Even without effective mechanisms for erecting cartels, the combination of foreign exchange rationing, loans from public intermediaries, and preferential tax deferrals and exemptions afforded a potent set of instruments for directing resources toward favored industries and protecting them from foreign competition. This regime ended with the high-growth era, and was succeeded by a new regime, in which liberalization of Japan's foreign trade and investment, particularly after 1964, diluted the effectiveness of industrial policy. With

---

[41] Using six years of monthly data for each industry, Weinstein estimated generic, structural supply and demand equations, and, using dummy variables, estimated the effects of cartels on both equations. Recession cartels, 1962–83, and the special cartels, 1966–88, exhibited almost no measurable effect on either supply or demand. For the special cartels 1958–62, in the initial year of sanction industry supply generally contracted by enough to raise price by around 1%, but with the passage of time this effect seemed to disappear.

[42] Tokyo University's Miwa Y(oshiro) has argued quite persuasively that MITI's persistent attempts to cartelize the steel industry through administrative guidance all failed abysmally: Yoshiro Miwa, "Economic Consequences of Investment Coordination in the Steel Industry", in Firms and Industrial Organization in Japan, London: Macmillan, 1996, ch. 8.

[43] Seiritsu Ogura and Naoyuki Yoshino, "The Tax System and the Fiscal Investment and Loan Program", in Ryutaro Komiya, Masahiro Okuno, and Kotaro Suzumura (eds.), Industrial Policy of Japan, New York: Academic Press, 1988, ch. 5, pp. 121–53.

Table 9.6. Reductions in interest burden arising from public loans and reductions in taxes resulting from special depreciation allowances, by industry, 1961–1980

| | % of total fixed investment | | | |
| | 1961–73 | | 1974–80 | |
	Reduced interest	Increased depreciation	Reduced interest	Increased depreciation
Manufacturing	1.0	0.95	1.6	0.57
Transportation machinery	6.9	1.3	6.4	0.7
Iron and steel	0.5	1.4	1.6	0.7
General machinery	3.6	1.4	2.6	0.5
Marine shipping	22.3	7.2	17.0	4.1
Electric power	5.9	0.36	2.8	0.9

Source: Seiritsu Ogura and Naoyuki Yoshino, "The Tax System and the Fiscal Investment and Loan Program", in Ryutaro Komiya, Masahiro Okuno, and Kotaro Suzumura (eds.), *Industrial Policy of Japan*, New York: Academic Press, 1988, table VI, p. 151.

trade opening, Japanese firms responded not only to the dictates of the government, but also to the imperatives of the world marketplace. The Japanese government continued protecting a few sectors, including textiles, transistors, and agriculture, but the general trend of the 1970s was toward openness, and Japan's industrial policy took on a new focus.

The recent decades, 1975–

After the mid-1970s, the Japanese government, perhaps bowing to the law of international comparative advantage, shifted the focus of its industrial policy away from encouragement of heavy industries like steel, shipbuilding, or petrochemicals, and toward active promotion of collaborative research efforts in the high tech industries, and assistance of firms and workers in declining sectors.

(i) Assistance to declining sectors In the mid-1970s, when Japan's macroeconomic growth slowed and world oil prices quadrupled, a number of Japanese industries faced permanent economic reversals, and became widely perceived as "troubled", "structurally depressed", and so on. Some of these industries were the very same ones earlier targeted as "strategic" or "priority" sectors and promoted with subsidies, special tax breaks, and all the rest. Steel, shipbuilding, chemical fertilizer, coal mining, and petrochemicals number among the Japanese industries promoted in the 1950s and 1960s but

threatened with bankruptcy in the late 1970s. These industries continued to attract government attention even after confronting hardship, only now the focus became managing the redeployment of resources so as to stave off bankruptcies and protect workers' livelihoods. The package of measures used to accomplish this included payments of special unemployment compensation, government payments to firms scrapping equipment, official sanctioning of cartels, and tax exemptions and loans from public intermediaries for firms exiting troubled industries and entering different ones. Japan's coal mining and cotton textiles industries had already begun to elicit these sorts of measures in the previous decade.

Japan's coal mining industry had faced secularly declining demand ever since the opening of Middle East oil fields after World War II began to steadily lower the world price of petroleum and reduce the demand for coal. Yet even as late as 1955, the Japanese government was continuing to promote added investment in coal mining, and it abandoned this policy only when private coal producers no longer found expansion profitable even with government subsidies.[44] Employment in Japan's coal

---

[44] On the political history of Japanese government coal policies, see Richard J. Samuels, *The Business of the Japanese State: Energy Markets in Comparative and Historical Perspective*, Cornell University Press, 1987.

207

mining industry peaked in 1957 at 340,904. By 1963 it had fallen below 200,000, and by 1975 below 50,000. The Law on Temporary Measures for Coal Mining Area Development, enacted in 1961, offered subsidies to lure new businesses to coal regions, the first of many such measures, continuing into the 1990s.

Japan's textile industries had been economically distressed since the 1960s. The emergence of foreign competitors, and Japan's rising real wage rate, reduced the international competitiveness of Japan's textile industries, particularly those using natural fibers (cotton and silk). Nevertheless, trade protection and government subsidies of various kinds delayed the withdrawal of resources from these industries, and Japan was still the world's largest exporter of cotton textiles as late as 1969. These policies generated trade friction and led to the implementation of voluntary export restraints of cotton textiles by agreements with the USA and Europe. (The US–Japan Short-Term Cotton Textile Agreement, in effect over 1957–61, was succeeded by the multinational Long-Term Textile Arrangement, in effect over 1962–74, and supplemented by a special government agreement with the Nixon administration in October 1971.) In implementing these international agreements, the Japanese government also adopted measures to ameliorate some of their harmful effects on the industry. The Law on Temporary Measures for Structural Improvement of Textile Industries 1967–73 offered government assistance for textile firms to switch over to other businesses. It was extended twice, for 1974–8 and again for 1979–84.[45] Coal mining and textiles are not the lone examples of economically distressed Japanese industries to receive government support.

The First Oil Shock in 1973, and the permanent slowdown in Japan's macroeconomic growth rate about the same time, induced economic reversals in an unprecedented range of Japanese industries. Japan's shipbuilding industry had by 1970 become the world's dominant producer of oil supertankers. Naturally, with the contraction of Middle East oil shipments, the world demand for supertankers declined, and Japan's largest shipbuilders suffered enormous losses. The oil shock also wreaked havoc on Japan's petrochemical industries. But more than this, the rise in oil prices enlarged the marginal cost of producing electricity, which induced a contrac-

tion in the supply of electricity and a rise in its price. Industries that use electricity intensely suffered severe economic losses. In Japan these included aluminum refining and the producers of chemical fertilizer using electrolytic processes. Finally, the general slowdown of economic growth after the mid-1970s left intermediate goods industries with excess capacity. Particularly hard hit were the steel producers using open hearth and electric-arc furnaces. Theirs was a double whammy—both falling demand and rising marginal costs. In contrast, the two oil shocks of the 1970s somewhat revived Japan's coal mining industry, but only to delay its inevitable ultimate extinction.

To specifically address the wide-ranging economic adjustments occurring after the mid-1970s, the Diet enacted the Law on Temporary Measures for Promoting and Stabilizing Specified Depressed Industries (industry stabilization law), in effect over 1978–83. The main thrust of this measure was to authorize government sanction of cartels, including export cartels, and to offer loans from public intermediaries, government loan guarantees, and other subsidies to assist businesses converting to new industries. The law pertained to fourteen industries, half of them identified in the statute itself and the other half subsequently added by cabinet order. These were: aluminum smelting, ferrosylicon, linerboard, open-hearth and electric arc producers of steel, four synthetic fiber industries, three fertilizer industries, shipbuilding, cotton textiles, and wool textiles. The public loans and loan guarantees directed by the statute were heavily concentrated on the shipbuilding industry.

The further rise in oil prices that attended the Iranian revolution of 1979 (the Second Oil Shock) prolonged and enlarged many adverse effects of the First Oil Shock in Japan, and led to the enactment of a new statute to succeed the expiring industry stabilization law. The Law on Temporary Measures for the Structural Improvement of Specified Industries, in effect over 1983–8, pertained to twenty-two industries, including most of the ones targeted before along with cement, electric wire, sugar refining,

---

45 On Japanese government policies toward the cotton textile industry, see Robert M. Uriu, *Troubled Industries: Confronting Economic Change in Japan*, Cornell University Press, 1996.

and a number of newly designated industries producing petrochemicals. It had similar provisions to the earlier law. At the 1988 expiration of this law, yet another was enacted to succeed it, the Law on Temporary Measures for Adjustment Facilitation. The measure provided for JDB loans, tax exemptions, and tax deferrals, all directed at firms scrapping eighteen specific types of equipment.

In addition to the measures already mentioned, the Japanese government enacted a number of laws directing subsidies and assistance to the structurally unemployed and to the numerous small subcontractors in the declining industries, and assisting in the economic development of the most severely distressed regions of the nation. As these laws expired over 1983–6, they were renewed or replaced with new statutes, almost all of which have now expired, bringing to a close this chapter in the history of Japan's industrial policy.[46] There remains one final element of Japan's recent industrial policy for us to discuss: special support for high tech industries.

(ii) Support for high technology industries The government of Japan, like that of other developed nations, has encouraged inventive activity in a variety of ways that should probably not be regarded as an industrial policy, defined as the targeting of specific sectors. These include public expenditures on basic scientific research, the award of patents, and preferential tax treatment of private research expenditures. In addition, some small portion of public support for research in Japan (less than 5 percent of public R&D expenditures) is directed at developing commercial applications in specific industries, and is indeed a kind of targeting. With the shift in focus of other elements of Japan's industrial policy from growing sectors to declining ones, this sort of government encouragement of industry has seemed more prominent. It is the major ongoing element of government support for Japan's high tech industries: semiconductors, computers, biotechnology, and robotics, among others.

Government support for developing commercial applications of new technologies is, of course, not a new policy in Japan. The Tomioka silk-reeling plant operated by the Meiji government was essentially that. In more recent times, the Japanese government has operated several national laboratories since the early 1950s including the Electronic Laboratory, under the direction of MITI, which produced the first transistors in Japan only a few years after their invention in the USA, and laboratories affiliated with Japan's nationalized telecommunications enterprise NTT, which developed new switching equipment and other related technologies. There are many other government research institutes, mostly devoted to energy, pollution abatement, and health. More significantly, since the 1960s, the Japanese government has also directly supported selected, applied research efforts of private firms themselves.

The Mining and Manufacturing Technology Research Association Law, enacted in 1961, authorized MITI to organize and contribute funds to joint research ventures involving firms in the industries within its provenance. To better implement these powers, MITI's "Agency" of Industrial Science and Technology was formed in 1966 to manage the funding of large-scale projects.[47] The most famous project under this program was the Very Large Scale Integrated Circuits (VLSI) Technology Research Association, 1976–9, which successfully developed processes for manufacturing certain kinds of semi-

---

46 These laws included the following: Law on Temporary Measures for Those Unemployed in Specified Depressed Industries 1978–83; Law on Temporary Measures for Those Unemployed in Specified Regions 1978–83; Law on Special Measures Concerning Stabilization of Employment in Specified Depressed Industries and in Specified Depressed Regions 1983–1986; Law on Special Measures for Employment Stabilization in Specified Industries 1987–1995; Law on Promotion of Regional Employment 1987–; Law on Temporary Measures for Assisting Small and Medium Enterprises to Cope with Yen Appreciation 1978–80; Law on Temporary Measures for Small and Medium Enterprises in Specified Depressed Regions 1978–83; Law on Temporary Measures for Small Firms in Specified Depressed Regions 1983–1988; Law on Temporary Measures for Business Conversion of Small Firms 1986–1993; Law on Temporary Measures for Dealing with Regions Related to Specified Depressed Industries 1983.

47 Scott Callon has noted that the Japanese name for the MITI subdivision officially translated "Agency for Industrial Science and Technology" (Kōgyō Gijutsu In) would be more accurately rendered in English as "Institute of Industrial Technology", but inserting the English words "agency" and "science" seems to place it more on a par with the Science and Technology Agency (Kagaku Gijutsu Chō), the cabinet-level entity charged with co-ordinating the public research expenditures of all the ministries. Most public research expenditures to universities are allocated by the Ministry of Education, while most public research expenditures to private businesses are allocated by MITI. See Scott Callon, *Divided Sun: MITI and the Breakdown of Japanese High-Tech Industrial Policy, 1975–1993*, Stanford University Press, 1995, pp. 34–5.

conductors. This project was 40 percent publicly funded and 60 percent privately funded, with a total budget of ¥74 billion (about $50 million). Japan's rise to dominance of the manufacture of dynamic random access memory (DRAM) silicone semiconductor chips, invented only in 1970 by Intel, an American company, is widely hailed, or condemned, as being a direct result of the VLSI project. On the basis of these arguments, the US government enacted legislation authorizing antitrust exemptions for similar research consortia (1984 National Cooperative Research Act). Under the antitrust protection afforded by this act, the US government in 1987 established a publicly funded research consortium of private semiconductor manufacturer firms, known as the Semiconductor Manufacturing Technology Corporation (Sematech), a direct analogue of MITI's VLSI project. As of this writing, Sematech seems to have been a costly failure.[48]

There have been well over a hundred research consortia organized by MITI. One of the better known ones, besides the VLSI consortium, was the Fifth Generation Consortium (1982–92). It never achieved its ambitious objective, the development of a computer able to simulate human thought. When, sooner or later, there is another stunning MITI "success" such as the VLSI project, the previous failures should also be recalled.

This completes the description of Japan's industrial policy and its many changes over the passing decades. It remains for us to consider whether any of it has mattered.

Analysis of Japanese industrial policy

There have been several serious attempts at empirical analysis of Japanese industrial policy, all focusing on the postwar era. The most comprehensive is that of Richard Beason and David Weinstein.[49] They collected annual time-series measuring the distribution across two-digit SIC mining and manufacturing industries of government transfers (per unit of output), tariff rates, average effective corporate tax rates, and relative dependence on JDB loans (JDB loans as a percentage of all loans to the sector) over 1955–90. They then sought contemporaneous and lagged statistical relations between these meas-

ures of government policy and their own sophisticated measures of the annual rates of technological advance in the same respective industries. They found no relation, either for any one industry or for the pooled set of industries, in the high-growth era 1955–74, in the more recent period 1975–90, or in the two together. Industrial policy made virtually no measurable contribution to Japan's postwar economic growth.

Industrial policy might still have enlarged Japan's national income, even without enhancing its total factor productivity, if it had improved its international terms of trade. For this to have occurred, Japanese targeting must have induced contrived scarcities that raised the prices of Japanese exports in foreign markets. Marcus Noland made a study of this possibility, focusing on the years between 1968 and 1984.[50] For the years 1968, 1976, and 1984, for the two-digit SIC mining and manufacturing sectors, he computed net subsidies on loans from public intermediaries, present value of tax deferrals resulting from the application of special depreciation rates, and effective tariff rates. He found significant, but somewhat idiosyncratic, contemporaneous and eight-year lagged statistical relations between the policy variables and the net exports of each sector. High tariff rates in a given sector, perversely, seemed to be associated with reduced net exports in the same sector. But tax preferences and loan subsidies seemed generally to stimulate sectoral net exports, with a lag. Further, Noland found that without these effects of industrial policy Japan would have been a net importer, rather than net exporter, of iron and steel, general machinery, precision machinery, chemicals, and transportation equipment, in at least some years between 1968 and 1974. That is, Japan's encouragement of steel, shipbuilding, chemical fertilizers, electronic calculators, and machine tools might indirectly have reduced Japan's net exports of other goods (automobiles?

48 Andrew Dick, *Industrial Policy and Semiconductors: Missing the Target*, Washington, DC: American Enterprise Institute, 1995, esp. ch. 8, "The Sematech Experiment".

49 Richard Beason and David E. Weinstein, "Growth, Economies of Scale, and Targeting in Japan (1955–1990)", *Review of Economics and Statistics*, vol. 88, no. 2 (May 1996), pp. 286–95.

50 Marcus Noland, "The Impact of Industrial Policy on Japan's Trade Specialization", *Review of Economics and Statistics*, vol. 75 (May 1993), pp. 241–8.

transistors?) and, conceivably, raised the relative prices of those other goods in foreign markets, to Japan's net benefit. This line of reasoning seems speculative in the extreme. Noland's evidence is unlikely to convince skeptics that Japan's industrial policy did improve the nation's terms of foreign trade.

Analyses focusing, narrowly, on the effects of industrial policy on specific sectors afford sharper assessments. Paul Krugman has evaluated government encouragement of Japan's steel industry.[51] He makes the simple observation that in 1971, after two decades of subsidized loans and special tax breaks for steel producers, Japan's steel industry was earning a rate of return on its assets well below the average for other Japanese manufacturing industries. This was not a case of industrial policy simulating the effects of Smith's invisible hand, but of its expanding the capacity to produce steel beyond what was narrowly profitable. For this to have been a wise policy, there would have had to exist external benefits from enlargement of the steel industry. But, as Krugman convincingly argues, there really were none. The technology of steel production has advanced little since 1950, and by 1960 had been completely assimilated by the Japanese producers—no neighborhood effects of expanded industry output here.

Industrial targeting made Japan's steel industry larger, but probably reduced Japan's national income. To put it another way, investments in the industry would have earned a higher social return elsewhere. In a clumsy attempt at rebutting Krugman's analysis, the journalist Robert Kuttner averred, "The most obvious benefit of Japanese steel targeting is that it gave Japan relatively cheap inputs for other major exports (cars, ships) and that it provided a winning export product in steel itself."[52] Careful readers of the early parts of this chapter will immediately recognize this for the specious claim that it is (cf. especially the section titled "Marshallian externalities"). Kuttner apparently mistakes a pecuniary externality for a technological one. Krugman's argument still stands, and almost surely applies not only to steel, but also to shipbuilding, chemical fertilizers, coal mining, petrochemicals, and the other "priority" sectors targeted by Japan's industrial policy for the two decades after 1945.

We turn finally to the semiconductor industry,

a high tech industry widely presumed to exhibit Marshallian externalities, learning effects, and oligopolistic tendencies. Furthermore, the research consortium organized by MITI that perfected the technology for producing DRAM chips is a clear example of Japanese targeting. Informal government protection of the industry from imports is a further possible element of Japanese industrial policy toward the industry: US semiconductor firms alleged that MITI had connived with domestic demanders of DRAM chips to effect a "buy Japanese" policy. By the mid-1980s Japanese producers had attained a near total dominance of the domestic DRAM market and held a significant share of the world market.

Baldwin and Krugman attempted to gauge the possible effects of market protection on the price of a particular kind of DRAM, the 16K DRAM, and on Japanese producer profits and consumer welfare.[53] Their analysis takes into account the plausible reductions in Japanese producers' marginal costs arising from the learning effects of the enlarged cumulative output that protection would have afforded. Their finding? The learning effects engendered by protection of the domestic market were indeed crucial to the Japanese export of semiconductors. They lowered the marginal costs of the Japanese producers, and, by constricting the cumulative output and learning effects of foreign producers, raised the foreign rivals' marginal costs by even more. But competition among the Japanese producers competed away any profits the industry might have realized from these effects. Furthermore, the world price of semiconductors would have actually been lower if foreigners had captured the Japanese market, and experienced the learning effects of their enlarged cumulative output. Protection of the domestic market was a loser for Japanese consumers and gained nothing for Japanese producers, claim Baldwin and Krugman. Their analysis

[51] Paul R. Krugman, "Targeted Industrial Policies: Theory and Evidence", in Dominick Salvatore (ed.), *The New Protectionist Threat to World Welfare*, Amsterdam: North-Holland, 1987.

[52] Robert Kuttner, "Commentary", in *Industrial Change and Public Policy: A Symposium Sponsored by the Federal Reserve Bank of Kansas City, Jackson Hole, Wyoming, August 24–26, 1983*, Kansas City, Kan.: FRB of Kansas City, p. 175.

[53] Richard Baldwin and Paul R. Krugman, "Market Access and International Competition: A Simulation Study of 16K Random Access Memories", in Robert Feenstra (ed.), *Empirical Studies of International Trade*, Cambridge, Mass.: MIT Press, 1988.

presumes that learning effects are confined within the respective nations. For example, Japanese marginal costs of producing semiconductors depend upon the cumulative output of the Japanese producers. This is the fundamental premise on which Japanese government targeting of semiconductors could even conceivably have been welfare enhancing for Japan.

Irwin and Klenow find this presumption to be refuted by data on the evolving prices of DRAM chips and market shares of individual producers.[54] They find that firms learn three times more from an increase in their own output as they do from an increase in the output of another firm, but that learning spills over just as much between firms of differing nationalities as it does between firms of the same nationality. If there exists a community of scientists and engineers within which the sharing of knowledge gives rise to propitious neighborhood effects, then that community appears to be an international one, based on this evidence for the semiconductor industry. The case for Japanese government promotion or protection of its semi-conductor industry having improved Japanese economic welfare is just not tenable.

Conclusion

The famous reputation of Japanese industrial policy owes much to the fact that the years before liberalization of foreign trade in the mid-1960s stripped MITI of some of its powers coincided exactly with the onset of Japan's remarkable postwar economic recovery. Yet the industries most favored by Japanese industrial policy prior to 1964—coal mining, steel, electric power, and shipbuilding—contributed relatively less to high growth than did other, less favored, industries. Nor did the favored industries exhibit the valid criteria for economically efficient targeting—Marshallian externality, rapid innovation, or international oligopoly.

---

[54] Douglas A. Irwin and Peter J. Klenow, "Learning-by-Doing Spillovers in the Semiconductor Industry", *Journal of Political Economy*, vol. 102, no. 6 (December 1994), pp. 1200–27.

FURTHER READING

■ Chalmers Johnson, *MITI and the Japanese Miracle, 1925–1975*, Stanford University Press, 1982. A detailed and insightful political history of MITI that did much to popularize the notion that industrial policy was a significant factor in Japan's successful economic development.

■ Ryutaro Komiya, Masahiro Okuno, and Kotaro Suzumura (eds.), *Industrial Policy of Japan*, New York: Academic Press, 1988. Description and empirical analysis of a wide range of Japanese government policies, written by professors of economics at Japanese universities.

■ Paul R. Krugman (ed.), *Strategic Trade Policy and the New International Economics*, Cambridge, Mass.: MIT Press, 1986. Economists discuss the theoretical case for government promotion of high tech industries and its relevance to actual policy, including some industrial policies of the Japanese government.

■ Robert S. Ozaki, *The Control of Imports and Foreign Capital in Japan*, New York: Praeger Publishers, 1972. Describes the procedure followed by the government of Japan in allocating foreign exchange from 1953 to 1964; an early recognition of the fact that the MITI bureaucrats rationing foreign exchange perceived themselves to be implementing an industrial policy.

■ Richard J. Samuels, *"Rich Nation, Strong Army": National Security and the Technological Transformation of Japan*, Cornell University Press, 1994. Convincingly argues that promotion of national defense has motivated most serious attempts at industrial targeting by the Japanese government, from the Meiji era to the present.

■ Hong W. Tan and Haruo Shimada (eds.), *Troubled Industries in the US and Japan*, New York: St Martin's Press, 1996. Theoretical and empirical analysis of government policies that assist declining sectors.

■ James E. Vestal, *Planning for Change: Industrial Policy and Japanese Economic Development, 1945–1990*, Oxford University Press, 1993. A chronological account of Japanese industrial policies since the Occupation era.

Public Finance | 10

In Japan as in other democracies, many of the most hotly debated political issues concern the public finances: taxes, the issuance and retirement of government debt, and the collective provision of goods and services including education, health care, social security, and national defense. We have touched briefly on Japanese taxation and government debt in some of the other chapters and will not delve further into those matters.[1] But here we shall briefly examine the expenditure side of Japan's public finances, with particular focus on the rationale and dimensions of Japanese government provision of goods and services.

Until quite recently, it would have been correct to say that the public sector of Japan was small compared with those of the other developed countries. This is no longer true. Largely as a result of social welfare legislation enacted in the 1970s, government expenditures in Japan have ballooned and now absorb as great a fraction of national income as does US public spending.

The public sector of Japan

The public sector encompasses two different economic roles of government: that of provider of goods and that of producer of goods.[2] A lot of collectively provided goods in Japan and elsewhere are also government-produced and vice versa, but there are many exceptions. For instance, governments also produce goods without providing them, that is they produce for sale. A long-time Japanese example is the government production and sale of industrial alcohol (recently privatized). There are also goods that governments provide but without themselves producing. For Japan this includes health care.

Government production in Japan

There are no perfectly satisfactory measures of the scale of government production. The major problem is that of valuing the output of public enterprise. Much of the output of government is not sold, so there are no market prices by which to value it. An alternative is to eschew attempts at measuring output and instead measure the government employment of productive inputs, the most important of which is labor.

Government employees as a fraction of the labor force for Japan and other countries, reported by separate categories, are given in Table 10.1. By this measure, the role of the Japanese government as producer of goods is quite small indeed compared

---

1 For a thorough description of Japanese taxes, both currently and historically, consult Hiromitsu Ishi, *The Japanese Tax System*, 2nd edn, Oxford: Clarendon Press, 1992. For a pithy critique of Japan's tax system from the standpoint of economic efficiency, see Alan Reynolds, "Toward Meaningful Tax Reform in Japan", presented at Keidanren–Cato Institute Symposium, Tokyo, April 6, 1998 (http://www.freetrade.org/pubs/speeches/ar-4-6-98.html).

2 There is also a third role performed by government: that of the setter and enforcer of rules. The government regulation of commerce, trade, and private finance are in this category. This important set of topics is reserved for the chapters on industrial policy (Ch. 9), environmental policy (11), industrial organization (12), financial institutions (13), and labor (15).

Table 10.1. Government employees as a percentage of all employment, Japan and selected other nations, 1988 and 1994

	Total employment[a] (mn)		Government service (except armed forces and public enterprise) (%)		Armed forces (%)		Public enterprise (%)	
	1988	1994	1988	1994	1988	1994	1975–9	1988
JAPAN	60.1	64.5	6.0	6.0	0.4	—	1.4	0.02
USA	116.7	124.5	13.0	13.4	1.5	1.1	1.6	
UK	25.9	25.3	19.5	15.0	1.2	—	8.2	
Germany	27.4	36.3	13.7	13.9	1.9	1.2	7.9	
France	21.7	22.3	20.7	13.8	2.6	2.4	4.4	
Canada	12.3	13.4	18.8	13.4	0.6	0.5	4.5	
Italy	21.5	20.0	13.0	16.2	2.6	—	5.7	
OECD	361.4	418.5	13.7	14.7	1.4	0.8	n.a.	

a Total employment includes both civilian and armed forces.

Sources: Total employment, government service, and armed forces: *OECD Economic Outlook Historical Statistics 1960–1988*, Paris: OECD, 1990, table 2.13, p. 42, and table D, p. 22; and OECD, *Historical Statistics 1960–1994*, Paris: OECD, 1996, table 2.13, p. 44, and table D, p. 22. Public enterprise: Leila Pathirane and Derek W. Blades, "Defining and Measuring the Public Sector: Some International Comparisons", *Review of Income and Wealth*, vol. 28, no. 3 (September 1982), pp. 261–89, table 4, and *Japan Statistical Yearbook 1990*, table 21–3.

with the governments of other countries including the United States. And with the privatization of the national railways, the nationalized telecommunications firm (NTT), and the monopoly of salt and tobacco, government production in Japan has shrunk even further. At the least, such comparisons belie the many commentaries to the effect that Japan's economy is based more on a principle of central planning and government direction than is that of the USA.

Is bureaucracy more efficient in Japan than elsewhere?

Japan's small employment in central and local government administration compared with the United States has indicated to some not Japan's limited production of administrative services, but its great efficiency of providing such services.[3] A comparison of the staff of MITI with its US counterparts is illustrative. Although most noted as the ministry responsible for executing the industrial policy of Japan—awarding tax credits, granting licenses to import, and monitoring compliance with industrial standards—it is also charged with the regulation of

Japan's ten electric power companies, and with the oversight of other energy industries including petroleum refining, gas and coal, conducting censuses of manufacturing and commerce, and awarding permission to open large stores. In the USA, these tasks devolve on a variety of agencies and commissions, including the Department of Commerce, the Department of Energy, the public utilities commissions of the various states, and even local zoning boards. In 1985 the staff of MITI was 17,763 while that of the US Department of Commerce was 35,150, of the Department of Energy 16,749, and of the state public utilities commissions about 5,000. Though the population of the United States is just twice that of Japan, the MITI bureaucrats performed tasks which in the USA required the services of about three times as many persons.

Three different reasons for claiming that bureaucrats are more productive in Japan than in other countries have been cited. The first is the rich tradition of bureaucratic government that flowed to

---

3 See e.g. K. Calder, "Japan's Minimalist Government", *Wall Street Journal*, February 13, 1981.

Japan from ancient China, achieving its ultimate refinement in the Tokugawa *baku-han* system. Even today, the civil service of Japan occupies an exalted position in society and attracts the ablest graduates of the top universities.[4] The second reason is the practice of retired government officials being posted to private firms, *amakudari*, literally "descent from heaven". Milton Friedman, no admirer of government bureaucracy, has commented favorably on this practice.[5] The notion here is that bureaucrats learn that a high paying job upon retirement depends on the display of exceptional diligence while still in the civil service. A third explanation may be more important than either of these. Fiscal authority in Japan is far more centralized than in the USA. The federal system in which local governments exercise autonomy in public spending and taxation allows wide differences across jurisdictions but requires duplication of many administrative procedures. To say that a unitary system in which control resides in the central government is more efficient than a federal system entails a judgment that local autonomy is not worth the added costs of fragmented administration. Such a claim is not easily proved.

Government provision of goods in Japan

As with government production, the value of government provision of goods is more precisely gauged by measuring outlays than by imputing a conjectural value to output. Quite simply, the value of resources that are absorbed in the collective provision of goods is indicated by government expenditure.

There are two kinds of government expenditure: government purchases, and transfers. *Transfers* are payments made without receipt of goods in return. Examples include subsidies, social security payments, public assistance, and interest payments on government debt. Purchases contribute directly to aggregate demand while transfers do not. But all government expenditures including transfer payments represent a collective provision of goods.

The political decision to collectively provide hospital services as through Britain's nationalized health industry results in government final purchases in the form of hospital buildings, doctors' salaries, and so on. But Japan's current system of covering privately incurred health care expenses on a fee-for-service basis gives rise to transfer payments. Both entail the collective provision of health services. To measure the value of all government-provided collective goods, we need to include all government expenditures for both final purchases and transfers.

Table 10.2 compares government expenditures relative to GNP for Japan and several other countries. By this measure, the collective provision of goods is smaller in Japan than in most other countries, but before 1974 it was much smaller. The growth of government spending since then in Japan consists overwhelmingly of payments for medical expenses and retirement pensions, both mandated by legislation enacted in 1973. As a result of these changes, not only the size but also the composition of government expenditures of Japan have come to closely match those of the other developed countries (with the exception of defense, which absorbs a rather smaller share of national income in Japan).

Japan, like the United States and the other countries in the table, devotes a significant fraction of its GDP to the collective provision of social security, education, health, and defense. And the largest component for each country is social security.

Politics, voting, and public choice

The sorts of goods to be collectively provided and their quantities are a political decision. But, to the extent politicians are constrained to act in the economic interests of their constituents, goods will be provided collectively only when they are socially valued above costs. Institutional features of the

---

4 For more on the social status of bureaucrats in Japan, see John Creighton Campbell, "Democracy and Bureaucracy in Japan", in Takeshi Ishida and Ellis S. Kraus (eds.), *Democracy in Japan*, University of Pittsburgh Press, 1989, pp. 113–38.

5 "We have an image of Japan incorporated as being government-industry collaboration . . . A very simple thing makes that arrangement work in Japan: It is retirement at age fifty-five, with top officials in the government bureaus then going to work for the private enterprises they were connected with before. That is what transfers the private incentives to the political level": Milton Friedman, "Market Mechanisms and Central Planning", the G. Warren Nutter Lecture in Political Economy, *American Enterprise Institute* (1981), pp. 125–6. For further elaboration of the incentives conferred on bureaucrats by *amakudari*, see M. Aoki, *Information, Incentives and Bargaining in the Japanese Economy*, Cambridge University Press, 1988, pp. 264–8; and Ulrike Schaede, "The 'Old Boy' Network and Government–Business Relationships in Japan", *Journal of Japanese Studies*, vol. 21, no. 2 (1995), pp. 293–317.

Table 10.2. Government expenditures relative to GDP, by purpose, Japan and selected other nations, 1972–1996

	JAPAN[a]	USA[b]	UK[c]	Germany	France	Italy[d]	Canada
Defense							
1973	0.9	6.3	5.2	2.9	1.6	2.2	1.7
1986	1.0	6.5	3.6	3.0	3.2	2.5	2.2
1994–7	0.9	3.2	3.2	1.6	4.0	1.7	n.a.
Education							
1973	4.2	5.0	6.1	4.7	4.5	5.3	5.9
1986	n.a.	n.a.	n.a.	n.a.	n.a.	n.a.	n.a.
1994–7	3.8	5.0	n.a.	4.5	5.6	n.a.	6.7
Health							
1973	3.0	1.5	4.6	5.5	5.6	1.2	4.9
1986	4.8	4.4	5.0	7.1	6.5	5.3	6.5
1994–7	5.7	6.5	5.8	8.2	7.8	5.3	6.7
Social security pensions							
1973	5.2	9.9	9.0	13.9	17.7	13.7	9.0
1986	11.2	10.8	13.6	15.9	21.9	17.2	12.3
1994–7	13.4	13.1	14.7	18.6	23.2	18.9	15.1
Interest on public debt							
1973	1.0	2.5	4.2	1.4	1.2	4.2	3.9
1986	n.a.	n.a.	n.a.	n.a.	n.a.	n.a.	n.a.
1994–7	5.6	5.2	3.6	5.2	6.4	n.a.	n.a.
Total							
1973	25.1	35.1	44.5	44.0	41.6	43.1	39.4
1986	31.9	33.1	42.4	59.6	51.3	51.0	44.6
1994–7	36.2	33.3	43.3	46.4	53.7	51.8	45.6

[a] 1972.   [b] 1974–5.   [c] 1973–4.   [d] 1973–5.

Sources: 1970s data: OECD, *Public Expenditure Trends* (June 1978), table 2, pp. 14–15, and table 5, pp. 29–31; 1986 data: OECD, *Historical Statistics 1960–1981*, table 6.3, p. 63 (social security transfers as a percentage of GDP); and *Statistical Abstract of the United States*, table 1486, p. 862 (military expenditures); 1986 and 1990s data: *OECD in Figures 1998* (http://www.oecd.org/publications/figures/index.htm); and International Department, Bank of Japan, *Comparative Economic and Financial Statistics, Japan and other Major Countries*, Tokyo, 1997, p. 114.

political decision process can either strengthen or weaken the alignment of interests between government officials and their constituents. Several features of Japan's political system are relevant here.

The national government: a parliamentary democracy

The Liberal Democratic Party and its precursor retained control of Japan's government continually from 1948 until 1993. In August 1993 the LDP failed to win a majority of seats in the lower house of the Diet, and a coalition government came to power led by a renegade party of defectors from the LDP (the so-called "New Party"). The LDP returned to power in April 1996 in coalition with its once arch-rival Socialist party, and in September 1997 it regained sole power; since July 1997 however it has not enjoyed a majority of seats in the upper house.

During the decades of LDP rule, the budgeting process came to reflect the autocratic decisions of the ruling councils of the party. The give-and-take of legislative debate and voting interfered little with budgets or appropriations of the national government. As a result, the Japanese budget process entailed consideration of the budget as a whole rather than of each item separately. This favored both efficiency and conservatism. Only items clearly valued above cost were likely to be adopted. Each ministry would in August of each year submit proposals to the budget committee of the cabinet, and the cabinet would return the proposals with recommendations. A second round of considerations then resulted in a recommendation to the Diet in December. The Diet generally accepted the proposals without amendment and little debate. Not surprisingly, year-to-year changes in budgets were small.

In contrast, the *ad hoc* budgeting process of the US Congress has always favored adoption individually of proposals that would not have received the endorsement of a majority if voted on as a package. Consider a numerical example from the leading textbook on the economics of public finance written by Nobel laureate James Buchanan and his student Marilyn Flowers.[6] The example goes like this. Suppose that the tax burden of each of three projects is $33.33 per person and that the benefits per person of each project accrue to the equally numerous constituents of legislative districts A, B, and C as follows:

	Project 1	Project 2	Project 3
Benefits to A	$35	$35	$ 0
Benefits to B	35	0	35
Benefits to C	0	35	35

No project is worth funding, yet all three receive the endorsement of a majority of the representatives if considered separately. If considered as a package, the three projects are rejected.

It is too soon to know in what fashion the advent of coalition government and the demise of the formerly dominant LDP will alter these important elements of the budgeting process in Japan. Other significant elements of the Japanese political system, to which we next turn, remain unchanged.

The government of Japan: a highly centralized, unified system

There are many political units within the nation of Japan. Besides the forty-eight prefectures (*to*, *dō*, *fu*, *ken*) there are cities (*shi*), towns (*chō*), and villages (*son*). These political units elect governors, mayors, and other local officials who direct local governing bodies. Articles 92–95 of Japan's constitution adopted in 1947 assure "local self-government". But the appearance of local autonomy is misleading. In matters of public finance the national government holds overriding authority. The basis for central government domination is control of financial resources.

Though two-thirds of government spending is typically channeled through local governing bodies,

only one-third of tax revenues are collected by them. A variety of tax transfers from the central to the local governments offsets this imbalance. But as Ishi,[7] Yonehara,[8] Reed,[9] and other commentators have documented, the tax transfers include extensive directions from central government officials as to how local spending is to be allocated. In practice, the policy is to stress uniformity of level of public services. It would be surprising indeed if Japanese of every different locality valued public works identically, in spite of regional variation in population density, incomes, education, and other things. More likely, national uniformity of government services is not efficient *per se* but arises instead because the unitary fiscal system of Japan is a poor vehicle for linking public spending to local preferences. Offsetting this is the lower overall cost of government administration in a unitary system compared with a federal one.

Overrepresentation of rural districts

Japan has experienced more rapid urbanization since 1920 than any other country of the world.[10] As in the United States and other countries in which urbanization is also occurring, albeit at a slower rate, the rural jurisdictions attain a growing overrepresentation in the national legislature. In the USA a Supreme Court decision of 1964 mandated judicial redistricting to assure a more equal representation in the national Congress. In like fashion, the Supreme Court of Japan has ruled that disparities of three times or more in representation in the lower house of the Diet are unconstitutional and require legislative redistricting. As the status quo generally favors the incumbents, there is little enthusiasm for redistricting by the Diet itself. The result is perpetuation of the rural imbalance, in flagrant defiance of the Supreme Court.

---

6 James M. Buchanan, and Marylin R. Flowers, *The Public Finances: An Introductory Textbook*, 6th edn, Homewood, Ill.: Richard D. Irwin, 1987, p. 135.

7 Hiromitsu Ishi, *The Japanese Tax System*, Oxford University Press, ch. 14, pp. 248–83.

8 Junshichiro Yonehara, *Local Public Finance in Japan*, Research Monograph no. 36, Centre for Research on Federal Financial Relations, Australian National University, 1981.

9 S. R. Reed, *Japanese Prefectures and Policy Making*, University of Pittsburgh Press, 1986.

10 Many details supporting this claim may be found in Norman J. Glickman, *The Growth and Management of the Japanese Urban System*, San Francisco: Academic Press, 1979.

Some tentative conclusions

The distinctive features of public choice in Japan favor efficient provision of national collective goods but not of local ones. In thinking about defense spending, foreign aid, and government support of basic scientific research, there is some basis for modeling these choices as broadly reflecting the general will of the people. But for local public works, including roads, sewers, parks, public housing and the like, claims of government failure are more credible. Many of the specific items of government spending just enumerated are what economists call "public goods".

Public goods

For ordinary goods, market prices are a reliable indication of social value and there is little advantage in collective provision. But parks, bridges, and sewers are not ordinary, for two reasons. The first is that, once the goods are available, there is little or no social gain in excluding anyone in the community from using them. Many can use the same park simultaneously without serious congestion. The second reason why goods like parks are different is that they are indivisible. The different members of the community cannot choose different amounts of parks, bridges, sewer systems, and so on. The quantity must be the same for all. Goods that have these two characteristics—noncongestion and indivisibility—are called "public goods".

Some public goods are privately provided, for instance non-cable TV broadcasts, private toll roads, and private parks. But there are two ways in which market allocation of public goods might be improved upon by government provision. The first is that government can collectively provide public goods that are valued above the costs but are unprofitable for anyone to produce privately. The second reason is that the government can make the services of public goods available to all; that is, it can finance the goods out of general taxes rather than by user fees. Private suppliers will instead set prices for the goods' use and exclude those unwilling to pay.

Besides these two advantages of government provision of public goods, there is also a major disadvantage. The political system may do a poor job of discouraging government provision of goods that are not valued above the costs.[11] In contrast, private production of goods valued below cost is unlikely to occur except by mistake, because of its unprofitability.

Some of the goods typically provided by government are not public goods at all, for instance education. But many of the goods collectively provided by governments *are* public goods, and these include national defense, roads, and parks, among many others.

Local public goods

The social value of a sewer system, a park, or a bridge is the summation of the values placed on it by all who would use it. As these goods tend to be used mainly by those who reside near to them, the goods may be described as *local*. If the cost of supplying local public goods is divided among members of the community in proportion to each person's respective willingness to pay for an additional increment of the good, then there will be unanimity as to which public goods should be collectively provided and in what amounts.[12]

As already discussed, Japan has a unitary fiscal system rather than a federal system. The nationwide configuration of local public goods is decided by the national polity rather than by local governing bodies. Local public goods are therefore not locally financed, as would be required by a matching of cost shares with each person's marginal willingness to

---

11 Adam Smith offered the example of "A great bridge . . . thrown over a river at a place where nobody passes, or merely to embellish the view for the windows of a neighboring palace: things which sometimes happen, in countries where works of this kind are carried on by any other revenue than that which they themselves are capable of affording" (*The Wealth of Nations*, University of Chicago Press, 1976 edn, p. 247). A modern Japanese example of wasteful government provision of goods is the amazing flow of public works projects to the home district of the charismatic politician Tanaka Kakuei, prime minister from July 1972 to December 1974, who was forced to resign as a result of the Lockheed bribery scandal.

12 This was first noted by the Swedish economist Knut Wicksell, who argued on this basis that collective provision of goods should require unanimous approval of the electorate. Wicksell's argument was refined by E. Lindahl, and the constellation of public goods and amounts receiving unanimous approval when costs are borne by each individual in proportion to his marginal valuation is referred to as the *Lindahl equilibrium*. For a modern statement of the argument, see Paul Samuelson, "The Pure Theory of Public Expenditure", *Review of Economics and Statistics*, vol. 36 (November 1954), pp. 387–9; and "Diagrammatic Exposition of a Theory of Public Expenditure", *Review of Economics and Statistics*, vol. 37 (November 1955), pp. 350–6.

pay. Policy stresses national uniformity in the level of public services even though average incomes and tax burdens are higher in urban centers. Consequently residents of Tokyo, Osaka, and Nagoya pay not only the costs of their own local public goods, but also a portion of the cost of local public goods elsewhere in the country. Such a rule—national uniformity of public services—possibly reflects the disproportionate under-representation in the Diet of the urban regions. Whatever the reason, given the implied sharing of costs, residents of Tokyo, Osaka, and Nagoya can be expected to favor smaller national amounts of local public goods than are efficient and citizens of the other communities to favor larger amounts than are efficient. But the efficient level itself is likely to be higher in the urban centers, where higher incomes and greater population sizes induce a higher willingness to pay. The end result is a nationally uniform level of local public goods that is less than the efficient amount in the urban centers but above the efficient amount elsewhere.[13]

In international comparisons, Japan has far less park space, a smaller fraction of houses with sewer connections, fewer public libraries, and fewer air-ports than any other developed country (see Table 10.3). This is particularly striking if the largest cities of Japan are compared with other large cities of the world. The peculiarities of Japanese public finance mentioned in the previous paragraph are probably not the sole reason for Japan's paucity of local public goods.

The US negotiators in the 1990 Japan–US trade talks (the Structural Impediments Initiative) claimed that the Japanese government was spending too little on local public goods and that this had diverted the private savings of the Japanese toward foreign investment. Japan's foreign investment, in this view, was distorting exchange rates and causing trade imbalances that were perhaps to Japan's advantage but were harmful to other countries and disruptive of world trade. Among the other questionable premises of this argument, it rests on the unproven

[13] This is approximately the same argument advanced by Japan's most noted authority on the economics of public finance: Yukio Noguchi, "The Failure of Government to Perform its Proper Task: A Case Study of Japan", *ORDO*, vol. 34 (1983), pp. 59–69.

Table 10.3. Government-provided local public goods, Japan, the USA, France, and the UK, 1980s

	Public parks (m²/person)		Public airports (no. per 1mn persons, 1987)	Sewers (% of population connected)		Public libraries (service points per 1mn persons)	
Japan	4.3	(1986)	6	44	(1988)	18.6	(1986)
Sapporo	5.2						
Tokyo	2.3						
Nagoya	4.9						
Osaka	2.9						
USA		(1984)	219	73	(1986)	67.0	(1985)
Chicago	23.9						
Los Angeles	21.5						
France		(1984)	55	64	(1983)	29.9	(1980)
Paris	12.2						
UK		(1976)	21	95	(1982)	250.4	(1986)
London	30.4						

Sources: Libraries (US): *Statistical Abstract of the US, 1989*, table 273, p. 160; (other than US): *UNESCO Statistical Yearbook, 1985–9*; parks (Japan): Statistics Bureau, Management and Coordination Agency, *Social Indicators by Prefecture*, Nov. 1988, p. 146; sewers: OECD, *OECD Economic Surveys—Japan, 1990–91*, table A1, p. 131; airports, parks (other than Japan): Economic Planning Agency, "Seikatsu kankyō kiban o chūshin ni seibi no okure ga medatsu shakai shihon" (Social capital for which the delay in improvement is striking, particularly when focusing on the basic living environment) *JCER Economic Journal* (Nihon keizai kenkyu), no. 20 (1990), table 11, p. 127, and table 19, p. 130.

principle known as Denison's law, which asserts that public investment absorbs private savings. As just argued, there are good reasons to believe that local public goods are under-provided in the urban centers of Japan but over-provided elsewhere in the country. The Japanese government agreed in the negotiations to increase national spending for public works over a ten-year period.

International public goods

Some public goods are not only national but international. Contributions to world knowledge obviously spill across country's borders. Also, Japan's contribution to the common defense of the Western alliance and to the alliance's other goals, including assistance of lesser developed countries, are additions to international public goods.

National defense is a pure public good. If national defense refers to actions that reduce the likelihood of a foreign invasion or attack, it is quite clear that no one citizen may obtain a different level of national defense from others. The level of defense must be the same for all. It is in this sense indivisible. Furthermore, no one residing in the country can opt out or be left out of the common defense. None can be excluded.

Japan and the USA are allies. What either contributes to its own defense therefore also adds to the defense of the other. The corollary is that, as one spends more on defense, the other can cut back with no loss in security. The United States is twice as populous as Japan and therefore likely to have a greater willingness to spend on defense. The inevitable result is that the USA contributes far more to the two nations' common defense than does Japan. As one spends more, the other has felt it needed to spend that much less. The result is friction between the governments of the two countries and US pressure on Japan to spend more. In the Reagan era, Japan devoted about 1 percent of its national income to defense compared with 6 percent of US national income. The long-term effects of the USA's greater spending on defense are difficult to quantify but undeniably present. These effects include fewer consumer goods and a reduced rate of innovation in the production of consumer goods in the United States, and the opposite in Japan. An example may clarify some of the issues.

Figure 10.1(a) shows the marginal social value of defense and the marginal cost of it in two countries, Big and Little. Big and Little are allies. Little desires that the combined total of their defense be Q_L^* and Big desires that the combined total be Q_B^*. Thus, the

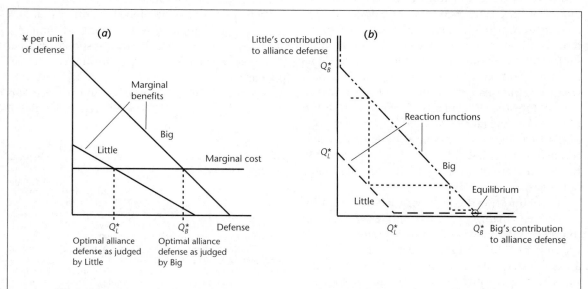

Figure 10.1. Marginal valuations of defense by allies "Big" and "Little", and implied reaction curves of each in choosing its contribution to the common defense

reaction functions of Big and Little that show the chosen contribution of each to the common defense given, that of the other, are as follows:

$$Q_B = Q_B^* - Q_L, \quad \text{if } Q_B^* > Q_L$$
$$= 0, \quad\quad\quad \text{if } Q_B^* \leq Q_L$$

and

$$Q_L = Q_L^* - Q_B, \quad \text{if } Q_L^* > Q_B$$
$$= 0, \quad\quad\quad \text{if } Q_L^* \leq Q_B$$

These are graphed in Figure 10.1(*b*). The only stable combination of defense spending by each ally is $Q_B = Q_B^*$ and $Q_L = 0$, as shown by the sequence of action–reaction starting at any point.

In the example, the "Little" country is a free-rider on the defense expenditures of its "Big" ally, though each applies the same narrowly selfish principles in determining its own contribution to their common defense. Does the example fit the facts of the Japan–US alliance?

Japan has a population about half that of the United States and, at least until recently, a lower per capita income. Both factors favor smaller social valuation of defense in Japan. Also, pre-1945 history prejudices the Japanese against a large defense establishment. These facts conform to the example, but there are other facts that conflict with it. The example presumes that neither country cares about the allocation of defense spending between them, but only about the combined total. The desire of each country to control the deployment of its own forces renders this assumption false. Also, Japan has been subject to US pressure and coercion to increase its defense spending, whereas the example has each country setting its own defense budget independently of the other.[14] Elements of cooperation within the alliance were most evident in allocation of costs of the 1990 Persian Gulf War. Although Japan contributed no troops, it did make a sizable payment to the government of the United States to defray some of the costs.

Contribution to the common defense of an international alliance is not the only example of an international public good. Other examples include funding the United Nations and its programs, assistance to lesser developed countries,[15] and contributions to the advance of science and technology. Japan contributes to all these activities, but, as with its contributions to alliance defense, it is often criticized for not contributing enough. Given the logic of independent contributions to the stock of an international public good, perhaps we should be surprised Japan contributes as much as it does. Tension between Japan and the USA on these issues reflects the fact that Japan is small relative to the United States, not that it is more parochial in pursuit of its national interests.

Other components of government expenditures

The largest components of government spending in Japan, as elsewhere, are for social security, health, education, and national defense. We now take up the issues pertaining specifically to the first three of these.

The social security system of Japan

In Japan, employees first became entitled to public pensions in 1941. Public pensions were extended to include the self-employed in 1959. However, pension benefits were quite modest until 1973, when they were increased so dramatically that the government soon developed an enormous fiscal deficit. In 1985 modifications were introduced, with the intent of reducing overall future pension benefits.

There are very few developed countries that lack social security programs,[16] and points of similarity are many. We may well ask why this should be. First, in simple terms, the retirement insurance schemes tax current workers and pay income to those who have retired from the workforce and to their survivors or dependents.[17] Three different rationales of

---

14 In spite of the obvious deficiencies of this naive model, it has been the basis for statistical estimation of the relation between defense spending of Japan and the USA: see Minoru Okamura, "Estimating the Impact of the Soviet Union's Threat on the United States–Japan Alliance: A Demand System Approach", *Review of Economics and Statistics*, vol. 73, no. 2 (May 1991).

15 For a critical evaluation of Japan's overseas development assistance, see Robert M. Orr, Jr, *The Emergence of Japan's Foreign Aid Power*, Columbia University Press, 1990.

16 New Zealand and Australia do not have social security; all other members of the OECD do.

17 Social security, as the term is usually understood, includes more than just retirement insurance, though that is its essence. In the USA, social security benefits have expanded to include disability payments, medical expenses, and in some instances unemployment compensation. A similar statement is true of Japan and many other countries.

such a policy have been advanced: (1) redistribution, (2) insurance, and (3) the intergenerational bargain.

Redistribution

Because the younger, still working, individuals are taxed to pay the public pension benefits of those retired, social security entails a redistribution of wealth. Such redistribution has often been most profound and most evident at the time a public pension scheme is first adopted or is greatly expanded. When the social security system of the United States was introduced in 1935, retirees immediately began to receive full pension benefits even though they of course had not earlier had to pay social security wage contributions. And when in 1973 public pensions were made more generous in Japan, those already fully vested (having been employed and having paid wage taxes for a minimum of twenty years) immediately became entitled to the now enriched benefits, a windfall redistribution from those younger than themselves. Is social security nothing more than a political palliative to those who are aged at the moment the system is initiated? Perhaps. But there are two further justifications for compulsory public pensions.

Insurance

A mature public pension scheme need not entail significant redistributions of wealth across generations. All pay wage taxes when young and receive pension benefits when old. If the taxes paid over a lifetime have equal value to the total stream of benefits for each person (in some expectant sense), then there is no redistribution of wealth across groups of individuals. But why should a public pension scheme of this sort—one that is "fully funded" in the argot of the social security experts—be compulsory? And why should it be necessary for government to provide it? Individuals themselves elect such a rearrangement of their own lifetime income stream whenever they purchase term life insurance from a private company. But life insurance benefits are not perfectly indexed to the cost-of-living. And in fact, it may not be profitable for any private insurer to offer such indexation because of the costs of hedging such a promise in futures markets. Government can offer pensioners real protection against cost-of-living inflation, backed by its power to levy taxes.[18] In Japan, as in the USA and other countries, public

pension benefits are adjusted upwards each year in accordance with movements in a consumer price index. But if public pensions are nothing more than inflation-proof retirement insurance, why make it compulsory for all to subscribe? The simplest answer is that they are in fact more than insurance.

The intergenerational bargain

Public pensions may be universal (compulsory) simply because citizens unanimously benefit from participation. This was first convincingly argued by Paul Samuelson.[19] In Samuelson's argument, if each successive generation receives more than it itself has paid to finance the benefits of its predecessor, there is a perpetual postponement of reckoning. It is perpetual because there is no "final generation" with no successor to leech off of. (As one wag put it, the only one to lose is posterity, and what has posterity done for us lately?) The inexorable upward adjustment of pension benefits is bounded only by the potential future output of the society; the upward adjustments of pension benefits may be slowed if such a bound is approached, but it need not be halted altogether. Furthermore, the process of economic growth, spurred by technological advance, may well mean that the future outputs of economies really are boundless. Each generation pays more taxes than the previous one but realizes an even greater increase in pension benefits than its increase in taxes, a kind of grand bargain across the generations unanimously enriching them all. The Samuelson argument would be an utterly compelling argument in favor of universal public pensions if only the wage contributions levied to finance them introduced no distortions that eroded national income.

The detailed provisions of Japan's social security program have fueled further public debate. The primary issue here is, what are the appropriate adjustments to make as the age structure of the population evolves? This is an issue also confronting the United States and other nations, but Japan's situation is unique because of its remarkably skewed

---

18 So claims Nicholas Barr, "Economic Theory and the Welfare State: A Survey and Interpretation", *Journal of Economic Literature*, vol. 30, no. 2 (June 1992), pp. 741–803, at p. 772.

19 Paul A. Samuelson, "An Exact Consumption-Loan Model of Interest with or without the Social Contrivance of Money", *Journal of Political Economy*, vol. 66 (December 1958), pp. 467–82.

population age profile. As the age structure of Japan's population approaches its steady state in the first decades of the twenty-first century, the percentage of the population over age 65 will increase quite dramatically: 1985, 10.3%; 1990, 12.0%; 2000, 17.2%; 2010, 22%; 2020, 26.9%.[20] This "aging" of the Japanese population is also expected to strain the government health system in coming decades.

The government health insurance system

A major portion of health care expenditures are provided by government in Japan: 73.5 percent in 1987. In the United States, one of the only developed countries still lacking a universal system of government-provided health care, the government programs known as "Medicare" and "Medicaid" account for about 40 percent of the total national spending on health care. The government of Japan has provided health insurance coverage for employees and their dependents since 1922, and for the self-employed, their dependents, and others since 1938. Coverage under national health insurance was made compulsory for all not already covered by employee health insurance in 1958, but at that time all except primary employees were still required to pay 30 percent of their own health expenses. In 1974 an annual ceiling of 30,000 yen was placed on the private payments for covered health expenses, a significant enrichment. The ceiling has since been raised, and in 1997 it reached 54,000 yen per month. Also, in 1973 patients aged 70 years or older and with incomes below a certain level were relieved of all personal expenses for covered medical benefits. From 1973 to 1982, health care expenses of the elderly grew at twice the rate as those of other age groups, an ineluctable consequence of having lowered the prices perceived by the aged without altering the prices paid (by government) to the providers. Amendments to the earlier law (Old Age Health and Medical Care Law) enacted in 1986 and taking effect in 1987 reinstated co-payments for the elderly at a somewhat modest 800 yen per month for outpatients and 300 or 400 yen per day for hospital patients.

Both employee health insurance and national health insurance in Japan operate on a similar principle. The government reimburses health care providers for the services they perform according to a fee schedule. The system is funded by wage taxes in the case of the employee health insurance and through general government revenues and assessments on members' households in the case of national health insurance.

Most of the developed countries of the world other than the USA have some system of comprehensive and universal government health insurance. Health insurance is not a public good. In the United States, where the government fails to provide it, many individuals themselves purchase it from private suppliers. Yet even in the USA there is growing political argument in favor of government provision. Proponents of government-provided health insurance argue that adverse selection makes it unprofitable to provide socially valuable health insurance. Adverse selection is the phenomenon in which insurance providers cannot distinguish between prospects that represent high risks and those that represent low risks but the prospects themselves do know their own risk class. If the premium is set at a high level, only the high-risk prospects subscribe. Depending on the details, this may render voluntary subscription unprofitable even where there exist terms under which compulsory subscription by all would add more to the gains of high-risk prospects than the losses it would impose on low-risk prospects.[21]

Whatever the reasons for government provision of health insurance, it is quite clear that specific aspects of such a policy themselves have important consequences. For instance, the Japanese practice of reimbursing for services according to fee schedules implies that government decisions regarding the levels of fees will influence the kinds and quantities of different services that physicians and hospitals provide. Compared with other nations, Japan enjoys a very high utilization of pharmaceutical preparations, frequent visits to doctors' offices, a very short average length of visit with a doctor, infrequent admissions to hospitals, lengthy stays in hospitals, fewer hospital attendants per patient, a very low

---

20 "Sōmuchō tōkei kyoku" (Statistic bureau, management and coordination agency of the Japanese government), *Nihon no tōkei 1998* (Statistical yearbook of Japan 1998), table 2–1, p. 9.

21 So argued the economic theorist George Akerlof in the seminal paper on the economics of adverse selection, "The Market for 'Lemons': Qualitative Uncertainty and the Market Mechanism", *Quarterly Journal of Economics*, vol. 84 (August 1970), pp. 488–500.

incidence of Cesarian sections, a high rate of appendectomy, a low rate of gall bladder surgery, almost no organ transplants, and a high utilization of CT scanners.[22] It is impossible to know for certain the extent to which the government fee schedules have induced these peculiarities, as opposed to demographics, diet, medical education, and other factors having done so. But there are many suggestions that the fee schedules are partly responsible. For instance, it is claimed that doctors in Japan deliberately prescribe small doses of medication so that patients will have to return for a refill, adding a further fee for an office visit.

An alternative to the Japanese practice of reimbursing health care providers according to a fee schedule is for government not only to provide health services but also to produce them. The US government Veterans' Administration (VA) hospitals and staffs produce health services for veterans as a form of compensation for past military service. Matt Lindsay has detailed the problems that arise.[23] The VA hospitals are operated so as to satisfy government officials. Privately produced health services must satisfy patients. The difference between these two alternatives speaks worlds about the disadvantages of government production. Government officials, however well intentioned and motivated, as outside observers have a different vantage point from that of the actual consumers of the goods. There is no perfect solution to the problem of efficient government provision of health services.

Education

The Japanese system of public education has elicited many admiring comments from Americans. Yet Japan devotes a smaller percentage of its national income to government provision of education (3.5 percent versus 4.6 percent in 1989). Much of the difference in levels of public spending has to do with the centralized national control of primary and secondary public education in Japan compared with the highly decentralized local administration characteristic of the United States. Also, there is much less public support for colleges and universities in Japan than in America. The centralization of authority over the curriculum, staffing, and even the school lunch menus, is yet another manifestation of the fact that Japan's government resembles a unitary more than federal system. While central control surely economizes on administrative costs, it lessens the sensitivity of public education to local preferences.

Education, like health insurance, is not a public good. The reasons for government provision of education are largely not economic, but are social and political.

Conclusion

The public sector of Japan's economy employs about 6 percent of its labor force, a considerably smaller percentage than is true of many other developed nations, and less even than the United States. Japanese government expenditures, both transfer payments and spending for goods and services, amount to around one-third of national income, again smaller than the corresponding fractions of most other developed nations. The Japanese government devotes a smaller fraction of national income to defense than do many of its allies, which might reflect Japan's relatively small valuation of alliance security, at least compared with the USA, which has twice its population. Japan also expends a smaller fraction of its national income on public support for health and education than does the United States, even though its national health insurance is broad in coverage and its system of primary and public education is widely regarded as highly effective. Japan's modest public expenditures on health and education partly reflect the centralized nature of its government administration, in which prefectural and local governments exercise only limited autonomy from the national government. Also, it

---

[22] R. Niki, "The Wide Distribution of CT Scanners in Japan", *Social Science and Medicine*, vol. 21, pp. 1131–7; Yoichi Yoshida and Katsumi Yoshida, "The High Rate of Appendectomy in Japan", *Medical Care*, vol. 14 (November 1976), pp. 950–7; Francis C. Notzon, Paul J. Placek, and Selma M. Taffel, "Comparisons of National Cesarean-Section Rates", *New England Journal of Medicine*, vol. 316, no. 7 (February 12, 1987), p. 387; Klim McPherson, "International Differences in Medical Care Practices", in *Health Care Systems in Transition*, OECD Social Policy Studies no. 7, 1990, pp. 17–28.

[23] Cotton Mather Lindsay, "A Theory of Government Enterprise", *Journal of Political Economy*, vol. 84 (February 1976), pp. 1061–77.

reflects the relatively youthful demographic profile of Japanese society, which is about to change in the ensuing decades. Japan's currently modest expenditures on social security pensions are a further consequence of this same demographic structure. In short, Japan's public expenditures have so far achieved essential aims while encroaching little on private economic activity.

FURTHER READING

■ James M. Buchanan and Marylin R. Flowers, *The Public Finances: An Introductory Textbook*, 6th edn, Homewood, Ill.: Richard D. Irwin, 1987. A superb introduction to the economics behind government expenditures, written by the Nobel laureate James Buchanan and one of his students.

■ Shafiqul Islam, "Foreign Aid and Burdensharing: Is Japan Free Riding to a Coprosperity Sphere in Pacific Asia?", in Jeffrey A. Frankel and Miles Kahler (eds.), *Regionalism and Rivalry: Japan and the United States in Pacific Asia*, University of Chicago Press, 1993, ch. 7, pp. 321–90. The author argues that Japanese and American expenditures lack the essential characteristics of an international public good, and that Japan's overseas development assistance is no less generous or unselfish than that of other nations.

■ James H. Schulz, Allen Borowski, and William H. Crown, with Akiko Kumashiro, Thomas Leavitt, and Kazuo Takada, *Economics of Population Aging: The "Graying" of Australia, Japan, and the United States*, New York: Auburn House, 1991. Wide-ranging discussion of the social security system of Japan, in comparative perspective.

■ Tokue Shibata (ed.), *Public Finance in Japan*, University of Tokyo Press, 1986. Essays on expenditure and tax policies of the Japanese government by leading Japanese scholars.

Environmental Policy | 11

Pollution of air and water, the erosion of scenic beauty, and the growing intrusion of noise and overcrowding have afflicted Japan as they have other countries. In recent decades, these assaults on the Japanese environment have provoked lawsuits and have led to the enactment of taxes on polluters to compensate victims and subsidies for pollution abatement. In considering Japan's environmental policies, though, one should not overlook the many ways in which environmental problems are resolved in the economy without a need for expanding the scope of government authority. Examples include the evolution, in Japan, of a legally recognized "right to sunshine", rules set not by government but by profit-seeking proprietors of restaurants, owners of rail lines, and landlords, and limitations on fishing that are self-imposed and self-enforced by private fishermen's cooperatives.

Some of the above examples have involved litigation. Japan has fewer lawyers per person and less litigation than the United States. In spite of these differences, the court system of Japan seems to have provided an adequate basis for resolving a lot of the environmental issues in a rather *laissez-faire* manner. Unfortunately, the *laissez-faire* approach occasionally fails horribly. Only after four widely publicized environmental disasters produced a political outcry did the government of Japan seriously intervene in the control of industrial pollution.

Four environmental crises

Mercury poisoning in Minamata

The name of Minamata, a small fishing village in the south of Japan, will forever be linked with the horrors of mercury poisoning—irreversible symptoms including tremors, paralysis, and dementia, in severe cases resulting in death. Minamata disease first showed up in cats and birds as early as 1953, and by 1959 was common in humans including congenital cases. We now know that the fertilizer company Chisso caused Minamata disease by discharging compounds of mercury into the sea where they were bioconcentrated in fish which were eaten by humans and animals. This was first learned in 1957 by researchers from nearby Kumamoto University and was confirmed through experiments on cats by a doctor in the employ of Chisso itself in 1959. In a pattern that was to be repeated elsewhere in Japan, Chisso executives sought to suppress knowledge of the company's culpability, stonewalling and dissembling in spite of growing protests by local fishermen and residents whose livelihoods and health were ruined. A negotiated settlement between Chisso and its victims included nominal compensation and an agreement (later invalidated by a court) precluding further claims against Chisso.

Mercury poisoning in Niigata

Mercury poisoning appeared again in 1965 in Niigata prefecture on the middle of the western coast of Japan, this time caused by the toxic effluent of Showa Denko, an industrial rival of Chisso using the same process as Chisso to produce nitrogen fertilizer. Fish taken from the Agano River and eaten by humans transmitted organic mercury to the unfortunate victims. Emboldened by the previous history of Minamata and by the defiant proclamations of the president of Showa Denko, thirteen victims filed suit in 1967. In 1971 the victims won the suit, which precipitated further litigation against Chisso, also ultimately successful.

Cadmium poisoning in Toyama

Itai-itai disease is the name for the painful effects of cadmium poisoning: decalcification that leads to brittle bones, acute sensitivity to pain, loss of appetite, and in severe cases death. In Japanese "Itai-itai!" is the cry of one in physical pain. Itai-itai disease appeared in the environs of Toyama on the western coast of Japan as early as the 1920s, but only in 1964 was it fully understood to be the result of cadmium poisoning caused by effluent of the mining and smelting of zinc and lead by the Mitsui Metal Mining Company. The cadmium toxins leached into the streams and eventually settled into the irrigated rice paddies where they were uptaken into the rice and soybeans which the people harvested and ate. In 1968 a group of twenty-eight victims sued and won an award for damages in 1971, and on appeal—by Mitsui—won an even larger award the following year. Mitsui promptly settled other claims out of court and agreed to alter its operations to prevent future contamination.

Industrial pollution in Yokkaichi

Yokkaichi is a city on the Ise peninsula south of Nagoya which after 1955 became re-established as a center for petroleum refining and processing. A number of companies established facilities in close proximity to one another including Shoseki (oil refining), Mitsubishi Monsanto (vinyl chloride), Mitsubishi Yuka (ethylene), Mitsubishi Kasei (chemicals), Ishihara (chemical fertilizer), and Chūden

(electric power). By 1960 local residents began to experience asthma-like symptoms which were clearly the result of air pollution by these companies including emissions of sulfur oxides. Fish in the surrounding waters had ceased to be fit for consumption. Local fishermen correctly associated this threat to their livelihoods with the discharge into the waters of untreated industrial effluent. In 1968, following inconclusive reports on the problem, half measures by local government, and stonewalling by the companies, nine of the many sufferers of Yokkaichi asthma filed a suit against the six companies and in 1972 won a sizable award.

The sad events just recounted galvanized the national government to act. In 1970 a special government agency for coordinating environmental policies was established and in subsequent years new environmental legislation was enacted. Two major policies merit attention: the establishment and continual strengthening of environmental controls, and the enactment, implementation, and eventual retrenchment of a law that established taxes on polluters to compensate individuals for their pollution related health injuries.

Policies for meeting environmental standards in Japan

Environmental quality standards were first established in Japan for ambient sulfur oxides in February 1969 and for water pollution in April 1970. These standards represent goals or targets for government policy-makers in Japan. They do not in themselves bind the decisions of businesses in any way. But there exists in Japan a constellation of policies that have induced firms to abate their toxic emissions and effluents. Since 1970 the standards have been steadily increased as environmental quality has improved in Japan. In this sense the standards represent moving targets. The policies that precipitated these improvements in air and water quality include a somewhat confusing mix of controls, subsidies, and government guidance.

With regard to sulfur oxides, the root cause of acid rain and a major component of air pollution, the government has established maximum allowable volumes of emissions according to formulae that impose tougher controls on facilities with lower stack heights, or that are in more densely inhabited or more polluted regions. And these so-called "*k*-value" controls (for *k* is the parameter of the formula that varies from area to area) are in some instances superseded by more strict controls imposed by prefectural governments. To meet these various controls, which apply to as many as 150,000 industrial boilers in Japan, firms have switched to fuels having lower sulfur content, have increased stack heights, and have installed scrubbers that remove toxins prior to emissions.

Nitrogen oxide emissions, a major component of photochemical air pollution, have also been the object of government controls in Japan. But the dramatic reductions in ambient levels of sulfur oxides in Japan since the early 1970s have not been duplicated for nitrogen oxides. Possibly this is because diesel truck engines are a major and growing source of nitrogen oxide emissions in Japan. Automotive emission controls are severe in Japan but will remain largely ineffective at reducing ambient nitrogen oxide unless and until technology affords a workable substitute for the diesel engine.

Water quality, as measured by the oxygen content of lakes, rivers, and streams, has steadily improved in Japan. Higher oxygen content indicates the greater presence of living organisms unable to coexist with high levels of toxins. The improving water quality reflects both the application of effluent controls to private businesses and the expansion of public investments in water and sewage treatment since the early 1970s.

Economic incentives for pollution abatement

Many commentators emphasize the role of administrative guidance in inducing firms in Japan to reduce their toxic discharges, but it is unlikely that government jawboning and cajoling would have been effective had firms not been convinced that the steps were in their own narrow interest. The Japanese environmental policy has provided economic incentives for pollution abatement, including extensive subsidies and tax credits contingent on the installation of abatement devices or upon relocating to less populated areas. Where these incentives are lacking, as in the case of nitrous oxides, the results have been noticeably less. The lion's share of private

investments in coal scrubbers were by Japan's ten regulated electric power companies. Government influence in this instance is unsurprising, as price regulation has afforded a way of rewarding compliance with environmental goals. In broad terms, the environmental policies of Japan combine elements of both subsidy and direct control.

The *subsidy* policy, which provides firms with positive rewards for abating air and water pollution, and the *control* approach, which requires firms to meet set levels of environmental performance or else face penalties, both substitute command and control mechanisms for the price system. Subsidies will guide firms to the least-cost method of reducing toxic discharges only if policy-makers are able to deduce what that method is. Often this is not possible. For instance, subsidies may be provided for installing specific abatement devices, even when relocating or some other action would attain equal reductions in pollution at lower cost. The control approach allows firms to choose their own methods of compliance, but generally fails to take full account of the differing costs of compliance of differing firms and industries. Any particular global level of pollution reduction is achieved at lower cost if those having low incremental costs of pollution reduction are held to higher standards than others.

The alternative to the subsidy policy and controls policy, which exploits the market principle most fully while nevertheless attaining given ambient reductions in pollution, is to issue pollution permits which firms can trade in the market. Those having the greatest cost of pollution abatement would be the highest bidders for the permits, and each firm would have an incentive to implement its own least-cost method of pollution abatement in order to minimize its outlays for permits. Such a policy is only now being introduced in the United States, but on a limited basis. There is little doubt that wider recourse to the tradable permits approach would greatly lower the costs of environmental improvement, yet there is little enthusiasm for it among politicians in the USA and perhaps even less in Japan. Why?

Subsidies shield firms from output restrictions and cause taxpayers to bear the cost of pollution abatement. Uniform controls force less efficient firms to shut down, which works to the advantage of surviving firms. Under the tradable permits policy, polluting firms and their customers would bear the costs of pollution. Relatively large firms that are likely to face output restrictions if tradable permits are issued, and are likely also to survive in competition with smaller firms if uniform controls are imposed, will favor both the subsidy policy and the controls policy over the tradable permits policy.[1] Environmental policy in Japan, and elsewhere, reflects the preferences of large and profitable firms, not those of taxpayers or of small marginal firms.

The 1973 Law for Compensation of Pollution-Related Health Injuries

Perhaps the most widely discussed response to the four major pollution crises was the enactment of a scheme that taxes polluters and compensates individuals who contract pollution-related diseases. Many outside observers have commented favorably on this law.[2]

The law establishing this policy, enacted in 1973, identified two classes of claimants. The first class included those residing in geographic areas designated by the government as subject to air pollution from non-specific sources and who later contracted respiratory diseases such as bronchitis, asthma, or emphysema. The second class included those residing in areas designated by government authorities as having been polluted by specific toxins and who contracted related illnesses including mercury poisoning (Minamata disease), cadmium poisoning (Itai-Itai disease), and PCB poisoning.

Designated claimants of both classes are entitled under the law to collect compensation from special funds financed through taxes levied on polluters. The compensation is according to a formula that is based on the age, sex, and severity of injury, and is to cover medical expenses and rehabilitation expenses and to compensate victims or their bereaved families for lost earnings resulting from disability or death.

The claims were financed through levies on polluters. (The costs of administering the levies and claims as opposed to the claims themselves have been financed largely by general government revenues.) In the case of Class Two claims—claims associated with specific toxins—the companies responsible for releasing the toxins have been assessed annual levies to finance the claims. In the case of Class One

claims, involving respiratory ailments of unspecific origin by residents of designated "high air pollution" regions, claims have been financed 20 percent from tonnage taxes paid by the owners of motor vehicles and 80 percent by taxes on large emitters of sulfur oxides. The base of the sulfur oxide tax is the firm's annual emission of such toxins as judged by its usage of fossil fuels and degree of pollution abatement. Only large[3] polluters have been taxed in this way, but these account for an overwhelming percentage of sulfur oxide emissions. Also, the tax rate per unit of toxic emission was stipulated to be nine times greater for facilities within the designated high pollution regions. The tax rates on sulfur oxides have been adjusted annually to assure that total collections are sufficient to meet all claims.

In 1986 the Compensation Law was greatly altered. First, the designation of further Class One claimants was permanently suspended as of March 1, 1988. Second, the tax rates on sulfur oxide emissions within designated regions and others were made equal to one another. Third, rather than only financing claims, the tax proceeds were now earmarked for research into pollution abatement, medical treatment of pollution-related illnesses, and dissemination of the results of such research. The Class Two claims, involving specific toxins and taxes on those responsible for having discharged the toxins, were left intact.

Economic analysis of the compensation law
Environmentalists and others lauded the 1973 law and sharply criticized its later alteration. But economics reveals two defects in the original law that the changes do in fact correct. The first is that, by providing compensation for pollution-related injuries, the law actually weakened the incentives of individuals themselves to avoid pollution sources. Continuing to tax sulfur oxide emissions but sus-

---

[1] This is approximately the argument of James M. Buchanan and Gordon Tullock, "Polluters' Profits and Political Response", *American Economic Review*, vol. 65, no. 1 (March 1975), pp. 82–3.

[2] For example, Ezra Vogel described this policy as "imaginative" and noted that "Some Americans concerned with pollution are beginning to urge that America consider similar measures": *Japan As Number One: Lessons for America*, London: Harper Colophon, 1979, pp. 82–3.

[3] "Large" is defined as having maximal emission more than 5,000Nm^3/hr if the facilities are located within a designated high pollution region and more than 10,000Nm^3/hr if not.

pending the future designation of Class One victims entitled to compensation may actually result in an improved allocation of resources.

A second defect in the original law was the provision that the sulfur oxide tax be readjusted annually so that collections would match disbursements for compensation. The prospect that, if enough individuals located their residences near pollution sources, future tax increases would drive the polluters away further inured individuals from themselves avoiding harm, an added distortion in their calculations beyond that already induced by the prospect of receiving compensation. In fact, the tax rate on sulfur oxide emissions was increased dramatically from 1974 to 1977 by a factor of 33, reaching a whopping ¥536.63 per cubic meter in the designated high pollution zones (the equivalent of a 30 percent tax rate on fossil fuels). As emissions of sulfur oxides declined and the number of legally designated Class One victims increased, it became necessary to increase the tax *rate* simply to maintain receipts at the intended level. This undoubtedly afforded a significant economic incentive for firms to either relocate, install abatement equipment, or cease operations. But that does not establish the economic desirability of the policy. An enlightened policy not only reduces environmental toxins, but does it in the least-cost way, and also respects the brutal fact that some pollution is more costly to eliminate than is worthwhile. At the very least, Japan's pollution taxes and emissions controls have, indeed, resulted in cleaner air; one can quibble about whether this was achieved at the least possible cost, or whether it was worth the cost.

The "polluter pays principle"

In 1975, the research staff of the OECD argued in a series of monographs that firms should be taxed for polluting, not rewarded for abating pollution.[4] Japan had just been admitted to the OECD, an international organization dedicated to the study of economic policies in the developed countries, which was widely touted in Japan as further evidence—if any were still needed—of Japan's status as a developed nation. Perhaps for this reason, the so-called "polluter pays principle" immediately attained wide currency in the popular press in Japan and was heartily endorsed by influential politicians there.

As distorted through the prism of mass culture, the "polluter pays principle" became nothing more than a "punish polluters principle".[5] In fact, the argument for pollution taxes rather than abatement subsidies is based on the idea that abatement subsidies may induce each individual firm to pollute less but, by encouraging new firms to enter, may draw resources toward polluting industries. In contrast, taxes on polluting industries induce firms to exit.

To call the tax policy a "polluter pays" policy is to label it falsely. As firms in an industry reduce their outputs in response to a tax, the industry supply shrinks and the product price rises. Ultimately, then, consumers of the products of polluting industries also bear the burden of a tax on pollution. Of course, to label the policy one of "consumers pay for pollution" is unlikely to generate wide support for it. In any case, Japan's sulfur oxide emission tax, automotive tonnage tax, and k-class controls do all exemplify the sort of policy that the OECD staff had advocated. No one seriously doubts that the policies have contributed to improved air quality in Japan, but, again, that may not be the decisive factor in evaluating the policies.

Spillovers

The serious pollution problems are examples of economic spillovers. There are many other examples. A spillover arises when one is oblivious to the effects on others of one's own actions. The emission of toxic fumes by a manufacturing firm is an example of spillover, and the emission of tobacco fumes by a smoker on a crowded train may be another. Other instances might include the erection of a tall building that enshades the adjoining property owned by a sunshine-loving neighbor, a loud mah jong party that annoys neighbors, harvesting fish from the ocean and thus depleting the future catch of other fishermen, entering an already crowded freeway and thereby slowing the travel of others when an alternate route is available, and so on.

---

4 OECD, *The Polluter Pays Principle: Definition, Analysis, Implementation*, Paris: OECD, 1975.

5 Remy Prud'homme, "Appraisal of Environmental Policies of Japan", in S. Tsuru (ed.), *Growth and Resource Problems Related to Japan*, New York: St Martin's Press, 1980, pp. 193–208 at p. 205.

Disciplined thinking about spillovers has been greatly advanced by the insight of Nobel laureate Ronald Coase that the absence of saleable ownership rights is the necessary premise of all spillovers.[6] If the right to smoke a cigarette in a crowded train were clearly assigned—to each person holding a seat, for instance—and could be easily traded, then smokers could not be described as oblivious to the effects of their smoking on others. If a person sitting nearby is offended by the smoke, she would offer a payment to buy the smoking right. Even if the offer is declined, the smoker has been made to consider the value of the harm his smoking inflicts—and has judged the value to himself of a relaxing smoke to be greater! A spillover is not present. For a spillover to arise, it must be that the one offended by the smoke declines to offer a payment, either because she believes the smoker should have to pay her for the right to smoke and the smoker thinks the opposite, or because such transactions are so unusual that the nuisance of reaching an accommodation through trading outweighs the likely benefits to either party.

Coase's analysis of spillovers directs attention to the many instances in which environmental problems are resolved by the creation of new saleable ownership rights rather than through taxation or government administration. One curious example of this is the Japanese "right to sunshine".

Right to sunshine

As a result of court cases decided in Japan in the last two decades, sunshine rights are now among the tradable economic goods there. In 1960, a resident of Tokyo named Suzuki added a second storey to his house. The new construction at midday completely enshaded the home of his neighbor named Mitamura. Because of the blockage of sunlight, Mitamura sold his home and moved elsewhere but sued Suzuki for damages. In 1972 the Supreme Court of Japan ruled in favor of Mitamura. There have been a number of similar cases in the years since. The result is that the outcome of such litigation has become rather predictable, though it is likely to depend upon details such as the changing angle of the sun's rays through the annual change of seasons, whether the building is in a densely populated or more rural setting, the purpose of the offending construction, and so. Nevertheless, as the outcome

of these cases has become predictable—whether it is an award of compensation or an injunction against building—litigation has become unnecessary in many instances. For instance, if new construction is expected to infringe on the sunshine rights of the owners of adjoining property, then the builder will first purchase a waiver of those rights before proceeding. The right to sunshine is, in effect, a saleable good.

Now that private tradable rights to sunshine are clearly assigned in Japan, there remains little further possibility that those undertaking new construction in residential areas will be oblivious to sunlight blockages. But this is also true in the United States, where the courts, generally speaking, have adopted a rule of never issuing injunctions against new building that enshades neighboring property and never awarding damages for deprivation of sunlight.[7] Builders in the USA will still not fail to consider the deprivation of sunshine that their building imposes on owners of adjoining property, because they are confronted with bids from those owners to forgo their offending construction. (Notice that this does not mean that the building will be suspended!) The crucial role of the court cases such as *Suzuki* vs. *Mitamura* is that they clearly assign sunshine rights to one party or the other; it matters little to the ultimate outcome of such disputes which one wins. Once a property right is assigned unambiguously to one person, market trading—if unimpeded by transactions costs—will then allocate the right to whoever values it the highest, a proposition known as "Coase's Law". But the transactions cost, which includes the cost of negotiating and enforcing private agreements, often does seriously impede trade. This is particularly so in trades that involve large groups of persons collectively. Even in these instances, government administration has occasionally introduced new distortions rather than offsetting existing ones.

Shinkansen noise

A large number of persons living next to the tracks

---

6 Ronald H. Coase, "The Problem of Social Cost", *The Journal of Law and Economics*, vol. 3 (1960), pp. 1–44.

7 For a closer comparison of the two countries' laws on this issue, see Steven S. Miller, "Let the Sunshine In: A Comparison of Japanese and American Solar Rights", *Harvard Environmental Law Review*, vol. 1 (1976), pp. 578–600.

of Japan's high speed bullet trains, the *shinkansen*, have sought through private entreaties and litigation to slow the trains to quiet the noise and vibration. In a series of court cases decided in the 1980s, the Japan National Railways (now Japan Railways) was ordered to slow the speed of its *shinkansen* in the heavily populated cities such as Nagoya. It is quite likely that the many passengers of the *shinkansen* would, as a group, be willing to pay far more to prevent delays in their travels than would be necessary to induce the relatively few who live next to the tracks to permit the trains to move speedily. But the costs of the railroad's reaching an agreement with the residents are prohibitive in this case because of the difficulties in obtaining the unanimous consent of the residents. The court decisions will therefore not be overridden by private agreements as in the sunshine cases.

Private versus public administration of spillover disputes

The *shinkansen* noise case indicates that administered "solutions" to spillover disputes can themselves cause new misallocations of economic resources. This is less likely to be true when rules are administered by private owners than when administered by judges or government employees. Consider, for instance, the calculations of the owner of a private rail line in setting no-smoking rules for passengers. If nonsmokers' willingness to pay for an expansion of no-smoking cars is greater than smokers' willingness to pay for smoking cars, then the rail line's profits are increased by expanding the no-smoking cars. Of course, smokers and nonsmokers may reach their own accommodations with one another that override the proprietor's designations, but the costs of such negotiations are apt to be prohibitive and are at the least troublesome.

In spite of the greater profits that efficient smoking rules would confer, the number of no-smoking cars on *shinkansen* has in fact been the subject of acrimonious dispute. At first, none of the sixteen cars on each *shinkansen* was so designated. Following public complaints, first one and then two cars were designated no-smoking. Why the controversy? Perhaps the prospect of greater profit was not a sufficient inducement to the national railways (JNR), a government enterprise, to seek efficient smoking rules.

Added JNR profit (actually a smaller loss) need not have meant greater rewards for the managers of JNR, but rather an enrichment of Japanese taxpayers. The lack of controversy surrounding smoking rules on the many private rail lines in Japan is an instructive contrast to the JNR experience in setting no-smoking rules on *shinkansen*.

Foreign visitors to Japan and others have remarked upon the extensive rules that owners of apartment complexes set for their tenants. Rules vary from landlord to landlord and might prohibit the flushing of toilets at certain hours for instance, or the playing of mah jong which is a game often accompanied by the loud sounds of tiles clacking together. The rules often pertain to behavior that is apt to have spillovers. As with the no-smoking example, the profit motive is an inducement to set efficient rules. Competition among landlords is a counterbalance to individual mistakes. For instance, if all landlords were to prohibit mah jong, then there would be a great profit for any that allowed it and attracted the few tenants willing to pay a great premium to clack the mah jong tiles in their own abodes rather than only at a mah jong parlor.

A final example of private resolution of a spillover dispute in Japan is the management of offshore fishing rights by co-ops. The harvest of fish from the ocean depletes the biomass, and diminishes the possibility of future harvest. Where many are fishing in the same area, each may be inclined to ignore the effects of his behavior on the others' future harvest, and may wastefully overfish. This sort of spillover has been offered as the justification for government limits on fish harvest. An analogous principle underlies the international treaties, to which Japan is a party, limiting the harvest of whales. But the Japanese fishery is a famous example in which individuals have evolved sophisticated rules of behavior that prevent overfishing without government regulation. These informal rules include *de facto* exclusive rights in particular fishing grounds, and self-imposed limits on harvest, agreed upon and enforced among fishermen themselves.[8]

---

8 For more on this topic, see Kenneth Ruddle and Tomoya Akimichi, "Sea Tenure in Japan and the Southwestern Ryukyus", and Kevin MacEwen Short, "Self-Management of Fishing Rights by Japanese Cooperative Associations: A Case Study from Hokkaido", chs. 11 and 12, respectively, in John Cordell (ed.), *A Sea of Small Boats*, Cultural Survival, 1989, pp. 337–87.

Law and lawyers in Japan

Infrequency of litigation in Japan

The four environmental crises mentioned before, the sunshine disputes, and the *shinkansen* noise dispute are all exceptional in Japan in that they involved litigation, which is generally a lot less frequent in Japan than in the United States and elsewhere. There are two reasons for the infrequency of litigation in Japan. First, litigation is more costly than in other countries because of the artificial scarcity of attorneys. Second, the outcome of litigation is more predictable than in other nations because Japanese law is based on a civil code rather than a common law, and because Japanese court cases are decided by judges rather than by juries.

Many have commented upon the cultural trait of the Japanese people of avoiding conflict and seeking consensus. But avoidance of conflict is a universal goal not a uniquely Japanese one. John Haley was among the first to question whether the infrequency of litigation in Japan demands a cultural explanation.[9] He conceded that litigation is infrequent in Japan, compared with other countries, but argued that this might just reflect the fact that the number of bar certified attorneys is far less in relation to the population in Japan than in other nations, and so attorney fees are higher there. Certification of attorneys in Japan is by competitive examination and as many take the bar exam in Japan each year as do in the USA, but the pass rate is drastically lower in Japan. Consequently, in 1994 there were about 18,400 bar certified attorneys in Japan compared to 840,000 in the USA. Limited supply of court attorneys implies a higher price for the services of such attorneys, and therefore lower demand. Of course, the scarcity of legal services is a government policy and would probably not be tolerated if it imposed extremely large social costs. Perhaps it does not impose large costs. Lawyers in Japan do not enjoy spectacularly large earnings compared with lawyers in the USA. A lot of legal work in Japan is performed by persons with legal training but without bar certification. In any case, infrequency of litigation in Japan has a more fundamental reason than the artificial scarcity of attorney services.

Compared with other nations, the outcome of litigation is more predictable in Japan, so that out-of-court settlement is more likely; this achieves approximately the same result but avoids court costs.[10] In Japan, as in Germany and other nations that have legal systems based upon a civil code, tort cases, including cases involving spillover disputes, are decided by judges according to statutes. In the United States and Great Britain tort cases are decided according to the common law, that is, according to the precedent cases rather than according to a statute. Statutory law affords a narrower scope for judicial interpretation. To the extent that this renders the outcome of torts more predictable, it promotes out-of-court settlements that avoid litigation costs. A further factor contributing to the predictability of litigation in Japan is that cases are decided by judges rather than by juries there. Judge's decision rules are more apt to be formulaic and predictable, not idiosyncratic and manipulable as with juries. Again, predictability of the outcome of litigation promotes out-of-court settlement.

The upshot of this discussion is that there are no cultural peculiarities or biases that render the court system of Japan incapable of performing its essential role in tort cases of enforcing clear assignments of property rights to one party or another. A final example in which they have done exactly that is in liability for defective products.

Product liability law

Until the enactment by the Diet of the Product Liability Law, which took effect in July 1995, the rule in tort cases involving liability for damages arising from product defects in Japan was one in which the plaintiff was obliged to demonstrate negligence on the part of the manufacturer. The new law shifts that burden of proof to the manufacturer. The plaintiff is still obliged to demonstrate the existence of a defect, that there was damage, and that the damage was a result of the defect, but under the new law she is no longer required to demonstrate

---

9 John O. Haley "The Myth of the Reluctant Litigant", *Journal of Japanese Studies*, vol. 4, no. 2 (Summer 1978), pp. 359–90.

10 This line of argument is developed by J. Mark Ramseyer, "Reluctant Litigant Revisited: Rationality and Disputes in Japan", *Journal of Japanese Studies*, vol. 14, no. 1 (Winter 1988), pp. 111–23; and J. Mark Ramseyer and Minoru Nakazato, "The Rational Litigant: Settlement Amounts and Verdict Rates in Japan", *Journal of Legal Studies*, vol. 28 (June 1989), pp. 263–90.

negligence on the part of the product manufacturer or that the negligence caused the defect.

Under the earlier regime, because of the inherent difficulties for a consumer to prove negligence on the part of a manufacturer, very few consumers were awarded compensation for damages. This meant, in effect, that consumers were generally liable for damages resulting from defective products, though there were some notable exceptions. In some widely publicized cases consumers did succeed in proving negligence and collected damages. These cases included ones involving the drug thalidomide, the mistaken admixture of arsenic into infant powdered milk by the Morinaga Milk Company, PCB (polychlorinated biphenal) contamination of cooking oil produced by Kanemi Rice Oil, and a diarrhea remedy that produced a neurological disorder known as SMON (subacute-myelo-optico-neuropathy). Except for these cases and a few others, all of which were long in settlement, consumers were liable for damages arising from defective products.

The publicity surrounding these cases was the original impetus for new legislation, which was discussed and debated for two decades before its eventual enactment in 1994. Under the new law, because consumers are no longer obliged to prove negligence, manufacturers are more likely than before to be held liable for damages resulting from defective products. But the placement of the rule of liability actually matters less than one might have supposed. This is a further instance of Coase's law.

As demonstrated by Hamada,[11] and by Demsetz,[12] if potential damage from defective products can be avoided when the manufacturer incurs an added cost, and if the consumers and the manufacturer are fully and accurately informed as to whether the manufacturer has incurred the added costs, and are informed also as to the extent of those costs and the likelihood and extent of damages thereby prevented, then placement of the rule of liability has no economic effect whatsoever. If the consumers are liable, then their willingness to pay for the presumptively safe products is greater than for unsafe ones by precisely the amount of the expected damages arising from the use of unsafe products. The manufacturer will decide to incur the added costs of producing a safe product if and only if the added value to consumers warrants it; that is the economically efficient criterion. In the opposite case, in which the

manufacturer is liable, consumers' willingness to pay is no greater for the presumptively safe product than for the unsafe one, but now manufacturers factor into their calculations their own expectation of greater costs resulting from compensation for damages in use of the unsafe product—just as, under the rule of strict consumer liability, the manufacturer incurs the added cost of producing a safe product only if the expected avoidance of damages warrants it, the economically efficient rule. In other words, if unsafe products are offered under the regime of consumer liability, then unsafe products will also be offered under the regime of producer liability, and it is economically efficient in each case. Since the enactment of the product liability law in Japan, manufacturers have hastened to purchase liability insurance. There is little evidence that products have been either redesigned or withdrawn from the market.

Conclusion

An environment free of toxins is one among the multitude of scarce goods. For society, more of any good necessarily requires the sacrifice of others. The upshot is that some pollution is indeed more costly to eliminate than is worthwhile. The challenge for governments everywhere is to enact policies that assure both that environmental degradation is actually permitted wherever its avoidance would entail the sacrifice of more highly valued other goods, and that whatever level of environmental quality is attained is conjoined with the maximum possible output of other goods. In other words, the goal of an enlightened policy is an economically efficient allocation of resources, not the elimination of pollution.

If property rights were of infinite scope, were clearly assigned to specific individuals, and could be traded costlessly, the only environmental policy capable of achieving an economically efficient allocation of resources would be one of complete *laissez-faire*. That is not the world in which we live. In

---

11 Koichi Hamada, "Liability Rules and Income Distribution in Product Liability", *American Economic Review*, vol. 66, no. 1 (March 1976), pp. 228–34.

12 Harold Demsetz, "Wealth Distribution and the Ownership of Rights", *Journal of Legal Studies*, vol. 1 (1972), pp. 223–32.

Japan, four highly publicized and outrageous cases of industrial pollution in the 1950s and 1960s were so obviously inconsistent with economic efficiency that the nation insisted upon a government response. The government-administered controls, subsidies or pollution abatement, and taxes on toxic emissions enacted in the 1970s may not have been perfect, but they are widely regarded as improvements.

Less profound departures from economic efficiency that are of the same fundamental nature as the problem of toxic emissions and effluents have been dealt with in Japan by expansions of the domain of private property rights. The right to sunshine is the most famous example. Broadly conceived, the environmental policy of Japan includes the nation's legal system.

FURTHER READING

■ William J. Baumol and Wallace E. Oates, *The Theory of Environmental Policy*, 2nd edn, Cambridge University Press, 1988. The standard textbook for courses in environmental economics.

■ Ronald H. Coase, "The Problem of Social Cost", *Journal of Law and Economics*, vol. 3 (1960), pp. 1–44. The original application of Coase's law to tort cases, one of the most cited articles ever written by an economist.

■ J. Gresser, K. Fujikura, and A. Morishima, *Environmental Law in Japan*, Cambridge, Mass.: MIT Press, 1981. Legal scholars discuss a wide variety of Japanese court cases and statutes, including all of the ones mentioned in this chapter and many others.

■ Koichi Hamada, "Product Liability Rules: A Consideration of Law and Economics in Japan", *Japanese Economic Review*, vol. 46, no. 1 (March 1995), pp. 2–22. Economic analysis of the Product Liability Law that took effect in Japan in 1995.

■ Norie Huddle and Michael Reich, with Nahum Stiskin, *Island of Dreams: Environmental Crisis in Japan*, 2nd edn, Cambridge, Mass.: Schenkman Books, 1987. The details of Japan's four most infamous environmental crises, written by journalists.

■ J. Mark Ramseyer, *Odd Markets in Japanese History*, Cambridge University Press, 1996, ch. 3, pp. 43–53. Argues that late nineteenth-century and earlier twentieth-century Japanese courts established rules for dealing with tort cases that were probably economically efficient, even though they permitted environmental abuses that would not be tolerated today.

■ Kimio Uno, *Japanese Industrial Performance*, New York: North-Holland, 1987, ch. 16, pp. 271–310. Documents the air and water pollution abatement expenditures of Japanese industries, 1960–80, and relates these to government regulations and subsidies, and to measured improvements in environmental quality; includes numerous tables and a floppy diskette with quantitative data.

Industrial Organization | 12

The notion that Japan's economy operates on the basis of unique principles may have gained currency because of the country's singular pattern of industrial organization. The business groups that have long been ubiquitous in Japan do pose challenges for economists. Japan's business groups include the prewar zaibatsu and their postwar manifestation known as the financial keiretsu, and also include the enterprise groups consisting of large manufacturing firms and their respective families of suppliers, subcontractors, wholesalers, and retailers.

What can explain the persistent self-organization of Japanese economic activity into affiliated groups of quasi-independent companies; and, if this way of arranging production is truly economical, then why does it seem to be confined to Japan? Other peculiarities of Japanese industrial organization have also attracted notice.

Many of the world-famous Japanese companies are industrial behemoths, quite distinct from the atomistic pygmies of the perfect competition model. Japan's industries are on average rather more concentrated than their US analogues. Why, and what if anything does this indicate about the allocative efficiency of Japan's industries?

A further set of issues, interrelated with those just mentioned, has to do with government policy toward competition and monopoly. Japan's anti-monopoly laws are a legacy of the American Occupation. The laws were first adopted in 1948 and significantly amended in 1953. Like the US statutes on which they are loosely based, Japan's anti-monopoly laws prohibit price-fixing, mergers for monopoly, and other practices economists generally equate with cartelization (and also many practices not equated with cartelization). However, unlike the US antitrust statutes, penalties for violating Japan's anti-monopoly laws are rather small, and significant exceptions to the laws have been extended to designated industries. Has the weakness of antitrust laws significantly affected the pricing and output of industries?

Besides anti-monopoly laws, Japan also has laws that specify government control of prices, investments, and entry in industries as diverse as telecommunications, railroads, electric power, and agriculture. Government regulation is typically implemented in a less transparent manner in Japan than elsewhere, although the sorts of industries subject to regulation are the same. Also, Japan, like the United States, has significantly deregulated its transport, telecommunications, and other industries in recent years. What have been the purposes and consequences of government regulation of industry in Japan, and what are the reasons for deregulation?

We begin our consideration of the industrial organization of Japan with the business groups.

Japan's business groups

Financial keiretsu

Business groups have been an important feature of Japan's industrial organization, at least since the beginning of this century. As early as the 1870s, there had already emerged the Yasuda banking complex, the Mitsubishi shipping conglomerate, and the Mitsui trading company, all of which later became cornerstones in the vast commercial empires known as the zaibatsu, precursors of the current-day financial keiretsu.

As detailed in Chapters 3 and 4, each zaibatsu consisted of disparate firms, including banks, trading companies, and manufacturing concerns, much of whose stock reposed in a common holding company *qua* head office that was itself controlled by a wealthy family. In 1948, the Occupation authorities dissolved the zaibatsu shareholding interlocks; at about the same time, the Anti-monopoly Laws of Japan (1947, amended in 1953) abolished holding companies. (In July 1997, the Anti-monopoly Law was again amended, finally removing the prohibition against holding companies.)

By the early 1960s, many of the companies previously associated with each of the four major zaibatsu had re-established shareholding ties with one another. These groups are widely referred to as the financial keiretsu, or just keiretsu. (But be warned that in Japanese the word *keiretsu* is also used to refer to other business groups, including subcontracting groups and directed marketing channels.) *Keiretsu* is a Japanese word that defies exact translation. A literal rendering into English might be "succession", in the sense of a sequence of entities joined together, as links in a chain. Besides the progeny of the big four zaibatsu—Mitsui, Mitsubishi, Sumitomo, and Fuyo (formerly Yasuda)—the six financial keiretsu include the Dai-Ichi Kangyo group, consisting mainly of former members of the smaller Kawasaki and Furukawa zaibatsu, and the Sanwa group, which had no prewar antecedent.

There are different ways of ascertaining which companies belong to which financial keiretsu. The clearest evidence of affiliation is appearance on the roster of monthly "presidents' club" meetings of any one of the six respective groups. These rosters are public, though the agendas of the meetings are not. The presidents' club members, as of October 1995, are listed by keiretsu affiliation and industry classification in Table 12.1. A few companies belong to more than one presidents' club—Hitachi belongs to three of them—but these are the rare exceptions. The rosters of the presidents' clubs exhibit little change from one year to the next, and the changes that do occur are mostly the result of mergers. Altogether, the members of the six presidents' clubs in 1995 numbered 185 companies, including most but not all of the largest companies in Japan. Some of the large companies not on the rosters of presidents' clubs include Honda Motor, Matsushita, Sony, and Fuji Film.

The presidents' club companies span a wide selection of industries. In fact, the economist Miyazaki Yoshikazu famously characterized the financial keiretsu as organized on the basis of the "complete-set principle" (*wan setto shugi*); that is, each of them included at least one company in each major industry.[1] It is readily apparent, from Table 12.1, that in industry after industry the members of the differing financial keiretsu compete with one another. For instance, Toyota, Mitsubishi Motors, Nissan, Daihatsu, and Isuzu are each affiliated with a different keiretsu; Kirin Brewery belongs to the Mitsubishi presidents' club, but Sapporo Breweries belongs to the Fuyo presidents' club. There are many other similar examples. The financial keiretsu are not simply cartels, coalitions of suppliers of similar products. Rather, they represent suppliers of differing products, and in many instances fellow members of the same presidents' club trade with one another. Japan's Fair Trade Commission has periodically surveyed the extent of transactions between fellow members of same presidents' clubs. In 1980 it reported that 20 percent of the sales of presidents' club manufacturing firms were to fellow members of the same clubs, and 12 percent of purchases were from fellow club members.[2] These are all very large companies, most of whose transactions are probably with smaller firms, outside the presidents' clubs, so the Fair Trade Commission data just reported do suggest a disposition toward trade between fellow members of the same financial keiretsu.

Presidents' club members borrow principally but not exclusively from fellow members. The single largest lender to each of them is usually the city bank that belongs to the same presidents' club as the company itself. In the usual pattern, loans from the presidents' club city bank account for 10–20 percent

---

[1] For an example of Miyazaki's dissection of the financial keiretsu, in English, see Yoshikazu Miyazaki, "Rapid Economic Growth in Post-War Japan—with Special Reference to 'Excessive Competition' and the Formation of 'Keiretsu'", *The Developing Economies*, vol. 5 (1967), pp. 329–50.

[2] Kosei Torihiki Iinkai, Keizaibu Jigyoka (Executive Office of the Fair Trade Commission of Japan, Enterprise Section, Economics Division) "Kigyō shudan no jittai ni tsuite" (Concerning the state of business groups), *Kosei Torihiki*, no. 394 (1983), pp. 20–4.

Table 12.1. Presidents' clubs of the six financial keiretsu, October 1995[a]

	Mitsui	Mitsubishi	Sumitomo	Fuyo	Sanwa	Dai-Ichi Kangyo
City banks	8314 Sakura Bank	8315 Mitsubishi Bank[b]	8318 Sumitomo Bank	8317 Fuji Bank	8320 Sanwa Bank	8311 Dai-Ichi Kangyo Bank
Trust banks	8401 Mitsui Trust and Banking	8402 Mitsubishi Trust and Banking	8403 Sumitomo Trust and Banking	8404 Yasuda Trust and Banking	8407 Toyo Trust and Banking	
Hazard insurance	8752 Taisho Marine and Fire Ins.	8751 Tokio Marine and Fire Insurance	8753 Sumitomo Marine and Fire Ins.	8755 Yasuda Fire and Marine Insurance		8756 Nissan Fire and Marine Insurance Taisei Fire and Marine Insurance
Life insurance	Mitsui Life Insurance Company	Meiji Life Insurance Co.	Sumitomo Life Insurance Co.	Yasuda Life Insurance Co.	Daido Life Insurance Co. Japan Life Insurance Co.	Fukoku Life Insurance Co. Asahi Life Insurance Co.
Forestry			1371 Sumitomo Forestry			
Mining	1501 Mitsui Mining 1505 Hokkaido Colliery & Steamship		1503 Sumitomo Mining			
Construction	1821 Mitsui Construction 1961 Sanki Engineering	1996 Mitsubishi Construction	1823 Sumitomo Construction	1801 Taisei	1802 Obayashi 1811 Zenitaka 1890 Toyo Construction 1928 Sekisui House	1803 Shimizu Construction
Foods	2001 Nippon Flour Mills	2503 Kirin Brewery		2002 Nisshin Flour Milling 2501 Sapporo Breweries 2871 Nippon Reizo	2284 Itoham Foods	
Textiles	3402 Toray Industries	3404 Mitsubishi Rayon		3105 Nisshin Spinning 3403 Toho Rayon	3103 Unitica 3401 Teijin	3407 Asahi Chemical Industry
Paper and pulp	3861 New Oji Paper *3863 Nippon Paper Industries	3864 Mitsubishi Paper Mills		*3863 Nippon Paper Industries		3862 Honshu Paper

(continued over)

239

Table 12.1. (cont.)

	Mitsui	Mitsubishi	Sumitomo	Fuyo	Sanwa	Dai-Ichi Kangyo
Chemicals	4001 Mitsui Toatsu Chemicals 4061 Denki Kagaku Kogyo 4183 Mitsui Petrochemical Ind.	4010 Mitsubishi Chemical Industries 4182 Mitsubishi Gas Chemical 4213 Mitsubishi Plastics Industries	4005 Sumitomo Chemical 4203 Sumitomo Bakelite	4004 Showa Denko 4023 Kureha Chemical Industry 4403 Nippon Oil and Fats	4043 Tokuyama Soda 4204 Sekisui Chemical 4208 Ube Inds. 4217 Hitachi Chemical 4508 Tanabe Seiyaku 4511 Fujisawa 4613 Kansai Paint	4061 Denki Kagaku Kogyo 4151 Kyowa Hakko Kogyo 4205 Nippon Zeon 4401 Asahi Denka Kogyo 4501 Sankyo 4911 Shiseido 4912 Lion
Oil and coal products		5004 Mitsubishi Oil		5005 Toa Nenryo Kogyo	5007 Cosmo Oil	5002 Showa Oil
Rubber goods					5105 Toyo Tire and Rubber	5101 The Yokohama Rubber
Glass and ceramics	*5233 Chichibu Onoda Cement	5201 Asahi Glass	5202 Nippon Sheet Glass *5232 Sumitomo Osaka Cement	5231 Nihon Cement	*5232 Sumitomo Osaka Cement	*5233 Chichibu Onoda Cement
Iron and steel	5631 The Japan Steel Works	5632 Mitsubishi Steel Mfg.	5405 Sumitomo Metal Industries	5404 NKK	*5406 Kobe Steel 5407 Nisshin Steel 5408 Nakayama Steel Works 5486 Hitachi Metals	5403 Kawasaki Steel *5406 Kobe Steel 5562 Japan Metals & Chemicals
Non-ferrous metals	5706 Mitsui Mining & Smelting	5711 Mitsubishi Materials 5771 Mitsubishi Shindoh 5804 Mitsubishi Cable Industries Mitsubishi Aluminum	5713 Sumitomo Metal Mining 5738 Sumitomo Light Metal Ind. 5802 Sumitomo Electric Industries		5812 Hitachi Cable	5701 Nippon Light Metal 5715 Furukawa 5801 Furukawa Electric
Machinery		6331 Mitsubishi Kakoki	6302 Sumitomo Heavy Industries	6326 Kubota 6471 Nippon Seiko	6472 NTN Toyo Bearing	6011 Niigata Engineering 6310 Iseki 6361 Ebara
Electric appliances	6502 Toshiba	6503 Mitsubishi Electric	6701 NEC	*6501 Hitachi	*6501 Hitachi	*6501 Hitachi

Transport equipment	7003 Mitsui Engineering & Shipbuilding *7013 Ishikawajima-Harima Heavy Industries 7203 Toyota Motor	7011 Mitsubishi Heavy Industries 7211 Mitsubishi Motors		6703 Oki Electric Industry 6841 Yokogawa Hokushin Electric 7201 Nissan Motor	6704 Iwatsu Electric 6753 Sharp 6971 Kyocera 6988 Nitto Denko 7004 Hitachi Zosen 7224 Shin Meiwa Industry 7262 Daihatsu Motor	6504 Fuji Electric 6506 Yaskawa Electric Mfg. 6702 Fujitsu 6791 Nippon Columbia 7012 Kawasaki Heavy Industries *7013 Ishikawajima-Harima Heavy Ind. 7202 Isuzu Motors
Precision machinery	7731 Nikon			7751 Canon	7741 Hoya	7750 Asahi Optical
Commerce	8031 Mitsui 8231 Mitsukoshi	8058 Mitsubishi	8053 Sumitomo	8002 Marubeni	8004 Nichimen *8063 Nissho Iwai 8088 Iwatani 8233 Takashimaya	8001 Itochu *8063 Nissho Iwai 8020 Kanematsu-Gosho 8110 Kawasho Seibu Department Store
Misc. financing						
Securities					8591 Orix	8607 Nippon Kangyo Kakumaru Securities
Real estate	8801 Mitsui Real Estate Development	8802 Mitsubishi Estate	8830 Sumitomo Realty & Development	8804 Tokyo Tatemono		
Transportation	9104 Mitsui O.S.K. Lines	9101 Nippon Yusen		9001 Tobu Railway 9006 Keihin Electric Express Rail 9126 Showa Line	9042 Hankyu 9062 Nippon Express 9105 Navix Line	9062 Nippon Express 9107 Kawasaki Kisen
Warehousing	9302 The Mitsui Warehouse	9301 Mitsubishi Warehouse & Transport	9303 The Sumitomo Warehouse			9304 The Shibusawa Warehouse
Services						9681 Tokyo Dome 9871 Itoki

[a] Number before company name is the securities identification code number.
[b] Since 1996: Bank of Tokyo-Mitsubishi.
* Indicates affiliation with more than one presidents' club.

Source: "Tōyō keizai" (Oriental economist), *Kigyō keiretsu sōran* (Handbook of keiretsu enterprises), 1996.

241

of any other fellow presidents' club member's total outstanding debt. The presidents' club trust bank holds another 5–10 percent of each fellow member's debt and the life insurance company, 1–5 percent. The balance of a typical presidents' club company's total borrowing is from outside the group, including borrowing from financial members of presidents' clubs other than the one of affiliation. Presidents' club members also borrow from the three long-term credit banks, the city banks not affiliated with the six financial keiretsu, and from the regional banks. Since 1980 large Japanese companies have been allowed access to international financial markets as a source of funds, but they still rely quite heavily upon domestic loans.

Another visible linkage among fellow presidents' club members is cross-shareholding. The average fractions of outstanding shares held within the respective presidents' clubs in 1994 were Sumitomo: 23.4 percent, Mitsubishi: 27.5 percent, Dai-Ichi Kango: 11.7 percent, Sanwa: 16 percent, Mitsui: 16.5 percent, and Fuyo: 14.6 percent, but about half of these shares were held by financial institutions of the respective groups. The Anti-monopoly Law of Japan limits the extent of shares that banks and insurance companies may hold in any one company. Since 1987 these limits have been set at 5 percent for banks and 7 percent for insurance companies. Few banks or insurance companies hold share interests approaching these limits. The shareholding of

banks in the companies to which they lend is an important aspect of Japan's bank-centered system of financial intermediation, a topic explored in detail in the next chapter. In any case, there does seem to be a bit more to the presidents' clubs than financial intermediation.

About one-third of the (non-ordered) pairs of nonfinancial companies belonging to a same presidents' club are directly linked with one another by cross-shareholding, and in about half of these instances the cross-shareholding is reciprocal. Typically, the share interest of any one presidents' club company in another lies around 1 percent. In other words, the cross-shareholding ties are usually insufficient to confer a controlling interest. Cross-shareholding between nonfinancial members of differing presidents' clubs is unusual. A convincing explanation for cross-shareholding between nonfinancial firms that are possibly trading partners would go a long way toward explaining the *raison d'être* of the financial keiretsu themselves—and, indeed, that of the other business groups in Japan.

The financial keiretsu occupy a sizable niche in the Japanese economy. Together, the six presidents' clubs in 1994 accounted for about one-eighth of the sales of nonfinancial businesses in Japan, one-seventh of the paid-in capital, and one-fifth of the net profit. These and other such data, broken down for each of the six financial keiretsu, are represented in Table 12.2.

Table 12.2. Scale of keiretsu presidents' club companies, excluding banks and insurance companies, in relation to the Japanese economy, 1994

	% of respective totals for all industrial companies in Japan[a]					
	Employees	Assets	Paid-in capital	Sales	Operating profit	Net profit
Mitsui	0.65	2.01	2.33	2.37	2.20	5.30
Mitsubishi	0.54	1.88	2.38	2.02	2.45	5.69
Sumitomo	0.31	1.14	1.60	1.57	0.67	1.15
Fuyo	0.75	1.98	2.91	2.17	1.40	2.09
Sanwa	0.94	2.50	3.25	2.50	3.14	4.52
Dai-Ichi Kangyo	1.11	3.29	3.71	3.80	2.46	2.46
All six	3.63	11.50	14.44	12.95	11.10	19.63

[a] 2.4mn companies in all.

Source: "Toyo keizai" (see Table 12.1), p. 25.

Attempts have been made to broaden the classification of the financial keiretsu beyond the rosters of the presidents' clubs, by identifying all the important loan clients of the presidents' club banks, and identifying the broader web of cross-shareholding linking presidents' club members to other companies. By focusing only on the presidents' club members, we may grossly understate their scale in relation to the Japanese economy.

Enterprise groups (*kigyō shudan*)

The financial keiretsu are not the sole identifiable business groups of Japan. There are also groups of firms centered, respectively, around several of the largest industrial companies. These might be referred to as enterprise groups, but there is no standard term of reference for them, and in Japanese, the phrase *kigyō shudan* (lit., "enterprise group") is also, somewhat confusingly, used to refer to the financial keiretsu. Here, let us reserve the name "enterprise group" for this other category, a number of representatives of which are listed in Table 12.3. Quite a few of the forty firms identified there as leaders of enterprise groups are themselves members of a keiretsu presidents' club.

The enterprise groups generally include myriad subsidiaries as well as independent subcontractors and other suppliers, and some also include wholesalers and retailers of the group's products. Trading ties within the respective enterprise groups may be presumed to be a lot more extensive than is generally true in the financial keiretsu. Also, the shareholding of the enterprise group leader in the other members is typically strong enough to confer *de facto* control, not merely a silent financial interest. The enterprise groups are more tightly knit than the financial keiretsu.

The combined assets of the forty enterprise groups listed in Table 12.3 approached 10 percent of the total assets of all industrial firms in Japan in 1994. In other words, the scale of the forty largest enterprise groups roughly corresponds to that of all the industrial members of the presidents' clubs of the six financial keiretsu.

The economics of cross-shareholding

Attempts to understand the economic rationale behind Japan's business groups have focused prin-cipally upon cross-shareholding. The advantages of banks holding stock in the firms to which they lend are fairly well understood, and are explored in detail in the next chapter. About half of the cross-shareholding within financial keiretsu presidents' clubs is of this sort, and roughly mirrors the pattern

Table 12.3. Companies heading the 40 most significant enterprise groups, 1996[a]

1801	Taisei (Fuyo)
2503	Kirin Brewery (Mitsubishi)
2914	Japan Tobacco
3402	Toray Industries (Mitsui)
3407	Asahi Chemical Industry (Dai-Ichi)
3863	Nippon Paper Industries (Mitsui, Fuyo)
4010	Mitsubishi Chemical Industries (Mitsubishi)
4204	Sekisui Chemical (Sanwa)
4452	Kao Corp.
4502	Takeda Chemical Industries
4901	Fuji Photo Film
5001	Nippon Oil Co.
5108	Bridgestone Corp.
5201	Asahi Glass (Mitsubishi)
5401	Nippon Steel
5404	NKK (Fuyo)
5711	Mitsubishi Materials (Mitsubishi)
5802	Sumitomo Electric Industries (Sumitomo)
6326	Kubota (Fuyo)
6501	Hitachi (Fuyo, Sanwa, Dai-Ichi)
6502	Toshiba (Mitsui)
6503	Mitsubishi Electric (Mitsubishi)
6701	NEC (Sumitomo)
6702	Fujitsu (Dai-Ichi)
6752	Matsushita Electric Industrial Co.
6758	Sony Corp.
7011	Mitsubishi Heavy Industries (Mitsubishi)
7201	Nissan Motor (Fuyo)
7203	Toyota Motor (Mitsui)
7267	Honda Motor Co.
7751	Canon (Fuyo)
8031	Mitsui (Mitsui)
8058	Mitsubishi (Mitsubishi)
8263	Daei
8264	Ito-Yokado Co.
8591	Orix (Sanwa)
8801	Mitsui Estate development (Mitsui)
9501	Tokyo Electric Power Co.
9613	NTT
	JR-Higashi Nihon

[a] Presidents' club memberships are stated in parentheses.

Source: see Table 12.1.

of lending by the banks. But bank stockholding in clients is not confined to the financial keiretsu. For instance, the smaller (regional) banks, too, hold stock in clients. Bank stockholding in clients appears not to be a defining characteristic of the financial keiretsu. In fact, the zaibatsu antecedents of the financial keiretsu predate Japan's bank-centered system of financial intermediation.

In Chapter 3 we speculated that the zaibatsu evolved as an efficient mode of corporate governance in selected industries, such as mining, trading, and banking, in which close monitoring of managerial decisions was relatively productive. By consolidating controlling share interests in close holding companies, the wealthy families of zaibatsu founders were able to oversee the enterprise managers, and to capture the rewards from doing so. With the 1948 dissolution of the zaibatsu holding companies and deconcentration of shareholding, governance of the former members of the zaibatsu was thrown into a state of disarray. Yet the enterprises had accumulated a number of valuable assets, including knowledgeable teams of employees, and so perpetuation of the enterprises as going concerns was worthwhile. One interpretation of the postwar reconfiguration of zaibatsu enterprises into the financial keiretsu is that it established a new mechanism of corporate governance. Eleanor Hadley, an economist on MacArthur's staff during the early Occupation era who helped to implement the zaibatsu dissolution, later argued in an influential monograph that in the financial keiretsu the large city banks had taken on essentially the same role as that of the holding companies in the zaibatsu.[3] As banks became the dominant financial intermediaries, a consequence of particular regulations of Japanese financial markets, it was natural that they should insinuate themselves into corporate governance. If this is true, then the organization of firms into bank-centered financial groups can have served an important purpose. Because any companies belonging to the same group had ongoing dealings with one another, banks' information about each of them was improved if the same bank was the close monitor of all of them. For many students of the subject, this is a satisfactory explanation for the financial keiretsu. And tied, as the explanation is, to the unique history of zaibatsu evolution and dissolution, it leaves little question why groups like the

financial keiretsu did not also develop in the United States or other nations. But there remain puzzles. For example, why are industrial members of the respective presidents' clubs so often linked to one another by cross-shareholding?

A leading explanation of keiretsu cross-shareholding, not altogether convincing, is that its purpose is to forestall any hostile takeover, the amassing of a controlling share interest by an outside investor that is opposed by the incumbent managers of the company. In one interpretation, the prevention of such takeovers is merely in the selfish interests of the company's managers, not necessarily in the interests of the company's incumbent shareholders.[4] In a more sophisticated version of the argument, the prevention of takeovers actually enhances the value of the firm by protecting the firm's long-term contracts from abrogation.[5] Takeovers are indeed quite rare events in Japan, but almost certainly not because company shares lie in the hands of fellow group members. For one thing, even companies outside the orbit of business groups in Japan are seldom acquired by other companies or outside investors. Takeovers, and the threat of takeovers, are simply not an important aspect of corporate governance in Japan.[6] And in the United States, where takeovers are frequent occurrences, many indisputable examples of takeover defenses have been observed but self-organization of firms into cross-shareholding groups is not among them. Cross-shareholding in Japan is not to forestall hostile takeovers. What, then, can be its purpose?

---

[3] Eleanor Hadley, *Antitrust in Japan*, Princeton University Press, 1970.

[4] For developments of this line of argument, see Odagiri H., "Kigyō shudan no riron" (A theory of industrial groups), *Kikan Riron Keizaigaku*, vol. 26 (1975), pp. 144–54; Kobayashi Y., "Kigyō shudan no bunseki" (Economic analysis of enterprise groups), Hokkaido University, Sapporo, 1980; and M. Aoki, "Shareholders' Non-unanimity on Investment Financing: Banks versus Individual Investors", in M. Aoki (ed.), *The Economic Analysis of the Japanese Firm*, Amsterdam: North-Holland, 1984.

[5] Examples of this kind of argument may be found in J. M. Ramseyer, "Takeovers in Japan: Opportunism, Ideology, and Corporate Control", *UCLA Law Review*, vol. 35 (1987), pp. 1–64; M. Aoki, "The Japanese Firm in Transition", in K. Yamamura and Y. Yasuba (eds.), *The Political Economy of Japan*, i, *The Domestic Transformation*, Stanford University Press, 1987, pp. 263–88; and Paul Sheard, "The Economics of Interlocking Shareholding in Japan", *Ricerche Economiche*, vol. 45 (1991), pp. 421–48.

[6] This, despite its title, is the essential theme of Carl Kester, *Japanese Takeovers: The Global Contest for Corporate Control*, Cambridge, Mass.: Harvard Business School, 1991.

One explanation for cross-shareholding[7] is that it slants the terms of trade between two firms in favor of the firm in which shares are held, and so gives the opposite firm a way of penalizing it, by divesting the stock, should things go wrong but allowing trade between the two to continue. Bargainers may be presumed to set terms of trade in such a way that they divide the gains equally. But if one firm holds stock in the other, then its own gains include a share interest in the other's gains. Consequently, equal division of the gains from trade actually enriches a party in which shares are held by the other, relative to the case in which there is no cross-shareholding. A small share interest in a trading partner might, in this way, impart a small bias to the terms of trade, which is narrowly disadvantageous to the shareholder, but can serve a useful purpose, bonding the other party to observe otherwise unenforceable stipulations. For instance, presidents' club members may pay slightly higher prices when buying from fellow members in which they hold stock than if purchasing from outsiders, but they are assured of special consideration on quality, service, truthful revelation of private information and the like, by the implicit threat of divesting the stock if the stockholder ever becomes dissatisfied.

This theory of cross-shareholding among presidents' club members is a bit speculative, but does explain why the cross-shareholding should be more likely to link trading partners than others (and there is some evidence that it does[8]). It also would explain why the cross-shareholding is often insufficient to confer anything other than a silent financial interest. The theory does not account for the configuration of trading partners into (nearly) mutually exclusive, share-interlocked groups. The existence, in Japan, of mutually interacting groups of firms owes a lot to the fact that, historically, each zaibatsu group of large companies was controlled by the same wealthy family. (The Sanwa financial keiretsu, lacking any zaibatsu antecedent, remains something of an anomaly.) That each of the large banks at the center of the respective groups economizes by insinuating itself into the governance of a set of mutually interacting companies, rather than unrelated ones, has probably also contributed to the perpetuation of the financial keiretsu. In further explaining the many peculiar features of the financial keiretsu, historical inquiries and detailed case studies may prove helpful.[9]

The enterprise groups pose a different set of challenges for economists. Here, the central issue is vertical integration.

Vertical integration

Each enterprise group represents a less vertically integrated structure than the one that would result if all of its activities were organized within a single firm, but is more vertically integrated than if each constituent enterprise were completely independent of the others, and not a subsidiary of the group leader or controlled directly by it. Vertical integration refers to the incorporation of successive steps of a production process within the same organization, and here production is defined in the broadest possible terms, including, for instance, the wholesaling and retailing of a product, as well as its manufacture. The question, what determines the extent of vertical integration in an economy, lies at the core of industrial organization, and also at the intellectual frontiers of it.

Because of the complicated web of technology, in which the output of each industry is also a productive input in every industry, complete vertical integration would require that the entire economy consist of a single enterprise, so that it becomes a command economy, or centrally planned economy. The opposite extreme, a complete absence of vertical integration, would require that each individual person in the economy be self-employed, and that her production behavior be coordinated with that of others only through a decentralized price system. Vertical integration on the economy-wide scale—central planning—is cumbersome and wasteful of resources, as evidenced by its crashing failure in every nation in which it has been attempted. Yet, the spontaneous self-organization of production into partially vertically integrated structures called business firms is a ubiquitous feature of every market economy. If central planning on the economy-wide scale wastes resources, then how can central plan-

---

[7] David Flath, "The Keiretsu Puzzle", *Journal of the Japanese and International Economies*, vol. 10 (1996), pp. 101–21.

[8] See Flath, "The Keiretsu Puzzle", for details.

[9] For a recent attempt, by a political scientist rather than an economist, see Michael Gerlach, *Alliance Capitalism: The Social Organization of Japanese Business*, University of California Press, 1993.

ning on a small scale, which is the nature of a business firm, conserve resources? The Nobel laureate Ronald Coase long ago gave a definitive answer to this question.[10] Just as there are costs of directing production that can be avoided by allowing the price system to coordinate things, so too are there costs of employing a price system that can be avoided by direct administration. The costs of employing a price system are the costs of activities that are either essential to trade or facilitate trade in some way. Such activities include the search for a trading partner, negotiation of mutually agreeable terms of trade, assurance of ownership rights in the traded items, evaluation of the characteristics of the traded items, and so on. Advertising, negotiation, search, and enforcement of exclusive ownership rights are all costly activities that can be dispensed with within a firm (not between firms), and so firms can be economical ways of organizing production, even though establishing and operating a firm itself gives rise to new costs.

In the market economy, vertical integration will proceed further, the greater are the costs of transacting through the price system, and the less are the costs of administering a directed system of production. One of the influences on the costs of transacting is the extent of the market. If a market is too small to allow middlemen to be profitable, or too small to allow more than a few sellers of similar goods to be profitable, then monopolistic distortions and limited gains from specialization in the costly activities that facilitate trading will elevate the costs of transacting and favor more complete vertical integration than otherwise. To put it another way, the division of labor is limited by the extent of the market.[11]

Vertically integrated production units are characteristic of the small economy with limited demand for final products, not the large economy. Japan's economy has grown large compared with those of most other nations, and so might have been expected to attain a quite decentralized organization of production. Whether the enterprise groups represent such a structure depends upon the object of comparison. The Japanese automobile manufacturers that lead enterprise groups are clearly less vertically integrated even than their American counterparts. Toyota relies on an extensive network of subcontractors to supply parts such as General

Motors manufactures itself, for instance. Yet, in thinking of the ways in which the Toyota group and Japan's other enterprise groups represent a more directed vertical structure than conceivable alternatives, one can be mindful of the added transactions costs that invariably accompany an expanded division of labor.

We next turn our attention to the horizontal integration of Japanese industry, the question of cartels, monopoly, and oligopoly.

Industrial concentration and oligopoly in Japan

Many of the world-famous Japanese companies hold even more commanding positions within Japan itself than they do in export markets. Kirin Beer, Fuji Film, Toyota, Matsushita, Nippon Steel, Bridgestone, Shiseido, and others are all Gullivers; their rivals within Japan are mere Lilliputians by comparison (see Table 12.4). But this is hardly distinctive. The United States has Gullivers that match many of the ones in Japan, including Kodak, GM, and US Steel.

Several authors have attempted systematic comparisons between the concentration of industries in Japan and in the USA. The general result is that if an industry is concentrated in the United States, it counterpart is likely to be relatively concentrated in Japan. To illustrate, let us consider a small but representative sample of industries. Scherer and Ross[12] report concentration measures for forty-four US manufacturing industries, a set that is "fairly representative, but excludes vaguely defined catch-all categories and favors the larger, more highly concentrated industries".[13] Of these, thirty-three can be matched with industries in Japan for which

---

10 Ronald H. Coase, "The Nature of the Firm", *Economica*, vol. 4 (1937), pp. 386–405.

11 The original author of this principle was Adam Smith, but it was George Stigler who reinterpreted it in roughly the terms expressed here: George Stigler, "The Division of Labor is Limited by the Extent of the Market", *Journal of Political Economy*, vol. 59, no. 3 (June 1951).

12 F. M. Scherer and D. Ross, *Industrial Market Structure and Economic Performance*, Boston: Houghton-Mifflin, 1990, table 3–6, p. 77; US Bureau of the Census, "Concentration Ratios in Manufacturing", *1982 Census of Manufacturers*, MC82-S-7 (April 1986).

13 Ibid. p. 76.

Table 12.4. Market shares of leading Japanese companies, 1996

Product	Company	Share of industry output in Japan (%)
Crude steel	Nippon Steel	25.5
Color TVs	Matsushita	16.5
Automobiles	Toyota	38.4
Tires	Bridgestone	50.7
Cosmetics	Shiseido	26.0
Beer	Kirin	44.4
Color film	Fuji	67.0

Source: http://satellite.nikkei.co.jp/enews/bb/ranking/share.html

because of the fixed costs of setting up production facilities or establishing a new enterprise, then the maximum number of firms that can profitably co-exist is less, the smaller the scale of demand. Of course, this ignores foreign demand, but recall that exports in both Japan and the USA absorb only around 10 percent of aggregate output.

What, if anything, does the pattern of concentration of Japanese industries imply about pricing and allocation of goods? The weight of expert opinion favors the view that concentration affects prices and allocation, but not as much as other factors, including government regulation, the nature of contractual arrangements between firms and their customers, and the degree of substitutability in demand among the products of competing firms. Some of the widely used theoretical models of oligopoly—such as the Cournot model—predict an inverse relationship between industry price and concentration, but in empirical investigations such a relationship has been detected only in the rare instances of

concentration data are available from Senō.[14] The measure of concentration for both countries is the Herfindahl index, the sum of squared shares of industry sales.[15] The Herfindahl indices are plotted in Figure 12.1 on page 248.

The figure reveals two rather unsurprising facts. First, the Japanese analogues of relatively concentrated American industries themselves tend to be relatively concentrated—points in the diagram tend to fall along a positively sloping ray from the origin. Second, most Japanese industries are more concentrated than their US analogues—points in the diagram tend to lie above the 45 degree line denoting matched industries of equal concentration in Japan and the United States.[16] Analyses of more global samples have yielded approximately similar conclusions to these.[17]

The similar patterns of industrial concentration in Japan and America no doubt reflect the likeness of technology in the corresponding industries of the two nations. Firms that use blast furnaces, refineries, or assembly lines have proportionately high fixed costs. Where methods of producing that have high fixed costs are profitable, firms tend to be large, and their industries concentrated, in both Japan and America.

The greater concentration of Japanese industries compared with their US counterparts is also unsurprising. Because Japan is a much less populous nation than the USA, the scale of demand facing each industry is correspondingly less in Japan than in the United States. Where there exist economies of scale over some initial range of output, for example

14 Senō Akira, "Gendai nihon no sangyo shuchu" (Industrial concentration in contemporary Japan), *Nihon Keizai Shinbunsha* (1983), table 42, pp. 239–99.

15 The Herfindahl index is bounded between 0 and 1, and in the symmetric case of n identical firms equals $1/n$. The Cournot model of firms producing homogeneous products implies that the industry price–cost margin equals the Herfindahl index divided by elasticity of demand facing the industry.

16 The regression equation is

$$H_J = 0.064 + 0.954 H_{US}, \quad \text{adj } R^2 = 0.468, n = 33.$$
$$(3.1) \quad (5.4)$$

The t-statistics are reported beneath coefficient estimates.

17 See e.g. Richard E. Caves and Masu Uekusa, *Industrial Organization in Japan*, Washington: Brookings Institution, 1972, table 2–3, p. 25. Caves and Uekusa, comparing US 3-digit SIC industries with their Japanese analogues in 1963, find that the average 4-firm concentration ratios (percentages of industry sales accounted for by the four largest in the industry, CR4) are 38.3% for US industries and 37.5% for Japanese ones and that the following regression relationship holds:

$$CR4_J = 13.2 + 0.573 CR4_{US}, \quad R^2 = 0.397, n = 99.$$
$$(4.2) \quad (8.1)$$

Also see Unotoro Keiko, "Shuchūdo no nichibei hikaku ni tsuite" (On comparing the degree of concentration in Japan and America), *Kosei Torihiki*, no. 448 (February 1988), pp. 75–9. Unotoro, using commodity-level data (5-digit SIC), for 1982: USA, 1984: Japan, finds that the Herfindahl indices (summation of squared shares of industry shipments, H) average 0.10514 for US industries and 0.15143 for Japanese ones, and that the following regression relationship holds:

$$H_{US} = 0.075 + 0.21 H_J, \quad R^2 = 0.35, n = 209.$$
$$(10.0) \quad (5.4)$$

The numbers in parentheses are t-statistics.

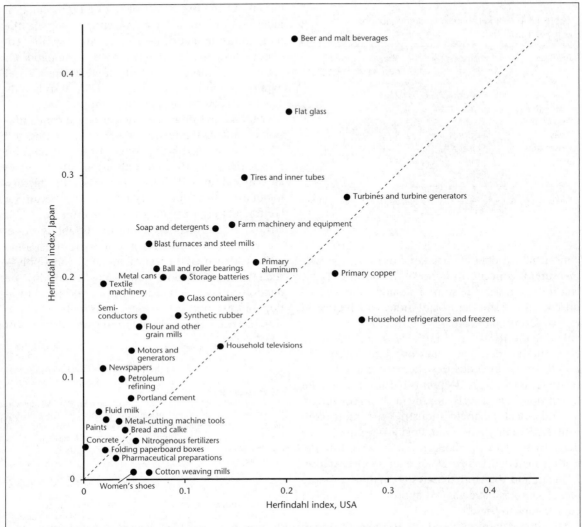

Figure 12.1. Herfindahl indices (summation of squared shares of industry sales) of matched industries in Japan and the United States, 1980

Sources: *USA*: F. M. Scherer and D. Ross, *Industrial Market Structure and Economic Performance*, Boston: Houghton-Mifflin, 1990, table 3–6, p. 77 (primary source: US Bureau of the Census, 1982 Census of Manufacturer, "Concentration Ratios in Manufacturing", MC82-S-7 (April 1986)); *Japan*: Senō Akira, *Gendai nihon no sangyō shūchū* (Industrial concentration in contemporary Japan), Tokyo: Nihon keizai shinbunsha, 1983, table 42, pp. 239–99.

natural experiment. For instance, positive relations between price and concentration may be discerned in the geographic pricing patterns of regional oligopolies in the United States.[18] Such patterns have been much less evident in cross-industry studies. Perhaps this is because concentration not only influences the strength of price competition but also reflects it. Concentrated industries may include those in which entry is perceived to be unprofitable

because price competition is already intense; less concentrated industries may be those in which

---

[18] For a fairly comprehensive survey of empirical studies of the relation between industry concentration, prices, and profits, see Richard Schmalensee, "Studies of Market Structure and Performance", in R. Schmalensee and Robert D. Willig (eds.), *Handbook of Industrial Organization*, ii, Amsterdam: North-Holland, 1988, ch. 16, pp. 951–1009. Schmalensee discusses the few studies to isolate the relationship between concentration and pricing at pp. 987–8.

entry was perceived as profitable because price competition was weak.[19] Consequently, more concentrated industries will not necessarily exhibit larger divergences between price and marginal cost than do other, less concentrated, ones.

Factors besides concentration that influence price competition in Japan

Because the relatively great industrial concentration of Japan affords a weak basis for judging the intensity of price competition there, attention may be directed to two factors that bear more directly on pricing behavior.

First, the antitrust laws of Japan are more permissive than those of the United States; the penalties for violating Japan's anti-monopoly laws are minute, and the resources devoted to their enforcement are rather minimal. To the extent that US antitrust laws do impede collusive practices, these considerations favor weaker price competition in Japan than in the United States.

Second, business firms in Japan are somewhat inclined to have long and persistent trading relations with one another. These relations are implicit—not detailed in written agreements—but are neither entered into lightly nor broken off abruptly. The most tangible manifestation of such long-term trading ties are the business groups of various kinds with which a large number of Japanese corporations are affiliated. But even households in Japan are far more likely than Americans to patronize the same shops repetitively and habitually. These durable ties between firms and their customers divert competition away from price reductions and toward higher product quality and more reliable service.

Both of these topics warrant further attention and to that we now turn.

Anti-monopoly laws of Japan

Japan's anti-monopoly laws are a legacy of the American Occupation. Originally enacted in 1948 as a part of the package of reforms that also included the breakup of the zaibatsu, the anti-monopoly laws of Japan have several features in common with the antitrust laws of the United States. First, some of the specific language of the Sherman Act and Clayton Act (the US antitrust laws) is incorporated into the Japanese statute—"conspiracy in restraint of trade",

"tend to monopolize", and so on. Second, the Act established a new government agency, the Fair Trade Commission of Japan, charged with the responsibility for investigating violations of the anti-monopoly laws, and also empowered to reach judgments and issue decrees. The Fair Trade Commission of Japan has an analogous role to that of the Federal Trade Commission of the USA. And third, many of the same practices that have been the subject of antitrust cases in the United States have also run afoul of anti-monopoly law in Japan—resale price maintenance, exclusive dealing, customer restrictions, price-fixing rings, and mergers.

For all the similarities, however, there are also striking differences between Japanese and US antitrust laws. First, there are significant exemptions to the anti-monopoly laws of Japan that have no counterpart in the US statutes. The Fair Trade Commission can designate an industry as in recession, and therefore temporarily exempt from anti-monopoly laws. Additionally, an industry may be granted exemption from anti-monopoly laws for the purpose of "rationalization". There is no intellectually respectable basis for either exemption; neither promotes an economically efficient allocation of resources. In the ensuing years there have been hundreds of industries designated either as recession cartels or rationalization cartels. Perhaps surprisingly, there is very little evidence that this widespread legalization of blatant price-fixing has actually resulted in contractions of output or rises in price in the designated industries. A cartel, legal or illegal, is a prisoners' dilemma: though it is mutually advantageous for firms in the same industry to contract output or raise prices, it is more profitable for any one of them to do the opposite. Legal authorization to form a cartel does not in itself change this.

A second difference between Japan's antitrust law and that of the USA is that the resources devoted to investigating potential violations of anti-monopoly laws are rather limited in Japan. The Fair Trade Commission is the only agency of the Japanese government authorized to pursue such cases. In the United States, not only the Federal Trade Commission (in many ways the model on which Japan's Fair Trade Commission was founded) but also the Justice

---

19 This idea is developed by John Sutton, *Sunk Costs and Market Structure*, Cambridge, Mass.: MIT Press, 1991.

Department and private citizens (if arguing that they themselves have been harmed) are empowered to bring suit against antitrust violators.[20] Private citizens are encouraged in this by the prospect of receiving treble damages—compensation equal to thrice the value of harm inflicted as judged by a court. In Japan the executive branch prosecutions of anti-monopoly cases are not strictly for violation of the anti-monopoly laws, but for failure to comply with a Fair Trade Commission order, always the end result of the Commission's own tortuous investigation and negotiations with the violator. The Fair Trade Commission has a meager staff (fewer than 200 inspectors), with limited powers of subpoena and a small operating budget. It is therefore hardly surprising that it brings few actions (a total of thirty in fiscal year 1992, for instance) compared with the hundreds of antitrust actions brought in the USA each year.

A final difference between antitrust laws in Japan and the USA is that the penalties for violating the anti-monopoly laws of Japan are both trivial and seldom even invoked. In 1977 the anti-monopoly laws were amended to raise the highest civil fine allowed by a factor of ten to 5 million yen (well under $50,000) and also to allow the FTC to set a surcharge of 0.5–2 percent of a cartel's earnings. The aggregate of such surcharges levied in 1997 totaled 5.9 billion yen. The highest fine that can be invoked against even the largest corporations is typically in thousands of dollars only. The criminal penalties for violation of a Fair Trade Commission order include imprisonment, but this penalty has never been applied. In contrast, the maximum fine for violating the US Sherman Act is currently set at $10 million, and treble damage awards in US antitrust cases are essentially boundless and have reached millions of dollars. The usual outcome of antitrust actions brought by Japan's Fair Trade Commission is either a consent decree or a cease and desist order, neither entailing any fine at all. US companies often employ in-house attorneys to determine that each aspect of their ongoing operations is in compliance with antitrust laws. Few Japanese corporations bother to do this. This is hardly surprising when the worst penalty likely to be invoked is whatever adverse publicity attends a public reprimand from the Fair Trade Commission.

The anti-monopoly laws of Japan have never re-ceived the enthusiastic support of the long-ruling Liberal Democratic Party. As early as 1953, the first year after the American Occupation ended, the anti-monopoly laws of Japan were significantly amended to weaken proscriptions against mergers of large firms and widen the explicit exceptions even from prohibitions on price fixing. Recently, the "weak" anti-monopoly laws of Japan have been the basis for US complaints in the ongoing Japan–US trade talks, and the government of Japan has promised to devote more resources to investigating violations. But so far, Japan's anti-monopoly laws are more permissive and less of a weight in the calculations of firms than is true of the US antitrust statutes. However, one can argue on this basis that price competition is weaker in Japan than in the United States only to the extent that US antitrust laws have proscribed collusive practices. And the many critics of antitrust laws argue, to the contrary, that their main effect on the operations of US companies has been to raise the costs of organizing production or informing customers about products.[21]

Besides antitrust laws, there is another important factor influencing price competition in Japan—the prevalence of long-term trading ties.

Long-term trading ties

Firms rely upon a variety of measures to assure that their trading partners comply fully with specifications pertaining to the characteristics of the product or service exchanged, the promptness of delivery, and so on. In the United States the threat of a lawsuit in event of contract breach is one of the important factors. But in Japan lawsuits are seldom resolved quickly, and even in the event of a favorable outcome are unlikely to fully compensate for business losses. The main protection against fraud in Japan, and to only a slightly smaller degree elsewhere, is the firm's diminished reputation. A reputation is, precisely, an expectation of a level of performance.

---

[20] There is a formal provision in the anti-monopoly laws of Japan that allows private suits, but in fact there have only ever been a handful of such suits and none has ever resulted in compensation of the plaintiff: J. Mark Ramseyer, "The Costs of the Consensual Myth: Antitrust Enforcement and Institutional Barriers to Litigation in Japan", *Yale Law Journal*, vol. 94 (1985), pp. 604–45.

[21] For a cogent statement of this position, see Harold Demsetz, "How Many Cheers for Antitrust's 100 Years?" *Economic Inquiry*, vol. 30 (1992), pp. 207–17.

As with expectations generally, reputations are based on the history of prior experiences. The longer the record of satisfactory performance, the greater is one's expectation of its continuance. There are, of course, other factors that contribute to reputation as well. The salesman who engages in small acts of kindness is seeking to enhance the prospective client's expectation of his future performance. But all is evaluated in light of the salesman's own narrow self-interest in raising such an expectation: "Is he buying me a drink only to set me up for his subsequent fraudulent deceit?" The salesman has to work doubly hard to convince us that the kindnesses reflect a virtuous disposition and are not a calculated deception.

There is much evidence that business reputations in Japan are neither easily acquired nor lightly discarded. Many Japanese companies have formed durable alliances with trading partners. The most visible examples are the various business groups with which many Japanese firms are affiliated, but there are other examples also. For instance, in their filing statements with the Tokyo stock exchange, Japanese corporations name their most important customers and suppliers. These public identifications of trading relationships that are durable and to the apparent mutual satisfaction of both firms contribute to reputation. A history of satisfactory performance raises the expectation of its continuation. The permanence of trading ties among companies is analogous also to the permanence of ties between firms and their employees, and between firms and their major creditors in Japan.

Development of a strong reputation lowers the costs of trading and enlarges the gains from trade. But if incumbents have strong reputations, their customers will remain loyal in the face of entry and will switch patronage only if offered large price discounts to do so. It might seem that this would place new entrants at a distinct disadvantage. But offsetting this apparent barrier to entry is the fact that, when customers tend to be loyal, the rewards to successful establishment of a new reputation become that much greater, and worth a greater sacrifice. The net effect of long-term trading ties on product prices and on seller concentration, enhanced reputations, and customer loyalty are, like the lack of a vigorous antitrust policy, uncertain. But, as we shall next discover, whatever allocative distortions result in Japan from the interplay among antitrust policy, private contractual arrangements, and pricing and entry decisions of firms are little evident in the aggregate profits of Japanese businesses.

Welfare losses arising from oligopolistic pricing in Japan

The welfare losses arising from oligopolistic distortions refer to the potential increase in national income that could result from reallocation of productive resources toward industries in which prices are above marginal costs. An industry's contribution to the welfare loss is the potential added value of its own output, the area of a triangular region under the demand curve and above the marginal cost curve (see Figure 12.2). In adding such welfare losses across industries to reach an economy-wide total, we should, to avoid double-counting, define industries as vertical chains of resource suppliers each of which faces a final demand only—for instance, the farmers, millers, and bakers facing a demand for bread. If economy-wide welfare losses are to be estimated, it is also necessary to make some presumption about how the demands for different final products are interrelated—the simplest of course being that they are unrelated, a fall in the price of one not affecting the demand for any other.

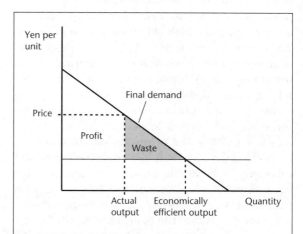

Figure 12.2. Welfare losses resulting from oligopoly

The area of the triangle labeled "waste" represents the net social value of having the industry produce the economically efficient output rather than its actual output.

It is surely beyond the limits of our knowledge to estimate the welfare losses resulting from oligopoly with any great precision, as to do this requires knowledge of the elasticity of demand for each final product as well as knowledge of the shape of the marginal cost curve of each industry. However, it seems likely that oligopoly welfare losses are of the same order of magnitude as the economic profits of all firms in the economy. (That is, we would be greatly astounded if welfare losses were as great as four or five times aggregate profits and not at all astounded if welfare losses were less than profits.) And Harberger and many others have argued, based on evidence, that the combined economic profits of all industries are no more than a mere 1 percent of national income.[22] This is true for Japan as well. Consider the following.

Economic profits are profits net of all costs, including costs that are implicit only and that do not give rise to accounting entries. In other words,

Economic profit = accounting profit – implicit costs.

In Japan, in 1988 wages and salaries paid represented 67.7 percent of value-added by corporations.[23] The value-added of corporations (that is final sales of corporations) represented 60.1 percent of gross domestic product in that year. Thus, $(1 - 0.677) \cdot 60.1\% = 19.4\%$ of GDP was the gross income of corporations before taxes, including both implicit competitive payments for owned assets and any economic profit. Total corporate assets—excluding financial investments to avoid double-counting—represented 2.371 times the value of GDP. If the entire amount of gross corporate profit were considered a return on investment, then it would constitute an 8.18 percent rate of return (before taxes and gross of depreciation). The accounting rate of depreciation on corporate assets was 3.26 percent. Thus, $8.18\% - 3.26\% = 4.92\%$ is the before-tax rate of return on corporate assets in 1988, net of depreciation. But this surely overstates the actual rate of return, as the book value of corporate assets likely understates their market value, the effects of both growth and inflation. Let us take the figure as an upper bound. In that year the average market rate of return on short-term debt (public and corporate bond transactions with repurchase agreement within a month (*gensaki*)) was 4.67 percent in Japan. Accordingly, the economic profits of corporations are estimated

to be just under two-thirds of a percent of GDP: $0.59\% = (4.92\% - 4.67\%) \cdot 2.371$.

To reach an estimate of welfare losses requires further assumptions. For instance, assume that all economic profits are earned by profit-maximizing cartels which produce subject to constant returns to scale, and that the demand facing each is approximately linear. Then the contribution of each to the welfare loss is half its economic profit. By these assumptions, the aggregate welfare losses are about one-third of a percent of GDP. Shinjo and Doi, analyzing 1980 data, reach slightly larger estimates but use a different strategy. (They count all advertising expenditures as contributing to waste, for instance.[24])

The reduction in Japan's national income caused by contrived scarcities is not great, judging from the modest levels of the economic profits of Japanese corporations. But we should not overlook the possibility that monopoly profits are capitalized into asset prices, and therefore not reflected in the profits of the firms that employ those assets. The phenomenon of profits capitalized into asset prices is exemplified by the firm that pays a market price for a government license, valuable only because the licenses are kept scarce by government policy. Collusive profits that are unprotected by government regulation seem far less likely to attach themselves to specific saleable assets.

We turn now to our next topic, the nature and scope of government regulation in Japan.

Regulation

The regulated industries are those in which government controls entry, price, and the quality or quant-

---

[22] Arnold C. Harberger, "Monopoly and Resource Allocation", *American Economic Review*, vol. 44 (May 1954), pp. 77–87. F. M. Scherer and David Ross, *Industrial Market Structure and Economic Performance*, 3rd edn, Boston: Houghton Mifflin, 1990, pp. 661–79, thoroughly review the many subsequent attempts to extend, refine, replicate, or criticize Harberger's original analysis of the oligopoly welfare losses of the US manufacturing sector.

[23] The figures cited in this paragraph are from the *Japan Statistical Yearbook, 1990*, table 11–1, pp. 368–71.

[24] Koji Shinjo and Noriyuki Doi, "Welfare Loss Calculations for Japanese Industries", *International Journal of Industrial Organization*, vol. 7 (1989), pp. 243–56.

ity of output. In Japan the regulated industries are, with a few exceptions, utilities, transport, banking and finance, and telecommunications. Similar industries are now or once were regulated in the United States and indeed in all the developed countries.

Regulatory institutions

In Japan regulations are administered by the national government, not by semi-autonomous national or local regulatory commissions as in the USA.[25] For instance, regulation of Japan's ten electric generating companies resides in MITI; the Ministry of Post and Telecommunications (MPT) administers regulations of broadcasting, telephones, and cable; the Ministry of Transport (MOT) regulates trucks, airlines, buses, taxis and railroads; the Ministry of Finance (MOF) regulates banks, securities markets, and insurance firms; and so on.

These ministries seem to have discretion regarding the manner in which to implement regulations, and this somewhat complicates attempts to describe the precise content of the regulations. For instance, the various statutes that vest ministries with the authority to regulate entry stipulate either permission (*kyoka*), licensure (*menkyo*), registration (*toroku*), or notification (*todoke*). Authority to regulate price entails either permission, authorization (*ninka*), guidance (*shidō*), or notification (*todoke*). In 1989 the Road Freight Law was revised so that entry into the trucking industry required a permit from the MOT rather than a license, and price changes required notification of MOT rather than authorization. This was widely hailed as a softening of regulation. Insiders seem to read meaning into these nuances. Outsiders are often hopelessly in the dark.

The history of regulation in Japan can be divided into three periods. The first period, from the Meiji Restoration to the 1930s, was a period of *laissez-faire* in most industries, including electric power, but government enterprises dominated in a few others, including rail, post, telecommunications, and broadcasting. The decade of the 1930s and continuing through the war years saw expanding state control, as Japan's military government commandeered resources. In some industries including electric power, private firms were nationalized. In others, government production orders subverted private choices. The final period, dating from the American Occu-

pation to the present, is one in which the utilities, transport, and finance sectors are either regulated or dominated by government enterprises, while other sectors are largely free of regulation. It may be that a fourth period is now commencing, a period of deregulation. Japan, like the USA, has loosened government regulations on pricing and entry in its airline, trucking, banking, and telecommunications industries. Also steps have been taken toward the privatization of the major government enterprises including JNR, NTT, JAL, and JTS.[26] Deregulation has not however been as far reaching in Japan as in the United States. Restrictions on entry and pricing remain in domestic airlines, long-distance telephone service, and stock brokerage, all of which have been completely freed from regulation in the USA.

Rationale for regulation

The fact that similar industries are regulated in Japan and elsewhere might indicate that regulations have a common rationale across nations. Explanations for regulation fall into two categories: public interest theories, and public choice theories. *Public interest theories* see regulation as correcting market failures, raising national income, or improving resource allocation. Public interest theories include the natural monopoly argument and network externality argument.

Public choice theories argue that regulation benefits politically effective special interests, perhaps to the detriment of national income. Public choice theories include the capture thesis, which holds that producers tend to be more politically effective than consumers and capture the organs of government

---

[25] An important reason why independent regulatory commissions are rarely created in Japan is that under the Japanese legal tradition, unlike that of America, authority does not reside primarily in coercive powers imparted by statutes. What authority the government has to regulate industry and trade resides not in its ability to prosecute violators, but only in its highly developed facility at persuading, bargaining, or cajoling firms into compliance. Statutory authority could be assigned to an independent commission, but facility at persuasion can clearly not be: John O. Haley, "Consensual Governance: A Study of Law, Culture, and the Political Economy of Postwar Japan", in Shumpei Kumon and Henry Rosovsky (eds.), *The Political Economy of Japan*, iii, *Cultural and Social Dynamics*, Stanford University Press, 1992, pp. 32–62.

[26] These are, respectively, Japan National Railways, Nippon Telephone and Telegraph, Japan Air Lines, and Japan Tobacco and Salt.

charged with formulating or implementing regulations.[27] The reason why producers of a good are effective is that they are less numerous than the consumers of the good and thus represent a more concentrated interest, one better able to overcome free-riding among its own members in mounting a political lobby.

The empirical difference between the public choice theories and public interest theories may be less profound than proponents of the strict capture thesis would imply. For Nobel laureate Gary Becker has argued that, all else the same, political lobbies in favor of government regulations that raise the national income or promote economic efficiency will encounter less strenuous opposition and thus be more effective: public choice considerations favor regulations that are in the public interest![28] Becker's argument rests on the premise that a political test favors the side that has amassed the larger "war chest" for lobbying. Any deadweight loss that accompanies a government program that transfers resources from one group of citizens to another imposes a wedge between the net benefits anticipated by the program's supporters and the losses that the opponents of the program seek to avoid. Thus, compared to the proponents, the opponents of policies that impose deadweight losses have a heightened incentive to contribute to a lobby. Proponents of such policies may nevertheless prevail, but they must overcome their inherent disadvantage in some way, either by superior facility at overcoming free-riding among their own members, superior rhetoric, or some other device. In other words, the general tenor of government regulation ought, in Becker's theory, to be toward economically efficient policies, but departures from that pattern ought not to surprise us very much. Let us consider some specific Japanese cases.

Electric power

The electric power industry is often cited as an example of a natural monopoly, an industry in which, because economical production entails large fixed costs, only one firm can be profitable. Government regulation of electric power, it is argued, assures that power companies do not exploit their monopolies by restricting output. But the history of regulation of electricity in Japan is unsupportive of the claim that the industry was a natural monopoly. In the first

three decades of this century, private power companies flourished in Japan, unimpeded by significant government regulation. Many of the urban centers were served by multiple companies. Vigorous competition kept prices low. Attempts to form effective cartels in the 1920s repeatedly failed because of price cutting by the colluders.[29] The private firms resisted the nationalization of power transmission (generation was nationalized) and survived the war to lobby for and obtain the reintegration of power and transmission and the division of the Japanese market for electricity into nine regional monopolies regulated by MITI. (The Okinawa Power Company became the tenth regional monopoly in 1972.) The practice of *amakudari* (bureaucrats regularly assuming jobs in the power companies upon retirement from the civil service) has cemented ties between the firms and the government bureaucracy.[30]

Telecommunications

Domestic telecommunications was a nationalized industry in Japan, practically from its inception in the late nineteenth century until 1985. Until 1952 the telecommunications monopoly was a section of the Ministry of Communications; and from 1952 to 1953 domestic telecommunications services were provided by the government corporation NTT and foreign telecommunications services were provided by the private corporation KDD (Kokusai Denshin Denwa). The 1985 Telecommunications Business Law mandated the privatization of NTT (which was

---

[27] The seminal articles developing the capture thesis are George Stigler, "The Theory of Economic Regulation", *Bell Journal of Economics and Management Science*, vol. 2 (Spring 1971), pp. 2–21; and Sam Peltzman, "Toward a More General Theory of Regulation", *Journal of Law and Economics*, vol. 19 (August 1976), pp. 211–40.

[28] Gary Becker, "A Theory of Competition among Pressure Groups for Political Influence", *Quarterly Journal of Economics*, vol. 98 (August 1983), pp. 371–400.

[29] By the early 1930s, "[c]ompetition between the five [leading] firms remained so fierce that some weak-willed Tokyo homeowners accepted contracts with two companies—one for the first floor and one for the second—while big companies alternated daily between Tokyo Electric Light and Tōhō Electricity in order to maintain peace with both suppliers": Laura E. Hein, *Fueling Growth: The Energy Revolution and Economic Policy in Postwar Japan*, Harvard University Press, 1990, p. 43.

[30] On the history of government regulation in the electric power industry of Japan, see Richard J. Samuels, *The Business of the State: Energy Markets in Comparative and Historical Perspective*, Cornell University Press, 1987.

still incomplete in 1993) and opened both domestic and international telecommunications to limited entry by new firms.

An often cited public interest rational for government control of telecommunications industries is the presence of network externalities. According to this argument, demanders place a higher value on phone service the greater the number of other subscribers, yet individually each fails to consider the value that others place upon their connecting to the system. The efficient network will be profitable only if higher prices are charged to those who attach greater value to expansion of the system, and lower prices to those subscribers who themselves value connection rather lightly. But such cross-subsidy pricing invites cream-skimming, entry by firms that only supply service to demanders who are charged high prices in order to cover the costs of extending service to other customers at prices below cost. The efficient network must be protected from entry if it is to remain profitable, and because such entry barriers invite contrived scarcity, prices and quantity must also be controlled. In Japan as in the USA, the government-controlled price of local telephone services has probably been below marginal cost, and the price of long-distance service above marginal cost. As long-distance callers would seem to value the expansion of the network more than local callers (there are closer substitutes for local calls than for long-distance ones), this pricing structure fits the argument just stated. The network externality argument is also invoked to rationalize regulation of postage and transport, and these industries also have set cross-subsidy pricing.

Railroads

Japan's first railroads were government-operated and in 1906 and 1907 most of the extant major private rail lines (seventeen in all) were nationalized. By 1940 the fraction of rail lines that were government-operated had steadily fallen from the 1906 peak of 91 percent to about two-thirds of the total in the country, based on kilometers of track. Following the war the government railways were organized into a public firm or *kosha* (*kokutetsu kosha*). The private rail lines were and continue to be subject to price and entry regulation. In principle, the ticket price or freight charge per kilometer of distance is the same for short trips as for long ones—a further instance of cross-subsidy pricing, as the marginal cost of providing rail service is greater in more densely inhabited regions.

In the 1970s the perennially unprofitable Japan National Railways (Kokutetsu) was among the infamous "three Ks" of government red ink, along with government purchases of rice (*kome*) and government-provided health insurance (*kenko hoken*). And in 1986 a law was enacted to split JNR into twelve different companies and eventually to privatize them.

Trucking [31]

The maintenance of effective price regulation of rail freight in Japan ultimately required the regulation of prices and entry in the trucking industry as well—just as was true in the USA—because some rail freight prices were kept above marginal costs, inviting cream-skimming by truckers. The Railway Express Enterprise Law of 1949 established price and entry regulation of the trucking services connected with rail shipments. The Road Transportation Law of 1951 divided remaining truckers into two categories: those licensed to serve particular routes on regular timetables, and those licensed to serve one customer at a time on consignment within a designated region. The Road Transport Law also forbade prices that "will probably cause unfair competition with other companies", and the Ministry of Transport acted on this mandate by posting elaborately detailed price schedules, which it updated annually, applicable to each specific category of service. It would appear on the face of it that the MOT, exercising the authority vested in it to restrict entry and set prices in commercial trucking, was the manager of a national cartel of the trucking industry.

Cartelizing regulations such as these have been the strongest evidence supporting the capture theory. And explaining the elimination of precisely such regulations has proved to be the greatest challenge facing proponents of the capture thesis.[32] But a big

---

[31] For more details on regulation of trucking in Japan, see David Flath, "Japanese Regulation of Truck Transport", Working Paper no. 119, Center on Japanese Economy and Business, Columbia Business School, June 1996.

[32] For a strong attempt at defending the capture thesis nevertheless, see Sam Peltzman, "The Economic Theory of Regulation after a Decade of Deregulation", *Brookings Papers on Economic Activity, Microeconomics* (1989), pp. 1–59.

difference between the government-administered trucking cartel of Japan and the one extant in the United States between 1935 and 1980 is that the price regulation was widely evaded in Japan, but fairly strictly observed in the USA.

In short, the US government-administered trucking cartel significantly restricted the supply of commercial trucking services and raised their prices, but the Japanese trucking cartel did so to a far smaller extent. The restriction on entry into commercial trucking in Japan was enforced rather strictly, but this became a significant impediment to commercial trucking only with the advent of parcel delivery service in the 1980s. To offer nationwide parcel delivery service, it was necessary to obtain separate licenses for each local area. In 1992 illegal political bribes, paid years before by a trucking company in pursuit of the licenses needed for it to offer expanded parcel delivery service, were exposed. But by then, legislation had already put an end to the artificial scarcity of licenses to conduct parcel delivery service. In December 1989, the Diet passed the Motor Vehicle Law that abolished licenses and instated a system of permits, which are more freely bestowed than the earlier licenses and which authorize truckers to supply more or less unlimited services within designated regions. The MOT still requires notification of price changes and retains the authority to disapprove them, but regulated prices were widely disregarded by the truckers anyway.

Airlines

Japan is among the many countries that has long been served by a state-owned airline. Airlines were forbidden by SCAP from operation in Japan during the American Occupation. JAL was formed the very year after the Occupation ended, coexisting with two private airlines, each authorized to provide domestic service only on specified and differing routes. In 1987 the government-owned shares in JAL were sold and the awarding of routes liberalized. As with trucking, the effects of these changes remain to be seen.

Deregulation: a new era?

In the 1980s not only Japan but also the United States and the major European countries all moved to deregulate telecommunications, transport, and financial service industries. It is natural to seek a common basis in the deregulation policies of the different countries. There are several common forces to consider: technological changes, demonstration effects, and international competition and cooperation. While all three forces seem to have played a role in the deregulation of telecommunications industries, technological changes played the main role. The development of microwave transmission in the 1960s obviated the need for costly switching stations. As the technology matured, it became economically feasible for large firms to erect their own transmission stations, avoiding the very high prices that government regulation required they pay to rent the use of transmission stations of authorized providers. The advent of computers further lowered the costs and expanded the capabilities of the new technology. The effect was that long-distance telecommunications had ceased to be a natural monopoly if indeed it ever was one.

The United States was the first country to deregulate long-distance telecommunications, perhaps as an indirect outcome of the antitrust suit that broke up AT&T. The beneficial effects on quality of service could be readily observed, increasing the likelihood of similar measures being taken elsewhere. Also, foreign companies were among the strongest proponents of breaking the KDD monopoly on international telecommunications in Japan, and since 1985 the two new entrants competing directly with KDD are both foreign companies.

Demonstration effects are apparent in the international movement to deregulate airlines. First, the United States deregulated its airline industry by a law enacted in 1978, with provisions coming into effect over the subsequent five years. The expansion of domestic air service and reduction in relative price of air travel that accompanied these changes were obvious to all by the mid-1980s. In 1986 Germany privatized Lufthansa, in 1986 Australia deregulated its domestic routes, in 1987 the UK privatized British Airways, and, as already mentioned, in 1987 Japan took steps to privatize JAL and liberalize its regulation of airlines. Here is an instance where the benefits of deregulation in the USA provided a strong impetus for deregulation in other countries.

The main basis for privatizing rail in Japan was that JNR had become a massive drain on public resources, owing to the escalating pension benefits the government was obliged to award JNR employees. Though it is illegal for government employees to strike in Japan, JNR employees had from time to time staged work slowdowns in support of their demands for enriched compensation. The division of JNR into twelve private companies was an attempt to weaken the bargaining power of the workers. There is no obvious parallel to the 1980 deregulation of rail in the USA, where air and trucking had long since eroded whatever benefits accrued to rail companies as a result of regulatory control of rail prices and routes, weakening industry support for perpetuating the regulation.

The deregulation of the banking and securities industries of the United States, European countries, and Japan in the 1980s is largely an indirect result of the liberalization of controls on international financial transactions. As the world economy has grown, the important trading countries have relaxed their regulations that interfered with international trading generally, perhaps spurred by the increasing gains from such trade. When international financial transactions became more free, domestic interest rates became tied to an unregulated international interest rate. Domestic regulation of banking became redundant at best and an encumbrance to banks and their customers at worst. Here is a case where international competition and cooperation was the driving force in deregulation as each country, Japan included, sought to protect its own citizens' gains from international transactions.

Convincing economic explanations for regulation that are also capable of explaining instances of deregulation do not in every case exist. Regulation, like politics generally, remains somewhat unpredictable, not strictly governed by economic considerations nor totally removed from the chance play of random events.

Conclusion

For all its peculiarities, the industrial organization of Japan exhibits some remarkable points of consistency with those of other developed nations. If an industry is dominated by large firms in Japan, then so is its analogue in the United States. The same market forces seem to be shaping the pattern of industrial concentration in both nations, even though Japan's large firms are self-organized into business groups and America's are not; the Anti-monopoly Laws of Japan impose weak penalties and are weakly enforced; and Japanese businesses are prone to form long-term trading ties. Also, economic profits are a trivial percentage of national income in Japan, as in the United States, which strongly suggests that oligopolistic pricing has not very much distorted the allocation of resources in either nation.

It is often suggested that the hand of government falls more heavily on industry in Japan than it does in other nations. This view is unsupported by careful observation. The incidence of government control of entry and pricing across Japanese industries is actually quite similar to that of the other developed nations. The regulated industries in Japan include public utilities, transport, telecommunications, banking, finance, and insurance. These are all regulated in some form or another by every developed nation.

FURTHER READING

■ Richard E. Caves and Masu Uekusa, *Industrial Organization in Japan*, Brookings Institution, 1976. The noted Harvard economist Caves joins with Tokyo University's Uekusa in exploring the structure, conduct, and performance of Japanese industries.

■ H(iroyuki) Iyori and A(kinori) Uesugi, *The Antimonopoly Laws of Japan*, New York: Federal Legal Publications, 1983. Details the specific stipulations of Japan's antimonopoly law.

■ David Weinstein, "Foreign Direct Investment and Keiretsu: Rethinking US and Japanese Policy", in Robert C. Feenstra (ed.), *The Effects of US Trade Protection and Promotion Policies*, University of Chicago Press, 1996, ch. 4, pp. 81–116. Argues that Japan's business groups exist mostly to take advantage of idiosyncratic features of Japanese government regulation and taxation; a useful counterbalance to the many other studies that identify them as novel forms of economic organization. Weinstein may be closer to the truth.

Finance | 13

Banks, insurance companies, and investment houses act as middlemen in the mediation of funds between those who save and those who invest in machines, buildings, and other such real assets. As with middlemen generally, financial intermediaries lower the costs of transacting and widen the gains from trade, in this case the trade of current income for future income.

Nations differ in the extent to which financial intermediation occurs through securities markets and investment houses rather than through banks. In Japan, banks have dominated the supply of funds to businesses ever since the 1930s. Almost every large corporation in Japan maintains a special relationship with some particular bank, the company's "main bank". The main bank typically holds more of the firm's debt than any other and also holds a significant equity interest in the firm; it is represented in the firm's management councils, and assumes special responsibilities for managing the company's affairs in times of financial distress. The main bank system of Japan contrasts sharply with practices in the United States in which corporations rely much upon the issue of stocks, bonds, and other securities, and maintain somewhat distant relations with banks. But similarities exist between the main bank system of Japan and the bank-centered financial systems of many other nations, Germany in particular. The dominance of banks in Japanese financial intermediation has had a long history.

In the wake of the 1927 financial crisis in which a number of banks failed, the government of Japan enacted laws empowering the Ministry of Finance to limit the number of commercial banks in Japan and to regulate banks' investments. In implementing these regulations, the MOF virtually suppressed corporate bond issues altogether. At the end of World War II, the American Occupation authorities directed enactment of additional legislation which further consolidated Ministry of Finance authority over financial intermediaries. Under these statutes, the banking industry became in effect a government-protected cartel. The dominant position of banks in Japan's financial intermediation originated in these policies.

In the 1970s the Japanese banking cartel began to unravel, a consequence of the increasing opportunities for Japanese firms to obtain funds in international markets. Because rapid growth in Japanese government debt in the mid-1970s threatened to make private borrowing more difficult, the government authorities began to widen the access of their nations' citizens to international financial markets, even though it made inevitable the extensive deregulation of domestic financial markets. With deregulation, banks' profits eroded and their lending practices became reckless. Bank loans fueled an unprecedented boom in Japan's real estate and stock markets in the late 1980s, and when the crash came in 1990–1, the banks, Japan's dominant intermediaries, were stuck with a mountain of depreciated collateral. Some banks have been allowed to fail and more may follow, but Japan's main bank system has so far shown remarkable resilience. This should not surprise us much, for the cornerstone proposition in the theory of corporate finance, named the

Modigliani–Miller thesis after its authors, holds that choice among channels of financial intermediation exhibits fundamental arbitrariness.

If one looks beyond the particulars of Japanese finance, the universals come into focus: in Japan as elsewhere, borrowers and lenders both gain from arrangements that align the interests of the one with that of the other. The elaborate mechanisms by which Japanese banks inform themselves about the firms to which they lend, and act on the information, solve the essential problems of corporate finance and corporate governance, but may not survive the ongoing deregulation.

Financial intermediaries

Discussions of Japan's financial markets can make the whole topic appear rather Byzantine, partly because there exist types of intermediary unique to Japan, such as long-term credit banks, trust banks, and securities finance companies. Also, the objects

traded by the intermediaries include financial assets either unique to Japan or at least somewhat removed from everyday experience. But behind all the complexity lies a simplicity: financial intermediaries fundamentally borrow from savers—mostly households—and lend to investors in machines, buildings, and other such real assets—mostly private businesses and government. Figure 13.1 depicts in a stylized way the main flows of funds from households through the financial intermediaries of Japan. The various kinds of intermediary represented in the figure all obtain funds from households and supply funds either to private businesses or government. And because some are more efficient at obtaining funds and others more efficient at using them, the intermediaries also trade with one another.

Figure 13.2 shows Japan's actual extent of financial intermediation from households to businesses, government, and foreigners. It depicts Japan's annual flow of funds from each sector as a percentage of GDP, from 1965 to 1997. In the figure, annual additions to a sector's stock of claims on the future

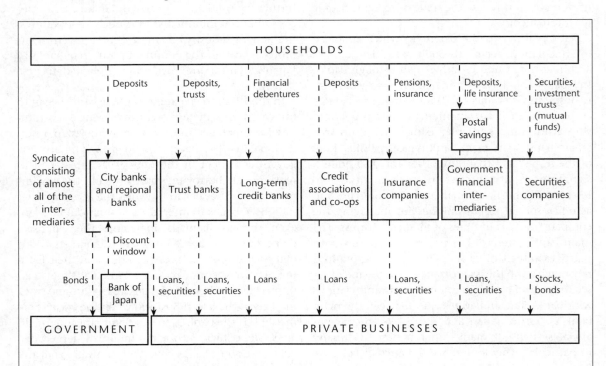

Figure 13.1. Financial intermediation in Japan

The diagram depicts the main flows of funds from households to private businesses and government, through intermediaries.

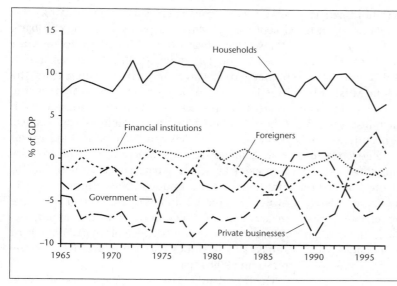

Figure 13.2. Annual flow of funds from each sector as a percentage of GDP, 1965–1997

Households are net suppliers of funds, and private business and government are net users. The financial institutions in effect borrow from households and lend to the other sectors.

Source: Bank of Japan, *Economic Statistics Annual*.

income of the other sectors or the diminution of the other sectors' stock of such claims on it (a financial surplus) is indicated by a positive entry, and the opposite (a financial deficit) is indicated by a negative entry. The claims include loans, shares of stock, and other securities—in other words, all financial instruments. Notice that beginning in 1994 Japanese businesses actually began to reduce their aggregate net financial liability to the other sectors, an unprecedented phenomenon and a manifestation of the slowdown in business investment that has so far characterized the decade. Also apparent in the figure, the massive increase in Japanese government borrowing after 1974 greatly displaced or "crowded-out" borrowing by private businesses. The relaxation of Japanese government controls on international capital account transactions after 1980 is widely regarded as a political response to the distress caused by the crowding-out of private borrowing. Before addressing these issues, we need first to describe the particulars of Japanese financial institutions, including the types of intermediary identified in Figure 13.1 and the sorts of financial assets they trade.

The distinctions among the differing categories of financial intermediary reflect regulatory constraints that have now been relaxed and are scheduled for elimination by the year 2001. The 1992 Financial System Reform Act, which took effect on April 1, 1993, permitted banks, securities companies, and insurance companies, by merging with one another

or establishing subsidiaries, each to offer selected services previously reserved for the others. And in November 1996 Prime Minister Hashimoto proposed the complete elimination of all regulatory partitions among financial intermediaries no later than 2001, dubbed Japan's version of the "Big Bang" that transformed the London financial markets in 1988. After these changes are fully implemented, the largest Japanese financial institutions will each fall into more than one of the various categories identified in Figure 13.1 and described below. (A chronological recapitulation of the regulations of financial markets discussed in this chapter may be found in the Appendix.)

Commercial banks

Banks are the financial intermediaries that accept deposits of various kinds and create new deposits by issuing loans. *City banks* are the large commercial banks with many branches nationwide (and in some cases worldwide), which for the most part extend short-term loans (maturities of one year or less) to large corporations. Prominent among the nine Japanese city banks are the six focal members of the financial keiretsu. Each of the six serves as the main bank to most of the core firms of its respective keiretsu group (that is, members of the presidents' club), and is a secondary lender to a lot of the core members of the other groups. The presidents' clubs encompass about 150 of the largest nonfinancial companies in Japan representing about one-seventh of all corporate assets in Japan.

One of the city banks, the Bank of Tokyo–Mitsubishi (known as the Bank of Tokyo prior to its 1996 merger with another city bank the Mitsubishi Bank), specializes more than the others in foreign operations, a reflection of its earlier history as a quasi-public bank, handling foreign currency exchange and helping to place Japanese government debt in foreign markets. From its founding in 1880, the Bank of Tokyo was known as the Yokohama Specie Bank, but after the Pacific war it was reorganized as a fully private bank and renamed. Prior to its merger with the Mitsubishi Bank, the Bank of Tokyo maintained more foreign branches than domestic ones and the majority of its loans were denominated in foreign currency.

The 120 or so banks referred to as *regional banks* typically have branches in only one prefecture, and lend to smaller, less prominent, companies than do the city banks. The regional banks are also substantial lenders of funds to the city banks through the interbank market. In this sense, the regional banks specialize in collecting deposits and the city banks specialize in extending loans. The banks that between 1989 and 1992 were converted from mutuals to joint-stock companies are also categorized as regional banks. The distinction between a regional bank and city bank is unambiguous but rather arbitrary, in the sense that the two engage in like activities. The largest regional banks are even comparable in size to the city banks.

Japan's seven *trust banks* primarily accept trust deposits and issue long-term loans. They also manage corporate pension funds, an activity in which they compete with life insurance companies. (Corporate pension funds received favorable tax treatment in Japan only beginning in 1962 and before then were virtually non-existent.) Trust deposits in Japan are of two types. "Money trust deposits" closely resemble passbook savings accounts; they are not themselves objects of trade. "Loan trust deposits" give rise to negotiable trust certificates of two or five-year maturities. The interest paid on both sorts of trust deposit have not closely reflected the market return on the trust assets, mostly medium and long-term loans to business. Since 1971, the trust banks have been allowed to expand their other types of

loan, even to consumer loans. The trust banks also accept some ordinary deposits, and one city bank (Daiwa) has always been allowed to accept trust deposits and has done so. Regulatory separation between trust banks and others dating from the American Occupation era was motivated by the prudence of restricting long-term lending to institutions that incur long-term liabilities. For instance, time deposits and debentures are rather longer-term than demand deposits. Since April 1993 ordinary commercial banks in Japan have been permitted to offer money trusts and loan trusts through wholly owned subsidiaries, and most of the city banks have in fact established such subsidiaries for that purpose. All regulatory barriers between ordinary banks, trust banks, and securities companies are slated for removal in 1999 as part of the "Big Bang".

The three banks classified as *long-term credit banks* extend long-term loans to private businesses (mostly of maturities five to seven years). These include Industrial Bank of Japan, Long-Term Credit Bank of Japan (LTCB), and Nippon Credit Bank. The LTCB encountered some financial distress and was nationalized in October 1998, and Nippon Credit Bank was nationalized in December 1998 after government inspections revealed sizable undisclosed losses. Both continue in operation under government direction but face liquidation within the next two years. The main source of funds of all the long-term credit banks has been the sale of one-year and five-year debentures (bearer bonds sold directly to the public and available in denominations as small as 10,000 yen, which is equivalent to about $100). The government authorities for a long time held the coupon rates on the debentures below a market-clearing level. In the early 1950s the national government purchased nearly half of these debentures. Other banks purchased most of the remainder for use as collateral on discount window borrowing from the Bank of Japan.[1] Over the ensuing years more and more of the financial debentures have been absorbed by individuals and by now almost all of them have been. The prewar antecedents of all three of the long-term credit banks were government banks

---

[1] On this point see Frank Packer, "The Role of Long-Term Credit Banks within the Main Bank System", in Masahiko Aoki and Hugh Patrick (eds.), *The Japanese Main Bank System: Its Relevance for Developing and Transforming Economies*, Oxford University Press, 1994, ch. 5, pp. 142–87 at pp. 155–6.

whose main function was to channel government funds toward heavy industry, public infrastructure investments and colonial development. In the early postwar period the loan activity of the long-term credit banks was closely coordinated with the Japan Development Bank, a government bank.

Credit associations and co-ops

Other depository institutions of Japan include credit associations and cooperatives. The four hundred or so *credit associations* (*shinkin*) are mutuals, which means that their depositors are actually equity-holders. Regulations allow them to lend only to small businesses (those employing fewer than 300 and with capital below a set amount), and further require that they lend primarily to their own members. Their members include a lot of small retailers and wholesalers. The National Federation of Credit Associations (*zenshinren*) acts as a kind of central bank and investor of surplus funds for all the credit associations in Japan. The *credit cooperatives* (*shinkumi*) very much resemble the credit associations but are less numerous and tend to be smaller and more insular. The National Federation of Credit Cooperatives (*zenshinsoren*) is a direct analogue of *zenshinren*. *Labor credit associations* are organized on the same principle as the other credit associations but their members are mostly labor unions. They act as agents for government-assured housing loans to individuals.

Rural cooperatives provide a number of supplies and business services to their members and extend loans to them and accept their deposits. They also provide life insurance to members. In Japan there are now about 3,000 *agricultural cooperatives* (*nōkyo*) and about 1,600 *fishery cooperatives* (*gyokyo*). The prefectural credit federations of agricultural and fishery co-ops respectively invest the surplus funds of members, depositing a significant portion in the Nōrin Chūkin bank (Central Depository for Agriculture and Forestry). In size of deposits, this is comparable to a city bank. Besides deposits funneled to it through the prefectural credit federations, the Nōrin Chūkin bank also issues financial debentures resembling those of the long-term credit banks. The Nōrin Chūkin bank has in the past been required to invest in low-yield government debt and loans to public utilities, recycling a portion of the heavy pub-

lic subsidies to Japanese agriculture, but in recent years it has also been permitted to invest in foreign securities. A somewhat analogous firm to the Nōrin Chūkin bank is the government-owned firm called Shōko Chūkin Ginko (Central Depository Bank for Commerce and Industry), which issues one and five-year debentures like those of the Nōrin Chūkin and is a major lender to small-business associations.

Insurance companies

Insurance policies exhibit some characteristics of a loan, for they represent current payment of a premium in return for promise of future payment of claims. And, in Japan, insurance of all kinds often promises repayments to policy-holders if held long enough (similar to "whole life insurance" in the USA). Insurance companies are in this sense borrowers, and in Japan are themselves major lenders to private businesses; they are important financial intermediaries.

All but five of the twenty-eight *life insurance companies* of Japan are mutuals rather than joint-stock companies. Only two of the twenty-six *non-life insurance companies* are mutuals. The presidents' clubs of the six financial keiretsu each include a life insurance company and non-life insurance company, and these hold significant amounts of both equity and debt in their fellow presidents' club members which include most of the largest corporations in Japan. Japanese personal assets include substantial holdings of life insurance and relatively little stock, but the life insurance companies themselves hold immense stock portfolios. In this way, the life insurance mutuals consolidate the asset-holdings of individuals and act on their collective behalf in aligning the interests of corporate managers with those of shareholders.[2] Life insurance companies also manage corporate pension funds.

In addition to the above activities, life insurance companies in Japan extend long-term loans to private industry, and since 1979 have been permitted to invest in foreign securities including yen-denominated bonds issued by foreigners in Japan

---

2 This aspect of Japan's life insurance mutuals is the main concern of Ryutaro Komiya, "The Life Insurance Company as a Business Enterprise", in Kenichi Imai and Ryutaro Komiya (eds.), *Business Enterprise in Japan: Views of Leading Japanese Economists*, Cambridge, Mass.: MIT Press, 1994, ch. 18, pp. 365–86.

(so-called "samurai bonds") and yen-denominated bonds issued in euromarkets (so-called "sushi bonds"). After 1990, Japan's life insurance companies invested heavily in the subordinated debt of banks and securities companies, and had to absorb massive losses when collapsing asset prices burdened those same institutions with bad loans of their own. As a result of such losses, in April 1997 Nissan Mutual became the first Japanese life insurance company in the postwar era to declare bankruptcy.

Non-life insurance in Japan is mostly automotive-related, followed by fire insurance and then marine insurance. Non-life insurance coverage is less in Japan in relation to GDP than in any of the other developed nations—exactly the opposite of the situation for life insurance. Non-life companies hold more deposits and securities and extend fewer loans than do the life insurance companies. Since 1980, the non-life companies have become significant holders of short-term US government debt. Since October 1996 life insurance companies have been allowed to sell property and casualty insurance policies, and other insurance companies have been allowed to sell life insurance, through subsidiaries. Regulatory barriers among insurance companies, banks, and securities companies are slated for complete removal in fiscal year 2000 as part of the "Big Bang". Until July 1998, premium rates on non-life insurance in Japan were set by insurance industry rating bureaus, which were actually government-authorized cartels. Since then insurance companies have been allowed to choose premium rates independently (though they still must notify the MOF of the precise rates they are setting).

Securities companies

Investment houses mediate trades of existing securities (brokerage), introduce new securities as agents for the issuing firms (underwriting), and trade in securities on their own account (dealing). In Japan almost all of the underwriting fees and the bulk of brokerage commissions have accrued to the three largest investment houses; in decreasing order of size, these are Nomura, Nikko, and Daiwa. In November 1997, the fourth largest investment house, Yamaichi, suspended operations, and most of its retail operations have been taken over by the American investment house Merrill Lynch. Another ten

smaller companies also do some underwriting as well as brokerage, and another couple hundred much smaller companies do no underwriting, only brokerage.

Each of the big investment houses and several of the smaller ones maintain links with other companies called *investment trust companies*, which offer financial assets called "investment trust certificates" that very much resemble shares in mutual funds. There are eleven investment trust companies in Japan. These were all once divisions of investment houses, but in 1962 the government authorities forced them to be split off in an attempt to forestall widely publicized abuses. From December 1998 banks in Japan have also been permitted to offer investment trust certificates to their customers, through subsidiaries.

The three companies in Japan known as *securities finance companies* borrow very short-term funds from the interbank market and lend to securities traders to cover margin transactions (securities trades using borrowed funds or borrowed securities). These companies lend primarily to investment houses, which then reloan to clients. The securities finance companies hold the actual securities or proceeds from sale of securities as collateral. Investment houses also extend credit directly to clients without the mediation of securities finance companies. And since 1985 individuals have been permitted to use securities as collateral on bank loans and in this way to obtain margin financing directly from banks.

Since April 1993, banks in Japan have been permitted to offer securities brokerage services through wholly owned subsidiaries, and most of the city banks have done so. And since 1997 securities companies have been allowed to offer "comprehensive accounts" which enable their customers to write checks. Regulatory barriers between banks and securities companies are slated for complete removal in fiscal year 1999 as part of the "Big Bang". After that time, banks will be permitted to underwrite securities as well as offer brokerage services. Brokerage commissions are also slated for complete deregulation at that time.

Government financial intermediaries

The largest depository institution in the world is a Japanese public institution, the *postal savings system*, established in 1875. Under this system individuals make time deposits and obtain life insurance at post office branches. Postal savings deposits expanded quite dramatically in the 1970s, growing as a percentage of all deposits in Japan (including postal savings deposits, deposits of city banks, regional banks, trust banks, long-term credit banks, and credit associations) from about 12 percent in 1965 to about 28 percent in 1980, and about 29 percent in 1992.

The funds accumulated from postal savings deposits are mainly transferred to the Ministry of Finance (Trust Fund Bureau), and the much smaller accumulated surplus from the sale of postal life insurance is invested directly by the Ministry of Posts and Telecommunications (MPT). Besides the postal savings deposits, the Trust Fund Bureau consolidates the social security surplus and other miscellaneous funds of the government. Under the process known as the "fiscal investment and loan program", these funds (both those controlled by the MOF Trust Fund Bureau and by the MPT Postal Life Insurance Fund) are lent to local governments and to a variety of government financial intermediaries —the Japan Development Bank, the Export–Import Bank, and nine[3] so-called "public corporations" (kōko).

The *Japan Development Bank* (JDB), founded in 1951, specializes in long-term loans at below-market interest rates. It has typically joined in loan syndicates with private banks to fund large-scale investments of private industry. Because its loans represent subsidies, the pattern of its lending reflects public policy, not profit-seeking by the officials of the bank. Politically influential but economically ailing industries such as textiles, shipbuilding, and coal mining have garnered the lion's share of JDB loans over the decades. Its outstanding loans amount to about the same extent as those of a city bank.

The *Export–Import Bank of Japan*, established in 1950, makes loans (often in syndicate with private banks) related to Japanese trade with other nations: loans to Japanese exporters, to cover deferred payments by foreign buyers (export credits); loans to Japanese importers, to hasten the settlement of international accounts (import credits); loans to finance foreign direct investment, including joint ventures between Japanese and foreign firms (investment credits); and loans to foreign governments and corporations, to finance their purchases of Japanese goods (direct loans). As with the Japan Development Bank, all of its loans are at below-market interest rates. The scale of the Export–Import Bank is roughly comparable to that of the Japan Development Bank, about the same as a city bank.

The other government intermediaries tied to the fiscal investment and loan program focus respectively on housing loans (*Housing Loan Corporation*); loans to small businesses (*People's Finance Corporation, Small Business Finance Corporation, Small Business Credit Insurance Public Corporation*); loans to rural businesses (*Agriculture, Forestry, and Fisheries Finance Corporation*); loans to garbage collection firms (*Environmental Sanitation Business Finance Corporation*); and loans to firms in the less developed regions of Japan (*Okinawa Development Finance Corporation, Hokkaido and Tohoku Development Corporation*). Altogether, the outstanding loans of these bodies are immense. The Housing Loan Corporation holds about half of the residential credit in Japan and by itself accounts for about half of the loans and discounts outstanding of all the government financial intermediaries, including the Japan Development Bank and Export–Import Bank. The outstanding loans of all the government intermediaries combined represent about one-fourth of all loans in Japan and about three-fourths as much as the loans of all the city banks combined.

Other intermediaries

Several other types of financial intermediary merit a brief mention. First are the companies that specialize in consumer and personal finance. These include companies mostly affiliated with department stores or other retailers, which finance the purchase of durable goods on installment. Personal finance is also the domain of companies called *sarakin* (lit. "salaryman finance"), which extend unsecured, high-interest loans to individuals and are notorious for their aggressive collection efforts.

Second, much trade credit is either absorbed by business firms themselves or else financed by the large general trading companies rather than by banks. The nine large general trading companies

---

[3] A tenth, the Medical Care Facilities Finance Corporation, was reconfigured in 1985, its link to the FILP broken.

borrow heavily from the city banks, and themselves lend (mostly to medium-sized firms) by extending trade credit. In fact, since their reorganization in the 1950s, this sort of financial intermediation is a major activity of the large general trading companies. Paul Sheard has detailed the particular advantages of the general trading companies in fulfilling this role. Given their widespread dealings in the economy, the large general trading companies are well informed regarding the creditworthiness of many firms, and can be trusted to act responsibly on such information whenever their own valuable reputations are at stake.[4]

Finally, a number of foreign banks maintain establishments in Japan and perform many of the same services as Japanese banks. They accept deposits, extend loans to private businesses (including but not limited to loans denominated in foreign currency, so-called "impact loans"), deal in securities, and so on. Their aggregate share of these various businesses is minuscule in comparison with the domestic banks. A number of foreign investment houses also maintain offices in Japan, and a few have seats on the Tokyo Stock Exchange. Mostly their clients are foreign traders of Japan-related financial assets and Japanese traders in foreign assets. A couple of the largest insurance companies in Japan are foreign-owned.

Table 13.1 identifies the financial assets and liabilities, as of end December 1997, of intermediaries operating in Japan. From the table one can glean the relative significance of deposits, trusts, financial debentures, securities investment trusts, pensions, and insurance as liabilities of each category of financial intermediary, and the relative importance of securities and loans among their assets. The table recapitulates in a precise way much of the preceding description of Japan's financial intermediaries.

We now turn our attention to the differing kinds of financial assets tradable in Japan.

Securities markets of Japan

Securities are tradable claims on future income, unlike bank loans, for instance, which generally are not transferable. Examples of securities include stocks, bonds, and notes. To complete our basic survey of Japanese financial intermediation, we need to briefly describe each of the major categories of security in Japan, noting the relevant regulatory constraints. This is a useful exercise, because without such background information much of the literature on Japanese finance would remain impenetrable. Somewhat arbitrarily, we divide the financial instruments into two groups: those having maturities of one year or less, and those of longer maturity. The markets for these are often referred to, respectively, as "money markets" and "capital markets".

Money markets

The money markets of Japan (markets for financial instruments with maturities of one year or less) include those restricted by regulation to financial institutions—the "interbank markets"—and those not so restricted—the "open markets".

Interbank markets

Six broker–dealers (called *tanshi gaisha*, lit. "short-term loan companies") act as intermediaries in the interbank market. The oldest of the interbank markets, as old as Japanese banking itself, is the *call market*, in which financial institutions trade very short-term funds, with maturities ranging from a few hours (9am–1pm or 1pm–3pm, called "half-day" loans) to one week. The Bank of Japan itself maintains accounts with the money market dealers and intervenes directly in the call market, both to smooth out temporary fluctuations and to influence monetary aggregates. Until April 1979, the call rate was set by the MOF. It was the first of the posted interest rates to be fully deregulated. Since 1972 a *dollar call market* has developed in which Japanese financial institutions trade very short-term claims on bank deposits denominated in US dollars through foreign exchange brokers.

An interbank market in securities of relatively longer maturity than call money was officially recognized in May 1971. (Before then, the posted rate on these instruments was identical to the call rate.) The objects of trade in this market are *discounted bills* (*tegata*). These instruments are either short-term notes of the Bank of Japan or commercial bank

---

4 Paul Sheard, "The Japanese General Trading Company as an Aspect of Inter-firm Risk-sharing", *Journal of the Japanese and International Economies*, vol. 3 (1989), pp. 308–22.

Table 13.1. Financial assets and liabilities of intermediaries in Japan, end-December 1997 (¥ trillions)

Banking accounts:	All banks		City banks		Regional banks		Long-term credit banks		Cooperatives and credit associations	
	Assets	Liab.	Assets	Liab.	Assets	Liab.	Assets	Liab.	Assets	Liab.
Currency & deposits at BOJ	10.3		n.a.		n.a.		n.a.		n.a.	
Deposits		687.1		249.2		233.2		14.3	6.6	211.5
Financial debentures	17.6	67.3	15.7	6.1	6.7		1.2	39.5	9.2	21.9
Trusts	11.1		1.4		5.5		0.5		4.7	
Pensions										
Life insurance										
Non-life insurance										
Securities investment trusts	5.9		2.6		1.5		1.1		3.7	
Gov' bonds	69.0		16.2		22.3		4.2		20.4	
Industrial bonds	12.7	0.2	1.9		1.3		0.3		6.9	
Stock	46.7		27.5		6.8		5.4		1.7	
Call money	21.5	42.7	2.7	31.0	5.8	5.2	0.8	1.7	8.0	1.0
Loans	629.8		214.1		184.1		45.6		157.2	0.4
Foreign claims and debts	46.6	53.9	10.0	1.0	4.6		3.6		11.1	0.1

Banking accounts:	Trust banking		Insurance companies		Securities companies		Public intermediaries		Total		Net surplus (+) or deficit (−)
	Assets	Liab.	Assets	Liab.	Assets	Liab.	Assets	Liab.	Assets	Liab.	
Currency & deposits at BOJ	3.5		14.3		6.9		0.9		11.2		−11.2
Deposits	4.4		12.6		5.3		10.7	238.0	35.4	925.1	889.7
Financial debentures		124.1	7.0				7.0		47.0	67.3	20.3
Trusts		32.3							18.1	124.1	106.0
Pensions				47.9				95.7		80.2	80.2
Life insurance				146.5						242.1	242.1
Non-life insurance				35.7						35.7	35.7
Securities investment trusts	25.3		2.5		1.2	45.5			9.6	45.5	35.9
Gov' bonds	6.4		44.6	0.4	17.9	0.8	56.2	23.2	213.0	23.2	−189.8
Industrial bonds	34.6		6.3	5.2	5.6	5.2	17.4		48.4	1.4	−47.0
Stock	8.5		35.9		7.8	0.5	0.2		125.2	10.4	−114.9
Call money			6.9		7.2	4.1			44.1	44.3	−0.8
Loans	22.2	0.1	67.3	1.0	1.2		168.4		889.1	5.9	−883.1
Foreign claims and debts	24.0	0.8	32.9		5.5		22.3		131.2	53.9	−77.4

Note: In this table, "banking accounts" include those of all such institutions, including foreign banks operating in Japan and the banking accounts of trust banks; "trust banking" includes money trust and loan trust accounts of all institutions, not only trust banks; "securities companies" include securities investment trust accounts (i.e. mutual funds) of all institutions; "public intermediaries" include the postal savings system and other government intermediaries but not the BOJ nor the "Trust Fund Bureau" account of the national government; "government bonds" include long-term and short-term bonds of the national and local governments and of government corporations; "industrial bonds" are domestic only; eurobonds and other foreign bonds are included under "foreign claims and debts".

Source: Bank of Japan, *Economic and Financial Data on CD-ROM 1998* (financial institutions accounts); and Bank of Japan web site (http://www.boj.or.jp/en/siryo/siryo_f.htm), preliminary estimates of flow of funds.

certificates with, as attached collateral, promissory notes that companies have given to the bank when borrowing money. The maturities range from one month to six months, and most of the trading activity (about four-fifths) is in two-month maturities. The bills market operates in the same fashion as the call market, with the money market dealers acting as brokers. The interest rates on discounted bills were completely freed from MOF control in October 1979.

Open markets

Open money markets are the markets for short-term financial instruments not limited to financial institutions. The earliest of the short-term financial instruments to be completely free of MOF price control—in fact, it was never subject to price control—were bond repurchase agreements, known as *gensaki*. The original seller of a *gensaki* offers a long-term bond with a promise to buy it back at a specified later date (usually three months hence) at a particular price. In other words, a *gensaki* transaction amounts to a short-term loan in which a long-term bond serves as collateral. The *gensaki* market is an over-the-counter market with securities companies acting as brokers.

From the market's beginnings in 1949, the MOF restricted the *gensaki* market to securities companies, at the same time barring them from participating in the call market. (From 1961, securities companies could lend call money but could not borrow it.) In 1977 it relaxed these restrictions and permitted banks to participate in *gensaki* and securities companies to participate fully in the call market; it also opened the *gensaki* market to nonfinancial institutions (but not individuals). At this time the market ballooned in activity. The minimum trading amount is large (currently ¥100 million) and individuals are still barred from trading *gensaki* by the MOF. The exchange of *gensaki* elicits a small transaction tax. Short-term financial instruments not subject to this tax have now crowded out *gensaki* somewhat, but securities companies continue to trade *gensaki* in order to manage their own asset portfolios. The *gensaki* rates represent the longest continuous time series of short-term interest rates in Japan that have remained free of government control, which accounts for their wide use in academic studies of Japan's macroeconomy. (The time series dates from 1977—before that the market was subject to re-

stricted access as just noted and therefore rather thin).

To recover some of the business that banks were losing to securities companies' burgeoning trade in *gensaki*, the banks lobbied for and obtained permission to offer additional short-term instruments: certificates of deposit (from May 1979), money market certificates (from March 1985), and bankers' acceptances (from June 1985).

Certificates of deposit (CDs) are issued by Japanese banks in maturities from one month to one year in fairly large denominations (reduced from a minimum denomination of ¥100 million to ¥50 million in April 1987), are tradable by anyone, are not subject to a transaction tax, and have never been subject to price control. The most widely followed Japanese monetary aggregate M2 + CDs includes currency, demand deposits, time deposits, and CDs. That is, CDs have some of the character of money, being highly liquid and a repository of the precautionary cash holdings of large corporations.

Money market certificates (MMCs) are bank time deposits (included in the monetary aggregate M2 and not really securities). At first they were available only in large denominations, but since June 1992 they are available in any denomination; until 1994 they were available only at legal maximum interest rates (tied to the market-determined CD rate). These certificates have not found wide demand in the market. Since June 1992 MMCs are lumped together with other large-denomination time deposits in official statistics.

Bankers' acceptances (BAs) are discounted bills that arise from the financing of imports or exports. The market for BAs in Japan was established in response to a direct request by the US government, apparently in the hope that it would increase the demand for yen in the settlement of international transactions, strengthen the yen relative to other currencies including the US dollar, and restrain Japanese exports. The yen BA market has never been very active.

Commercial paper (CP), the name for short-term, negotiable promissory notes issued without collateral by high-grade corporations, was first permitted in Japan in November 1987. The Japanese banks for years successfully opposed authorization of a commercial paper market; even now, only companies meeting specific criteria are permitted to issue it. The CP market remains small compared with that for CDs and compared with the CP market in the United States, but Colin McKenzie has examined the properties of CP rates and the incidence of issue in Japan and finds little evidence of regulatory constraint.[5] Perhaps the relative thinness of the Japanese CP market is due to factors other than regulation. For instance, public information regarding large companies in Japan remains highly imperfect. The BOJ acquires CP as part of its open market operations and as of December 1997 held ¥4.6 trillion, an astounding 38 percent of the ¥12 trillion outstanding.

So far in Japan short-term government debt instruments have yet to attain wide circulation. *Government financing bills* (FBs) with 60-day maturities have long been sold by the government to the Bank of Japan to cover seasonal or temporary shortfalls of government funds. No law precludes private institutions purchasing FBs from the government, but the prices have been set below the market level making it unprofitable for them to do so. (The government has announced its intention to begin auction pricing of FBs in 1999.) From May 1981 the BOJ began to sell FBs out of its own holdings rather than redeeming them itself. From February 1986 the national government has auctioned *Treasury bills* (TBs) with six-month maturities, and from September 1989 with three-month maturities. The amounts issued remain small. The BOJ also sells out of its holdings of TBs. The simple explanation for the retarded development of the market for short-term government debt in Japan is that Japanese banks oppose its expansion, fearing it would cut into their own business.

Capital markets

The markets for securities with maturity longer than one year, that is to say, the markets for bonds and stocks, are widely known as the capital markets. We begin with the bond markets, starting with government debt instruments.

Bond markets

In 1965 the national government issued long-term bonds (called *kokusai*, lit. "national debt (certificates)") for the first time since World War II, before then having adhered to an annually balanced fiscal budget. The 1947 Fiscal Law (Art. 5), to inhibit inflationary finance, precludes the purchase of government bonds by the Bank of Japan sooner than one year after issue. To comply with this stipulation, the government began in 1965 to place bonds with a syndicate consisting of nearly all the financial institutions in Japan, including not only banks but also insurance and securities companies. Securities companies succeeded in brokering only about 10 percent of the bonds to individual investors, sufficient for the emergence of a secondary market in government bonds on the stock exchanges, albeit a small one. Banks were at this time prohibited from selling the bonds (by the 1948 Securities Law—the stipulation was relaxed in 1977). The issue price was set below a market level, but the BOJ, by prior arrangement with the syndicate, bought nearly all the bonds one year after issue at a predetermined price which insulated syndicate members from significant loss.

At first, the BOJ bond purchases were completely fungible to its discount window lending. That is, the bond purchases were small relative to the BOJ direct lending, and a rise in the former could be offset yen-for-yen by a curtailment of the latter. The massive expansion of Japanese government debt from the mid-1970s changed this and induced significant policy adjustments. The expansion of social security and national health insurance enacted in 1974 without commensurate taxes happened to coincide with the first oil shock and a permanent reduction in Japan's natural rate of macroeconomic growth. The result was an explosion of national government debt.

In 1976 the outstanding long-term bonds of the national government finally became so extensive that the BOJ could no longer repurchase all of them a year after issue and still maintain complete control of the money supply. The old system of indirectly placing government bonds was unworkable. Soon after this the authorities initiated steps toward market placement of long-term government debt. In April 1977 the banks were for the first time permitted to sell on the open market the bonds held for at least a year and not repurchased by the BOJ. (In April 1981, the minimum holding period was reduced to 100 days.) In January 1978 the MOF began the sale of certain classes of bond by auction rather

---

5 Colin McKenzie, "The Commercial Paper Market in Japan", Working Paper no. 118, Center on Japanese Economy and Business, Columbia Business School, June 1996.

than private placement. And in June 1978 the BOJ began to purchase bonds from the syndicate by spot bid rather than by the execution of repurchase agreements at predetermined prices. Even in 1998, the process of establishing a totally uncontrolled market for Japanese government debt remained incomplete; only financial institutions are allowed to bid on new issues—they are not placed on the open market. Trading activity in Japanese government bonds is not uniformly distributed across issues but is concentrated instead on selected "benchmark issues", not by regulation but by free choice. The benchmark issues command a liquidity premium.[6]

As in other nations, local governments in Japan have long issued bonds to finance capital investments. Only the largest prefectures and municipalities meet MOF standards of eligibility to issue *local government bonds*. The others must borrow directly from government financial institutions. Also, selected government-owned enterprises are authorized to issue *government-guaranteed bonds* and do so. Local government bonds are either publicly offered or privately placed in syndicates of local financial institutions. Government-guaranteed bonds are publicly offered. Both local government bonds and government-guaranteed bonds are sold over the counter through securities companies, and a few issues are also listed on the exchanges.

The market for bonds of private nonfinancial corporations in Japan was long hampered by nearly prohibitive eligibility requirements. Since 1985, however, these regulations have been greatly relaxed and corporate bonds of several types now trade in Japanese capital markets. *Straight bonds*, sometimes called industrial bonds, simply promise the holder a stream of payments. *Convertible bonds* also promise a stream of payments, but they may be exchanged for some specified number of shares of stock of the issuing company. The first company to issue convertible bonds in Japan was Nippon Express in September 1966. Many Japanese companies issued convertible bonds in the late 1980s. *Warrant bonds* are industrial bonds issued along with warrants, i.e. rights to purchase some number of shares of stock of the issuing company at a specified price. Detachable warrants may be traded independently of the bonds with which issued. Warrant bonds were first authorized in Japan in 1981, and detachable warrants were first authorized in April 1989.

Statistics on corporate bonds in Japan often include the financial debentures of the long-term credit banks and selected other banks, but these are bearer bonds issued in small denominations, are not underwritten, and are a lot less risky and more liquid than the bonds issued by nonfinancial corporations. Some foreign companies, foreign governments, and international public bodies (such as the Asian Development Bank and the World Bank) have issued *yen-denominated foreign bonds* that trade in Japan, popularly known as "samurai bonds".[7] The first of these was in 1970. Since 1985 samurai bonds have been somewhat displaced by yen-denominated Eurobonds (known as "daimyo bonds"—see fn. 7), which are yen-denominated bonds offered outside of Japan and therefore not directly subject to domestic regulations. Over-the-counter trading of corporate bonds, that is through securities dealers who sell from their own inventories, is far more pervasive in Japan than brokered trading of bonds through the exchanges. This is quite natural, given the relative thinness of the market for most types of bond in Japan compared with the markets for equities.

Stock markets

Stock markets have existed in Japan since the late Meiji era. The Tokyo Stock Exchange, the oldest in Japan, was established in 1878. One curious feature of stock trading in Japan prior to 1948 was the predominance of futures transactions.[8] Just as in commodities futures trading, the objects of trade were not the shares themselves but, rather, promises

---

6 For a close analysis of benchmark issues, see Toshiharu Takahashi, "The Secondary Government Bond Market in Japan", in Shinji Takagi (ed.), *Japanese Capital Markets*, Oxford: Basil Blackwell, 1993, ch. 7, pp. 249–76.

7 The popular terms of reference for international securities reflect a predilection for inside jokes. Direct analogues of the so-called "samurai bonds" include "Yankee bonds" (dollar-denominated bonds issued by foreigners in the USA) and "bulldog bonds" (pound-denominated bonds issued by foreigners in the UK); "shogun bonds" refer to foreign currency bonds issued in Japan by nonresidents; "daimyo bonds" are euroyen bonds, yen-denominated bonds issued on the euromarkets including the Tokyo offshore market; "sushi bonds" are non-yen-denominated bonds issued abroad by Japanese corporations.

8 On this point see Ichirō Kawamoto, "Regulation of Exchange Markets", in Louis Loss, Makoto Yazawa, and Barbara Ann Banoff (eds.), *Japanese Securities Regulation*, University of Tokyo Press/ Little, Brown, 1983, ch. 6; Kawamoto discusses the history of trading practices on pp. 106–7. Also see Shinji Takagi, "The Japanese Equity Market, Past and Present", *Journal of Banking and Finance*, vol. 13 (1987), pp. 537–70.

to deliver shares by a specified settlement date. Clearing agents in these transactions secured the traders against breach of contract and accepted commissions from brokers. And, just as is typical in commodities futures trading, the promise to deliver shares was usually repurchased by its original issuer some time prior to the settlement date, so that actual transfer of stock ownership did not occur: only the risk associated with unforeseen movements in the market value of the stock was transferred. New share issues were generally not sold on the exchanges, but instead were privately placed. Most companies, including many large ones, remained closely held. For instance, the zaibatsu companies' shares reposed largely in holding companies, which in turn were owned by a few wealthy families.

The Securities Exchange Law of 1948 outlawed stock futures trading (*teiki torihiki*; lit. "arbitrage transactions") and enacted spot trading. Nevertheless, the actual turnover of shares, even now, remains low in Japan compared with the stock markets of other nations. Large percentages of outstanding shares reside in the hands of "stable shareholders". These are trading partners, creditors, fellow members of same keiretsu groups and the like, who rarely divest their shareholdings.

Compared with the United States, disclosure requirements for stock listing and issue are weak in Japan. The MOF requires the submission of financial statements which it publishes (*Yūka Shoken Hōkokushō*), but the accounting standards underlying these statements are far less strict than is true of their US counterpart (10-K reports filed with the Securities Exchange Commission). Steps are currently underway to change this. For instance, beginning with fiscal year 2001 Japanese corporations for the first time ever will be required to report consolidated financial statements.

Sanctions against insider trading in Japan are notoriously weak and seldom if ever invoked.[9] But the case for prohibition of insider trading is less compelling than many suppose. The prospect of trading on inside information surely elicits an expanded supply of managers, pushing down the equilibrium level of other forms of managerial compensation. This means that top managers and other insiders obtain more compensation from trading on information, and obtain correspondingly less compensation in other forms, than do their counterparts in the USA where insider trading is strictly prohibited.

Until 1969, all seasoned equity issues (common stock issues by firms whose shares already trade on the exchanges) were rights offerings to existing shareholders, usually at par value, which for many firms was 50 yen per share. In rights offerings, incumbent shareholders are given the opportunity to purchase new shares at a set price. Rights offering avoids underwriting fees altogether and is less disruptive of concentrated ownership. Nevertheless, in the last twenty-five years underwritten public offerings have displaced rights offerings, perhaps because firms wish to avoid increasing their dividend payout rates. Rights offering at a price less than that of the secondary market amounts to the award of a stock dividend. Many Japanese companies have set their dividend rates at or near the minimum required for listing on the Tokyo Stock Exchange (10 percent of par), and keep them there.

In principle, all listed securities are tradable only on the exchanges, not over the counter. Until very recently, brokerage commission schedules were set by the exchange and approved by the MOF. It was widely reported that these posted commission rates were renegotiable downward by at least 20 percent on large transactions. Complete deregulation of brokerage commissions is slated to occur in 1999.

So far we have discussed Japan's domestic markets and institutions. Many of the securities traded in domestic markets have exact analogues in international financial markets. And the most important of these by far is the Euromarket.

The Euromarket

The Euromarket exploits a major loophole: many domestic regulations of each nation pertain only to trading in financial assets denominated in the

---

9 Consider the following quotation from an essay describing relevant securities laws of Japan: "Although insider trading is generally condemned in the United States, and although US cases imposing civil liability for such trading have drawn attention in Japanese business circles, most Japanese do not believe that insider trading is immoral. Thus, although the Securities and Exchange Law contains several provisions that could be used to recover profits from short-swing trading, those provisions are not enforced": Misao Tatsuta, "Proxy Regulation, Tender Offers, and Insider Trading", in Loss, Yazawa, and Banoff, *Japanese Securities Regulation*, ch. 8, pp. 191–2.

domestic currency. Euro-assets are any assets denominated in a currency other than that of the nation in which offered. For instance, *eurobonds* might be corporate debentures denominated in yen but offered in London, Zurich, and New York rather than in Tokyo.

Eurocurrencies are bank deposits denominated in a currency other than that of the country in which the bank resides. Eurocurrencies need not be deposits at European bank offices. For instance, Singapore, Hong Kong, New York, and Tokyo are all the repositories of eurocurrencies, which, depending on the currency of denomination, are also referred to as eurodollars, euroyen, europounds, and so on.

Both the United States (since 1981) and Japan (since 1986) permit the establishment of banking facilities that, although physically located within the respective nations' borders and allowed to accept deposits and issue loans denominated in the domestic currency, are not regarded by the government authorities as "resident"; i.e., they are exempted from domestic regulations including reserve requirements, deposit rate ceilings, and levies for deposit insurance. These so-called "offshore" banking facilities are permitted to transact only with foreigners. In the USA these special banks are referred to as "International Banking Facilities" (IBFs). Their analogues in Japan are referred to as the *Japan Offshore Market* (JOM). Both the IBFs and the JOM are clearly part of the Euromarket, the nexus of transactions in euro-assets.

The banks that accept eurocurrency deposits (so-called eurobanks) typically also act as investment banks, underwriting the flotation of eurobonds, i.e. bonds not denominated in the currency of the financial center in which they are offered. Corporations issue *euronotes* and *euro-commercial paper*, i.e. short-term (three to six months) tradable fixed interest securities, denominated in a currency other than that of the financial centers in which they are offered.

The main impetus for the development of euromarkets has been the evasion of domestic banking regulations including interest rate ceilings, restrictions on international lending of domestic currency, and domestic rules requiring the withholding of tax on interest payments. In most instances a euromarket transaction could have instead been consummated in the traditional financial markets, but

different government regulations would then have applied. For this reason, the Euromarket is sometimes described as a parallel market to the more traditional financial markets. The Euromarket first developed in the 1950s and 1960s, then expanded dramatically in the 1970s when the OPEC nations placed substantial wealth in eurodollar deposits and other such euro-assets.

Widened Japanese participation has further enlarged euromarkets. Before 1980, the MOF severely restricted access of Japanese companies to euromarkets and other foreign financial markets. For instance, it required Japanese companies to meet stringent eligibility standards before authorizing eurobond flotations; it limited the holdings of euro-assets by Japanese insurance companies and other large Japanese institutional investors; and it limited the participation of Japanese banks in euroloan syndicates and eurobond flotations. The MOF lifted all these restrictions over a period of years up to 1986, and in so doing integrated Japan's domestic capital markets with international ones. The new arbitrage opportunities this entails have hastened the dismantlement of Japan's extensive web of domestic interest rate controls, portfolio constraints, narrow rules of eligibility for issuing certain classes of securities, and other such financial regulations.

This leads us naturally to the next topic, the variety of ways in which regulatory constraints have shaped Japanese banking and finance.

Regulation of financial markets

Not only Japan, but most nations, regulate banks and investment houses and do so for essentially the same reason: to protect the collective interests of those who lend to them. The inevitably numerous small depositors in a bank themselves have no effective way of monitoring the bank's investments and assuring that it remains solvent. Similarly, the small investors in stocks or mutual funds have little effective way of monitoring the performance of brokers or fund managers. For these reasons, the imposition of government standards of prudential investment by banks and public disclosure of information by issuers and brokers of securities might be thought to prove economical. Perhaps this accounts for the pervasiveness of regulation of financial markets the world over.[10]

Origins of banking regulation

Significant regulation of banking in Japan was first established as a direct result of the financial crisis of 1927. Failure of a large Japanese bank, the Bank of Taiwan, led to runs on other banks, including a number of smaller ones which themselves failed. In 1927 there were 1,280 commercial banks, and in 1929 only 878. In the immediate wake of the 1927 crisis a new "Bank Law" was promulgated to take effect January 1928. The new law empowered the Ministry of Finance to limit entry into commercial banking. Control of entry, including authorization of new branches, in effect heightened MOF authority to regulate all activities of banks. The MOF exercised its new authority by encouraging bank mergers, which resulted in a steady decline in the number of banks. In 1947 in Japan there were only 69 banks, just short of the MOF goal of "one bank per prefecture". The professed MOF object in promoting a concentration of banking was to create an industry consisting of banks that were both sounder and more easily monitored by the MOF than before.

Also under authority of the Bank Law, the MOF established in 1933 a para-public advisory council to make ongoing recommendations concerning requests by corporations for official permission to float new bonds, recommendations that it invariably followed. The Council for Regulating Bond Issues (Kisai Chōsei Kyōgikai) was dominated by the large commercial banks whose top executives held a decisive block of seats. Loans from banks compete with bond issues as a source of corporate funds. And, as one might expect, the Bond Council enacted measures that greatly discouraged bond flotation: it authorized only the largest and most profitable corporations to float bonds, and these were required to meet stringent collateral requirements in the form of low rate deposits—with banks, of course! Though debentures had been an important source of corporate finance before 1933, in the years afterward they were not. Only electric utilities and a few other blue chip companies continued to issue industrial bonds.

Occupation reforms of Japanese financial markets

At the war's end, the US Occupation authorities set about establishing in Japan laws and regulations similar to those of the United States itself. The Securities Exchange Act of 1948, modeled somewhat on America's Banking Act of 1933 (also called the "Glass–Steagall Law" after its congressional sponsors), prohibited banks in Japan from underwriting securities and prohibited banks from themselves investing in securities. This latter provision was repealed after the Occupation ended, however, so that the relevant restriction on banks' investing in stocks after 1953 became a provision of Japan's anti-monopoly law limiting such investments to no more than 10 percent of the shares in any one company. (In 1987 the limit was lowered to 5 percent for banks and 7 percent for insurance companies.) Underwriting and brokering of securities became the exclusive purview of investment houses. The further elaborate segmentation of intermediaries into those specializing in long-term loans versus short-term loans, trust accounts versus banking accounts, life insurance versus property and casualty insurance, and so on—all now slated for removal— also dates from the Occupation era. Additional Occupation reforms perpetuated and strengthened the government protection of banks.

The Interest Control Law of 1948, analogue of America's Regulation Q of the Federal Reserve Act, empowered the MOF to regulate interest rates. In characteristic fashion, the MOF implemented this authority through the device of para-public advisory councils. The Interest Rate Regulation Council (Kinri Chōsei Shingi Kai) issued recommendations to the Bank of Japan Policy Committee (Nihon Ginkō Seisaku Iinkai), which issued recommendations to the MOF, recommendations it invariably followed. Both of these councils, like the Bond Council, were heavily weighted with representatives of the major banks. The professed guiding principle in implementing the Interest Control Law was to maintain low interest rates on loans in Japan to promote investment. Arguably, it did the virtual

---

[10] For an elaboration of this view of financial market regulation, see Mathias Dewatripont and Jean Tirole, *The Prudential Regulation of Banks*, Cambridge, Mass.: MIT Press, 1994.

opposite of this by enabling the banks to cartelize financial markets.

The object of the bank cartel was to maintain low rates of interest on bank deposits while elevating the interest rates on bank loans, in other words to exercise monopsony power in acquiring deposits and monopoly power in supplying loans. Figure 13.3 illustrates the operation of the bank cartel. Under the Interest Control Law, interest rates on bank deposits were indeed suppressed,[11] but the interest rates on bank loans, although also nominally suppressed, were effectively raised toward market-clearing levels by the device of compensating balances (*kōsoku yokin*). Here, compensating balances refer to the minimum deposits that a borrower is obliged, by stipulations of a bank loan, to maintain at the lending bank. The market for bank loans under this regime has been characterized as a "gray" market, as distinct from the "black" markets that price controls foster.[12] The nuance is that black markets are completely hidden from public view, whereas gray markets are hidden only from the view of the unperceptive. According to estimates released by Japan's Fair Trade Commission, compensating balances have been as large as 50 percent of all balances, which would entail effective interest rates on loans approximately double the nominal rate. In this way, banks continued to set market-determined interest rates on loans while remaining in compliance with the legal ceiling on loan rates.

Besides being cartelized and protected, the Japanese banking industry also received subsidies. First,

banks that borrowed from the Bank of Japan paid a low rate of interest (official discount rate). To maintain this policy, the BOJ found it necessary to limit the amount each bank borrowed from it, simply to prevent expansion of the nation's money supply. These credit limits, and the ancillary stipulations referred to as "window guidance", were communicated to each bank privately, an example of the administrative guidance so ubiquitous in the Japanese bureaucracy. Between 1954 and 1974, BOJ outstanding loans to banks ranged between 3 and 5 percent of banks' total demand deposit liabilities. If the discount rate had been set at the higher level of the call rate (also a posted rate), bank profits would have been substantially reduced (by as much as 0.25 percent of total bank assets per year). Besides this, interest on ordinary bank deposits was exempt from individual income taxes. Nominally, interest income in excess of 3 million yen per year was tax-

---

[11] One piece of evidence that interest rates on bank deposits were suppressed resides in the fact that such rates were consistently held below the non-regulated interest rate on overnight interbank loans (the "call" rate, i.e. interest rate on banks' loans to one another). Deposit rates would tend to exceed the call rate if both were freely determined because deposits are of longer average maturity than call money and therefore are more sensitive to unpredictable movements in interest rates, and to that extent in unregulated markets elicit a greater risk premium than do call loans. On this point see Yoshio Suzuki, *Money and Banking in Contemporary Japan*, Yale University Press, 1980, esp. pp. 44–5.

[12] Hugh Patrick, "Japan's Interest Rates and the 'Grey' Financial Market", *Pacific Affairs*, vol. 38, nos. 3 and 4 (Fall–Winter 1965–6), pp. 326–44.

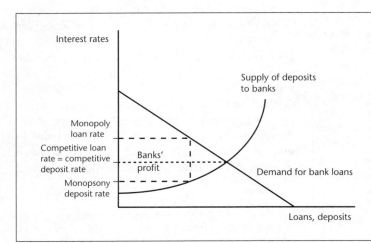

Figure 13.3. Implementation of the Interest Control Law of 1948

The MOF permitted the banking industry to cartelize the markets for loans and deposits. By suppressing the deposit rate while allowing the loan rate to reach a market-clearing level, the banking industry realized greater profit than if both these rates had been set competitively.

able, but individuals could open multiple accounts under fictitious names to evade all taxes without detection.

Finally, bank deposits were safe. No banks were allowed by the MOF to fail no matter how badly mismanaged. No depositors lost their investments. Each of the policies just described lowered the banks' incremental costs of obtaining loanable funds and contributed to their profits. Recent years have witnessed the devolution of this regulatory regime, and far sooner than many expected, given the proven political effectiveness of the Japanese banking lobby. Japanese firms now enjoy wide access to bond markets, money markets, and foreign financial markets including euromarkets; and in 1994 even the ceilings on deposit rates were officially discontinued. The dismantlement of the government-managed Japanese banking cartel began in earnest about 1980.

Deregulation of financial markets

Prior to the mid-1970s, even in spite of cartelization of domestic bank loans, few Japanese companies sought foreign sources of funds. Quite simply, Japanese laws and regulations did not permit it. The Foreign Exchange and Foreign Trade Control Law, which remained in effect from 1949 until 1981, in principle prohibited virtually all international financial transactions, with exceptions granted on a case-by-case basis. Initially under this regime, the Japanese government used its allocation of foreign exchange to control the nation's pattern of imports and exports, as well as to insulate the domestic financial system from international arbitrage. It abandoned the practice of rationing foreign exchange for current account transactions in April 1964, in accordance with the IMF charter (Article 8), but continued to control capital account transactions. For example, Japanese private companies were disallowed from issuing foreign bonds of any kind; foreign companies were generally deemed ineligible to place yen bonds in Japan (the first to do so was the American retailer Sears and Roebuck in March 1979); Japanese financial institutions were restrained from including foreign securities in their asset portfolios; the foreign loans of Japanese banks with overseas branches were subject to limits. These restrictions and others continued to insulate Japan's

financial markets from foreign ones. As intended, the restrictions prevented international arbitrage from constraining domestic regulation of interest rates and protected Japanese banks from foreign competition, but at a cost—the sacrifice of gains from international trade. And, with the explosion of Japanese government debt in the 1970s, the cost of financial insularity finally grew intolerably large, forcing a change. This probably would have happened even without the expansion of Japanese government debt, though not as soon.

Around 1974, the gaping Japanese fiscal deficit, the recent doubling of world oil prices, and contractionary monetary policy all contributed to record-high interest rates on loans in Japan. Japanese companies in pursuit of low interest loans would no longer be denied access to foreign markets. From about this time, the MOF began expanding the number of Japanese companies eligible to float eurobonds. The types of eurobonds actually issued by Japanese corporations continued to reflect idiosyncrasies of MOF regulations. So, for instance, most of the eurobonds were denominated in Swiss francs (and swapped into yen), only because MOF restrictions on Japanese financial institution participation in eurobond underwriting syndicates made the issue of yen-denominated eurobonds (euroyen bonds) less convenient. Also, more companies met MOF eligibility requirements to issue convertible bonds than straight bonds, so in the early 1980s Japanese companies greatly expanded their issues of convertible eurobonds, a further example of regulatory distortion. The new Foreign Exchange and Foreign Trade Control Law, which in 1981 replaced the old one, in principle allowed all international financial transactions unless specifically prohibited. In fact, prohibitions and eligibility requirements on the issue of euroyen bonds and restrictions on Japanese participation in euroloan syndicates and eurobond underwriting syndicates remained in place until 1984.

Once Japanese companies gained expanded access to euromarkets, continued suppression of domestic bond markets in Japan lost a lot of its value to Japanese banks. The Bond Council relaxed its eligibility rules for issuing domestic bonds and relaxed collateral requirements. By 1988, 180 companies had become eligible to issue domestic straight bonds with no collateral, and by 1993, 800 companies were eligible. Finally, in 1996 all corporations were permitted to issue bonds.

Japanese banks' loss of government protection from competition by investment houses meant that, even with government complicity, the banks no longer enjoyed significant monopsony power in setting deposit rates. The government-managed ceiling on bank deposit rates thus lost much of its advantage to banks, and was ultimately phased out over the early 1990s (and was finally abolished in October 1994). With deregulation of bank deposit rates, the analogous restraints on the intermediaries that compete domestically with banks—stipulated legal minimum insurance premiums, minimum stock brokerage commissions, and so on—also lost much of their point (which had been the effective cartelization of banking), and these too began to be phased out in the final years of the twentieth century. All of this is anticlimactic. Even by the late 1980s, the gales of competition that accompanied deregulation were already eroding the profits of Japanese banks, and therein lay the seeds of a major crisis.

Financial crisis and government response

Where the government insures bank depositors against losses, as in Japan and indeed all of the developed nations, banks themselves may be tempted to undertake riskier investments than is economically efficient. An important protection against such moral hazard is the requirement that banks place their own net worth at risk and do not merely invest the government-insured deposits. Under the previous regulatory regime in Japan, government protection and cartelization of banking *de facto* assured the substantial net worth of banks. But with the abandonment of that regulatory regime in the 1980s, the banks' net worth proceeded to erode. In spite of the banks' diminished net worth, the expansion of Japan's money supply following the February 1987 Louvre accord had left them flush with reserves. This turned out to be an unfortunate mixture. Japanese banks became more aggressive in their evaluation of loan collateral and default risk, and their reckless lending was the essential catalyst in the unprecedented and unsustainable runup in Japanese real estate and equity prices known ever since as the "Bubble". When the crash came in 1990–1, the banks were left with a mountain of bad loans that has strained Japan's system of prudential regulation of banks in ways previously unimaginable.

Even before the crash, international bankers were complaining that Japan's prudential standards were less strict than those of other nations, and that this afforded Japanese banks an unfair advantage in euromarket operations. The complaints led to the multilateral negotiation of minimum capital adequacy standards binding on any banks participating in the euromarkets. Here "capital" is the name for the net worth of banks, that is, the difference between a bank's assets and liabilities, the value of its stockholders' equity. Under the Basle accord of 1988 (so named because the venue for the negotiations was the headquarters of the Bank for International Settlements (BIS) in Basle, Switzerland), twelve nations including Japan agreed to impose common minimum capital standards on multinational banks. The "BIS standards",[13] which banks are now required to meet in order to participate fully in international markets, require that the book value of each bank's common equity ("tier 1 capital"), plus supplemental ("tier 2") capital no greater in value than the tier 1 capital and comprising a risk-weighted average of its preferred stock, subordinated debt, and unrealized capital gains on securities ("undisclosed reserves"), exceeds 8 percent of a risk-weighted average of the bank's assets. Put succinctly, tier 1 capital plus tier 2 capital up to the same value as the tier 1 capital must exceed 8 percent of a risk-weighted average of the bank's assets. Regarding the risk weights of the sizable items, a risk weight of 1.0 is assigned to business loans by the bank, a weight of 0.5 to residential mortgages, and a weight of 0 is assigned to government bonds. Undisclosed reserves receive a weight of 0.45. Bank assets denominated in foreign currency are valued in domestic currency units based on the current exchange rate at the end of the fiscal year (in Japan, March 31).

The BIS standards were phased in over two years, with international banks each required to attain a 7.5 percent risk-weighted capital ratio by January 1,

---

13 For complete details on the BIS standards, see Maximilian J. B. Hall, *Banking Regulation and Supervision: A Comparative Study of the UK, USA, and Japan*, Aldershot, Hants, and Brookfield, Vt: Edward Elgar, 1993.

1991, and the full 8 percent ratio by January 1, 1993 (extended until April 1, 1993 for Japanese banks). Meeting these standards became more difficult for the Japanese banks when, in 1990, the market values of their stock portfolios dropped precipitously (depleting their tier 2 capital). In the end, all of the large Japanese banks did, initially, meet the standards, but many of them had to issue substantial amounts of new stock and convertible bonds to do so. Then, in April 1997, Nippon Credit Bank (the smallest of Japan's three long-term credit banks) failed to meet the BIS standard and terminated its international operations. The same month, Hokkaido Takushoku Bank (a city bank, nicknamed "Takugin"), which was known to be in financial distress, announced that it was abandoning its international operations as an austerity measure. Seven months later, in November 1997, Takugin actually went into liquidation, the only city bank ever allowed to fail, an event that underscored the seriousness of the bad loan crisis confronting Japan's banking system as a whole. Nippon Credit Bank, for a time, remained afloat, thanks to an infusion of public funds (¥70 billion in special loans from the BOJ) which enabled it to place a new issue of common stock with other banks and a new issue of convertible bonds with insurance companies. Nippon Credit Bank was not the only large bank to receive an injection of public capital. Under a special law enacted in February 1998 (the Financial Stabilization Law), ¥13 trillion in public funds (= 2.6 percent of 1997 GDP) was earmarked for purchase of subordinated bonds and preferred stock in solvent but undercapitalized Japanese banks, including the largest ones. About ¥2 trillion of these funds were actually spent (as of March 1998). Even with these added infusions, some of Japan's leading international banks seem to have met the BIS standard only by dint of the fact that their failure to declare losses on bad loans from the "Bubble" era inflated the book value of their common equity (tier 1 capital).

In August 1998 the Long Term Credit Bank of Japan (LTCB), largest of the three long-term credit banks, and known to be in extreme financial distress, became the latest Japanese bank to announce the suspension of its international operations. It was widely evident that LTCB was about to become the largest Japanese bank ever to fail; its assets of ¥26 trillion were three times as great as those of Takugin

at the time of its failure. It was thus also clear that further measures were needed to assure the solvency of the banking system as a whole. In October 1998 the Diet appropriated ¥25 trillion for the purchase of banks' preferred stock and subordinated debt (replacing the previous appropriation of ¥13 trillion yen earmarked for the same purpose), and another ¥18 trillion for government purchases of shares in failed banks. At this time it also created a new entity called the Financial Reconstruction Commission (FRC) to oversee the nationalization and liquidation of failed banks. To the surprise of no one, the first act of the new authorities was to nationalize the LTCB, in October 1998. Two months later, in a move that was a bit of a surprise, the FRC also nationalized the Nippon Credit Bank, asserting that government inspections had uncovered massive undisclosed losses there. Both LTCB and Nippon Credit Bank are scheduled for liquidation. So far, there have not been any further instances of this kind, although a few of the large banks remain in dire straits. Daiwa, for instance, has withdrawn from international operations. In March 1999 the government authorities (the Financial Supervisory Agency) expended ¥7.5 trillion to purchase preferred stock and subordinated debt issued by fifteen of the largest banks, all of which they declared were undercapitalized but commercially viable. (The Bank of Tokyo–Mitsubishi was the only city bank not included.) This may not be the last public infusion of capital into the major banks.

The banks in Japan have used questionable, but apparently legal, accounting practices to avoid writing off bad loans. Banks have hesitated to write off their bad loans because the write-offs would reduce their BIS capital ratios and could also precipitate withdrawal of deposits (in spite of government guarantees).

But the bad loan problem should not be exaggerated. Undisclosed losses of the city banks, trust banks, and long-term credit banks are of unknown extent, but at the end of the 1997 fiscal year probably averaged about 2 percent of their total risk-weighted assets. In figures released by the Financial Supervisory Agency (a cabinet-level entity established in June 1998 to monitor banks), the banks acknowledged, as of March 1998, ¥87.5 trillion in bad loans (11 percent of their total loans outstanding), of which ¥50.2 trillion or about two-thirds of the total was held by Japan's nineteen largest banks (the nine city banks, seven trust banks and three long-term credit banks).[14] But only about one-tenth of the bad loans are classified as already in default, and, based on evidence from recent bank liquidations and government assisted bank mergers, as much as two-thirds of the remaining bad loans are likely to be eventually repaid. This places the undisclosed losses of all the banks at around ¥30 trillion, or about 3 percent of their total loans (and 6 percent of national income) and about six times all banks' annual average operating profit 1993FY–1997FY. This is an immense figure, but it is only two-thirds as great as the ¥45.7 trillion in bad loans that Japanese banks had already written off from 1992FY to 1997FY. The public infusions of bank capital are expected to accelerate the writing off of bad loans; indeed, that is their avowed purpose. Japan's bad loan crisis is at least in the order of magnitude of America's savings and loan crisis, which in 1989 required an appropriation of public funds equal to $40 billion (around 1 percent of US national income).

For several (and possibly even many) of Japan's agricultural cooperatives, credit cooperatives and credit associations, and smaller or weaker banks, the burden of non-performing loans from the "Bubble" era was sufficient to erase their net worth altogether. When the government insures deposits, insolvent banks can often still continue operations, but, as already described, their incentives to invest prudently will be severely attenuated. (For example, this is the fundamental motivation behind the BIS standards.) To avoid such situations, the MOF has typically arranged for insolvent or chronically undercapitalized financial institutions to be acquired by stronger ones, and these instances have become more frequent since the emergence of the bad loan crisis. The acquiring firms have usually needed special inducements of some kind, either special loans from the BOJ or side-payments from the Deposit Insurance Corporation (DIC), the entity ultimately responsible for insuring bank deposits in Japan (established in 1971).[15] To facilitate these and other operations, in the February 1998 Financial Stabilization Law, already mentioned, the DIC received an additional ¥17 trillion in public funds (= 3.4 percent of 1997 GDP), and the deposit insurance levies on banks were also increased. So far, the largest demands on DIC funds have arisen from failed credit cooperatives.

The credit cooperatives and credit associations had been subject to the supervisory oversight of prefectural governments rather than the MOF, and were particularly susceptible to moral hazard and outright fraud. In December 1994 the BOJ organized a new entity known as the Tokyo Kyōdo Bank, capitalized by it, the DIC, and a consortium of private banks, to oversee the liquidation of assets in two fraudulently mismanaged and insolvent credit cooperatives in Tokyo. After it became apparent that far more credit cooperatives and credit associations had become insolvent (not necessarily the result of fraud), the government in September 1996 added still more capital to the Tokyo Kyōdo Bank (¥120 billion from the DIC) and renamed it the Resolution and Collection Bank (RCB). By August 1998, the RCB had taken over more than twenty credit cooperatives (of the more than three hundred in Japan) and either liquidated them or hived them off, with side-payments, to stronger credit co-ops.

The insolvent agricultural cooperatives posed special problems. Their difficulties were largely the result of imprudent loans to housing finance companies (*jūsen*[16]), loans made in the "Bubble era" at the behest of government officials who were possibly themselves motivated by the prospect of lucrative employment in the *jūsen* upon retirement from government. The *jūsen* were not depository institutions, and consequently lay beyond the purview of the MOF. Yet each of them had been capitalized by a large commercial bank. Although the *jūsen* had been created in the 1970s, they did not balloon in size until after March 1990, when the founding banks each began to steer their own customers to their *jūsen* affiliates to evade newly established MOF limits on the banks' own real estate loans. With the collapse of real estate prices in 1991, seven of the eight *jūsen* became insolvent. This posed no imminent threat to the survival of the founding banks, but

---

14 The latest figures are posted on the web site of the Financial Supervision Agency of the Japanese government, under "press releases": [http://www.fsa.go.jp].

15 For recent examples of insolvent banks either acquired by stronger banks with side-payments from the Deposit Insurance Corporation, reorganized, or liquidated, see Appendix B.

16 The Japanese word *jūsen* is a contraction for *jūtaku kinyū senmon kaisha*, lit. "companies specializing in housing finance".

it did jeopardize the numerous small agricultural cooperatives that had also been induced to loan heavily to the *jūsen*. It became clear in 1995 that, as a result of this situation, a sizable appropriation would be necessary to make good on the (implicit) government guarantee of deposits in the agricultural co-ops. The Agricultural and Fisheries Cooperative Savings Insurance Corporation, the nominal guarantor of these deposits, financed by levies on the cooperatives, itself held far too little capital to fully cover the impending losses. After rancorous debate in the Diet, a bill was enacted in June 1996 that liquidated the *jūsen* and reimbursed the agricultural co-ops for a substantial portion of their *jūsen*-related losses, financed by special levies on the founding banks and an appropriation of ¥685 billion in public funds. This by no means ended the problems of Japan's agricultural cooperatives, however.

The MOF had announced in 1997 that after April 1998 all of Japan's depository institutions would be required to have BIS capital ratios of at least 4 percent or else face "prompt corrective action". As this date approached, however, the MOF liberally bestowed year-long extensions to institutions not in compliance, almost all of them co-ops of one sort or another. Of the 1,900 agricultural cooperatives in Japan, 82 acknowledged insolvency as of October 1997, and all of them have been allowed to continue operating. The Japanese government's delay in closing chronically undercapitalized depository institutions, including large banks as well as small co-ops, may enlarge the ultimate costs of the crisis by precipitating further moral hazard and delaying the reallocation of collateral on defaulted but not foreclosed loans (usually real estate) to higher-valued uses.

Nobody yet knows the ultimate outcome of the current bad loan problem. But one thing is apparent. It has not so far dislodged banks as the dominant financial intermediaries of Japan. Japan's bank-centered system of financial intermediation is our next topic.

The main bank system

Not every Japanese company listed on the stock exchanges has a main bank, but most do. And for these, loans from the main bank always comprise the largest source of external funds. The main bank also holds a significant equity interest in the corporation, is represented in the corporation's management councils, and assumes special responsibilities for managing the corporation's affairs in times of financial distress. Companies that belong to the same financial keiretsu group often also share the same main bank, and partly for this reason the financial keiretsu are occasionally described as bank-centered groups. But the financial keiretsu have prewar antecedents, the zaibatsu, while the main bank system is largely a postwar phenomenon.

Origins of the main bank system

Before the Pacific war, few large companies in Japan depended much on bank loans as a source of funds. Private placement of equity was a common source of venture capital. Banks' role as intermediaries was more or less limited to the supply of loans to individuals to finance their equity holdings. Most firms including the very largest were rather closely held, so banks had little role in corporate governance, either. Bond markets were active until the 1930s, when the Bond Council suppressed them, and many small banks invested heavily in bonds, trade credit, and other speculative assets. The large banks served as clearing houses for transactions within their own zaibatsu groups but attracted few deposits from outside. Many going concerns drew on their considerable flows of retained earnings, avoiding capital markets and banks altogether.

After the financial crisis of 1927, things began to change. Under the Bank Law enacted in 1928, small banks were either shut down or consolidated with larger ones. Industrial bonds were curtailed. Large companies now turned a little more to the stock market and bank loans for external funds. After 1937, military procurement spending filled the coffers of manufacturing firms and supplied most of the reserves needed for further investment.

During the war years, the Japanese government used banks as conduits for the payment of funds to munitions producers. For this purpose, industrial firms were assigned by the government authorities to specific banks, which then became the designated leaders of syndicated loans to the assigned firms. The pattern of loans was dictated by the military planners, not determined independently by the banks. Nevertheless, the wartime loan syndicates exhibited in incipient form some aspects of the main bank system. And in later years, the main banks of many firms were the same banks to which the firms had been assigned by military planners during the war.[17]

Government back payments to munitions firms at first continued even after the war's end, but were soon prohibited by the Occupation authorities. Stock market trading was suspended until 1948, by which time concentrated equity holdings in zaibatsu enterprises had been expropriated and dispersed. Rigid controls on foreign exchange transactions insulated Japan from international capital markets, and the banking and securities industries now operated under new laws and regulations which assured that banks would be protected and subsidized. With industrial bonds suppressed and stockholders made ineffective at governing by the deconcentration of large blocks, the way was open for banks to dominate the intermediation of funds between households and businesses.

In the 1950s, Japanese companies began to take on tremendous debt, largely in the form of loans from banks. About this time also, Japanese banks first became significant equity-holders in the firms to which they were lending, which for the six largest city banks (Mitsui, Mitsubishi, Fuji, Sanwa, Sumitomo, and Dai-Ichi Kangyo) included most of the members of their same financial keiretsu groups. By 1960, most large companies were relying on bank loans as their leading source of external funds, and all essential elements of the main bank system were clearly in evidence.

Character of the main bank relationship

For most large Japanese companies, the main bank, besides being the largest debtholder in the firm, is also among the leading stockholders in the firm. In a typical pattern, the main bank holds 10–20 percent of the firm's debt, and 1–3 percent of the stock. Other banks, insurance companies, and so on each hold smaller amounts of both debt and stock. The debt of most large Japanese companies is not highly concentrated in any single creditor. This insulates the creditors from excessive risk and protects the client firm from monopoly exploitation by the banks.

As already mentioned, the Anti-monopoly Law of Japan (as amended in 1953) limits shareholding in any one firm by each bank and insurance company. In 1987 the limit was lowered from 10 to 5 percent. (The limit remains at 7 percent for insurance companies.) Few instances of bank shareholding have approached these limits. Nevertheless, banks in Japan do often place themselves among the leading shareholders in the firms to which they lend, and gain representation on the boards of directors. For the largest companies a 1–3 percent equity interest suffices.

A couple of things other than its being the largest debtholder in a firm, and a major shareholder, differentiate the main bank from other creditors. First, the main bank handles a disproportionately large share of the client firm's daily transactions. For instance, the main bank might set up a teller window on the client firm's premises to handle deposits and withdrawals by the client's employees, all of whom maintain accounts with it. Second, in times of financial distress, the main bank is likely to intervene in the management of the firm. Arguably, these aspects of the main bank relation are corollaries of the main bank's position as largest debtholder and best informed party regarding the firm's management decisions. We will return to this point shortly. But first, let us consider the problems facing borrowing firms generally.

Borrowing firms everywhere must confront the same problems: how to assure lenders of their creditworthiness, and how to assure lenders that the act of borrowing itself will not precipitate imprudent actions. (Why be careful if the funds at stake are someone else's?) Stockholding by Japanese banks in the companies to which they lend resolves both problems and lowers the costs of financial intermediation. Two simple examples illustrate the problems and the manner in which bank stockholding mitigates the problems. The first example highlights the distorting effect of borrowing on investment choice, the temptation of borrowers to substitute risky assets for safer ones.

---

17 On this point, see Juro Teranishi, "Loan Syndication in Wartime Japan and the Origins of the Main Bank System", in Aoki and Patrick, *The Japanese Main Bank System*, ch. 2, pp. 51–88; and Takeo Hoshi, "Evolution of the Main Bank System", in Mitsuaki Okabe (ed.), *The Structure of the Japanese Economy: Changes in the Domestic and International Fronts*, London: Macmillan, 1995, ch. 11, pp. 287–322.

Asset substitution [18]

Risky investments have outcomes that vary randomly across possible future "states". (Each state represents a possible contingency with probability less than or equal to one, and the probabilities summed over all states equal one.) The risk-neutral investor (such as a firm with diffuse stockholding) seeks the maximum expected return, an average of the returns in all possible states weighted by their probabilities of occurrence.

The distorting effect of borrowing resides in the fact that a borrower attaches the same zero value to states in which partial default occurs and to states of full default, but the lender clearly prefers partial default to complete default. Investments that maximize the expected value of the firm but that risk partial default may therefore be passed over in favor of riskier projects.[19] To put it a little differently, borrowers are not as averse to default as lenders would like them to be.

An example illustrates the problem. Suppose that debt commits the firm to the payment of interest = ¥50 and that its managers must choose one of three projects, each of which has two equally likely payoffs (see Table A). The stockholders own a residual claim on earnings—whatever remains, if anything, after interest payments, belongs to them. So, for instance, if project A is adopted, the stockholders will claim ¥50 if state 1 attains (= ¥100 earnings – ¥50 interest), and will claim nothing if state 2 attains (earnings = ¥30, which is all expended toward the ¥50 interest that is owed). Each of the states is equally likely, so the expected claims of stockholders if project A is adopted equal ¥25 (= ½¥50 + ½¥0). The other entries in the last three columns of the table are deduced in a like fashion.

The stockholders prefer project B. The debtholders prefer project C. Firm value is maximized by choosing A. Investors holding both debt and stock (not necessarily in equal proportions) will prefer the value-maximizing project. The reason? The combination of debt plus equity more closely resembles an unencumbered claim on the firm's assets than does either just debt or just equity. If banks hold both stock and debt in companies, it can therefore be mutually advantageous for other investors to defer to their judgment in evaluating projects. In other words, bank stockholding in the firms to which they lend confers control over the firm's choices, not merely because the banks gain voting power, but because the capital markets reward the firm's other securities-holders for placing corporate governance in the banks' hands.

Bank stockholding often implies representation on the board of directors, which, because it assures access to privileged or inside information, can resolve additional problems, those emanating from asymmetries between what is privately known and what is publicly known about the firm's creditworthiness.

Information asymmetry [20]

Loans must be acceptable to both borrower and lender based on their respective private information. The prudent lender will not rely on borrowers' truthfully revealing information that is damaging, and will instead assume the worst. If this credibility problem cannot be resolved, then external financing may be unprofitable for all except those who actually *are* poor credit risks (an extreme case of "adverse selection": the market "selects" the least

---

Table A

	Payoffs		NPV*	NPV* to stock-holders	NPV* to debt-holders
	State 1 (prob. = 0.5) (¥)	State 2 (prob. = 0.5) (¥)	(¥)	(¥)	(¥)
Project A	100	30	65	25	40
Project B	120	0	60	35	25
Project C	50	50	50	0	50

* NPV = net present value.

---

[18] For an early discussion of the asset substitution problem, see Michael C. Jensen and William H. Meckling, "Theory of the Firm: Managerial Behavior, Agency Costs and Ownership Structure", *Journal of Financial Economics*, vol. 3, no. 4 (1976), pp. 305–60.

[19] There is a symmetric distortion that would arise if lenders rather than borrowers chose investments. But because stockholders vote while debtholders do not, the manager is usually considered to be under the control of the stockholders; in other words, both the stockholders and manager are agents of the firm's debtholders.

[20] Myers and Majluf were among the first to develop the implications of asymmetric information in financial markets: Stewart C. Myers and Nicholas S. Majluf, "Corporate Financing and Investment Decisions when Firms Have Information that Investors Do Not Have", *Journal of Financial Economics*, vol. 13 (1984), pp. 187–221.

Table B

| | Value of the firm | | NPV | NPV of debt that promises interest = $50 |
| | State 1 (prob. = 0.5) | State 2 (prob. = 0.5) | | |
	(¥)	(¥)	(¥)	(¥)
High-risk firm	100	0	50	25
Low-risk firm	50	50	50	50

attractive prospects). Stockholding by the lender can resolve the problem, either by hedging the risk or by conferring access to inside information.

An example like the one used to illustrate the asset substitution problem may be helpful. Suppose here that firms are committed to particular real investments but that the firms are of two types: one is high-risk and the other low-risk. The manager of a firm knows his own firm's true characteristics but outsiders do not. If debt commits the firm to the payment of interest = ¥50, then the debt of the high-risk firm has a lower net present value (NPV) than that of the low-risk firm (see Table B). If the low-risk firm is unable to differentiate itself from the high-risk firm, then it can sell its debt only at the ¥25 that is the net present value of debt in the high-risk firm. On these terms, the low-risk firm cannot profitably borrow to finance its investments: only high-risk firms will borrow. Notice however that a combination of debt and equity has the same NPV in both firms. Additionally, banks that own sufficient stock to gain representation in the management councils of the firm will have access to inside information that enables them to distinguish the true risk of debt. Further notice in this example that it is the low-risk firms that gain from these aspects of bank stockholding, not the high-risk firms. Can this be why not all firms in Japan form main bank relationships? If so, then it holds an implication for academic studies that seek differences in the financial statements of Japanese firms that have main banks and those that do not.[21] Although we predict that the firms with main banks are in a lower-risk class, we also predict that this fact cannot be discerned from the publicly available information about the firms. We must rely on indirect evidence to confirm that bank stockholding separates out low-risk firms.

There is one further implication. In the example,

any mechanism that automatically transfers wealth from stockholders to debtholders in event of default raises the value of debt in the high-risk firm, narrowing the difference in value of debt between it and the low-risk firm. Bankruptcy rules that transfer control of the firm from debtholders to stockholders in event of default represents such a mechanism. Where such laws are well established and swiftly implemented, bank stockholding loses some of its point.

Stockholding by banks

Shareholding by lenders including banks is effective at resolving the problems just detailed. By holding shares, lenders gain inside information about the firm's dealings and also gain the power to act on the information. And, as detailed above, banks that hold both stock and debt have efficient incentives in evaluating the firm's real investments. Banks that hold stock can accurately assess risk and can forestall asset substitution. Researchers have accumulated much evidence that shows that shareholding by banks in Japan has indeed lowered the costs of debt, removed liquidity constraints, and promoted greater borrowing.

The first item of evidence, due to Hoshi, Kashyap, and Scharfstein, is that companies with close ties to banks are less liquidity-constrained than other companies, controlling for differences in real investment prospects.[22] Furthermore, based on a study by Prowse, Japanese banks hold more stock in companies that are prone to agency problems than in others, and borrowing by such companies is not constrained by agency problems as it is in the USA.[23] Prowse also found that in Japan, unlike the United States, companies with high R&D expenses, high growth, intangible assets, and the like do not have lower debt-to-equity ratios. The interpretation is

---

[21] The first to identify sets of firms that have main banks and those that do not, and to seek differences in their financial statements, was Iwao Nakatani, "The Economic Role of Financial Corporate Grouping", in Masahiko Aoki (ed.), *The Economic Analysis of the Japanese Firm*, Amsterdam: North-Holland, 1984, pp. 227–58.

[22] Takeo Hoshi, Anil Kashyap, and David Scharfstein, "Corporate Structure, Liquidity, and Investment: Evidence from Japanese Industrial Groups", *Quarterly Journal of Economics*, vol. 106 (1991), pp. 33–60.

[23] Stephen D. Prowse, "Institutional Investment Patterns and Corporate Financial Behavior in the US and Japan", *Journal of Financial Economics*, vol. 27, no. 1 (1990), pp. 43–66.

that, because Japanese banks hold stock in firms that are prone to agency problems, such firms are less impeded in borrowing in Japan than in the United States.

My own estimates of structural equations explaining both debt-to-asset ratios and stockholding by largest lenders add further weight to arguments that stockholding by Japanese banks lowers the costs of their financial intermediation.[24] These estimates indicate that the largest debtholders in keiretsu presidents' club firms hold more stock if the firms borrow heavily or have weaker collateral, greater prospects of growth, or high levels of spending on research and development or on advertising—precisely the companies most prone to the agency problems of debt which stockholding by a main bank can help resolve. The estimates further demonstrate that keiretsu presidents' club companies in which debtholders hold more stock borrow more, *ceteris paribus*. This effect is not significantly stronger for larger debtholders than for lesser ones, which suggests that it is advantageous also for debtholders other than main banks to hold stock in clients. This is a satisfying result, because in Japan debtholders often do hold stock in clients even if they are not the main banks.

Main banks and financial distress

Tens of thousands of small firms in Japan fail every year, and few if any have main banks. Typically, they declare bankruptcy and the courts supervise the liquidation of their assets. When large Japanese firms without main banks fail, they, too, often seek the protection of bankruptcy and face reorganization under court supervision, though these cases are rare indeed. In the years 1971–82, among firms listed on the stock exchange, only thirty-one went bankrupt, and none seemed to have had close relations with any particular bank. When large, listed firms that do have main banks fail, instead of bankruptcy proceedings, the main bank itself intervenes in the company's affairs, acts as a liaison with other debtholders, and supervises the reconstruction or liquidation of the firm.

There were only a few instances before 1990 where firms with main banks became financially distressed. Paul Sheard identified forty-two cases over the three decades from 1960 to 1990, and

found that these cases exhibited a number of common features.[25] For instance, the main bank usually dispatched its own employees to take on top management posts in the distressed firms. Furthermore, the main bank usually assumed the pivotal role in formulating a recovery plan and restructuring claims on the firms. If the plan called for additional external funds, the main bank usually provided them; and if the plan called for liquidation of assets, the main bank supervised it. In short, main banks performed functions that the courts undertake in instances of failure by firms that do not have main banks. They did this not for altruistic reasons: rather, they took the lead when firms failed because they, as largest debtholders, had the most to gain from setting things right.

The management of financial distress is a local public good among the firm's debtholders; all of them benefit from its being handled well. But the largest debtholder has the most at stake if matters are handled ably and, to just that extent, can be expected to undertake most or even all of the costly supervision and oversight activities that attend intervention in the affairs of the failing firm.[26] Court-supervised reorganization would spread costs among debtholders, but the costs themselves are likely to be greater than if a company insider with its own wealth at stake were deciding matters. The additional costs are not so much the direct costs embodied in court fees and the like, as the indirect costs arising from inappropriate liquidation, failure to appoint competent management, and so on. One important purpose of the main bank system is to avoid these costs of bankruptcy if the worst should happen. A portion of the anticipated cost savings is passed on to the main bank itself, well before failure occurs. This is why, in spite of the anticipated special burdens that fall on the largest debtholder should a firm fail, each lender to a large, important

24 David Flath, "Shareholding in the Keiretsu, Japan's Financial Groups", *Review of Economics and Statistics*, vol. 75, no. 2 (May 1993), pp. 249–57.

25 Paul Sheard, "Main Banks and the Governance of Financial Distress", in Aoki and Patrick, *The Japanese Main Bank System*, ch. 6, pp. 188–230.

26 There is a direct analogy here to the contributions of allies to their common defense. In the absence of cooperation, only the one that values the common defense most highly contributes anything. See the discussion of alliance defense expenditures in Ch. 10.

Table 13.2. Sources of funding for the nonfinancial corporate sector, 1965–1997

	Fund-raising by the nonfinancial corporate sector (% of private investment)									(1997 ¥ trillions)	
	Total corporate external fund-raising	Private loans	Public loans	Commercial paper	Stock	Industrial bonds	Foreign bonds	Other foreign sources (FDI, trade credit, and other)	Private investment	Total corporate external fund-raising	Internal fund-raising
1965–67	53.9	42.1	5.1	0.0	3.4	2.6	0.0	0.7	63.5	34.2	29.3
1968–70	47.8	36.5	4.0	0.0	4.0	1.4	0.2	1.6	115.6	55.2	60.4
1971–73	65.8	53.4	4.1	0.0	4.2	2.3	−0.1	2.2	147.0	96.8	50.2
1974–76	45.5	33.8	4.5	0.0	2.6	2.2	0.6	1.1	147.3	67.0	80.3
1977–79	30.6	20.8	3.7	0.0	2.7	1.7	0.5	0.7	154.8	47.4	107.4
1980–82	38.0	27.9	4.0	0.0	3.3	1.3	0.8	−0.2	171.4	65.2	106.3
1983–85	44.8	32.9	2.1	0.0	3.1	1.0	2.7	0.2	184.9	82.8	102.1
1986–88	59.9	34.9	2.7	4.0	4.9	2.4	4.5	2.0	237.7	142.4	95.3
1989–91	60.7	30.9	6.0	1.0	4.9	2.5	6.1	3.3	319.6	194.1	125.5
1992–94	14.7	6.6	8.1	−0.9	0.7	4.3	−1.4	−1.5	291.4	42.7	248.7
1995–97	4.1	−3.9	0.1	0.7	1.5	3.3	−2.3	6.6	305.4	12.6	292.9
1997									104.9	4.3	103.6
Outstanding, end Dec. 1997 (¥tr.)	459.0		95.2	11.8	245.0	66.3	23.9				

Sources: *fund-raising and outstanding amounts,* end December 1997: Bank of Japan, *Economic and Financial Data on CD-ROM 1998* (financial institutions accounts) and Bank of Japan web site (http://www.boj.or.jp/en/siryo/siryo_f.htm) (preliminary estimates of flow of funds); *private investment:* Economic Planning Agency web site (http://www.epa.go.jp/ e-e/eri/menu.html) (system of national accounts).

Japanese firm covets the position of main bank. In particular, the main bank takes the lion's share of the company's profitable business; it handles its payment accounts; it acts as the lead bank in its eurobond floats; it leads the private placement of its domestic bonds. In short, the main bank system serves the interest of the large Japanese commercial banks as well as that of their clients.

But the system is clearly undergoing severe strain. When in November 1998 Yamaichi Securities collapsed, its main bank Fuji was unable to save it from liquidation. However, Fuji Bank did arrange a ¥100 billion rescue of Yasuda Trust the very next month. For now at least, the main bank system survives.

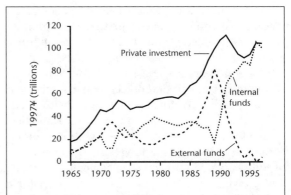

Figure 13.4. Sources of funds, nonfinancial corporate sector, 1965–1997

Source: Bank of Japan, *Economic Statistics Annual*.

Resilience of the main bank system

As Japanese regulatory constraints on euromarket finance and domestic bond finance were lifted in the mid-1980s, many observers predicted that the main bank system would unravel. So far it has not, even in the face of the unprecedented solvency crisis faced by the banks themselves since the 1990–1 fall-off in Japan's real estate and stock prices. Perhaps the massive infusion of public capital into the major banks has helped to perpetuate the main bank system. Its ultimate fate will not be known until the current recession ends and Japanese corporations again seek increased funds to finance their investment.

Table 13.2 describes the sources of funding of private investment in Japan in recent years. At the end of December 1997, outstanding private loans to Japan's nonfinancial corporate businesses remained large relative to stocks, bonds, and other securities, in spite of the fact that outstanding private loans had actually diminished over the interval 1995–7. Much of the reduction in outstanding loans may be attributed to the write-offs of bad loans from the late 1980s. From FY1992 to FY1997, the Japanese banks wrote off ¥45.7 trillion in bad loans.[27]

The recent reduction in outstanding loans has not been accompanied by any significant expansion of outstanding securities. Rather, businesses have forgone added external funding of all kinds. This is depicted graphically in Figure 13.4. Journalists and other analysts have argued that the astringency of external funding, and of bank loans in particular, has caused the stagnation of private investment since 1990 that is also evident in the figure. But such

a "credit crunch" must not exist; for if it did then interest rates in Japan would be high, yet the opposite is manifestly true. In September 1998 the call rate reached the astonishingly low level of 0.25 percent, while the short-term prime lending rate stood at 1.625 percent and the long-term prime rate at 2.5 percent. It appears that it is the demand for external funds, and not the supply, that must be temporarily low in Japan. Only after private investment revives will we learn whether the Japanese banks have finally retained their place as the dominant source of external funds, and whether the main bank system can persist.

The ultimate fate of the main bank system may be of less moment than is often supposed. Economists have long been aware that the corporate choice among sources of finance is largely arbitrary. And this pertains not only to the choice among different debt instruments—loans versus securities—but between debt itself and equity.

Debt versus equity

Debt and equity divide the sources of corporate finance into two broad categories. Debt encompasses bank loans, debentures, trade credit, notes, com-

27 Financial Supervisory Agency, Government of Japan, "The Current Status of Risk Management Loans held by Deposit-Taking Financial Institutions", July 17, 1998 (table: "Loss on Disposal of Bad Loans of All Japanese Banks").

mercial paper, and other such fixed claims on corporate earnings—"fixed" in that they promise specific, scheduled payments. Debt claims on firms' earnings hold priority over equity. That is, the property of equity-holders consists only of the residual earnings of the corporation, i.e. what remains (if anything) after scheduled payments to debtholders. Residual earnings may be remitted to stockholders as dividend payments or retained within the firm. Retention of earnings has long been a greater source of equity finance than new share issues for profitable and growing Japanese firms. To state the point a little bit differently, the dividend payout rate of Japanese corporations is typically quite low both in an absolute sense and in comparison with that of corporations in the United States and elsewhere.

In corporate finance, the choice among sources of funds is the nub of the matter. The fundamental arbitrariness of it all may thus come as a bit of a surprise.

The M–M thesis

Among the most celebrated propositions in economics is the Modigliani–Miller (M–M) thesis that, in the absence of market frictions or tax distortions, the market value of a firm's assets is unrelated to its financial structure.[28] Both authors of this thesis have been awarded Nobel prizes. It might seem a little strange to contemplate the market value of a firm, including all its assets, lock, stock, and barrel. For firms themselves, in their entirety, seldom represent objects of trade. Far more commonplace are trades of financial claims on firms' earnings. To purchase outright ownership of all the assets of a firm, one would have to purchase *all* the outstanding claims on the firms' earnings, including both debt and equity claims. The market value of the firm's assets V, then, equals the market value of outstanding debt D plus the market value of outstanding stock E:

$$V = D + E.$$

The M–M thesis holds that, *unless the firm's extent of debt financing affects gross earnings directly—either by affecting its tax liabilities, costs of governance, or in some other way—then the market value of the firm is independent of its extent of debt financing: V is independent of D/E.*

The veracity of the M–M thesis rests on the fact that, where its premises are true, combinations of debt and equity held in proportion to their market values represent a composite asset whose income stream is independent of the firm's extent of debt financing. Arbitragers will ensure that such composite asset has an unchanging market value. The composite asset's implicit rate of return is the firm's cost of capital. Consequently, arbitrage ensures that the firm's cost of capital is unrelated to its reliance on debt financing.

Notice that the M–M thesis has wide applicability to corporate finance. For instance, by forgoing a dividend, the firm maintains the value of its outstanding equity at a higher level than otherwise, and can retire a portion of its debt. The dividend payout decision thus amounts to a choice between debt and equity. Also, where the premises of the M–M thesis hold, the choice among different forms of debt or equity is as irrelevant to the value of the firm's assets as is the choice of overall extent of debt. It matters not whether the firm finances largely with bank loans, as is typical of large corporations in Japan, or issues securities, both debentures and stock, as is more typical of America's large corporations. Regulations, provisions of the tax code, institutions for governing corporations and for monitoring corporate investment behavior—all of which lie outside the premises of the M–M thesis—surely influence corporate finance, and account for the persistent differences across nations. But underlying it all is an element of arbitrariness.

Taxes and corporate finance

Many of the factors that first gave rise to the banks' dominance of corporate finance in Japan have already been described. Provisions of the tax code are also known to influence corporate finance. Contrary to the premises of the Modigliani–Miller thesis, reliance on debt financing alters the tax liabilities of the firm and its investors, in Japan as elsewhere. Interest payments on debt represent tax-deductible expenses of corporations, whereas accruals to equity-holders do not. Consequently, debt financing

---

[28] Franco Modigliani and H. Merton Miller, "The Cost of Capital, Corporate Finance and the Theory of Investment", *American Economic Review*, vol. 48 (June 1958), pp. 261–97.

reduces corporate income tax liabilities.[29] But dividends, capital gains, and interest are all subject to further taxation as they accrue to the firm's investors as taxable income. Because capital gains income generally is taxed at a lower rate than other forms of income, investors' individual tax liabilities are in aggregate lower if the firm finances with equity rather than debt, even though corporate income tax liabilities are made greater.[30] If, as appears to have been true in both Japan and America, the corporate income tax rate is significantly larger than the difference in tax rates on investors' ordinary and capital gains incomes, then the reduction in corporate income tax liabilities arising from financing with debt rather than equity more than offsets the implied increase in investors' tax liabilities as corporate distributions accrue to them as ordinary income rather than capital gains.

The tax advantage of corporate debt financing may have been slightly larger in Japan than in the United States. Corporate income tax rates are comparably large in Japan and America. In Japan they lie near 50 percent for the largest corporations (taking into account prefectural as well as national taxation). In the USA the corporate federal income tax rate was 46 percent until 1986 when it was lowered to 34 percent, and then raised again to 35 percent in 1993. So, for example, before 1986, paying out an extra 100 yen as interest rather than awarding it to equity-holders reduced corporate income tax liabilities by about 50 yen, in either nation. But more of such reductions in corporate income tax liabilities survived taxation of investors' incomes in Japan than in the USA because of the generally lower personal income tax rates in Japan. On the basis of 1980 tax rates and the incidence of corporate distributions to investors weighted by tax bracket, each 100 yen paid as interest rather than equity income reduced Japanese investors' cumulative tax liabilities by 40 yen;[31] and each dollar paid as interest rather than equity income reduced American investors' tax liabilities by 30 cents. Hence the tax advantage was larger in Japan.

Corporate governance and the monitoring of corporate investments

The preceding discussion suggests that tax considerations absolutely favor debt over equity financing

in Japan, America, and other nations whose tax codes include similar provisions—essentially all the developed nations. Equity financing does nevertheless persist. Why? The question is not as silly as it may seem, for corporations could so burden themselves with debt that default is a near certainty and residual claims on earnings have essentially no value.

The reason firms typically do not finance only with debt is that there are special costs uniquely associated with debt finance that are avoided by equity finance: namely, the costs of resolving difficulties posed by the asset substitution problem and by asymmetric information. As firms borrow more they become more likely to default on scheduled debt repayments even if they were to behave exactly as the lenders would prefer, which exacerbates both of these problems. By refraining from borrowing, firms may conserve resources that would otherwise be dissipated in activities needed to assure lenders of their creditworthiness and reliability. In Japan these activities include establishing and maintaining a close relationship with a main bank. Additionally, the prospect of formal bankruptcy proceedings in the event of default facilitates borrowing by assuring that lenders' interests will be protected, but in a way that imposes some costs on stockholders. Costs associated with anticipated bankruptcy proceedings in the event of default are thus like the costs of other activities essential to borrowing, and can be avoided only by refraining from borrowing.

Equity financing too entails unique costs—the costs of aligning the corporate managers' interests with those of the stockholders, and the costs of assuring investors that the firm's future prospects are favorable. The costs of aligning managerial incentives include the costs of monitoring managerial performance, and the costs of establishing and maintaining reputations as stockholders for rewarding managerial actions that enhance stockholder

[29] This was first noted by Modigliani and Miller themselves: see Franco Modigliani and H. Merton Miller, "Corporate Income Taxes and the Cost of Capital: A Correction", *American Economic Review*, vol. 53 (June 1963).

[30] See H. Merton Miller, "Debt and Taxes", *Journal of Finance*, vol. 33 (May 1977), pp. 261–75.

[31] David Flath, "Debt and Taxes: Japan Compared with the US", *International Journal of Industrial Organization*, vol. 2 (1984), pp. 311–26.

wealth. Managers of corporations encumbered with debt find their spheres of authority limited by the firms' lenders. For this reason, costly procedures of stockholder monitoring and control of managerial behavior are less essential for highly levered corporations than for all-equity corporations.[32] Additionally, in the event that a firm expands its equity by the sale of new stock (rather than by retaining earnings), it needs to assure investors that the firms' prospects are favorable—if indeed they are! New stock issues will net greater paid-in capital if outside auditors or underwriters certify the firm's prospects, but such certification is costly. For this reason, corporations the world over typically resort to new stock issues only when earnings are insufficient to meet desired amounts of equity financing.[33]

Japan's corporate governance practices evolved along with its main bank system, and complement it. Before the Pacific war, much of the corporate equity reposed in zaibatsu holding companies which consolidated the personal fortunes of the wealthy few. The zaibatsu enterprises were financed largely through retained earnings rather than bank loans, and the founding families, through delegated agents, closely monitored and controlled the companies.[34] The forced dissolution of zaibatsu holding companies in 1948 permanently disrupted these old modes of corporate governance, and elicited new ones. From the 1950s, as banks became the dominant intermediaries, they also insinuated themselves into the governance of their corporate clients. Because main banks could be counted upon to closely monitor the investment choices of their client firms, other stakeholders could disengage from these activities with little fear of adverse consequences. Companies in Japan hold general stockholders' meetings annually, in compliance with securities laws, but these are notorious charades having little or nothing to do with the actual governance of the corporations. Extortionists known as *sōkaiya* (lit., general meeting specialists) acquire small stock positions in Japanese companies and then threaten to disrupt the meetings through long harangues, embarrassing questions, or other such legal but annoying actions, unless paid by the managers. There have also been instances in which *sōkaiya* have received payments from managers to prevent other shareholders from raising legitimate points embarrassing to the managers, for instance complaints

about the pollution practices of the company. All of this amounts to a sideshow. Actual corporate governance in Japan is conducted in private, largely by the main bank, if there is one.

The most careful empirical study of corporate governance in Japan has been concluded by Steven Kaplan.[35] Examining 1980s data, he found that Japan's top corporate executives were about as likely as their US counterparts to be dismissed should their firm's stock price decline by 50 percent, its earnings become negative, or its sales decline by 50 percent. He also found that Japanese and American top corporate executives' compensation exhibited about the same sensitivity to a two-standard deviation change in stock price. In other words, although the institutions of corporate governance differ very much between Japan and the United States, Kaplan found that the relation between managerial rewards and firm performance was very similar in the two nations.

Conclusion

The very great dependence of Japanese corporations on bank loans during the 1950s, 1960s, and 1970s clearly owed a great deal to regulations. The banks were subsidized and protected. The bond market was suppressed, and foreign capital markets were placed off limits for Japanese firms. Given all this, it is unsurprising that banks should have taken a leading role in supplying funds to businesses, and, in doing so, seeing that their own interests were protected by establishing close relationships with clients. In

---

[32] For the original statement of this view, see Michael C. Jensen, "Eclipse of the Public Corporation", *Harvard Business Review*, vol. 86, no. 9 (Sept.–Oct. 1989), pp. 61–74.

[33] This fact was first noted by Stewart Myers who labeled it the "pecking order" thesis. See e.g. Myers and Majluf, "Corporate Financing and Investment Decisions when Firms Have Information that Investors Do Not Have".

[34] For discussion of the origins and nature of the zaibatsu, refer to Ch. 3.

[35] Steven N. Kaplan, "Top Executive Rewards and Firm Performance: A Comparison of Japan and the US", *Journal of Political Economy*, vol. 102 (June 1994), pp. 510–46. Also see Steven N. Kaplan, "Corporate Governance and Corporate Performance: A Comparison of Germany, Japan and the US", in Donald H. Chew (ed.), *Studies in International Corporate Finance and Governance Systems: A Comparison of the US, Japan, and Europe*, Oxford University Press, 1997, pp. 251–8.

short, government cartelization and protection of banks led to the main bank system.

When Japanese regulatory constraints on euromarket finance were lifted in the mid-1980s, the Japanese domestic banking cartel began to unravel. Quite simply, if Japanese banks were no longer to be protected from competition by euro-intermediaries, then a cartel of domestic channels of intermediation was no longer valuable. Deposit rate ceilings, restrictions on the issue of domestic bonds and commercial paper, artificially high brokerage commissions, and so on all lost their essential point—the cartelization of Japanese banking—and all were, or soon will be, eliminated. With decartelization, Japanese banks'

profits eroded and their lending grew reckless. This was particularly so under the expansionary Japanese monetary policy following the February 1987 Louvre Accord. The resulting run-up in asset prices in 1988–9 was followed by a crash in 1990–1 that left the Japanese banks' net worth in a precarious state. And, because of the 1990s slowdown in macroeconomic growth and investment, many Japanese banks are still flirting with insolvency nearly a decade later. In spite of it all, bank loans for now remain the most important source of external funds to Japanese businesses. In other words, Japan's main bank system continues to display remarkable resilience, even though its ultimate fate is very much in doubt.

Appendix A   Chronology of changes in regulation of Japanese financial markets

Prewar era

Under authority of the 1927 Bank Law, the MOF in 1933 established a para-public advisory council to make ongoing recommendations concerning requests by corporations for official permission to float new bonds, recommendations that it invariably followed. The Bond Council (Kisai Chōsei Kyōgikai), which was dominated by the large banks, authorized only the largest and most profitable corporations to float bonds, and these were required to meet stringent collateral requirements in the form of low-rate bank deposits. Though debentures had been an important source of corporate finance before 1933, in the years afterward only electric utilities and a few other blue-chip companies continued to issue industrial bonds.

Occupation era and afterwards

The Securities Exchange Act of 1948, modeled on America's Banking Act of 1933 (the Glass–Steagall Law), prohibited banks in Japan from underwriting securities and prohibited banks from themselves from investing in securities. But this latter provision was repealed after the Occupation ended, so that the relevant restriction on banks' investing in stocks after 1953 became a provision of Japan's anti-monopoly law limiting such investments to no more than 10 percent of the shares in any one company. (In 1987 the limit was lowered to 5 percent for banks and 7 percent for insurance companies.) Underwriting and brokering of securities became the exclusive purview of investment houses. Intermediaries were further segmented into those specializing in long-term loans versus

short-term loans, trust accounts versus banking accounts, life insurance versus property and casualty insurance, and so on.

The Interest Control Law of 1948, counterpart of the US Regulation Q of the Federal Reserve Act, empowered the MOF to regulate interest rates. Under this authority, the MOF suppressed interest rates on bank deposits, but tacitly permitted interest rates on bank loans to reach market-clearing levels.

The Foreign Exchange and Foreign Trade Control Law, which remained in effect from 1949 until 1981, prohibited in principle virtually all international financial transactions, with exceptions granted on a case-by-case basis. Under this regime, Japanese private companies were disallowed from issuing foreign bonds of any kind, including eurobonds. Foreign companies were, until 1979, generally deemed ineligible to place yen bonds in Japan. Japanese financial institutions were restrained from including foreign securities in their asset portfolios. The foreign loans of Japanese banks with overseas branches were subject to limits. These restrictions and others insulated Japan's financial markets from foreign ones and protected Japanese banks from foreign competition.

First steps toward deregulation

The dismantlement of the government-managed Japanese banking cartel began in earnest with the enactment of the new Foreign Exchange and Foreign Trade Control Law in 1981, which in principle allowed all international financial transactions unless specifically prohibited. In fact, prohibitions and eligibility requirements on the issue of euroyen bonds and restrictions on Japanese participation in euroloan syndicates and eurobond underwriting syndicates remained in place until 1984, but were then phased out completely.

Once Japanese companies gained expanded access to euromarkets, continued suppression of domestic bond markets in Japan lost a lot of its value to Japanese banks. The Bond Council relaxed its eligibility rules for issuing domestic bonds and relaxed collateral requirements. By 1988, 180 companies had become eligible to issue domestic straight bonds with no collateral, and by 1993, 800 companies were eligible. Finally, in 1996 all corporations were permitted to issue bonds.

Commercial paper, the name for short-term, negotiable promissory notes issued without collateral by high grade-corporations, was first permitted in Japan November 1987, and eligibility requirements have been gradually relaxed since then.

In 1994 ceilings on deposit rates, having been gradually relaxed over the previous few years, were officially discontinued altogether.

BIS capital adequacy standards

Under the Basle accord of 1988, twelve nations including Japan agreed to impose common minimum capital standards on multinational banks. The BIS standards, which banks are now required to meet in order to participate fully in international markets, require that the book value of each bank's common equity plus a risk-weighted average (up to that same amount) of its preferred stock, subordinated debt, and unrealized capital gains on securities exceeds 8 percent of a risk-weighted average of the bank's assets. The BIS standards were phased in over two years, with international banks each required to attain a 7.5 percent risk-weighted capital ratio by January 1, 1991, and the full 8 percent ratio by January 1, 1993 (extended until April 1, 1993 for Japanese banks).

Financial System Reform Act

The 1992 Financial System Reform Act, which took effect on April 1, 1993, permitted banks, securities companies, and insurance companies, by merging with one another or by establishing subsidiaries, each to offer selected services previously reserved for the others.

■ Since April 1993, ordinary commercial banks in Japan have been permitted to offer money trusts and loan trusts through wholly owned subsidiaries, and most of the city banks have in fact established such subsidiaries for that purpose.

■ Since April 1993, banks in Japan have been permitted to offer securities brokerage services through wholly owned subsidiaries and most of the city banks have done so.

■ Since October 1996, life insurance companies have been allowed to sell property and casualty insurance policies and other insurance companies to sell life insurance, through subsidiaries.

The "Big Bang"

In November 1996 Prime Minister Hashimoto proposed the complete elimination of all regulatory partitions among financial intermediaries no later than 2001, dubbed Japan's version of the "big bang" that transformed the London financial markets in 1988.

■ Since 1997, securities companies have been allowed to offer "comprehensive accounts" which enable their customers to write checks.

■ From December 1998 banks in Japan are permitted to offer investment trust certificates (mutual funds) to their customers, through subsidiaries.

■ Until July 1998, premium rates on non-life insurance in Japan were set by insurance industry rating bureaus, which were actually government authorized cartels. Since then insurance companies have been allowed to choose premium rates independently (though they still must notify the MOF of the precise rates they are setting).

■ All regulatory barriers between ordinary banks, trust banks, and securities companies are slated for removal in 1999. After that time banks will be permitted to underwrite securities as well as offer brokerage services. Brokerage commissions are also slated for complete deregulation at that time.

■ Remaining regulatory barriers among insurance companies, banks, and securities companies are slated for removal in fiscal year 2000, completing the "Big Bang".

Appendix B Failed regional banks (August 1998) and their disposition

Date of execution	Failed bank (and assets, in ¥bn)	Disposition; acquiring bank or newly formed bank (and assets, in ¥bn)	Side-payment from DIC (¥bn)
4/92	Toho Sogo Bank (213.1)	Acquired by Iyo Bank (2,890.7)	2
10/92	Toyo Shinkin Bank (304.2)	Acquired by Sanwa Bank (35,349.7)	20
1/96	Hyogo Bank Ltd (3,400)	Taken over by newly formed and government-operated bridge bank Midori Bank, to be merged with Hanshin Bank Ltd in April 1999	approx. 550
9/96	Taiheiyo Bank	Recapitalized and renamed Wakashio Bank	117
10/97	Fukutoku Bank and Bank of Naniwa, Ltd	Two weak banks merged (after DIC purchase of bad loans) to form Nanihaya Bank	n.a.
10/97	Kyoto Kyoei Bank, Ltd	Acquired by Kofuku Bank, Ltd	n.a.
11/97	Hanwa Bank (438)	Liquidated	
11/97	Tokuyo City Bank	Liquidated	

FURTHER READING

■ Masahiko Aoki and Hugh Patrick (eds.), *The Japanese Main Bank System*, Oxford University Press, 1994. Economists describe and analyze the main bank system, from both historical and comparative perspectives.

■ Dick Beason and Jason James, *The Political Economy of Japanese Financial Markets: Myths Versus Reality*, New York: St Martin's Press, 1999. Description and analysis of the most recent developments in the regulation of the Japanese financial market.

■ Stephen Bronte, *Japanese Finance: Markets and Institutions*, Euromoney Publications, 1982. An excellent journalistic description of the various kinds of financial intermediaries and securities markets of Japan with many points of comparison to the United States.

■ Frances McCall Rosenbluth, *Financial Politics in Contemporary Japan*, Cornell University Press, 1989. A political scientist analyzes why Japan's government-administered bank cartel began to unravel in the face of the post-1974 Japanese government deficits.

■ Paul Sheard (ed.), *Japanese Firms, Finance and Markets*, Sydney: Addison-Wesley, 1996. Essays on Japanese corporate governance and corporate finance, written by economists.

■ Shinji Takagi (ed.), *Japanese Capital Markets*, Oxford: Basil Blackwell, 1993. Descriptive and analytic studies of Japanese securities markets.

■ Yoshio Suzuki (ed.), *The Japanese Financial System*, Oxford University Press, 1987. An English translation of the official Bank of Japan overview of Japanese financial markets and institutions.

Marketing | 14

Many have claimed that the marketing of products in Japan is hampered by anachronistic, outmoded, and backwards customs and institutions and by practices that enlarge or perpetuate monopolistic distortions. What are the facts?

Japan's marketing system does indeed exhibit a number of peculiarities. Japan has far more retail stores per person than do most other developed countries, more than twice as many stores per person as the United States. Furthermore, Japan, more than other countries, exhibits convoluted marketing channels. Products typically pass through the hands of two separate wholesalers before reaching retail shops or industrial customers, and often through more—occasionally a lot more. In the USA passage through the hands of a single wholesaler is more typical. Finally, manufacturers, wholesalers, and retailers in Japan very frequently enter complicated contractual arrangements with one another. Minimum resale prices, customer restrictions, exclusive dealing stipulations, and other such "vertical restraints" have frequently run afoul of anti-monopoly laws in Japan but nevertheless remain pervasive there. So is the conventional view correct? Is Japan's distribution sector hopelessly mired in waste and inefficiency? Careful analysis argues generally against it.

The ubiquity of retail stores in Japan reflects its geography, transport system, and the relative scarcity of living space. The proliferation of small stores affords Japanese households the added convenience of next-door shopping, which they particularly value because it enables them to make more frequent shopping trips, maintain low household inventories, and thus economize on scarce living space. At the same time, the geographic centricity of Japan and superabundance of commercial vehicles there imply that the added costs of restocking a multiplicity of small stores as opposed to a smaller number of large ones are less in Japan than they would be in many other nations. In short, the ubiquity of stores is an economic response to the peculiar local conditions of Japan. A retail structure in Japan resembling that of the USA, which is dominated by large "superstores", would waste resources, rather than economizing, as so many have claimed. The complex marketing channels that often include multiples of wholesale steps are corollaries of the ubiquity of stores; when final destinations are more numerous, the efficient logistical artery has more branches. All this is very logical—and we shall explore the logic in a bit more detail—but in pondering Japan's retail structure, government regulations also merit attention.

Regulations restricting the building of new stores having large floor space have long been a fixture of Japanese law, even predating the Pacific war. More recently, Japan's so-called Large Store Law was fingered by US trade negotiators as a "structural impediment" to the sale of US products in Japan. In 1998 this law was repealed, leaving the regulation of store sizes and locations entirely to the prefectural governments. But evidence and reason indicate that the Large Store Law more reflected the structure of Japan's distribution sector than shaped it. Given that small stores are ubiquitous in Japan anyway, for the reasons mentioned above, regulations that protect small stores from competition by large stores imply only small economic distortions and encounter little effective resistance. If small stores had not predominated already, the Large Store Law could not have survived in Japan's political marketplace.

Economics also has a lot to say about the rationale for vertical restraints, and most of it is unsupportive of the conventional view that the ubiquity of these practices in Japan indicates the presence of monopolistic distortions there. Firms bound to one another by vertical restraints—in Japan referred to as "distribution keiretsu"—may run afoul of antimonopoly law, but in fact they are seldom seeking to exploit or perpetuate market power. More usual motivations for customer restrictions, price stipulations, exclusive dealing, and the like are to improve the incentives of firms to promote products, inform customers about products, or maintain the quality of products. The pervasiveness of vertical restraints in Japan may be a sign that marketing there is relatively unconstrained by inappropriate laws and regulations—and to that extent is more economically efficient than elsewhere, not less so.

Structure of Japan's distribution sector

The starting point in understanding the many apparent peculiarities of Japan's marketing system is the myriad of small retail stores there. Anyone who walks along an urban street in Japan for the first time is likely to be struck by the numerousness, smallness, and remarkable degree of specialization of retail shops. Here is a shop, which is little more than a stall, selling mainly shampoo, soap, and other toiletries. Here is another right next to it, the same small size, selling only vegetables. And here is yet another, selling electric appliances of the season—space heaters and the like in winter and electric fans in summer.

In most cities of the United States, zoning laws separate residential and commercial establishments. In Japan, on the contrary, residential dwellings and commercial establishments are interspersed. Many residents of Japan, perhaps even most, are able to purchase daily necessities by shopping on foot in their own neighborhoods. It is as difficult to imagine daily life in Japan without small and familiar retail

stores, where the proprietors are also neighbors, as it is to imagine daily life in the USA without trips to the nearest chain supermarket in the family car. Perhaps this is why cultural explanations for Japan's ubiquity of small stores are so often offered: "The Japanese people have a decided preference for fresh produce, which necessitates daily shopping trips"; "The Japanese people prefer dealing with friends rather than strangers"; and so on, as if other people in the world did not also enjoy fresh produce or congeniality. A more analytic approach is productive here. We begin by describing numbers that bear out the casual impression: Japan does have particularly many retail stores relative to its population.

Density of retail stores in Japan compared with other nations

Table 14.1 details the numbers of stores per thousand persons in Japan and selected other nations, based on censuses of business conducted by the nations' respective governments. The figures for the 1980s exclude eating and drinking establishments, to focus narrowly on "stores". (It is unclear from the source document whether the 1990 figures exclude restaurants and bars.)

Japan has about twice as many stores per person as

Table 14.1. Numbers of stores per thousand persons in Japan and selected other nations

Country	Retail stores per 1,000 persons	
	around 1985[a]	1990
JAPAN	14.3 (1982)	13.2
USA	6.1 (1987)	7.9
UK	6.2 (1982)	8.1
France	10.3 (1982)	9.7
Germany	6.6 (1984–5)	8.5
Greece	16.2 (1978)	18.4

a Excluding eating and drinking establishments.

Sources: 1985 figures: David Flath and Tatsuhiko Nariu, "Is Japan's Retail Sector Truly Distinctive?" *Journal of Comparative Economics*, vol. 23 (1996), pp. 181–91 (primary source: Censuses of commerce of the respective nations); 1990 figures: Dirk Pilat, "Regulation and Performance of the Distribution Sector", *OECD Working Papers*, vol. 5 (1997), table 2.3, p. 19.

does the USA, the UK, or Germany. In this respect, Japan, and not the USA, may be unusual. But notice that Greece seems to have even more stores per thousand persons than does Japan. Japan's fragmented retail sector may be peculiar, but is not unique.

The relative ubiquity of stores in Japan is not limited to stores of a particular type. It is characteristic both of stores selling daily necessities like food and toiletries, and of stores selling durable goods like furniture or apparel. The relative ubiquity of retail stores in Japan is pervasive with one glaring exception: department stores. Though Japan has more than four times as many food stores per thousand persons as does the United States, it has only one-fifth as many department stores. This may come as a surprise to anyone who has patronized and admired the upscale, opulent, and seemingly omnipresent Japanese department stores in Osaka, Tokyo, or other major cities of Japan. But "department stores" also include the low-end discount stores (any large stores selling a wide array of merchandise are classified as department stores), and these are far less numerous in Japan than in the USA. The reason is regulation.

The Large Store Law

A succession of Japanese laws over the last half-century have imposed bureaucratic obstacles to the establishment of large stores. The Department Store Act of 1937, which was suspended in 1947 and then reinstated in 1956, required approval of the national government (Ministry of Commerce and Industry, prewar/Ministry of International Trade and Industry, postwar) for the opening of a new department store anywhere in Japan. In 1973 the Large Scale Retail Store Law replaced the Department Store Act and made the extent of floor space of proposed stores, rather than the nature of the stores, the criterion for necessitating MITI approval. The cutoffs were $3,000m^2$ in the largest cities and $1,500m^2$ everywhere else; in fact, almost all stores having larger floor space than these had been department stores. In 1978 this law was completely revamped so as to broaden its coverage to include all proposed new stores with floor space above $500m^2$. In May 1998, the Diet replaced the old law with a new one that places all details of the regulation of large stores

under the control of the prefectural governments. Some prefectures may enact more severe restraints on the opening of large stores, and others may remove the restraints altogether.

Prior to 1998, the process of securing MITI approval to open a large store was torturous and, if successful, typically required two years or more to obtain. The process involved hearings before local panels that included owners of existing stores whose businesses would suffer if the particular proposed large store was established. These panels tended either to recommend against MITI approval or else propose restrictions on the hours or days of the week that a new large store could operate. In many cases they proposed onerous requirements, such as the requirement that the large store offer classes in cultural activities such as calligraphy or floral arrangement, at prices that would fail to cover costs. MITI tended to adopt these recommendations and proposals. Consequently, following the adoption of the 1978 amendments to the Large Store Act, the number of applications to open new stores with floor space in excess of $500m^2$ dropped in 1984 to less than 500 applications in all of Japan, a nation of 120 million persons.[1]

In 1989, the US government identified the Large Store Law as a "structural impediment" to the sale of US-made consumer products in Japan, and argued in trade negotiations with the government of Japan for a repeal or relaxation of the law. Whatever the merits of the claim that expansion of the number of large stores in Japan would expand commercial opportunities for US businesses, the government of Japan did agree to expedite the process of approving the opening of large stores. But the law remained in force, and the actual numbers of large stores showed little signs of increase. It is too early to know whether the shift from national government control to prefectural government control of the regulation of large stores, enacted in 1998, will matter. At least for now, the Large Store Law remains the essential reason why Japan has far fewer department stores per person than the USA when at the same time it

---

[1] McCraw and O'Brien offer this fact as evidence of the profound effects of the Large Store Law: Thomas K. McCraw and Patricia A. O'Brien, "Production and Distribution: Competition Policy and Industrial Structure", in Thomas K. McCraw (ed.), *American Versus Japan: A Comparative Study*, Boston: Harvard Business School Press, 1986, ch. 3, pp. 77–116.

has far more of most other kinds of stores per person.

We will shortly examine the political economy of the Large Store Law, but first we need to understand the basic economics of retail structure and how it applies to Japan.

Economics of retail density

Those who leap to the unwarranted conclusion that a marketing system like Japan's with a ubiquity of stores must be burdened with unnecessary costs—the added costs of maintaining and restocking a multiplicity of small stores as opposed to a few large ones—perhaps overlook the benefits of a proliferation of stores. These benefits reside in the economies on household transport and storage of goods that result from shortening the distance between the representative household and nearest store.

For nondurable daily necessities like groceries and toiletries, lowering the costs of shopping trips induces households to shop more frequently and buy smaller quantities of the goods each time, so they can maintain smaller household inventories and economize on storage space. This describes the basic logic of the *economic order quantity model*, first developed by William Baumol. The model is relatively simple and, because of its wide applicability in economics, is worth learning independently of its application to the present issue. (For example, Baumol applied it to the demand for money.)

Economic order quantity model

Let us presume that a household consumes some good at a continuous rate of q units per week, shopping when its holdings are just exhausted. The household's maximal inventory equals the amount it obtains each time m, and it makes q/m shopping trips per week. Let the household's reorder costs be r per shopping trip, and let its storage costs be k per maximal inventory. Then the household's combined storage and reorder costs are

$$r(q/m) + km.$$

Now the household chooses its reorder quantity m, and by implication its frequency of shopping q/m, so as to minimize its combined storage and reorder costs. That is, it chooses m so that the derivative with respect to m of combined storage and reorder

costs equals zero. This leads immediately to the so-called square root rule:

$$m^* = (qr/k)^{1/2}.$$

The optimal reorder quantity is proportionate to the square root of the costs of a single shopping trip and is inversely proportionate to the square root of storage cost per unit of inventory. As storage costs k rise or the costs of a shopping trip r fall, the household reduces the quantity m it obtains on each shopping trip, shopping more frequently and reducing its maximal inventory.

The economic order quantity model is depicted diagrammatically in Figures 14.1(*a*) and 14.1(*b*). This model reveals why Japanese households shop more frequently than American households do. Because retail stores are so numerous in Japan, the cost of a single shopping trip is less. And because Japanese households tend to live in small dwellings, household storage space commands a premium, and so a greater frequency of shopping trips is necessary. Furthermore, the economic order quantity model reveals that where household storage costs are high, as in Japan, households derive a greater benefit from a proliferation of stores and are willing to pay a bit more for the added convenience of next-door shopping than if their storage costs were lower.

The above paragraph gives us one reason for

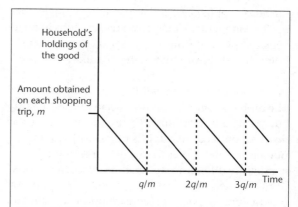

Figure 14.1(*a*). Economic order quantity model

The household consumes continually at the rate of q units per week, shopping only when its holdings are just exhausted. Maximum holdings exactly equal the amount obtained on each shopping trip. More frequent shopping trips mean that less is obtained on each shopping trip.

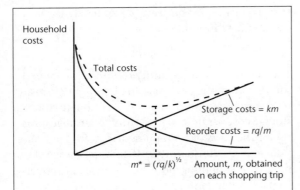

Figure 14.1(b). Economic order quantity model, continued

Household reorder costs are proportionate to the frequency of shopping trips, which becomes less and less as the amount obtained on each trip is allowed to rise. Household storage costs are proportionate to maximal holdings, which grow *pari passu* with the amount obtained on each shopping trip. The optimal reorder quantity balances the marginal increase in shopping costs and the marginal reduction in storage costs. If the costs of a single shopping trip become less, the optimal reorder quantity also becomes less—the household shops more frequently, thereby economizing on storage costs.

Japan's ubiquity of stores, but it is not the only reason. For instance, Japan has not only more stores per person selling daily necessities like groceries, but also relatively more stores selling durables like furniture, appliances, and apparel. Why might that be? To complete the picture we need to look at retail density not only from the point of view of households, but also from that of the distribution sector.

Why are there so many retail stores in Japan?

The proliferation of retail stores benefits households but at the same time raises the logistical costs of the distribution sector itself. It is more costly to restock numerous small stores than a few large ones. To put it a slightly different way, as stores proliferate, some of the burden of transporting goods from point of production to point of consumption are shifted away from households and on to the distribution sector. Just how far such shifting will go, that is just how dense retail outlets will become, depends upon the households' and distribution sector's relative efficiencies at storing and transporting goods. This is because new stores can be profitable only if the

added benefits that their presence confers are greater than their costs. As already mentioned, factors like scarcity of living space that raise all households' costs of storing goods lead households to offer higher price premia to retailers who locate closer to their dwellings, which makes a greater profusion of stores profitable. Similarly, factors that lower retailers' costs render it more profitable for them to accommodate households' preferences for shorter shopping trips and increase the profitability of a profusion of stores.

The vast majority of Japan's population resides in the coastal plains of Kanto, Chubu, and Kansai that encompass Tokyo, Nagoya, and Osaka, respectively. Accordingly, the geographic distance between point of production and point of final consumption is typically much less in Japan than in most other developed nations. For this reason, the costs of restocking a multiplicity of retail stores are less in geographically compact Japan than in the vast United States or the expanses of western Europe. Over the decades, Japan has developed a system of roads and rail lines that further lower the costs of maintaining its proliferation of stores. By the 1980s Japan had more commercial vehicles per person than any other nation besides the United States.

Other factors influence retail density in the same basic way as does scarcity of living space and efficiency of distribution sector logistics. For example, if owning and operating a personal vehicle is more expensive, then households will place more value on the convenience of nearby shopping, and proliferation of stores will become more profitable and more likely. Also, population density itself affects the relative profitability of retailer proliferation, independently of any effects it may have on the scarcity value of household (or retailer!) storage space. For if population density is great, any given number of retail stores per person corresponds to a shorter average distance between each household and the nearest store, and the marginal reductions in that average distance caused by the entry of a new store is also correspondingly less. In regions of greater population density, therefore, the benefits to households of store proliferation are smaller and proliferation of stores becomes less profitable and less likely. Japan is more densely inhabited than America or the nations of Western Europe, and on this ground we might expect it to have fewer stores per person rather than more. Sorting out the various influences on Japan's density of retail stores, including the Large Store Law, scarcity of household storage space, geographic centrism, costs of maintaining personal vehicles, and population density, requires careful statistical investigation. Up to now there have been only a few such studies, but their findings support the tentative conclusion that regulation matters less than the other factors just mentioned.

A couple of studies have explored the prefecture-by-prefecture variation within Japan itself in numbers of stores of different kinds. Here population density matters a great deal and in the way we would expect, with Tokyo, the most densely inhabited prefecture, having the least number of stores per person. A similar pattern is evident within the United States, with New York City exhibiting fewer stores per person than most any other city. The author[2] and Jeroen Potjes[3] report statistical regressions in which not only population density, but also household floor space per person and extent of ownership of personal vehicles, significantly influence the number of stores per person in each prefecture. I also included as an explanatory variable the number of department stores per person in each prefecture. If department stores are relatively less numerous, then the Large Store Law may be presumed to impose more severe constraints on the opening of large stores (almost all of which in Japan are "department stores"). Based on this investigation, prefectures with fewer department stores seem also to have rather more of other stores of various types, including food, liquor, and apparel, all of which are items that Japanese department stores sell in great quantities.

However, the sensitivity of numbers of other stores to prefectural differences in numbers of department stores is far smaller than would need to be the case if Japan's Large Store Law were the main reason for its ubiquity of stores compared with other nations. For instance, the regression equation predicts that, if Japan's number of department stores were to quintuple, its number of food stores would fall by one-fourth. But then Japan would still have more than twice as many food stores as the USA. An international study of retail density bears out the point.

In a recent paper by the author and Nariu Tatsuhiko,[4] numbers of retail stores per person in each of seventeen nations including Japan and the USA are statistically related to each nation's population density, household floor space per person, the "length" of the country (defined as the square root of its land area), cars per person, and trucks per person—all of which in some way reflect factors that bear on the economic advantages of a retail system that exhibits a ubiquity of stores. And all these factors significantly influence retail density across the nations in the way we would expect. Nor is this all. Japan is not a regression outlier. Rather, its relative ubiquity of stores is correctly predicted on the basis of its small length, relative paucity of household floor space, and superabundance of trucks, controlling for population density, all as suggested at various points in the preceding discussion.

In light of all this, we return attention to Japan's Large Store Law.

Political economy of the Large Store Law

The Large Store Law of Japan and its antecedents have protected small stores there from competition with larger ones. Government regulations in the USA have tended to favor large stores. Local zoning in almost every city in the United States has had the effect of separating residential and commercial activities, which promotes car ownership and favors large stores over smaller ones. Many scholars and others have correctly deplored Japan's Large Store Law as imposing unnecessary constraints on the marketing of goods in Japan, but they may have both exaggerated the extent to which Japan's marketing system reflects the heavy hand of government regulation, and overlooked the extent to which the US marketing system and those of other nations are also influenced by government regulations.

Government policies that transfer income encounter less strenuous political opposition if the deadweight losses they impose are small in relation

2 David Flath, "Why Are There So Many Retail Stores in Japan?" *Japan and the World Economy*, vol. 2 (1991), pp. 365–86.
3 Jeroen C. A. Potjes (1993), *Empirical Studies in Japanese Retailing*, Tinbergen Institute Research Series no. 41, Amsterdam: Thesis Publishers.
4 David Flath and Tatsuhiko Nariu, "Is Japan's Retail Sector Truly Distinctive?" *Journal of Comparative Economics*, vol. 23 (1996), pp. 181–91.

to the net subsidy.[5] Given that small stores are ubiquitous in Japan anyway for the reasons mentioned in the previous section, regulations that protect small stores from competition by large stores imply only small economic distortions and encounter little effective resistance. If small stores had not been predominant already, the Large Store Law could not have survived in Japan's political marketplace. Geographic factors in the USA have favored large chain stores, and slanted the political marketplace in favor of regulations that benefit them instead. Government limitations on large stores can survive the give-and-take of political competition in Japan but not in the United States. For local zoning that favors large stores over small ones, the reverse is true. In each case, regulation ends up exaggerating the inherent tendencies rather than fundamentally influencing them.

Given that Japan's ubiquity of stores fundamentally reflects the country's geography, other aspects of Japan's marketing system also appear logical. In particular, Japan's convoluted marketing channels, which exhibit multiple wholesale steps, are corollaries of its multiplicity of retail stores.

The complexity of wholesale marketing channels in Japan

Wholesalers are middlemen who purchase only to resell, and whose customers are often not final demanders but instead retailers or other wholesalers. Any sensible analysis of wholesaling needs to begin by recognizing that middlemen of all sorts lower the costs of trading rather than adding to them; otherwise they could not charge prices that their customers willingly pay and that cover their own costs. The costs of middlemen are transactions costs by definition; they are costs of activities that are either essential to trade or that facilitate trade. These include the costs of assuring ownership rights, detecting the quality of traded goods, discovering valuable trading opportunities, negotiating mutually agreeable terms, and so on. Those who can perform these services at costs that are lower than the middleman's price spread do so; many cannot. Competition among middlemen forces their price spread (difference between bid price and asking price) to the lowest level that just covers their own costs. In all these respects, wholesaling in Japan

surely resembles wholesaling in other nations; but there is one thing about wholesaling in Japan that stands out.

The peculiar thing about wholesaling in Japan is the often large number of separate wholesalers through whose hands goods pass before reaching their ultimate destinations on the shelves of retail stores. One indication of this fact is the large percentage of merchant wholesalers' sales that are to other wholesalers: 41.9 percent for Japan versus 24.8 percent for the United States and 16.2 percent for West Germany (all in 1985–6).[6] A more precise indication of the numbers of wholesale steps in Japan can be constructed from data on the gross markup of retailers' prices over manufacturers' prices and from the average price spreads of all wholesalers. Dividing the total price markup in a wholesale chain by the average price spread of all wholesalers gives an estimate of the number of wholesalers in the chain. The average total price markup in wholesale chains is in fact less in Japan than in the United States: 24 percent of manufacturers' price in Japan versus 35 percent in the USA (again based on 1985 data).[7] But the average price markup of each wholesaler is also less in Japan than in the USA, so we infer that on average Japanese marketing channels have a greater number of wholesale steps, 1.8 in Japan versus 1.4 in the USA.[8] If we round these to the nearest integers, we could say that the typical or average marketing channel in Japan includes two wholesalers in sequence while that in the United States includes only one. The commonly held view that wholesale marketing channels are longer or have more steps in Japan than in the USA is thus supported. What are the reasons for this peculiarity?

Japan's multiplicity of wholesale steps reflects its proliferation of retail outlets. Retail businesses like

5 So argues Gary Becker, "A Theory of Competition among Pressure Groups for Political Influence", *Quarterly Journal of Economics*, vol. 98, no. 3 (August 1983), pp. 371–400.

6 Takatoshi Ito and M. Maruyama, "Is the Japanese Distribution System Really Inefficient?" in Paul Krugman (ed.), *Trade With Japan: Has the Door Opened Wider?* University of Chicago Press/ NBER, 1991, pp. 149–74.

7 Ibid.

8 See table 6–1, p. 86, in Tatsuhiko Nariu and David Flath, "The Complexity of Wholesale Distribution Channels in Japan", in M. Kotabe and M. Czinkota (eds.), *The Japanese Distribution System*, Probus, 1991, pp. 83–98.

food, liquor, and toiletries that have vastly more outlets per person in Japan than in the USA also tend to have more wholesale steps in Japan.[9] In thinking about the reasons for this, reflect for a moment on the human circulatory system. The arteries that have many branches before reaching the finest capillaries are far more efficient at delivering oxygen to the body's numerous small cells than would be a system of arteries with few branches leading more directly from heart to each cell. In the same fashion, the simple logistics of transporting goods to multiple destinations dictates the shipment of goods to intermediate collection points in order to exploit the cost savings that arise from consolidating shipments. The post office exploits the same principle in delivering mail. And although, as the post office example indicates, there is no necessity that titular ownership changes hands at the point where goods are delivered to logistical collection points, it is quite natural that goods often do pass from one wholesaler to another at precisely such a point.

One further fact about wholesale marketing channels in Japan is worth iterating. Marketing channels that have particularly many wholesale steps in Japan are likely also to have relatively many wholesale steps in the United States.[10] For instance, fresh fish, meat, and vegetables all have more wholesale steps than most other kinds of business in both nations. Shoes and apparel have relatively few wholesale steps in both countries. Common forces appear to be operative in the economies of both Japan and America. Marketing channels in Japan and elsewhere reflect the calculated attempts of profit-seeking entrepreneurs to economize on transport costs, to avert spoilage, and to collect and act on information about the local demands for goods. The same is true of other aspects of Japanese marketing channels, including that which we next address, the contractual arrangements among channel members.

Vertical restraints

Manufacturers, wholesalers, and retailers linked to one another by contracts stipulating maximum or minimum resale prices, exclusive dealing, customer assignments, and so on are referred to in Japan as *distribution keiretsu*. Typical examples include the well-known manufacturers of home electronics

(Matsushita, Toshiba), cameras (Nikon), cosmetics (Shiseido), and the members of their respective marketing channels. In Japan, as in the United States, antitrust laws proscribe contractual stipulations of the sort just mentioned, which in antitrust law are referred to generically as "vertical restraints". For instance, Japanese anti-monopoly laws explicitly proscribe "unjust" customer restrictions and exclusive dealing stipulations. But there are significant exemptions from Japan's anti-monopoly laws. For instance, in Japan contracts stipulating minimum resale prices for copyrighted works are legal, while in the United States such contracts have been illegal since 1976. And in any case, the penalties for violating anti-monopoly laws in Japan are largely inconsequential, and the resources devoted to investigating and prosecuting anti-monopoly cases are also small. All this has contributed to the view that vertical restraints remain prevalent in Japan.

We learn of the details of vertical restraints in Japan in the same way as we do for the United States, in the annals of antitrust cases. Economists have devised convincing explanations for many of the US antitrust cases involving vertical restraints, and often these same explanations also fit Japanese cases that exhibit similar patterns. Here, an economic explanation is a logical argument that identifies the basis of profitability of the offending practice and that also accounts for other facts of a particular case, including ones that at first may have seemed unrelated to the practice in question. In other words, the goal is to understand the rationale for practices like vertical restraints, and only secondarily to judge the merits or demerits of laws that proscribe these practices. That said, many of the convincing explanations of specific instances of vertical restraints suggest that, rather than creating and perpetuating contrived scarcities, vertical restraints more often reflect attempts by manufacturers and wholesalers to align the interests of other members of the marketing channel with their own interest, and thereby lower the costs of informing customers about products or the costs of maintaining the

---

9 Ibid. table 6–3, p. 94.
10 Ibid. Estimates of average numbers of wholesale steps in Japan (and in the USA) are fresh fish, 2.56 (2.27); meat and poultry, 1.68 (1.67); vegetables and fruit, 1.86 (1.73); men's apparel, 1.22 (1.12); shoes, 1.14 (1.31).

quality of products. To make this point, we shall take up several Japanese examples of vertical restraints drawn from anti-monopoly cases there. But first we need to lay out some fundamental considerations common to all sorts of arrangements between manufacturers and the distributors of their products.

Monopolistic manufacturer and independent distributors

The large manufacturers of consumer goods very typically offer unique products that command a loyal following of customers. Such manufacturers face downward-sloping demand curves; they can continue to make sales even if they raise prices. In this somewhat narrow sense, they are monopolists. They can be expected to set prices to customers that exceed their own marginal cost. And for this reason, activities such as advertising and quality assurance that push out the demand at each price add to the manufacturer's own profits.

If a monopolistic manufacturer distributes its own products itself, then it can adjust prices, promotional activities, the density of retail outlets, and so on to maximize its own profits. But more commonly, manufacturers prefer not to distribute their own products themselves but instead sell to independent wholesalers or retailers. These independent distributors in turn become responsible for many of the activities affecting the final demand for the products and the quantities ultimately sold. In this situation, the independent distributors in maximizing their own profits will not necessarily make choices that maximize the manufacturer's profit. The simplest illustration of this involves choosing the price.

Suppose that a manufacturer with constant unit costs of producing faces a downward-sloping linear final demand. To keep matters simple, suppose that the manufacturer sells to an independent retail industry whose costs consist solely of its payments to the manufacturer. The manufacturer attains maximum profit only if retail profit is zero, which it will be if competition among retailers forces the price they set all the way down to the same level as the price the manufacturer charges them. But any attenuation of competition among retailers drives a wedge between the manufacturer's price and the retail price that inevitably diminishes the manu-

facturer's profit by more than the amount by which it enlarges the retailers' profits. For instance, in the extreme case in which the retail industry itself is a monopoly (a perfect cartel for example), it sets a price to final demanders such that it sells exactly half the quantity that would be demanded of it if it were to set the same price as it pays the manufacturer. Recognizing this fact, the manufacturer sets a price that leaves it with profits only half as great as it could realize if it were vertically integrated, and the independent retail monopoly ends up with profits one-fourth as great as this. Figure 14.2 illustrates the geometric logic of these statements.

The conclusion to draw is more general than the geometric example: a monopolistic manufacturer selling to an independent monopoly distributor will impose constraints on the distributor's pricing or purchases that eliminate or counteract any price wedge and preserve the manufacturer's profit. Examples of such manufacturer-imposed constraints include a resale price ceiling, minimum purchase quantity (sometimes referred to as a sales quota), and imposition of a flat fee followed by marginal cost pricing.

A Japanese example of a manufacturer imposing a maximum resale price to prevent a downstream price wedge from eroding its profit appears in the anti-monopoly case involving Takeya miso.[11] (Miso is soybean paste used in Japanese cuisine.) Takeya's

---

[11] The legal citation to the case is as follows: KK Takeya, 25 *Shinketsushu* 32 [FTC (recommendation) no. 10, 1978], Feb. 13, 1979. This refers to the Fair Trade Commission of Japan's published decision (a few paragraphs setting out the basic facts and findings in the case), the tenth decision of 1978, published in vol. 25, p. 32, of *Shinketsushu* (lit. "compilation of decisions"). The decision in this case was a "recommendation" decision (*kankoku shinketsu*), which means that the FTC investigated and found a violation of anti-monopoly law and the respondent agreed to take remedial action without recourse to a formal hearing. Other types of decisions include "consent" decisions (*doi shinketsu*), in which the FTC has held a formal hearing and found a violation, and the respondent agreed to take remedial action and not appeal through the courts; and "formal" decision (*seishiki shinketsu*), in which the FTC has held a formal hearing and has found either that no violation occurred or else that it did and has issued an order to desist which the respondent may appeal through the courts. Besides the published decision, the Takeya miso case is also discussed in a slightly more expansive manner in an article authored by a staffer of the FTC, in *Kosei torihiki*, the monthly publication of the Fair Trade Commission of Japan: M. Izumisawa, "KK Takeya no kosoku joken tsuki torihiki ni kan suru dokkin ho no mondai ten" (Anti-monopoly law issues pertaining to Takeya Co.'s attachment of restrictive conditions to its transactions), *Kosei torihiki*, no. 342 (1979), pp. 54–7.

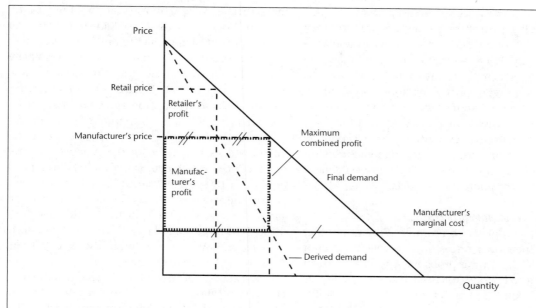

Figure 14.2. Successive monopolies

A monopolistic manufacturer with constant unit costs and facing linear final demand sells to an independent retail monopoly whose costs consist solely of payments to the manufacturer. The wedge between the manufacturer's price and the retail price confers only half as much profit on the retailer as it takes away from the manufacturer. (Geometrically, rectangles of maximum area inscribed in right triangles form identical residual triangles. Consequently, the retail-profit rectangle has sides half as great as the corresponding sides of the maximum-combined-profit rectangle, and thus has area one-fourth as great. The manufacturer-profit rectangle has half the area of the maximum-combined-profit rectangle.)

miso "monopoly" (its national market share was never higher than about 4 percent but its nearest rival's market share was only 2 percent) was based on its distinctive flavor and reputation for quality supported by television advertising. The distribution channel for Takeya miso encountered a bottleneck at the wholesale level, with only five primary wholesalers in the Kanto area. To prevent these wholesalers from exploiting Takeya's monopoly, Takeya imposed maximum resale prices on the wholesalers and devoted extensive effort to enforcing the stipulation, including resort to an elaborate system of record-keeping, circuitous methods of payment, and detailed assignments of retailers to specific wholesalers, and of secondary wholesalers to specific primary wholesalers. The FTC found Takeya's price ceiling to violate anti-monopoly laws and ordered it to withdraw the stipulation. Takeya complied, and in the months following the decision in the case Takeya's production fell about 4 percent

while that of the nine other largest Miso producers either rose slightly or remained the same. That is, Takeya produced more output when it was imposing price ceilings on wholesalers than when it was not imposing price ceilings, just as we would expect. The basic logic of a monopolistic manufacturer's arrangements with independent distributors, clearly evident in the Takeya case, forms an essential starting point in understanding more complicated cases, including those involving manufacturer-imposed price floors.

Resale price maintenance

Resale price maintenance (RPM) refers to retailers' agreement with a manufacturer (or wholesaler) not to resell the products of a manufacturer at prices below some stipulated level—a manufacturer-imposed price floor. Such a price floor would on first thought seem counter to the manufacturer's own self-interest. If distributors set higher prices then they face a smaller quantity demanded and, in turn, they themselves buy smaller quantities from the manufacturer, which erodes rather than enlarges the manufacturer's profits. And in fact, the impetus for minimum retail price stipulations occasionally comes not from a manufacturer, but from retailers.[12] But such instances are rare indeed. More commonly, resale price maintenance is either part of a collusive conspiracy among two or more manufacturers (or wholesalers), or else is intended to improve retailers' incentives to promote the products.

RPM as a device for cartelization

Competing suppliers who collude with one another to raise their own prices and enlarge their joint profit face a cheating problem. Any one of them attains greater profits for itself if it secretly lowers price and expands sales; but this reduces the profits of the other conspirators by more than it adds to the profits of the chiseller. Sophisticated colluders will therefore establish mechanisms for preventing one another from secretly lowering prices, so that price discounting induces swift retaliation and is effectively discouraged. Resale price maintenance has occasionally served as such a mechanism. Retail prices are easier to monitor than wholesale prices or manufacturer prices. Collusive schemes that assign each retailer to only one supplier and stipulate minimum retail prices are likely to succeed because secret price discounts to retailers become ineffective at expanding sales when retailers are prevented either from lowering their prices or from substituting products of one supplier for that of others. (They each handle the products of only one supplier.)

Resale price maintenance has been a central component in only a few collusive schemes exposed over the years by Japan's Fair Trade Commission. These include attempts at cartelization by the Tokyo wholesalers of the products of the leading producer of stationery, by the Tokyo suppliers and wholesalers of automotive replacement glass, and by the producers of infant powdered milk. In each of these cases, competing suppliers acted in concert to stipulate minimum retail prices and assigned each retailer to a single supplier.

In the case involving stationery,[13] in September 1964 the fourteen Tokyo wholesalers of Kokuyo KK, the leading producer of stationery with a 17 percent market share, formed an association known as the Kokuyo Association (Kokuyo Kai) and agreed to assignments of each retailer to only one wholesaler and to a schedule of retail prices and wholesale prices. In October 1966 the FTC found these arrangements to violate Japan's anti-monopoly law and the Kokuyo Association agreed to desist from the offending practices. One curious feature of this case is that it represents an attempt to cartelize the Tokyo wholesale market for the products of only one producer, which demonstrates that a firm need not hold a 100 percent market share to be a monopoly in the economic sense. Also note that, had the cartel of wholesalers succeeded, it would have diminished the profits of Kokuyo, the original producer. Perhaps the swift response of the FTC reflects Kokuyo's influence in the case.

In the auto glass case,[14] the ten secondary manufacturers of glass for automotive repairs acted in concert in 1965 to establish minimum prices at the fifty-eight Tokyo retail outlets for such glass, and made elaborate customer assignments which involved primary and secondary wholesalers as well as the retailers. This cartel, if successful, would have been harmful to the interests of the three primary manufacturers of automotive glass in Japan who were the suppliers of raw materials to the secondary manufacturers. Just as in the Kokuyo Kai case, the FTC acted quickly to nip the cartel in the bud.

The powdered milk cases[15] are the only cases

---

12 For instance, in California in the 1930s an association of retail druggists coerced toothpaste suppliers into enforcing retail price stipulations. Pepsident resisted and was confronted with a boycott by the association. The courts found the boycott to be illegal.

13 Tokyo Kokuyo Kai, 14 *Shinketsushu* 46 [FTC (recommendation) no. 14, 1966], Oct. 27, 1966.

14 KK Ishizuka tokushu gurasu seisakujo hoka shuri jidosha gurasu seizo mata wa hanbai gyosha 15-mei oyobi Tokyo-to jidosha gurasu bukai ni tai suru ken (Case against Tokyo Auto Glass Association, Ishizuka KK Specialty Glass Works, and [9] other makers of glass for automotive repairs and [6] wholesalers), 14 *Shinketsushu* 79 [FTC (recommendation) no. 7, 1972], June 30, 1972.

15 There were two series of related cases involving essentially all the leading producers of infant powdered milk. The first series involved the sales subsidiaries of Morinaga, Meiji, and Sankyo and resulted in formal decisions against all of the companies which were upheld on appeal (by two of the three) to the Tokyo High Court and the Supreme Court of Japan: Meiji Shoji KK 15 *Shinketsushu* 67 [FTC (decision) no. 1 1966], Oct. 11, 1968, affirmed on second appeal (*jokoku*), 29 *Minshu* 951 (Sup. Ct. 2d P.B., July 11, 1975); and Wakodo KK, 15 *Shiketsushu* 84 [FTC (decision) No. 3, 1966], Oct. 11, 1968, affirmed on second appeal

involving RPM ever to be appealed to the Supreme Court of Japan, and are generally regarded as establishing the *per se* illegality of RPM except where explicitly exempted from Japan's anti-monopoly laws. We should hasten to add that the exemptions are significant (they include all copyrighted works); and, because penalties for violating anti-monopoly laws in Japan are so small, the laws seem to be widely flouted anyway.

The facts of the powdered milk cases are as follows. Beginning in 1963 and 1964, essentially all the leading producers of infant formula acted in concert to stipulate retail prices, assign each wholesaler to only one producer, and assign retailers to wholesalers. The producers closely monitored these arrangements and each instituted elaborate systems of rebates to wholesalers contingent on their complying with the various stipulations. The producers instigated these arrangements by acting through their sales subsidiaries, and, when this was found to violate anti-monopoly law, acted directly to perpetuate the same practices, which were again found to violate anti-monopoly law. At about the same time these practices occurred, the top executives of the same producers of infant formula conspired to form a monopsony in the purchase of raw milk, which was also found to violate anti-monopoly law.[16] One curious item pertinent to this case is the much more recent unraveling of a price-fixing conspiracy involving some US producers of infant powdered milk.[17] Coincidence? Or is there some generic property of the market for infant powdered milk that induces attempts at cartelization? For reasons of protecting public health, the governments of Japan, the United States, and other nations restrict entry in the production of infant formula. Whatever the merits of these policies, and they may be considerable, the government restrictions enlarge the reward to successful cartelization by assuring that profits will not quickly be competed away by new entrants. For this reason, the infant powdered milk industries of Japan and the United States were both more likely than other industries in the two nations to nurture price-fixing conspiracies.

Cases in which RPM occupies a central place in a cartel scheme are few in number in both Japan and elsewhere. Interesting as these cases may be, they are exceptional. There are many more instances of record in which manufacturers have stipulated minimum resale prices not as part of collusive conspiracies in concert with rivals, but individually, in attempts to encourage retailer efforts at promoting their own products. These too have run afoul of antitrust laws, and not only in the USA but in Japan as well.

RPM and retailers' incentives to provide special services

The fundamental logic of retailer provision of presale demonstrations, "special services", was first articulated in a famous article by the economist Lester Telser.[18] Telser argued that manufacturers will often desire that presale demonstrations be given because some customers who would otherwise not buy the product at all will do so if they are given a presale demonstration of the product. But retailers cannot recover the costs of the demonstrations if they must compete in price with free-riding rivals who avoid giving demonstrations themselves but attract customers who have seen the demonstrations elsewhere. In this instance retailers will eventually stop providing the demonstrations. If however the manufacturer maintains a minimum retail price sufficiently above the wholesale price to compensate retailers for the costs of providing demonstrations, then retailers find that they can attract customers and be profitable only if they provide the demonstrations. (Customers will buy from the retailer who provided them with the presale demonstration if his price is not greater than that of his

---

(*jokoku*) 29 *minshu* 888 (Sup. Ct. 1st P.B., July 10, 1975). The second series of cases involved the continuation of the same offending practices as in the earlier cases, only by the parent companies: Yukijirushi Nyugyo KK, 24 *Shinketsushu* 65 [FTC (decision) no. 2, 1974], Nov. 28, 1977. Meiji Nyugyo KK 24 *Shinketsushu* 86 [FTC (decision) no. 3, 1974], Nov. 24, 1977. Morinaga Nyugyo KK, 24 *Shinketsushu* 106 [FTC (decision) no. 4, 1974], Nov. 28, 1977.

16 Yuki Jirushi KK hoka gyunyu seizo gyosha 4-mei ni tai suru ken (Case against Yuki Jirushi KK and four other makers of drinking milk), 21 *Shinketsushu* 30 [FTC (consent) no. 18, 1974], May 22, 1974.

17 In June 1992 the FTC charged Abbott Laboratories, Mead Johnson & Co., and American Home Products with collusion and price fixing in the sale of infant formula. These and related cases filed by various state attorney generals eventually led to consent decrees involving the payment of substantial penalties by the companies.

18 Lester Telser, "Why Should Manufacturers Want Fair Trade?" *Journal of Law and Economics*, vol. 3 (1960), pp. 86–105. (*Re.* the odd title: manufacturer-imposed minimum retail prices have sometimes been referred to as "fair trade" prices).

rivals.) Resale price maintenance can therefore induce retailers to provide presale demonstrations. This argument is most compelling for products that are somewhat complicated or unfamiliar, or for which there exist many optional features or gradations of quality and so on. Japanese examples for which the argument seems to fit well include antitrust cases involving Matsushita, Nikon, and France Bed, involving cameras, electric appliances, and furniture, respectively.

France Bed KK, a major producer of beds in Japan (40 percent market share in 1974), sold directly to 2,525 independent retailers which it organized into a formal association consisting of three hierarchical categories. The most exalted of the three categories was reserved for retailers with the largest and most diverse sales of France Bed products. Most of these sold France Bed products exclusively. Around 1965 France Bed began to insist that all of its retailers adhere to suggested retail prices which France Bed advertised to customers. Nevertheless, some retailers persisted in price discounting, and France Bed seemed to regard this as a problem. Why? The special services argument fits this case perfectly. Price discounting tended to erode the incentives of retailers to maintain showrooms with display pieces. By price discounting, retailers could attract customers who examined the beds at other outlets and could themselves avoid the considerable costs of maintaining showrooms. Unless price discounting was curbed, eventually few if any retailers would find it profitable to maintain showrooms, damaging the business prospects of the entire chain as well as eroding France Bed's own profits. It is rather clear that these arrangements can have had nothing to do with cartelization of the retailers, as this would have been counter to France Bed's own self-interest, and it was France Bed rather than the retailers that instigated the scheme. Nevertheless, the FTC found these arrangements to violate anti-monopoly laws.[19]

The Nikon case[20] resembles the France bed case in essential respects, except that the products were cameras and camera lenses and the special services consisted not of maintaining showrooms, but rather of employing knowledgeable salesmen to demonstrate the products and answer customer's queries. In fact, Nikon had been officially authorized to practice resale price maintenance in the sale of cameras, but this authorization was withdrawn in 1966. Nikon continued its price maintenance even after 1966. Nippon Kogaku Kogyo KK (Nikon) sold its products in Japan through four designated wholesalers who in turn sold to 1,200 retailers in 1972. The retailers were designated by Nikon as belonging to one of three categories: "Nikon stores", "Nikon outlets", or "Nikon apprentices". The "stores" tended to have greater sales and in turn received more support from Nikon. Just as in the Takeya miso case, Nikon sought to prevent wholesalers from raising prices and eroding its own profits, imposing price ceilings on the wholesalers. But, as in the France Bed case, Nikon also sought to maintain retail prices to make it less profitable for retailers to refrain from sales promotion activities and attract customers who had obtained product demonstrations from other retailers. Further, Nikon prevailed on wholesalers to assist it in enforcing minimum retail price stipulations, introduced a system of rebates to retailers and wholesalers contingent on their observance of its policies, and assigned each retailer to a specific wholesaler. Nikon dispatched monitors to discover instances of retail sales of Nikon products below stipulated minimum prices. Repeated instances of price discounting were understood to result in discontinuance of shipments. Nikon can have had no desire to cartelize the wholesaling or retailing of its products, as this would have eroded its own profits. These arrangements were clearly meant to encourage more extensive efforts by retailers at promoting its products and to prevent wholesalers from introducing a price wedge. Nevertheless, in June 1974, the FTC found Nikon's practices to violate anti-monopoly laws.

The Matsushita case[21] differs from the Nikon case only in the much greater number of retailers and wholesalers involved. Matsushita Denki KK was in 1965 the largest producer of home electronic products such as televisions, radios, vacuum cleaners,

---

[19] France Bed KK, 22 *Shinketsushu* 127 [FTC (recommendation) no. 2, 1976], Feb. 20, 1976. For additional facts regarding this case, see Y. Tazaki, "Beddo hanbai ni kan suru saihanbai kakaku iji oyobi senbaiten seido" (Exclusive outlets and resale price maintenance in the sale of beds), *Kosei Torihiki*, no. 305 (1976), pp. 28–31.

[20] Nihon Kogaku Kogyo KK, 19 *Shinketsushu* 25 [FTC (recommendation) no. 7, 1972], June 30, 1972.

[21] Matsushita Denki Sangyo KK, 17 *Shinketsushu* 187 [FTC (consent) no. 4, 1967], Mar. 12, 1971.

refrigerators, fans, and heaters, with a roughly 20 percent market share of each. It sold these products under the "National" brand name through a network of 180 wholesalers and 30,000 retailers. Beginning in 1964, it introduced a system of minimum retail prices which wholesalers were held responsible for enforcing. To make it easier to monitor wholesalers' compliance with these stipulations, Matsushita assigned each wholesaler an exclusive geographic territory, and to prevent a wholesale–retail price wedge from eroding its own profits, it also stipulated (maximum) wholesale prices. Matsushita's motivation for stipulating minimum retail prices was to encourage presale demonstrations by retailers, not to cartelize wholesalers and retailers. Nevertheless, the FTC found Matsushita's practices to violate Japan's anti-monopoly laws.

The France Bed, Nikon, and Matsushita cases expose some features of Japan's distribution keiretsu usually hidden from public view. In spite of the FTC findings of illegality in these instances and others like them, the anti-monopoly laws of Japan pose few significant obstacles to the activities of distribution keiretsu. This is because resources devoted to enforcement of the laws are quite limited and penalties for violations are inconsequential. On the basis of the examples just discussed, to the extent that manufacturers of consumer products in Japan persist in illegally maintaining retail prices, they are likely to attain lower costs of marketing, which results in improved resource allocation. Careful consideration of instances of customer assignment and exclusive dealing stipulations support analogous conclusions.

Customer assignments/exclusive territories/ exclusive agency

In both the Nikon and the Matsushita cases, the manufacturer assigned each retailer to a specific wholesaler, in effect conferring on each wholesaler a virtual monopoly in sales of the product to the retailers assigned to it. The reason in both instances was to facilitate manufacturers' monitoring of wholesalers' arrangements with retailers, not to cartelize the wholesalers. Other examples of customer assignment are motivated by the desire on the part of manufacturers to align the interests of distributors of their products with their own interests. And as in the Nikon and Matsushita cases, these customer assignments are invariably accompanied by additional stipulations such as price ceilings or sales quotas, intended to prevent distributors from exploiting their monopolies in ways that are detrimental to the manufacturer. A Japanese example is the Yakult case.[22]

KK Yakuruto honsha (Yakult) owned a valuable patent on the process for making a yoghurt drink. It produced the undiluted liquid for this drink and sold it to licensees, who diluted it, put it in bottles carrying the Yakult trademark, and sold the drink to retailers. Yakult assigned exclusive geographic territories to the bottlers and also specified their sales quantities to the retailers. The problem that Yakult sought to address with these arrangements was the following. If bottlers were permitted to sell to the same customers, then their incentives to maintain quality would be attenuated. For in that case, costly efforts by any one bottler to maintain quality would result in enhanced future sales of rival bottlers and thus would not have been undertaken for optimal investment in quality: bottlers selling in the same territory would tend to dilute the drinks, cutting their own costs but diminishing future demand facing not only themselves but rivals. Yakult assigned exclusive territories to the bottlers to prevent this problem from arising.

Further Japanese examples of customer assignment include the many instances in which foreign manufacturers have each assigned a single Japanese importer the exclusive rights to sell their products within Japan. Foreign cosmetics, foreign beer and liquor, and many other branded consumer products have been introduced into Japan under such exclusive agency contracts, disallowing "parallel imports" by non-designated agents. Why would foreign manufacturers want to create independent, downstream, Japan-based monopolies in the distribution of their products? A sole importer, one that is a Japan-wide monopolist in the sale of a particular foreign brand of merchandise, may have a better incentive to act on private information in setting order quantities, or a better incentive to manage marketing channels appropriately so as to assure

22 KK Yakuruto Honsha, 13 *Shinketsushu* 72 [FTC (recommendation) no. 19, 1965], Sept. 13, 1965.

optimal promotion efforts, than would a competitive industry of importers.[23] This may account for some examples of sole agency contracts between foreign manufacturers and distributors in Japan. For instance, in spring 1995, unauthorized parallel imports of foreign cosmetics, sold through discount department stores in Japan, greatly lowered the retail prices of the products but also made it impossible for the designated Japanese importer to maintain the extensive network of point-of-sale product demonstration and promotion (special services) that it, and the manufacturers, had apparently considered to be essential to the successful marketing of the products. The end result of the parallel imports was probably to constrict sales of the products rather than expand them.

Exclusive dealing

Manufacturers occasionally stipulate that retailers of their products must not handle rivals' products. In particular, they do this when they intend to assist retailers in their selling efforts and wish to assure that the benefits redound on themselves rather than on rivals. For example, Gakken, the leading Japanese publisher of educational materials and encyclopedias, insisted that independent salesmen of its educational books and magazines deal with it exclusively, in order that the sales leads it provided not be used by the salesmen to benefit rivals.[24] The leads were generated from subscriber lists and responses to tear-out cards in Gakken's many related educational publications. In other words, Gakken had incurred significant costs in gathering leads and would have been less inclined to incur such costs if its returns from these activities had been diminished. Nevertheless, the FTC found that Gakken's exclusive dealing stipulations violated anti-monopoly laws.

Antitrust rules pertaining to exclusive dealing, not only in Japan but also in the United States, reflect a preoccupation with the possibility that exclusive dealing stipulations might foreclose entry. But in fact, foreclosure is unlikely to be the motivation for exclusive dealing stipulations. Customers would typically not agree to stipulations that conferred monopoly on an incumbent supplier unless compensated in advance for the likely future reduction in their own gains from trade that would result from monopoly pricing; but, because monopoly pricing reduces customers' gains from trade more than it adds to the monopolist's profits, the compensation required before the customers will consent to foreclosing stipulations exceeds what the incumbent supplier is willing to pay. Clever economists have constructed two exceptions to this argument. The first exception, due to Rasmussen, Ramseyer, and Wiley,[25] holds that, where entry is unprofitable unless some minimum efficient scale is assured, the incumbent supplier need not obtain the consent of all its customers in order to blockade entry. In this instance, exclusive dealing stipulations can be profitable for the monopolist. The second exception, due to Aghion and Bolton,[26] resides in the fact that, if an incumbent monopolist can join with its customers and levy fees on new entrants, they may profit from doing so, and if they do not know entrants' costs exactly they may inadvertently but unavoidably set fees that blockade efficient entry. Nobody has so far demonstrated that either qualification corresponds to actual cases of exclusive dealing. For instance, Gakken itself faced rivals; it was not an incumbent monopolist as these qualifications require.

In a recent complaint, Kodak, a US manufacturer of photographic film, alleged that its leading Japanese rival Fuji had foreclosed it from some marketing channels in Japan by entering exclusive dealing arrangements with wholesalers. The US government presented Kodak's complaint to the World Trade Organization, which ruled in December 1997 that the charges were without merit. This case awaits further study by economists before a definitive explanation may be offered.

---

[23] Rey and Tirole explore the incentive effects of exclusive agency stipulations: Patrick Rey and Jean Tirole, "The Logic of Vertical Restraints", *American Economic Review*, vol. 76 (1986), pp. 221–33.

[24] For a parallel example in the USA involving the sale of hearing aids through independent exclusive sales agents, see Howard Marvel, "Hearing Aides", in R. N. Lafferty, R. H. Lande, and J. Kirkwood (eds.), *Impact Evaluations of Federal Trade Commission Vertical Restraints Cases*, Washington DC: Bureau of Economics, Federal Trade Commission, 1984, pp. 270–385.

[25] Eric Rasmussen, J. Mark Ramseyer, and John S. Wiley Jr, "Naked Exclusion", *American Economic Review* (December 1991), pp. 1137–45.

[26] Phillipe Aghion and Patrick Bolton, "Contracts as a Barrier to Entry", *American Economic Review* (1987), pp. 38–401.

Manufacturer acceptance of returns

Our final example of a special arrangement between the manufacturer of a product and downstream distributors of it is the practice, common in Japan, of the manufacturer accepting returns of unsold merchandise. The practice is widely noted as pertaining to books, magazines, wearing apparel, cosmetics, and electric appliances. The returned merchandise is, for the most part, not damaged or defective but merely unsold, yet after its return the manufacturers typically destroy it; they do not hold it in inventory for sale at a later time. To understand this practice, one should first note that it has the effect of placing a floor under the resale price, for no retailer will sell merchandise at a discount below the price it can receive from the manufacturer if it returns the items. Manufacturer acceptance of returns, in this way, resembles resale price maintenance and can have a similar motivation; it might simply be one way of administering RPM. But there is an additional aspect to manufacturer acceptance of returns. It can be part of an optimal price-setting policy under conditions of demand uncertainty.[27]

A manufacturer that must produce before learning the true state of demand will want to disallow sales at prices below the level consistent with maximum total receipts even if it leaves some items unsold. It will generally be possible to sell the entire production run by allowing the price to fall, but it won't be worth it if the discount on merchandise that could have been sold at a higher price subtracts more from sales revenue than the larger quantity sold adds to it. By accepting returns of unsold merchandise, the manufacturer can prevent this kind of corrosive price discounting. A manufacturer-stipulated minimum resale price can, in principle, achieve the same result, but it will be difficult to enforce, for it requires that retailers fully absorb the losses attending their unsold merchandise.[28] The rationales for RPM discussed earlier in the chapter, including the special services argument, do not presume that retailers will order more merchandise than they can actually sell at the stipulated resale price and so do not give rise to this kind of enforcement problem.

This explanation for manufacturer acceptance of returns—that it is to forestall revenue-reducing price discounts—is most persuasive for products that are easily returnable, are subject to demand uncertainty, and have distinctive attributes. Good examples are magazines, newspapers, books, and cosmetic jewelry, and all of them are marketed with liberal return privileges, not only in Japan, but also in the USA and elsewhere. If, as often suggested, the acceptance of returns is more common in Japan than elsewhere, the reason is likely to be found in the greater uncertainty in predicting demand at each of the numerous retail outlets.[29]

Conclusion

Japan's distribution system, though frequently labeled "inefficient", manifestly is not. Japan's fragmented and complex distribution sector is uniquely suited to its own particular geography. The scarcity of living space in Japan, and the inconvenience there of owning and operating a car, enhance Japanese households' willingness to pay for the added convenience of next-door shopping. And Japan's geographic centricity and highly developed transport system lower the costs of a distribution sector that accommodates this preference, a distribution sector having a proliferation of retail outlets that must be continually restocked through complex logistical arteries. These factors combine to make a proliferation of stores in Japan not only inevitable, but desirable. And, given this, regulations such as the Large Store Law that protect small stores from competition by large ones imply only minor economic distortions and encounter little effective political resistance. The Large Store Law more reflected than shaped the structure of Japan's distribution sector.

Also, manufacturers in Japan have been free to enter contractual arrangements with wholesale and retail distributors of their products little en-

---

[27] David Flath and T. Nariu, "Returns Policy in the Japanese Marketing System", *Journal of the Japanese and International Economies*, vol. 3 (1989), pp. 49–63.

[28] Nevertheless, Deneckere *et al.* offer this as a possible explanation for RPM: see Raymond Deneckere, Howard P. Marvel, and James Peck, "Demand Uncertainty and Price Maintenance: Markdowns as Destructive Competition", *American Economic Review*, vol. 87, no. 4 (September 1997), pp. 619–41.

[29] For an elaboration of this view, see Howard P. Marvel and James Peck, "Demand Uncertainty and Returns Policies", *International Economic Review*, vol. 36, no. 3 (August 1995), pp. 691–714.

cumbered by the anti-monopoly laws which are weakly enforced. Vertical restraints, including minimum retail price stipulations, customer assignments, and exclusive dealing, have all been used by manufacturers in Japan to provide distributors with appropriate incentives or to otherwise lower the costs of marketing products. Tougher antitrust rules or penalties effectively discouraging Japanese firms from imposing vertical restraints would distort resource allocation, not improve it.

FURTHER READING

■ David Flath, "Vertical Restraints in Japan", *Japan and the World Economy,* vol. 1 (1989), pp. 187–203. Discusses selected anti-monopoly cases of Japan including the ones described in this chapter.

■ David Flath, "Why Are There So Many Retail Stores in Japan?" *Japan and the World Economy,* vol. 2 (1990), pp. 365–86. More on the ubiquity of retail stores in Japan.

■ David Flath and Tatsuhiko Nariu, "Is Japan's Retail Sector Truly Distinctive?" *Journal of Comparative Economics,* vol. 23 (1996), pp. 181–91. Answers the title's question in the negative.

■ Maruyama Masayoshi, Sakai Kyohei, Togawa Yoko, Sakamoto Nobuo, Yamashita Michio, Arakawa Masaharu, and Ijo Hiroyuki, "Nihon no ryūtsū shisutemu: riron to jissho" (The distribution system of Japan: theory and empirics), *Keizai bunseki,* vol. 123 (May 1991). Japanese economists analyze the nation's distribution system.

■ Nariu Tatsuhiko, *Ryūtsū no keizai riron* (The economic theory of marketing), Nagoya daigaku shuppankai, 1994. Theoretical and econometric analysis of Japanese marketing channels by a leading expert on the topic.

Labor | 15

Compared with Americans and some Europeans, the Japanese typically work for fewer different employers over the courses of their lives and receive a larger component of pay based strictly on years of continual service. These facts were first recognized by the anthropologist James Abegglen, who conducted field study at manufacturing plants in Japan in 1955–6.[1] Abegglen's characterizations were quickly affirmed by others (including Dore[2]), and references to "Japanese-style employment practices" were soon understood to refer to lifetime employment and seniority-based wages. The academic literature on these topics continues to explore the historical origins of these practices, their prevalence in Japan today, and their reasons for being.

Although the compensation systems of the large Japanese companies in particular at first seemed to Abegglen and others to be peculiar in the extreme, and completely divorced from economic logic, the weight of current opinion holds that they are neither unique to Japan nor irrational. Pay systems that both reward employees for more years of service and defer compensation until after employee performance has been thoroughly evaluated are used to control and motivate the employees of large companies in most developed nations, not only in Japan. Seniority-based pay, by discouraging quits and also increasing the onerousness of early dismissal, has enabled large Japanese companies to economize on the costs of training employees in skills that are specific to their respective workplaces while preserving employee incentives to exert effort.

Other important aspects of Japanese labor markets have evolved in tandem with the lifetime employment/seniority-based pay and promotion systems of the large companies. These include the practice of awarding a significant fraction of pay in the form of biannual bonuses, the organization of workers into enterprise-based unions rather than industry-wide unions or occupational-based craft unions, and the differing career paths of Japan's male and female workers. Examined in toto, the peculiar aspects of the Japanese employment system can be understood as a sophisticated response to the universal problems inherent in recruiting, training, organizing, and motivating workers.

Lifetime employment and seniority-based wages

Abegglen's original description of the employment practices of Japanese manufacturing firms was based on his extensive interviews of personnel officers and others at nineteen large factories in a spectrum of heavy industries and thirty-four smaller factories, mainly in the textile industry, over the period 1955–6. He found that employment in the Japanese factory represented a lifetime commitment:

At whatever level of organization in the Japanese factory,

---

[1] James G. Abegglen, *The Japanese Factory*, Glencoe, Ill.: Free Press, 1958.
[2] Ronald Dore, *British Factory–Japanese Factory*, University of California Press, 1973.

the worker commits himself on entrance to the company for the remainder of his working career. The company will not discharge him even temporarily except in the most extreme circumstances. He will not quit the company for industrial employment elsewhere. . . . This rule of a lifetime commitment is truly proved by its rare exceptions . . . (*The Japanese Factory*, 1958, p. 11)

Abegglen cited the case of an Osaka-based electric equipment manufacturer employing 4,530 persons, in which only about five or six were fired each year and these for the most egregious reasons such as absenteeism or thievery. The company had a quit rate of only between 2 and 3 percent per year for men, and two-thirds of this was due to retirement. The annual quit rate for women was 10 percent.

With regard to pay scales in the factories he investigated, Abegglen found that steady service was strongly rewarded but that other factors more obviously related to productivity were not:

It is not at all difficult to find situations where workers doing identical work at an identical pace receive markedly different salaries, or where a skilled workman is paid at a rate below that of a sweeper or doorman. The position occupied and the amount produced do not determine the reward provided. . . . The importance given to education, age, length of service, and similar factors in the total wage scale means that a worker is heavily penalized for job mobility and strongly rewarded for steady service. (*The Japanese Factory*, 1958, pp. 67–8)

Abegglen illustrated this by relating in detail the pay system of an Osaka/Kobe materials processing firm which he declared to be typical of large manufacturing companies in Japan. The rules the company used to determine the base bay, bonus, and fringe benefits of shop-floor workers as well as senior executives had almost no obvious tie to individuals' performances since entering employment with the firm, but did reward those employees having more years of service with the firm.

Abegglen argued that the system of lifetime employment and seniority-based pay, by failing to link pay and performance, was hampering the productivity of Japanese factories, but that it was nevertheless very much in harmony with aspects of Japanese culture. He described the Japanese employment system as paternalistic, even feudalistic, one in which the employment relation entails permanent membership in a hierarchical group, as opposed

to Western employment systems which embody nothing more than an arms'-length, ongoing exchange of labor services for money.

The Abegglen book was translated into Japanese where it became a best-seller (*Nihon no keiei*, Daiyamondo-sha, 1958), eventually going through twenty printings. Its impact on academic thinking in America concerning Japan's business and economy has also been enormous as judged by the immense number of citations to the book itself, and even more numerous references, without citation, to the employment practices that the book first exposed.

As matters stand currently, it appears that Abegglen was right on some points and wrong on others. As skeptics have been careful to demonstrate, the phenomena of lifetime employment and seniority-based wages are not universal in Japan nor completely unknown in other developed countries.[3] The practices that Abegglen exposed are little evident in the small firms of Japan, but are somewhat evident in the large firms of other nations. Nevertheless, it seems that Abegglen was basically correct in that lifetime employment and seniority-based wages have been far more prevalent in Japan than in the United States or elsewhere, particularly with respect to the male employees of large firms. However, Abegglen was wide of the mark in suggesting that Japanese companies' seniority-based pay systems fail to preserve performance incentives. Before examining the economic rationale for lifetime employment and seniority-based pay, we first offer some supporting evidence for these last few declarations.

Lifetime employment

The Ministry of Labor of Japan and its counterparts in other countries, such as the US Department of Labor, from time to time have surveyed their countries' respective workforces regarding earnings, education, age, tenure of employment, and so on and published summaries of the results. Such cross-section data reflect age, year, and cohort effects and

---

[3] The skeptics include eminent Japanese scholars; see e.g. Kazuo Koike, "Human Resource Development and Labor-Management Relations", in Kozo Yamamura and Yasukichi Yasuba (eds.), *The Political Economy of Japan*, i, *The Domestic Transformation*, Stanford University Press, 1987, pp. 289–330; and Haruo Shimada, "The Perception and the Reality of Japanese Industrial Relations", in Lester C. Thurow (ed.), *The Management Challenge: Japanese Views*, Cambridge, Mass.: MIT Press, 1986, pp. 42–68.

must therefore be interpreted with a measure of caution. The experience of the representative worker over a career, an amalgam of the experiences of different kinds of cohorts in various years, is evident in the age effect only.

A crude estimate of the expected ultimate tenure of employment of incumbent workers, accurate if year and cohort effects are not present, may be gleaned by doubling the current average tenure. Such estimates, for various countries and years, are reported in Table 15.1. Japan exhibits the longest expected tenure of employment of all the countries listed in the table, and the United States exhibits the shortest. But expected tenure seems not to differ much between Japan, Germany, France, and Spain; it is about twenty years in all of them. The expected tenure is around fifteen years for most of the other nations listed in the table, including the USA. Finland lies between the two extremes. Perhaps the employment practices of Japan and the United States are each representative of a type or category, also manifested in other nations. Workers' careers in Japan (and in Germany, France, and Spain) manifest lifetime employment, while those in the USA (and Australia, Netherlands, Canada, and the UK) exhibit successive temporary employments. A more detailed comparison of male workers' careers in Japan and the USA is even more revealing.

Japanese workers of all ages are less likely to have accepted a new job within the most recent year than is true of US workers. Table 15.2 indicates the percentage of male workers in each age group reporting having accepted a new job within the most recent year in Japan and the USA in 1966 and 1977–8. We can extract from these data a crude estimate of the cumulative number of different jobs the representative male worker in each country could expect to have held at each age, an estimate that would be exact if, again, year and cohort effects were not present.

It is apparent from the last entries in the last four columns of Table 15.2 that male workers in Japan hold fewer different jobs over their careers than do their US counterparts. By these estimates, in 1966 Japanese male workers could expect to hold 4.23 different jobs over their careers and US male workers, 10.19 different jobs; on the basis of the 1977–8 data, Japanese male workers might expect to hold 4.91 jobs over their careers and Americans 11.16 jobs. In both Japan and the United States, it appears that younger workers switch jobs more frequently than do older ones, which is to be expected, as younger workers are still acquiring skills and may not have settled into a permanent career, nor have they had as much opportunity as older workers to have discovered an employer with whom they have a mutually satisfying arrangement.

In both Japan and the United States, average tenure of employment tends to be longer in large firms than in smaller ones. Masanori Hashimoto and John Raisian find that in both countries the effect of tenure on earnings is weaker and peaks earlier for small firms than for large ones; their estimated expected tenures for firms of different sizes in Japan and the USA, based on workforce surveys of 1979, are reported in Table 15.3. Their procedure was simply to double the average tenures of employees in each category.

From these data, it is apparent that the ultimate tenures of workers in small firms in Japan has been comparable to that in large firms in the United States. There is perhaps then some basis for claiming, as many have, that the distinctive employment practices are characteristic only of large firms in Japan, those that employ about a third of the workforce. But other commentators have emphasized instead that the contrast between the employment

Table 15.1. Average ultimate expected tenure of employment in selected countries

	Ave. no. of expected years of service[a]		
	1979	1985	1991
JAPAN	17.8	20.6 (1984)	21.8 (1990)
Germany		22.2 (1984)	20.8 (1990)
France		21.4 (1983)	20.2
Spain		22.4 (1987)	19.6 (1992)
Finland	15.6	16.8	18
UK		16.6	15.8
Canada	14.6	15.2 (1983)	15.6
Netherlands		17.8	14 (1990)
Australia	13	13.2	13.6
USA	12.8 (1978)	15.4 (1983)	13.4

[a] Average ultimate tenure is estimated by doubling the average tenure of incumbent employees as of the year of observation.

Source: "Enterprise Tenure, Labour Turnover and Skill Training", in OECD Employment Outlook, July 1993, table 4.2, p. 123.

Table 15.2. Job-switching by male workers in Japan and the United States, 1966 and 1977–8

Age	% of male workers starting new jobs in the most recent year				Cumulative number of jobs male workers would expect to have held by each age if it were the same for all cohorts[a]			
	Japan		USA		Japan		USA	
	1966	1977	1966	1978	1966	1977	1966	1978
16–17	—	19	—	50		0.36		1.00
18–19	20.4	19	31.7	50	0.41	0.72	1.27	2.00
20–24	15.0	26	28.5	48	1.16	2.06	4.12	4.40
25–29	8.8	13	13.8	35	1.60	2.71	5.50	6.15
30–34	8.8	8	13.8	25	2.04	3.11	6.88	7.40
35–39	6.6	7	7.4	18	2.36	3.46	8.36	8.30
40–54	5.6	5	5.2	13	3.20	4.21	9.40	10.25
55–64	1.0	7	3.8	7	4.20	4.91	10.16	10.95
65–69	0.6	—	2.7	4	4.23		10.19	11.15
70+	0.6	—	2.7	1	4.23		10.19	11.16

[a] Computed by multiplying the percentages in the corresponding left-hand columns by the number of year intervals in the respective age brackets and cumulating.

Sources: Japan 1966: Economic Planning Agency, *Economic Survey of Japan*, Tokyo: Japan Times, 1968, p. 152; *Japan 1977*: *Basic Survey of Employment*; *USA 1966*: *Monthly Labor Review*, vol. 89 (1966); *USA 1978*: *Special Labor Force Reports*, no. 238 (1978). Also see Robert E. Cole, "Permanent Employment in Japan: Facts and Fantasies", *Industrial and Labor Relations Review*, vol. 26, no. 1 (October 1972), table 8, p. 627, and Masanori Hashimoto and John Raisian, "Employment Tenure and Earnings Profiles in Japan and the United States", *American Economic Review*, vol. 75, no. 4 (September 1985), table 2, p. 724.

practices of large firms and small ones is present in the United States as well as Japan. For instance, Robert Hall[4] demonstrates that a significant fraction of US male employees of large firms work for the same employer from entry into the labor market until retirement.

The phrase "lifetime employment" may not be strictly accurate for the representative Japanese male worker; but it is certainly consistent with the data just reviewed that some subset of the workers, perhaps a majority of the male employees of the largest manufacturing firms, do in fact enter employment upon completion of their formal educations and do not switch employers until reaching the age of mandatory retirement, which until recently was 55 for most Japanese male employees. (The age of mandatory retirement has been rising in Japan lately, for reasons not well understood.)

Seniority-based wages

The differences in earnings among Japanese workers are more completely explained by the differences in their lengths of service to their current employers than is true of US or European workers. To identify the extent to which seniority alone enhances earn-

Table 15.3. Expected ultimate tenure of employment of employees of different sized firms, Japan and the United States, 1979

	No. of employees		
	1–100	101–1,000	1,001–
Japan (yrs)	23	24	31
USA (yrs)	10	15	21

Source: Masanori Hashimoto and John Raisian, "Employment Tenure and Earnings Profiles in Japan and the United States", *American Economic Review*, vol. 75, no. 4 (September 1985), table 3, p. 726.

[4] Robert E. Hall, "The Importance of Lifetime Jobs in the US Economy", *American Economic Review*, vol. 72 (September 1982), pp. 716–24; see also Manuelita Ureta, "The Importance of Lifetime Jobs in the US Economy Revisited", *American Economic Review*, vol. 82, no. 1 (March 1992), pp. 322–35.

ings, one must also account for the effects of other factors that can be expected to enhance workers' earnings, too. Workers with more years of formal education and workers having longer experience in an occupation have more skills, and so contribute more to the output and revenues of their employers; consequently their services are in greater demand. The costs of acquiring skills either by extending one's formal education, by gaining work experience, or by some other way impede others from supplying competing labor services and, together with the greater demand for skilled labor, assure that the earnings of workers that possess skills will remain above those of workers who lack them.

A number of investigators have identified components of the earnings of US, European, and Japanese workers that are explained not by years of education or years of experience in the same occupation, but by tenure of service to the current employer.[5] The effect of tenure on earnings is larger for Japanese workers than for Americans or Europeans. How much larger? Hashimoto and Raisian,[6] analyzing 1980 data, have estimated statistical regression equations in which workers' earnings depend upon years of education, years of occupational experience, and tenure of service with the current employer. Based on these estimates, a representative male worker in a large firm in either Japan or the United States having the average number of years of formal education and remaining with the same employer from the outset of his career would attain maximum earnings after about thirty years. But the American worker's earnings would have doubled, half of which would be the result of tenure, while the Japanese worker's earnings would have tripled, four-fifths of which would be the result of tenure.

Consider a specific example of a pay system that incorporates seniority-based elements. The labor economist Koike K(azuo) has described in detail the remuneration system for blue-collar employees of one of Japan's large automobile manufacturers.[7] Each worker's pay is comprised of four elements which on average contribute to earnings as follows:

Job grade rate:	40%
Basic rate:	30%
Age rate:	25%
Merit rate:	7%

The *job grade rate* is the largest contributor to earn-

ings. The job grade is the hierarchy of classifications identifying workers' depth and breadth of skills, and the degree of responsibility they assume over the work of others. Job grades range from junior worker to team leader to sub-foreman and, ultimately, to foreman. The total number of grades is approximately eight. The job rate for sub-foreman, the second highest grade, is 26 percent higher than that of the lowest-grade junior worker; the job rate for the foreman is 61 percent higher than that of the lowest-grade worker.

The *basic rate* consists of the entry wage and a cumulation of annual increments. The entry wage is heavily dependent upon education and prior experience. The *age rate*, on the other hand, is strictly determined by chronological age, completely independent of individual performance.

The effect of both tenure and seniority upon earnings operate through the annual increments to the basic rate and also through the job grade rate. This is because workers are considered for upgrades only after accumulating sufficient years of service, and high-grade positions are generally filled by internal promotion rather than by hiring from outside. The promotion ladder thus resembles a career-long

---

5 For *Japan*, see Jacob Mincer and Yoshio Higuchi, "Wage Structure and Labor Turnover in the United States and Japan", *Journal of the Japanese and International Economies*, vol. 2 (1988), pp. 97–133; Haruo Shimada, *Earnings Structure and Human Investment*, Tokyo: Kogakush, 1981; Masanori Hashimoto and John Raisian, "Employment Tenure and Earnings Profiles in Japan and the United States", *American Economic Review*, vol. 75, no. 4 (September 1985), pp. 721–35; Robert Clark and Naohiro Ogawa, "Employment Tenure and Earnings Profiles in Japan and the United States: Comment", *American Economic Review*, vol. 82, no. 1 (March 1992), pp. 336–45. For the *USA*, see Jacob Mincer, *Schooling, Experience, and Earnings*, Columbia University Press, 1974; Robert Topel, "Wages Rise with Seniority", unpublished paper, University of Chicago, November 1987. For comparisons of the earnings vs tenure profiles of European and Japanese workers, see Kazuo Koike, "Seniority Wages?" in Kazuo Koike, *Understanding Industrial Relations in Modern Japan*, New York: St Martin's Press, 1988, ch. 1, pp. 16–56.

6 Masanori Hashimoto and John Raisian, "Employment Tenure and Earnings Profiles in Japan and the United States", *American Economic Review*, vol. 75, no. 4 (September 1985), pp. 721–35. The effect of tenure on the earnings of male Japanese workers in years since 1980 is explored in Robert L. Clark and N(aohiro) Ogawa, "Comment", and M. Hashimori and J. Raisian, "Reply", *American Economic Review*, vol. 82, no. 1 (March 1991), pp. 336–54.

7 K(azuo) Koike, "Learning and Incentive Systems in Japanese Industry", in Ronald Dore and Masahiko Aoki (eds.), *The Japanese Firm: The Sources of Competitive Strength*, Oxford University Press, 1994, ch. 2, pp. 41–65 (esp. p. 57).

tournament, perhaps one in which most participants advance through the early rounds. In other words, elevation from "junior worker" to "senior worker" after a set number of years may be nearly universal, even though not automatic. (Of course, only a few ever advance all the way to foreman.) The Japanese term of reference for seniority-based pay systems is *nenkō-joretsu*, which literally translated means "ranking by seniority". This example demonstrates how the pay system of a large Japanese company can attach a high reward to longer years of service and still preserve incentives to exert effort and acquire greater proficiency. According to Koike, the pay system for managerial employees of the same automobile company resembles in essential respects the one for its blue-collar employees just described.

Economic rationale for lifetime employment and seniority-based wages

There are two differing economic rationales for earnings that rise with tenure of service and that induce longer average tenure: (1) to promote efficient acquisition and use of company-specific skills, and (2) to provide incentives for workers, as agents of their employers, to be diligent in their efforts on the employers' behalf. Let us refer to these respectively as the *company-specific skills* and *agency* theories.

Company-specific skills
General skills such as basic literacy, punctuality, and the ability to draw upon a well established body of knowledge are widely applicable in the workplace and render the possessor's services more valuable to many competing employers. But company-specific skills such as derive from familiarity with particular coworkers, or from familiarity with machines or production methods that are unique to a particular firm, render a worker's services more valuable to a particular employer.

The basic logic of investment in skills was developed by the Nobel laureate Gary Becker.[8] Because competition among employers equates the market wage rate of workers using general skills with the value of their marginal contributions to any firm's revenues, employers will be disinclined to subsidize employees' acquisition of general skills. Therefore workers themselves must bear the full costs of acquiring general skills; but, because the competitive labor market fully rewards them for doing, so they can be expected to make economically efficient choices. With regard to company-specific skills, matters are different.

Workers who acquire skills that are specific to their employing company can incrementally contribute more to their employer's revenues, but will not have increased their potential for contributing to the revenues of competing employers. Consequently, employees, in the absence of special assurances, will hesitate to incur costs in acquiring company-specific skills because they would then be in the vulnerable position of depending upon the employer's largesse to reward them for having done so. And the employer may hesitate to incur costs in training workers because if the workers quit it will have had only a short time in which to profit from the greater productivity that the training confers. But trained employees can be dissuaded from quitting, by the prospect of earning more in the one job than in alternate employment. And an employer who develops a reputation for avoiding layoffs and paying senior workers more than they could earn elsewhere can pay its novice employees lower wages than they could immediately earn elsewhere. Figure 15.1 illustrates possible paths of earnings over the workers' careers where competition in the labor market assures that the present value of expected career earnings is the same across employers.

The basic point here is that employers who retain and reward senior employees are likely to realize a greater profit from their training of workers in company-specific skills than they would if they were paying only spot market wages throughout the workers' careers. For, by paying senior (trained) employees more than they could earn elsewhere, the firm discourages trained employees from quitting so that their skills contribute to the firm's revenue for a longer period of time; and, once the firm establishes a reputation for retaining and rewarding senior employees, labor market competition will push down the wages it is necessary for that firm to pay novice employees.

---

8 Gary S. Becker, *Human Capital: A Theoretical and Empirical Analysis with Special Reference to Education*, 2nd edn, New York: NBER, 1975.

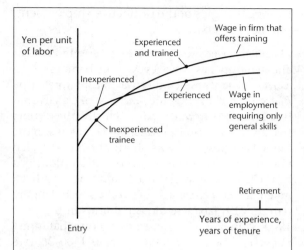

Figure 15.1. Wages over workers' careers

An employer that provides training in skills that are specific to it is likely to pay seniority-based wages to discourage trained workers from quitting. Once it has a reputation for retaining and rewarding senior employees, it will be able to pay novice employees less, further steepening the earnings–tenure profile.

Agency

An additional explanation for earnings that rise with tenure, after accounting for other factors, emerges from analysis of mandatory retirement. As the economist Edward Lazear has pointed out, firms that require their employees to retire upon reaching a certain age must be paying senior employees wages that exceed their incremental contributions to the firm's revenue.[9] For in the opposite case firms would be pleased if their senior employees extended their service indefinitely: mandatory retirement would not be in the firms' own interests. As many as 88 percent of all firms having more than thirty employees in Japan, in fact, have mandatory retirement at set ages,[10] and until it became illegal (as a result of amendments to the Age Discrimination in Employment Acts of 1978 and 1986) as many as 45 percent of the firms in the United States did, too.[11] Why have these firms been paying senior employees not only more than they could earn elsewhere (as would be entailed by optimal training in company-specific skills), but more even than the employees incrementally contribute to revenues? Lazear offers a convincing answer.

Unless a worker suffers a penalty upon dismissal, she can be expected to shirk. But if she receives as wages exactly her marginal contribution to her employer's revenues, then wherein lies the penalty? If dismissed by one employer, she would merely be hired by another at a comparable pay scale—unless, that is, she had posted a bond with the first employer which is forfeit upon her dismissal. But then, absent any instance of shirking, the bond must be returned to the worker upon her retirement or voluntary departure from the firm; otherwise the bond is not the worker's to forfeit. Wages that are expected to rise with seniority serve as just such a bond against shirking. That is, the anticipation of earning more than she contributes to her employer's revenue (more than she could earn in the spot labor market) *late* in her career leads the worker to fear dismissal *earlier* in her career. In such a regime, competition in the labor market drives down wages early in workers' careers, so that over their entire tenures of employment non-shirking workers are fully remunerated. But then mandatory retirement policies are sensible, for workers late in their careers would want to extend indefinitely. The argument identifies an advantage of seniority-based wages and also accounts for the existence of mandatory retirement.

Figure 15.2 illustrates a possible wage scheme. Retirement occurs at the economically efficient date, when the worker's marginal valuation of leisure has risen to equal her marginal contribution to an employer's earnings. Wages that rise with seniority rather than always equaling the marginal contribution to the employer's revenues assure that the worker is averse to dismissal and avoids shirking. But then wages late in the career exceed the worker's incremental contribution to the employer's revenues, and if retirement is to be at the efficient date it must be mandatory.

Here then are two explanations for seniority-based

9 Edward P. Lazear, "Why is there Mandatory Retirement?" *Journal of Political Economy*, vol. 87 (December 1979), pp. 1261–84.
10 Murakami Kiyoshi, "Retirement Benefits and Pension Plans in Japan", Business Series no. 135, Sophia University Press, 1991.
11 Richard Burkhauser and Joseph Quinn, "Is Mandatory Retirement Overrated? Evidence from the 1970s", *Journal of Human Resources*, vol. 19 (1984), pp. 512–31.

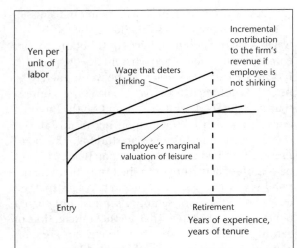

Figure 15.2. A wage scheme that deters shirking

A wage higher than a non-shirker's incremental contribution to revenues late in the worker's career can assure that the worker has at each instant more to lose by shirking and being fired than by not shirking and remaining with the firm. Mandatory retirement is optimally imposed at the point at which the worker's marginal valuation of leisure equals her incremental contribution to the firm's revenues.

Source: based on Edward P. Lazear, "Labor Economics and the Psychology of Organizations", *Journal of Economic Perspectives*, vol. 5, no. 2 (Spring 1991), pp. 89–110, figure 1, at p. 91.

wages, and they are not mutually exclusive. Notice however that the agency theory does not require lifetime employment. If non-shirking workers who quit or are dismissed receive severance pay equal to the discounted present value of the firm's accumulated liabilities to them, then shirking will still be deterred. Workers trained in company-specific skills, and who are paid more as a result, will be less likely to separate from their employer than are workers not so trained, so the company-specific skills theory does explain both lifetime employment and seniority-based wages. But the company-specific skills theory does not by itself imply that the wages of senior employees will exceed their incremental contributions to the firm's revenue and so is not a good explanation for the existence of mandatory retirement. Not surprisingly, historical and other evidence supports the validity of both the company-specific skills theory and the agency theory as explanations of Japan's distinctive employment practices.

Historical origins of the distinctive employment practices of Japanese firms

Abegglen's suggestion that lifetime employment and seniority-based wages were in harmony with aspects of Japanese culture was misinterpreted by many as implying that the practices were anachronistic holdovers from the past. Actually, the distinctive practices became prevalent in Japan only in the immediate postwar years shortly before Abegglen undertook his study. Government statistics described by the labor relations scholar Taira[12] indicate that a much lower percentage of workers had lengthy tenures with Japanese industrial firms in the years 1900–39 than in 1957, and also indicate that hiring rates and separation rates in the years 1900–36 were about twice as great as those that prevailed in the years 1949–66.

Factory employment became widespread in Japan only with the industrialization that occurred in the late nineteenth century. Textiles, the first major industry of Japan, accounted for one-fourth of Japan's manufacturing output by 1885 and for a third of its manufacturing output by the end of the century and as late as 1926. Saxonhouse has carefully documented the high turnover among workers in Japan's textile industry during the early twentieth century.[13] As late as 1930, a majority of Japan's factory workers, and as much as 80 percent of textile factory workers, were women. Typically, the employees of Japan's textile factories were teenage girls who came from the countryside, lived in company dormitories, worked for no more than a year or two, and then returned to their homes permanently to marry and raise families. Though the differing outputs of textile factories employing workers of varying degrees of occupational experience reveal that the longer the employees worked the more productive they became, Saxonhouse argues that, owing to the remarkable uniformity of the firms' machinery and production methods, the relevant

12 Koji Taira, *Economic Development and the Labor Market in Japan*, Columbia University Press, 1970, tables 19–20, pp. 154–5.

13 Gary R. Saxonhouse, "Country Girls and Communication among Competitors in the Japanese Cotton-Spinning Industry", in Hugh Patrick (ed.), *Japanese Industrialization and Its Social Consequences*, University of California Press, 1976, pp. 97–125.

labor skills were general, not company-specific. That this labor market operated as a spot market, with little indication of long-term contracting, deferred compensation, or premiums for seniority, might therefore suggest that company-specific skills were a necessary requisite for the evolution of life-time employment and seniority-based wages.[14] But women's career patterns in Japan remain rather different from men's. In a real sense, the female employees of Japanese firms have never experienced lifetime employment, so perhaps we should con-sider industries other than textiles. Here, too, the historical record points away from tradition, culture, or backwardness as facile explanations for the dis-tinctive employment practices of Japanese firms in the postwar era.

The historian Andrew Gordon has examined company histories and other contemporary sources for information regarding the evolving employment practices of five large companies in heavy industries, including shipbuilding, electronics, and steel, all based on the coastline south-west of Tokyo.[15] These companies, unlike the textile factories, throughout their existence have largely employed male workers, many of whom have devoted their careers to the companies' respective industries. The history of these companies' employment relations includes evidence that supports both the agency theory and the company-specific skills theory.

When at first (roughly from 1853 to 1900) the companies hired workers on a spot market basis through labor bosses acting as brokers and overseers, they encountered repeated problems in imposing workplace discipline, identifying and rewarding good performance, and cultivating the loyalty of skilled workers. In the years leading up to the Pacific war, these companies, in uneasy tandem with in-cipient unions, proceeded to establish a structure of pay in which good performance would be rewarded and skilled workers retained. But this evolution was temporarily interrupted by the growing involve-ment of the military-led government bureaucracy in the affairs of heavy industrial firms. It is not difficult to see in these events evidence for both the company-specific skills and agency theories, for apparently seniority-based pay evolved through trial-and-error attempts not only to retain experienced workers trained at company expense, but also to ensure diligent efforts by workers.

Further evidence

Too often, the company-specific skills and agency theories have been cast by their proponents as mutually exclusive alternatives.[16] They are not mu-tually exclusive. There is ample evidence of their joint validity in explaining Japan's system of life-time employment and seniority-based wages.

There exists convincing evidence that workers in Japanese firms tend to accumulate company-specific skills. First, in Japanese industries that have steeper earnings–tenure profiles, workers have longer aver-age tenures of employment.[17] As already mentioned, the company-specific skills theory accounts for this but the agency theory does not. The socially effi-cient arrangements will assure optimal mobility. Employment contracts that deter shirking do not alter the socially efficient degree of mobility; we expect severance payments to preserve mobility if the sole reason for seniority-based wages is to deter shirking. But the efficient degree of mobility is less if workers possess company-specific skills than if they do not, so investment in company-specific skills affords a rationale for lifetime employment as well as seniority-based wages.

Second, upon formally retiring, many persons in Japan continue to work. A significant fraction of

---

[14] The payment system in silk-reeling was actually a modified piece-rate system in which the total compensation of the collec-tion of employees was set in advance but its allocation across individuals was according to their relative rankings of produc-tivity. See Masanori Nakamura and Corrado Molteni, "Silk-reeling Technology and Female Labour", in Masanori Nakamura (ed.), *Technology Change and Female Labor in Japan*, Tokyo: United Nations University Press, 1994, ch. 1, pp. 25–58, at pp. 48–9. The desirable incentive properties of such a tournament-based com-pensation system have only recently been fully appreciated by economic theorists; see e.g. Edward P. Lazear and Sherwin Rosen, "Rank-Order Tournaments as Optimal Labor Contracts", *Journal of Political Economy*, vol. 89 (1981), pp. 841–64.

[15] Andrew Gordon, *The Evolution of Labor Relations in Japan: Heavy Industry, 1853–1955*, Harvard University Press, 1985. For a short summary of this work, see Andrew Gordon, "Japanese Labor Relations in the Twentieth Century", *Journal of Labor Research*, vol. 11, no. 3 (Summer 1990), pp. 239–52.

[16] There is an ongoing and lively conversation between pro-ponents of the company-specific skills and agency theories. This discussion is focused primarily on explaining the employment practices of US companies. For a review of recent literature see Robert M. Hutchens, "Seniority, Wages and Productivity: A Turbulent Decade", *Journal of Economic Perspectives*, vol. 3, no. 4 (Fall 1989), pp. 49–64.

[17] Jacob Mincer and Yoshio Higuchi, "Wage Structures and Labor Turnover in the United States and Japan", *Journal of the Japanese and International Economies*, vol. 2 (1988), pp. 97–133.

these are in fact re-employed by the firms from which they have ostensibly retired. As many as four out of five firms in Japan re-employ their own retirees.[18] This would be mildly puzzling unless the retirees' skills were to a degree company-specific.

Additional evidence that Japan's seniority-based wages are associated with investment in company-specific skills resides in the observation that the Japanese industries experiencing the most rapid technical change also tend to have the steepest earnings–tenure profiles.[19] New technologies are at first incompletely diffused through an industry, so rapid technical advance implies that companies are unlikely to settle on standard ways of doing things and workers' skills tend to be company-specific. There is no obvious association between technical change and the advantages of Lazear-type incentive contracts.

Final evidence that Japanese workers acquire company-specific skills may be discovered in the ample documentation of formal on-the-job training programs in numerous Japanese firms. These include initiation programs for new employees, which very typically include hazing rituals intended to instill a group ethos among workers. This surely enhances the productivity of cooperative efforts but in a way that is unlikely to be transferable to other firms.

That Japan's seniority-based wages are also intended to deter shirking, as the agency theory implies, is revealed by further evidence. Mandatory retirement is more common in Japan than it ever was in the United States and is more common among large firms in Japan than among smaller ones.[20] That is, steeper earnings–tenure profiles are associated with mandatory retirement, as the agency theory predicts. Also, severance payments by Japanese companies rise with tenure and are higher when separation is for company reasons than when it is for personal reasons.[21] In other words, some component of anticipated future compensation is treated as the accumulated property of the employee, just as the agency theory requires. Seniority-based pay is not merely an inducement for trained employees to prolong their years of service.

Additionally, industries in Japan with later ages of mandatory retirement have flatter earnings–tenure profiles.[22] This is consistent with the deterrence of shirking as the reason for earnings rising with tenure: where retirement is later, the reservation wages (marginal valuation of leisure) of workers must be rising more slowly, so shirking late in the career is less of a temptation and requires a smaller deterrent. This argument only applies to the workers for whom retirement from the particular job coincides with retirement from the labor force.

None of the evidence just related points directly to factors that have caused Japan, more than other countries, to be a fertile environment either for investing in company-specific skills or for promoting Lazear-type labor contracts, though the evidence does imply that such factors exist. What are these factors? The truth is that nobody really knows. Perhaps the rapid and somewhat varied assimilation of new technologies in the postwar period led firms to adopt idiosyncratic ways of operating, which meant that job skills tended to be company-specific. Additionally, in the rapid growth era firms were expanding and the costs of assuring job security were correspondingly less. To that extent, the net reward to investment in company-specific skills was temporarily high. A further conjecture is that the undeniable prevalence in Japan of team production methods was eventually discovered to have fostered company-specific skills.

No one has yet suggested factors likely to have precipitated greater reliance on Lazear-type agency

---

18 Y. Nodera, "Japanese Employment Policies for Older Workers", *Aging and Work*, vol. 4, no. 2 (Spring 1981); and S. Sekiguchi "The Problems Faced in the Japanese Industrial Workplace", in J. C. Campbell (ed.), *The Aging Labor Force: Implications for Japan and the United States: A Seminar Report*, New York: Japan Society, 1980.

19 Mincer and Higuchi, "Wage Structures and Labor Turnover" (n. 17); and Hong W. Tan, "Technical Change and Human Capital Acquisition in the US and Japanese Labor Markets", in Charles R. Hulten (ed.), *Productivity Growth in Japan and the United States*, NBER Studies of Income and Wealth, vol. 53, University of Chicago Press, 1990, pp. 385–409.

20 Ronald Dore, Jean Bounine-Cabalé, and Kari Tapiola, *Japan at Work: Markets, Management and Flexibility*, Paris: OECD, 1989: "Already 1967 surveys showed that 95 percent of firms with more than 1000 workers had formal retirement rules . . . But only half of firms with 30–99 workers had such rules. By 1985 that last proportion and reached 83 percent; 96 percent in firms with 100–299 workers and only just short of 100 percent in the largest firms" (pp. 56–7).

21 Hideshi Itoh, "Japanese Human Resource Management from the Viewpoint of Incentive Theory", in Ronald Dore and Masahiko Aoki (eds.), *The Japanese Firm: The Sources of Competitive Strength*, Oxford University Press, 1994, pp. 233–64, at p. 248.

22 Robert L. Clark and Naohiro Ogawa, "The Effect of Mandatory Retirement on Earnings Profiles in Japan", *Industrial and Labor Relations Review*, vol. 45, no. 2 (January 1992), pp. 258–66.

contracts in Japan than elsewhere, but let us venture a guess nevertheless. May it not be the case that the prevalence in Japan of company-specific skills weakened the credibility of dismissal as a sanction for shirking? Companies, after all, will be somewhat loathe to dismiss workers already trained in company-specific skills. Further steepening of the wage–tenure profile offsets this effect by making dismissal more onerous to workers, but necessitates the introduction of mandatory retirement policies.

Other aspects of Japanese labor markets and labor relations, to which we now turn, are intertwined with seniority-based wages and lifetime employment.

Bonuses

The practice, widespread in Japan, of awarding employees bonuses in June or July and again in December evolved contemporaneously with lifetime employment. The awarding of such bonuses is now nearly universal in Japan; even the Prime Minister receives a bonus, as do college professors, factory workers, secretaries, and almost all other workers. In the United States bonuses are common for senior executives but for few others. The bonuses have grown to represent a sizable component of annual earnings, as much as four times monthly base wages on average, as shown in the top half of Table 15.4. Bonuses do vary from year to year, but they do not seem to be closely linked to individual performance. Rather, they reflect the general state of a company's fortunes. When business is booming bonuses tend to be large, and when slack they tend to be small.

Table 15.4 gives a fair representation of the substantial inertia in the size of bonuses awarded. The variation across firm sizes and across industries vastly outweighs the variation from one year to the next. Freeman and Weitzman[23] explored the statistical correlation between bonuses and profits in Japan and concluded that, on average, 91 percent of the typical bonus was stationary, a constant amount, and the remaining 9 percent was proportionate to two-digit industry profits. As bonuses average about one-fourth of earnings, this means that, overall, workers might be viewed as earning a constant base wage plus a share in profits that amounts to about 2.25 percent (= 9% ÷ 4) of their overall earnings. Of course, bonuses might be more sensitive to the

profits of employing firms, as opposed merely to the profits of very broadly defined industries of which the firms are members. Because of the payment of bonuses as just described, Weitzman has identified wages in Japan as qualitatively conforming to his utopian scheme called the "share economy".[24] Weitzman argued that workers should (whether by government edict or merely by they and their employers embracing his argument is unclear) be assured of a share in profits, because then they would be somewhat insulated from the effects of the business cycle. Firms would tend to retain workers in downturns and would not be inefficiently attached to workers in upturns. In the "share economy" wages would vary pro-cyclically and thus act to stabilize employment rates at high levels. This rather begs the question as to why the practice of awarding bonuses that vary with profits evolved in Japan.

Hashimoto has related bonuses to the problem of retaining the services of workers whose skills are company-specific.[25] The wage flexibility that bonuses represent enables firms to discourage inefficient quits. As argued above, Japanese firms pre-commit to paying senior workers premium wages, in part to discourage quits and thus extend the returns from the firms' having trained the workers in company-specific skills. But firms' assessment of workers' incremental contributions to revenues is likely to be more accurate than that of the workers themselves. Workers therefore have less ability than their employers to predict their future stream of earnings if they do remain with the firm. The firm's attempts to retain the services of trained workers will be defeated if misinformed workers quit simply because they have underestimated the lucrativeness of their remaining. If, however, workers come to trust their employers to adjust wages in light of the employers' information regarding their productivity, and em-

---

[23] R. Freeman and M. L. Weitzman, "Bonuses and Employment in Japan", *Journal of the Japanese and International Economies*, vol. 1 (1987), pp. 168–94.

[24] Martin Weitzman, "Macroeconomic Implications of Profit Sharing", in S. Fischer (ed.), *Macroeconomics Annual*, Cambridge, Mass.: MIT Press, 1986; Martin Weitzman, "The Simple Macroeconomics of Profit Sharing", *American Economic Review*, vol. 75, pp. 937–53; Martin Weitzman, *The Share Economy*, Harvard University Press, 1984.

[25] Masanori Hashimoto, "Bonus Payments, On-the-job Training, and Lifetime Employment in Japan", *Journal of Political Economy*, vol. 87, no. 5 (October 1979), pp. 1086–1104.

Table 15.4. Bonuses awarded, across industries and over time[a]

Industry	1991 base earnings (¥1,000/mo.)			1991 summer and year-end bonuses (×base)		
	Large	Medium	Small	Large	Medium	Small
All industries	350	285	257	4.4	3.5	2.7
Mining	374	320	268	4.0	3.7	2.3
Construction	405	324	242	4.9	3.6	2.7
Manufacturing	346	271	259	4.3	3.5	2.8
Retailing and wholesaling	330	280	153	4.6	3.5	2.4
Finance and insurance	346	299	291	4.9	4.8	4.2
Realty	357	310	292	4.7	3.6	3.4
Transport and communications	369	324	301	3.8	2.5	1.8
Electric and gas	391	348	311	4.3	4.5	4.4
Service	339	286	248	4.3	3.5	3.0

Year	Principal enterprises			Small and medium enterprises		
	Base earnings (¥1,000/mo.)	Summer bonus (×base)	Year-end bonus (×base)	Base earnings (¥1,000/mo.)	Summer bonus (×base)	Year-end bonus (×base)
1983	204	2.5	2.7	163	2.0	2.3
1984	210	2.5	2.7	168	2.0	2.4
1985	216	2.6	2.8	174	2.1	2.3
1986 R	223	2.5	2.7	179	2.0	2.3
1987	232	2.5	2.7	184	2.0	2.3
1988	238	2.5	2.8	188	2.1	2.4
1989	246	2.6	2.9	192	2.2	2.5
1990	253	2.8	3.0	200	2.2	2.6
1991 R	264	2.8	3.0	207	2.3	2.6
1992 R	276	2.8	2.9	214	2.2	

[a] Large = >1,000 employees; medium = 100–999 employees; small = 10–99 employees.
R = recession year.

Source: Toyo keizai (see Table 12.1), tables 64 and 66, p. 148, and table 73, p. 152.

ployers are faithful in doing so, then wages will reveal the employer's information. And quits will occur only if judged to be gainful in the light of all available information—that of the employer as well as the worker. If this is true, then bonuses should vary over time according to the changing marginal productivity of labor in firms and industries, and should on average be larger in relation to base wages the greater is the incidence of company-specific skills as indirectly evidenced by firm size and employees' average tenure. Hashimoto's statistical evidence confirms these implications.

Klein, Crawford, and Alchian have extended the argument by suggesting that Japan's expanding economy during the postwar recovery strengthened the trustworthiness of employers in setting flexible wages.[26] Employers might have been tempted to set bonuses at a lower level than their private information warranted, given the employees' understand-

---

[26] Benjamin Klein, Robert G. Crawford, and Armen Alchian, "Vertical Integration, Appropriable Rents, and the Competitive Contracting Process", *Journal of Law and Economics*, vol. 21, no. 2 (October 1978), pp. 297–326 at p. 319.

ing of the rule used in setting bonuses. The firm would at first reap a windfall, but once workers discovered the deceit flexible wages would lose their effectiveness in discouraging inefficient quits. Where the firm is expanding, however, its future losses from such deceit are large in relation to the potential one-time gains and the firm is less likely to behave fraudulently. This may be why the bonus system became so pervasive in postwar Japan, and not in the United States and elsewhere where seniority-based wages have also been observed. But it is not altogether convincing.

Actually, the bonuses may have a much simpler interpretation. They are paid at the two times each year when Japanese people typically lavish seasonal gifts on relatives and acquaintances. The Japanese bonuses resemble the "Christmas bonuses" that some US companies bestow on their employees more than they do the incentive-laden "executive bonuses" paid to the top managers of many more US companies. Perhaps the bonuses in Japan, like the Christmas bonuses in the United States, amount to a kind of employee saving plan, with the employing company acting as financial intermediary. The ubiquity of bonuses in Japan then has a straightforward interpretation. The distorting and cartelizing effects of Japanese government regulation of banks and other financial institutions has created an opening for what would otherwise appear to be a somewhat costly and inefficient channel of financial intermediation.

Our discussion to this point has centered on arrangements between employers and individual workers. We next address the ways that workers in Japan have banded together to act collectively in their dealings with employers.

Enterprise unions

Labor unions are a common feature of industrial employment the world over and Japan is no exception. But Japanese labor relations do exhibit two distinctive characteristics. The first is that the typical Japanese labor union collects the employees of a single firm, not employees of different firms in the same industry or workers of similar crafts employed in different industries. That is, most Japanese labor unions are *enterprise unions*, not industry-wide unions or craft unions. The second distinctive feature is that the percentage of total working time lost because of strikes is far less in Japan than in most other nations. The key questions about Japan's labor unions center on the underlying reasons for the two distinctive aspects just mentioned, and on whether the distinctive features necessarily mean that the Japanese unions are ineffective at protecting workers' interests. A further issue is the precise interrelation between enterprise unions and Japan's other employment practices, for union members in Japan are mostly the permanent employees of the large firms, exactly the same workers most subject to lifetime employment and seniority-based wages.

Nature and extent of unionization

As discussed in Chapter 4, the history of Japan's labor union movement before 1945 was not a happy one. In the absence of effective legal protection, unions enjoyed little success. The prewar unionization rate peaked in 1931, when only 8 percent of Japan's industrial workers belonged to unions, and these were relatively concentrated in smaller firms. The military-dominated governments of the 1930s regarded the labor movement as political anathema and imprisoned many of the union leaders, and, in 1940 the second Konoe administration completely abolished independent labor unions. The labor laws enacted in the Occupation era changed everything and remain in effect today, without substantial amendment.

The Labor Union Law, enacted December 1945 (and amended in 1949), officially recognizes labor unions with elected leaders as bargaining agents for their members, protects the right to strike, and *ipso facto* extends the terms of union agreements to other employees of the same factory if three-fourths of the employees are members of the particular union. It also established national and prefectural labor commissions to conciliate, mediate, and arbitrate labor disputes. The Labor Relations Adjustment Law, enacted September 1946, details the procedures the labor commissions are to follow. The last of the three basic laws, the Labor Standards Law, enacted April 1947, stipulates terms applicable to all labor contracts, including provisions for overtime pay, prior notice of dismissal, prohibition of child labor, employer compensation for on-the-job accidents, and standards of workplace safety and sanitation. Besides the three laws, the Constitution of Japan, promulgated in November 1946, includes a stipulation (Article 28) guaranteeing "the right of workers to organize and to bargain and act collectively". In spite of Article 28, however, strikes by government employees are prohibited in Japan.

Japanese labor unions have evolved within the framework of these laws, and they are, overwhelmingly, enterprise unions. They organize the employees of a single company, or of merely one plant within a company. As Table 15.5 shows, more than 90 percent of union members in Japan belong to enterprise unions. These are not mere "locals" of larger unions. They enjoy (or "endure", depending on how one views it) complete autonomy in bargaining. Japan's national confederations of labor unions, of which currently the largest by far is the one known as Rengō (lit. "the alliance"), have concerned themselves mainly with national politics, not with collective bargaining or strike activity. The national confederations are not therefore proper analogues of the industry-wide unions of other nations, such as the US United Auto Workers' Union, United Mineworkers' Union, or Steelworkers' Union. The only large industry-wide union in Japan is the Seamen's Union. The unions of public workers also exhibit some aspects of industry-wide unions, but are classified as enterprise unions. These include the Japan Railway Workers' Union, Telecommunication Workers' Union, Postal Workers' Union, Teachers' Union, and Municipal Workers' Union. There are no large craft unions in Japan. The few union members identified in the table as belonging to "other" types of union are, for the most part, casual day-laborers registered at government unemployment insurance offices, who belong to the Day-Workers' Union, a large union that does not fit easily into the other categories.

The bottom row of Table 15.6 indicates some of the movements in the overall unionization rate of Japan. The great expansion in unionization after enactment of the labor laws is evident, as is the more recent secular decline in unionization. As the table illustrates, unionization rates not only in Japan, but also of other developed nations, declined in the last decade. Perhaps the slowing of macroeconomic growth since the mid-1970s has stiffened management resistance to union organizing efforts. In support of such a conjecture, the decline in unionization in Japan since 1975 largely mirrors a drop in the rate at which unions have organized the workers in new establishments. It is not simply the result of a shifting pattern of employment across industries, toward the less unionized sectors.[27]

---

[27] The conjecture and its supporting evidence are both based on Richard B. Freeman and Marcus E. Rebick, "Crumbling Pillar? Declining Union Density in Japan", *Journal of Japanese and International Economies*, vol. 3 (1989), pp. 578–605.

Table 15.5. Composition of union membership by type of union, 1930–1988

	1930	1947	1964	1975	1988	1995
% of all union members belonging to:						
Enterprise unions	36	82	91	91	91	—
Industrial unions	46	6	5	5	4	—
Craft unions	7	10	1	1	3	—
Other	10	2	3	2	2	—
All unions	100	100	100	100	100	
Numbers (mn)	0.35	6.27	9.65	12.47	12.16	12.61
% of labor force	1.2	18.0	20.5	23.4	19.7	18.9

Sources: Ministry of Labor, *Trade Unions Basic Survey*; and David E. Weinstein, "United We Stand: Firms and Enterprise Unions in Japan", *Journal of Japanese and International Economies*, vol. 8 (1994), table 1, p. 55 (primary sources: *Rodō kumiai kihon chōsa 30 nen shi* (30 year history of the trade unions basic survey); and *Nihon no rodō kumiai no genjō* (State of labor unions in Japan)).

Table 15.6. Union membership in Japan and other nations, 1970–1990

	Union membership (% of wage and salary earners)			Coverage (% of workers covered by union contracts)
	1970	1980	1990	
France	22	18	10	92 (1985)
USA	23	22	16	18 (1990)
JAPAN	35	31	25	23 (1985)
Germany	33	45	33	90 (1985)
Canada	31	36	36	38 (1990)
Italy	36	49	39	n.a.
UK	45	50	39	47 (1990)

Source: OECD, *Employment Outlook* (1994), table 5.7, p. 184, and table 5.8, p. 185.

Currently, Japan's overall unionization rate lies in the mid-range for developed nations. The percentage of industrial workers belonging to unions in Japan is more than that of the USA but less than that of some European countries. However, the last column of Table 15.6 reveals a way in which Japan is distinctive. In some nations—Germany and France in particular—many workers who are not union members are nevertheless covered by labor contracts negotiated by unions. In Japan, however, matters are actually reversed: fewer workers are covered by union contracts than are union members. In Germany union organizing activity is afforded only weak legal protection, but industry-wide negotiation of labor contracts is enshrined in law and amounts to monopsonistic cartelization of employers in the respective industries. In France, *de jure* extension of selected terms of union labor contracts to nonunion employees in the same firms, industries, or regions is pervasive, even though unionization itself is quite low. Extension mechanisms like those of Germany or France actually discourage union membership—why should employees pay union dues if they obtain no special benefits from membership?

As already mentioned, the Labor Union Law of Japan *ipso facto* extends the terms of union agreements to other employees of the same factory if three-fourths of the employees are members of the particular union. The analogous stipulation of the relevant US statute (the Wagner Act) requires that a simple majority of workers in the same "bargaining unit" vote by secret ballot in favor of exclusive representation by one union.[28] The extension of the terms of union labor contracts to non-members is thus significantly weaker in Japan than in the United States. Almost all of Japan's incumbent enterprise unions organize far more than the three-fourths needed for extension of coverage to other employees of their same unit, which is often an establishment only, not an entire firm. Nevertheless, the three-fourths rule may well have impeded efforts in Japan organize any new union not favored by management. This difference between US and Japanese labor law thus corresponds to the fact that industry-wide unions, although opposed by employers, could still form in the United States; but only enterprise unions could form in Japan, where employer resistance to industry-wide unions was more effective.[29] This rather begs the question as to why these legal stipulations were allowed to persist in the respective nations. An appealing conjecture is that Japan's labor laws and its tendency to form enterprise unions are both subject to the same economic forces, i.e. the prevalence of company-specific skills at large firms.

Japan's unions tend to organize the employees of large firms, not small ones. Thus, industries with large firms like mining, public utilities, and heavy manufacturing industries are the most unionized in Japan, and wholesaling, retailing, agriculture, and the construction industry are the least unionized. Table 15.7 illustrates the profound difference in unionization across firms of differing sizes in Japan. It is obvious that the typical union member in Japan is a permanent employee of a large manufacturing firm. And few such employees are not members of an enterprise union. These are the same workers who are most subject to lifetime employment and seniority-based wages. This fact underlies explanations for Japan's tendency to form enterprise unions rather than industry-wide or craft unions.

---

28 In the USA, a "bargaining unit" is a set of workers designated a domain for union representation elections and collective bargaining, by the government commission known as the National Labor Relations Board.

29 William B. Gould IV, *Japan's Reshaping of American Labor Law*, Cambridge, Mass.: MIT Press, 1984, esp. the discussion on pp. 37–8. Also see Richard B. Freeman and Marcus E. Rebick, "Crumbling Pillar? Declining Union Density in Japan", *Journal of Japanese and International Economies*, vol. 3 (1989), pp. 578–605, esp. pp. 589–92.

Table 15.7. Unionization by firm size and industry, 1991

	No. of union members ('000)[a]			
	Total	No. of employees per firm		
		300+	30–299	1–29
Agriculture, forestry, and fishery	51 (19.7)	4 (44.4)	1 (0.1)	16 (10.3)
Mining	17 (21.8)	13 (72.2)	3 (0.8)	1 (2.2)
Construction	886 (16.8)	249 (64.0)	20 (0.1)	597 (16.9)
Manufacturing	3977 (28.2)	2908 (63.1)	555 (0.7)	106 (2.1)
Electric, gas, heating, and water	225 (71.9)	159 (100.0)	5 (0.2)	4 (6.1)
Transport and telecommunications	1645 (44.7)	1009 (100.0)	245 (0.9)	127 (11.4)
Wholesaling, retailing, and restaurants	1089 (6.4)	854 (91.2)	174 (0.3)	60 (0.5)
Finance and insurance	1171 (56.2)	1116 (100.0)	43 (0.3)	3 (0.4)
Real estate	17 (1.8)	12 (22.2)	5 (0.2)	1 (0.1)
Services	1888 (12.9)	529 (18.7)	329 (0.4)	87 (1.2)
Public administration	1322 (74.4)	—	—	—
All industries	12323 (20.5)	7253 (64.5)	1380 (0.4)	1036 (3.3)

a Union members as a percentage of all employees are given in parentheses.

Source: *Nihon no tōkei* (1992/3), table 69, p. 49, and table 74, p. 56.

Rationale and implications of enterprise unionism

The goals of a labor union include both the economic enrichment of its members and the expansion of its ranks. These two goals often conflict with one another, for union wages can generally be raised by constricting employment, that is by monopolizing the supply of labor and effecting a contrived scarcity of it. But unions can also perform actions that increase the demand for their members' services, which would, in principle, allow both higher wages and expanded employment. Actions that a union can perform to enlarge the demand for its members' services include providing services that facilitate negotiation and enforcement of efficient labor contracts. Such services might have to do with the screening of job applicants. (Here one thinks of the internationally ubiquitous union hiring hall for seamen.) Also, collective negotiation of contracts may afford cost savings when compared to case-by-case negotiations. Grievance procedures and other such contract-monitoring activities are also logically subject to economies of scale. Unions that perform these services thus enlarge the effective demand for labor. Additionally, David Weinstein has pointed out that an enterprise union might actually induce an enlarged demand for its members' services merely by insisting upon expanded employment if, as in the Cournot model, it causes the firm's oligopolistic rivals to shrink their outputs.[30] Of course, the enterprise unions of the rival firms will adopt the same ploy, greatly reducing the overall effectiveness of each union's insistence upon expanded employment as a way of increasing its employer's willingness to pay for labor services; the situation resembles an arms race that none win but that none can avoid.

The preceding discussion opens a range of possible implications of Japan's enterprise unions. As labor monopolies, the unions would have constricted employment and raised the wages in the unionized sector. As suppliers of valuable services, they would have expanded employment in the

30 David Weinstein, "United We Stand: Firms and Enterprise Unions in Japan", *Journal of the Japanese and International Economies*, vol. 8 (1994), pp. 53–71. The Cournot model on which Weinstein's model turns, the standard model for the behavior of manufacturing oligopolies, presumes that firms in the same industry choose outputs to maximize their own respective profits, given the imputed output decisions of rivals. If a union labor contract "forces" enlarged output by one firm, it reduces the profit-maximizing outputs of the others, who thus concede a larger share of the industry output and profit to the one.

unionized sector and, by bargaining effectively for a share of the resulting benefits, raised the wage rate. Finally, as adjuncts to the oligopolistic rivalry of the large firms, enterprise unions would have expanded output and employment in unionized industries, but without necessarily raising the wage rate, or without raising it by much.

Direct evidence pertaining to Japanese unions' effects on wages and employment is scant. Because nearly all of the large employers in Japan and few of the small ones have enterprise unions, it is most difficult to distinguish a union wage effect from a firm-size effect. However, one study by Giorgio Brunello,[31] examining mostly small and medium-sized Japanese manufacturing firms, did find that unionized firms tended to achieve much smaller profit-to-sales ratios, slightly smaller rates of return on equity, and much smaller value-added per worker than similar but nonunionized firms in the same industries. Another study by a team of Japanese labor economists[32] found that unionization in small and medium-sized manufacturing firms tended to be associated with enlarged bonuses and severance pay, higher wages for female employees, and increased inclination of employees to refrain from working on paid holidays. While hardly conclusive, these two studies together support the finding that Japan's enterprise unions enlarge wages and reduce their employing firms' profits. The unions-as-labor-monopolies story receives qualified support.

An enterprise union is not a valuable monopoly of general labor, but it is, potentially, a valuable monopoly of the services of workers with skills specific to the one company. And, as argued earlier in the chapter, lifetime employment and seniority-based wages evolved in Japan to promote the acquisition of company-specific skills and to discourage shirking by workers who, having acquired such skills, were unlikely to be dismissed. The fact that the employees of the large manufacturing firms in Japan are the locus of these practices and also are the most unionized reinforces the idea that investment in company-specific skills has given rise to union labor monopolies in Japan at the enterprise level. Industry-wide labor monopolies would of course be more valuable than enterprise labor monopolies, but not by enough in Japan, where enterprise labor monopolies are themselves relatively valuable, to overcome employer resistance or political opposi-

tion to the necessary adjustments in labor laws. None of this precludes Japan's enterprise unions having actually provided valuable contract enforcement services. And here also, the employment practices of large firms have a significant bearing. Labor contracts assuring that workers have efficient incentives to acquire company-specific skills and avoid shirking necessarily depend upon the workers' belief that the employer will fulfill promises to compensate them late in their careers for services rendered earlier. An enterprise union that can hold an employer to account strengthens workers' credence in these implicitly long-term labor contracts, to the enrichment of both employer and workers.

Whether a union effects a contrived scarcity of labor services or enlarges the employer's effective demand for those services, its members will obtain little of the resulting economic rent unless it can bargain effectively. Union success in bargaining depends very much upon the credible threat to impose losses on a recalcitrant employer by striking. We next examine just how effective Japanese unions have been in this regard.

Bargaining and strikes

Paradoxical as it might seem, the effectiveness of a union at extracting higher wages for its members cannot be judged by the frequency or duration of strikes. The purpose of a strike is to reveal the employer's true willingness to pay a premium for the labor services of union members. A strike will occur whenever the union believes that an employer might be understating the size of that premium. And the strike will continue until the union is satisfied that the employer has admitted the truth. If the employer's willingness to pay is already known by the union, a strike is unnecessary: union and employer will reach an immediate accommodation with one another without a strike.

All of this can be made very precise. Suppose that

---

[31] Giorgio Brunello, "The Effect of Unions on Firm Performance in Japanese Manufacturing", *Industrial and Labor Relations Review*, vol. 45, no. 3 (April 1992), pp. 471–87.

[32] Nakamura Kasuke, Sato Hiroshige, and Kamiya Takatoshi, "Rōdō kumiai wa, hontō ni yaku ni tatteiru no ka" (Do labor unions really have a useful role?) *Sōgō rōdō kenkyūjo*, 1988. The authors surveyed small and medium-sized manufacturing firms in the Tokyo area in 1982.

a union and an employer are bargaining over the wage the employer is to pay. Suppose also that the value to the employer of the union's labor exceeds the nonunion wage by some set amount v, and that the object of their bargaining is simply what portion of that amount the employer pays in the form of a premium p in excess of the market wage for non-union labor. The employer and union proceed by an alternating sequence of offers and counter-offers. Each round of bargaining is costly to both. If the costs are known to both, then the first party will make an offer that the other is just sure to accept, that is, one that would leave it just as well off whether it accepts the offer or proposes the symmetric counter-offer. For instance, if prolonging the bargaining by one round imposes a cost of Δ, which is borne by the parties in proportion to their respective shares of the gain from trade (if each applies the discount factor $1 - \Delta$ in determining the present values of shares to be received one period ahead), then the first party will propose terms that imply its own share of the gain is

$$s = 1/(2 - \Delta),$$

and the other party will accept. The reason? If the other party declines the offer, it can propose a symmetric offer in the next round, which would confer on it a share, net of costs, of having prolonged the bargaining for a round, equal to

$$s - \Delta s = (1 - \Delta)/(2 - \Delta),$$

that is, exactly the share it would receive if it had accepted the initial offer:

$$1 - s = 1 - 1/(2 - \Delta).$$

In the limit, as Δ grows small (for instance, as each round of bargaining takes less time), s approaches 1/2: they divide the gain equally.[33] The union and employer agree immediately on a union wage premium: $p = v/2$. There is no strike.

Yet even in this case, the threat of a strike is crucial to the outcome. If, instead of an open-ended bargaining process as just described, the bargainers are limited to just one round of offers, after which failure to agree means that neither party realizes any gain from trade, then the party that makes the last offer secures all of the gain. A regime that allows employer lockouts but disallows strikes, in effect, limits bargaining to a single round and confers the

right of last offer on the employer. The employer makes a single take-it-or-leave-it offer and captures the entire gain from employing the incumbent workers rather than others. This roughly describes the industrial relations regime of Japan prior to World War I, in which strikes resulted in the incarceration of union members, and the threat of a strike therefore generally lacked credibility. But what about Japan's current industrial relations regime in which strikes are allowed? Strikes, although somewhat rare, do nevertheless occur. An extension of the previous example reveals why.[34]

Suppose that, although the employer (of course) knows its own maximum willingness to pay a premium for union labor, the union does not know it; the true value of v is the employer's private knowledge. To keep matters simple, suppose that, initially, the union knows only that v lies in an interval $(\underline{v}, \bar{v})$. In this case, by prolonging bargaining (allowing a strike to continue), the employer "signals" that the true value of v is low. To put it another way, as time elapses without agreement, the union will infer that the true value of v must be lower than it had previously hoped and will continually revise its wage offer downward. Upon some reflection, the following will be seen to represent optimal decisions by both union and employer, each given the respective choice of the other.

The union's initial wage offer is a wage premium $p = \bar{v}/2$. As time elapses without agreement, the union will continually revise its wage offer downward, so that

$$p = (1/2)\bar{v}e^{-rt},$$

where t is the elapsed time and r is the continuous

33 By similar reasoning, if the costs of delaying agreement differ between the two parties (but are still proportionate to their respective ultimate shares of the gain), then the initial offer, which the second party accepts, equals $s_1 = \Delta_2/(\Delta_1 + \Delta_2 - \Delta_1\Delta_2)$, where $1 - \Delta_i$ represents the discount factor of party i. In other words, for either, the share obtained becomes larger, the greater is the opposite party's cost of prolonging bargaining. This reasoning was first developed by Ariel Rubenstein, "Perfect Equilibrium in a Bargaining Model", *Econometrica*, vol. 50, no. 1 (1982), pp. 97–109.

34 Models like the one sketched here are discussed at length in the excellent survey by John Kennan and Robert Wilson, "Bargaining and Private Information", *Journal of Economic Literature*, vol. 31 (March 1993), pp. 45–104. Also see Peter C. Cramton, "Delay in Bargaining with Two-Sided Uncertainty", *Review of Economic Studies*, vol. 59, no. 1 (January 1992), pp. 205–25.

discount rate. (For example, $\bar{v}e^{-rt}$ happens to be the discounted present value of amount $\bar{v}$ to be realized t periods hence.) If the true value of v lies at the high end of the interval, the employer can do no better than accept the initial offer, and will do so. But if the true value of v lies below $\bar{v}$, the employer will hold out until the union wage offer has declined to the point where it divides the true gain from trade equally between them. Then it will accept the offer and the strike will end.

The union and employer reason as follows. If the union wage offer is continually revised downward ("decays") at the same rate as the employer's time rate of discount, then the employer will, at any given instant, reject the current offer if that offer leaves the employer with less than half of the true gain from trade. The reason? With this particular decay rate, if the wage offer of a given instant leaves the employer with less than half of the gain, then the onerousness of postponing realization is more than offset by the ensuing downward revision of the union's wage offer. And, precisely because the employer calculates in this manner, the union can do no better for itself than by, in fact, allowing its wage offer to decay at exactly the same rate as the time rate of discount (its own and the employer's, here presumed to be identical). A faster decay rate might hasten agreement but at too high a cost to the union, and a slower decay rate might ultimately leave the union with a larger share, but would take too long to be worthwhile. Furthermore, the union's initial wage offer should be one that the employer accepts only if the true gain is at the top of the interval, for any lower initial offer would needlessly sacrifice the potential advantages to the union of ultimate discovery of the truth, and any higher offer would be sure to be rejected.

The upshot of all this is quite simple. A strike will occur only if the employer's maximum willingness to pay a premium for union labor is known only to the employer itself. Also, strikes will last longer, the greater is the discrepancy between the employer's maximum willingness to pay for union labor and the union's initial perception of how high the employer's maximum willingness to pay might be.

Percentage of working time lost due to strikes
Strikes are rare events in all the developed nations, including Japan. Table 15.8 describes the incidence,

Table 15.8. Strikes in Japan and selected other nations, 1992

	% of total working time lost	Incidence (% of total employed)	Mean duration (days)
JAPAN	0.002	0.17	2.1
UK	0.01	1.5	1.7
France	0.01	0.02	13.9
USA (1993)	0.014	0.15	21.4
Germany	0.02	2.0	2.6
Canada (1993)	0.02	0.73	7.8
Italy	0.05	14.7	0.9

Note: Canada excludes strikes involving fewer than 500 workers; USA excludes strikes involving fewer than 1,000 workers or lasting less than half of a working day; Japan excludes strikes lasting less than half a working day.

Source: Randall K. Filer, Daniel S. Hamermesh, and Albert Reese, *The Economics of Work and Pay*, 6th edn, London: Harper Collins, 1996, table 12.3, p. 475 (primary source: International Labour Organization, *Yearbook of Labour Statistics*, 1994, tables 3 and 31).

duration, and costliness of strikes in Japan and a few other countries. Only seventeen in 10,000 employees were involved in strikes in Japan in 1992, slightly more than in the United States but significantly less than in the other nations. Furthermore, the mean duration of strikes was much less in Japan in that year—two days in Japan compared with three weeks in the USA. The percentage of total working time lost because of strikes in Japan in 1992 was a mere 0.002 percent, much lower than in any other nation listed in the table, including the United States.

In Japan union labor contracts are nearly always for the upcoming year, and are negotiated in the spring each year, an event known as the "spring labor offensive" or *shuntō* (short for *shun-ki chin-ageru kyōdō tōsō*, lit. the springtime cooperative struggle to hike wages). April is the beginning of the annual school year in Japan, and also the time when new graduates take up their first jobs, and so it is the logical month for concluding labor contracts. Beginning in 1955, a large number of Japanese labor unions have attempted annually to cooperate with one another to coordinate the timing and substance of their contract negotiations. Only since then have the annual spring labor negotiations been referred to as *shuntō*. These annual displays of cooperation across unions have actually achieved very little. The locus of contract negotiation and strike activity in

Japan is, quite emphatically, the enterprise. Synchronicity of negotiations across enterprises did not require cooperation, for it is more or less assured by the predominance of one-year contracts. About half of the strikes in Japan occur in the months leading up to the "spring offensive", in February–May. Most other strikes tend to occur around the times bonuses are paid, mid-summer and December, and involve disputes about the levels of bonus payments.

Careful readers of the previous sections will know that Japan's infrequency and short duration in strikes is a poor indication of the relative effectiveness of its labor unions at obtaining higher wages for their members. Really, the insignificance of losses resulting from strikes in Japan means only that there is little discrepancy between the unions' and employers' information regarding the employers' maximum willingness to pay a premium for union members' services. It does not necessarily mean that the premium itself is small. Enterprise union members in Japan mainly consist of the regular employees of large firms, trained in company-specific skills and expecting to enjoy long tenures of service. Compared with members of a typical industry-wide union in the United States or elsewhere, the members of a Japanese enterprise union are relatively homogeneous and have had a longer time in which to observe the behavior of their employer. For both these reasons, it is quite natural to suppose that union members in Japan should be relatively well-informed regarding their employers' willingness to pay a premium for their services.

Up to this point in our discussion of Japanese labor markets, our focus has been nearly exclusively on male workers, about two-thirds of whom in Japan are the regular employees of large firms. We next examine the experiences of female workers in Japan, of whom about two-thirds work for small and medium firms or are self-employed.

Japanese women and the labor market

The percentage of women over 15 years in age who are members of the labor force—that is, the women's labor force participation rate—is as large in Japan as in most other developed nations, and has exhibited little overall change since 1920 when reliable statistics first became available: throughout the past eight decades, and the many accompanying changes in Japan's economy and society, it has remained near 50 percent. In other developed nations, particularly the USA, the women's labor force participation rate has displayed a dramatic upward trend through most of the twentieth century. The data in Table 15.9 document the secular rise in women's labor force participation rates in the United States and Europe, and the relatively stable women's labor force participation rate in Japan.

Table 15.9. Labor force participation rates of persons aged 15–64, Japan and selected other countries, 1956, 1976, and 1994 (%)

	Total			Men			Women		
	1956	1976	1994	1956	1976	1994	1956	1976	1994
JAPAN	70.5	61.6	76.4	85.8	81.2	90.6	56.4	45.8	62.1
USA	58.7	59.7	77.9	82.6	74.9	85.3	35.7	44.5	70.5
Canada	54.3	60.1	74.0	82.9	60.1	82.6	25.1	44.3	67.8
UK	62.5	60.3	75.2	88.2	78.5	83.3	39.2	43.6	65.6
France*	56.9	55.9	67.5	79.3	71.9	75.9	36.4	41.1	59.1
Italy*	57.7	50.2	60.0	92.2	72.1	76.9	33.8	29.9	43.4

* Figures for Italy 1962 rather than 1956, and figures for France 1959 and 1977 rather than 1956 and 1976.

Source: OECD, *Labour Force Statistics* (1956–67 and 1966–86); and OECD, *Historical Statistics, 1960–1994* (1996), tables 2.6, 2.7, and 2.8, pp. 40–1.

Table 15.10. Composition of labor force by type of employment and by sex, 1920–1995

	Women				Men			
	Female participation rate (%)	Employees	Self-employed	Family enterprise	Male participation rate (%)	Employees	Self-employed	Family enterprise
1920	53.4				92.2			
1930	49.1	—	—	—	90.5	—	—	—
1940	52.6	0.304	0.100	0.596	90.1	0.490	0.369	0.141
1950	48.6	0.264	0.122	0.613	83.4	0.477	0.348	0.175
1955	50.6	0.332	0.117	0.551	85.3	0.539	0.318	0.144
1960	50.9	0.419	0.135	0.447	85.0	0.617	0.276	0.107
1965	49.8	0.492	0.121	0.386	83.4	0.681	0.244	0.073
1970	50.9	0.532	0.139	0.329	84.4	0.713	0.230	0.057
1975	46.1	0.597	0.120	0.281	83.4	0.746	0.211	0.042
1980	46.9	0.638	0.115	0.246	82.1	0.758	0.205	0.037
1985	47.6	0.705	0.103	0.193	80.4	0.790	0.182	0.028
1990	50.1	0.725	0.107	0.168	77.2	0.811	0.164	0.025
1995	50.0	0.785	0.090	0.125	77.6	0.838	0.143	0.018

Source: 1920–85: population census; Japan Statistical Association, *Historical Statistics of Japan*, vol. 1, table 3–6, p. 388; 1990, 1995: labor force survey, *Japan Statistical Yearbook* (1997), tables 3–2, 3–3, pp. 82–5. The population census bases labor force membership upon a criterion of usual status, while the labor force survey bases it upon actual status in the most recent month. The two do not match exactly. The participation rates for Japan in the previous table are based on the labor force survey.

Labor market choices entail more than just deciding whether to participate in the labor force. With the shift of resources from agriculture to manufacturing in Japan over the postwar decades, a rising percentage of both men and women have hired on as employees, rather than seeking self-employment or working in a family enterprise. As Table 15.10 shows, the percentage of Japanese women laborers hiring on as employees has risen from 26 percent in 1950 to 78 percent in 1995. The percentage of Japanese male workers hiring on as employees also rose, from 48 percent in 1950 to 84 percent in 1995. Thus, the trend toward work as an employee pertains to both men and women, but it pertains more strongly to women, for a disproportionately large number of the self-employed and workers in family enterprise in Japan, particularly in the agricultural sector, have always been women.

The core question that motivates analysis of women's labor market opportunities and choices in Japan, the USA, and elsewhere is the same: to what extent are economic considerations the decisive factors, and to what extent are cultural and sociological factors important?

Career choices

Women who join the labor force forgo opportunities to engage in non-paid household production or leisure. Generally speaking, the higher the market wage rate that women can earn, the more likely they are to choose paid employment over the alternatives. But the values placed upon leisure and upon household production also influence the decision to enter the labor force. Most persons value leisure more highly, the higher their incomes are—leisure is what economists refer to as a "normal" good. Consequently, female members of a family tend to value leisure more, and therefore to be less inclined to enter the labor force, the higher are the incomes of the other members of their families. Labor force participation is not the only alternative to leisure. Another possible use of one's time is household production, which includes such tasks as meal preparation, cleaning, shopping, and child care. Women with small children in Japan are less likely than others to forgo household chores and enter the labor force. In fact, a substantial number of Japanese women have exited the labor force during their years of child rearing, re-entering when their children have reached school age. The labor force participation rates of Japanese women at successive ages are therefore often described as resembling the letter "M".

Various changes over time have altered both the rewards and the costs to Japanese women of engaging in paid labor. The advance of technology and the improved educational status of women have increased women's labor productivity, and induced increases in their market wage rate, which would, by itself, have elicited greater participation. Furthermore, the general decline in fertility in Japan since the 1940s has lowered the cost of labor force participation for the representative adult Japanese woman.[35] Offsetting both factors just mentioned, the growth in earnings of women's family members has enlarged the value to them of leisure, and discouraged them from participating in the labor force.[36]

Over the past several decades, more of the women in Japan aged 15–19 have remained in school and postponed entry into the labor market. This trend is

clearly evident in Figure 15.3. The rising labor force participation rate of women aged 20–24 is perhaps also an implication of higher average education. Having stayed in school, women have been enabled to earn more in the labor market and so have become more inclined to seek paid employment. Participation rates of women at later ages have also displayed upward trends, particularly since 1985, but not sufficiently so to raise the overall average participation rate of Japanese women over the age of 15.

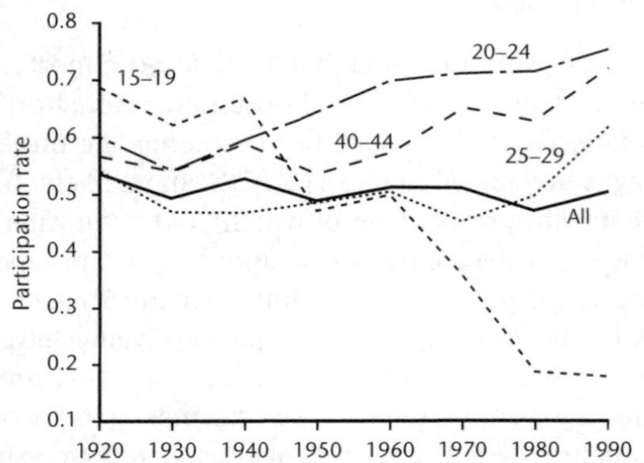

Changes in the labor force participation of Japanese women are more evident in the experiences of separate birth cohorts. A birth cohort is the set of women born within the same interval, such as 1951–5 or 1926–30. Figure 15.4 plots the participation rates of selected birth cohorts of Japanese women at various ages. The figure clearly indicates the tendency, already discussed, for later cohorts to forgo labor force participation in the teen years but to increase it in later years, particularly the years of prime maturity, their mid-40s. The M-shaped pattern of labor force participation over the life cycle is very strongly evident for the earlier cohorts, but appears to be flattening somewhat in the most recent cohorts.

We would very much like to know the extent to which the changes in Japanese women's careers are explainable strictly in terms of the forces already described—secular increase in the market wage rates of women and in the wage rates of their family members, and changes in fertility—as opposed, say, to some more fundamental shift over time in the responsiveness of Japanese women to the rewards

Figure 15.3. Japanese women's labor force participation rates at selected ages, 1920–1990

Sources: 1920–80: Japanese Statistical Association, *Historical Statistics of Japan*, i, *1987*, table 3–2, pp. 366–72; *1990*: Japanese *Statistics Annual*, 1992, based on population census.

35 Economists have interpreted Japan's postwar decline in fertility as itself due in part to increases in the market wages of women: see Robert W. Hodge and Naohiro Ogawa, *Fertility Change in Contemporary Japan*, University of Chicago Press, 1991; and Masanori Hashimoto, "Economics of Postwar Fertility Decline in Japan: Differentials and Trends", *Journal of Political Economy*, vol. 83, no. 2 (March/April 1974), pp. S170–s194.

36 Two econometric studies report estimates of the responsiveness of women's labor force participation as employees (not self-employed or workers in family enterprises), to husband's income and to the market wage rate for women's labor services. Both confirm that Japanese women are more likely to work as employees, the lower their husband's income and the higher the market wage rate for their own services. See Haruo Shimada and Yoshio Higuchi, "An Analysis of Trends in Female Labor Force Participation in Japan", *Journal of Labor Economics*, vol. 3, no. 1 (1985), pp. S355–S374; and Naohiro Ogawa and John F. Ermisch, "Family Structure, Home Time Demands, and the Employment Patterns of Japanese Married Women", *Journal of Labor Economics*, vol. 14, no. 4 (October 1996), pp. 677–702.

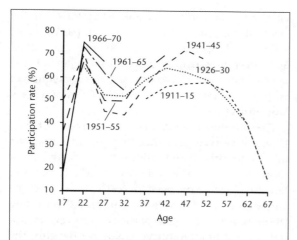

Figure 15.4. Japanese women's labor force participation over the life cycles of selected birth cohorts
Sources: as for Figure 15.3.

and costs of paid employment. Few would deny that both kinds of changes have been occurring and are mutually reinforcing.

Equal employment opportunities

Japanese women earn substantially less than Japanese men, roughly 50 percent less. In large part this is a reflection of women's generally smaller investments in formal education, smaller incidence of on-the-job-training, and shorter average tenures of employment than men. Women in Japan who have adopted the M-shaped life-cycle labor force participation pattern have not been included in the lifetime employment system of large Japanese companies described earlier in this chapter. By the same token, Japanese women are over-represented in family enterprise and self-employment.

Exit from the labor force during the years of child rearing is a common thread that runs through the many ways in which Japanese women's educational and labor market choices differ from men's. In anticipation of such a career pattern, investments in education and in company-specific skills are expected to yield a low economic return. And when such a pattern is the norm, employers become naturally reluctant to offer the same training to their women employees that they routinely offer to men. Such policies need not reflect misogyny or prejudice

against women, but they do limit the career opportunities for women. Sex-differentiated personnel policies that are profitable for the companies that maintain them, may, nevertheless, inefficiently inhibit women in the pursuit of education and training. A vicious cycle exists: the sex-differentiated personnel rules are profitable because relatively few women are well educated or career-minded, but few women become well educated or career-minded because of the proliferation of such rules. Such inefficiencies invite regulatory or judicial remedy, and in Japan there are already examples of both kinds of response.

A series of court rulings in Japan have invalidated such sex-differentiated personnel policies as mandatory retirement of females upon marriage (*Sumitomo Cement*, December 1966), mandatory retirement upon becoming pregnant (*Mitsui Engineering and Shipbuilding*, March 1977), and ten-year-earlier ages of mandatory retirement for women than for men (age 47 for women versus 57 for men: *Izu Cactus Park*, August 1975).[37]

The Equal Employment Opportunities Law, enacted in Japan in May 1985, went considerably further than court rulings such as those just mentioned, making it altogether illegal for Japanese companies to maintain sex-differentiated policies for employee recruitment, training, promotion, and retirement. This legislation also abolished the various sex-differentiated stipulations in the Labor Standards Law, including severe restrictions on overtime, late night, and early morning work by women. Although the Equal Employment Opportunity Law embodied no explicit penalties for noncompliance, it does seem to have altered the personnel policies of the large companies and government agencies in one respect. These now require all new hires, men and women, to choose between career tracks. Nearly all male university graduates choose a general track, while most women university graduates choose the alternative ("mommy") track, affording greater flexibility regarding leave-time and working hours but fewer opportunities for career advancement. That women are offered the choice at all is a new

---

37 These and other similar cases are discussed in Alice H. Cook and Hiroko Hayashi, *Working Women in Japan: Discrimination, Resistance, and Reform*, Cornell International Industrial and Labor Relations Report No. 10, Cornell University Press, 1980.

development, and one that could eventually be followed by dramatic changes in the career patterns of Japanese women. For example, labor economist Linda Edwards draws our attention to the substantial rise in percentage of female students at Japan's four-year colleges and the decline in fertility rates in the years since the equal Employment Opportunity Law was enacted.[38] The widening incidence of child care leave in Japan is another sign of change.

A number of laws have expanded the incidence of unpaid child care leave in Japan, and promoted the establishment of child daycare facilities. The Working Women's Welfare Law of 1972 directed the Labor Ministry and other government bodies to encourage employers to provide unpaid child care leave and to provide child care facilities for the convenience of working mothers. Under provisions of this law, many prefectures and municipalities have established daycare centers for young children, with below-cost fees. The Law concerning Child Care Leave, enacted in 1975, mandated one year's unpaid child care leave for female teachers and nurses. Finally, the Child Care Leave Law, enacted in May 1991, mandated the provision of one year's unpaid leave with guarantee of return to the original job for most female employees with young children.[39]

Conclusion

The economist Edward Lazear has argued convincingly that the personnel practices of a company should be viewed as a set of interrelated institutions, and not as a list of items to be evaluated in isolation from one another.[40] The characteristic personnel practices of the large Japanese companies exhibit a range of features which, considered in toto, induce efficient choices by employees. These features include seniority-based pay and promotion ladders, mandatory retirement, on-the-job training, semiannual bonuses, annual renegotiation of labor contracts with an enterprise union, and separate career tracks for women and men.

Seniority-based compensation schemes, which discourage quits and also enlarge the onerousness to employees of early dismissal, economize on the costs of training employees in company-specific skills, while preserving performance incentives. Such an employment system evolved in Japan in the postwar era and induced the long average tenures of employment characteristic of the male employees of large firms there.

The strong attachments that formed between Japanese workers and their incumbent employers made enterprise-based unions more effective labor monopolies than they otherwise would have been, but also obviated the need for costly strikes. Lifetime employees are relatively well informed regarding the employer's valuation of their services even without the test of a prolonged strike. Besides this, the biannual bonuses, so ubiquitous in Japan, credibly signal changes in employers' valuations of workers' services, and also introduce an element of needed flexibility into what otherwise might be a rigidly predetermined permanent employment system.

Women in Japan have tended to exit from the labor force during the years of child rearing, adopting an M-shaped life-cycle pattern of labor force participation. For this reason, employers have hesitated to make the same investments in the training of female employees that they do for their male employees. In recent years, Japanese women have been attaining superior educations and choosing to have fewer children, and more and more of them are seeking career tracks, formerly reserved only for Japanese men, that entail lifelong attachment to a single employer. Equal employment opportunities for women and men in Japan are being encouraged by these economic forces as well by laws and regulations.

---

[38] Linda N. Edwards, "The Status of Women in Japan: Has the Equal Employment Opportunity Law Made a Difference?" *Journal of Asian Economics*, vol. 5, no. 2 (Summer 1994), pp. 217–40.

[39] The economic effects of the 1991 law are analyzed by Margaret K. Pasquale, "Child Care Leave and its Impact on Retention in the Firm for Married Women Employees in Japan", paper presented to the Japan economic seminar, November 18, 1995, mimeo.

[40] Edward P. Lazear, *Personnel Economics*, Cambridge, Mass.: MIT Press, 1995, pp. 2–3.

FURTHER READING

■ Randall K. Filer, Daniel S. Hamermesh, and Albert Reese, *The Economics of Work and Pay*, 6th edn, London: Harper Collins, 1996. An excellent college textbook for courses in labor economics, with much attention to international variations in practices and institutions.

■ Masanori Hashimoto, *The Japanese Labor Market in a Comparative Perspective with the United States: A Transaction-Cost Interpretation*, Kalamazoo, Mich.: W. E. Upjohn Institute for Employment Research, 1990. Analyzes Japanese employment practices and labor market institutions largely from the perspective of greater investment in company-specific skills in Japan than in the USA.

■ Hideshi Itoh, "Japanese Human Resource Management from the Viewpoint of Incentive Theory", in Ronald Dore and Masahiko Aoki (eds.), *The Japanese Firm: The Sources of Competitive Strength*, Oxford University Press, 1994, ch. 9, pp. 233–64. Discusses applications of the economic theories of tournaments, teams, and principal–agent contracts to Japanese employment practices, with numerous references to the relevant academic literature.

■ Kazuo Koike, *Understanding Industrial Relations in Modern Japan*, New York: St Martin's Press, 1988. A collection of essays on Japanese employment practices by Japan's most noted labor economist.

■ Edward P. Lazear, *Personnel Economics*, Cambridge, Mass.: MIT Press, 1995. Wide-ranging discussion of the economics of hiring, organizing, and motivating employees, by the originator of the "agency" theory of mandatory retirement and seniority-based wages. Highly recommended.

■ Masanori Nakamura (ed.), *Technology Change and Female Labor in Japan*, Tokyo: United Nations University Press, 1994. A very detailed discussion of the work of Japanese women from 1890 to 1985, with particular attention to the implications of Japan's changing economic structure, away from light industry, agriculture, fisheries, and mining and toward heavy industry.

Technology | 16

In this final chapter, we take a brief look at the economic aspects of Japanese inventive activity. Once slandered as a nation of copycats, Japan is now widely recognized as an innovator, particularly in production management. Because Japan was a late developer among the industrial countries, it adopted science and technology policies that hastened the diffusion and dissemination of existing discoveries rather than promoting new discoveries. For example, Japan's patent system encourages the early revelation of new discoveries, promotes patent licensing on terms favorable for users, and affords patent-holders only limited rights of exclusivity. In spite of it, Japanese firms, particularly the large ones, have always devoted substantial resources to research and development, relying upon secrecy and imitation lags, as well as upon patents, to protect their discoveries. Most of the private research efforts of Japanese firms have been directed toward the development of process innovations with immediate commercial application, not toward basic scientific advances. Public support for research in Japan also reflects some of the same biases as its patent system. In Japan, a lot of the publicly funded research is actually conducted by the private sector, as opposed to being conducted by public universities or government research institutes as is more typical of the United States and some other countries. Also, less of the government-supported research is directly related to national defense in Japan than is true of the USA.

Extent of resources devoted to invention and discovery

All the advanced countries, including Japan, devote substantial resources to research and development. Furthermore, research efforts are heavily focused on the same few industries. Table 16.1 details spending on research and development in Japan in fiscal year 1995, both in aggregate and in selected broadly defined industries. In Japan the chemicals, electric machinery, and transportation equipment industries absorbed more than two-thirds of all public and private resources devoted to invention and discovery. These same "high technology" industries have been the focus of research and development efforts in the United States and other countries, also. The total funds devoted to research in Japan amounted to approximately 3 percent of fiscal year 1995 GDP, of which 78 percent were the result of private contributions and 22 percent, government contributions. Spending by corporations accounted for 71 percent of all spending.

In these data, spending by corporations is categorized by purpose according to the following criteria. "Applied" research is devoted to the general pursuit of commercial applications, whereas "developmental" spending is that which leads directly to commercial products. "Basic" research is any that is pre-commercial.

Table 16.2 compares research spending in Japan with that of other nations. Japan's overall spending

Table 16.1. Research and development spending in Japan, 1995

	Expenditures on research, f.y. 1991 (¥bn)	% composition		
		Basic	Applied	Developmental
Spending by private corporations in selected industries				
Chemicals	1,555	14.3	26.1	59.6
Electric machinery	3,274	4.1	20.1	75.8
Transportation equipment	1,361	4.2	13.4	82.4
All other industries	3,206	6.5	25.8	67.7
Total	9,396	6.6	22.0	71.3
Spending by research institutes	1,920			
Spending by universities	1,875			
Total spending	**13,191**			
Sources of funds				
Government	2,866	(21.7% of total)		
Private	10,310	(78.2% of total)		
Foreign	15	(0.1% of total)		

Source: Science and Technology Agency, *Kagaku gijutusu yōran* (Indicators of science and technology), 1997, table 1–4 (pp. 34–5), and table 2–2 (pp. 58–9).

Table 16.2. International comparison of R&D spending, 1985 and 1995

	Expenditures on research and development, (% of GDP)[a]		% composition by source					
			Government				Private	
			Non-defense		Defense			
	1985	1995	1985	1995	1985	1995	1985	1995
JAPAN	2.71	2.95	20.4	22.0	0.6	0.9	79.0	77.1
USA	2.72	2.46	20.6	17.3	29.7	19.8	49.7	62.9
Germany	2.75	2.28	33.1	35.0	4.5	0.5	62.4	64.5
France	2.23	2.34	34.4	33.4	18.5	11.2	47.1	55.4
UK	2.25	2.05	21.5	21.0	20.7	12.3	57.8	66.7
Italy	1.1		40.6		5.1		48.3	
Canada	1.4		46.0		2.9		51.1	
OECD	2.3		24.9		18.1		57.0	

[a] For Italy, Canada, and OECD: % of GNP.

Sources: for Italy, Canada, and OECD: OECD, *OECD Science and Technology Indicators Report no. 3: R&D, Production, and Diffusion of Technology*, Paris: OECD, 1989; all others: Science and Technology Agency, *Kagaku gijutusu yōran* (Indicators of science and technology), 1997, fig. 2, p. 4, and fig. 4, p. 6.

in relation to its GNP is commensurate with that of other developed countries. But a larger percentage of research spending in Japan is privately rather than government financed, and a significantly smaller percentage of government-financed research expenditure is dedicated to national defense.

The rationale for government spending on research is quite transparent. Knowledge is the classic example of a public good. Its value to the nation often exceeds whatever revenues an inventor himself might hope to capture, even under a patent system as exclusionary as that of the United States. The pursuit of knowledge, like the erection of bridges, lighthouses, and national defenses, may be privately unprofitable yet socially beneficial. For this reason governments that themselves provide research and development can hope to raise the national income.

There have been many attempts to evaluate the actual contribution of both private and public research expenditures to national income, in both Japan and the USA. Our next task is to examine these estimates.

Measuring the returns to research and development

In economics, technological advance means a shift in the production function. The production function indicates the maximum value of output derivable from given inputs if the most effective known method is used. For instance, the Cobb–Douglas production function

$$Q = aK^bL^{1-b}, \qquad \text{where } a > 0, \text{ and } 1 > b > 0,$$

indicates the maximum output Q that can be produced with K units of capital and L of labor. An increase in the parameter a is an unambiguous advance in technology ("neutral" technological change). A shift in the production function that entailed changes in b would be an advance for some combinations (K, L) but not all. Such a change in technology is referred to as "biased" (in favor of using capital, or labor-saving, if $db/dt > 0$; and in favor of using labor, or capital-saving, if $db/dt < 0$).

Economists measure technological advance by estimating the production function of firms in an industry. Changes in output not attributable to changes in capital or labor are adduced to be shifts in the production function. Following this logic, a precise measure of the rate of technological advance under the Cobb–Douglas production function is

$$\frac{1}{Q}\frac{dQ}{dt} - b\frac{1}{K}\frac{dK}{dt} - (1-b)\frac{1}{L}\frac{dL}{dt},$$

which is called the rate of change in total factor productivity.[1] If technical change is neutral ($db/dt = 0$), then the rate of change in total factor productivity equals the rate of change in parameter a of the production function: $(1/a)(da/dt)$.

Industries that invest more heavily in research and development have the fastest rates of technical change. The economist Mansfield (and others including Minasian, Terleckyj, and Griliches) have discovered a statistical relation between the rate of change in total factor productivity and R&D spending as follows. Define the accumulated stock of knowledge R as an input analogous to capital or labor, so that the production function becomes

$$Q = \alpha R^\theta K^b L^{1-b}, \qquad \text{or, equivalently,} \qquad \alpha R^\theta = a.$$

Now if technical change is not biased toward capital or labor ($db/dt = 0$), then the rate of change in total factor productivity becomes

$$(1/\alpha)(d\alpha/dt) + (\theta Q/R)(1/Q)(dR/dt).$$

Of course, the "stock of knowledge" R is itself not directly measurable. However, an industry or firm's incremental advance in knowledge dR/dt relative to its output Q can be equated to its annual *spending* on research and development relative to the *market value* of its final output (that is, its value-added). The parameter $\theta Q/R$ is estimated by regressing estimates of rate of change in total factor productivity on annual expenditures on research and development relative to value-added. Because θ is defined as the elasticity of output with respect to accumulated knowledge ($\theta \equiv (\partial Q/\partial R)R/Q$), it follows that $\theta Q/R = \partial Q/\partial R$ represents the *perpetual addition to annual output* associated with an added increment of knowledge, *the result of expending one unit of current output on research and development*. We can refer to estimates of $\theta Q/R$ as the rate of return from R&D spending.

---

[1] A "factor" is a productive input such as labor or capital. Labor productivity is output per unit of labor. Total factor productivity is a geometric weighted average of the productivities of all factors of production.

A number of scholars have estimated the rate of return from R&D spending for firms and industries in the United States and Japan using Mansfield's method as just outlined. First, the rate of change in total factor productivity is constructed as a residual rate of change in value of final output unexplained by a regression of output on capital and labor inputs. Then the rate of change in total factor productivity is regressed on R&D spending relative to value of final output. The slope coefficient from this regression is an estimate of the rate of return from R&D spending. Table 16.3 reports such estimates for American and Japanese firms and industries.

The estimates in Table 16.3 reveal two things. First, individual firms' rates of return from their own respective R&D spending are rather less than broadly defined industries' rates of return from their respective R&D spending. An explanation for this resides in the fact that research and development by one firm often leads to advances that other firms then imitate without themselves incurring costs of discovery. These intra-industry spillovers contribute to the industry's rate of return from R&D spending but not to that of individual firms.

Second, the industry-wide rate of return from R&D spending is consistently estimated to be higher in Japan than in the United States when overlapping periods are studied. This suggests that imitation or licensed use of new discoveries is more prevalent in Japan than in the USA. To understand the reasons for this, we need to explore aspects of the patent system of Japan.

Japan's patent system

Invention and innovation clearly benefit society. But once a new technology is introduced, others can observe and imitate it without themselves incurring the costs of initial discovery. As imitative rivals learn how to produce at lower cost, they expand output, depressing product price and eroding whatever rewards might have been captured by the original innovator. As Andrew Carnegie once said, "Pioneer'n don't pay." If this were the whole story, it would be puzzling indeed that many companies devote substantial resources to research and development. But of course it is not the whole story. To spur innovation, most countries, including Japan,

award patents to inventors. A patent is an exclusive government franchise for the use or sale of rights to a new product or new method of producing, in effect a monopoly. One of the reasons that private companies can hope to capture some rewards from their own new discoveries is the prospect of receiving a patent.

Japan's first patent law was enacted at the beginning of the twentieth century and its last significant amendment was in 1959. The US Constitution empowers Congress to authorize patents "to promote the progress of Science and the useful Arts", and America's first patent laws were enacted in 1790, 1793, and 1836. The last of these established the US Patent Office and encoded the basic principles upon which current US patent laws still rest. British patent laws originated in the seventeenth century.

Under the laws of both Japan and the United States, an invention must meet standards of novelty, utility, and non-obviousness if it is to be patentable. But the novelty requirement is rather diluted in Japan compared with other countries.[2] A minor modification of an already patented invention is far more likely to be considered new and, to that extent, itself worthy of patent protection in Japan. The acquisition of significant rights of exclusivity under the patent system of Japan therefore requires multiple patents, "boxing in" the new invention. This is particularly so because until 1988 each patent application could make at most one claim. And in fact, the number of patents applied for and issued in Japan has been quite large in comparison to the numbers applied for and issued in other countries.[3]

The patent system of Japan promotes the early revelation of new discoveries. In Japan, as in the European countries but unlike America, the first to file for a patent gains priority. In the United States the first to invent holds priority; that is only the inventor may apply for a patent in the first year after

---

[2] For some of the details of Japan's patent laws that bear on the novelty requirement, see Arthur Wineberg, "The Japanese Patent System: A Non-Tariff Barrier to Foreign Businesses?" *Journal of World Trade Law*, vol. 22, no. 1 (1988), pp. 11–22.

[3] Because the Japanese patent system induces applicants to follow the "boxing in" strategy, the number of patents issued in Japan, unadjusted for the breadth of the rights they confer, surely gives an inflated measure of Japan's inventiveness relative to that of other nations. See Earl H. Kinmouth, "Japanese Patents: Olympic Gold or Public Relations Brass?" *Pacific Affairs*, vol. 60, no. 2 (Summer 1987), pp. 173–99.

Table 16.3. Estimates of the rate of return from R&D spending in Japan and the United States

Study	Sample period	Rate of return (%)	Object of analysis
JAPAN			
Odagiri (1985)	1960–66	30	15 manufacturing industries
	1966–73	60	15 manufacturing industries
	1973–77	30	15 manufacturing industries
Yaginuma *et al.* (1982)	1973–79	54	10 manufacturing industries
Suzuki & Miyagiwa (1986)	1974–79	52	50 manufacturing industries
Miyagawa (1983)	1971–81	81	12 manufacturing industries
Goto *et al.* (1986)	1976–80	22–51	50 manufacturing industries
Mansfield (1988)	1960–79	33–42	17 manufacturing industries
Goto and Wakasugi (1988)	1976–79	39	17 manufacturing industries
Goto and Suzuki (1989)	1976–84	40	7 manufacturing industries
Odagiri and Iwata (1986)	1966–73	20	135 companies
	1974–82	17	168 companies
USA			
Minasian (1969)	1948–57	54	chemical industry
Griliches (1973)	1958–63	40	85 manufacturing industries
Terleckyj (1974)	1948–66	37	20 manufacturing industries
Nadiri (1980)	1958–75	22	11 manufacturing industries
Grilliches and Lichtenberg (1984)	1964–73	11	193 manufacturing industries
	1968–78	31	193 manufacturing industries
Griliches (1980)	1957–65	17	883 large companies
Mansfield (1980)	1960–76	27	10 petroleum firms and 6 chemical firms
Link (1982)	1975–79	31	97 firms in the petroleum, chemicals and machinery industries

Sources: JAPAN: H. Odagiri, "Research Activity, Output Growth, and Productivity Increase in Japanese Manufacturing Industries", *Research Policy*, vol. 14, no. 3 (1985), pp. 117–30; H. Yaginuma, K. Horiuchi, M. Nakanishi, and T. Miyagiwa, "Setsubi toshi kenkyū '81" (Business investment survey '81), *Keizai keiei kenkyū*, 3–4 (1982), Japan Development Bank; K. Suzuki and T. Miyagiwa, "Nihon no kigyo toshi to kenkyū kaihatsu senryaku" (Research and development strategy and Japanese industrial investment), *Toyo keizai shinposha*, (1986); T. Miyagawa, "Kenkyū kaihatsu shishutsu no keizai koka to seifu no yakuwari" (The government's role in the economic effects of R&D expenditures), *Kikan gendai keizai*, vol. 55 (1983), pp. 139–50; A. Goto, N. Honjo, K. Suzuki, and M. Takinosawa, "Kenkyū kaihatsu to gijutsu shinpo no keizai bunseki" (Economic analysis of technical progress and research and development), *Keizai bunseki*, no. 103 (1986), (Keizai kikakucho); E. Mansfield, "Industrial R&D in Japan and the United States: A Comparative Study", *American Economic Review*, vol. 78, no. 2 (1988), pp. 223–8; A. Goto and R. Wakasugi, "Technology Policy", in R. Komiya, M. Okuno, and K. Suzumura *Industrial Policy of Japan*, New York: Academic Press, 1988, ch. 7, pp. 183–204; A. Goto and K. Suzuki, "R&D Capital, Rate of Return on R&D Investment and Spillover of R&D in Japanese Manufacturing Industries", *Review of Economics and Statistics*, vol. 71, no. 4 (1989), pp. 555–64; H. Odagiri and H. Iwata, "The Impact of R&D on Productivity Increase in Japanese Manufacturing Industries", *Research Policy*, 15 (1986), pp. 13–19.

UNITED STATES: J. Minasian, "Research and Development, Production Functions and Rates of Returns", *American Economic Review*, vol. 59 (1969), pp. 80–5; Z. Griliches, "Research Expenditures and Growth Accounting", in B. R. Williams (ed.), *Science and Technology in Economic Growth*, New York: John Wiley, 1973, pp. 59–83; N. E. Terleckyj, "Effects of R&D on the Productivity Growth of Industries: An Exploratory Study", Washington DC: National Planning Association, 1974; M. I. Nadiri, "Contributions and Developments of Research and Development Expenditures in the US Manufacturing Industries", in G. M. Furstenberg (ed.), *Capital, Efficiency and Growth*, Cambridge, Mass.: Ballinger, 1980, pp. 362–92; Z. Griliches and F. Lichtenberg, "Interindustry Technology Flows and Productivity Growth: A Reexamination", *Review of Economics and Statistics*, (May 1984), pp. 324–9; Z. Griliches, "Returns to Research and Development Expenditures in the Private Sector", in J. W. Kendrick and B. N. Vaccara (eds.), *New Developments in Productivity Measurement and Analysis*, University of Chicago Press, 1980; Mansfield, "Basic Research and Productivity Increase in Manufacturing", *American Economic Review*, vol. 70 (1980), pp. 863–73; A. Link, "Productivity Growth, Environmental Regulations, and the Composition of R&D", *Bell Journal of Economics*, vol. 13, no. 2 (1982), pp. 548–54.

announcing his invention. Granting priority to the first to file, as in Japan, encourages inventors to apply for patents quickly to pre-empt other claims. And in Japan patent applications are not secret as in the United States. Japan's patent office publishes all the applications eighteen months after it receives them. Upon a request for examination of the application (by the applicant, by an opponent, or another party), the patent application is published a second time. Those who would challenge the originality or obviousness of the patent claim may then state their cases to the authorities. The applicant has three months to respond to each pre-grant challenge. Once a patent has been issued, challenges are both more costly and less likely to succeed. The US patent office publishes patent applications only after it issues a patent, and patents can be opposed only after they are issued.

Japan's system of allowing opposition to patents before they are even issued promotes the licensing out of new inventions on terms favorable to users. If not offered favorable licensing terms, competitors can threaten to oppose an application, greatly prolonging and complicating the process of receiving a patent. The pre-grant opposition places a burden on the patent examiners in Japan to which their numbers and resources are not commensurate—a calculated policy of the government. The time from application to grant in Japan can be as long as ten years; and patent rights expire twenty years from the date of application or fifteen years from the date of grant, whichever is shorter. (In the USA, patent rights extend seventeen years from the date of grant.) In Japan, pre-grant commercial uses of an eventually patented invention are not considered infringements but do entitle the patent-holder to retroactive licensing fees. This amounts to a form of compulsory licensing of new inventions. In the USA, patents are granted more quickly and competitors therefore have less opportunity to employ a pending patent; also, competitors are unable to threaten pre-grant opposition as a bargaining lever in obtaining favorable terms for licensed use of pending patents.

In summary, Japan's patent system promotes the issuance of patents that are narrower in breadth than the patents issued in the United States; it also encourages the early revelation of new discoveries, and the licensing of inventions on terms favorable to users. By promoting licensing and imitation of inventions, Japan's patent system contributes to the larger industry-wide rate of return on resources devoted to research and development in Japan than elsewhere.

Effects of licensing and imitation on the allocation of resources to invention

Though the patent system of Japan affords smaller rewards for inventors than does that of the USA, it is nevertheless one spur to Japanese companies' investments in research and development documented earlier. But there are also other inducements. A discovery may prove profitable even if it does not result in the issuance of a patent. For one thing, imitation itself is neither costless nor instantaneous. There is little doubt that much of the R&D spending by corporations in Japan (and elsewhere!) is directed at understanding and adapting new products and technologies developed by others.

Licensed uses avoid the costs of imitation but entail payment of fees to the inventor. Licensing therefore preserves some incentives for invention while simultaneously promoting diffusion. Compulsory licensing on terms favorable to users is an even greater spur to the diffusion of new inventions.

Because Japan's patent system encourages licensing on terms favorable to users and allows ample opportunity for imitation, it shifts many of the advantages of innovation away from the inventor and toward other firms in the same industry as the inventor. For this reason, research and development in Japan can take the form of a waiting game rather than a race, each firm standing back and hoping for the others to develop an innovation rather than rushing to be the first to develop it. But this is more likely to be true of major innovations that drastically transform production methods and greatly reduce costs than it is of minor innovations that allow only incremental reductions in marginal costs. Katz and Shapiro have demonstrated an algebraic example of innovation in a duopoly, a simple model that artfully incorporates the relevant issues.[4]

---

[4] Michael L. Katz and Carl Shapiro, "R&D Rivalry with Licensing or Imitation", *American Economic Review*, vol. 77, no. 3 (June 1987), pp. 402–20.

In the Katz–Shapiro example, a large firm gains more than a small rival from being the first to introduce a minor innovation, whether or not licensing or imitation is present. The greater output over which a large firm realizes a cost reduction is decisive for minor innovations. The minor innovation game is a race and the large firms win. But the major innovation game can take the form of a waiting game rather than a race. If imitation is relatively easy (or, equivalently, if compulsory licensing on terms favorable to users is present), large firms will wait for smaller firms or outsiders to introduce major innovations. With imitation, major innovations sweep through an industry and erode the profits of the large firms by displacing the technologies in which they have established superiority. Nor can small firms expect to reap a bonanza by introducing major innovations because, although only they will have incurred the development costs, the technology will be available to all.

By encouraging imitation, Japan's patent system erodes the incentive to develop major innovations but probably does not greatly damage the incentive to develop minor ones, and at the same time it promotes the rapid, efficient, and widespread adoption of new technologies of either kind once they are introduced. In this way, the patent system of Japan makes the greatest advantage of Japan's historical position as a late developer, a borrower and adapter of foreign technology rather than a technology leader.[5] Nevertheless, Japan's contributions to the world stock of knowledge should not be slighted. We next examine a supporting example.

Japan as a technological innovator

There are many possible avenues of invention and discovery. Inventors will tend to choose only the avenues they expect will confer the greatest economic rewards. Historically, Japan has experienced relative scarcity of land and natural resources. Technological advances that economize on space and energy, and exploit other inputs more fully, have therefore long had a larger payoff in Japan than in other countries. And this is reflected in the actual path of technical change in Japan. The important innovations originating in Japan in this century have been labor-using but land-and-energy-saving—in other words, not neutral but biased in favor of the inputs having lower relative prices in Japan than in other countries. In agriculture, Japan was the first in the world to develop hybrid varieties of crops complementary to the heavy use of fertilizer and also the first to develop chemical fertilizers.[6] In manufacturing, the production management system developed at Toyota since the 1950s has, among other improvements, enabled drastic reductions in the use of space on assembly lines, and thus has economized on resources more scarce in Japan than elsewhere. Though first developed in Japan, the Toyota production system is now transforming manufacturing enterprises throughout the world. This merits closer analysis. In particular, the arrangements between Toyota and its subcontractors are now widely recognized as a path-breaking technological advance.

The Toyota system of production management

Japanese firms, beginning with Toyota, have developed novel, innovative, and efficient new ways of implementing and enforcing agreements with subcontractors. Subcontractors are firms that supply parts to other firms according to order. There are close complementarities between Toyota's innovations in production management and its growing reliance on a complex hierarchy of subcontractors.

The Toyota production management system entails the use of *kanban* or "signboards" attached to work in progress on the assembly line. When a subassembly is completed, its signboard is detached and returned to the previous workstation. Signboards released from the next workstation are attached to newly started subassemblies. A dearth of such signboards (released from the next station) indicates a bottleneck at the next station and is a signal for workers to move from other stations to that one. A

---

5 So argues Janusz A. Ordover, "A Patent System for Both Diffusion and Exclusion", *Journal of Economic Perspectives*, vol. 5, no. 1 (Winter 1991), pp. 43–60.

6 Hayami and Ruttan argue that the land and energy-saving bias of technological advance in Japanese agriculture reflects calculated attempts to economize on the productive resources that have been relatively most scarce in Japan: see Yujiro Hayami and V. W. Ruttan, "Factor Prices and Technical Change in Agricultural Development: The United States and Japan, 1880–1960", *Journal of Political Economy*, vol. 78, no. 5 (Sept./Oct. 1970), pp. 1115–41.

plethora of signboards released from the next station is a sign that a bottleneck is forming at one's own station and is a signal to hasten efforts. Toyota uses this system not only on the assembly line but also with subcontractors. That is, subcontractors time their deliveries of parts according to the number of signboards released by the first station on the assembly line. Efficient implementation of the *kanban* system of inventory control requires frequent and timely delivery of parts produced to fine tolerances and with a minimum of defects. This has required the development of a finely tuned system of subcontracting agreements in which Toyota's expectations are communicated in detail to subcontractors and made to be in the self-interest of the subcontractors to fulfill. Other firms have imitated Toyota's successful innovations.

Subcontracting

Though arrangements between manufacturing firms in Japan and their subcontractors are seldom prescribed in writing, it would be wrong to infer from this that the arrangements are ambiguous, loose, or subject to the whims of one party or the other. On the contrary, these contractual stipulations require the agreement of both parties, are quite precise, and are seldom abrogated. The subcontracting agreements in the automobile industry typically specify the prices to be paid for parts over the subsequent four years as a linear transformation of the buyer's own later estimates of components of the subcontractor's unit cost (including energy, materials, and labor).[7]

The specific parameters of these pricing rules reflect a subtle calculation. If the price is made to be simply proportionate to unit costs, then the subcontractor will have no incentive to seek cost reductions. Yet, if the price is completely divorced from costs, then the subcontractor will bear all the risk associated with factors that shift costs and are beyond his control, even though the customer is likely to be a large firm better equipped to bear such risks than the subcontractor, which may well be a small family enterprise.

Contracts between Japanese firms and their subcontractors do indeed reflect these considerations. Kawasaki and McMillan[8] have demonstrated that subcontractors that are small (measured by number of employees), and therefore likely to be highly averse to risk, experience less variation in profits than larger subcontractors. This indicates that price stipulations are gauged to more fully reward subcontractors for their cost-reducing efforts the less is their aversion to the risk that such rewards inevitably entail. Kawasaki and McMillan also find that price is more sensitive to changes in unit cost not only for subcontractors that are smaller or more risk-averse, but also for those who experience less predictable cost changes or who secure a smaller portion of inputs themselves and therefore have less discretion in determining their unit costs. This is a further indication that, where incentives for cost reduction are either more costly or less valuable, they are less likely to be present.

Managers dictate the organization of production within the firm. When firms instead contract out for parts and services, organization is not imposed by anyone but nevertheless emerges out of self-interest-directed behavior in response to market incentives. Subcontracting is most viable where command and control is cumbersome and ineffective and where the costs of assuring compliance with the terms of agreements is least. Not all Japanese auto manufacturers rely on subcontractors to the same extent. Toyota has the most subcontractors and Honda the least. Automobiles have thousands of small parts, many of which can be identified as defective without observing the process by which they were produced. Command and control of every detail of manufacture is therefore cumbersome and in many cases inessential. Nevertheless, subcontracting is sometimes still not viable because opportunism cannot be easily forestalled.

Opportunism can mean failing to make investments that reduce the costs of serving a customer, after having received a payment from the customer in anticipation of the investment. Opportunism can also mean substituting products or services of inferior quality after having received a payment from a customer in anticipation of superior products or services. Of course, prudent customers will antici-

7 Asanuma Banri, "The Organization of Parts Purchases in the Japanese Automotive Industry", and "The Contractual Practice for Parts Supply in the Japanese Automotive Industry", *Japanese Economic Studies*, vol. 14 (Summer 1985), pp. 32–78.

8 Seiichi Kawasaki and John McMillan, "The Design of Contracts: Evidence from Japanese Subcontracting", *Journal of the Japanese and International Economies*, vol. 1 (1987), pp. 327–49.

pate opportunism and take steps to forestall it. But where countermeasures are either ineffective or prohibitively costly, production of the parts within the firm itself may be the only viable alternative. For instance, the supplier who contemplates behaving opportunistically can expect an immediate benefit but losses in the future. The immediate benefit arises from avoiding costs. The future losses arise from the reduced demands of customers who, having failed to anticipate opportunism once, are unlikely to do so again. Generally, opportunism is less likely to be in the narrow self-interest of suppliers where (1) frequency of transactions is great—so that the scope for immediate benefits from avoiding costs is smaller, (2) duration of trade is long—so that future losses attending a reputation for behaving opportunistically are likely to be great, and (3) interest rates are low—so that future losses have a greater present value.

The main Toyota assembly plants in Aichi prefecture are in close geographic proximity to the subcontractors. In contrast, the suppliers of parts to Honda are geographically scattered. For this reason, suppliers deliver parts more frequently and in smaller loads to Toyota than to Honda. Also, Toyota has been an innovator in developing arrangements with subcontractors but Honda is an imitator or latecomer. Toyota therefore has a stronger reputation than Honda for maintaining lasting relations with subcontractors. Both are factors that account for the more extensive reliance on subcontracting by Toyota than Honda.

Conclusion

Many aspects of technological innovation in Japan reflect local considerations. As a late developer, Japan derived great benefit from borrowing and adapting foreign technology. This process has been abetted by a patent system that promotes the early revelation of new discoveries, encourages licensing and imitation, and affords weak ownership rights in inventions. Not surprisingly, given these aspects of the Japanese patent system, most private inventive activity in Japan is directed at incremental advances and conducted by large firms who stand to profit the most from small reductions in unit costs. The government of Japan also devotes significant resources to research, but mostly applied research rather than basic scientific discovery, very little of which is directed at the development of weapons systems.

The myth that Japan is a nation incapable of original innovation is soundly refuted by counterexamples, including the development of hybrid varieties of crops early in this century, decades before the United States, and the recent perfection and diffusion of the Toyota production management system, which includes very sophisticated and finely calibrated arrangements with subcontractors.

FURTHER READING

■ Zvi Griliches, "Issues in Assessing the Contribution of Research and Development to Productivity Growth", *Bell Journal of Economics*, vol. 10 (Spring 1979), pp. 92–116. A leading econometrician discusses conceptual problems in measuring the rate of return from R&D spending.

■ Janusz A. Ordover, "A Patent System for Both Diffusion and Exclusion", *Journal of Economic Perspectives*, vol. 5, no. 1 (Winter 1991), pp. 43–60. Argues that Japan's patent system is well suited to the nation's historical position as a late developer—a borrower and adapter of foreign technology, rather than a technology leader.

■ D. Eleanor Westney, "The Evolution of Japan's Industrial Research and Development", in Masahiko Aoki and Ronald Dore (eds.), *The Japanese Firm: The Sources of Its Competitive Strength*, Oxford University Press, 1994, ch. 6. Documents Japan's enlarged research expenditures during the 1980s and comments on the funding and organization of research in Japan compared to the other developed nations.

■ James P. Womack, Daniel T. Jones, and Daniel Roos, *The Machine that Changed the World*, London: Harper Perennial, 1991. The leaders of a team of researchers focusing on the world-wide automobile industry, and based at the Massachusetts Institute of Technology, describe the dramatic cost savings attained by the Toyota production management system, and the state of complete surprise in which American and European automakers learned of it.

Glossary

administrative guidance (*gyōsei shidō*)

Private communications between bureaucrats and businesses, widely thought to have projected Japanese government influence beyond the legally prescribed domains of regulation. *See also* window guidance.

agency theory

The theory that earnings are deferred and thus made contingent on satisfactory job performance, to provide incentives for workers, as agents of their employers, to be diligent in their efforts on the employers' behalf. A possible explanation for seniority-based wages in Japan's large corporations. (cf. company-specific skills theory.)

aggregate demand

Summed final purchases of domestic output by the nation's households, businesses and government, and by foreigners. In nominal amount it depends upon the size of the nation's money stock and upon the willingness of the nation's citizens to hold wealth in the form of money.

aggregate supply

The economy-wide production of goods and services, equal to real GDP. Its extent depends upon the state of technology and upon the efficiency with which the productive resources of the nation are allocated.

alternate attendance (*sankin kōtai*)

The requirement, formally proclaimed by the Tokugawa shogunate in 1635 and continued until 1862, that the *daimyō* spend half their time in Edo and that their families reside there year round. *Daimyō* whose *han* were close to Edo were required to rotate back and forth at six month intervals, while those whose *han* were remote rotated at longer intervals up to two years in length.

amakudari

Literally "descent from heaven". The practice of retired Japanese government officials being posted to private firms.

amenities

Valued items such as sunshine, beautiful scenery, and clean air that are present in the environment, not the result of human artifice. Like other non-market goods, these contribute to economic well-being but are not included in GDP or national income. (cf. household production.)

Baker–Miyazawa agreement

In October 1986, Japanese Minister of Finance Miyazawa Kiichi agreed that Japan would comply with the request of US Treasury Secretary James Baker that the Bank of Japan undertake expansionary monetary policy to weaken the yen relative to the US dollar. *See also* bubble economy.

baku-han system

Based on a contraction of the words *bakufu* and *han*. The political system established by Tokugawa Ieyasu in 1603 and continued until the Meiji Restoration in 1868. A feudal system with the Tokugawa *shogun* as overlord, leader of the *bakufu* (lit. "tent government") and absolute ruler of domains known as the *tenryō*. Directly under the *shogun* stood the *daimyō*, the military rulers of the next largest suzerains, known as *han*, and below them still others of the samurai class—in effect, an hereditary and hierarchical civil bureaucracy.

345

Glossary

balance of payments
Official accounts of the transactions between all citizens of one country and those of others. *See also* capital account balance, current account balance.

Balassa–Samuelson effect
Gradual real appreciation of the home currency caused by growth in productivity of the country's export sector relative to the productivity of its nontrade sectors.

bank capital
The net worth of banks; that is, the difference between a bank's assets and liabilities, the value of its stockholders' equity. *See also* BIS standards.

Bank of Japan (BOJ)
The central bank of Japan, founded in 1882.

bankers' acceptances
Discounted bills that arise from the financing of imports or exports.

biased technological change
A shift in the production function that is not neutral, one that does not increase the marginal productivity of all inputs equally. For instance, a labor-saving technological advance is biased in favor of using capital; it reduces the marginal productivity of labor relative to that of capital.

"Big Bang"
The complete elimination of all regulatory partitions between Japanese financial intermediaries, proposed by Prime Minister Hashimoto in November 1996 to be implemented in steps over the subsequent five years. The Japanese analogue of the "big bang" that transformed the London financial markets in 1988.

BIS standards
As agreed under the Basle accord of 1988 (negotiated by twelve nations including Japan at the headquarters of the Bank for International Settlements (BIS) in Basle, Switzerland, and phased in over the years 1991–3), if any bank is to fully participate in international markets then the book value of its common equity plus a risk-weighted average of its preferred stock, subordinated debt, and unrealized capital gains on securities must exceed 8 percent of a risk-weighted average of its assets.

Board of Trade (*boeki-cho*)
An agency of the Japanese government under the American occupation through which almost all foreign trade with Japan was channeled at subsidized prices and artificial exchange rates. In May 1949 the Board of Trade was reconfigured as a bureau within the Ministry of Commerce and Industry, now renamed the Ministry of International Trade and Industry (MITI), and the Japanese government then withdrew from participating directly in foreign trade.

Bond Council (*kisai chōsei kyōgikai*)
A para-public advisory council first established in 1933 to make ongoing recommendations to the Ministry of Finance concerning requests by corporations for official permission to float new bonds—recommendations that it invariably followed and that had the effect of limiting the issue of industrial bonds in Japan to electric utilities and a few other blue chip companies. Only after 1985 did the Bond Council gradually relax the eligibility requirements for issuing industrial bonds; in 1996 it completely eliminated them.

bonuses
In Japan, biannual payments to employees of amounts not stipulated in advance but that regularly comprise about one-fourth of wages each year. These bonuses are quite ubiquitous and are awarded to employees at the two times each year when the Japanese typically bestow seasonal gifts upon their friends, co-workers, and relatives, that is in June or July and in December.

Bretton Woods system
International monetary regime conceived at an international conference in Bretton Woods, New Hampshire in July 1944 and continued until August 1971, in which the United States government maintained the international price of gold at $32 per ounce and the governments of other participating countries maintained fixed exchange rates between their currencies and the US dollar. *See also* Nixon shock.

bubble economy
The period in Japan from 1987 to 1990 during which speeding of the growth of Japan's money supply, in accordance with the Baker–Miyazawa agreement and Louvre agreement, fueled massive increases in Japanese land and equity prices.

business cycles
Alternating periods of recession and expansion. The economy's temporary deviations from its long-term growth path.

Cabinet Planning Board
The central coordinator of Japan's wartime

industrial policy, established in October 1937 to draw up materials mobilization plans and administer controls on foreign trade. In November 1943 consolidated with the Ministry of Commerce and Industry (temporarily renamed the Munitions Ministry).

call market
Japan's interbank market in which financial institutions trade very-short-term funds (with maturities ranging from a few hours to one week) through broker-dealers known as *tanshi gaisha*.

call rate
The interest rate in Japan's interbank market. The principle operating target currently used by the Bank of Japan in conducting monetary policy.

capital account balance
The balance of those accounts of a country's balance of payments in which activity does not directly affect the nation's income in the current year: direct investment, portfolio investment, debt instruments, securities, foreign currency, and monetary gold, all of which represent claims on future income. (cf. current account balance.)

capital markets
The markets for stocks and bonds.

cartel
A group of suppliers of similar products who cooperate with one another.

caste system
Hierarchical stratification of Japanese society by birth, imposed by government throughout the Tokugawa era. Shinto and Buddhist priests, and doctors, were outside the caste system, but nearly everyone else fell into one of four groups. Listed from highest to lowest, these were samurai, farmer, artisan, and merchant (*shi-nō-kō-shō*). There were other categories as well, the emperor and his family and the court nobles on the one extreme, and the outcasts on the other extreme, but these groups did not include a significant fraction of the general population.

central bank
The government bank that implements monetary policy by controlling the size of the monetary base. For Japan this is the Bank of Japan (BOJ), for America it is the Federal Reserve Bank, and for the UK it is the Bank of England.

certificates of deposit (CDs)
Securities issued by Japanese banks in maturities

from one month to one year, in fairly large denominations (reduced from a minimum denomination of ¥100 million, to ¥50 million in April 1987), and tradable by anyone at market-determined prices.

chiso kaisei
Replacement of the Tokugawa era rice tax with a monetary land tax, implemented over the years 1873–80 and establishing private ownership of agricultural land for the first time in Japan.

chitsuroku shobun
Literally, "stipend measures". The series of steps by which the Meiji government terminated payment of the samurai stipends. In 1873 and in 1874 samurai were offered government bonds in commutation of their stipends, but few accepted the offer, and in 1876 replacement of samurai stipends with government bonds was made compulsory.

city banks
The large commercial banks in Japan with many branches nationwide.

Coase's law
The economic proposition that once a property right is assigned unambiguously to one person, market trading—if unimpeded by transactions costs—will then allocate the right to whoever values it the highest.

Cobb–Douglas production function
A production function exhibiting constant returns to scale and constant elasticities. For example: $Q = aK^bL^{1-b}$, where $a > 0$ and $1 > b > 0$, indicating the maximum output Q that can be produced with K units of capital and L of labor. Here, b is the elasticity of Q with respect to changes in K, and $(1 - b)$ is the elasticity of Q with respect to changes in L.

commercial paper
Short-term, negotiable promissory notes issued without collateral by high-grade corporations. Only permitted at all in Japan since November 1987.

company-specific skills theory
The theory that Japanese companies pay their employees seniority-based wages to promote efficient acquisition and use of company-specific skills. By paying senior employees that it has trained in company-specific skills more than they could earn elsewhere the firm discourages them from quitting and so avoids the costs of training replacement workers. (cf. agency theory.)

Glossary

comparative advantage
When one has a lower marginal cost of producing something than does anyone else. Specialization according to comparative advantage represents an optimal division of labor, one that fully realizes the possible gains from trade.

compensation principle
The principle that government policies which would elicit unanimity if implemented along with some pattern of lump-sum transfers should be adopted even without the lump-sum transfers.

constant returns-to-scale
Homogeneity of the production function in the sense that proportionate expansion of the employment of all inputs supports an equiproportionate enlargement of output. (cf. increasing returns-to-scale.)

convertibility of currency
The situation in which the government supplies foreign currency in exchange for domestic currency at the market price to anyone who requests it.

credit associations (*shinkin*)
Four hundred or so mutuals in Japan, allowed by regulations to lend only to small businesses that are primarily their own members, mostly small retailers and wholesalers. Labor credit associations, whose members are labor unions, are organized on the same principle. The National Federation of Credit Associations (*zenshinren*) acts as a kind of central bank and investor of surplus funds for all the credit associations in Japan.

credit cooperatives (*shinkumi*)
These are mutuals that much resemble credit associations but are less numerous and tend to be smaller and more insular. The National Federation of Credit Cooperatives (*zenshinsoren*) is a direct analogue of the credit associations' *zenshinren*. *See also* rural cooperatives.

cross-shareholding (*kabushiki mochiai*)
The practice widespread in Japan, but most evident within the financial keiretsu, in which a company maintains a small partial equity interest in a trading partner (5 percent of the outstanding shares or less).

current account balance
The balance of those accounts in a nation's balance of payments for which activity affects the current year's income: merchandise, services (including payments for the services of foreign assets, in other words dividends and interest payments on foreign assets), and unilateral transfers. (cf. capital account balance.)

daimyō
Literally, "great names". The 250 or so feudal lords of the Tokugawa era, the sovereign and dynastic rulers of *han*. The historical, and in many cases literal, descendants of the locally powerful warriors who emerged during Japan's warring states period (*sengogku jidai*) in the sixteenth century.

dajōkan
The ruling council of government in Japan from the 1868 Meiji Restoration until the promulgation of the Meiji constitution in 1889.

demand for money
The portion of the nation's wealth that its citizens desire to hold in the form of money.

Diet
The parliament of Japan, which originally, under the Meiji constitution promulgated in 1889, was a bicameral assembly, including an elected Lower House and non-elected House of Peers, with few actual powers. Under the current constitution promulgated in 1946 it is a bicameral assembly that includes a lower house (House of Representatives, *shūgi-in*) comprising representatives elected for four-year terms that elects the Prime Minister and can be dissolved at any time the Prime Minister calls a new election, and an upper house (House of Councilors, *sangi-in*) comprising a smaller number of members who serve for six-year terms, half standing for reelection every three years. The Prime Minister and a majority of the Cabinet must be Diet members.

diffusion index
An index of leading, coincident, and lagging indicators of economic activity on which the Economic Planning Agency bases its dating of business cycle turning points in Japan.

direct investment
The acquisition or enlargement of a controlling interest in an item of real estate, a business establishment, or a corporation in its entirety. Investments that confer merely a financial interest, and not control, are called portfolio investments. Direct investment that crosses national borders is called foreign direct investment.

discount rate
The interest rate pertaining to loans from the Bank of Japan to private commercial banks. Such loans

entail commercial banks offering their own promissory notes to the BOJ, secured by various sorts of high-quality collateral. Changes in the official discount rate have generally accompanied, and heralded, changes in monetary policy. *See also* window guidance.

discounted bills (*tegata*)

Short-term notes of the Bank of Japan, or commercial bank certificates with, as attached collateral, promissory notes companies have given to the bank when borrowing money. *See also* bankers' acceptances.

distribution keiretsu

A directed marketing channel in Japan, one in which the manufacturer has entered a contractual agreement with the wholesalers and retailers of its products that, for example, stipulates maximum or minimum permissible resale prices, makes customer assignments, or mandates exclusivity. *See also* vertical restraints.

Dodge line

The fiscal austerity measures and reforms introduced in 1949 at the suggestion of Joseph M. Dodge, President Truman's special emissary to Japan. The Dodge line included an end to price controls, elimination of inflation-financed subsidies, restoration of private foreign trade at a single exchange rate, and eventual elimination of US aid to Japan. *See also* reverse course in US policy toward Japan.

dual economy

An economy with two sectors, only one of which, the modern sector, exhibits a sensitive response to economic incentives. Formally represented by the disguised unemployment model of Nobel laureate W. Arthur Lewis.

dumping

The sale of imports at a lower price than in the country of origin. The basis for special protection measures as authorized under the GATT article 6.

economic order quantity model

A simple model that relates economic behavior to storage and reorder costs. An economic model in which the optimal reorder quantity is proportionate to the square root of the costs of a single reorder and inversely proportionate to the square root of storage cost per unit of inventory.

Economic Planning Agency

The agency of the government of Japan that com-

piles Japan's national income and product accounts, constructs economic forecasts, dates business cycle turning-points, and publishes economic analyses including the annual "white paper" on the Japanese economy.

Economic Stabilization Board

Japanese government agency established in August 1946 to administer price controls and coordinate other economic regulations of the early occupation era, in essence a revival of the Cabinet Planning Board.

economic profit

Profit net of all costs, including costs that are implicit only and that do not give rise to accounting entries. Equals accounting profit minus implicit costs.

Edo

The original name for Tokyo. It became the center of Japanese culture as well as government during the Tokugawa era, which is therefore also referred to as the Edo period.

enterprise groups

Groups of firms centered, respectively, around forty or so of the largest industrial companies in Japan, and that generally include myriad subsidiaries of these companies as well as independent subcontractors and other suppliers or distributors.

enterprise union

A labor union whose members are all employees of the same company, or perhaps even work at one establishment of a company. The most common type of labor union in Japan by far.

euromarket

The market for financial assets denominated in currencies other than those of the respective nations in which the assets are offered, such as corporate debentures denominated in yen but offered in London, Zurich, and New York rather than in Tokyo.

exchange rate overshooting

The tendency of an exchange rate to at first move in the opposite direction to its ultimate trajectory in response to a permanent change in monetary policy, a consequence of interest parity and price stickiness.

Export–Import Bank of Japan

A Japanese government bank established in 1950 to make loans related to Japanese trade with other nations. In 1999 consolidated with another

Glossary

Japanese government entity (the Japanese Overseas Economic Cooperation Fund) and renamed the Japan Bank for International Cooperation.

externalities

Costs or benefits of one's actions that, because they accrue to bystanders, do not enter one's calculations. Also referred to as neighborhood effects, or spillovers.

factor price equalization theorem

The proposition that if nations have the same technology and do not differ too much in their relative abundances of productive factors, then commodities trade by itself suffices to fully exhaust international gains from trade and bring about equalization of factor prices across nations.

Fair Trade Commission of Japan

The Japanese government agency responsible for investigating violations of the nation's anti-monopoly law, and empowered to reach judgments and issue decrees in such cases.

February 26 incident (1936)

In which young Japanese military officers leading 1,400 troops attempted a coup d'etat but were suppressed after three days. The rebels occupied a number of government offices in the center of Tokyo and conducted a wave of assassinations whose victims included the finance minister Takahashi, the former prime minister Saitō, and the brother-in-law of the current prime minister Okada who was mistaken for Okada.

financial crisis of 1927

Failure of a large Japanese bank, called the Bank of Taiwan, led to runs on other banks, including a number of smaller ones that themselves failed.

financial debentures

One-year and five-year bearer bonds sold directly to the public and available in very small denominations (as small as 10,000 yen), the main source of funds for Japan's three long-term credit banks.

financial keiretsu

The six business groups centered around Japan's largest commercial banks. The Mitsui, Mitsubishi, Sumitomo, and Fuyo (formerly Yasuda) financial keiretsu comprise a lot of the same companies that historically were affiliated with the corresponding four major zaibatsu. The Dai-Ichi Kangyo keiretsu consists mainly of former members of the smaller Kawasaki and Furukawa zaibatsu, and the Sanwa keiretsu had no prewar antecedent.

Financial Reconstruction Commission

A Japanese government agency created in October 1998 to oversee the nationalization and liquidation of failed banks.

Financial Supervisory Agency

A cabinet level entity in Japan, established in June 1998 to monitor banks.

financing bills (FBs)

Japanese government debt instruments with 60-day maturities, sold by the government to the Bank of Japan to cover seasonal or temporary shortfalls of government funds. The BOJ occasionally sells from its own holdings of FBs and in April 1999 the government also initiated sales of FBs directly to the public.

fiscal investment and loan program (*zaisei toyūshi*)

The annual budget (compiled in every year since 1953) for the portion of Japan's public sector that engages in financial intermediation, including the Postal Saving System, the Export–Import Bank of Japan, Japan Development Bank, and other government financial intermediaries.

fiscal policy

Changes in government spending and taxation.

furikomi

Authorized transfers between ordinary bank accounts in Japan, somewhat resembling payment by check.

gaiatsu

Literally, "foreign pressure". Often identified as necessary for the elimination of protectionist trade policies of the Japanese government.

GATT

The General Agreement on Tariffs and Trade, launched in October 1947, its fundamental principles being that signatories would accord one another most-favored-nation status (that is, would not apply a higher tariff rate to imports from any of them than was applied to imports from any other, nor a lower duty on exports to one signatory nation than to another) and would meet annually in Geneva and at irregular intervals in special conferences like the original one to seek multilateral tariff-reduction agreements.

GDP deflator

A broad-based price index that measures the inflation component in the growth of nominal GDP.

general trading companies (*sōgō shōsha*)
>The nine large Japanese companies that broker a significant amount of Japan's international trade, extend a substantial amount of trade credit within Japan itself, and act as intermediaries in a wide variety of business ventures.

genrō (elder statesmen)
>The extralegal role assumed by the Meiji oligarchs in advising the emperor on selection of prime ministers.

gensaki
>A bond repurchase agreement; in effect, a short-term loan in which a long-term bond serves as collateral.

Gerschenkron thesis
>The proposition that in economically backward nations, if industrial development occurs at all it is likely to draw on government direction and public funds.

Gini coefficient
>The minimum percentage of national income that would have to be redistributed if all of a nation's citizens were to have equal income.

gold standard
>Government pegging of the price of gold in terms of the home currency on international markets, thereby fixing the exchange value of the home currency in terms of the currencies of other gold standard nations.

government saving
>The accumulation of public wealth, equal to government income minus government purchases of goods and services used up during the current year.

gross domestic product (GDP)
>The value at current market prices of all final goods and services produced by a nation in a given year, where the nation is defined as encompassed by its geographic borders.

gross national product (GNP)
>The analogue of gross domestic product corresponding to the definition of the nation as comprising the citizens of the country, whether or not resident within the country's borders.

haihan chiken
>Proclamation of the Meiji government in July 1871 that abolished the *han* and replaced them with new political units, 3 *fu* and 302 *ken*, both called "prefectures" in English. In November the same year it consolidated these into 3 *fu* and 72 *ken*.

han
>The sovereign domains of the 250 or so Tokugawa era *daimyō*. *See also baku-han* system.

Heckscher–Ohlin theorem
>The proposition that a nation tends to export the goods for which its endowment of productive resources is best suited and import the goods for which its productive resources are least suited. *See also* Leontief paradox.

high-powered money, *see* monetary base.

honbyakushō system
>A system of collecting rice taxes that was quite uniform throughout Japan during the Tokugawa era. The *honbyakushō* (lit. "original farmers") were the heads of extended families each identified as responsible for paying taxes on a specified parcel of land in the cadastral surveys undertaken by Hideyoshi in 1582–98. These *honbyakushō* and later their familial successors and analogues were divided into groups of five members. Within each such group all members were held responsible for shortcomings in tax payments by any one. Each village had a designated headman, in some instances elected and in others hereditary, who was the official tax collector and intermediary between the samurai and all the groups in the village.

household production
>Goods and services produced and consumed within the household, such as preparation of meals at home, child-rearing, care of aged parents at home, cleaning one's own house, shopping, and so on. They are nonmarket goods and not included in GDP even though they do of course contribute to economic well-being. (cf. amenities.)

hysteresis
>Weak supply response to real exchange rate movements, due to the inherent noisiness in exchange rate movements having weakened their effectiveness at signaling permanently changed underlying conditions.

ie
>Literally, "house". The natural unit of social organization during the Edo period. An extended Japanese family, that is a group of persons related to one another by ties of blood or marriage and with a single patriarchal head.

Glossary

import price
: The price of an internationally traded good in terms of output of the importing country.

increasing returns-to-scale
: Technologies in which doubling of all inputs more than doubles output, so that average cost per unit declines as output expands. (cf. constant returns-to-scale.)

index number problem
: The impossibility of constructing, from externally observed data alone (in other words, from prices and quantities), a single statistic that will in all cases correctly rank consumption bundles in the order of preference of the one whose choices are being observed.

industrial policy
: Government authorities' use of subsidies, tax credits, trade restrictions, antitrust exemptions, and other such measures to direct resources toward or away from specific, targeted industries.

interest parity
: A situation in which the difference in nominal interest rates between a pair of countries either equals the expected appreciation of the one's currency relative to that of the other (covered interest parity) or equals the actual subsequent appreciation of the one's currency relative to that of the other (uncovered interest parity). International arbitrage, if unimpeded by government regulations or transactions costs, will bring about covered interest parity.

intra-industry trade
: Import and export of apparently similar goods by the same country.

investment trust certificates
: Financial assets in Japan that very much resemble mutual fund shares.

IS–LM model
: The Keynesian model as most often represented in economics textbooks.

J-curve
: The pattern in which real depreciation of the home currency, fully passed through to import prices, at first worsens the current account balance, but after a year or more improves it. Fundamentally due to the slowness of the demand response to real exchange rate movements. *See also* Marshall–Lerner condition.

Japan Development Bank
: Japanese government bank founded in 1951 that has extended long-term loans to businesses at below-market interest rates, many of them to politically influential but economically ailing industries such as textiles, shipbuilding, coal mining, and the like.

Japan Offshore Market (JOM)
: A part of the euromarket first authorized in 1986 and consisting of facilities that, although physically located within Japan and allowed to accept deposits and issue loans denominated in yen, are only permitted to transact with foreigners and are not regarded by the Japanese government authorities as "resident"; i.e. they are exempted from domestic regulations including reserve requirements, deposit rate ceilings, and levies for deposit insurance.

jūsen
: A contraction for *jūtaku kinyū senmon kaisha*, lit. "companies specializing in housing finance". The eight *jūsen* were each capitalized by large commercial banks in the 1970s but only attained great size after March 1990, when the banks began to steer their own customers to their *jūsen* affiliates to evade newly established MOF limits on the banks' own real estate loans. With the collapse of real estate prices in 1991, seven of the eight *jūsen* became insolvent, jeopardizing the numerous small agricultural cooperatives that had been induced by government officials to loan heavily to them. Ultimately a bill was enacted in June 1996 that liquidated the *jūsen* and reimbursed the agricultural coops for a substantial portion of their *jūsen*-related losses, financed by special levies on the founding banks and an appropriation of ¥685 billion in public funds.

keiretsu, *see* financial keiretsu

Keynesian model
: An economic model of the business cycle of the sort first articulated by John Maynard Keynes (*The General Theory of Employment, Interest, and Money*, 1936), in which, because of the stickiness of money prices, fluctuations in aggregate demand induce fluctuations in output and employment.

Keynesian multiplier effect
: Changes in aggregate spending that arise because consumption spending by one agent is income for another, so that changes in spending beget changes in income which beget still more changes in spending and so on, ad infinitum. If one denotes

the marginal propensity to consume out of income as b, then, in equilibrium, income y equals expenditures $c_0 + by$, and so $y = c_0/(1 - b)$, and an autonomous increase in expenditures Δc_0 ultimately precipitates an increase in income $\Delta y/\Delta c_0 = 1/(1 - b)$, the Keynesian multiplier.

kodan

Fifteen public corporations set up by the Japanese government in 1946 to purchase major commodities from producers at controlled prices, and resell in rationed amounts to demanders at lower prices. Dissolved after the 1949 implementation of the Dodge line.

kokudaka

Aggregate officially assessed annual average rice yield of the land one was authorized to tax during the Tokugawa era, a status token for the *daimyō* and some lesser samurai, since by shogunal design, the size of each's *kokudaka* comported with his place in the social hierarchy. The units of measurement were *koku*; 1 *koku* = 180 liters (5.1 bushels), nominally the amount of rice thought necessary to sustain an adult for one year.

labor's share

The fraction of national income that accrues as wages, in Japan approximately equal to three-fourths on average.

land reform

Measures introduced during the American occupation of Japan that expropriated the holdings of absentee landlords and awarded these to the tenant cultivators.

Large Store Law (1973)

A law, with antecedents going back to the Department Store Act of 1937, necessitating approval of the national government of Japan prior to opening a store with floor space above set amounts, approval which was never liberally bestowed. In May 1998, the Diet repealed the Large Store Law and placed all details of the regulation of large stores under the control of the prefectural governments.

law of diminishing marginal returns

The proposition that successive additions to output due to expanded employment of any one input are progressively smaller. Implied by the obvious existence of an upper bound on how much output is possible from expanding the employment of one input only (for example, the impossibility of feeding the entire world out of a flower pot).

learning effects

Improvements in technology that arise as a direct result of learning by doing, and so are more profound the greater the cumulative output.

Leontief paradox

The fact, first unveiled by Nobel laureate Wassily Leontief, that the United States in 1947 and 1951, though richly endowed with capital compared to other nations, was tending to export, not capital-intensive manufactured goods, so much as labor-intensive agricultural goods.

life-cycle model of saving

The model in which individuals arrange their lifetime patterns of consumption so as to completely exhaust their available wealth, saving while young and dissaving after retirement, enjoying balanced consumption throughout life and leaving nothing to their heirs.

lifetime employment (*shūshin koyō*)

Shorthand reference to the fact that the large Japanese companies avoid dismissals and have adopted wage schemes that discourage quits by their regular employees. The representative male Japanese worker can expect to hold fewer than five different jobs over his lifetime, his American counterpart as many as eleven. Lifetime employment became prevalent in Japan only in the postwar era.

liquidity trap

A situation in which the nation's citizens are satiated with money-holdings in the sense that they have no attractive alternative repositories of their wealth, and monetary policy is marginally ineffective at increasing aggregate demand.

long-term credit banks

The three commercial banks in Japan set up to extend long-term loans to private businesses: the Industrial Bank of Japan, Long-Term Credit Bank of Japan, and Nippon Credit Bank.

Louvre agreement

Agreement among the central banks of the G-7 nations (Japan, USA, UK, West Germany, France—the G-5, plus Canada and Italy), participants at the February 1987 Louvre conference, to make concerted actions to effect appreciation of the dollar. *See also* bubble economy.

M2 + CDs

The money aggregate in Japan consisting of currency held by the public, demand deposits, time

Glossary

deposits, and certificates of deposits (very large
denomination negotiable bank notes mainly held
by corporate investors).

main bank
The bank, if there is one, with which a Japanese
company has developed a special long-term
relationship. The main bank is the largest single
lender to the corporation, holds a significant equity
interest in the corporation, is represented in the
corporation's management councils, and assumes
special responsibilities for managing the
corporation's affairs in times of financial distress.

marginal cost
The added cost of producing one more increment
of output.

marginal product of labor
The added output due to employing one more
increment of labor.

Marshall–Lerner condition
The necessary and sufficient condition for a real
depreciation of the home currency that is fully
passed through to import prices to improve the
current account: the nation's elasticity of demand
for imports plus the elasticity of demand by
foreigners for the nation's exports is greater than 1.

May 15 incident (1932)
In which a group of young naval officers
confronted Prime Minister Inukai in his official
residence and shot him to death. Their co-
conspirators, on the same day, attempted to
sabotage Tokyo's electric power station and
attacked the Bank of Japan building, *seiyūkai*
headquarters, and other official installations. In the
ensuing military trials, the prosecutors and judges
permitted the assassins of Inukai and their co-
conspirators to deliver long-winded harangues
claiming patriotic motivations for everything, and
then meted out shockingly lenient sentences. These
events effectively ended government by the
political parties in Japan until after the Pacific War.

Meiji era
The period in Japan from the Meiji Restoration in
1868 to the death of the Meiji emperor in 1912.

Meiji Restoration
The culmination of a political revolution that
overthrew the Tokugawa shogunate on January 3,
1868. On that day armies of several *han* from the
southwest of Japan entered Kyoto and announced
the establishment of direct rule by the Meiji

emperor, then a boy of fifteen, a "restoration" of
the form of government historically assumed to
have existed in Japan of the seventh century. In
fact, the new government was a virtual oligarchy
primarily comprised of the leading figures of the
Satsuma and Chōshū *han* governments which had
spearheaded the rebellion.

MITI
The Ministry of International Trade and Industry,
the agency of the Japanese government most
directly responsible for implementing industrial
policy in the postwar era.

model factories
Pilot plants set up in Japan between 1872 and 1877
by foreign advisors hired by the Meiji government.
An early example of Japanese industrial policy. In
1884–7 the factories were sold to private investors
as an austerity measure.

modern economic growth
A sustained rise in per capita output made possible
by the continual application of scientific advances
to the technology of manufacturing, characteristic
of Japan since the last decades of the nineteenth
century.

Modigliani–Miller thesis
The thesis that unless a firm's extent of debt
financing affects its gross earnings directly—either
by affecting its tax liabilities or costs of governance,
or in some other way—then the market value of the
firm is independent of its extent of debt financing.

monetary base
Currency held by the public plus banks' vault cash
and deposits at the central bank (Bank of Japan).
Potential and actual reserves of commercial banks.

monetary policy
The government's adjustments in the size or rate of
growth of the nation's money stock.

money markets
Markets for short-term securities.

money multiplier
The ratio of the money supply to the monetary
base.

multinational enterprise
A company that produces goods in more than one
nation.

Mundell–Fleming model
The open-economy, in other words international,
variant of the Keynesian model.

354

national income
Sometimes called Net Domestic Product (Net National Product). The income of all citizens, computed by subtracting depreciation expenses and indirect taxes net of subsidies from Gross Domestic Product (Gross National Product). The amount that if consumed would leave the nation's wealth unchanged from the previous year.

natural monopoly
An industry in which, because economical production entails large fixed costs, only one firm can be profitable.

natural rate of unemployment
The unemployment rate consistent with acyclic economic activity.

Net Domestic Product (NDP), *see* national income.

Net National Product (NNP), *see* national income.

network externalities
Externalities that arise because one individual's purchase of a service enhances others' value of the same service.

New Trade Theory
The theory that identifies scale economies and oligopoly rather than comparative advantage as an important basis for international trade. Helpful in understanding the rationale for intra-industry trade.

new zaibatsu
Companies including Nippon sangyō (antecedent of today's Nissan) and Nakajima aircraft (antecedent of Fuji Heavy Industries) that had been induced by government subsidies to invest in Manchuria and other territories subdued and occupied by Japan's military forces during the Pacific War.

Nixon shock
Announcement by the US government in August 1971 that rather than devalue the dollar relative to virtually all other currencies, it would instead unilaterally abandon participation in the fixed exchange rate system and no longer maintain the international price of gold in terms of the dollar at a fixed level. *See also* Bretton Woods system.

Occupation era
The six year, eight and a half month period from Japan's capitulation in August 1945 until the restoration of Japanese sovereignty in April 1952, during which Japan's government, completely

subordinate to the USA, ratified and implemented policies dictated to it by Washington through the office of SCAP.

oil shocks
The doubling of world oil prices effected by the Organization of Petroleum Exporting Countries (OPEC) in the months following the Middle Eastern War of October 1973, "the first oil shock"; and the dramatic rise in world oil prices later precipitated by the 1979 Iranian revolution, "the second oil shock".

open market operations
Sales and purchases of assets by the central bank, which result in changes in the size of the money base.

Pacific War
The Japanese term of reference for Japan's engagement in the Second World War, starting with the hostilities with China that began on July 7, 1937 at the Marco Polo bridge near Peking and ending with Japan's acceptance of the Potsdam declaration on August 15, 1945.

pass-through
Changes in import prices that accompany exchange rate movements. The result of a foreign supply response to exchange rate movements. Full pass-through, the result of an infinitely elastic supply response, is a change in import prices that is exactly proportionate to the change in real exchange rate.

permanent income hypothesis
The proposition that individuals base their annual consumption on their own perception of their lifetime income, a perception that they update continually and that may differ considerably from their income in the current year.

Plaza accord
An agreement among representatives of the monetary authorities of the USA, Japan, UK, West Germany and France (the G-5, or group of five), meeting at the Plaza Hotel of New York City in September 1985, to coordinate their policies so as to effect a depreciation of the US dollar relative to other currencies.

postal savings system
A Japanese public institution established in 1875 through which individuals make time deposits and obtain life insurance at post office establishments. The funds accumulated in this way are channeled through Japan's other public financial

intermediaries in the process known as the fiscal investment and loan program.

prefectures (*to, dō, fu, ken*)
The forty-eight provinces within the nation of Japan.

presidents' clubs
The membership rosters of companies represented at the monthly meetings of the six financial keiretsu, widely regarded as the core set of companies in each. Altogether, the members of the six presidents' clubs in 1995 numbered 185 companies, including most but not all of the largest companies in Japan, spanning a wide selection of industries.

priority production scheme (*keisha seisan hōshiki*)
The industrial policy of Japan in the early occupation era: the subsidy and promotion of the coal mining, electric power, steel, and chemical fertilizer industries, based on principles enunciated by then finance minister Ishibashi Tanzan and his advisors.

Product Liability Law (1995)
A law making Japanese manufacturers liable for damages arising from product defects.

production function
A function that indicates the maximum output that can be obtained from employing each combination of productive inputs. A mathematical representation of the state of a technology. *See also* Cobb–Douglas production function.

public good
A good that many can consume simultaneously without serious congestion and for which the amount available is necessarily identical for all members of the community. Examples include parks, roads, bridges, and national defense.

purchasing power parity
The situation in which exchange rates are such that the market values of equivalent baskets of goods in differing countries, reckoned in the currency of any one of them, are identical. This is sometimes referred to as "absolute purchasing power parity" as distinct from the situation known as "relative purchasing power parity" in which the rate of appreciation of one currency relative to another just equals the difference in the two countries' domestic inflation rates.

quantity theory
The proposition that the nation's nominal GDP is proportionate to the size of its money stock.

rationalization cartel
A Japanese industry made temporarily exempt from the normal prohibitions against collusion and price-fixing in order to effect "technical promotion, quality improvement, cost reduction, efficiency increase, or other enterprise rationalization", as provided in Article 24-4 of the Antimonopoly Law as amended in 1953. (cf. recession cartel.)

real exchange rate
The quantity of goods produced in one country that exchange for one unit of identical such goods produced in another country. The nominal exchange rate divided by the ratio of domestic price level in the one country to that in the other.

real wage rate
The money wage rate divided by the price level. The wage rate expressed as units of output of equivalent market value to the money wage rate, in other words the wage rate expressed in purchasing power units.

recession cartel
A Japanese industry made temporarily exempt from the normal prohibitions against collusion and price-fixing because of the imminent bankruptcy of firms in the industry, as provided in Article 24-3 of the Antimonopoly Law as amended in 1953. (cf. rationalization cartel.)

Reconstruction Finance Bank (RFB)
A Japanese government bank of the early occupation era that provided heavily subsidized loans to private companies and was itself financed by borrowing from the Bank of Japan. The RFB was shut down in 1949 as part of the Dodge line.

regional banks
The 120 or so banks that typically have branches in only one prefecture, and lend to smaller, less prominent companies than do the city banks.

replacement rate
The ratio of initial maximum allowable unemployment insurance compensation to the previous wage income of an unemployed person.

resale price maintenance (r.p.m.)
Retailers' agreement with a manufacturer (or wholesaler) not to resell its products at prices below some stipulated level.

returns policy
The practice, common in Japan, of the manufacturer accepting returns of unsold merchandise from retailers, with full reimbursement.

revealed preference

The principle that one's choice of a consumption bundle reveals that one prefers it over any other that one could have instead purchased but did not.

reverse course in US policy toward Japan

After the Communist revolution succeeded in mainland China it became clear in Washington that Japan could be an important US ally in Asia and that if Japan's economy failed to recover, the Japan–US alliance would perpetually drain US government resources. In accordance with these developments, in 1949 at American insistence the extensive price controls, inflation-financed government subsidies, and state control of foreign trade that bedeviled Japan's early postwar years were precipitously aborted. (cf. Dodge line.)

Ricardian theory of saving

The theory that an important motivation for saving is the desire to leave a bequest for one's heirs. If it is true, then government programs that transfer private wealth across generations could precipitate offsetting voluntary transfers within families, and therefore be largely ineffectual.

right to sunshine (*nisshō ken*)

The legally recognized saleable right of Japanese property owners to enjoy the rays of sunlight that fall on their property, free of obstruction from the buildings of adjoining property owners.

rural cooperatives

Mutuals that provide a number of supplies and business services to their members and also extend loans and life insurance to them and accept their deposits. These include about 3,000 agricultural cooperatives (*nōkyo*) and about 1,600 fishery cooperatives (*gyokyo*). The prefectural credit federations of agricultural and fishery coops in turn invest the surplus funds of members, depositing a significant portion in the *nōrin chūkin* bank (Central Depository for Agriculture and Forestry).

samurai

The warriors, the top one of the four major castes of the Tokugawa era, comprising about 7 percent of the Japanese population. These included the *daimyō* as well as their retinues of vassals, advisors, and military retainers. Ostensibly the samurai's role in society was that of soldier, but with no wars to fight the samurai assumed the tasks of civil bureaucracy, mainly tasks associated with the enforcement and collection of taxes. Each samurai *ie* was assigned by the *daimyō* a set annual income to be paid in rice out of the taxes collected. *See also chitsuroku shobun.*

sarakin

Literally, "salaryman finance". The Japanese companies that extend unsecured, high-interest loans to individuals and are notorious for their aggressive collection efforts.

saving

Increase in wealth from one year to the next, equal to income minus consumption. National saving consists of private saving plus government saving.

SCAP

Supreme Commander of Allied Powers. The US official charged with governing Japan under the American occupation. From August 1945 to April 1951, General Douglas MacArthur, and from April 1951 to April 1952, General Mathew B. Ridgway.

seclusion policy (*sakoku*)

Order for the closing of the country issued in 1642 by the third *shōgun*, Iemitsu, grandson of Ieyasu. Dutch and Chinese were allowed continued contact through the Southern port at Nagasaki but were not allowed free transit within Japan. All other foreigners were denied entry into Japan under threat of death, and no Japanese were permitted to go abroad. These draconian decrees were strictly enforced for two centuries, ending only with the opening of Japan by Perry in 1853.

seniority-based wages (*nenkō-joretsu*)

A shorthand way of referring to the fact that the pay and promotion systems of the large Japanese companies reward regular employees for prolonging their tenures of service.

shōgun

The title assumed by Tokugawa Ieyasu in 1603, a revival of an ancient title assigned Yoritomo, the founder of the first warrior government in 1185, and claimed also by the Ashikaga in the fourteenth century. The political authority vested in Ieyasu and his heirs is referred to in English as the shogunate or as the *bakufu* (lit. "tent government"), both also used to refer to the earlier warrior governments of Japan.

shūntō

A contraction for: *shun-ki chin-ageru kyōdō tōsō*, lit. "the Springtime cooperative struggle to hike wages". The period of renegotiation of annual labor

Glossary

contracts in Japan, always in April, the beginning of the annual school year in Japan and also the time of accession of new graduates into jobs. First dubbed *shūntō* in 1955 by the labor unions.

sōkaiya
Literally, "general meeting-(special)ists". Extortionists who acquire small stock positions in Japanese companies and then threaten to disrupt annual general meetings through long harangues, embarrassing questions, or other such legal but annoying actions, unless paid by the managers.

Solow growth model
Model of a growing economy in which markets allocate resources efficiently and the nation saves a constant fraction of its annual output.

specialization
Producing more of a good than one consumes.

spillovers, *see* externalities.

stagflation
The phenomenon of a business cycle recession coinciding with rising inflation, such as occurred in Japan and the other developed nations at the time of the first oil shock.

steady-state growth path
Equilibrium path along which real GDP grows at the same rate as the labor force, a path to which real GDP will return following a temporary disturbance. Characteristic of a nation that devotes a constant fraction of its output to saving and in which markets allocate resources efficiently, as expressed by the Solow growth model.

super 301
A provision attached to US trade law intended to mandate the threat of trade sanctions against recalcitrant foreign nations, Japan in particular. It requires the US Trade Representative to publicly identify foreign countries impeding US exports and then to impose retaliatory sanctions if the situation is not addressed. In effect by an act of Congress, 1988–9, and by the executive order of President Clinton since 1994.

tanshi gaisha
Literally, "short-term loan companies". The six broker-dealers that act as intermediaries in Japan's interbank market (the call market).

tenryō
Literally, "emperor's realm". The lands under the direct control of the shogunate during the Tokugawa period, encompassing about a fifth of the entire land area of Japan including the major cities of Edo (now Tokyo), Osaka, and Kyo (now Kyoto) and in which about a third of the population of Japan came to reside.

terms of trade
The price of a nation's exports in terms of its imports; operationally, the ratio of export price index to import price index.

textile wrangle
An early episode of Japan–US trade friction that continued for the three years, 1969–71, and culminated in the Japanese government acceding to the American request that it administer a restraint on Japanese exports of synthetic textiles to the USA.

Tokugawa era
Also known as the Edo period. The time in Japan from the founding of the *baku-han* political system by Tokugawa Ieyasu in 1603 to the overthrow of that system in the Meiji Restoration of 1868.

total factor productivity
Output divided by a weighted average of the intensity of employment of all inputs, an index that measures the extent of technological advance.

treasury bills
Short-term securities of the national government of Japan which it has issued since the late 1980s; the amounts issued have never been large.

treaty ports
Specific cities (Kanagawa (now known as Yokohama), Nagasaki, Niigata, and Hyōgo (now Kobe), as well as Shimoda and Hakodate) within which foreigners were permitted to reside and remain subject to the laws of their own nations rather than Japan, designated in Japan's 1858 Treaty of Amity and Commerce with the USA and in nearly identical treaties it entered into with Britain, France, Russia, and the Netherlands later that same year.

trigger price mechanism
A US government regulation, in effect January 1978–March 1980 and October 1980–January 1982, under which steel imports sold below a stipulated legal minimum price would automatically trigger the imposition of special anti-dumping penalties.

Triple Intervention
The incident in which France, Russia, and Germany jointly prevented Japan from taking control of the

Kwantung peninsula of South Manchuria as agreed under the original terms of the 1895 Shimonoseki treaty concluding the Sino-Japanese War.

trust banks
The Japanese banks that primarily accept trust deposits, issue long-term loans, and manage corporate pension funds.

Twenty-One Demands
The Japanese government demand in 1915 that the Chinese republican government recognize special Japanese commercial and political privileges in China

underground economy
Economic activity that is deliberately concealed from government authorities (often because of its illegality), and thus not reflected in the national income and product accounts, even though in principle it should be included.

value-added
The difference between the market value of an industry's output and its payments for intermediate goods. An industry's payments to the suppliers of its productive inputs plus any economic profit it earns. An industry's contribution to the value of national output.

value of marginal product of labor
The market value of the added output made possible by employment of an additional increment of labor. The added revenue of a competitive firm that hires an additional unit of labor, and sells output at the market price (which it takes as given because its output is such a small component of the total industry supply).

vertical integration
Incorporation of successive stages of a production process within the same organization.

vertical restraints
Conditions that manufacturers insist distributors of their products observe. These include such stipulations as maximum resale price (resale price

maintenance), sales only to designated customers (customer assignment), and nonsale of rival's products (exclusive dealing). (cf. distribution keiretsu.)

voluntary export restraints (VERs)
Government-administered limitations on exports of specific products to particular nations. A frequent response of the Japanese government to trade friction with the USA and Europe throughout the postwar era and particularly in the 1980s. As a result of the GATT Uruguay Round agreement, existing voluntary export restraints will be allowed to lapse and new ones will not be imposed.

window guidance
The practice, officially suspended in June 1991, in which the Bank of Japan lent more to the banks that complied with its administrative guidance than to those that did not. In the postwar era the official discount rate was held below the call rate, affording a riskless arbitrage opportunity to any bank able to borrow from the BOJ discount window and lend on the interbank market. The BOJ limited the amount that it would loan to each bank and privately communicated that limit to it, presumably a higher limit if the bank's own loan portfolios included loans to the industries targeted by industrial policy.

World Trade Organization (WTO)
An international body established in the Uruguay Round of the GATT to adjudicate trade disputes among GATT signatories and carry forward the other activities that emanated from GATT.

yakuza
Organized criminals of Japan.

zaibatsu
The closely held and vast commercial empires that emerged in the Meiji era, grew to prominence during the World War I boom, and were dissolved by the American occupation authorities following the Pacific War. The four major zaibatsu were the Mitsui, Mitsubishi, Yasuda, and Sumitomo ones.

Index

Note: Page references in *italics* indicate tables or figures.